UNKNOWN WORLDS

UNKNOWN WORLDS

Tales from Beyond

Edited by
Stanley Schmidt
Martin H. Greenberg

Many thanks to Howard DeVore for his generous help
including the use of his complete collection of UNKNOWN
and too much else to mention . . .

Copyright © 1988 by Davis Publications, Inc.

Published in 1988 by
Galahad Books, a division of LDAP, Inc.
166 Fifth Avenue
New York, NY 10010

By arrangement with Davis Publications, Inc.

Library of Congress Catalog Card Number: 88-80836
ISBN: 0-88365-728-7

Printed in the United States of America

ACKNOWLEDGMENTS

Grateful acknowledgment is made to the following for their permission to reprint their copyrighted stories, all of which originally appeared in *Unknown Worlds:*

Mr. Jinx by Robert Arthur, copyright 1941 by Street & Smith Publications, Inc., reprinted by permission of Scott Meredith Literary Agency, Inc.

Hell is Forever by Alfred Bester, copyright 1942 by Street & Smith Publications, Inc., reprinted by permission of Kirby McCauley, Ltd.

The Cloak by Robert Bloch, copyright 1939 by Robert Bloch, reprinted by permission of Kirby McCauley, Ltd.

Armageddon by Fredric Brown, copyright 1941 by Fredric Brown, reprinted by permission of Scott Meredith Literary Agency, Inc.

Snulbug by Anthony Boucher, copyright 1941 by Street & Smith Publications, Inc., renewed © 1968 by The Condé Nast Publications, Inc., reprinted by permission of Curtis Brown Ltd.

Hell Hath Fury by Cleve Cartmill, copyright 1943 by Street & Smith Publications, Inc., reprinted by permission of Forrest J. Ackerman

The Gnarly Man by L. Sprague de Camp, copyright 1939, 1967 by L. Sprague de Camp, reprinted by permission of Blassingame-Spectrum Corp.

The Wheels of If by L. Sprague de Camp, copyright 1940 by L. Sprague de Camp, reprinted by permission of Blassingame-Spectrum Corp.

Hereafter, Inc. by Lester del Rey, copyright 1941 by Street & Smith Publications, Inc., reprinted by permission of Scott Meredith Literary Agency, Inc.

The Pipes of Pan by Lester del Rey, copyright 1940 by Street & Smith Publications, Inc., reprinted by permission of Scott Meredith Literary Agency, Inc.

Trouble with Water by H. L. Gold, copyright 1939 by Horace L. Gold, reprinted by permission of Muriel N. Gold

They by Robert A. Heinlein, copyright 1941 by Street & Smith Publications, Inc., renewed © 1968 by Robert A. Heinlein, reprinted by permission of the author

Blind Alley by Malcolm Jameson, copyright 1945 by Street & Smith Publications, Inc., reprinted by permission of Forrest J. Ackerman

A Gnome There Was by Henry Kuttner, copyright 1941 by Street & Smith Publications, Inc., renewed © 1968 by Catherine Reggie, reprinted by permission of Don Congdon Associates, Inc.

The Misguided Halo by Henry Kuttner, copyright 1939 by Street & Smith Publications, Inc., renewed © 1966 by Catherine Reggie, reprinted by permission of Don Congdon Associates, Inc.

The Bleak Shore and *Two Sought Adventure* by Fritz Leiber, copyright 1939 by Street & Smith Publications, Inc., reprinted by permission of Richard Curtis Associates, Inc.

The Refugees by Frank Belknap Long, copyright 1942 by Frank Belknap Long, reprinted by permission of Kirby McCauley, Ltd.

Fruit of Knowledge by C. L. Moore, copyright 1940 by Street & Smith Publications, Inc., renewed © 1967 by Catherine Reggie, reprinted by permission of Don Congdon Associates, Inc.

Greenface by James H. Schmitz, copyright 1943 by Street & Smith Publications, Inc., reprinted by permission of Scott Meredith Literary Agency, Inc.

The Hag Seleen by Theodore Sturgeon, copyright 1942 by Theodore Sturgeon, reprinted by permission of Kirby McCauley, Ltd.

CONTENTS

INTRODUCTION

Once upon a time—between 1939 and 1943, to be precise—there was a very special magazine. Originally it was called *Unknown,* later *Unknown Worlds.* Either way, it was the first, if not the only, fantasy magazine whose direct ancestor was a science fiction magazine. That unique parentage, blending the subject matter of traditional fantasy and the rational attitudes of modern science fiction, gave *Unknown* a most distinctive, highly individual flavor. True, some of the characters roaming its pages were gods or genies, werewolves or witches, demons or dryads. But the world in which they did their things, more often than not, was not some fairy-tale kingdom in a hazy time that never was, but the everyday world the magazine's twentieth-century readers lived in, with all the logical and illogical constraints, trials, and tribulations that come with that territory. Only in *Unknown* would you find gnomes being unionized, or the ultimate showdown between Good and Evil happening in Cincinnati, Ohio.

Sometimes those stories were light and zany, sometimes dark and sinister, but always they were entertaining. That was editor John W. Campbell's avowed One Absolute Requirement for *Unknown,* and most of the readers it attracted during its brief life would agree that it met that goal in a uniquely refreshing, imagination-tickling way. Unfortunately, it was unable to survive the wartime paper shortage, so many readers today have never seen a copy—though they may well have heard of it. If you are one of the lucky few who knew *Unknown* in its first incarnation, this book offers you a chance to renew an old friendship. If you're one of the younger ones encountering *Unknown* for the first time, it offers an introduction to something new, fun, and no longer generally available. Either way, I think you're going to enjoy these stories.

Stanley Schmidt

H. L. GOLD

Trouble With Water

Greenberg did not deserve his surroundings. He was the first fisherman of the season, which guaranteed him a fine catch; he sat in a dry boat—one without a single leak—far out on a lake that was ruffled only enough to agitate his artificial fly. The sun was warm, the air was cool; he sat comfortably on a cushion; he had brought a hearty lunch; and two bottles of beer hung over the stern in the cold water.

Any other man would have been soaked with joy to be fishing on such a splendid day. Normally, Greenberg himself would have been ecstatic, but instead of relaxing and waiting for a nibble, he was plagued by worries.

This short, slightly gross, definitely bald, eminently respectable businessman lived a gypsy life. During the summer he lived in a hotel with kitchen privileges in Rockaway; winters he lived in a hotel with kitchen privileges in Florida; and in both places he operated concessions. For years now, rain had fallen on schedule every week end, and there had been storms and floods on Decoration Day, July 4th and Labor Day. He did not love his life, but it was a way of making a living.

He closed his eyes and groaned. If he had only had a son instead of his Rosie! Then things would have been mighty different—

For one thing, a son could run the hot dog and hamburger griddle, Esther could draw beer, and he would make soft drinks. There would be small difference in the profits, Greenberg admitted to himself; but at least those profits could be put aside for old age, instead of toward a dowry for his miserably ugly, dumpy, pitifully eager Rosie.

"All right—so what do I care if she don't get married?" he had cried to his wife a thousand times. "I'll support her. Other men can set up boys in candy stores with soda fountains that have only two spigots. Why should I have to give a boy a regular International Casino?"

"May your tongue rot in your head, you no-good piker!" she would scream. "It ain't right for a girl to be an old maid. If we have to die in the poor-house, I'll get my poor Rosie a husband. Every penny we don't need for living goes to her dowry!"

Greenberg did not hate his daughter, nor did he blame her for his misfortunes; yet, because of her, he was fishing with a broken rod that he had to tape together.

That morning his wife opened her eyes and saw him packing his equipment.

1

She instantly came awake. "Go ahead!" she shrilled—speaking in a conversational tone was not one of her accomplishments—"Go fishing, you loafer! Leave me here alone. I can connect the beer pipes and the gas for soda water. I can buy ice cream, frankfurters, rolls, sirup, and watch the gas and electric men at the same time. Go ahead—go fishing!"

"I ordered everything," he mumbled soothingly. "The gas and electric won't be turned on today. I only wanted to go fishing—it's my last chance. Tomorrow we open the concession. Tell the truth, Esther, can I go fishing after we open?"

"I don't care about that. Am I your wife or ain't I, that you should go ordering everything without asking me—"

He defended his actions. It was a tactical mistake. While she was still in bed, he should have picked up his equipment and left. By the time the argument got around to Rosie's dowry, she stood facing him.

"For myself I don't care," she yelled. "What kind of a monster are you that you can go fishing while your daughter eats her heart out? And on a day like this yet! You should only have to make supper and dress Rosie up. A lot you care that a nice boy is coming to supper tonight and maybe take Rosie out, you no-good father, you!"

From that point it was only one hot protest and a shrill curse to find himself clutching half a broken rod, with the other half being flung at his head.

Now he sat in his beautifully dry boat on an excellent game lake far out on Long Island, desperately aware that any average fish might collapse his taped rod.

What else could he expect? He had missed his train; he had had to wait for the boathouse proprietor; his favorite dry fly was missing; and, since morning, not a fish struck at the bait. Not a single fish!

And it was getting late. He had no more patience. He ripped the cap off a bottle of beer and drank it, in order to gain courage to change his fly for a less sporting bloodworm. It hurt him, but he wanted a fish.

The hook and the squirming worm sank. Before it came to rest, he felt a nibble. He sucked in his breath exultantly and snapped the hook deep into the fish's mouth. Sometimes, he thought philosophically, they just won't take artificial bait. He reeled in slowly.

"Oh, Lord," he prayed, "a dollar for charity—just don't let the rod bend in half where I taped it!"

It was sagging dangerously. He looked at it unhappily and raised his ante to five dollars; even at that price it looked impossible. He dipped his rod into the water, parallel with the line, to remove the strain. He was glad no one could see him do it. The line reeled in without a fight.

"Have I—God forbid!—got an eel or something not kosher?" he mumbled. "A plague on you—why don't you fight?"

He did not really care what it was—even an eel—anything at all.

He pulled in a long, pointed, brimless green hat.

For a moment he glared at it. His mouth hardened. Then, viciously, he yanked the hat off the hook, threw it on the floor and trampled on it. He rubbed his hands together in anguish.

"All day I fish," he wailed, "two dollars for train fare, a dollar for a boat, a quarter for bait, a new rod I got to buy—and a five-dollar-mortgage charity has got on me. For what? For you, you hat, you!"

Out in the water an extremely civil voice asked politely: "May I have my hat, please?"

Greenberg glowered up. He saw a little man come swimming vigorously through the water toward him: small arms crossed with enormous dignity, vast ears on a pointed face propelling him quite rapidly and efficiently. With serious determination he drove through the water, and, at the starboard rail, his amazing ears kept him stationary while he looked gravely at Greenberg.

"You are stamping on my hat," he pointed out without anger.

To Greenberg this was highly unimportant. "With the ears you're swimming," he grinned in a superior way. "Do you look funny!"

"How else could I swim?" the little man asked politely.

"With the arms and legs, like a regular human being, of course."

"But I am not a human being. I am a water gnome, a relative of the more common mining gnome. I cannot swim with my arms, because they must be crossed to give an appearance of dignity suitable to a water gnome; and my feet are used for writing and holding things. On the other hand, my ears are perfectly adapted for propulsion in water. Consequently, I employ them for that purpose. But please, my hat—there are several matters requiring my immediate attention, and I must not waste time."

Greenberg's unpleasant attitude toward the remarkably civil gnome is easily understandable. He had found someone he could feel superior to, and, by insulting him, his depressed ego could expand. The water gnome certainly looked inoffensive enough, being only two feet tall.

"What you got that's so important to do, Big Ears?" he asked nastily.

Greenberg hoped the gnome would be offended. He was not, since his ears, to him, were perfectly normal, just as you would not be insulted if a member of a race of atrophied beings were to call you "Big Muscles." You might even feel flattered.

"I really must hurry," the gnome said, almost anxiously. "But if I have to answer your questions in order to get back my hat—we are engaged in restocking the Eastern waters with fish. Last year there was quite a drain. The bureau of fisheries is coöperating with us to some extent, but, of course, we cannot depend too much on them. Until the population rises to normal, every fish has instructions not to nibble."

Greenberg allowed himself to smile, an annoyingly skeptical smile.

"My main work," the gnome went on resignedly, "is control of the rainfall over the Eastern seaboard. Our fact-finding committee, which is scientifically situated in the meteorological center of the continent, coördinates the rainfall needs of the entire continent; and when they determine the amount of rain needed in particular spots of the East, I make it rain to that extent. Now may I have my hat, please?"

Greenberg laughed coarsely. "The first lie was big enough—about telling the fish not to bite. You make it rain like I'm President of the United States!'' He bent toward the gnome slyly. ''How's about proof?''

''Certainly, if you insist.'' The gnome raised his patient, triangular face toward a particularly clear blue spot in the sky, a trifle to one side of Greenberg. ''Watch that bit of the sky.''

Greenberg looked up humorously. Even when a small dark cloud rapidly formed in the previously clear spot, his grin remained broad. It could have been coincidental. But then large drops of undeniable rain fell over a twenty-foot circle; and Greenberg's mocking grin shrank and grew sour.

He glared hatred at the gnome, finally convinced. ''So you're the dirty crook who makes it rain on week ends!''

''Usually on week ends during the summer,'' the gnome admitted. ''Ninety-two percent of water consumption is on weekdays. Obviously we must replace that water. The week ends, of course, are the logical time.''

''But, you thief!'' Greenberg cried hysterically, ''you murderer! What do you care what you do to my concession with your rain? It ain't bad enough business would be rotten even without rain, you got to make floods!''

''I'm sorry,'' the gnome replied, untouched by Greenberg's rhetoric. ''We do not create rainfall for the benefit of men. We are here to protect the fish.

''Now please give me my hat. I have wasted enough time, when I should be preparing the extremely heavy rain needed for this coming week end.''

Greenberg jumped to his feet in the unsteady boat. ''Rain this week end—when I can maybe make a profit for a change! A lot you care if you ruin business. May you and your fish die a horrible, lingering death.''

And he furiously ripped the green hat to pieces and hurled them at the gnome.

''I'm really sorry you did that,'' the little fellow said calmly, his huge ears treading water without the slightest increase of pace to indicate his anger. ''We Little Folk have no tempers to lose. Nevertheless, occasionally we find it necessary to discipline certain of your people, in order to retain our dignity. I am not malignant; but, since you hate water and those who live in it, water and those who live in it will keep away from you.''

With his arms still folded in great dignity, the tiny water gnome flipped his vast ears and disappeared in a neat surface dive.

Greenberg glowered at the spreading circles of waves. He did not grasp the gnome's final restraining order; he did not even attempt to interpret it. Instead he glared angrily out of the corner of his eye at the phenomenal circle of rain that fell from a perfectly clear sky. The gnome must have remembered it at length, for a moment later the rain stopped. Like shutting off a faucet, Greenberg unwillingly thought.

''Good-by, week-end business,'' he growled. ''If Esther finds out I got into an argument with the guy who makes it rain—''

He made an underhand cast, hoping for just one fish. The line flew out over the water; then the hook arched upward and came to rest several inches above the surface, hanging quite steadily and without support in the air.

''Well, go down in the water, damn you!'' Greenberg said viciously, and he swished his rod back and forth to pull the hook down from its ridiculous levitation. It refused.

Muttering something incoherent about being hanged before he'd give in, Greenberg hurled his useless rod at the water. By this time he was not surprised when it hovered in the air above the lake. He merely glanced red-eyed at it, tossed out the remains of the gnome's hat, and snatched up the oars.

When he pulled back on them to row to land, they did not touch the water—naturally. Instead they flashed unimpeded through the air, and Greenberg tumbled into the bow.

"A-ha!" he grated. "Here's where the trouble begins." He bent over the side. As he had suspected, the keel floated a remarkable distance above the lake.

By rowing against the air, he moved with maddening slowness toward shore, like a medieval conception of a flying machine. His main concern was that no one should see him in his humiliating position.

At the hotel he tried to sneak past the kitchen to the bathroom. He knew that Esther waited to curse him for fishing the day before opening, but more especially on the very day that a nice boy was coming to see her Rosie. If he could dress in a hurry, she might have less to say—

"Oh, there you are, you good-for-nothing!"

He froze to a halt.

"Look at you!" she screamed shrilly. "Filthy—you stink from fish!"

"I didn't catch anything, darling," he protested timidly.

"You stink anyhow. Go take a bath, may you drown in it! Get dressed in two minutes or less, and entertain the boy when he gets here. Hurry!"

He locked himself in, happy to escape her voice, started the water in the tub, and stripped from the waist up. A hot bath, he hoped, would rid him of his depressed feeling.

First, no fish; now, rain on week ends! What would Esther say—if she knew, of course. And, of course, he would not tell her.

"Let myself in for a lifetime of curses!" he sneered. "Ha!"

He clamped a new blade into his razor, opened the tube of shaving cream, and stared objectively at the mirror. The dominant feature of the soft, chubby face that stared back was its ugly black stubble; but he set his stubborn chin and glowered. He really looked quite fierce and indomitable. Unfortunately, Esther never saw his face in that uncharacteristic pose, otherwise she would speak more softly.

"Herman Greenberg never gives in!" he whispered between savagely hardened lips. "Rain on week ends, no fish—anything he wants; a lot I care! Believe me, he'll come crawling to me before I go to him."

He gradually became aware that his shaving brush was not getting wet. When he looked down and saw the water dividing into streams that flowed around it, his determined face slipped and grew desperately anxious. He tried to trap the water—by catching it in his cupped hands, by creeping up on it from behind, as if it were some shy animal, and shoving his brush at it—but it broke and ran away from his touch. Then he jammed his palm against the faucet. Defeated, he heard it gurgle back down the pipe, probably as far as the main.

"What do I do now?" he groaned. "Will Esther give it to me if I don't take a shave! But how? . . . I can't shave without water."

Glumly, he shut off the bath, undressed and stepped into the tub. He lay down to soak. It took a moment of horrified stupor to realize that he was completely dry and that he lay in a waterless bathtub. The water, in one surge of revulsion, had swept out onto the floor.

"Herman, stop splashing!" his wife yelled. "I just washed the floor. If I find one little puddle I'll murder you!"

Greenberg surveyed the instep-deep pool over the bathroom floor. "Yes, my love," he croaked unhappily.

With an inadequate washrag he chased the elusive water, hoping to mop it all up before it could seep through to the apartment below. His washrag remained dry, however, and he knew that the ceiling underneath was dripping. The water was still on the floor.

In despair, he sat on the edge of the bathtub. For some time he sat in silence. Then his wife banged on the door, urging him to come out. He started and dressed moodily.

When he sneaked out and shut the bathroom door tightly on the flood inside, he was extremely dirty and his face *was* raw where he had experimentally attempted to shave with a dry razor.

"Rosie!" he called in a hoarse whisper. "Sh! Where's mamma?"

His daughter sat on the studio couch and applied nail-polish to her stubby fingers. "You look terrible," she said in a conversational tone. "Aren't you going to shave?"

He recoiled at the sound of her voice, which, to him, roared out like a siren. "Quiet, Rosie! Sh!" And for further emphasis, he shoved his lips out against a warning finger. He heard his wife striding heavily around the kitchen. "Rosie," he cooed, "I'll give you a dollar if you'll mop up the water I spilled in the bathroom."

"I can't papa," she stated firmly. "I'm all dressed."

"Two dollars, Rosie—all right, two and a half, you blackmailer."

He flinched when he heard her gasp in the bathroom; but, when she came out with soaked shoes, he fled downstairs. He wandered aimlessly toward the village.

Now he was in for it, he thought; screams from Esther, tears from Rosie—plus a new pair of shoes for Rosie and two and a half dollars. It would be worse, though, if he could not get rid of his whiskers—

Rubbing the tender spots where his dry razor had raked his face, he mused blankly at a drugstore window. He saw nothing to help him, but he went inside anyhow and stood hopefully at the drug counter. A face peered at him through a space scratched in the wall case mirror, and the druggist came out. A nice-looking, intelligent fellow, Greenberg saw at a glance.

"What you got for shaving that I can use without water?" he asked.

"Skin irritation, eh?" the pharmacist replied. "I got something very good for that."

"No. It's just— Well, I don't like to shave with water."

The druggist seemed disappointed. "Well, I got brushless shaving cream." Then he brightened. "But I got an electric razor—much better."

"How much?" Greenberg asked cautiously.

"Only fifteen dollars, and it lasts a lifetime."

"Give me the shaving cream," Greenberg said coldly.

With the tactical science of a military expert, he walked around until some time after dark. Only then did he go back to the hotel, to wait outside. It was after seven, he was getting hungry, and the people who entered the hotel he knew as permanent summer guests. At last a stranger passed him and ran up the stairs.

Greenberg hesitated for a moment. The stranger was scarcely a boy, as Esther had definitely termed him, but Greenberg reasoned that her term was merely wish-fulfillment, and he jauntily ran up behind him.

He allowed a few minutes to pass, for the man to introduce himself and let Esther and Rosie don their company manners. Then, secure in the knowledge that there would be no scene until the guest left, he entered.

He waded through a hostile atmosphere, urbanely shook hands with Sammie Katz, who was a doctor—probably, Greenberg thought shrewdly, in search of an office—and excused himself.

In the bathroom he carefully read the direction for using brushless shaving cream. He felt less confident when he realized that he had to wash his face thoroughly with soap and water, but without benefit of either, he spread the cream on, patted it, and waited for his beard to soften. It did not, as he discovered while shaving. He wiped his face dry. The towel was sticky and black, with whiskers suspended in paste, and, for that, he knew, there would be more hell to pay. He shrugged resignedly. He would have to spend fifteen dollars for an electric razor after all; this foolishness was costing him a fortune!

That they were waiting for him before beginning supper, was, he knew, only a gesture for the sake of company. Without changing her hard, brilliant smile, Esther whispered: "Wait! I'll get you later—"

He smiled back, his tortured, slashed face creasing painfully. All that could be changed by his being enormously pleasant to Rosie's young man. If he could slip Sammie a few dollars—more expense, he groaned—to take Rosie out, Esther would forgive everything.

He was too engaged in beaming and putting Sammie at ease to think of what would happen after he ate caviar canapes. Under other circumstances Greenberg would have been repulsed by Sammie's ultra-professional waxed mustache—an offensively small, pointed thing—and his commercial attitude toward poor Rosie; but Greenberg regarded him as a potential savior.

"You open an office yet, Doctor Katz?"

"Not yet. You know how things are. Anyhow, call me Sammie."

Greenberg recognized the gambit with satisfaction, since it seemed to please Esther so much. At one stroke Sammie had ingratiated himself and begun bargaining negotiations.

Without another word, Greenberg lifted his spoon to attack the soup. It would be easy to snare this eager doctor. A *doctor!* No wonder Esther and Rosie were so puffed with joy.

In the proper company way, he pushed his spoon away from him. The soup spilled onto the tablecloth.

"Not so hard, you dope," Esther hissed.

He drew the spoon toward him. The soup leaned off it like a live thing and splashed over him—turning, just before contact, to fall on the floor. He gulped and pushed the bowl away. This time the soup poured over the side of the plate and lay in a huge puddle on the table.

"I didn't want any soup anyhow," he said in a horrible attempt at levity. Lucky for him, he thought wildly, that Sammie was there to pacify Esther with his smooth college talk—not a bad fellow, Sammie, in spite of his mustache; he'd come in handy at times.

Greenberg lapsed into a paralysis of fear. He was thirsty after having eaten the caviar, which beats herring any time as a thirst raiser. But the knowledge that he could not touch water without having it recoil and perhaps spill, made his thirst a monumental raving. He attacked the problem cunningly.

The others were talking rapidly and rather hysterically. He waited until his courage was equal to his thirst; then he leaned over the table with a glass in his hand. "Sammie, do you mind—a little water, huh?"

Sammie poured from a pitcher while Esther watched for more of his tricks. It was to be expected, but still he was shocked when the water exploded out of the glass directly at Sammie's only suit.

"If you'll excuse me," Sammie said angrily, "I don't like to eat with lunatics."

And he left, though Esther cried and begged him to stay. Rosie was too stunned to move. But when the door closed, Greenberg raised his agonized eyes to watch his wife stalk murderously toward him.

Greenberg stood on the boardwalk outside his concession and glared blearily at the peaceful, blue, highly unpleasant ocean. He wondered what would happen if he started at the edge of the water and strode out. He could probably walk right to Europe on dry land.

It was early—much too early for business—and he was tired. Neither he nor Esther had slept; and it was practically certain that the neighbors hadn't either. But above all he was incredibly thirsty.

In a spirit of experimentation, he mixed a soda. Of course its high water content made it slop onto the floor. For breakfast he had surreptitiously tried fruit juice and coffee, without success.

With his tongue dry to the point of furriness, he sat weakly on a boardwalk bench in front of his concession. It was Friday morning, which meant that the day was clear, with a promise of intense heat. Had it been Saturday, it naturally would have been raining.

"This year," he moaned, "I'll be wiped out. If I can't mix sodas, why should beer stay in a glass for me? I thought I could hire a boy for ten dollars a week to run the hot-dog griddle; I could make sodas, and Esther could draw beer. All I can do is make hot dogs, Esther can still draw beer; but twenty or maybe twenty-five a week I got to pay a sodaman. I won't even come out square—a fortune I'll lose!"

The situation really was desperate. Concessions depend on too many factors to be anything but capriciously profitable.

His throat was fiery and his soft brown eyes held a fierce glaze when the gas and electric were turned on, the beer pipes connected, the tank of carbon dioxide hitched to the pump, and the refrigerator started.

Gradually, the beach was filling with bathers. Greenberg writhed on his bench and envied them. They could swim and drink without having liquids draw away from them as if in horror. They were not thirsty—

And then he saw his first customers approach. His business experience was that morning customers buy only soft drinks. In a mad haste he put up the shutters and fled to the hotel.

"Esther!" he cried. "I got to tell you! I can't stand it—"

Threateningly, his wife held her broom like a baseball bat. "Go back to the concession, you crazy fool. Ain't you done enough already?"

He could not be hurt more than he had been. For once he did not cringe. "You got to help me, Esther."

"Why didn't you shave, you no-good bum? Is that any way—"

"That's what I got to tell you. Yesterday I got into an argument with a water gnome—"

"A what?" Esther looked at him suspiciously.

"A water gnome," he babbled in a rush of words. "A little man so high, with big ears that he swims with, and he makes it rain—"

"Herman!" she screamed. "Stop that nonsense. You're crazy!"

Greenberg pounded his forehead with his fist. "I *ain't* crazy. Look, Esther. Come with me into the kitchen."

She followed him readily enough, but her attitude made him feel more helpless and alone than ever. With her fists on her plump hips and her feet set wide, she cautiously watched him try to fill a glass of water.

"Don't you see?" he wailed. "It won't go in the glass. It spills over. It runs away from me."

She was puzzled. "What happened to you?"

Brokenly, Greenberg told of his encounter with the water gnome, leaving out no single degrading detail. "And now I can't touch water," he ended. "I can't drink it. I can't make sodas. On top of it all, I got such a thirst, it's killing me."

Esther's reaction was instantaneous. She threw her arms around him, drew his head down to her shoulder, and patted him comfortingly as if he were a child. "Herman, my poor Herman!" she breathed tenderly. "What did we ever do to deserve such a curse?"

"What shall I do, Esther?" he cried helplessly.

She held him at arm's length. "You got to go to a doctor," she said firmly.

"How long can you go without drinking? Without water you'll die. Maybe sometimes I am a little hard on you, but you know I love you—"

"I know, mamma," he sighed. "But how can a doctor help me?"

"Am I a doctor that I should know? Go anyhow. What can you lose?"

He hesitated. "I need fifteen dollars for an electric razor," he said in a low, weak voice.

"So?" she replied. "If you got to, you got to. Go, darling. I'll take care of the concession."

Greenberg no longer felt deserted and alone. He walked almost confidently to a doctor's office. Manfully, he explained his symptoms. The doctor listened with professional sympathy, until Greenberg reached his description of the water gnome.

Then his eyes glittered and narrowed. "I know just the thing for you, Mr. Greenberg," he interrupted. "Sit there until I come back."

Greenberg sat quietly. He even permitted himself a surge of hope. But it seemed only a moment later that he was vaguely conscious of a siren screaming toward him; and then he was overwhelmed by the doctor and two internes who pounced on him and tried to squeeze him into a bag.

He resisted, of course, He was terrified enough to punch wildly. "What are you doing to me?" he shrieked. "Don't put that thing on me!"

"Easy now," the doctor soothed. "Everything will be all right."

It was on that humiliating scene that the policeman, required by law to accompany public ambulances, appeared. "What's up?" he asked.

"Don't stand there, you fathead," an interne shouted. "This man's crazy. Help us get him into this strait jacket."

But the policeman approached indecisively. "Take it easy, Mr. Greenberg. They ain't gonna hurt you while I'm here. What's it all about?"

"Mike!" Greenberg cried, and clung to his protector's sleeve. "They think I'm crazy—"

"Of course he's crazy," the doctor stated. "He came in here with a fantastic yarn about a water gnome putting a curse on him."

"What kind of a curse, Mr. Greenberg?" Mike asked cautiously.

"I got into an argument with the water gnome who makes it rain and takes care of the fish," Greenberg blurted. "I tore up his hat. Now he won't let water touch me. I can't drink, or anything—"

The doctor nodded. "There you are. Absolutely insane."

"Shut up." For a long moment Mike stared curiously at Greenberg. Then: "Did any of you scientists think of testing him? Here, Mr. Greenberg." He poured water into a paper cup and held it out.

Greenberg moved to take it. The water back up against the cup's far lip; when he took it in his hand, the water shot out into the air.

"Crazy, is he?" Mike asked with heavy irony. "I guess you don't know there's things like gnomes and elves. Come with me, Mr. Greenberg."

They went out together and walked toward the boardwalk. Greenberg told Mike the entire story and explained how, besides being so uncomfortable to him personally, it would ruin him financially.

"Well, doctors can't help you," Mike said at length. "What do they know about the Little Folk? And I can't say I blame you for sassing the gnome. You ain't Irish or you'd have spoke with more respect to him. Anyhow, you're thirsty. Can't you drink *anything?*"

"Not a thing," Greenberg said mournfully.

They entered the concession. A single glance told Greenberg that business was very quiet, but even that could not lower his feelings more than they already were. Esther clutched him as soon as she saw them.

"Well?" she asked anxiously.

Greenberg shrugged in despair. "Nothing. He thought I was crazy."

Mike stared at the bar. Memory seemed to struggle behind his reflective eyes. "Sure," he said after a long pause. "Did you try beer, Mr. Greenberg? When I was a boy my old mother told me all about elves and gnomes and the rest of the Little Folk. She knew them, all right. They don't touch alcohol, you know. Try drawing a glass of beer—"

Greenberg trudged obediently behind the bar and held a glass under the spigot. Suddenly his despondent face brightened. Beer creamed into the glass—and stayed there! Mike and Esther grinned at each other as Greenberg threw back his head and furiously drank.

"Mike!" he crowed. "I'm saved. You got to drink with me!"

"Well—" Mike protested feebly.

By late afternoon, Esther had to close the concession and take her husband and Mike to the hotel.

The following day, being Saturday, brought a flood of rain. Greenberg nursed an imposing hang-over that was constantly aggravated by his having to drink beer in order to satisfy his recurring thirst. He thought of forbidden icebags and alkaline drinks in an agony of longing.

"I can't stand it!" he groaned. "Beer for breakfast—phooey!"

"It's better than nothing," Esther said fatalistically.

"So help me, I don't know if it is. But, darling, you ain't mad at me on account of Sammie, are you?"

She smiled gently, "Poo! Talk dowry and he'll come back quick."

"That's what I thought. But what am I going to do about my curse?"

Cheerfully, Mike furled an umbrella and strode in with a little old woman, whom he introduced as his mother. Greenberg enviously saw evidence of the effectiveness of icebags and alkaline drinks, for Mike had been just as high as he the day before.

"Mike told me about you and the gnome," the old lady said. "Now I know the Little Folk well, and I don't hold you to blame for insulting him, seeing you never met a gnome before. But I suppose you want to get rid of your curse. Are you repentant?"

Greenberg shuddered. "Beer for breakfast! Can you ask?"

"Well, just you go to this lake and give the gnome proof."

"What kind of proof?" Greenberg asked eagerly.

"Bring him sugar. The Little Folk love the stuff—"

Greenberg beamed. "Did you hear that, Esther? I'll get a barrel—"

"They love sugar, but they can't eat it," the old lady broke in. "It melts in water. You got to figure out a way so it won't. Then the little gentleman'll know you're repentant for real."

"A-ha!" Greenberg cried. "I knew there was a catch!"

There was a sympathetic silence while his agitated mind attacked the problem from all angles. Then the old lady said in awe: "The minute I saw your place I knew Mike had told the truth. I never seen a sight like it in my life—rain coming down, like the flood, everywhere else; but all around this place, in a big circle, it's dry as a bone!"

While Greenberg scarcely heard her, Mike nodded and Esther seemed peculiarly interested in the phenomenon. When he admitted defeat and came out of his reflected stupor, he was alone in the concession, with only a vague memory of Esther's saying she would not be back for several hours.

"What am I going to do?" he muttered. "Sugar that won't melt—" He drew a glass of beer and drank it thoughtfully. "Particular they got to be yet. Ain't it good enough if I bring simple sirup—that's sweet."

He pottered about the place, looking for something to do. He could not polish the fountain on the bar, and the few frankfurters boiling on the griddle probably would go to waste. The floor had already been swept. So he sat uneasily and worried his problem.

"Monday, no matter what," he resolved, "I'll go to the lake. It don't pay to go tomorrow. I'll only catch a cold because it'll rain."

At last Esther returned, smiling in a strange way. She was extremely gentle, tender and thoughtful; and for that he was appreciative. But that night and all day Sunday he understood the reason for her happiness.

She had spread word that, while it rained in every other place all over town, their concession was miraculously dry. So, besides a headache that made his body throb in rhythm to its vast pulse, Greenberg had to work like six men satisfying the crowd who mobbed the place to see the miracle and enjoy the dry warmth.

How much they took in will never be known. Greenberg made it a practice not to discuss such personal matters. But it is quite definite that not even in 1929 had he done so well over a single week end.

Very early Monday morning he was dressing quietly, not to disturb his wife. Esther, however, raised herself on her elbow and looked at him doubtfully.

"Herman," she called softly, "do you really have to go?"

He turned, puzzled. "What do you mean—do I have to go?"

"Well—" She hesitated. Then: "Couldn't you wait until the end of the season, Herman, darling?"

He staggered back a step, his face working in horror. "What kind of an idea is that for my own wife to have?" he croaked. "Beer I have to drink instead of water. How can I stand it? Do you think I *like* beer? I can't wash myself. Already people don't like to stand near me; and how will they act at the end of the season? I go around looking like a bum because my beard is too tough for an electric razor, and I'm all the time drunk—the first Greenberg to be a drunkard. I want to be respected—''

"I know, Herman, darling," she sighed. "But I thought for the sake of our Rosie— Such a business we've never done like we did this week end. If it rains every Saturday and Sunday, but not on our concession, we'll make a *fortune!*''

"Esther!" Herman cried, shocked. "Doesn't my health mean anything?"

"Of course, darling. Only I thought maybe you could stand it for—"

He snatched his hat, tie and jacket, and slammed the door. Outside, though, he stood indeterminedly. He could hear his wife crying, and he realized that, if he succeeded in getting the gnome to remove the curse, he would forfeit an opportunity to make a great deal of money.

He finished dressing more slowly. Esther was right, to a certain extent. If he could tolerate his waterless condition—

"No!" he gritted decisively. "Already my friends avoid me. It isn't right that a respectable man like me should always be drunk and not take a bath. So we'll make less money. Money isn't everything—"

And with great determination he went to the lake.

But that evening, before going home, Mike walked out of his way to stop in at the concession. He found Greenberg sitting on a chair, his head in his hands, and his body rocking slowly in anguish.

"What is it, Mr. Greenberg?" he asked gently.

Greenberg looked up. His eyes were dazed. "Oh, you, Mike," he said blankly. Then his gaze cleared, grew more intelligent, and he stood up and led Mike to the bar. Silently, they drank beer. "I went to the lake today," he said hollowly. "I walked all around it hollering like mad. The gnome didn't stick his head out of the water once."

"I know," Mike nodded sadly. "They're busy all the time."

Greenberg spread his hands imploringly. "So what can I do? I can't write him a letter or send him a telegram; he ain't got a door to knock on or a bell for me to ring. How do I get him to come up and talk?"

His shoulders sagged. "Here, Mike. Have a cigar. You been a real good friend, but I guess we're licked."

They stood in an awkward silence. Finally Mike blurted: "Real hot, today. A regular scorcher."

"Yeah. Esther says business was pretty good, if it keeps up."

Mike fumbled at the Cellophane wrapper. Greenberg said: "Anyhow, suppose I did talk to the gnome. What about the sugar?"

The silence dragged itself out, became tense and uncomfortable. Mike was distinctly embarrassed. His brusque nature was not adapted for comforting discouraged friends. With immense concentration he rolled the cigar between his fingers and listened for a rustle.

"Day like this's hell on cigars," he mumbled, for the sake of conversation. "Dries them like nobody's business. This one ain't, though."

"Yeah," Greenberg said abstractedly. "Cellophane keeps them—"

They looked suddenly at each other, their faces clean of expression.

"Holy smoke!" Mike yelled.

"Cellophane on sugar!" Greenberg choked out.

"Yeah," Mike whispered in awe. "I'll switch my day off with Joe, and I'll go to the lake with you tomorrow. I'll call for you early."

Greenberg pressed his hand, too strangled by emotion for speech. When Esther came to relieve him, he left her at the concession with only the inexperienced griddle boy to assist her, while he searched the village for cubes of sugar wrapped in Cellophane.

The sun had scarcely risen when Mike reached the hotel, but Greenberg had long been dressed and stood on the porch waiting impatiently. Mike was genuinely anxious for his friend. Greenberg staggered along toward the station, his eyes almost crossed with the pain of a terrific hang-over.

They stopped at a cafeteria for breakfast. Mike ordered orange juice, bacon and eggs, and coffee half-and-half. When he heard the order, Greenberg had to gag down a lump in his throat.

"What'll you have?" the counterman asked.

Greenberg flushed. "Beer," he said hoarsely.

"You kidding me?" Greenberg shook his head, unable to speak. "Want anything with it? Cereal, pie, toast—"

"Just beer." And he forced himself to swallow it. "So help me," he hissed at Mike, "another beer for breakfast will kill me!"

"I know how it is," Mike said around a mouthful of food.

On the train they attempted to make plans. But they were faced by a phenomenon that neither had encountered before, and so they got nowhere. They walked glumly to the lake, fully aware that they would have to employ the empirical method of discarding tactics that did not work.

"How about a boat?" Mike suggested.

"It won't stay in the water with me in it. And you can't row it."

"Well, what'll we do then?"

Greenberg bit his lip and stared at the beautiful blue lake. There the gnome lived, so near to them. "Go through the woods along the shore, and holler like hell. I'll go the opposite way. We'll pass each other and meet at the boathouse. If the gnome comes up, yell for me."

"O. K.," Mike said, not very confidently.

The lake was quite large and they walked slowly around it, pausing often to get the proper stance for particularly emphatic shouts. But two hours later, when they stood opposite each other with the full diameter of the lake between them, Greenberg heard Mike's hoarse voice: "Hey, gnome!"

"Hey, gnome!" Greenberg yelled. "Come on up!"

An hour later they crossed paths. They were tired, discouraged, and their throats burned; and only fishermen disturbed the lake's surface.

"The hell with this," Mike said. "It ain't doing any good. Let's go back to the boathouse."

"What'll we do?" Greenberg rasped. "I can't give up!"

They trudged back around the lake, shouting half-heartedly. At the boathouse, Greenberg had to admit that he was beaten. The boathouse owner marched threateningly toward him.

"Why don't you maniacs get away from here?" he barked. "What's the idea of hollering and scaring away the fish? The guys are sore—"

"We're not going to holler any more," Greenberg said. "It's no use."

When they bought beer and Mike, on an impulse, hired a boat, the owner cooled off with amazing rapidity, and went off to unpack bait.

"What did you get a boat for?" Greenberg asked. "I can't ride in it."

"You're not going to. You're gonna walk."

"Around the lake again?" Greenberg cried.

"Nope. Look, Mr. Greenberg. Maybe the gnome can't hear us through all that water. Gnomes ain't hardhearted. If he heard us and thought you were sorry, he'd take his curse off you in a jiffy."

"Maybe." Greenberg was not convinced. "So where do I come in?"

"The way I figure it, some way or other you push water away, but the water pushes you away just as hard. Anyhow, I hope so. If it does, you can walk on the lake." As he spoke, Mike had been lifting large stones and dumping them on the bottom of the boat. "Give me a hand with these."

Any activity, however useless, was better than none, Greenberg felt. He helped Mike fill the boat until just the gunwales were above water. Then Mike got in and shoved off.

"Come on," Mike said. "Try to walk on the water."

Greenberg hesitated. "Suppose I can't?"

"Nothing'll happen to you. You can't get wet; so you won't drown."

The logic of Mike's statement reassured Greenberg. He stepped out boldly. He experienced a peculiar sense of accomplishment when the water hastily retreated under his feet into pressure bowls, and an unseen, powerful force buoyed him upright across the lake's surface. Though his footing was not too secure, with care he was able to walk quite swiftly.

"Now what?" he asked, almost happily.

Mike had kept pace with him in the boat. He shipped his oars and passed Greenberg a rock. "We'll drop them all over the lake—make it damned noisy down there and upset the place. That'll get him up."

They were more hopeful now, and their comments, "Here's one that'll wake him," and "I'll hit him right on the noodle with this one," served to cheer them still further. And less than half the rocks had been dropped when Greenberg halted, a boulder in his hands. Something inside him wrapped itself tightly around his heart and his jaw dropped.

Mike followed his awed, joyful gaze. To himself, Mike had to admit that the gnome, propelling himself through the water with his ears, arms folded in tremendous dignity, was a funny sight.

"Must you drop rocks and disturb us at our work?" the gnome asked.

Greenberg gulped. "I'm sorry, Mr. Gnome," he said nervously. "I couldn't get you to come up by yelling."

The gnome looked at him. "Oh. You are the mortal who was disciplined. Why did you return?"

"To tell you that I'm sorry, and I won't insult you again."

"Have you proof of your sincerity?" the gnome asked quietly.

Greenberg fished furiously in his pocket and brought out a handful of sugar wrapped in Cellophane, which he tremblingly handed to the gnome.

"Ah, very clever, indeed," the little man said, unwrapping a cube and popping it eagerly into his mouth. "Long time since I've had some."

A moment later Greenberg spluttered and floundered under the surface. Even if Mike had not caught his jacket and helped him up, he could almost have enjoyed the sensation of being able to drown.

ROBERT BLOCH

The Cloak

SCENE: A hotel corridor.

OCCASION: A science fiction convention.

ANTHONY BOUCHER: . . . and when she was being admitted to the hospital they asked what her religion was and she said, "None." And they wrote down, "Protestant"!

WALTER BREEN: *Humph!* If they asked me what my religion was, I'd tell them "Druid"!

ROBERT BLOCH: Oh don't do that, they'd send you to a treesurgeon.

This is all 100% true and I was there and heard it; perhaps it may give you some notion of the Basic Bob Bloch: quick-witted, good-humored, and with a dash of wormwood. Attributed to him (I wasn't there) is a phrase now famous; when it was said that someone else had an unjustly bad name, when, really, after all, you know, "he has the heart of a small boy." Bloch said, "Yes, and he keeps it on his desk in a jar of formaldehyde"—thus settling that.

Born in 1917, Robert Bloch grew up in the wholesome heart of the upper Midwest, and, as for his own small boyhood, we rather assume it must have been over by the time he was seventeen, at which age he sold his first story to *Weird Tales*. But this is not it. Stories of his have been in four hundred anthologies in a dozen languages. He has written approximately fifty books, and has screen credits on at least ten films. He is the author of *Psycho*. Many awards. A flyer announcing his speaking appearance at the Third Annual Emory [University] Science Fiction and Fantasy Symposium included the significant line, *Tickets for Robert Bloch may be purchased separately*. . . . Robert and Eleanor Bloch live in Los Angeles.

The sun was dying, and its blood spattered the sky as it crept into a sepulcher behind the hills. The keening wind sent the dry, fallen leaves scurrying toward the west, as though hastening them to the funeral of the sun.

"Nuts!" said Henderson to himself, and stopped thinking.

The sun was setting in a dingy red sky, and a dirty raw wind was kicking up the half-rotten leaves in a filthy gutter. Why should he waste time with cheap imagery?

"Nuts!" said Henderson, again.

It was probably a mood evoked by the day, he mused. After all, this was the sunset of Halloween. Tonight was the dreaded All Hallows' Eve, when spirits walked in and skulls cried out from their graves beneath the earth.

Either that, or tonight was just another rotten cold fall day. Henderson sighed. There was a time, he reflected, when the coming of this night meant something. A dark Europe, groaning in superstitious fear, dedicated this Eve to the grinning Unknown. A million doors had once been barred against the evil visitants, a million prayers mumbled, a million candles lit. There was something majestic about the idea, Henderson reflected. Life had been an adventure in those times, and men walked in terror of what the next turn of a midnight road might bring. They had lived in a world of demons and ghouls and elementals who sought their souls— and by Heaven, in those days a man's soul meant something. This new skepticism had take a profound meaning away from life. Men no longer revered their souls.

"Nuts!" said Henderson again, quite automatically. There was something crude and twentieth-century about the coarse expression which always checked his introspective flights of fancy.

The voice in his brain that said "nuts" took the place of humanity to Henderson—common humanity which would echo the same sentiment upon hearing his secret thoughts. So now Henderson uttered the word and endeavored to forget problems and purple patches alike.

He was walking down the street at sunset to buy a costume for the masquerade party tonight, and he had much better concentrate on finding the costumer's before it closed than waste his time daydreaming about Halloween.

His eyes searched the darkening shadows of the dingy buildings lining the narrow thoroughfare. Once again he peered at the address he had scribbled down after finding it in the phone book.

Why the devil didn't they light up the shops when it got dark? He couldn't make out numbers. This was a poor, rundown neighborhood, but after all—

Abruptly, Henderson spied the place across the street and started over. He passed the window and glanced in. The last rays of the sun slanted over the top of the building across the wall and fell directly on the window and its display. Henderson drew a sharp intake of breath.

He was staring at a costumer's window—not looking through a fissure into hell. Then why was it all red fire, lighting the grinning visages of fiends?

"Sunset," Henderson muttered aloud. Of course it was, and the faces were merely clever masks such as would be displayed in this sort of place. Still, it gave the imaginative man a start. He opened the door and entered.

The place was dark and still. There was a smell of loneliness in the air—the smell that haunts all places long undisturbed; tombs, and graves in deep woods, and caverns in the earth, and—

"Nuts."

What the devil was wrong with him, anyway? Henderson smiled apologetically at the empty darkness. This was the smell of the costumer's shop, and it carried him back to college days of amateur theatricals. Henderson had known this smell of moth balls, decayed furs, grease paint and oils. He had played amateur Hamlet and in his hands he had held a smirking skull that hid all knowledge in its empty eyes—a skull, from the costumer's.

Well, here he was again, and the skull gave him the idea. After all, Halloween night it was. Certainly in this mood of his he didn't want to go as a rajah, or a Turk, or a pirate—they all did that. Why not go as a fiend, or a warlock, or a werewolf? He could see Lindstrom's face when he walked into the elegant penthouse wearing rags of some sort. The fellow would have a fit, with his society crowd wearing their expensive Elsa Maxwell take-offs. Henderson didn't greatly care for Lindstrom's sophisticated friends anyway; a gang of amateur Noel Cowards and horsy women wearing harnesses of jewels. Why not carry out the spirit of Halloween and go as a monster?

Henderson stood there in the dusk, waiting for someone to turn on the lights, come out from the back room and serve him. After a minute or so he grew impatient and rapped sharply on the counter.

"Say in there! Service!"

Silence. And a shuffling noise from the rear, then—an unpleasant noise to hear in the gloom. There was a banging from downstairs and then the heavy clump of footsteps. Suddenly Henderson gasped. A black hulk was rising from the floor!

It was, of course, only the opening of the trapdoor from the basement. A man shuffled behind the counter, carrying a lamp. In that light his eyes blinked drowsily.

The man's yellowish face crinkled into a smile.

"I was sleeping, I'm afraid," said the man softly. "Can I serve you, sir?"

"I was looking for a Halloween costume."

"Oh, yes. And what was it you had in mind?"

The voice was weary, infinitely weary. The eyes continued to blink in the flabby yellow face.

"Nothing usual, I'm afraid. You see, I rather fancied some sort of monster getup for a party—don't suppose you carry anything in that line?"

"I could show you masks."

"No. I meant werewolf outfits, something out of the sort. More of the authentic."

"So. The *authentic*."

"Yes." Why did this old dunce stress the word?

"I might—yes. I might have just the thing for you, sir." The eyes blinked, but the thin mouth pursed in a smile. "Just the thing for Halloween."

"What's that?"

"Have you ever considered the possibility of being a vampire?"

"Like Dracula?"

"Ah—yes, I suppose—Dracula."

"Not a bad idea. Do you think I'm the type for that, though?"

The man appraised him with the tight smile. "Vampires are of all types, I understand. You would do nicely."

"Hardly a compliment," Henderson chuckled. "But why not? What's the outfit?"

"Outfit? Merely evening clothes, or what you wear. I will furnish you with the authentic cloak."

"Just a cloak—is that all?"

"Just a cloak. But it is worn like a shroud. It *is* shroudcloth, you know. Wait, I'll get it for you."

The shuffling feet carried the man into the rear of the shop again. Down the trapdoor entrance he went, and Henderson waited. There was more banging, and presently the old man reappeared carrying the cloak. He was shaking dust from it in the darkness.

"Here it is—the genuine cloak."

"Genuine?"

"Allow me to adjust it for you—it will work wonders, I'm sure."

The cold, heavy cloth hung draped about Henderson's shoulders. The faint odor rose mustily in his nostrils as he stepped back and surveyed himself in the mirror. The lamp was poor, but Henderson saw that the cloak effected a striking transformation in his appearance. His long face seemed thinner, his eyes were accentuated in the facial pallor heightened by the somber cloak he wore. It was a big, black shroud.

"Genuine," murmured the old man. He must have come up suddenly, for Henderson hadn't noticed him in the glass.

"I'll take it," Henderson said. "How much?"

"You'll find it quite entertaining, I'm sure."

"How much?"

"Oh. Shall we say five dollars?"

"Here."

The old man took the money, blinking, and drew the cloak from Henderson's shoulders. When it slid away he felt suddenly warm again. It must be cold in the basement—the cloth was icy.

The old man wrapped the garment, smiling, and handed it over.

"I'll have it back tomorrow," Henderson promised.

"No need. You purchased it. It is yours."

"But—"

"I am leaving business shortly. Keep it. You will find more use for it than I, surely."

"But—"

"A pleasant evening to you."

Henderson made his way to the door in confusion, then turned to salute the blinking old man in the dimness.

Two eyes were burning at him from across the counter—two eyes that did not blink.

"Good night," said Henderson, and closed the door quickly. He wondered if he were going just a trifle mad.

At eight, Henderson nearly called up Lindstrom to tell him he couldn't make it. The cold chills came the minute he put on the damned cloak, and when he looked at himself in the mirror his blurred eyes could scarcely make out the reflection.

But after a few drinks he felt better about it. He hadn't eaten, and the liquor warmed his blood. He paced the floor, attitudinizing with the cloak—sweeping it about him and scowling in what he thought was a ferocious manner. Damn it, he was going to be a vampire all right! He called a cab, went down to the lobby. The driver came in, and Henderson was waiting, black cloak furled.

"I wish you to drive me," he said in a low voice.

The cabman took one look at him in the cloak and turned pale.

"Whazzat?"

"I ordered you to come," said Henderson gutturally, while he quaked with inner mirth. He leered ferociously and swept the cloak back.

"Yeah, yeah. O.K."

The driver almost ran outside. Henderson stalked after him.

"Where to, boss—I mean, sir?"

The frightened face didn't turn as Henderson intoned the address and sat back.

The cab started with a lurch that set Henderson to chuckling deeply, in character. At the sound of laughter the driver got panicky and raced his engine up to the limit set by the governor. Henderson laughed loudly, and the impressionable driver fairly quivered in his seat. It was quite a ride, but Henderson was entirely unprepared to open the door and find it slammed after him as the cabman drove hastily away without collecting a fare.

"I must look the part," he thought complacently, as he took the elevator up to the penthouse apartment.

There were three or four others in the elevator; Henderson had seen them before at other affairs Lindstrom had invited him to attend, but nobody seemed to recognize him. It rather pleased him to think how his wearing of an unfamiliar cloak and an unfamiliar scowl seemed to change his entire personality and appearance. Here the other guests had donned elaborate disguises—one woman wore the costume of a Watteau shepherdess, another was attired as a Spanish ballerina, a tall man dressed as Pagliacci, and his companion had donned a toreador outfit. Yet Henderson recognized them all; knew that their expensive habiliments were not truly disguises at all, but merely elaborations calculated to enhance their appearance. Most people at costume parties gave vent to suppressed desires. The women showed off their figures, the men either accentuated their masculinity as the toreador did, or clowned it. Such things were pitiful; these conventional fools eagerly doffing their dismal business suits and rushing off to a lodge, or amateur theatrical, or mask ball in order to satisfy their starving imaginations. Why didn't they dress in garish colors on the street? Henderson often pondered the question.

Surely, these society folk in the elevator were fine-looking men and women in their outfits—so healthy, so red-faced, and full of vitality. They had such robust throats and necks. Henderson looked at the plump arms of the woman next to him. He stared, without realizing it, for a long moment. And then, he saw that the occupants of the car had drawn away from him. They were standing in the corner, as though they feared his cloak and scowl, and his eyes fixed on the woman. Their chatter had ceased abruptly. The woman looked at him, as though she were about to speak, when the elevator doors opened and afforded Henderson a welcome respite.

What the devil was wrong? First the cab driver, then the woman. Had he drunk too much?

Well, no chance to consider that. Here was Marcus Lindstrom, and he was thrusting a glass into Henderson's hand.

"What have we here? Ah, a bogy-man!" It needed no second glance to perceive that Lindstrom, as usual at such affairs, was already quite bottle-dizzy. The fat host was positively swimming in alcohol.

"Have a drink, Henderson, my lad! I'll take mine from the bottle. That outfit of yours gave me a shock. Where'd you get the make-up?"

"Make-up? I'm not wearing any make-up."

"Oh. So you're not. How . . . silly of me."

Henderson wondered if he were crazy. Had Lindstrom really drawn back? Were his eyes actually filled with a certain dismay? Oh, the man was obviously intoxicated.

"I'll . . . I'll see you later," babbled Lindstrom, edging away and quickly turning to the other arrivals. Henderson watched the back of Lindstrom's neck. It was fat and white. It bulged over the collar of his costume and there was a vein in it. A vein in Lindstrom's fat neck. Frightened Lindstrom.

Henderson stood alone in the ante-room. From the parlor beyond came the sound of music and laughter; party noises. Henderson hesitated before entering. He drank from the glass in his hand—Bacardi rum, and powerful. On top of his other drinks it almost made the man reel. But he drank, wondering. What was wrong with him and his costume? Why did he frighten people? Was he unconsciously acting his vampire role? That crack of Lindstrom's about make-up now—

Acting on impulse, Henderson stepped over to the long panel mirror in the hall. He lurched a little, then stood in the harsh light before it. He faced the glass, stared into the mirror, and saw nothing.

He looked at himself in the mirror, and there was no one there!

Henderson began to laugh softly, evilly, deep in his throat. And as he gazed into the empty, unreflecting glass, his laughter rose in black glee.

"I'm drunk," he whispered. "I must be drunk. Mirror in my apartment made me blurred. Now I'm so far gone I can't see straight. Sure I'm drunk. Been acting ridiculously, scaring people. Now I'm seeing hallucinations—or not seeing them, rather. Visions. Angels."

His voice lowered. "Sure, angels. Standing right in back of me, now. Hello, angel."

"Hello."

Henderson whirled. There she stood, in the dark cloak, her hair a shimmering halo above her white, proud face, her eyes celestial blue, and her lips infernal red.

"Are you real?" asked Henderson, gently. "Or am I a fool to believe in miracles?"

"This miracle's name is Sheila Darrly, and it would like to powder its nose if you please."

"Kindly use this mirror through the courtesy of Stephen Henderson," replied the cloaked man, with a grin. He stepped back a ways, eyes intent.

The girl turned her head and favored him with a slow, impish smile. "Haven't you ever seen powder used before?" she asked.

"Didn't know angels indulged in cosmetics," Henderson replied. "But then there's a lot I don't know about angels. From now on I shall make them a special study of mine. There's so much I want to find out. So you'll probably find me following you around with a notebook all evening."

"Notebooks for a vampire?"

"Oh, but I'm a very intelligent vampire—not one of those backwoods Transylvanian types. You'll find me charming, I'm sure."

"Yes, you look like the sure type," the girl mocked. "But an angel and a vampire—that's a queer combination."

"We can reform one another," Henderson pointed out. "Besides, I have a suspicion that there's a bit of the devil in you. That dark cloak over your angel costume; dark angel, you know. Instead of heaven you might hail from my home town."

Henderson was flippant, but underneath his banter cyclonic thoughts whirled. He recalled discussions in the past; cynical observations he had made and believed.

Once, Henderson had declared that there was no such thing as love at first sight, save in books or plays where such a dramatic device served to speed up action. He asserted that people learned about romance from books and plays and accordingly adopted a belief in love at first sight when all one could possibly feel was desire.

And now this Sheila—this blond angel—had to come along and drive out all thoughts of morbidity, all thoughts of drunkenness and foolish gazings into mirrors, from his mind; had to send him madly plunging into dreams of red lips, ethereal blue eyes and slim white arms.

Something of his feeling had swept into his eyes, and as the girl gazed up at him she felt the truth.

"Well," she breathed, "I hope the inspection pleases."

"A miracle of understatement, that. But there was something I wanted to find out particularly about divinity. Do angels dance?"

"Tactful vampire! The next room?"

Arm in arm they entered the parlor. The merrymakers were in full swing. Liquor had already pitched gaiety at its height, but there was no dancing any longer.

Boisterous little grouped couples laughed arm in arm about the room. The usual party gagsters were performing their antics in corners. The superficial atmosphere, which Henderson detested, was fully in evidence.

It was reaction which made Henderson draw himself up to full height and sweep the cloak about his shoulders. Reaction brought the scowl to his pale face, caused him to stalk along in brooding silence. Sheila seemed to regard this as a great joke.

"Pull a vampire act on them," she giggled, clutching his arm. Henderson accordingly scowled at the couples, sneered horrendously at the woman. And his progress was marked by the turning of heads, the abrupt cessation of chatter. He walked through the long room like Red Death incarnate. Whispers trailed in his wake.

"Who is that man?"

"His eyes—"

"Vampire!"

"Hello, Dracula!" It was Marcus Lindstrom and a sullen-looking brunette in Cleopatra costume who lurched toward Henderson. Host Lindstrom could scarcely stand, and his companion in cups was equally at a loss. Henderson liked the man when sober at the club, but his behavior at parties had always irritated him. Lindstrom was particularly objectionable in his present condition—it made him boorish.

"M'dear, I want you t' meet a very dear friend of mine. Yessir, it being Halloween and all, I invited Count Dracula here, t'gether with his daughter. Asked his grandmother, but she's busy tonight at a Black Sabbath—along with Aunt Jemima. Ha! Count, meet my little playmate."

The woman leered up at Henderson.

"Oooh Dracula, what big eyes you have! Oooh, what big teeth you have! Oooh—"

"Really, Marcus," Henderson protested. But the host had turned and shouted to the room.

"Folks, meet the real goods—only genuine living vampire in captivity! Dracula Henderson, only existing vampire with false teeth."

In any other circumstance Henderson would have given Lindstrom a quick, efficient punch in the jaw. But Sheila was at his side, it was a public gathering; better to humor the man's clumsy jest. Why not be a vampire?

Smiling quickly at the girl, Henderson drew himself erect, faced the crowd, and frowned. His hands brushed the cloak. Funny, it still felt cold. Looking down he noticed for the first time that it was a little dirty at the edges; muddy or dusty. But the cold silk slid through his fingers as he drew it across his breast with one long hand. The feeling seemed to inspire him. He opened his eyes wide and let them blaze. His mouth opened. A sense of dramatic power filled him. And he looked at Marcus Lindstrom's soft, fat neck with the vein standing in the whiteness. He looked at the neck, saw the crowd watching him, and then the impulse seized him. He turned, eyes on that creasy neck—that wabbling, creasy neck of the fat man.

Hands darted out. Lindstrom squeaked like a frightened rat. He was a plump, sleek white rat, bursting with blood. Vampires liked blood. Blood from the rat, from the neck of the rat, from the vein in the neck of the rat, from the vein in the back of the squeaking rat.

"Warm blood."

The deep voice was Henderson's own.

The hands were Henderson's own.

The hands that went around Lindstrom's neck as he spoke, the hands that felt the warmth, that searched out the vein. Henderson's face was bending for the neck, and, as Lindstrom struggled, his grip tightened. Lindstrom's face was turning, turning purple. Blood was rushing to his head. That was good. Blood!

Henderson's mouth opened. He felt the air on his teeth. He bent down toward that fat neck, and then—

"Stop! That's plenty!"

The voice, the cooling voice of Sheila. Her fingers on his arm. Henderson looked up, startled. He released Lindstrom, who sagged with open mouth.

The crowd was staring, and their mouths were all shaped in the instinctive O of amazement.

Sheila whispered, "Bravo! Served him right—but you frightened him!"

Henderson struggled a moment to collect himself. Then he smiled and turned.

"Ladies and gentlemen," he said, "I have just given a slight demonstration to prove to you what our host said of me was entirely correct. I *am* a vampire. Now that you have been given fair warning, I am sure you will be in no further danger. If there is a doctor in the house I can, perhaps, arrange for a blood transfusion."

The O's relaxed and laughter came from startled throats. Hysterical laughter, in part then genuine. Henderson had carried it off. Marcus Lindstrom alone still stared with eyes that held utter fear. *He* knew.

And then the moment broke, for one of the gagsters ran into the room from the elevator. He had gone downstairs and borrowed the apron and cap of a newsboy. Now he raced through the crowd with a bundle of papers under his arm.

"Extra! Extra! Read all about it! Big Halloween Horror! Extra!"

Laughing guests purchased papers. A woman approached Sheila, and Henderson watched the girl walk away in a daze.

"See you later," she called, and her glance sent fire through his veins. Still, he could not forget the terrible feeling that came over him when he had seized Lindstrom. Why?

Automatically, he accepted a paper from the shouting pseudonewsboy. "Big Halloween Horror," he had shouted. What was that?

Blurred eyes searched the paper.

Then Henderson reeled back. That headline! It was an *Extra* after all. Henderson scanned the columns with mounting dread.

"Fire in costumer's . . . shortly after 8 p.m. firemen were summoned to the shop of . . . flames beyond control . . . completely demolished . . . damage estimated at . . . peculiarly enough, name of proprietor unknown . . . skeleton found in—"

"No!" gasped Henderson aloud.

He read, reread *that* closely. The skeleton had been found in a box of earth in the cellar beneath the shop. The box was a coffin. There had been two other boxes, empty. The skeleton had been wrapped in a cloak, undamaged by the flames—

And in the hastily penned box at the bottom of the column were eye-witness comments, written up under scareheads of heavy black type. Neighbors had feared the place. Hungarian neighborhood, hints of vampirism, of strangers who entered the shop. One man spoke of a cult believed to have held meetings in the place. Superstition about things sold there—love philters, outlandish charms and weird disguises.

Weird disguises—vampires—cloaks—*his eyes!*

"This is an authentic cloak."

"I will not be using this much longer. Keep it."

Memories of these words screamed through Henderson's brain. He plunged out of the room and rushed to the panel mirror.

A moment, then he flung one arm before his face to shield his eyes from the image that was not there—the missing reflection. *Vampires have no reflections.*

No wonder he looked strange. No wonder arms and necks invited him. He had wanted Lindstrom. Good God!

The cloak had done that, the dark cloak with the stains. The stains of earth, grave-earth. The wearing of the cloak, the cold cloak, had given him the feelings of a true vampire. It was a garment accursed, a thing that had lain on the body of one undead. The rusty stain along one sleeve was blood.

Blood. It would be nice to see blood. To taste its warmth, its red life, flowing.

No. That was insane. He was drunk, crazy.

"Ah. My pale friend, the vampire."

It was Sheila again. And above all horror rose the beating of Henderson's heart. As he looked at her shining eyes, her warm mouth shaped in red invitation, Henderson felt a wave of warmth. He looked at her white throat rising above her dark, shimmering cloak, and another kind of warmth rose. Love, desire, and a— hunger.

She must have seen it in his eyes, but she did not flinch. Instead, her own gaze burned in return.

Sheila loved him, too!

With an impulsive gesture, Henderson ripped the cloak from about his throat. The icy weight lifted. He was free. Somehow, he hadn't wanted to take the cloak off, but he had to. It was a cursed thing, and in another minute he might have taken the girl in his arms, taken her for a kiss and remained to—

But he dared not think of that.

"Tired of masquerading?" she asked. With a similar gesture she, too, removed her cloak and stood revealed in the glory of her angel robe. Her blond, statuesque perfection forced a gasp to Henderson's throat.

"Angel," he whispered.

"Devil," she mocked.

And suddenly they were embracing. Henderson had taken her cloak in his arm with his own. They stood with lips seeking rapture until Lindstrom and a group moved noisily into the anteroom.

At the sight of Henderson the fat host recoiled.

"You—" he whispered. "You are—"

"Just leaving," Henderson smiled. Grasping the girl's arm, he drew her toward the empty elevator. The door shut on Lindstrom's pale, fear-filled face.

"Were we leaving?" Sheila whispered, snuggling against his shoulder.

"We were. But not for earth. We do not go down into my realm, but up—into yours."

"The roof garden?"

"Exactly, my angelic one. I want to talk to you against the background of your own heavens, kiss you amidst the clouds, and—"

Her lips found his as the car rose.

"Angel and devil. What a match!"

"I thought so, too," the girl confessed. "Will our children have halos or horns?"

"Both, I'm sure."

They stepped out onto the deserted rooftop. And once again it was Halloween.

Henderson felt it. Downstairs it was Lindstrom and his society friends, in a drunken costume party. Here it was night, silence, gloom. No light, no music, no drinking, no chatter which made one party identical with another; one night like all the rest. This night was individual here.

The sky was not blue, but black. Clouds hung like the gray beards of hovering giants peering at the round orange globe of the moon. A cold wind blew from the sea, and filled the air with tiny murmurings from afar.

This was the sky that witches flew through to their Sabbath. This was the moon of wizardry, the sable silence of black prayers and whispered invocations. The clouds hid monstrous Presences shambling in summons from afar. It was Halloween.

It was also quite cold.

"Give me my cloak," Sheila whispered. Automatically, Henderson extended the garment, and the girl's body swirled under the dark splendor of the cloth. Her eyes burned up at Henderson with a call he could not resist. He kissed her, trembling.

"You're cold," the girl said. "Put on your cloak."

Yes, Henderson, he thought to himself. Put on your cloak while you stare at her throat. Then, the next time you kiss her you will want her throat and she will give it in love and you will take it in—hunger.

"Put it on, darling—I insist," the girl whispered. Her eyes were impatient, burning with an eagerness to match his own.

Henderson trembled.

Put on the cloak of darkness? The cloak of the grave, the cloak of death, the cloak of the vampire? The evil cloak, filled with a cold life of its own that transformed his face, transformed his mind, made his soul instinct with awful hunger?

"Here."

The girl's slim arms were about him, pushing the cloak onto his shoulders. Her fingers brushed his neck, caressingly, as she linked the cloak about his throat.

Henderson shivered.

Then he felt it—through him—that icy coldness turning to a more dreadful heat. He felt himself expand, felt the sneer cross his face. This was Power!

And the girl before him, her eyes taunting, inviting. He saw her ivory neck, her warm slim neck, waiting. It was waiting for him, for his lips.

For his teeth.

No—it couldn't be. He loved her. His love must conquer this madness. Yes, wear the cloak, defy its power, and take her in his arms as a man, not as a fiend. He must. It was the test.

"Sheila." Funny how his voice deepened.

"Yes, dear."

"Sheila, I must tell you this."

Her eyes—so alluring. It would be easy!

"Sheila, please. You read the paper tonight."

"Yes."

"I . . . I got my cloak there. I can't explain it. You saw how I took Lindstrom. I wanted to go through with it. Do you understand me? I meant to . . . to bite him. Wearing this damnable thing makes me feel like one of those creatures."

Why didn't her stare change? Why didn't she recoil in horror? Such trusting innocence! Didn't she understand? Why didn't she run? Any moment now he might lose control, seize her.

"I love you, Sheila. Believe that. I love you."

"I know." Her eyes gleamed in the moonlight.

"I want to test it. I want to kiss you, wearing this cloak. I want to feel that my love is stronger than this—thing. If I weaken, promise me you'll break away and run, quickly. But don't misunderstand. I must face this feeling and fight it; I want my love for you to be that pure, that secure. Are you afraid?"

"No." Still she stared at him, just as he stared at her throat. If she knew what was in his mind!

"You don't think I'm crazy? I went to this costumer's—he was a horrible little old man—and he gave me the cloak. Actually told me it was a real vampire's. I thought he was joking, but tonight I didn't see myself in the mirror, and I wanted Lindstrom's neck, and I want you. But I must test it."

"You're not crazy. I know. I'm not afraid."

"Then—"

The girl's face mocked. Henderson summoned his strength. He bent forward, his impulses battling. For a moment he stood there under the ghastly orange moon, and his face was twisted in struggle.

And the girl lured.

Her odd, incredibly red lips parted in a silvery, chuckly laugh as her white arms rose from the black cloak she wore to circle his neck gently. "I know—I knew when I looked in the mirror. I knew you had a cloak like mine—got yours where I got mine—''

Queerly, her lips seemed to elude his as he stood frozen for an instant of shock. Then he felt the icy hardness of her sharp little teeth on his throat, a strangely soothing sting, and an engulfing blackness rising over him.

L. SPRAGUE DE CAMP

The Gnarly Man

D r. Matilda Saddler first saw the gnarly man on the evening of June 14, 1946, at Coney Island.

The spring meeting of the Eastern Section of the American Anthropological Association had broken up, and Dr. Saddler had had dinner with two of her professional colleagues, Blue of Columbia and Jeffcott of Yale. She mentioned that she had never visited Coney, and meant to go there that evening. She urged Blue and Jeffcott to come along, but they begged off.

Watching Dr. Saddler's retreating back, Blue of Columbia cackled: "The Wild Woman from Wichita. Wonder if she's hunting another husband?" He was a thin man with a small gray beard and a who-the-hell-are-you-sir expression.

"How many has she had?" asked Jeffcott of Yale.

"Two to date. Don't know why anthropologists lead the most disorderly private lives of any scientists. Must be that they study the customs and morals of all these different peoples, and ask themselves, 'If the Eskimos can do it, why can't we?' I'm old enough to be safe, thank God."

"I'm not afraid of her," said Jeffcott. He was in his early forties and looked like a farmer uneasy in store clothes. "I'm so very thoroughly married."

"Yeah? Ought to have been at Stanford a few years ago, when she was there. Wasn't safe to walk across the campus, with Tuthill chasing all the females and Saddler all the males."

Dr. Saddler had to fight her way off the subway train, as the adolescents who infest the platform of the B. M. T.'s Stillwell Avenue station are probably the worst-mannered people on earth, possibly excepting the Dobu Islanders, of the western Pacific. She didn't much mind. She was a tall, strongly built woman in her late thirties, who had been kept in trim by the outdoor rigors of her profession. Besides, some of the inane remarks in Swift's paper on acculturation among the Arapaho Indians had gotten her fighting blood up.

Walking down Surf Avenue toward Brighton Beach, she looked at the concessions without trying them, preferring to watch the human types that did and the other human types that took their money. She did try a shooting gallery, but found knocking tin owls off their perch with a .22 too easy to be much fun. Long-range work with an army rifle was her idea of shooting.

The concession next to the shooting gallery would have been called a side show if there had been a main show for it to be a side show to. The usual lurid banner proclaimed the uniqueness of the two-headed calf, the bearded woman, Arachne the spider girl, and other marvels. The pièce de resistance was Ungo-Bungo, the ferocious ape-man, captured in the Congo at a cost of twenty-seven lives. The picture showed an enormous Ungo-Bungo squeezing a hapless Negro in each hand, while others sought to throw a net over him.

Dr. Saddler knew perfectly well that the ferocious ape-man would turn out to be an ordinary Caucasian with false hair on his chest. But a streak of whimsicality impelled her to go in. Perhaps, she thought, she could have some fun with her colleagues about it.

The spieler went through his leather-lunged harangue. Dr. Saddler guessed from his expression that his feet hurt. The tattooed lady didn't interest her, as her decorations obviously had no cultural significance, as they have among the Polynesians. As for the ancient Mayan, Dr. Saddler thought it in questionable taste to exhibit a poor microcephalic idiot that way. Professor Yoki's legerdemain and fire eating weren't bad.

There was a curtain in front of Ungo-Bungo's cage. At the appropriate moment there were growls and the sound of a length of chain being slapped against a metal plate. The spieler wound up on a high note: "—ladies and gentlemen, the one and only UNGO-BUNGO!" The curtain dropped.

The ape-man was squatting at the back of his cage. He dropped his chain, got up, and shuffled forward. He grasped two of the bars and shook them. They were appropriately loose and rattled alarmingly. Ungo-Bungo snarled at the patrons, showing his even, yellow teeth.

Dr. Saddler stared hard. This was something new in the ape-man line. Ungo-Bungo was about five feet three, but very massive, with enormous hunched shoulders. Above and below his blue swimming trunks thick, grizzled hair covered him from crown to ankle. His short, stout-muscled arms ended in big hands with thick, gnarled fingers. His neck projected slightly forward, so that from the front he seemed to have but little neck at all.

His face—well, thought Dr. Saddler, she knew all the living races of men, and all the types of freak brought about by glandular maladjustment, and none of them had a face like *that*. It was deeply lined. The forehead between the short scalp hair and the brows on the huge supraorbital ridges receded sharply. The nose, although wide, was not apelike; it was a shortened version of the thick, hooked Armenoid nose, so often miscalled Jewish. The face ended in a long upper lip and a retreating chin. And the yellowish skin apparently belonged to Ungo-Bungo.

The curtain was whisked up again.

Dr. Saddler went out with the others, but paid another dime, and soon was back inside. She paid no attention to the spieler, but got a good position in front of Ungo-Bungo's cage before the rest of the crowd arrived.

Ungo-Bungo repeated his performance with mechanical precision. Dr. Saddler noticed that he limped a little as he came forward to rattle the bars, and that the skin under his mat of hair bore several big whitish scars. The last joint of his left ring finger was missing. She noted certain things about the proportions of his shin and thigh, of his forearm and upper arm, and his big splay feet.

Dr. Saddler paid a third dime. An idea was knocking at her mind somewhere. If she let it in, either she was crazy or physical anthropology was haywire or— something. But she knew that if she did the sensible thing, which was to go home, the idea would plague her from now on.

After the third performance she spoke to the spieler. "I think your Mr. Ungo-Bungo used to be a friend of mine. Could you arrange for me to see him after he finishes?"

The spieler checked his sarcasm. His questioner was so obviously not a—not the sort of dame who asks to see guys after they finish.

"Oh, him," he said. "Calls himself Gaffney—Clarence Aloysius Gaffney. That the guy you want?"

"Why, yes."

"I guess you can." He looked at his watch. "He's got four more turns to do before we close. I'll have to ask the boss. He popped through a curtain and called, "Hey, Morrie!" Then he was back. "It's O. K. Morrie says you can wait in his office. Foist door to the right."

Morrie was stout, bald, and hospitable. "Sure, sure," he said, waving his cigar. "Glad to be of soivice, Miss Saddler. Chust a min while I talk to Gaffney's manager." He stuck his head out. "Hey, Pappas! Lady wants to talk to your ape-man later. I meant *lady*. O. K." He returned to orate on the difficulties besetting the freak business. "You take this Gaffney, now. He's the best damn ape-man in the business; all that hair rilly grows outa him. And the poor guy rilly has a face like that. But do people believe it? No! I hear 'em going out, saying about how the hair is pasted on, and the whole thing is a fake. It's mawtifying." He cocked his head, listening. "That rumble wasn't no rolly-coaster; it's gonna rain. Hope it's over by tomorrow. You wouldn't believe the way a rain can knock ya receipts off. If you drew a coive, it would be like this." He drew his finger horizontally through space, jerking it down sharply to indicate the effect of rain. "But as I said, people don't appreciate what you try to do for 'em. It's not just the money; I think of myself as an ottist. A creative ottist. A show like this got to have balance and propawtion, like any other ott—"

It must have been an hour later when a slow, deep voice at the door said: "Did somebody want to see me?"

The gnarly man was in the doorway. In street clothes, with the collar of his raincoat turned up and his hat brim pulled down, he looked more or less human, though the coat fitted his great, sloping shoulders badly. He had a thick, knobby walking stick with a leather loop near the top end. A small, dark man fidgeted behind him.

"Yeah," said Morrie, interrupting his lecture. "Clarence, this is Miss Saddler. Miss Saddler, this is Mr. Gaffney, one of our outstanding creative ottists."

"Pleased to meetcha," said the gnarly man. "This is my manager, Mr. Pappas."

Dr. Saddler explained, and said she'd like to talk to Mr. Gaffney if she might. She was tactful; you had to be to pry into the private affairs of Naga headhunters, for instance. The gnarly man said he'd be glad to have a cup of coffee with Miss Saddler; there was a place around the corner that they could reach without getting wet.

As they started out, Pappas followed, fidgeting more and more. The gnarly man said: "Oh, go home to bed, John. Don't worry about me." He grinned at Dr. Saddler. The effect would have been unnerving to anyone but an anthropologist. "Every time he sees me talking to anybody, he thinks it's some other manager trying to steal me." He spoke general American, with a suggestion of Irish brogue in the lowering of the vowels in words like "man" and "talk." "I made the lawyer who drew up our contract fix it so it can be ended on short notice."

Pappas departed, still looking suspicious. The rain had practically ceased. The gnarly man stepped along smartly despite his limp.

A woman passed with a fox terrier on a leash. The dog sniffed in the direction of the gnarly man, and then to all appearances went crazy, yelping and slavering. The gnarly man shifted his grip on the massive stick and said quietly, "Better hand onto him, ma'am." The woman departed hastily. "They just don't like me," commented Gaffney. "Dogs, that is."

They found a table and ordered their coffee. When the gnarly man took off his raincoat, Dr. Saddler became aware of a strong smell of cheap perfume. He got out a pipe with a big knobby bowl. It suited him, just as the walking stick did. Dr. Saddler noticed that the deepsunk eyes under the beetling arches were light hazel.

"Well?" he said in his rumbling drawl.

She began her questions.

"My parents were Irish," he answered. "But I was born in South Boston . . . let's see . . . forty-six years ago. I can get you a copy of my birth certificate. Clarence Aloysius Gaffney, May 2, 1900." He seemed to get some secret amusement out of that statement.

"Were either of your parents of your somewhat unusual physical type?"

He paused before answering. He always did, it seemed. "Uh-huh. Both of 'em. Glands, I suppose."

"Were they both born in Ireland?"

"Yep. County Sligo." Again that mysterious twinkle

She thought. "Mr. Gaffney, you wouldn't mind having some photographs and measurements made, would you? You could use the photographs in your business."

"Maybe." He took a sip. "Ouch! Gazooks, that's hot!"

"*What?*"

"I said the coffee's hot."

"I mean, before that."

The gnarly man looked a little embarrassed. "Oh, you mean the 'gazooks'? Well, I . . . uh . . . once knew a man who used to say that."

"Mr. Gaffney, I'm a scientist, and I'm not trying to get anything out of you for my own sake. You can be frank with me."

There was something remote and impersonal in his stare that gave her a slight spinal chill. "Meaning that I haven't been so far?"

"Yes. When I saw you I decided that there was something extraordinary in your background. I still think there is. Now, if you think I'm crazy, say so and we'll drop the subject. But I want to get to the bottom of this."

He took his time about answering. "That would depend." There was another pause. Then he said: "With your connections, do you know any really first-class surgeons?"

"But . . . yes, I know Dunbar."

"The guy who wears a purple gown when he operates? The guy who wrote a book on 'God, Man, and the Universe'?"

"Yes, He's a good man, in spite of his theatrical mannerisms. Why? What would you want of him?"

"Not what you're thinking. I'm satisfied with my . . . uh . . . unusual physical type. But I have some old injuries—broken bones that didn't knit properly—that I want fixed up. He'd have to be a good man, though. I have a couple of thousand dollars in the savings bank, but I know the sort of fees those guys charge. If you could make the necessary arrangements—"

"Why, yes, I'm sure I could. In fact, I could guarantee it. Then I *was* right? And you'll—" She hesitated.

"Come clean? Uh-huh. But remember, I can still prove I'm Clarence Aloysius if I have to."

"Who *are* you, then?"

Again there was a long pause. Then the gnarly man said: "Might as well tell you. As soon as you repeat any of it, you'll have put your professional reputation in my hands, remember.

"First off, I wasn't born in Massachusetts. I was born on the upper Rhine, near Mommenheim. And I was born, as nearly as I can figure out, about the year 50,000 B.C."

Matilda Saddler wondered whether she'd stumbled on the biggest thing in anthropology, or whether this bizarre personality was making Baron Munchausen look like a piker.

He seemed to guess her thoughts. "I can't prove that, of course. But so long as you arrange about that operation, I don't care whether you believe me or not."

"But . . . but . . . *how?*"

"I think the lightning did it. We were out trying to drive some bison into a pit. Well, this big thunderstorm came up, and the bison bolted in the wrong direction. So we gave up and tried to find shelter. And the next thing I knew I was lying on the ground with the rain running over me, and the rest of the clan standing around wailing about what had they done to get the storm god sore at them, so he made a bull's-eye on one of their best hunters. They'd never said *that* about me before. It's funny how you're never appreciated while you're alive.

"But I was alive, all right. My nerves were pretty well shot for a few weeks, but otherwise I was O. K., except for some burns on the soles of my feet. I don't know just what happened, except I was reading a couple of years ago that scientists had located the machinery that controls the replacement of tissue in the medulla oblongata. I think maybe the lightning did something to my medulla to speed it up. Anyway, I never got any older after that. Physically, that is. I was thirty-three at the time, more or less. We didn't keep track of ages. I look older now, because the lines in your face are bound to get sort of set after a few thousand years, and because our hair was always gray at the ends. But I can still tie an ordinary *Homo sapiens* in a knot if I want to."

"Then you're . . . you mean to say you're . . . you're trying to tell me you're—"

"A Neanderthal man? *Homo neanderthalensis?* That's right."

Matilda Saddler's hotel room was a bit crowded, with the gnarly man, the frosty Blue, the rustic Jeffcott, Dr. Saddler herself, and Harold McGannon, the historian. This McGannon was a small man, very neat and pink-skinned. He looked more like a New York Central director than a professor. Just now his expression was one of fascination. Dr. Saddler looked full of pride; Professor Jeffcott looked interested but puzzled; Dr. Blue looked bored—he hadn't wanted to come in the first place. The gnarly man, stretched out in the most comfortable chair and puffing his overgrown pipe, seemed to be enjoying himself.

McGannon was formulating a question. "Well, Mr.—Gaffney? I suppose that's your name as much as any."

"You might say so," said the gnarly man. "My original name meant something like Shining Hawk. But I've gone under hundreds of names since then. If you register in a hotel as 'Shining Hawk,' it's apt to attract attention. And I try to avoid that."

"Why?" asked McGannon.

The gnarly man looked at his audience as one might look at willfully stupid children. "I don't like trouble. The best way to keep out of trouble is not to attract attention. That's why I have to pull up stakes and move every ten or fifteen years. People might get curious as to why I never got any older."

"Pathological liar," murmured Blue. The words were barely audible, but the gnarly man heard them.

"You're entitled to your opinion, Dr. Blue," he said affably. "Dr. Saddler's doing me a favor, so in return I'm letting you all shoot questions at me. And I'm answering. I don't give a damn whether you believe me or not."

McGannon hastily threw in another question. "How is it that you have a birth certificate, as you say you have?"

"Oh, I knew a man named Clarence Gaffney once. He got killed by an automobile, and I took his name."

"Was there any reason for picking this Irish background?"

"Are you Irish, Dr. McGannon?"

"Not enough to matter."

"O. K. I didn't want to hurt any feelings. It's my best bet. There are real Irishmen with upper lips like mine."

Dr. Saddler broke in. "I meant to ask you, Clarence." She put a lot of warmth into his name. "There's an argument as to whether your people interbred with mine, when mine overran Europe at the end of the Mousterian. Some scientists have thought that some modern Europeans, especially along the west coast of Ireland, might have a little Neanderthal blood."

He grinned slightly. "Well—yes and no. There never was any back in the stone age, as far as I know. But these long-lipped Irish are my fault."

"How?"

"Believe it or not, but in the last fifty centuries there have been some women of your species that didn't find me too repulsive. Usually there were no offspring. But in the sixteenth century I went to Ireland to live. They were burning too many people for witchcraft in the rest of Europe to suit me at that time. And there was a woman. The result this time was a flock of hybrids—cute little devils, they were. So the Irishmen who look like me are my descendants."

"What did happen to your people?" asked McGannon. "Were they killed off?"

The gnarly man shrugged. "Some of them. We weren't at all warlike. But then the tall ones, as we called them, weren't either. Some of the tribes of the tall ones looked on us as legitimate prey, but most of them let us severely alone. I guess they were almost as scared of us as we were of them. Savages as primitive as that are really pretty peaceable people. You have to work so hard to keep fed, and there are so few of you, that there's no object in fighting wars. That comes later, when you get agriculture and livestock, so you have something worth stealing.

"I remember that a hundred years after the tall ones had come, there were still Neanderthalers living in my part of the country. But they died out. I think it was that they lost their ambition. The tall ones were pretty crude, but they were so far ahead of us that our things and our customs seemed silly. Finally we just sat around and lived on the scraps we could beg from the tall ones' camps. You might say we died of an inferiority complex."

"What happened to you?" asked McGannon.

"Oh, I was a god among my own people by then, and naturally I represented them in their dealings with the tall ones. I got to know the tall ones pretty well, and they were willing to put up with me after all my own clan were dead. Then in a couple of hundred years they'd forgotten all about my people, and took me for a hunchback or something. I got to be pretty good at flint working, so I could earn my keep. When metal came in, I went into that, and finally into black-smithing. If you'd put all the horseshoes I've made in a pile, they'd—well, you'd have a damn big pile of horseshoes, anyway."

"Did you . . . ah . . . limp at that time?" asked McGannon.

"Uh-huh. I busted my leg back in the Neolithic. Fell out of a tree, and had to set it myself, because there wasn't anybody around. Why?"

"Vulcan," said McGannon softly.

"Vulcan?" repeated the gnarly man. "Wasn't he a Greek god or something?"

"Yes. He was the lame blacksmith of the gods."

"You mean you think that maybe somebody got the idea from me? That's an interesting theory. Little late to check up on it, though."

Blue leaned forward and said crisply: "Mr. Gaffney, no real Neanderthal man could talk as fluently and entertainingly as you do. That's shown by the poor development of the frontal lobes of the brain and the attachments of the tongue muscles."

The gnarly man shrugged again. "You can believe what you like. My own clan considered me pretty smart, and then you're bound to learn something in fifty thousand years."

Dr. Saddler beamed. "Tell them about your teeth, Clarence."

The gnarly man grinned. "They're false, of course. My own lasted a long time, but they still wore out somewhere back in the Paleolithic. I grew a third set, and they wore out, too. So I had to invent soup."

"You *what?*" It was the usually taciturn Jeffcott.

"I had to invent soup, to keep alive. You know, the bark-dish-and-hot-stones method. My gums got pretty tough after a while, but they still weren't much good for chewing hard stuff. So after a few thousand years I got pretty sick of soup and mushy foods generally. And when metal came in I began experimenting with false teeth. Bone teeth in copper plates. You might say I invented them, too. I tried often to sell them, but they never really caught on until around 1750 A. D. I was living in Paris then, and I built up quite a little business before I moved on." He pulled the handkerchief out of his breast pocket to wipe his forehead; Blue made a face as the wave of perfume reached him.

"Well, Mr. Shining Hawk," snapped Blue with a trace of sarcasm, "How do you like our machine age?"

The gnarly man ignored the tone of the question. "It's not bad. Lots of interesting things happen. The main trouble is the shirts."

"Shirts?"

"Uh-huh. Just try to buy a shirt with a twenty neck and a twenty-nine sleeve. I have to order 'em special. It's almost as bad with hats and shoes. I wear an eight and one half hat and a thirteen shoe." He looked at his watch. "I've got to get back to Coney to work."

McGannon jumped up. "Where can I get in touch with you again, Mr. Gaffney? There's lots of things I'd like to ask you."

The gnarly man told him. "I'm free mornings. My working hours are two to midnight on weekdays, with a couple of hours off for dinner. Union rules, you know."

"You mean there's a union for you show people?"

"Sure. Only they call it a guild. They think they're artists, you know. Artists don't have unions; they have guilds. But it amounts to the same thing."

Blue and Jeffcott saw the gnarly man and the historian walking slowly toward the subway together. Blue said: "Poor old Mac! Always thought he had sense.

Looks like he's swallowed this Gaffney's ravings, hook, line, and sinker.''

"I'm not so sure," said Jeffcott, frowning. "There's something funny about the business."

"What?" barked Blue. "Don't tell me that *you* believe this story of being alive fifty thousand years? A caveman who uses perfume! Good God!"

"N-no," said Jeffcott. "Not the fifty thousand part. But I don't think it's a simple case of paranoia or plain lying, either. And the perfume's quite logical, if he were telling the truth."

"Huh?"

"Body odor. Saddler told us how dogs hate him. He'd have a smell different from ours. We're so used to ours that we don't even know we have one, unless somebody goes without a bath for a month. But we might notice his if he didn't disguise it."

Blue snorted. "You'll be believing him yourself in a minute. It's an obvious glandular case, and he's made up this story to fit. All that talk about not caring whether we believe him or not is just bluff. Come on, let's get some lunch. Say, see the way Saddler looked at him every time she said 'Clarence'? Like a hungry wolf. Wonder what she thinks she's going to do with him?"

Jeffcott thought. "I can guess. And if he *is* telling the truth, I think there's something in Deuteronomy against it."

The great surgeon made a point of looking like a great surgeon, to pince-nez and Vandyke. He waved the X-ray negatives at the gnarly man, pointing out this and that.

"We'd better take the leg first," he said. "Suppose we do that next Thursday. When you've recovered from that we can tackle the shoulder. It'll all take time, you know."

The gnarly man agreed, and shuffled out of the little private hospital to where McGannon awaited him in his car. The gnarly man described the tentative schedule of operations, and mentioned that he had made arrangements to quit his job. "Those two are the main thing," he said. "I'd like to try professional wrestling again some day, and I can't unless I get this shoulder fixed so I can raise my left arm over my head."

"What happened to it?" asked McGannon.

The gnarly man closed his eyes, thinking. "Let me see. I get things mixed up sometimes. People do when they're only fifty years old, so you can imagine what it's like for me.

"In 42 B. C. I was living with the Bituriges in Gaul. You remember that Cæsar shut up Werkinghetorich—Vercingetorix to you—in Alesia, and the confederacy raised an army of relief under Caswollon."

"Caswollon?"

The gnarly man laughed shortly. "I meant Wercaswollon. Caswollon was a Briton, wasn't he? I'm always getting those two mixed up.

"Anyhow, I got drafted. That's all you can call it; I didn't want to go. It wasn't exactly *my* war. But they wanted me because I could pull twice as heavy a bow as anybody else.

"When the final attack on Cæsar's ring of fortifications came, they sent me forward with some other archers to provide a covering fire for their infantry. At least, that was the plan. Actually, I never saw such a hopeless muddle in my life. And before I even got within bowshot, I fell into one of the Romans' covered pits. I didn't land on the point of the stake, but I fetched up against the side of it and busted my shoulder. There wasn't any help, because the Gauls were too busy running away from Cæsar's German cavalry to bother about wounded men.''

The author of "God, Man, and the Universe" gazed after his departing patient. He spoke to his head assistant: "What do you think of him?"

"I think it's so," said the assistant. "I looked over those X rays pretty closely. That skeleton never belonged to a human being. And it has more healed fractures than you'd think possible."

"Hm-m-m," said Dunbar. "That's right, he wouldn't be human, would he? Hm-m-m. You know, if anything happened to him—"

The assistant grinned understandingly. "Of course, there's the S. P. C. A."

"We needn't worry about *them*. Hm-m-m." He thought, you've been slipping; nothing big in the papers for a year. But if you published a complete anatomical description of a Neanderthal man—or if you found out why his medulla functions the way it does—Hm-m-m. Of course, it would have to be managed properly—"

"Let's have lunch at the Natural History Museum," said McGannon. "Some of the people there ought to know you."

"O. K.," drawled the gnarly man. "Only I've still got to get back to Coney afterward. This is my last day. Tomorrow, Pappas and I are going up to see our lawyer about ending our contract. Guy named Robinette. It's a dirty trick on poor old John, but I warned him at the start that this might happen."

"I suppose we can come up to interview you while you're . . . ah . . . con-valescing? Fine. Have you ever been to the museum, by the way?"

"Sure," said the gnarly man. "I get around."

"What did you . . . ah . . . think of their stuff in the Hall of the Age of Man?"

"Pretty good. There's a little mistake in one of those big wall paintings. The second horn on the woolly rhinoceros ought to slant forward more. I thought of writing them a letter. But you know how it is. They'd say: 'Were you there?' and I'd say, 'Uh-huh,' and they'd say, 'Another nut.' "

"How about the pictures and busts of Paleolithic men?"

"Pretty good. But they have some funny ideas. They always show us with skins wrapped around our middles. In summer we didn't wear skins, and in winter we hung them around our shoulders, where they'd do some good.

"And then they show those tall ones that you call Cro-Magnon men clean-shaven. As I remember, they all had whiskers. What would they shave with?"

"I think," said McGannon, "that they leave the beards off the busts to . . . ah . . . show the shape of the chins. With the beards they'd all look too much alike."

"Is that the reason? They might say so on the labels." The gnarly man rubbed his own chin, such as it was. "I wish beards would come back into style. I look much more human with a beard. I got along fine in the sixteenth century when everybody had whiskers.

"That's one of the ways I remember when things happened, by the haircuts and whiskers that people had. I remember when a wagon I was driving in Milan lost a wheel and spilled flour bags from hell to breakfast. That must have been in the sixteenth century, before I went to Ireland, because I remember that most of the men in the crowd that collected had beards. Now—wait a minute—maybe that was the fourteenth. There were a lot of beards then, too."

"Why, why didn't you keep a diary?" asked McGannon with a groan of exasperation.

The gnarly man shrugged characteristically. "And pack around six trunks full of paper every time I moved? No, thanks."

"I . . . ah . . . don't suppose you could give me the real story of Richard III and the princes in the tower?"

"Why should I? I was just a poor blacksmith, or farmer, or something most of the time. I didn't go around with the big shots. I gave up all my ideas of ambition a long time before that. I had to, being so different from other people. As far as I can remember, the only real king I ever got a good look at was Charlemagne, when he made a speech in Paris one day. He was just a big, tall man with Santa Claus whiskers and a squeaky voice."

Next morning McGannon and the gnarly man had a session with Svedberg at the museum. Then McGannon drove Gaffney around to the lawyer's office, on the third floor of a seedy office building in the West Fifties. James Robinette looked something like a movie actor and something like a chipmunk. He looked at his watch and said to McGannon: "This won't take long. If you'd like to stick around, I'd be glad to have lunch with you." The fact was that he was feeling just a trifle queasy about being left with this damn queer client, this circus freak or whatever he was, with his barrel body and his funny slow drawl.

When the business had been completed, and the gnarly man had gone off with his manager to wind up his affairs at Coney, Robinette said: "Whew! I thought he was a half-wit, from his looks. But there was nothing half-witted about the way he went over those clauses. You'd have thought the damn contract was for building a subway system. What *is* he, anyhow?"

McGannon told him what he knew.

The lawyer's eyebrows went up. "Do you *believe* his yarn? Oh, I'll take tomato juice and filet of sole with tartar sauce—only without the tartar sauce—on the lunch, please."

"The same for me. Answering your question, Robinette, I do. So does Saddler. So does Svedberg up at the museum. They're both topnotchers in their respective

fields. Saddler and I have interviewed him, and Svedberg's examined him physically. But it's just opinion. Fred Blue still swears it's a hoax or . . . ah . . .
some sort of dementia. Neither of us can prove anything.''

"Why not?''

"Well . . . ah . . . how are you going to prove that he was, or was not, alive
a hundred years ago? Take one case: Clarence says he ran a sawmill in Fairbanks,
Alaska, in 1906 and '07, under the name of Michael Shawn. How are you going
to find out whether there was a sawmill operator in Fairbanks at that time? And if
you did stumble on a record of a Michael Shawn, how would you know whether
he and Clarence were the same? There's not a chance in a thousand that there'd
be a photograph or a detailed description that you could check with. And you'd
have an awful time trying to find anybody who remembered him at this late date.

"Then, Svedberg poked around Clarence's face, yesterday, and said that no
Homo sapiens ever had a pair of zygomatic arches like that. But when I told Blue
that, he offered to produce photographs of a human skull that did. I know what'll
happen. Blue will say that the arches are practically the same, and Svedberg will
say that they're obviously different. So there we'll be.''

Robinette mused, "He does seem damned intelligent for an ape-man.''

"He's not an ape-man, really. The Neanderthal race was a separate branch of
the human stock; they were more primitive in some ways and more advanced in
others than we are. Clarence may be slow, but he usually grinds out the right
answer. I imagine that he was . . . ah . . . brilliant, for one of his kind, to begin
with. And he's had the benefit of so much experience. He knows an incredible
lot. He knows us; he sees through us and our motives.''

The little pink man puckered up his forehead. "I do hope nothing happens to
him. He's carrying around a lot of priceless information in that big head of his.
Simply priceless. Not much about war and politics; he kept clear of those as a
matter of self-preservation. But little things, about how people lived and how they
thought thousands of years ago. He gets his periods mixed up sometimes, but he
gets them straightened out if you give him time.

"I'll have to get hold of Pell, the linguist. Clarence knows dozens of ancient
languages, such as Gothic and Gaulish. I was able to check him on some of them,
like vulgar Latin; that was one of the things that convinced me. And there are
archeologists and psychologists—

"If only something doesn't happen to scare him off. We'd never find him. I
don't know. Between a man-crazy female scientist and a publicity-mad surgeon—
I wonder how it'll work out—''

The gnarly man innocently entered the waiting room of Dunbar's hospital. He,
as usual, spotted the most comfortable chair and settled luxuriously into it.

Dunbar stood before him. His keen eyes gleamed with anticipation behind their
pince-nez. "There'll be a wait of about half an hour, Mr. Gaffney,'' he said.
"We're all tied up now, you know. I'll send Mahler in; he'll see that you have
anything you want.'' Dunbar's eyes ran lovingly over the gnarly man's stumpy
frame. What fascinating secrets mightn't he discover once he got inside it?

Mahler appeared, a healthy-looking youngster. Was there anything Mr. Gaffney would like? The gnarly man paused as usual to let his massive mental machinery grind. A vagrant impulse moved him to ask to see the instruments that were to be used on him.

Mahler had his orders, but this seemed a harmless enough request. He went and returned with a tray full of gleaming steel. "You see," he said, "these are called scalpels."

Presently the gnarly man asked: "What's this?" He picked up a peculiar-looking instrument.

"Oh, that's the boss's own invention. For getting at the mid-brain."

"Mid-brain? What's that doing here?"

"Why, that's for getting at your— That must be there by mistake—"

Little lines tightened around the queer hazel eyes. "Yeah?" He remembered the look Dunbar had given him, and Dunbar's general reputation. "Say, could I use your phone a minute?"

"Why . . . I suppose . . . what do you want to phone for?"

"I want to call my lawyer. Any objections?"

"No, of course not. But there isn't any phone here."

"What do you call that?" The gnarly man got up and walked toward the instrument in plain sight on a table. But Mahler was there before him, standing in front of it.

"This one doesn't work. It's being fixed."

"Can't I try it?"

"No, not till it's fixed. It doesn't work, I tell you."

The gnarly man studied the young physician for a few seconds. "O. K., then I'll find one that does." He started for the door.

"Hey, you can't go out now!" cried Mahler.

"Can't I? Just watch me!"

"Hey!" It was a full-throated yell. Like magic more men in white coats appeared.

Behind them was the great surgeon. "Be reasonable, Mr. Gaffney," he said. "There's no reason why you should go out now, you know. We'll be ready for you in a little while."

"Any reason why I shouldn't?" The gnarly man's big face swung on his thick neck, and his hazel eyes swiveled. All the exits were blocked. "I'm going."

"Grab him!" said Dunbar.

The white coats moved. The gnarly man got his hands on the back of a chair. The chair whirled, and became a dissolving blur as the men closed on him. Pieces of chair flew about the room, to fall with the dry, sharp *ping* of short lengths of wood. When the gnarly man stopped swinging, having only a short piece of the chair back left in each fist. One assistant was out cold. Another leaned whitely against the wall and nursed a broken arm.

"Go on!" shouted Dunbar when he could make himself heard. The white wave closed over the gnarly man, then broke. The gnarly man was on his feet, and held young Mahler by the ankles. He spread his feet and swung the shrieking Mahler like a club, clearing the way to the door. He turned, whirled Mahler around his head like a hammer thrower, and let the now mercifully unconscious body fly. His assailants went down in a yammering tangle.

One was still up. Under Dunbar's urging he sprang after the gnarly man. The latter had gotten his stick out of the umbrella stand in the vestibule. The knobby upper end went *whoosh* past the assistant's nose. The assistant jumped back and fell over one of the casualties. The front door slammed, and there was a deep roar of "Taxi!"

"Come on!" shrieked Dunbar. "Get the ambulance out!"

James Robinette was sitting in his office, thinking the thoughts that lawyers do in moments of relaxation, when there was a pounding of large feet in the corridor, a startled protest from Miss Spevak in the outer office, and the strange client of the day before was at Robinette's desk, breathing hard.

"I'm Gaffney," he growled between gasps. "Remember me? I think they followed me down here. They'll be up any minute. I want your help."

"They? Who's they?" Robinette winced at the impact of that damn perfume.

The gnarly man launched into his misfortunes. He was going well when there were more protests from Miss Spevak, and Dr. Dunbar and four assistants burst into the office.

"He's ours," said Dunbar, his glasses agleam.

"He's an ape-man," said the assistant with the black eye.

"He's a dangerous lunatic," said the assistant with the cut lip.

"We've come to take him away," said the assistant with the torn coat.

The gnarly man spread his feet and gripped his stick like a baseball bat by the small end.

Robinette opened a desk drawer and got out a large pistol. "One move toward him and I'll use this. The use of extreme violence is justified to prevent commission of a felony, to wit: kidnaping."

The five men backed up a little. Dunbar said: "This isn't kidnaping. You can only kidnap a person, you know. He isn't a human being, and I can prove it."

The assistant with the black eye snickered. "If he wants protection, he better see a game warden instead of a lawyer."

"Maybe that's what *you* think," said Robinette. "You aren't a lawyer. According to the law, he's human. Even corporations, idiots, and unborn children are legally persons, and he's a damn sight more human than they are."

"Then he's a dangerous lunatic," said Dunbar.

"Yeah? Where's your commitment order? The only persons who can apply for one are: (a) close relatives and (b) public officials charged with the maintenance of order. You're neither."

Dunbar continued stubbornly: "He ran amuck in my hospital and nearly killed a couple of my men, you know. I guess that gives us some rights."

"Sure," said Robinette. "You can step down to the nearest station and swear out a warrant." He turned to the gnarly man. "Shall we throw the book at 'em, Gaffney?"

"I'm all right," said that individual, his speech returning to its normal slowness. "I just want to make sure these guys don't pester me any more."

"O. K. Now listen, Dunbar. One hostile move out of you and we'll have a warrant out for you for false arrest, assault and battery, attempted kidnaping, criminal conspiracy, and disorderly conduct. *And* we'll slap on a civil suit for damages for sundry torts, to wit: assault, deprivation of civil rights, placing in jeopardy of life and limb, menace, and a few more I may think of later."

"You'll never make that stick," snarled Dunbar. "We have all the witnesses."

"Yeah? And wouldn't the great Evan Dunbar look sweet defending such actions? Some of the ladies who gush over your books might suspect that maybe you weren't such a damn knight in shining armor. We can make a prize monkey of you, and you know it."

"You're destroying the possibility of a great scientific discovery, you know, Robinette."

"To hell with that. My duty is to protect my client. Now beat it, all of you, before I call a cop." His left hand moved suggestively to the telephone.

Dunbar grasped at a last straw. "Hm-m-m. Have you got a permit for that gun?"

"Damn right. Want to see it?"

Dunbar sighed. "Never mind. You *would* have." His greatest opportunity for fame was slipping out of his fingers. He drooped toward the door.

The gnarly man spoke up. "If you don't mind, Dr. Dunbar, I left my hat at your place. I wish you'd send it to Mr. Robinette here. I have a hard time getting hats to fit me."

Dunbar looked at him silently and left with his cohorts.

The gnarly man was giving the lawyer further details when the telephone rang. Robinette answered: "Yes. . . . Saddler? Yes, he's here. . . . Your Dr. Dunbar was going to murder him so he could dissect him. . . . O. K." He turned to the gnarly man. "Your friend Dr. Saddler is looking for you. She's on her way up here."

"Zounds!" said Gaffney. "I'm going."

"Don't you want to see her? She was phoning from around the corner. If you go out now you'll run into her. How did she know where to call?"

"I gave her your number. I suppose she called the hospital and my boarding-house, and tried you as a last resort. This door goes into the hall, doesn't it? Well, when she comes in the regular door I'm going out this one. And I don't want you saying where I've gone. It's nice to have known you, Mr. Robinette."

"Why? What's the matter? You're not going to run out now, are you? Dunbar's harmless, and you've got friends. I'm your friend."

"You're durn tootin' I'm going to run out. There's too much trouble. I've kept alive all these centuries by staying away from trouble. I let down my guard with Dr. Saddler, and went to the surgeon she recommended. First he plots to take me apart to see what makes me tick. If that brain instrument hadn't made me suspicious, I'd have been on my way to the alcohol jars by now. Then there's a fight, and it's just pure luck I didn't kill a couple of those internes, or whatever they are, and get sent up for manslaughter. Now Matilda's after me with a more-than-friendly interest. I know what it means when a woman looks at you that way and calls you 'dear.' I wouldn't mind if she weren't a prominent person of the kind that's always in some sort of garboil. That would mean more trouble, sooner or later. You don't suppose I *like* trouble, do you?''

''But look here, Gaffney, you're getting steamed up over a lot of damn—''

''*Ssst!*'' The gnarly man took his stick and tiptoed over to the private entrance. As Dr. Saddler's clear voice sounded in the outer office, he sneaked out. He was closing the door behind him when the scientist entered the inner office.

Matilda Saddler was a quick thinker. Robinette hardly had time to open his mouth when she flung herself at and through the private door with a cry of ''Clarence!''

Robinette heard the clatter of feet on the stairs. Neither the pursued nor the pursuer had waited for the creaky elevator. Looking out the window, he saw Gaffney leap into a taxi. Matilda Saddler sprinted after the cab, calling: ''Clarence! Come back!'' But the traffic was light and the chase correspondingly hopeless.

They did hear from the gnarly man once more. Three months later Robinette got a letter whose envelope contained, to his vast astonishment, ten ten-dollar bills. The single sheet was typed, even to the signature.

DEAR MR. ROBINETTE:

I do not know what your regular fees are, but I hope that the inclosed will cover your services to me of last June.

Since leaving New York I have had several jobs. I pushed a hack—as we say—in Chicago, and I tried out as pitcher on a bush league baseball team. Once I made my living by knocking over rabbits and things with stones, and I can still throw fairly well. Nor am I bad at swinging a club, such as a baseball bat. But my lameness makes me too slow for a baseball career, and it will be some time before I try any remedial operations again.

I now have a job whose nature I cannot disclose because I do not wish to be traced. You need pay no attention to the postmark; I am not living in Kansas City, but had a friend post this letter there.

Ambition would be foolish for one in my peculiar position. I am satisfied with a job that furnishes me with the essentials, and allows me to go to an occasional movie, and a few friends with whom I can drink beer and talk.

I was sorry to leave New York without saying good-by to Dr. Harold McGannon, who treated me very nicely. I wish you would explain to him why I had to leave as I did. You can get in touch with him through Columbia University.

If Dunbar sent you my hat as I requested, please mail it to me: General Delivery, Kansas City, Mo. My friend will pick it up. There is not a hat store in this town where I live that can fit me. With best wishes, I remain.

Yours sincerely,
SHINING HAWK
Alias CLARENCE ALOYSIUS GAFFNEY.

HENRY KUTTNER

The Misguided Halo

The youngest angel could scarcely be blamed for the error. They had given him a brand-new, shining halo and pointed down to the particular planet they meant. He had followed directions implicitly, feeling quite proud of the responsibility. This was the first time the youngest angel had ever been commissioned to bestow sainthood on a human.

So he swooped down to the earth, located Asia, and came to rest at the mouth of a cavern that gaped halfway up a Himalayan peak. He entered the cave, his heart beating wildly with excitement, preparing to materialize and give the holy lama his richly earned reward. For ten years the ascetic Tibetan Kai Yung had sat motionless, thinking holy thoughts. For ten more years he had dwelt on top of a pillar, acquiring additional merit. And for the last decade he had lived in this cave, a hermit, forsaking fleshly things.

The youngest angel crossed the threshold and stopped with a gasp of amazement. Obviously he was in the wrong place. An overpowering odor of fragrant *sake* assailed his nostrils, and he stared aghast at the wizened, drunken little man who squatted happily beside a fire, roasting a bit of goat flesh. A den of iniquity!

Naturally, the youngest angel, knowing little of the ways of the world, could not understand what had led to the lama's fall from grace. The great pot of *sake* that some misguidedly pious one had left at the cave mouth was an offering, and the lama had tasted, and tasted again. And by this time he was clearly not a suitable candidate for sainthood.

The youngest angel hesitated. The directions had been explicit. But surely this tippling reprobate could not be intended to wear a halo. The lama hiccuped loudly and reached for another cup of *sake* and thereby decided the angel, who unfurled his wings and departed with an air of outraged dignity.

Now, in a Midwestern State of North America there is a town called Tibbett. Who can blame the angel if he alighted there, and, after a brief search, discovered a man apparently ripe for sainthood, whose name, as stated on the door of his small suburban home, was K. Young?

"I may have got it wrong," the youngest angel thought. "They said it was Kai Yung. But this is Tibbett, all right. He must be the man. Looks holy enough, anyway.

"Well," said the youngest angel, "here goes. Now, where's that halo?"

Mr. Young sat on the edge of his bed, with head lowered, brooding. A depressing spectacle. At length he arose and donned various garments. This done, and shaved and washed and combed, he descended the stairway to breakfast.

Jill Young, his wife, sat examining the paper and sipping orange juice. She was a small, scarcely middle-aged, and quite pretty woman who had long ago given up trying to understand life. It was, she decided, much too complicated. Strange things were continually happening. Much better to remain a bystander and simply let them happen. As a result of this attitude, she kept her charming face unwrinkled and added numerous gray hairs to her husband's head.

More will be said presently of Mr. Young's head. It had, of course, been transfigured during the night. But as yet he was unaware of this, and Jill drank orange juice and placidly approved a silly-looking hat in an advertisement.

"Hello, Filthy," said Young. "Morning."

He was not addressing his wife. A small and raffish Scotty had made its appearance, capering hysterically about its master's feet, and going into a fit of sheer madness when the man pulled its hairy ears. The raffish Scotty flung its head sidewise upon the carpet and skated about the room on its muzzle, uttering strangled squeaks of delight. Growing tired of this at last, the Scotty, whose name was Filthy McNasty, began thumping its head on the floor with the apparent intention of dashing out its brains, if any.

Young ignored the familiar sight. He sat down, unfolded his napkin, and examined his food. With a slight grunt of appreciation he began to eat.

He became aware that his wife was eying him with an odd and distrait expression. Hastily he dabbed at his lips with the napkin. But Jill still stared.

Young scrutinized his shirt front. It was, if not immaculate, at least free from stray shreds of bacon or egg. He looked at his wife, and realized that she was staring at a point slightly above his head. He looked up.

Jill started slightly. She whispered, "Kenneth, what *is* that?"

Young smoothed his hair. "Er . . . what, dear?"

"That thing on your head."

The man ran exploring fingers across his scalp. "My head? How do you mean?"

"It's shining," Jill explained. "What on earth have you been doing to yourself?"

Mr. Young felt slightly irritated. "I have been doing nothing to myself. A man grows bald eventually."

Jill frowned and drank orange juice. Her fascinated gaze crept up again. Finally she said, "Kenneth, I wish you'd—"

"What?"

She pointed to a mirror on the wall.

With a disgusted grunt Young arose and faced the image in the glass. At first he saw nothing unusual. It was the same face he had been seeing in mirrors for years. Not an extraordinary face—not one at which a man could point with pride and say: "Look. *My face.*" But, on the other hand, certainly not a countenance which would cause consternation. All in all, an ordinary, clean, well-shaved, and rosy face. Long association with it had given Mr. Young a feeling of tolerance, if not of actual admiration.

But topped by a halo it acquired a certain eerieness.

The halo hung unsuspended about five inches from the scalp. It measured perhaps seven inches in diameter, and seemed like a glowing, luminous ring of white light. It was impalpable, and Young passed his hand through it several times in a dazed manner.

"It's a . . . halo," he said at last, and turned to stare at Jill.

The Scotty, Filthy McNasty, noticed the luminous adornment for the first time. He was greatly interested. He did not, of course, know what it was, but there was always a chance that it might be edible. He was not a very bright dog.

Filthy sat up and whined. He was ignored. Barking loudly, he sprang forward and attempted to climb up his master's body in a mad attempt to reach and rend the halo. Since it had made no hostile move, it was evidently fair prey.

Young defended himself, clutched the Scotty by the nape of its neck, and carried the yelping dog into another room, where he left it. Then he returned and once more looked at Jill.

At length she observed, "Angels wear halos."

"Do I look like an angel?" Young asked. "It's a . . . a scientific manifestation. Like . . . like that girl whose bed kept bouncing around. You read about that."

Jill had. "She did it with her muscles."

"Well, I'm not," Young said definitely. "How could I? It's scientific. Lots of things shine by themselves."

"Oh, yes. Toadstools."

The man winced and rubbed his head. "Thank you, my dear. I suppose you know you're being no help at all."

"Angels have halos," Jill said with a sort of dreadful insistence.

Young was at the mirror again. "Darling, would you mind keeping your trap shut for a while? I'm scared as hell, and you're far from encouraging."

Jill burst into tears, left the room, and was presently heard talking in a low voice to Filthy.

Young finished his coffee, but it was tasteless. He was not as frightened as he had indicated. The manifestation was strange, weird, but in no way terrible. Horns, perhaps, would have caused horror and consternation. But a halo— Mr. Young read the Sunday newspaper supplements, and had learned that everything odd could be attributed to the bizarre workings of science. Somewhere he had heard that all mythology had a basis in scientific fact. This comforted him, until he was ready to leave for the office.

He donned a derby. Unfortunately the halo was too large. The hat seemed to have two brims, the upper one whitely luminous.

"Damn!" said Young in a heartfelt manner. He searched the closet and tried on one hat after another. None would hide the halo. Certainly he could not enter a crowded bus in such a state.

A large furry object in a corner caught his gaze. He dragged it out and eyed the thing with loathing. It was a deformed, gigantic woolly headpiece, resembling a shako, which had once formed a part of a masquerade costume. The suit itself had long since vanished, but the hat remained to the comfort of Filthy, who sometimes slept on it.

Yet it would hide the halo. Gingerly Young drew the monstrosity on his head and crept toward the mirror. One glance was enough. Mouthing a brief prayer, he opened the door and fled.

Choosing between two evils is often difficult. More than once during that nightmare ride downtown Young decided he had made the wrong choice. Yet, somehow, he could not bring himself to tear off the hat and stamp it underfoot, though he was longing to do so. Huddled in a corner of the bus, he steadily contemplated his fingernails and wished he was dead. He heard titters and muffled laughter, and was conscious of probing glances riveted on his shrinking head.

A small child tore open the scar tissue on Young's heart and scrabbled about in the open wound with rosy, ruthless fingers.

"Mamma," said the small child piercingly, "look at the funny man."

"Yes, honey," came a woman's voice. "Be quiet."

"What's that on his head?" the brat demanded.

There was a significant pause. Finally the woman said, "Well, I don't really know," in a baffled manner.

"What's he got it on for?"

No answer.

"Mamma!"

"Yes, honey."

"Is he crazy?"

"Be quiet," said the woman, dodging the issue.

"But what *is* it?"

Young could stand it no longer. He arose and made his way with dignity through the bus, his glazed eyes seeing nothing. Standing on the outer platform, he kept his face averted from the fascinated gaze of the conductor.

As the vehicle slowed down Young felt a hand laid on his arm. He turned. The small child's mother was standing there, frowning.

"Well?" Young inquired snappishly.

"It's Billy," the woman said. "I try to keep nothing from him. Would you mind telling me just what that is on your head?"

"It's Rasputin's beard," Young grated. "He willed it to me." The man leaped from the bus and, ignoring a half-heard question from the still-puzzled woman, tried to lose himself in the crowd.

This was difficult. Many were intrigued by the remarkable hat. But, luckily, Young was only a few blocks from his office, and at last, breathing hoarsely, he stepped into the elevator, glared murderously at the operator, and said, "Ninth floor."

"Excuse me, Mr. Young," the boy said mildly. "There's something on your head."

"I know," Young replied. "I put it there."

This seemed to settle the question. But after the passenger had left the elevator, the boy grinned widely. When he saw the janitor a few minutes later he said:

"You know Mr. Young? The guy—"

"I know him. So what?"

"Drunk as a lord."

"Him? You're screwy."

"Tighter'n a drum," declared the youth, "swelp me Gawd."

Meanwhile, the sainted Mr. Young made his way to the office of Dr. French, a physician whom he knew slightly, and who was conveniently located in the same building. He had not long to wait. The nurse, after one startled glance at the remarkable hat, vanished, and almost immediately reappeared to usher the patient into the inner sanctum.

Dr. French, a large, bland man with a waxed, yellow mustache, greeted Young almost effusively.

"Come in, come in. How are you today? Nothing wrong, I hope. Let me take your hat."

"Wait," Young said, fending off the physician. "First let me explain. There's something on my head."

"Cut, bruise or fracture?" the literal-minded doctor inquired. "I'll fix you up in a jiffy."

"I'm not *sick,*" said Young. "At least, I hope not. I've got a . . . um . . . a halo."

"Ha, ha," Dr. French applauded. "A halo, eh? Surely you're not that good."

"Oh, the hell with it!" Young snapped, and snatched off his hat. The doctor retreated a step. Then, interested, he approached and tried to finger the halo. He failed.

"I'll be— This is odd," he said at last. "Does look rather like one, doesn't it?"

"What is it? That's what I want to know."

French hesitated. He plucked at his mustache. "Well, it's rather out of my line. A physicist might— No. Perhaps Mayo's. Does it come off?"

"Of course not. You can't even touch the thing."

"Ah. I see. Well, I should like some specialists' opinions. In the meantime, let me see—" There was orderly tumult. Young's heart, temperature, blood, saliva and epidermis were tested and approved.

At length French said: "You're fit as a fiddle. Come in tomorrow, at ten. I'll have some other specialists here then."

"You . . . uh . . . you can't get rid of this?"

"I'd rather not try just yet. It's obviously some form of radioactivity. A radium treatment may be necessary—"

Young left the man mumbling about alpha and gamma rays. Discouraged, he donned his strange hat and went down the hall to his own office.

The Atlas Advertising Agency was the most conservative of all advertising agencies. Two brothers with white whiskers had started the firm in 1820, and the company still seemed to wear dignified mental whiskers. Changes were frowned upon by the board of directors, who, in 1938, were finally convinced that radio had come to stay, and had accepted contracts for advertising broadcasts.

Once a junior vice president had been discharged for wearing a red necktie.

Young slunk into his office. It was vacant. He slid into his chair behind the desk, removed his hat, and gazed at it with loathing. The headpiece seemed to have grown even more horrid than it had appeared at first. It was shedding, and, moreover, gave off a faint but unmistakable aroma of unbathed Scotties.

After investigating the halo, and realizing that it was still firmly fixed in its place, Young turned to his work. But the Norns were casting baleful glances in his direction, for presently the door opened and Edwin G. Kipp, president of Atlas, entered. Young barely had time to duck his head beneath the desk and hide the halo.

Kipp was a small, dapper, and dignified man who wore pince-nez and Vandyke with the air of a reserved fish. His blood had long since been metamorphosed into ammonia. He moved, if not in beauty, at least in an almost visible aura of grim conservatism.

"Good morning. Mr. Young," he aid. "Er . . . is that you?"

"Yes," said the invisible Young. "Good morning. I'm tying my shoelace."

To this Kipp made no reply save for an almost inaudible cough. Time passed. The desk was silent.

"Er . . . Mr. Young?"

"I'm . . . still here," said the wretched Young. "It's knotted. The shoelace, I mean. Did you want me?"

"Yes."

Kipp waited with gradually increasing impatience. There were no signs of a forthcoming emergence. The president considered the advisability of his advancing to the desk and peering under it. But the mental picture of a conversation conducted in so grotesque a manner was harrowing. He simply gave up and told Young what he wanted.

"Mr. Devlin has just telephoned," Kipp observed. "He will arrive shortly. He wishes to . . . er . . . to be shown the town, as he put it."

The invisible Young nodded. Devlin was one of their best clients. Or, rather, he had been until last year, when he suddenly began to do business with another firm, to the discomfiture of Kipp and the board of directors.

The president went on. "He told me he is hesitating about his new contract. He had planned to give it to World, but I had some correspondence with him on the matter, and suggested that a personal discussion might be of value. So he is visiting our city, and wishes to go . . . er . . . sightseeing."

Kipp grew confidential. "I may say that Mr. Devlin told me rather definitely that he prefers a less conservative firm. 'Stodgy,' his term was. He will dine with me tonight, and I shall endeavor to convince him that our service will be of value. Yet"—Kipp coughed again—"yet diplomacy is, of course, important. I should appreciate your entertaining Mr. Devlin today."

The desk had remained silent during this oration. Now it said convulsively: "I'm sick. I can't—"

"You are ill? Shall I summon a physician?"

Young hastily refused the offer, but remained in hiding. "No, I . . . but I mean—"

"You are behaving most strangely," Kipp said with commendable restraint. "There is something you should know, Mr. Young. I had not intended to tell you as yet, but . . . at any rate, the board has taken notice of you. There was a discussion at the last meeting. We have planned to offer you a vice presidency in the firm."

The desk was stricken dumb.

"You have upheld our standards for fifteen years," said Kipp. "There has been no hint of scandal attached to your name. I congratulate you, Mr. Young."

The president stepped forward, extending his hand. An arm emerged from beneath the desk, shook Kipp's, and quickly vanished.

Nothing further happened. Young tenaciously remained in his sanctuary. Kipp realized that, short of dragging the man out bodily, he could not hope to view an entire Kenneth Young for the present. With an admonitory cough he withdrew.

The miserable Young emerged, wincing as his cramped muscles relaxed. A pretty kettle of fish. How could be entertain Devlin while he wore a halo? And it was vitally necessary that Devlin be entertained, else the elusive vice presidency would be immediately withdrawn. Young knew only too well that employees of Atlas Advertising Agency trod a perilous pathway.

His reverie was interrupted by the sudden appearance of an angel atop the bookcase.

It was not a high bookcase, and the supernatural visitor sat there calmly enough, heels dangling and wings furled. A scanty robe of white samite made up the angel's wardrobe—that and a shining halo, at sight of which Young felt a wave of nausea sweep him.

"This," he said with rigid restraint, "is the end. A halo may be due to mass hypnotism. But when I start seeing angels—"

"Don't be afraid," said the other. "I'm real enough."

Young's eyes were wild. "How do I know? I'm obviously talking to empty air. It's schizo-something. Go away."

The angel wriggled his toes and looked embarrassed. "I can't, just yet. The fact is, I made a bad mistake. You may have noticed that you've a slight halo—"

Young gave a short, bitter laugh. "Oh, yes. I've *noticed* it."

Before the angel could reply the door opened. Kipp looked in, saw that Young was engaged, and murmured, "Excuse me," as he withdrew.

The angel scratched his golden curls. "Well, your halo was intended for somebody else—a Tibetan lama, in fact. But through a certain chain of circumstances I was led to believe that you were the candidate for sainthood. So—" The visitor made a comprehensive gesture.

Young was baffled. "I don't quite—"

"The lama . . . well, sinned. No sinner may wear a halo. And, as I say, I gave it to you through error."

"Then you can take it away again?" Amazed delight suffused Young's face. But the angel raised a benevolent hand.

"Fear not. I have checked with the recording angel. You have led a blameless life. As a reward, you will be permitted to keep the halo of sainthood."

The horrified man sprang to his feet, making feeble swimming motions with his arms. "But . . . but . . . but—"

"Peace and blessings be upon you," said the angel, and vanished.

Young fell back into his chair and massaged his aching brow. Simultaneously the door opened and Kipp stood on the threshold. Luckily Young's hands temporarily hid the halo.

"Mr. Devlin is here," the president said. "Er . . . who was that on the bookcase?"

Young was too crushed to lie plausibly. He muttered, "An angel."

Kipp nodded in satisfaction. "Yes, of course . . . *What?* You say an angel . . . an angel? Oh, my gosh!" The man turned quite white and hastily took his departure.

Young contemplated his hat. The thing still lay on the desk, wincing slightly under the baleful stare directed at it. To go through life wearing a halo was only less endurable than the thought of continually wearing the loathsome hat. Young brought his fist down viciously on the desk.

"I won't stand it! I . . . I don't have to—" He stopped abruptly. A dazed look grew in his eyes.

"I'll be . . . that's right! I don't *have* to stand it. If that lama got out of it . . . of course. 'No sinner may wear a halo.' " Young's round face twisted into a mask of sheer evil. "I'll be a sinner, then! I'll break all the Commandments—"

He pondered. At the moment he couldn't remember what they were. "Thou shalt not covet thy neighbor's wife." That was one.

Young thought of his neighbor's wife—a certain Mrs. Clay, a behemothic damsel of some fifty summers, with a face like a desiccated pudding. That was one Commandment he had no intention of breaking.

But probably one good, healthy sin would bring back the angel in a hurry to remove the halo. What crimes would result in the least inconvenience? Young furrowed his brow.

Nothing occurred to him. He decided to go for a walk. No doubt some sinful opportunity would present itself.

He forced himself to don the shako and had reached the elevator when a hoarse voice was heard hallooing after him. Racing along the hall was a fat man.

Young knew instinctively that this was Mr. Devlin.

The adjective "fat," as applied to Devlin, was a considerable understatement. The man bulged. His feet, strangled in biliously yellow shoes, burst out at the ankles like blossoming flowers. They merged into calves that seemed to gather momentum as they spread and mounted, flung themselves up with mad abandon, and revealed themselves in their complete, unrestrained glory at Devlin's middle. The man resembled, in silhouette, a pineapple with elephantiasis. A great mass of flesh poured out of his collar, forming a pale, sagging lump in which Young discerned some vague resemblance to a face.

Such was Devlin, and he charged along the hall, as mammoths thunder by, with earth-shaking tramplings of his crashing hoofs.

"You're Young!" he wheezed. "Almost missed me, eh? I was waiting in the office—" Devlin paused, his fascinated gaze upon the hat. Then, with an effort at politeness, he laughed falsely and glanced away. "Well, I'm all ready and r'aring to go."

Young felt himself impaled painfully on the horns of a dilemma. Failure to entertain Devlin would mean the loss of that vice presidency. But the halo weighed like a flatiron on Young's throbbing head. One thought was foremost in his mind: he *had* to get rid of the blessed thing.

Once he had done that, he would trust to luck and diplomacy. Obviously, to take out his guest now would be fatal insanity. The hat alone would be fatal.

"Sorry," Young grunted. "Got an important engagement. I'll be back for you as soon as I can."

Wheezing laughter, Devlin attached himself firmly to the other's arm. "No, you don't. You're showing me the town! Right now!" An unmistakable alcoholic odor was wafted to Young's nostrils. He thought quickly.

"All right," he said at last. "Come along. There's a bar downstairs. We'll have a drink, eh?"

"Now you're talking," said the jovial Devlin, almost incapacitating Young with a comradely slap on the back. "Here's the elevator."

They crowded into the cage. Young shut his eyes and suffered as interested stares were directed upon the hat. He fell into a state of coma, arousing only at the ground floor, where Devlin dragged him out and into the adjacent bar.

Now Young's plan was this: he would pour drink after drink down his companion's capacious gullet, and await his chance to slip away unobserved. It was a shrewd scheme, but it had one flaw—Devlin refused to drink alone.

"One for you and one for me," he said. "That's fair. Have another."

Young could not refuse, under the circumstances. The worst of it was that Devlin's liquor seemed to seep into every cell of his huge body, leaving him, finally, in the same state of glowing happiness which had been his originally. But poor Young was, to put it as charitably as possible, tight.

He sat quietly in a booth, glaring across at Devlin. Each time the waiter arrived, Young knew that the man's eyes were riveted upon the hat. And each round made the thought of that more irritating.

Also, Young worried about his halo. He brooded over sins. Arson, burglary, sabotage, and murder passed in quick review through his befuddled mind. Once he attempted to snatch the waiter's change, but the man was too alert. He laughed pleasantly and placed a fresh glass before Young.

The latter eyed it with distaste. Suddenly coming to a decision, he arose and wavered toward the door. Devlin overtook him on the sidewalk.

"What's the matter? Let's have another—"

"I have work to do," said Young with painful distinctness. He snatched a walking cane from a passing pedestrian and made threatening gestures with it until the remonstrating victim fled hurriedly. Hefting the stick in his hand, he brooded blackly.

"But why work?" Devlin inquired largely. "Show me the town."

"I have important matters to attend to." Young scrutinized a small child who had halted by the curb and was returning the stare with interest. The tot looked remarkably like the brat who had been so insulting on the bus.

"What's important?" Devlin demanded. "Important matters, eh? Such as what?"

"Beating small children," said Young, and rushed upon the startled child, brandishing his cane. The youngster uttered a shrill scream and fled. Young pursued for a few feet and then became entangled with a lamp-post. The lamp-post was impolite and dictatorial. It refused to allow Young to pass. The man remonstrated and, finally, argued, but to no avail.

The child had long since disappeared. Administering a brusque and snappy rebuke to the lamp-post, Young turned away.

"What in Pete's name are you trying to do?" Devlin inquired. "That cop's looking at us. Come along." He took the other's arm and led him along the crowded sidewalk.

"What am I trying to do?" Young sneered. "It's obvious, isn't it? I wish to sin."

"Er . . . sin?"

"Sin."

"Why?"

Young tapped his hat meaningly, but Devlin put an altogether wrong interpretation on the gesture. "You're nuts?"

"Oh, shut up," Young snapped in a sudden burst of rage, and thrust his cane between the legs of a passing bank president whom he knew slightly. The unfortunate man fell heavily to the cement, but arose without injury save to his dignity.

"I beg your pardon!" he barked.

Young was going through a strange series of gestures. He had fled to a show-window mirror and was doing fantastic things to his hat, apparently trying to lift it in order to catch a glimpse of the top of his head—a sight, it seemed, to be shielded jealously from profane eyes. At length he cursed loudly, turned, gave the bank president a contemptuous stare, and hurried away, trailing the puzzled Devlin like a captive balloon.

Young was muttering thickly to himself.

"Got to sin—really sin. Something big. Burn down an orphan asylum. Kill m' mother-in-law. Kill . . . anybody!" He looked quickly at Devlin, and the latter shrank back in sudden fear. But finally Young gave a disgusted grunt.

"Nrgh. Too much blubber. Couldn't use a gun or a knife. Have to blast— Look!" Young said, clutching Devlin's arm. "Stealing's a sin, isn't it?"

"Sure is," the diplomatic Devlin agreed. "But you're not—"

Young shook his head. "No. Too crowded here. No use going to jail. Come on!"

He plunged forward. Devlin followed. And Young fulfilled his promise to show his guest the town, though afterward neither of them could remember exactly what had happened. Presently Devlin paused in a liquor store for refueling, and emerged with bottles protruding here and there from his clothing.

Hours merged into an alcoholic haze. Life began to assume an air of foggy unreality to the unfortunate Devlin. He sank presently into a coma, dimly conscious of various events which marched with celerity through the afternoon and long into the night. Finally he roused himself sufficiently to realize that he was standing with Young confronting a wooden Indian which stood quietly outside a cigar store. It was, perhaps, the last of the wooden Indians. The outworn relic of a bygone day, it seemed to stare with faded glass eyes at the bundle of wooden cigars it held in an extended hand.

Young was no longer wearing a hat. And Devlin suddenly noticed something decidedly peculiar about his companion.

He said softly, "You've got a halo."

Young started slightly. "Yes," he replied, "I've got a halo. This Indian—" He paused.

Devlin eyed the image with disfavor. To his somewhat fuzzy brain the wooden Indian appeared even more horrid than the surprising halo. He shuddered and hastily averted his gaze.

"Stealing's a sin," Young said under his breath, and then, with an elated cry, stooped to lift the Indian. He fell immediately under its weight, emitting a string of smoking oaths as he attempted to dislodge the incubus.

"Heavy," he said, rising at last. "Give me a hand."

Devlin had long since given up any hope of finding sanity in this madman's actions. Young was obviously determined to sin, and the fact that he possessed a halo was somewhat disquieting, even to the drunken Devlin. As a result, the two men proceeded down the street, bearing with them the rigid body of a wooden Indian.

The proprietor of the cigar shop came out and looked after them, rubbing his hands. His eyes followed the departing statue with unmitigated joy.

"For ten years I've tried to get rid of that thing," he whispered gleefully. "And now . . . aha!"

He re-entered the store and lit a Corona to celebrate his emancipation.

Meanwhile, Young and Devlin found a taxi stand. One cab stood there; the driver sat puffing a cigarette and listening to his radio. Young hailed the man.

"Cab, sir?" The driver sprang to life, bounced out of the car, and flung open the door. Then he remained frozen in a half-crouching position, his eyes revolving wildly in their sockets.

He had never believed in ghosts. He was, in fact, somewhat of a cynic. But in the face of a bulbous ghoul and a decadent angel bearing the stiff corpse of an Indian, he felt with a sudden, blinding shock of realization that beyond life lies a black abyss teeming with horror unimaginable. Whining shrilly, the terrified man leaped back into his cab, got the thing into motion, and vanished as smoke before the gale.

Young and Devlin looked at one another ruefully.

"What now?" the latter asked.

"Well," said Young, "I don't live far from here. Only ten blocks or so. Come on!"

It was very late, and few pedestrians were abroad. These few, for the sake of their sanity, were quite willing to ignore the wanderers and go their separate ways. So eventually Young, Devlin, and the wooden Indian arrived at their destination.

The door of Young's home was locked, and he could not locate the key. He was curiously averse to arousing Jill. But, for some strange reason, he felt it vitally necessary that the wooden Indian be concealed. The cellar was the logical place. He dragged his two companions to a basement window, smashed it as quietly as possible, and slid the image through the gap.

"Do you really live here?" asked Devlin, who had his doubts.

"Hush!" Young said warningly. "Come on!"

He followed the wooden Indian, landing with a crash in a heap of coal. Devlin joined him after much wheezing and grunting. It was not dark. The halo provided about as much illumination as a twenty-five-watt globe.

Young left Devlin to nurse his bruises and began searching for the wooden Indian. It had unaccountably vanished. But he found it at last cowering beneath a washtub, dragged the object out, and set it up in a corner. Then he stepped back and faced it, swaying a little.

"That's a sin, all right," he chuckled. "Theft. It isn't the amount that matters. It's the principle of the thing. A wooden Indian is just as important as a million dollars, eh, Devlin?"

"I'd like to chop that Indian into fragments," said Devlin with passion. "You made me carry if for three miles." He paused, listening. "What in heaven's name is that?"

A small tumult was approaching. Filthy, having been instructed often in his duties as a watchdog, now faced opportunity. Noises were proceeding from the cellar. Burglars, no doubt. The raffish Scotty cascaded down the stairs in a babel of frightful threats and oaths. Loudly declaring his intention of eviscerating the intruders, he flung himself upon Young, who made hasty clucking sounds intended to soothe the Scotty's aroused passions.

Filthy had other ideas. He spun like a dervish, yelling bloody murder. Young wavered, made a vain snatch at the air, and fell prostrate to the ground. He remained face down, while Filthy, seeing the halo, rushed at it and trampled upon his master's head.

The wretched Young felt the ghosts of a dozen and more drinks rising to confront him. He clutched at the dog, missed, and gripped instead the feet of the wooden Indian. The image swayed perilously. Filthy cocked up an apprehensive eye and fled down the length of his master's body, pausing halfway as he remembered his duty. With a muffled curse he sank his teeth into the nearest portion of Young and attempted to yank off the miserable man's pants.

Meanwhile, Young remained face down, clutching the feet of the wooden Indian in a despairing grip.

There was a resounding clap of thunder. White light blazed through the cellar. The angel appeared.

Devlin's legs gave way. He sat down in a plump heap, shut his eyes, and began chattering quietly to himself. Filthy swore at the intruder, made an unsuccessful attempt to attain a firm grasp on one of the gently fanning wings, and went back to think it over, arguing throatily. The wing had an unsatisfying lack of substantiality.

The angel stood over Young with golden fires glowing in his eyes, and a benign look of pleasure molding his noble features. "This," he said quietly, "shall be taken as a symbol of your first successful good deed since your enhaloment." A wingtip brushed the dark and grimy visage of the Indian. Forthwith, there was no Indian. "You have lightened the heart of a fellow man—little, to be sure, but some, and at a cost of much labor on your part.

"For a day you have struggled with this sort to redeem him, but for this no success has rewarded you, albeit the morrow's pains will afflict you.

"Go forth, K. Young, rewarded and protected from all sin alike by your halo." The youngest angel faded quietly, for which alone Young was grateful. His head was beginning to ache and he'd feared a possible thunderous vanishment.

Filthy laughed nastily, and renewed his attack on the halo. Young found the unpleasant act of standing upright necessary. While it made the walls and tubs spin round like all the hosts of heaven, it made impossible Filthy's dervish dance on his face.

Some time later he awoke, cold sober and regretful of the fact. He lay between cool sheets, watching morning sunlight lance through the windows, his eyes, and feeling it splinter in jagged bits in his brain. His stomach was making spasmodic attempts to leap up and squeeze itself out through his burning throat.

Simultaneous with awakening came realization of three things: the pains of the morrow had indeed afflicted him; the halo mirrored still in the glass above the dressing table—and the parting words of the angel.

He groaned a heartfelt triple groan. The headache would pass, but the halo, he knew, would not. Only by sinning could one become unworthy of it, and—shining protector!—it made him unlike other men. His deeds must all be good, his works a help to men. He could not sin!

FRITZ LEIBER

Two Sought Adventure

It was the Year of the Behemoth, the Month of the Hedgehog, the Day of the Toad. A hot, late summer sun was sinking down toward evening over the somber, fertile land of Lankhmar, the most civilized country in a world which history forgets. Peasants toiling in the endless grain fields paused for a moment, and lifted their earth-stained faces, and noted that it would soon be time to commence lesser chores. Cattle cropping the stubble began to move in the general direction of home. Sweaty merchants and shopkeepers decided to wait a little longer before tasting the pleasures of the bath. Thieves and astrologers moved restlessly in their sleep, sensing that the hours of night and work were drawing near.

At the southernmost limit of the land of Lankhmar, a day's ride beyond the village of Soreev, where the grain fields gave way to rolling forests of maple and oak, two horsemen cantered leisurely along a narrow, dusty road. They presented a sharp contrast. The larger wore a tunic of unbleached linen, drawn tight at the waist by a very broad leather belt. A fold of linen cloak was looped over his head as a protection against the sun. A long sword with a pomegranate-shaped golden pommel was strapped to his side. Behind his right shoulder a quiver of arrows jutted up. Half sheathed in a saddlecase was a thick yew bow, unstrung. His great, lissom muscles, white skin, copper hair, green eyes, and above all the pleasant, yet untamed, expression of his massive countenance, all hinted at a land of origin colder, rougher, and more barbarous than that of Lankhmar.

Even as everything about the larger man suggested the wilderness, so the general appearance of the smaller man—and he was considerably smaller—spoke of the city. His dark face was that of a jester. Bright, black eyes, snub nose, and little lines of irony about the mouth. Hands of a conjurer. Something about the set of his wiry frame betokening exceptional competence in street fights and tavern brawls. He was clad from head to foot in garments of gray silk, soft, and curiously loose of weave. His slim sword, cased in gray mouse skin, was slightly curved toward the tip. From his belt hung a sling and a pouch of missiles.

Despite their many dissimilarities, it was obvious that the two men were comrades, that they were united by a bond of subtle mutual understanding. The smaller rode a dappled gray mare; the larger, a chestnut gelding.

They were nearing a point where the narrow road came to the end of a rise, made a slight turn, and wound down into the next valley. Green walls of leaves pressed in on either side. The heat was considerable, but not oppressive. It brought to mind thoughts of satyrs and centaurs dozing in hidden glades.

Then the gray mare, slightly in the lead, whinnied. The smaller man tightened his hold on the reins, his black eyes darting quick, alert glances, first to one side of the road and then to the other. There was a faint scraping sound, as of wood on wood.

Without warning the two men ducked down, clinging to the side harness of their horses. Simultaneously came the musical twang of bowstrings, like the prelude of some forest concert, and several arrows buzzed angrily through the spaces that had just been vacated. Then the mare and the gelding were around the turn and galloping like the wind, their hoofs striking up great puffs of dust.

From behind came excited shouts and answers as the pursuit got under way. There seemed to have been fully seven or eight men in the ambuscade—squat, sturdy rogues wearing chain-mail shirts and steel caps. Before the mare and the gelding had gone a stone's throw down the road, they were out and after, a black horse in the lead.

But those pursued were not wasting time. The larger man rose to a stand in his stirrups, whipping the yew bow from its case. With his left hand he bent it against the stirrup, with his right he drew the upper loop of the string into place. Then his left hand slipped down the bow to the grip and his right reached smoothly back over his shoulder for an arrow. Still guiding his horse with his knees, he rose even higher and turned in his saddle—it was a sight for the gods—and sent an eagle-feathered shaft whirring. Meanwhile his comrade had placed a small leaden ball in his sling, whirled it twice about his head, so that it hummed stridently, and loosed his cast.

Arrow and missile sped and struck together. The one pierced the shoulder of the leading horseman and the other smote the second on his steel cap, and tumbled him from his saddle. The pursuit halted abruptly in a tangle of plunging and rearing horses. The men who had caused this confusion pulled up at the next bend in the road and turned back to watch.

"By the Hedgehog," said the smaller, grinning wickedly, "but they will think twice before they play at ambuscades again!"

"Blundering fools," said the larger. "Haven't they even learned to shoot from their saddle? I tell you, Gray Mouser, it takes a barbarian to fight his horse properly."

"Except for myself and a few other people," replied the one who bore the strangely appropriate nickname of Gray Mouser. "But look, Fafhrd, the rogues retreat bearing their wounded, and one gallops far ahead. *Tcha,* but I dinted black beard's pate for him. He hangs over his nag like a bag of meal. If he'd have known who we were, he wouldn't have been so hot on the chase."

There was some truth to this last boast. The names of the Gray Mouser and the northerner Fafhrd were already something to conjure with in the lands around Lankhmar and in proud Lankhmar, too. Their taste for strange adventure, their mysterious comings and goings, and their odd sense of humor were matters that puzzled almost all men alike.

Abruptly Fafhrd unstrung his bow and turned forward in his saddle.

"This should be the very valley we are seeking," he said. "See, there are the two double-humped hills of which the document speaks. Let's have another look at it, to test my guess."

The Gray Mouser reached into his capacious leather pouch and withdrew a page of thick vellum, which was curiously greenish with extreme age. Three edges were frayed and worn; the fourth showed a clean and recent cut. It was inscribed with the intricate hieroglyphs of Lankhmarian writing, done in the black ink of the squid. But it was not to these that the Mouser turned his attention, but to several faint lines of diminutive red script, written into the margin. These he read.

"Let kings stack their treasure houses ceiling-high, and merchants burst their vaults with hoarded coin, and fools envy them. I have a treasure that outvalues theirs. A diamond as big as a man's skull. Twelve rubies each as big as the skull of a cat. Seventeen emeralds each as big as the skull of a mole. And certain rods of crystal and bars of orichalchum. Let overlords swagger jewel-bedecked and queens load themselves with gems, and fools adore them. I have a treasure that will outlast theirs. A treasure house have I built for it in the far southern forest, where the two hills hump double, like sleeping camels, a day's ride beyond the village of Soreev.

"A great treasure house with a high tower, fit for a king's dwelling—yet no king may dwell there. Immediately below the keystone of the chief dome my treasure lies hid, eternal as the glittering stars. It will outlast me and my name, I, Urgaan of Angarngi. It is my hold on the future. Let fools seek it. They shall win it not. For although my treasure house be empty as air, yet have I left a guardian there. Let the wise read this riddle and forbear."

"The man's mind runs to skulls," muttered the Mouser. "He must have been a gravedigger or a necromancer."

"Or an architect," observed Fafhrd thoughtfully, "in those past days when graven images of the skulls of men and animals served as the chief architectural ornament."

"Perhaps," agreed the Mouser. "Surely the writing and ink are old enough. They date at least as far back as the Century of the Wars with the East—five long life-spans."

The Mouser was an accomplished forger, both of handwriting and of objects of art. He knew what he was talking about.

Satisfied that they were near the goal of their quest, the two comrades gazed through a break in the foliage down into the valley. It was shaped like the inside of a pod—shallow, long, and narrow. They were viewing it from one of the narrow ends. The two peculiarly humped hills formed the long sides. The whole of the valley was green with maple and oak, save for a small gap toward the middle. That, thought the Mouser, might mark a peasant's dwelling and the cleared space around it.

Beyond the gap he could make out something dark and squarish rising a little above the treetops. He called his companion's attention to it, but they could not decide whether it was indeed a tower such as the document mentioned, or just a peculiar shadow, or perhaps even the dead, limbless trunk of a gigantic oak. It was too far away.

"Almost sufficient time has passed," said Fafhrd, after a pause, "for one of those rogues to have sneaked up through the forest for another shot at us. Evening draws near."

They spoke to their horses and moved on, slowly, as if not to disturb the arboreal quiet. They tried to keep their eyes fixed on the thing that looked like a tower, but since they were descending, it almost immediately dropped out of sight below the treetops. There would be no further chance of seeing it until they were quite close at hand.

The Mouser felt a subdued excitement running through his flesh. Soon they would discover if there were a treasure to be had or not. A diamond as big as a man's skull—rubies—emeralds— He found an almost nostalgic delight in prolonging and savoring to the full this last, leisurely stage of their quest. The recent ambuscade served as a necessary spice.

He thought of how he had slit the interesting-looking vellum page from the ancient book on architecture that reposed in the library of the rapacious and overbearing Lord Rannarsh. Of how, half in jest, he had sought out and interrogated several peddlers from the South. Of how he had found one who had recently passed through a village named Soreev. Of how that one had told him of a stone structure in the forest south of Soreev, called by the peasants the House of Angarngi, and reputed to be long deserted. The peddler had seen a high tower rising above the trees. The Mouser recalled the man's wizened, cunning face and chuckled. And that brought to mind the greedy, sallow face of Lord Rannarsh, and a new thought occurred to him.

"Fafhrd," he said, "those rogues we just now put to flight—what did you take them for?"

The northerner grunted humorous contempt.

"Run-of-the-manger ruffians. Waylayers of fat merchants. Pasture bravos. Bumpkin bandits!"

"Still, they were all well armed, and armed alike—as if they were in some rich man's service. And that one who rode far ahead. Mightn't he have been hastening to report failure to some master?"

"What is your thought?"

The Mouser did not reply for some moments.

"I was thinking," he said, "that Lord Rannarsh is a rich man and a greedy one, who slavers at the thought of jewels. And I was wondering if he ever read those faint lines of red lettering and made a copy of them, and if my theft of the original sharpened his interest."

The northerner shook his head.

"I doubt it. You are oversubtle. But if he did, and if he seeks to rival us in this treasure quest, he'd best watch each step twice—and choose servitors who can fight on horseback."

They were moving so slowly that the hoofs of the mare and the gelding hardly stirred up the dust. They had no fear of danger from the rear. A well-laid ambuscade might surprise them, but not a man or horse in motion. The narrow road wound along in a rather purposeless fashion. Leaves brushed their faces, and occasionally they had to swing their bodies out of the way of encroaching branches. The ripe, dryish scent of the late summer forest was intensified now that they were below the rim of the valley. Mingled with it were whiffs of wild berries and aromatic shrubs. Shadows imperceptibly lengthened.

"Nine chances out of ten," murmured the Mouser dreamily, "the treasure house of Urgaan of Angarngi was looted some hundred years ago, by men whose bodies are already dust."

"It may be so," agreed Fafhrd. "Unlike men, rubies and emeralds do not rest quietly in their graves."

This possibility, which they had discussed several times before, did not disturb them now, or make them impatient. Rather did it impart to their quest the pleasant melancholy of a lost hope. They drank in the rich air and let their horses munch random mouthfuls of leaves. A jay called shrilly from overhead and off in the forest a catbird was chattering, their sharp voices breaking in on the low buzzing and droning of the insects. Night was drawning near. The almost horizontal rays of the sun gilded the treetops. Then Fafhrd's sharp ears caught the hollow lowing of a cow.

A few more turns brought them into the clearing they had spied. In line with their surmise, it proved to contain a peasant's cottage—a neat little low-eaved house of weathered wood, situated in the midst of an acre of grain. To one side was a bean patch; to the other, a woodpile which almost dwarfed the house. In front of the cottage stood a wiry old man, his skin as brown as his homespun tunic. He had evidently just heard the horses and turned around to look.

"Ho, father," called the Mouser, "it's a good day to be abroad in, and a good home you have here."

The peasant considered these statements and then nodded his head in agreement.

"We are two weary travelers," continued the Mouser.

Again the peasant nodded gravely.

"In return for two silver coins will you give us lodging for the night?"

The peasant rubbed his chin and then held up three fingers.

"Very well, you shall have three silver coins," said the Mouser, slipping from his horse. Fafhrd followed suit.

Only after giving the old man a coin to seal the bargain, did the Mouser question casually, "Is there not an old, deserted place near your dwelling called the House of Angarngi?"

The peasant nodded.

"What's it like?"

The peasant shrugged his shoulders.

"Don't you know?"

The peasant shook his head.

"But haven't you ever seen the place?" The Mouser's voice carried a note of amazement he did not bother to conceal.

He was answered by another headshake.

"But father, it's only a few minutes' walk from your dwelling, isn't it?"

The peasant nodded tranquilly, as if the whole business were very obvious and no matter for surprise.

A muscular young man, who had come from behind the cottage to take their horses, offered a suggestion.

"You can see tower from other side the house. I can point her out."

At this the old man proved he was not completely speechless by saying in a dry, expressionless voice: "Go ahead. Look at her all you want."

And he stepped into the cottage. Fafhrd and the Mouser caught a glimpse of a child peering around the door, an old woman stirring a pot, and someone hunched in a big chair before the tiny fire.

The upper part of the tower proved to be just barely visible through a break in the trees. The last rays of the sun touched it with deep red. It looked about four or five bowshots distant. And then, even as they watched, the sun dipped under and it became a featureless square of blackish stone.

"She's an old place," explained the young man vaguely. "I been all around her. Father, he's just never bothered to look."

"You've been inside?" questioned the Mouser.

The young man scratched his head doubtfully.

"No. She's just an old place. No good for anything."

"There'll be a fairly long twilight," said Fafhrd, his wide green eyes drawn to the tower as if by a lodestone. "Long enough for us to have a closer look."

"I'd show the way," said the young man, "save I got water to fetch."

"No matter," replied Fafhrd. "When's supper?"

"When first stars show."

They left him holding their horses and walked straight into the woods. Immediately it became much darker, as if twilight were almost over, rather than just begun. The vegetation proved to be somewhat thicker than they had anticipated. There were vines and thorns to be avoided. Irregular, pale patches of sky appeared and disappeared overhead.

The Mouser let Fafhrd lead the way. His mind was occupied with a queer sort of reverie about the peasants. It tickled his fancy to think how they had stolidly lived their toilsome lives, generation after generation, only a few steps from what might be one of the greatest treasure-troves in the world. It seemed an incredible contrast. How could people sleep so near jewels and not dream of them? But probably they never dreamed.

So the Gray Mouser was sharply aware of few things during the journey through the woods, save that Fafhrd seemed to be taking a long time—which was strange, since the barbarian was an accomplished woodsman.

Finally a deeper and more solid shadow loomed up through the trees, and in a moment they were standing in the margin of a small, boulder-studded clearing, most of which was occupied by the bulky structure they sought. Abruptly, even before his eyes took in the details of the place, the Mouser's mind was filled with a hundred petty perturbations. Weren't they making a mistake in leaving their horses with those strange peasants? And mightn't those rogues have followed them to the cottage? And wasn't this the Day of the Toad, an unlucky day for entering deserted houses? And shouldn't they have a short spear along, in case they met a forest leopard? And wasn't that a whippoorwill he heard crying on his left hand, an augury of ill omen?

The treasure house of Urgaan of Angarngi was a peculiar structure. The main feature was a large, shallow dome, resting on walls that formed an octagon. In front, and merging into it, were two lesser domes. Between these gaped a great square doorway. The tower rose asymmetrically from the rear part of the chief dome. The eyes of the Mouser sought hurriedly through the dimming twilight for the cause of the salient peculiarity of the structure, and decided it lay in the utter simplicity. There were no pillars, no outjutting cornices, no friezes, no architectural ornaments of any sort, skull-embellished or otherwise. Save for the doorway and a few tiny windows set in unexpected places, the House of Angarngi was a compact mass of uniformly dark gray stones.

But now Fafhrd was striding up the short flight of terraced steps that led toward the open door, and the Mouser perforce followed him, although he would have liked to spy around a little longer. With every step he took forward he sensed an odd reluctance growing within him. His earlier mood of pleasant expectancy vanished as suddenly as if he'd stepped into quicksand. It seemed to him that the black doorway yawned like a toothless mouth. And then a little shudder went through him, for he saw the mouth had a tooth—a bit of ghostly white that jutted up from the floor. Fafhrd was reaching down toward the object.

"I wonder whose skull this may be?" said the northerner calmly.

The Mouser regarded the thing, and the scattering of bones and fragments of bone beside it. His feeling of uneasiness was fast growing toward a climax, and he had the unpleasant conviction that, once it did reach a climax, something would happen. What was the answer to Fafhrd's question? What form of death had struck down that earlier intruder? It was so dark inside the treasure house. Didn't the manuscript mention something about a guardian? It was hard to think of a flesh-and-blood guardian persisting for three hundred years, but there were things that were immortal or nearly immortal. He could tell that Fafhrd was not in the least affected by any premonitory disquietude, and was quite capable of instituting an immediate search for the treasure. That must be prevented at all costs. But how? He remembered that the northerner loathed snakes.

"This cold, damp stone," he observed casually. "Just the place for snakes."

"Nothing of the sort," replied Fafhrd angrily. "I'm willing to wager there's not a single serpent inside."

But a moment later he was agreeing it would be well to postpone the search until daylight returned, now that the treasure house was located.

As they re-entered the woods, the Mouser heard a little inner voice whispering to him, "Just in time. Just in time." Then the sense of uneasiness departed as suddenly as it had come, and he began to feel somewhat ridiculous. This caused him to sing a bawdy ballad of his own invention, wherein demons and other supernatural agents were ridiculed obscenely. Fafhrd chimed in good-naturedly on the choruses.

It was not as dark as they expected when they reached the cottage. They saw to their horses, found they had been well cared for, and then fell to the savory mess of beans, porridge, and pot herbs that the peasant's wife ladled into oak bowls. Fresh milk to wash it down was provided in quaintly carved oak goblets. The meal was a satisfying one and the interior of the house was neat and clean, despite its stamped earthen floor and low beams, which Fafhrd had to duck.

There turned out to be six in the family, all told. The father, his equally thin and weather-beaten wife, the older son, a young boy, a daughter, and a mumbling grandfather, whom extreme age confined to a chair before the fire. The last two were the most interesting of the lot.

The girl was in that usually gawkish age of mid-adolescence, but there was a wild, coltish grace to the way she moved her lanky legs and the slim arms with their prominent elbows. She was very shy, and gave the impression that at any moment she might dart out the door and into the woods.

In order to amuse her and win her confidence, the Mouser began to perform small feats of legerdemain, plucking copper coins out of the ears of the astonished peasant, and bone needles from the nose of his giggling wife. Using sleight of hand and other tricks of illusion, he turned beans into buttons and back again into beans, swallowed a large fork, made a tiny wooden manikin jig on the palm of his hand, and utterly bewildered the cat by pulling what seemed to be a mouse out of its mouth. All the while he kept up a stream of convulsively nonsensical chatter.

The old folks gaped and grinned. The little boy became frantic with excitement. His sister watched everything with concentrated interest, and even smiled warmly when the Mouser presented her with a square of fine, green linen he had conjured from the air, although she was still too shy to speak.

Then Fafhrd roared sea-chanteys that rocked the roof and sang lusty songs that set the old grandfather gurgling with delight. Meanwhile the Mouser fetched a small wine-skin from his saddlebags, concealed it under his cloak, and filled the oak goblets as if by magic. These rapidly fuddled the peasants, who were unused to so potent a beverage, and by the time Fafhrd had finished telling a bloodcurling tale of the frozen north, they were all nodding, save the girl and the grandfather.

The latter looked up at the merry-making adventurers, his watery eyes filled with a kind of impish, senile glee, and mumbled, "You two be right clever men. Maybe beast won't get you." But before this remark could be elucidated, his eyes had gone vacant again, and in a few moments he was snoring.

Soon all were asleep, Fafhrd and the Mouser keeping their weapons close at
hand, and only variegated snores and occasional snaps from the dying embers
disturbed the silence of the cottage.

The Day of the Cat dawned clear and cool. The Mouser stretched himself luxuriously and, catlike, flexed his muscles and sucked in the sweet, dewy air. He
felt exceptionally cheerful and eager to be up and doing. Was not this *his* day,
the day of the Gray Mouser, a day in which luck could not fail him?

His slight movements awakened Fafhrd and together they stole silently from the
cottage so as not to disturb the peasants, who were oversleeping with the wine
they had taken. They refreshed their faces and hands in the wet grass and paid a
visit to the stable. Then they munched some bread, washed it down with drafts of
cool well water flavored with wine, and made ready to depart.

This time their preparations were well thought out. The Mouser carried a mallet
and a stout steel pry-bar, in case they had to attack masonry, and made certain
that candles, flint, wedges, chisels, and several other small tools were in his pouch.
Fafhrd borrowed a pick from the peasant's implements and tucked a coil of thin,
strong rope in his belt. He also took his bow and quiver of arrows.

The forest was delightful at this early hour. Bird cries and chatterings came
from overhead, and once they glimpsed a black, squirrellike animal scampering
along a bough. A couple of chipmunks scurried under a bush dotted with red
berries. What had been shadow the evening before was now a variety of green-
leafed beauty. The two adventurers trod softly.

They had hardly gone more than a bowshot into the woods, when they heard a
faint rustling behind them. The rustling came rapidly nearer, and suddenly the
peasant girl burst into view. She stood breathless and poised, one hand touching
a tree trunk, the other pressing aside some leaves, ready to fly away at the first
sudden move. Fafhrd and the Mouser stood as stock-still as if she were a doe or
a dryad. Finally she managed to conquer her shyness and speak.

"You go there?" she questioned, indicating the direction of the treasure house
with a quick, ducking nod. Her dark eyes were serious.

"Yes, we go there," answered Fafhrd, smiling.

"Don't." This word was accompanied by a rapid headshake.

"But why shouldn't we, girl?" Fafhrd's voice was gentle and sonorous, like
an integral part of the forest. It seemed to touch some spring within the girl that
enabled her to feel more at ease. She gulped a big breath and began.

"Because I watch it from edge of the forest, but never go close. Never, never,
never. I say to myself there be a magic circle I must not cross. And I say to
myself there be a giant inside. Queer and fearsome giant." Her words were coming rapidly now, like an undammed stream. "All gray he be, like the stone of his
house. All gray—eyes and hair and fingernails, too. And he has a stone club as
big as a tree. And he be big, bigger than you, twice as big." Here she nodded at
Fafhrd. "And with his club he kills, kills, kills. But only if you go close. Every
day, almost, I play a game with him. I pretend to be going to cross the magic
circle. And he watches from inside the door, where I can't see him, and he think

I'm going to cross. And I dance through the forest all around the house, and he follows me, peering from the little windows. And I get closer and closer to the circle, closer and closer. But I never cross. And he be very angry and gnash his teeth, like rocks rubbing rocks, so that the house shakes. And I run, run, run away. But you mustn't go inside. Oh, you mustn't.''

She paused, as if startled by her own daring. Her eyes were fixed anxiously on Fafhrd. She seemed drawn toward him. The northerner's reply was serious and carried no overtone of patronizing laughter at her childish fantasy.

"But you've never actually seen the gray giant, have you?"

"Oh, no. He be too cunning. But I say to myself he must be there inside. And that's the same thing, isn't it? Grandfather knows about him. We used to talk about him, when I was little. Grandfather calls him the beast. But the others laugh at me, so I don't tell."

Here was another astounding paradox, thought the Mouser with an inward grin. Imagination was such a rare commodity with the peasants that this girl unhesitatingly took it for reality.

"Don't worry about us, girl. We'll be on the watch for your gray giant," he started to say, but he had less success than Fafhrd in keeping his voice completely natural or else the cadence of his words didn't chime so well with the forest setting.

The girl uttered one more warning, "Don't go inside, oh, please," and turned and darted away.

The two adventurers looked at each other and smiled. Somehow the unexpected fairy tale, with its conventional ogre and its charmingly naïve narrator, added to the delight of the dewy morning. Without a comment they resumed their soft-stepping progress. And it was well that they went quietly, for when they had gotten within a stone's throw of the clearing, they heard low voices that seemed to be grumbling in altercation. Immediately they cached the pick and pry-bar and mallet under a clump of bushes, and stole forward, taking advantage of the natural cover and watching where they planted their feet.

On the edge of the clearing stood half a dozen stocky men in black chain-mail shirts, bows on their backs, short swords at their sides. They were immediately recognizable as the rogues who had laid the ambuscade. They seemed to be arguing about something. Two of them started for the treasure house, only to be recalled by a comrade. Whereupon the argument apparently started afresh.

"That red-haired one," whispered the Mouser after an unhurried look. "I can swear I've seen him in the stables of Lord Rannarsh. My guess was right. It seems we have a rival."

"Why do they wait, and keep pointing at the house?" whispered Fafhrd. "Is it because some of their comrades are already at work inside?"

The Mouser shook his head. "That cannot be. See those picks and shovels and levers they have rested on the ground? No, they wait for someone—for a leader. Some of them want to examine the house before he arrives. Others counsel against it. And I will bet my head against a bowling ball that the leader is Rannarsh himself. He is much too greedy and suspicious to intrust a treasure quest to any henchman.''

"What's to do?" murmured Fafhrd. "We cannot enter the house unseen, even if it were the wise course, which it isn't. Once in, we'd be trapped."

"I've half a mind to loose my sling at them right now and teach them something about the art of ambuscade," replied the Mouser ferociously. "Only then the survivors would flee into the house and hold us off until, mayhap, Rannarsh came, and more men with him."

"We might circle part way round the clearing," said Fafhrd, after a moment's pause, "all the time keeping to the woods. Then we can enter the clearing unseen and shelter ourselves behind one of the small domes. In that way we become masters of the doorway, and can prevent their taking cover inside. Thereafter I will address them suddenly and try to frighten them off, you meanwhile staying hid and giving substance to my threats by making enough racket for ten men."

This seemed the handiest plan to both of them, and they managed the first part of it without a single hitch. The Mouser crouched behind the small dome, his sword, sling, daggers, and a couple of sticks of wood laid ready for either noise-making or fight. Then Fafhrd strode briskly forward, his bow held carelessly in front of him, an arrow fitted to the string. It was done so casually that it was a few moments before Rannarsh's benchmen noticed him. Then they quickly reached for their own bows and as quickly desisted when they saw that the huge newcomer had the advantage of them. They scowled in irritated perplexity.

"Ho, rogues!" began Fafhrd, "we allow you just as much time as it will take you to make yourselves scarce, and no more. Don't think to resist or come skulking back. My men are scattered through the woods. At a sign from me they will feather you with arrows."

Meanwhile the Mouser had begun a low din and was slowly and artistically working it up in volume. Rapidly varying the pitch and intonation of his voice and making it echo first from some part of the building and then from the forest wall, he created the illusion of a whole squad of bloodthirsty bowmen. Nasty cries of "Shall we let fly?" "You take the redhead," and "Try for the belly shot; it's surest," kept coming now from one point and now another, until it was all Fafhrd could do to refrain from laughing at the woebegone, startled glances the six rogues kept darting around. But his merriment was extinguished when, just as the rogues were starting to slink shamefacedly away, an arrow arched erratically out of the woods, passing a spear's length above his head.

"Curse that branch!" came a deep, grunty voice the Mouser recognized as issuing from the throat of Lord Rannarsh. Immediately after, it began to bark commands.

"At them, you fools! It's all a trick. There are only two of them. Rush them!"

Fafhrd turned without warning and loosed point-blank at the voice, but did not silence it. Then he dodged back behind the small dome and ran with the Mouser for the woods.

The six rogues, wisely deciding that a charge with drawn swords would be overly heroic, followed suit, unslinging their bows as they went. One of them turned before he had reached sufficient cover, nocking an arrow. It was a mistake. A ball from the Mouser's sling took him low in the forehead, and he toppled forward dead.

The sound of that hit and fall was the last heard in the clearing for quite a long time, save for the inevitable bird cries, some of which were genuine, and some of which were communications between Fafhrd and the Mouser. The conditions of the death-dealing contest were obvious. Once it had fairly begun, no one dared enter the clearing, since he would become a fatally easy mark; and the Mouser was sure that none of the five remaining rogues had taken shelter in the treasure house. Nor did either side dare withdraw all its men out of sight of the doorway, since that would allow someone to take a commanding position in the top of the tower, providing the tower had a negotiable stair. Therefore it was a case of sneaking about near the edge of the clearing, circling and counter-circling, with a great deal of squatting in a good place and waiting for somebody to come along and be shot.

The Mouser and Fafhrd began by adopting the latter strategy, first moving about twenty paces nearer the point at which the rogues had disappeared. Evidently their patience was a little better than that of their opponents. For after about ten minutes of nerve-racking waiting, during which pointed seed pods had a queer way of looking like arrowheads, Fafhrd got the red-haired henchman full in the throat just as he was bending his bow for a shot at the Mouser. That left four besides Rannarsh himself. Immediately they changed their tactics and separated, the Mouser circling rapidly around the treasure house and Fafhrd drawing as far back from the open space as he dared.

Rannarsh's men must have decided on the same plan, for the Mouser almost bumped into a scar-faced rogue as soft-footed as himself. At such close range, bow and sling were both useless—in their normal function. Scar-face attempted to jab the barbed arrow he held into the Mouser's eye. The Mouser weaved his body to one side, swung his sling like a whip, and felled the man senseless with a blow from the horn handle. Then he retreated a few paces, thanked the Day of the Cat that there had not been two of them, and took to the trees as being a safer, though slower method of progress. Keeping to the middle heights, he scurried along with the sure-footedness of a rope walker, swinging from branch to branch only when it was necessary, making sure he always had more than one way of retreat open.

He had completed three quarters of his circuit when he heard the clash of swords a few trees ahead. He increased his speed and was soon looking down on a sweet little combat. Fafhrd, his back to a great oak, had his broadsword out and was holding off two of Rannarsh's henchmen, who were attacking with their shorter weapons. It was a tight spot and the northerner realized it. He knew that ancient sagas told of heroes who could best four or more men at swordplay. He also knew that such sagas were lies, providing the hero's opponents were reasonably competent.

And Rannarsh's men were veterans. They attacked cautiously, but incessantly, keeping their swords well in front of them and never slashing wildly. Their breath whistled through their nostrils, but they were grimly confident, knowing the northerner dared not lunge strongly at one of them because it would lay him wide open to a thrust by the other. Their game was to get one on each side of him and then attack simultaneously.

Fafhrd's counter was to shift position quickly and attack the nearer one murderously before the other could get back in range. In that way he managed to keep them side by side, where he could hold their blades in check by swift feints and crosswise sweeps. Sweat beaded his face and blood dripped from a scratch on his left thigh. A fearsome grin showed his white teeth, which occasionally parted to let slip a base, primitive insult.

The Mouser took in the situation at a glance, descended rapidly to a lower bough, and poised himself, aiming a dagger at the back of one of Fafhrd's adversaries. He was, however, standing very close to the thick trunk, and round this trunk darted a horny hand tipped with a short sword. The third henchman had also thought it wise to take to the trees. Fortunately for the Mouser, the man was uncertain of his footing and therefore his thrust, although well aimed, came a shade slow. As it was the little gray-clad man only managed to dodge by dropping off.

Thereupon he startled his opponent with a modest acrobatic feat. He did not drop to the ground, knowing that would put everyone at the mercy of the man in the tree. Instead, he grabbed hold of the branch on which he had been standing, swung himself smartly up again, and grappled. Steadying themselves now with one hand, now another, they drove for each other's throat, ramming with knees and elbows whenever they got a chance. At the first onset both dagger and sword were dropped, the latter sticking point down in the ground directly between the two battling henchmen and startling them so that Fafhrd almost got home an attack.

The Mouser and his man surged and rolled along the branch away from the trunk, inflicting little damage on each other since it was hard to keep balance. Finally they slid off at the same time, still gripping the branch with their hands. The puffing henchman aimed a vicious kick. The Mouser escaped it by yanking up his body and doubling up his legs. The latter he let fly violently, taking the henchman full in the chest with a dull thump. The unfortunate retainer of Rannarsh fell to the ground, and had the wind knocked out of him for a second time.

At the same time one of Fafhrd's opponents tried a trick that might have turned out well. Choosing a moment when his companion was pressing the northerner closely, he snatched for the sword sticking in the ground, intending to hurl it underhanded as if it were a javelin. But Fafhrd, whose superior endurance was rapidly giving him an advantage in speed, anticipated the movement and simultaneously made a brilliant counterattack against the other man. There were two thrust, both lightninglike, a first a fent at the belly, the second a slicing stab that sheared through the throat to the spine. Then he whirled around and, with a quick sweep, knocked both weapons out of the hands of the first man, who looked up in bewilderment and promptly collapsed into a sitting position, panting in almost utter exhaustion.

To cap the situation, the Mouser dropped lightly down, as if out of the sky. Fafhrd automatically started to raise his sword, for a backhand swipe. Then he stared at the Mouser for as long a time as it took the man sitting on the ground to give three tremendous gasps. Then he began to laugh, first uncontrollable snickers and later thundering peals of hysterical violence. It was a laughter in which battle-begotten madness, completely sated anger, and relief at escape from death were equally mingled.

"Oh, by Glaggerk and by Kos!" he roared, "By the Behemoth! Oh, by the Cold Waste and the guts of the Red God! Oh! Oh! Oh!" Again the insane bellowing burst explosively. "Oh, by the Killer Whale and the Cold Woman and her spawn!" By degrees the laughter died away, choking in his throat. He rubbed his forehead painfully with the palm of his hand, as if he were blind, and his face became starkly grave. Then he knelt beside the man he had just slain, and straightened his limbs, and closed his eyes, and began to weep in a dignified, almost stoic way that would have seemed ridiculous and hypocritical in anyone but a barbarian.

Meanwhile the Mouser's reactions were nowhere near as primitive. He felt worried, ironic, and slightly sick. He understood Fafhrd's emotions, but knew that he would not feel the full force of his own for some time yet, and by then they would be deadened and somewhat inhibited. He peered about anxiously, fearful of an anticlimactic attack that would find his companion helpless. He counted over the tally of their opponents. Yes, the six henchmen were all accounted for. But Rannarsh himself, where was Rannarsh? He fumbled in his pouch to make sure he had not lost his good-luck talismans and amulets. His lips moved rapidly as he murmured two or three prayers and cantrips. But all the while he held his sling ready, and his eyes never once ceased their quick shifting.

From the middle of a thick clump of bushes he heard a series of agonized gasps, as the man he had felled from the tree began to regain his wind. The henchman whom Fafhrd had disarmed, his face ashy pale from exhaustion rather than fright, was slowly edging back into the forest. The Mouser watched him carelessly, noting the comical way in which the steel cap had slipped down over his forehead and rested against the bridge of his nose. Meanwhile the gasps of the man in the bushes were taking on a less agonized and more vocal quality. At almost the same instant, the two rose to their feet and stumbled off into the forest.

The Mouser listened to their blundering retreat. He was sure that there was nothing more to fear from them. *They* wouldn't come back. And then a little smile stole into his face, for he heard the sounds of a third person joining them in their flight. That would be Rannarsh, thought the Mouser, a man cowardly at heart and incapable of carrying on single-handed. It did not occur to him at the moment that the third person might be the man he had stunned with his sling handle.

* * *

Mostly just to be doing something, he followed them leisurely for a couple of bowshots into the forest. Their trail was easy to follow, being marked by trampled bushes and thorns bearing tatters of cloth. It led in a beeline directly away from the clearing, hardly deviating a yard anywhere. Satisfied, he returned, going out of his way to regain the mallet, pick, and pry-bar.

He found Fafhrd tying a loose bandage around the scratch on his thigh. The northerner's emotions had run their gamut and he was himself again. The dead man for whom he had been somberly grieving now meant no more to him than food for beetles and birds. Whereas for the Mouser it continued to be a somewhat frightening and sickening object.

"And now do we proceed with our interrupted business?" the Mouser asked.

Fafhrd nodded in a matter-of-fact manner and rose to his feet. Together they entered the rocky clearing. It came to them as a surprise how little time the fight had taken. True, the sun had moved somewhat higher, but the atmosphere was still that of rather early morning. The birds were still singing fitfully. The dew had not dried yet. The treasure house of Urgaan of Angarngi stood massive, featureless, grotesquely impressive, and unaltered. Save for a feeling of emptiness and emotional exhaustion, they might be just arriving from the cottage.

"The peasant girl predicted the truth without knowing it," said Mouser with a smile. "We played her game of 'circle-the-clearing and don't-cross-the-magic-circle,' didn't we?"

The treasure house had no fears for him today. He recalled his perturbations of the previous evening, but was unable to understand them or see any reason for them—doubtless they were a delayed reaction from the shock of the ambuscade. The very idea of a guardian seemed somewhat ridiculous. There were a hundred other ways of explaining the skeleton inside the doorway.

So this time it was the Mouser who skipped into the treasure house ahead of Fafhrd, The interior was disappointing, being empty of any furnishings and as bare and unornamented as the outside walls. Just a large, low room. To either side square doorways led to the smaller domes, while to the rear a long hallway was dimly apparent, and the beginnings of a stair leading to the upper part of the main dome.

With only a casual glance at the skull and the broken skeleton, the Mouser made his way toward the stair.

"Our document," he said to Fafhrd, who was now beside him, "speaks of the treasure as resting just below the keystone of the chief dome. Therefore we must seek in the room or rooms above."

"True," answered the northerner, glancing around. "But I wonder, Mouser, just what use this structure served. A man who builds a house solely to hide a treasure is shouting to the world that he *has* a treasure. Do you think it might have been a temple?"

The Mouser suddenly shrank back with a sibilant exclamation. Sprawled a little way up the stair was another skeleton, the major bones hanging together in a somewhat lifelike fashion. The whole upper half of the skull was smashed to fragments.

"Our hosts are overly ancient and indecently naked," hissed the Mouser, angry with himself for being badly startled. Then he darted up the stairs to examine the grisly find. His sharp eyes picked out several sharp objects among the bones. A rusty dagger, a tarnished gold ring that looped a knucklebone, a handful of horn buttons, and a slim, green-eaten copper cylinder. The last awakened his curiosity. He picked it up, dislodging the bones in the process, so that they fell apart, rattling dryly. He managed to pry off the cap of the cylinder with his dagger point, and shook out a tightly rolled sheet of ancient parchment. This he gingerly un-wound. Fafhrd and he scanned the lines of diminutive red lettering by the light from a small window on the landing above.

Mine is a secret treasure. Orichalchum have I, and crystal, and blood-red amber. Rubies and emeralds that demons would war for, and a diamond as big as the skull of a man. Yet none have seen them save I. I, Urgaan of Angarngi, scorn the flattery and the envy of fools. A fittingly lonely treasure house have I builded for my jewels. There, hidden under the keystone, they may dream unperturbed until earth and sky wear away. A day's ride beyond the village of Soreev, in the valley of the two double-humped hills, lies that house, domed and single-towered. It is empty. Any fool may enter. Let him. I care not.

"The details differ slightly," murmured the Mouser, "but the phrases have the same ring as in our document."

"The man must have been mad," asserted Fafhrd, scowling. "Or else why should he carefully hide a treasure and then, with equal care, leave directions for finding it?"

"We thought *our* document was a memorandum or an oversight," said the Mouser thoughtfully. "Such a notion can hardly explain *two* documents." Lost in strange speculation, he turned toward the remaining section of the stair, only to find still another skull grinning at him from a shadowy angle. This time he was not startled, yet he experienced the same feeling that a fly must experience, when, enmeshed in a spider's web, it sees the dangling, empty corpses of a dozen of its brothers. But the feeling was only momentary. He began to speak rapidly.

"Nor can such a notion explain *three* or *four* or mayhap a *dozen* such documents. For how came these other questers here, unless each had found a written message? Urgaan of Angarngi may have been mad, but he sought deliberately to lure men here. One thing is certain. This house conceals—or did conceal—some deadly trap. Some guardian. Some giant beast, say. Or perhaps the very stones distill a poison. Perhaps hidden springs released sword blades which stab out through cracks in the walls and then return."

"That cannot be," answered Fafhrd. "These men were killed by great, bashing blows. The ribs and spine of the first were splintered. The second had his skull cracked open. And that third one there. See! His pelvic bones are smashed."

The Mouser started to reply. Then his face broke into an unexpected smile. He could see the conclusion to which Fafhrd's arguments were unconsciously lead-ing—and he knew that that conclusion was ridiculous. What thing would kill with great, bashing blows? What thing but the gray giant the peasant girl had told them about? The gray giant twice as tall as a man, with his great stone club—a giant fit only for fairy tales and fantasies.

And Fafhrd returned the Mouser's smile. It seemed to him that they were making a great deal of fuss about nothing. These skeletons were suggestive enough, to be sure, but did they not represent men who had died many, many years ago—centuries ago? What guardian could outlast three centuries? Why, that was a long enough time to weary the patience of a demon! And there were no such things as demons, anyhow. And there was no earthly use in mucking around about ancient fears and horrors that were as dead as dust. The whole matter, thought Fafhrd, boiled down to something very simple. They had come to an empty house to see if there was a treasure in it. Well then, shouldn't they just go ahead and get the business over with?

Agreed upon this point, the two comrades made their way up the remaining section of stair that led to the dimmer regions of the House of Angarngi. Despite their confidence, they moved cautiously and kept sharp watch on the shadows lying ahead. This was wise.

Just as they reached the top, a flash of steel spun out of the darkness. It nicked the Mouser in the shoulder as he twisted to one side. There was a metallic clank as it fell to the stone floor. The Mouser, gripped by a sudden spasm of anger and fright, ducked down and dashed rapidly through the door from which the weapon had come, straight at the danger, whatever it was.

"Dagger-tossing in the dark, eh, you slick-bellied worm?" Fafhrd heard the Mouser cry, and then he, too, had plunged through the door.

Lord Rannarsh cowered against the wall, his rich hunting garb dusty and disordered, his black, wavy hair pushed back from his forehead, his cruelly handsome face a sallow mask of hate and extreme terror. For the moment the latter emotion seemed to predominate and, oddly enough, it did not appear to be directed toward the men he had just assailed, but toward something else, something unapparent.

"O gods!" he cried, "let me go from here. The treasure is yours. Let me out of this place. Else I am doomed. The thing has played at cat and mouse with me. I cannot bear it. I cannot bear it!"

"So now we pipe a different tune, do we?" hissed the Mouser furiously. "First dagger-tossing, then fright and pleas!"

"Filthy coward tricks," added Fafhrd succinctly. "Skulking here safe while your henchmen died bravely."

"Safe? Safe, you say? O gods!" Rannarsh almost screamed. Then a subtle change became apparent in his rigid-muscled face. It was not that his terror decreased. If anything, that became greater. But there was added to it, over and above, a consciousness of desperate shame, a realization that he had demeaned himself uneradicably in the eyes of these two ruffians. His lips began to writhe, showing tight-clenched teeth. A look of insane cunning crept into his white-rimmed eyes. He extended his left hand in a gesture of supplication.

"Oh, mercy, have mercy," he cried piteously, and his right hand twitched a second dagger from his belt and hurled it underhand at Fafhrd.

The northerner knocked aside the weapon with a swift blow of his palm, then said deliberately, "He is yours, Mouser. Kill the man."

And now it was cat against cornered rat indeed. Lord Rannarsh whipped a gleaming sword from its gold-worked scabbard and rushed in, cutting, thrusting, stabbing. The Mouser gave ground slightly, his slim blade flickering in a defensive counterattack that was wavering and elusive, yet deadly. He brought Rannarsh's rush to a standstill. His blade moved so quickly that it seemed to weave a net of steel around the man. Then it leaped forward three times in rapid succession. At the first thrust it bent nearly double against a concealed shirt of chain mail. The second thrust pierced the belly. The third transfixed the throat. Lord Rannarsh fell to the floor, spitting and gagging, his fingers clawing at his neck. There he died.

"Butchery," said Fafhrd somberly, "simple butchery. Although he had fairer play than he deserved, and handled his sword well. Mouser, I like not this killing, although there was surely more justice to it than the others."

The Mouser, wiping his weapon against his opponent's thigh, understood what Fafhrd meant. He felt no elation at his victory, only a cold, queasy disgust. A moment before he had been raging, but now there was no anger left in him. He pulled open his gray jerkin and inspected the dagger wound in his left shoulder. A little blood was still welling from it and trickling down his arm. Not much. The flow had almost stopped.

"Lord Rannarsh was no coward," he said slowly. "He killed himself, or at least caused his own death, because we had seen him terrified and heard him cry in fright."

And at these words, without any warning whatsoever, stark terror fell like an icy eclipse upon the hearts of the Gray Mouser and Fafhrd. It was as if Lord Rannarsh had left them a legacy of fear, which passed to them immediately upon his death. And the unmanning thing about it was that they had no premonitory apprehension, no hint of its approach. It did not take root and grow gradually greater, like normal fear. It came all at once, paralyzing, overwhelming. Worse still, there was no discernible cause. One moment they were looking down with something of indifference upon the twisted corpse of Lord Rannarsh. The next moment their legs were weak, their guts were cold, their spines prickling, their teeth clicking, their hearts pounding, their hair lifting at the roots.

Fafhrd felt as if he had walked unsuspecting into the jaws of a gigantic serpent. His barbaric mind was stirred to the deeps. He thought of the grim god Kos brooding alone in the icy silence of the Cold Waste. He thought of the masked powers Fate and Chance, and of the game they play for the blood and brains of men. And he did not will these thoughts. Rather did the intense fear seem to liberate them, so that they rose into consciousness unbidden.

Slowly he regained control over his quaking limbs and twitching muscles. As if in a nightmare, he looked around him slowly, taking in the details of his surroundings. The room they were in was semicircular, forming half of the great dome. Two small windows, high in the curving ceiling, let in light.

An inner voice kept repeating. "Don't make a sudden move. Slowly. Slowly. Above all, don't run. The others did. That was why they died so quickly. Slowly. Slowly."

He saw the Mouser's face. It reflected his own terror. How much longer would this last? How much longer could he stand it without running amuck? How much longer could he passively endure this feeling of a great invisible paw reaching out over him, inch by inch, implacably?

The faint sound of footsteps came from the room below. Regular and unhurried footsteps. Now they were crossing into the rear hallway below. And now they were on the stairs. And now they had reached the landing, and were advancing up the second section of the stairs.

The man who entered the room was tall and frail and old and very gaunt. Scant locks of intensely black hair straggled down over his high-domed forehead. His sunken, waxy cheeks showed clearly the outlines of his long jawbone, and waxy skin was pulled tight over his small nose. Fanatical eyes burned in deep, bony sockets. He wore the simple, sleeveless robe of a holy man. A pouch hung from the cord round his waist.

He fixed his eyes upon Fafhrd and the Gray Mouser.

"I greet you, men of blood," he said in a hollow voice.

Then his gaze fell with displeasure upon the corpse of Rannarsh.

"More blood has been shed. It is not well."

And with the bony forefinger of his left hand he traced in the air a curious triple square, the sign sacred to the Great God of Lankhmar.

"Do not speak," his calm, toneless voice continued, "for I know your purposes. You have come to take treasure from this house. Others have sought to do the same. They have failed. You will fail. As for myself, I have no lust for treasure. For forty years I have lived on crusts and water, devoting my spirit to the Great God." Again he traced the curious sign. "The gems and ornaments of this world and the jewels and gauds of the world of demons cannot tempt or corrupt me. My purpose in coming here is to destroy an evil thing.

"I"—and here he touched his chest—"I am Arvlan of Angarngi, the ninth lineal descendant of Urgaan of Angarngi. This I always knew, and sorrowed for, because Urgaan of Angarngi was a man of evil. But not until fifteen days ago, on the Day of the Spider, did I discover from ancient documents that Urgaan had builded this house, and builded it to be an eternal trap for the unwise and venturesome. He has left a guardian here, and that guardian has endured.

"Cunning was my accursed ancestor, Urgaan, cunning and evil. The most skillful architect in all Lankhmar was Urgaan, a man wise in the ways of stone and learned in geometrical lore. But he scorned the Great God. He lusted after improper powers. He had commerce with demons, and won from them an unnatural treasure. This he hid, but hid in such a way that it would wreck endless evil on the world. It is my purpose and my right to destroy that evil.

"Seek not to dissuade me, lest doom fall upon you. As for me, no harm can befall me. The hand of the Great God is poised above me, ready to ward off any danger that may threaten his faithful servant. His will is my will. Do not speak, men of blood! I go to destroy the treasure of Urgaan of Angarngi.''

And with these words the gaunt holy man walked calmly on, with measured stride, like an apparition, and disappeared through the narrow doorway that led into the forward part of the great dome.

Fafhrd stared after him, his green eyes wide, feeling no desire to follow or to interfere. His terror had not left him, but it was transmuted in a queer way. He was still aware of a dreadful threat, but it no longer seemed to be directed against him personally.

Meanwhile, a most curious notion had lodged in the mind of the Mouser. He felt that he had just now seen, not a venerable holy man, but a dim reflection of the centuries-dead Urgaan of Angarngi. Was not this Arvlan a lineal descendant? Surely Urgaan had that same high-domed forehead, that same secret pride, that same air of command! And those locks of youthfully black hair, which contrasted so ill with the aged face. Were they too not part of a picture looming from the past? A picture dimmed and distorted by time, but retaining something of the power and individuality of the ancient original?

They heard the footsteps of the holy man proceed a little way into the other room. Then for the space of a dozen heartbeats there was complete silence. Then the floor began to tremble slightly under their feet, as if the earth were quaking, or as if a giant were treading near. Then there came a single quavering cry from the next room, cut off in the middle of a single sickening crash that made them lurch. Then, once again, utter silence.

Fafhrd and the Mouser looked at one another in blank amazement—not so much because of what they had just heard but because, almost at the moment of the crash, the pall of terror had lifted from them completely. They jerked out their swords and hurried into the next room.

It was a duplicate of the one they had just quitted, save that instead of two small windows, there were three, one of them near the floor. Also, there was but a single door, the one through which they had just entered.

Near the thick center wall, which bisected the dome, lay the body of the holy man. Only "lay" was not the right word. Left shoulder and chest were mashed against the floor.

Set in the wall near his head was a stone about two feet square, jutting out a little from the rest. On this was boldly engraved, in antique Lankhmarian hieroglyphs: "Here rests the treasure of Urgaan of Angarngi."

The sight of that stone was like a blow in the face. It roused every ounce of obstinacy and reckless determination in them. What matter that an old man sprawled smashed beside it? They had their swords! What matter they now had proof some grim guardian resided in the treasure house? They could take care of themselves! Run away and leave that stone unmoved, with its insultingly provocative inscription? No, by Kos and the Behemoth! They'd see themselves in Hades first!

Fafhrd ran to fetch the pick and the other large tools, which had been dropped on the stairs when Lord Rannarsh tossed his first dagger. The Mouser looked more closely at the jutting stone. The cracks around it were wide and filled with a dark, tarry mixture. It gave out a slightly hollow sound when he tapped it with his sword hilt. He calculated that the wall was about six feet thick at this point— enough to contain a sizable cavity. He tapped experimentally along the wall in both directions, but the hollow ring quickly ceased. Evidently the cavity was a fairly small one. He noted that the crevices between all the other stones were very fine, showing no evidence of any cementing substance whatsoever. In fact, he couldn't be sure that they weren't false crevices, superficial cuts in the surface of solid rock. But that hardly seemed possible. He heard Fafhrd returning, but continued his minute examination.

The state of the Mouser's mind was peculiar. A dogged determination to get at the treasure overshadowed other emotions. The inexplicably sudden vanishing of his former terror had left certain parts of his mind benumbed. It was as if he had unconsciously decided to hold his thoughts in leash until he had seen what the treasure cavity contained. For example, although his examination of the room assured him that the possibility of a secret panel or door was most unlikely, he did not ask himself how the creature or entity that struck down the holy man had entered and escaped. He was content to keep his mind occupied with material details, and yet make no deductions from them. A delayed emotional reaction to the fights in the forest and the slaying of Rannarsh undoubtedly contributed to this attitude.

His calmness gave him a feeling of safety—at least temporary safety. His experiences had vaguely convinced him that the guardian, whatever it was, which had smashed the holy man and played cat and mouse with Rannarsh and themselves, did not strike without first inspiring a premonitory terror in its victims.

Fafhrd felt very much the same way, except that he was even more single-minded in his determination to solve the riddle of the inscribed stone.

They attacked the wide crevices with chisel and mallet. The dark tarry mixture came away fairly easily, first in hard lumps, later in slightly rubbery, gouged strips. After they had cleared it away to the depth of a finger, Fafhrd inserted the pick and managed to move the stone slightly. Thus the Mouser was enabled to gouge a little more deeply on that side. Then Fafhrd subjected the other side of the stone to the leverage of the pick. So the work proceeded, with alternate pryings and gougings.

They concentrated on each detail of the job with unnecessary intensity, mainly to keep their imaginations in check. What good could come of letting your thoughts be haunted by the image of a man more than two hundred years dead? A man with high-domed forehead, sunken cheeks, nose of a skull—that is, if the dead thing on the floor was a true type of the breed of Angarngi. A man who had somehow won a great treasure, and then hid it away from all eyes, seeking to obtain neither glory nor material profit from it. Who said he scorned the envy of fools, and who yet wrote many provocative notes in diminutive red lettering in order to inform fools of his treasure, and make them envious. Who seemed to be reaching out across the dusty centuries to grapple with you, like a spider spinning a web to catch a fly on the other side of the world. No, best not think of him until you had more to go on!

And yet, he was a skillful architect, the holy man had said. Could such an architect build a stone automaton twice as tall as a tall man? A gray stone automaton with a great club? Could he make a hiding place for such an automaton, and from which it could emerge, deal death, and then return? No, no, such notions were childish, not to be entertained! Stick to the job in hand. First find what lay behind the inscribed stone. Leave thoughts until afterward.

The store was beginning to give more easily to the pressure of the pick. Soon they would be able to get a good purchase on it and edge it out.

Meanwhile an entirely new sensation was growing on the Mouser—not one of terror at all, but of physical revulsion. The air he breathed seemed thick and sickening, although he noted no special odor. He found himself disliking the texture and consistency of the tarry mixture, which somehow he could only liken to wholly imaginary substances, such as the dung of dragons or the solidified vomit of the behemoth. He avoided touching it with his fingers, and he kicked away the litter of chunks and strips that had gathered around his feet. The sensation of queasy loathing became difficult to endure.

He tried to fight it, but had no more success than if it had been seasickness, which in some ways it resembled. He felt unpleasantly dizzy. His mouth kept filling with saliva. The cold sweat of nausea beaded his forehead. He could tell that Fafhrd was unaffected, and he hesitated to mention the matter; it seemed ridiculously out of place, especially as it was unaccompanied by any fear or fright. Finally the stone itself began to have the same effect on him as the tarry mixture, filling him with a seemingly causeless, but none the less sickening revulsion. Then he could bear it no longer. With a vaguely apologetic nod to Fafhrd, he dropped his chisel and went to the low window for a breath of fresh air.

This did not seem to help matters much. He pushed his head through the window and gulped deeply. His mental processes were overshadowed by the general indifference of extreme nausea, and everything seemed very far away. Therefore when he saw that the peasant girl was standing in the middle of the clearing, it was some time before he began to consider the import of the fact. When he did, part of his sickness left him; or at least he was enabled to overpower it sufficiently to stare at her with gathering interest.

Her face was white as a sheet. Her fists were clenched, her arms held rigid at her sides. Even at the distance he could catch something of the mingled terror and determination with which her eyes were fixed on the great doorway. Toward this doorway she was forcing herself to move, one jerking step after another, pausing between each step, as if she had to keep screwing her courage to a higher pitch. Suddenly the Mouser began to feel frightened, not for himself at all, but for the girl. Her terror was obviously intense, and yet she must be doing what she was doing—braving her "queer and fearsome gray giant"—for his sake and Fafhrd's.

At all costs, he thought, she must be prevented from coming closer. It was wrong that she be subjected for one moment longer to such a horribly intense terror.

His mind was confused by his abominable nausea, yet he knew what he must do. He hurried toward the stairs with shaky strides, waving Fafhrd another vague gesture. Just as he was going out of the room he chanced to turn up his eyes, and spied something peculiar on the ceiling. What it was he did not fully realize for some moments.

Fafhrd hardly noticed the Mouser's movements, much less his gestures. The block of stone was rapidly yielding to his efforts. He had previously experienced a faint suggestion of the Mouser's nausea, but perhaps because of his greater single-mindedness, it had not become seriously bothersome. And now his attention was wholly concentrated on the stone. Persistent prying had edged it out a palm's breadth from the wall. Seizing it firmly in his two powerful hands, he tugged it from one side to the other, back and forth. The dark, viscous stuff clung to it tenaciously, but with each sidewise jerk it moved forward a little.

The Mouser lurched hastily down the stairs, fighting vertigo. His feet kicked bones and sent them knocking against the walls. What was it he had seen on the ceiling? Somehow, it seemed to mean something. But he must get the girl out of the clearing. She mustn't come any closer to the house. She mustn't enter.

Fafhrd began to feel the weight of the stone, and knew that it was nearly clear. It was damnably heavy—almost a foot thick. Two carefully gauged heaves finished the job. The stone overbalanced. He stepped back to avoid having his feet crushed. The stone crashed ponderously on the floor. A faint, jewellike glitter came from the cavity that had been revealed. Fafhrd eagerly thrust his head into it.

The Mouser staggered toward the doorway. It was a bloody smear. That was it, a bloody smear he had seen against the ceiling. And just above the corpse of the holy man. But why should that be? He'd been smashed against the floor, hadn't he? The girl. He must get to the girl. He must. There she was, almost at the doorway. He could see her. He felt the stone floor vibrating slightly beneath his feet.

But that was his dizziness, wasn't it?

Fafhrd felt the vibration, too. But any thought he might have had about it was lost in his wonder at what he saw. The cavity seemed to be about four feet square. It was filled, to a level just below the surface of the opening, with a heavy metallic liquid that resembled mercury, except that it was night-black. Resting on this liquid was the most wondrous group of gems Fafhrd had ever imagined. They were indeed the gems the document mentioned.

In the center was a titan diamond, cut with a myriad of oddly angled facets. Around it were two irregular circles, the inner formed of twelve rubies, each a decahedron, the outer formed of seventeen emeralds, each an irregular octahedron. Lying between these gems, touching some of them, sometimes connecting them with each other, were thin, fragile-looking bars of crystal, amber, greenish tourmaline, and honey-pale orichalchum. All these objects did not seem to be floating in the metallic liquid, so much as resting upon it, their weight pressing down the surface into shallow depressions, some cup-shaped, others troughlike. The rods glowed faintly, while each of the gems glittered coldly with a light that Fafhrd's mind was strangely forced to believe was refracted starlight.

His gaze shifted to the mercurous, heavy fluid, where it bulged up between, and he saw distorted reflections of stars and constellations which he recognized, stars and constellations which would be visible now in the sky overhead, were it not for the concealing brilliance of the sun. An awesome wonder engulfed him. His gaze shifted back to the gems. There was something tremendously meaningful about their complex arrangement, something that seemed to speak of over-whelming truths, but in an alien symbolism. More, there was a compelling impression of inner movement, or sluggish thought, of inorganic consciousness. It was like what the eyes see when they close at night—not utter blackness, but a shifting, fluid pattern of many-colored points of light. Feeling that he was reach-ing impiously into the core of a thinking mind, Fafhrd gripped with his right hand for the diamond as big as a man's skull.

The Mouser blundered through the doorway. There could be no mistaking it now. The stones were trembling. That bloody smear, as if the ceiling had champed down upon the holy man, crushing him against the floor, or as if the floor had struck upward. What could it mean? But there was the girl, her terror-wide eyes fastened upon him, her mouth open for a scream that did not come. He must drag her away, out of the clearing.

Buy why should he feel that a fearful threat was now directed at himself as well? Why should he feel that something was poised above him, threatening? As he stumbled down the terraced steps, he looked over his shoulder and up. The tower. O gods! The tower! It was falling. It was falling toward him. It was dip-ping at him over the dome. But look, there were no fractures along its length. It was not breaking. It was not falling. It was bending. It couldn't. O gods, it couldn't!

Fafhrd's hand jerked back, clutching the great, strangely faceted jewel, so heavy that he had difficulty in keeping his hold upon it. Immediately the surface of the metallic, star-reflecting fluid was disturbed. It bobbed and shook. Surely the whole house was shaking, too. The other jewels began to dart about erratically, like water insects on the surface of a puddle. The various crystalline and metallic bars began to spin, their tips attracted now to one jewel and now to another, as if they were lodestones. The whole surface of the fluid was in a whirling, jerking confu-sion that suggested a mind gone mad because of loss of its chief part.

For an agonizing instant the Mouser stared up amazement-frozen at the club-like top of the tower, ponderously hurling itself down upon him. Then he ducked his head and lunged forward at the girl, tackling her, rapidly rolling over and over with her, over and over. The tower top struck a sword's length behind them, with a thump that jolted them momentarily off the ground. Then it jerked itself up from the pitlike depression it had made.

Fafhrd tore his gaze away from the incredible, alien beauty of the jewel-confused cavity. His right hand—it was burning. The diamond was hot. Or, no, no, it was cold, cold beyond belief. What was happening to the room? Kos! It was changing shape! The ceiling was bulging downward at a point. He made for the door, then stopped dead in his tracks. The door was closing down, like a stony mouth. He turned and took a few steps over the quaking floor toward the small, low window. It snapped shut, like a sphincter. He tried to drop the diamond. It clung painfully to the inside of his hand. With a snap of his wrist he whipped it away from him. It hit the floor and began to bounce about like a living star.

The Mouser and the peasant girl rolled toward the edge of the clearing. The tower made two more tremendous bashes at them but both went yards wide, like the blows of a blind madman. Now they were out of range. The Mouser lay sprawled on his side, watching a house that hunched and heaved like a beast, and a tower that bent double as it thumped grave-deep pits into the ground. It crashed into a group of boulders and its top broke off, but the jaggedly fractured end continued to beat the boulders in wanton anger, smashing them into fragments. The Mouser felt a compulsive urge to take out his dagger and stab himself in the heart. It couldn't be. It couldn't be. A man had to die when he saw something like that. Fafhrd! Fafhrd!

Fafhrd clung to sanity because he was threatened from a new direction at every minute and because he could say to himself, "I know. I know. The house is a beast, and the jewels are its mind. Now that mind is mad. I know. I know." Walls, ceiling, and floor quaked and heaved, but their movements did not seem to be directed especially at him. Occasional crashes almost deafened him. He staggered over rocky swells, dodging stony advances that were half bulges and half blows, but that lacked the speed and directness of the tower's first smash at the Mouser. The corpse of the holy man was jolted about in grotesque mechanical reanimation.

Only the great diamond seemed aware of Fafhrd. Exhibiting a fretful intelligence, it kept bounding at him viciously, sometimes leaping high as his head. He involuntarily made for the door as his only hope. It was champing up and down with convulsive regularity. Watching his chance, he dived at it just as it was opening, and writhed clear. The diamond followed him, striking at his legs. The carcass of Rannarsh was flung sprawling in his path. He jumped over it, then slid, lurched, stumbled, fell down stairs in earthquake, where dry bones danced. Surely the beast must die, the house must crash and crush him flat. The diamond leaped for his skull, missed, hurtled through the air, and struck a wall. Thereupon it burst with an explosive crack into a great puff of iridescent dust, like a tension-laden drop of glass that has been cooled by being dipped into water.

Immediately the rhythm of the shaking of the house began to increase. Fafhrd raced across the vibrating floor, escaped by inches the embrace of the great doorway, plunged across the clearing—passing a dozen feet from the spot where the tower was beating boulders into crushed rock—and then leaped over two pits in the ground. His face was rigid and white. His eyes were vacant. He blundered bull-like into two or three trees, and only came to a halt because he knocked himself flat against one of them.

The house had ceased most of its random movements, and the whole of it was shaking like a hugh dark jelly. Suddenly its forward part heaved up. A behemoth in death agony. The two smaller domes were jerked ponderously a dozen feet off the ground, as if they were the paws. The tower whipped into convulsive rigidity. The main dome contracted sharply, like a stupendous lung. For a moment it hung there, poised. Then it crashed to the ground in a heap of gigantic stone shards. The earth shook. The forest resounded. Escaping air whipped branches and leaves. Suddenly, all was still. Only from the fractures in the stone a tarry, black liquid was slowing oozing, and there and there iridescent puffs of air suggested jewel-dust.

Along a narrow, dusty road two horsemen were cantering slowly toward the village of Soreev in the southern most limits of the land of Lankhmar. They presented a somewhat battered appearance. The limbs of the larger, who was mounted on a chestnut gelding, showed several bruises, and there was a bandage around his thigh and another around the palm of his right hand. The smaller man, the one mounted on a gray mare, seemed to have suffered an equal number of injuries.

"Do you know where we're headed?" said the latter, breaking a long silence. "We're headed for a city. And in that city are endless houses of stone, stone towers without numbers, streets paved with stone, domes, arches, stairs. *Tcha,* if I feel then as I feel now, I'll never go within a bowshot of its walls."

His large companion smiled.

"What now, little man? Don't tell me you're afraid of—earthquakes?"

MANLY WADE WELLMAN

When It Was Moonlight

Let my heart be still a moment, and this mystery explore.
                                                    —*The Raven*

His hand, as slim as a white claw, dipped a quillful of ink and wrote in one corner of the page the date—March 3, 1842. Then:

THE PREMATURE BURIAL
BY EDGAR A. POE

He hated his middle name, the name of his miserly and spiteful stepfather. For a moment he considered crossing out even the initial; then he told himself that he was only wool-gathering, putting off the drudgery of writing. And write he must, or starve—the Philadelphia *Dollar Newspaper* was clamoring for the story he had promised. Well, today he had heard a tag of gossip—his mother-in-law had it from a neighbor—that revived in his mind a subject always fascinating.

He began rapidly to write, in a fine copperplate hand:

There are certain themes of which the interest is all-absorbing, but which are entirely too horrible for the purposes of legitimate fiction—

This would really be an essay, not a tale, and he could do it justice. Ofter he thought of the whole world as a vast fat cemetery, close set with tombs in which not all the occupants were at rest—too many struggled unavailingly against their smothering shrouds, their locked and weighted coffin lids. What were his own literary labors, he mused, but a struggle against being shut down and throttled by a society as heavy and grim and senseless as clods heaped by a sexton's spade?

He paused, and went to the slate mantelshelf for a candle. His kerosene lamp had long ago been pawned, and it was dark for midafternoon, even in March. Elsewhere in the house his mother-in-law swept busily, and in the room next to his sounded the quiet breathing of his invalid wife. Poor Virginia slept, and for the moment knew no pain. Returning with his light, he dipped more ink and continued down the sheet:

To be buried while alive is, beyond question, the most terrific of these extremes which has ever fallen to the lot of mere mortality. That it has frequently, very frequently, fallen will scarcely be denied—

Again his dark imagination savored the tale he had heard that day. It had happened here in Philadelphia, in this very quarter, less than a month ago. A widower had gone, after weeks of mourning, to his wife's tomb, with flowers. Stopping to place them on the marble slab, he had heard noise beneath. At once joyful and aghast, he fetched men and crowbars, and recovered the body, all untouched by decay. At home that night, the woman returned to consciousness.

So said the gossip, perhaps exaggerated, perhaps not. And the house was only six blocks away from Spring Garden Street, where he sat.

Poe fetched out his notebooks and began to marshal bits of narrative for his composition—a gloomy tale of resurrection in Baltimore, another from France, a genuinely creepy citation from the *Chirurgical Journal* of Leipzig; a sworn case of revival, by electrical impulses, of a dead man in London. Then he added an experience of his own, romantically embellished, a dream adventure of his boyhood in Virginia. Just as he thought to make an end, he had a new inspiration.

Why not learn more about that reputed Philadelphia burial and the one who rose from seeming death? It would point up his piece, give it a timely local climax, insure acceptance—he could hardly risk a rejection. Too, it would satisfy his own curiosity. Laying down the pen, Poe got up. From a peg he took his wide black hat, his old military cloak that he had worn since his ill-fated cadet days at West Point. Huddling it round his slim little body, he opened the front door and went out.

March had come in like a lion and, lionlike, roared and rampaged over Philadelphia. Dry, cold dust blew up into Poe's full gray eyes, and he hardened his mouth under the gay dark mustache. His shins felt goosefleshy; his striped trousers were unseasonably thin and his shoes badly needed mending. Which way lay his journey?

He remembered the name of the street, and something about a ruined garden. Eventually he came to the place, or what must be the place—the garden was certainly ruined, full of dry, hardy weeds that still stood in great ragged clumps after the hard winter. Poe forced open the creaky gate, went up the rough-flagged path to the stoop. He saw a bronzed nameplate—"Gauber," it said. Yes, that was the name he had heard. He swung the knocker loudly, and thought he caught a whisper of movement inside. But the door did not open.

"Nobody lives there, Mr. Poe," said someone from the street. It was a grocery boy, with a heavy basket on his arm. Poe left the doorstep. He knew the lad; indeed he owed the grocer eleven dollars.

"Are you sure?" Poe prompted.

"Well"—and the boy shifted the weight of his burden—"if anybody lived here, they'd buy from our shop, wouldn't they? And I'd deliver, wouldn't I? But I've had this job for six months, and never set foot inside that door."

Poe thanked him and walked down the street, but did not take the turn that would lead home. Instead he sought the shop of one Pemberton, a printer and a friend, to pass the time of day and ask for a loan.

Pemberton could not lend even one dollar—times were hard—but he offered a drink of Monongahela whiskey, which Poe forced himself to refuse; then a supper of crackers, cheese and garlic sausage, which Poe thankfully shared. At home, unless his mother-in-law had begged or borrowed from the neighbors, would be only bread and molasses. It was past sundown when the writer shook hands with Pemberton, thanked him with warm courtesy for his hospitality, and ventured into the evening.

Thank Heaven, it did not rain. Poe was saddened by storms. The wind had abated and the March sky was clear save for a tiny fluff of scudding cloud and a banked dark line at the horizon, while up rose a full moon the color of frozen cream. Poe squinted from his hat brim at the shadow-pattern on the disk. Might he not write another story of a lunar voyage—like the one about Hans Pfaal, but dead serious this time? Musing thus, he walked along the dusk-filling street until he came again opposite the ruined garden, the creaky gate, and the house with the doorplate marked: "Gauber."

Hello, the grocery boy had been wrong. There was light inside the front window, water-blue light—or was there? Anyway, motion—yes, a figure stooped there, as if to peer out at him.

Poe turned in at the gate, and knocked at the door once again.

Four or five moments of silence; then he heard the old lock grating. The door moved inward, slowly and noisily. Poe fancied that he had been wrong about the blue light, for he saw only darkness inside. A voice spoke:

"Well, sir?"

The two words came huskily but softly, as though the door-opener scarcely breathed. Poe swept off his broad black hat and made one of his graceful bows.

"If you will pardon me—" He paused, not knowing whether he addressed man or woman. "This is the Gauber residence?"

"It is," was the reply, soft, hoarse and sexless. "Your business, sir?"

Poe spoke with official crispness; he had been a sergeant-major of artillery before he was twenty-one, and knew how to inject the proper note. "I am here on public duty," he announced. "I am a journalist, tracing a strange report."

"Journalist?" repeated his interrogator. "Strange report? Come in, sir."

Poe complied, and the door closed abruptly behind him, with a rusty snick of the lock. He remembered being in jail once, and how the door of his cell had slammed just so. It was not a pleasant memory. But he saw more clearly, now he was inside—his eyes got used to the tiny trickle of moonlight.

He stood in a dark hallway, all paneled in wood, with no furniture, drapes or pictures. With him was a woman, in full skirt and downdrawn lace cap, a woman as tall as he and with intent eyes that glowed as from within. She neither moved nor spoke, but waited for him to tell her more of his errand.

Poe did so, giving his name and, stretching a point, claiming to be a subeditor of the *Dollar Newspaper,* definitely assigned to the interview. "And now, madam, concerning this story that is rife concerning a premature burial—"

She had moved very close, but as his face turned toward her she drew back. Poe fancied that his breath had blown her away like a feather; then, remembering Pemberton's garlic sausage, he was chagrined. To confirm his new thought, the woman was offering him wine—to sweeten his breath.

"Would you take a glass of canary, Mr. Poe?" she invited, and opened a side door. He followed her into a room papered in pale blue. Moonglow, drenching it, reflected from that paper and seemed an artifical light. That was what he had seen from outside. From an undraped table his hostess lifted a bottle, poured wine into a metal goblet and offered it.

Poe wanted that wine, but he had recently promised his sick wife, solemnly and honestly, to abstain from even a sip of the drink that so easily upset him. Through thirsty lips he said: "I thank you kindly, but I am a temperance man."

"Oh," and she smiled. Poe saw white teeth. Then: "I am Elva Gauber—Mrs. John Gauber. The matter of which you ask I cannot explain clearly, but it is true. My husband was buried, in the Eastman Lutheran Churchyard—"

"I had heard, Mrs. Gauber, that the burial concerned a woman."

"No, my husband. He had been ill. He felt cold and quiet. A physician, a Dr. Mechem, pronounced him dead, and he was interred beneath a marble slab in his family vault." She sounded weary, but her voice was calm. "This happened shortly after the New Year. On Valentine's Day, I brought flowers. Beneath his slab he stirred and struggled. I had him brought forth. And he lives—after a fashion—today."

"Lives today?" repeated Poe. "In this house?"

"Would you care to see him? Interview him?"

Poe's heart raced, his spine chilled. It was his peculiarity that such sensations gave him pleasure. "I would like nothing better," he assured her, and she went to another door, an inner one.

Opening it, she paused on the threshold, as though summoning her resolution for a plunge into cold, swift water. Then she started down a flight of steps.

Poe followed, unconsciously drawing the door shut behind him.

The gloom of midnight, of prison—yes, of the tomb—fell at once upon those stairs. He heard Elva Gauber gasp:

"No—the moonlight—let it in—" And then she fell, heavily and limply, rolling downstairs.

Aghast, Poe quickly groped his way after her. She lay against a door at the foot of the flight, wedged against the panel. He touched her—she was cold and rigid, without motion or elasticity of life. His thin hand groped for and found the knob of the lower door, flung it open. More dim reflected moonlight, and he made shift to drag the woman into it.

Almost at once she sighed heavily, lifted her head, and rose. "How stupid of me," she apologized hoarsely.

"The fault was mine," protested Poe. "Your nerves, your health, have naturally suffered. The sudden dark—the closeness—overcame you." He fumbled in his pocket for a tinderbox. "Suffer me to strike a light."

But she held out a hand to stop him. "No, no. The moon is sufficient." She walked to a small, oblong pane set in the wall. Her hands, thin as Poe's own, with long grubby nails, hooked on the sill. Her face, bathed in the full light of the moon, strengthened and grew calm. She breathed deeply, almost voluptously. "I am quite recovered," she said. "Do not fear for me. You need not stand so near, sir."

He had forgotten that garlic odor, and drew back contritely. She must be as sensitive to the smell as . . . as . . . what was it that was sickened and driven away by garlic? Poe could not remember, and took time to note that they were in a basement, stone-walled and with a floor of dirt. In one corner water seemed to drip, forming a dank pool of mud. Close to this, set into the wall, showed a latched trapdoor of planks, thick and wide, cleated crosswise, as though to cover a window. But no window would be set so low. Everything smelt earthy and close, as though fresh air had been shut out for decades.

"Your husband is here?" he inquired.

"Yes." She walked to the shutter-like trap, unlatched it and drew it open.

The recess beyond was as black as ink, and from it came a feeble mutter. Poe followed Elva Gauber, and strained his eyes. In a little stone flagged nook a bed had been made up. Upon it lay a man, stripped almost naked. His skin was as white as dead bone, and only his eyes, now opening, had life. He gazed at Elva Gauber, and past her at Poe.

"Go away," he mumbled.

"Sir," ventured Poe formally, "I have come to hear of how you came to life in the grave—"

"It's a lie," broke in the man on the pallet. He writhed halfway to a sitting posture, laboring upward as against a crushing weight. The wash of moonlight showed how wasted and fragile he was. His face stared and snarled bare-toothed, like a skull. "A lie, I say!" he cried, with a sudden strength that might well have been his last. "Told by this monster who is not—my wife—"

The shutter-trap slammed upon his cries. Elva Gauber faced Poe, withdrawing a pace to avoid his garlic breath.

"You have seen my husband," she said. "Was it a pretty sight, sir?"

He did not answer, and she moved across the dirt to the stair doorway. "Will you go up first?" She asked. "At the top, hold the door open, that I may have—" She said "life," or, perhaps, "light." Poe could not be sure which.

Plainly she, who had almost welcomed his intrusion at first, now sought to lead him away. Her eyes, compelling as shouted commands, were fixed upon him. He felt their power, and bowed to it.

Obediently he mounted the stairs, and stood with the upper door wide. Elva Gauber came up after him. At the top her eyes again seized his. Suddenly Poe knew more than ever before about the mesmeric impulses he loved to write about.

"I hope," she said measuredly, "that you have not found your visit fruitless. I live here alone—seeing nobody, caring for the poor thing that was once my husband, John Gauber. My mind is not clear. Perhaps my manners are not good. Forgive me, and good night.''

Poe found himself ushered from the house, and outside the wind was howling once again. The front door closed behind him, and the lock grated.

The fresh air, the whip of gale in his face, and the absence of Elva Gauber's impelling gaze suddenly brought him back, as though from sleep, to a realization of what had happened—or what had not happened.

He had come out, on this uncomfortable March evening, to investigate the report of a premature burial. He had seen a ghastly sick thing, that had called the gossip a lie. Somehow, then, he had been drawn abruptly away—stopped from full study of what might be one of the strangest adventures it was ever a writer's good fortune to know. Why was he letting things drop at this stage?

He decided not to let them drop. That would be worse than staying away altogether.

He made up his mind, formed quickly a plan. Leaving the doorstep, he turned from the gate, slipped quickly around the house. He knelt by the foundation at the side, just where a small oblong pane was set flush with the ground.

Bending his head, he found that he could see plainly inside, by reason of the flood of moonlight—a phenomenon, he realized, for generally an apartment was disclosed only by light within. The open doorway to the stairs, the swamp mess of mud in the corner, the out-flung trapdoor, were discernible. And something stood or huddled at the exposed niche—something that bent itself upon and above the frail white body of John Gauber.

Full skirt, white cap—it was Elva Gauber. She bent herself down, her face was touching the face or shoulder of her husband.

Poe's heart, never the healthiest of organs, began to drum and race. He pressed closer to the pane, for a better glimpse of what went on in the cellar. His shadow cut away some of the light. Elva Gauber turned to look.

Her face was as pale as the moon itself. Like the moon, it was shadowed in irregular patches. She came quickly, almost running, toward the pane where Poe crouched. He saw her, plainly and at close hand.

Dark, wet, sticky stains lay upon her mouth and cheeks. Her tongue roved out, licking at the stains—

Blood!

Poe sprang up and ran to the front of the house. He forced his thin, trembling fingers to seize the knocker, to swing it heavily again and again. When there was no answer, he pushed heavily against the door itself—it did not give. He moved to a window, rapped on it, pried at the sill, lifted his fist to smash the glass.

A silhouette moved beyond the pane, and threw it up. Something shot out at him like a pale snake striking—before he could move back, fingers had twisted in the front of his coat. Elva Gauber's eyes glared into his.

Her cap was off, her dark hair fallen in disorder. Blood still smeared and dewed her mouth and jowls.

''You have pried too far,'' she said, in a voice as measured and cold as the drip from icicles. "I was going to spare you, because of the odor about you that repelled me—the garlic. I showed you a little, enough to warn any wise person, and let you go. Now—"

Poe struggled to free himself. Her grip was immovable, like the clutch of a steel trap. She grimaced in triumph, yet she could not quite face him—the garlic still clung to his breath.

"Look in my eyes," she bade him. "Look—you cannot refuse, you cannot escape. You will die, with John—and the two of you, dying, shall rise again like me. I'll have two fountains of life while you remain—two companions after you die."

"Woman," said Poe, fighting against her stabbing gaze, "you are mad."

She snickered gustily. "I am sane, and so are you. We both know that I speak the truth. We both know the futility of your struggle." Her voice rose a little. "Through a chink in the tomb, as I lay dead, a ray of moonlight streamed and struck my eyes. I woke. I struggled. I was set free. Now at night, when the moon shines—*Ugh!* Don't breathe that herb in my face!"

She turned her head away. At that instant it seemed to Poe that a curtain of utter darkness fell, and with it sank down the form of Elva Gauber.

He peered in the sudden gloom. She was collapsed across the window sill, like a discarded puppet in its booth. Her hand still twisted in the bosom of his coat, and he pried himself loose from it, finger by steely, cold finger. Then he turned to flee from this place of shadowed peril to body and soul.

As he turned, he saw whence had come the dark. A cloud had come up from its place on the horizon—the fat, sooty bank he had noted there at sundown—and now it obscured the moon. Poe paused, in midretreat, gazing.

His thoughtful eye gauged the speed and size of the cloud. It curtained the moon, would continue to curtain it for—well, ten minutes. And for that ten minutes Elva Gauber would lie motionless, lifeless. She had told the truth about the moon giving her life. Hadn't she fallen like one slain on the stairs when they were darkened. Poe began grimly to string the evidence together.

It was Elva Gauber, not her husband, who had died and gone to the family vault. She had come back to life, or a mockery of life, by touch of the moon's rays. Such light was an unpredictable force—it made dogs howl, it flogged madmen to violence, it brought fear, or black sorrow, or ecstasy. Old legends said that it was the birth of fairies, the transformation of werewolves, the motive power of broom-riding witches. It was surely the source of the strength and evil animating what had been the corpse of Elva Gauber—and he, Poe, must not stand there dreaming.

He summoned all the courage that was his, and scrambled in at the window through which slumped the woman's form. He groped across the room to the cellar door, opened it and went down the stairs, through the door at the bottom, and into the stone-walled basement.

It was dark, moonless still. Poe paused only to bring forth his tinder box, strike a light and kindle the end of a tightly twisted linen rag. It gave a feeble steady light, and he found his way to the shutter, opened it and touched the naked, wasted shoulder of John Gauber.

"Get up," he said. "I've come to save you."

The skullface feebly shifted its position to meet his gaze. The man managed to speak, moaningly:

"Useless. I can't move—unless she lets me. Her eyes keep me here—half alive. I'd have died long ago, but somehow—"

Poe thought of a wretched spider, paralyzed by the sting of a mudwasp, lying helpless in its captive's close den until the hour of feeding comes. He bent down, holding his blazing tinder close. He could see Gauber's neck, and it was a mass of tiny puncture wounds, some of them still beaded with blood drops fresh or dried. He winced, but bode firm in his purpose.

"Let me guess the truth," he said quickly. "Your wife was brought home from the grave, came back to a seeming of life. She put a spell on you, or played a trick—made you a helpless prisoner. That isn't contrary to nature, that last. I've studied mesmerism."

"It's true," John Gauber mumbled.

"And nightly she comes to drink your blood?"

Gauber weakly nodded. "Yes. She was beginning just now, but ran upstairs. She will be coming back."

"Good," said Poe bleakly. "Perhaps she will come back to more than she expects. Have you ever heard of vampires? Probably not, but I have studied them, too. I began to guess, I think, when first she was so repelled by the odor of garlic. Vampires lie motionless by day, and walk and feed at night. They are creatures of the moon—their food is blood. Come."

Poe broke off, put out his light, and lifted the man in his arms. Gauber was as light as a child. The writer carried him to the slanting shelter of the closed-in staircase, and there set him against the wall. Over him Poe spread his old cadet cloak. In the gloom, the gray of the cloak harmonized with the gray of the wall stones. The poor fellow would be well hidden.

Next Poe flung off his coat, waistcoat and shirt. Heaping his clothing in a deeper shadow of the stairway, he stood up, stripped to the waist. His skin was almost as bloodlessly pale as Gauber's, his chest and arms almost as gaunt. He dared believe that he might pass momentarily for the unfortunate man.

The cellar sprang full of light again. The cloud must be passing from the moon. Poe listened. There was a dragging sound above, then footsteps.

Elva Gauber, the blood drinker by night, had revived.

Now for it. Poe hurried to the niche, thrust himself in and pulled the trapdoor shut after him.

He grinned, sharing a horrid paradox with the blackness around him. He had heard all the fabled ways of destroying vampires—transfixing stakes, holy water, prayer, fire. But he, Edgar Allan Poe, had evolved a new way. Myriads of tales whispered frighteningly of fiends lying in wait for normal men, but who ever heard of a normal man lying in wait for a fiend? Well, he had never considered himself normal, in spirit, or brain, or taste.

He stretched out, feet together, hands crossed on his bare midriff. Thus it would be in the tomb, he found himself thinking. To his mind came a snatch of poetry by a man named Bryant, published long ago in a New England review—*Breathless darkness, and the narrow house.* It was breathless and dark enough in this hole, Heaven knew, and narrow as well. He rejected, almost hysterically, the implication of being buried. To break the ugly spell, that daunted him where thought of Elva Gauber failed, he turned sideways to face the wall, his naked arm lying across his cheek and temple.

As his ear touched the musty bedding, it brought to him once again the echo of footsteps, footsteps descending stairs. They were rhythmic, confident. They were eager.

Elva Gauber was coming to seek again her interrupted repast.

Now she was crossing the floor. She did not pause or turn aside—she had not noticed her husband, lying under the cadet cloak in the shadow of the stairs. The noise came straight to the trapdoor, and he heard her fumbling for the latch.

Light, blue as skimmed milk, poured into his nook. A shadow fell in the midst of it, full upon him. His imagination, ever outstripping reality, whispered that the shadow had weight, like lead—oppressive, baleful.

"John," said the voice of Elva Gauber in his ear, "I've come back. You know why—you know what for." Her voice sounded greedy, as though it came through loose, trembling lips. "You're my only source of strength now. I thought tonight, that a stranger—but he got away. He had a cursed odor about him, anyway."

Her hand touched the skin of his neck. She was prodding him, like a butcher fingering a doomed beast.

"Don't hold yourself away from me, John," she was commanding, in a voice of harsh mockery. "You know it won't do any good. This is the night of the full moon, and I have power for anything, anything!" She was trying to drag his arm away from his face. "You won't gain by—" She broke off, aghast. Then, in a wild-dry-throated scream:

"You're not John!"

Poe whipped over on his back, and his bird-claw hands shot out and seized her—one hand clinching upon her snaky disorder of dark hair, the other digging its fingertips into the chill flesh of her arm.

The scream quivered away into a horrible breathless rattle. Poe dragged his captive violently inward, throwing all his collected strength into the effort. Her feet were jerked from the floor and she flew into the recess, hurtling above and beyond Poe's recumbent body. She struck the inner stones with a crashing force that might break bones, and would have collapsed upon Poe; but, at the same moment, he had released her and slid swiftly out upon the floor of the cellar.

With frantic haste he seized the edge of the back-flung trapdoor. Elva Gauber struggled up on hands and knees, among the tumbled bedclothes in the niche; then Poe had slammed the panel shut.

She threw herself against it from within, yammering and wailing like an animal in a trap. She was almost as strong as he, and for a moment he thought that she would win out of the niche. But, sweating and wheezing, he bore against the planks with his shoulder, bracing his feet against the earth. His fingers found the latch, lifted it, forced it into place.

"Dark," moaned Elva Gauber from inside. "Dark—no moon—" Her voice trailed off.

Poe went to the muddy pool in the corner, thrust in his hands. The muck was slimy but workable. He pushed a double handful of it against the trapdoor, sealing cracks and edges. Another handful, another. Using his palms like trowels, he coated the boards with thick mud.

"Gauber," he said breathlessly, "how are you?"

"All right—I think." The voice was strangely strong and clear. Looking over his shoulder, Poe saw that Gauber had come upright of himself, still pale but apparently steady. "What are you doing?" Gauber asked.

"Walling her up," jerked out Poe, scooping still more mud. "Walling her up forever, with her devil."

He had a momentary flash of inspiration, a symbolic germ of a story; in it a man sealed a woman into such a nook of the wall, and with her an embodiment of active evil—perhaps in the form of a black cat.

Pausing at last to breathe deeply, he smiled to himself. Even in the direst of danger, the most heartbreaking moment of toil and fear, he must ever be coining new plots for stories.

"I cannot thank you enough," Gauber was saying to him. "I feel that all will be well—if only she stays there."

Poe put his ear to the wall. "Not a whisper of motion, sir. She's shut off from moonlight—from life and power. Can you help me with my clothes? I fell terribly chilled."

His mother-in-law met him on the threshold when he returned to the house in Spring Garden Street. Under the white widow's cap, her strong-boned face was drawn with worry.

"Eddie, are you ill?" She was really asking if he had been drinking. A look reassured her. "No," she answered herself, "but you've been away from home so long. And you're dirty, Eddie—filthy. You must wash."

He let her lead him in, pour hot water into a basin. As he scrubbed himself, he formed excuses, a banal lie about a long walk for inspiration, a moment of dizzy weariness, a stumble into a mud puddle.

"I'll make you some nice hot coffee, Eddie," his mother-in-law offered.

"Please," he responded, and went back to his room with the slate mantelpiece. Again he lighted the candle, sat down and took up his pen.

His mind was embellishing the story inspiration that had come to him at such a black moment, in the cellar of the Gauber house. He'd work on that tomorrow. The *United States Saturday Post* would take it, he hoped. Title? He would call it simply "The Black Cat."

But to finish the present task! He dipped his pen in ink. How to begin? How to end? How, after writing and publishing such an account, to defend himself against the growing whisper of his insanity?

He decided to forget it, if he could—at least to seek healthy company, comfort, quiet—perhaps even to write some light verse, some humorous articles and stories. For the first time in his life, he had had enough of the macabre.

Quickly he wrote a final paragraph:

There are moments when, even to the sober eye of Reason, the world of our sad Humanity may assume the semblance of a Hell—but the imagination of man is no Carathis, to explore with impunity its every cavern. Alas! The grim legion of sepulchral terrors cannot be regarded as altogether fanciful—but, like the Demons in whose company Afrasiab made his voyage down the Oxus, they must sleep, or they will devour us—they must be suffered to slumber, or we will perish.

That would do for the public, decided Edgar Allan Poe. In any case, it would do for the Philadelphia *Dollar Newspaper*.

His mother-in-law brought in the coffee.

LESTER DEL REY

The Pipes of Pan

Beyond the woods on either side were kept fields and fertile farm land, but here the undergrowth ran down to the dirt road and hid the small plot of tilled ground, already overrun with weeds. Behind that, concealed by thicker scrub timber lay a rude log house. Only the trees around, that had sheltered it from the heavy winds, had kept it from crumbling long before.

Pan recognized the lazy retreat to nature that had replaced his strong worship of old. He moved carefully through the tangled growth that made way for him, his cloven hoofs clicking sharply on the stones. It was a thin and saddened god that approached the house and gazed in through a hole that served as a window.

Inside, Frank Emmet lay on a rude pallet on the floor, a bag of his possessions beside him. Across from him was a stone fireplace, and between the two, nothing. A weak hand moved listlessly, brushing aside the vermin that knew his sickness; perhaps they sensed that the man was dying, and their time was short. He gave up and reached for a broken crock that contained water, but the effort was too great.

"Pan!" The man's voice reached out, and the god stepped away from the window and through the warped doorway. He moved to the pallet and leaned over his follower. The man looked up.

"Pan!" Emmet's words were startled, but there was a reverent note in his labored voice, though another might have mistaken the god for a devil. The tangled locks of Pan's head were separated by two goat horns and the thin sharp face ended in a ragged beard that seemed the worse for the weather. Then the neck led down to a bronzed torso that might have graced Hercules, only to end in the hips and legs of a goat, covered with shaggy hair. Horror and comedy mingled grotesquely, except for the eyes, which were deep and old, filled now with pity.

Pan nodded. "You've been calling me, Frank Emmet, and it's a poor god that wouldn't answer the appeal of his last worshiper. All the others of your kind have deserted me for newer gods, and only you are left, now."

It was true enough. Over the years, Pan had seen his followers fall off and dwindle until his great body grew lean and his lordly capering among the hills became a slow march toward extinction. Now even this man was dying. He lifted the tired head and held the crock of water to Emmet's mouth.

"Thanks!" The man mulled it over slowly. "So when I'm gone, there's no others. If I'd 'a' known, Pan, I might have raised up kids to honor your name, but I thought there were others. Am I—"

"Dying," the god answered. The blunt truth was easier than half-believed lies.

"Then take me outside, where the sun can shine on me."

Pan nodded and lifted him easily, bearing him out as gently as a mother might her child, but a spasm of pain shot over the man's face as Pan laid him down. The time was almost up, the god knew. From a pocket in his tattered loincloth he drew out a small syrinx, or pipe of seven reeds, and blew softly across it. A bird heard the low murmuring melody and improvised a harmony, while a cricket marked time in slow chirps.

Emmet's face relaxed slowly and one of his hands came out to lie on the hairy thigh. "Thanks, Pan. You've always been a good god to me, and I'm hoping you'll have good 1—" The voice trailed away and disappeared into the melody of the syrinx. Pan rose slowly, drawing a last lingering note from it, dropped the arm over the still chest and closed the eyes. Nearby was a rusty spade, and the earth was soft and moist.

Pan's great shoulders drooped as he wiped the last of the earth from his hands. Experimentally, he chirped at the cricket, but there was no response, and he knew that the law governing all gods still applied. When the last of their worshipers were gone, they either died or were forced to eke out their living in the world of men by some human activity. Now there would be hunger to satisfy, and in satisfying it, other needs of a life among men would present themselves.

Apollo was gone, long since, choosing in his pride to die, and the other gods had followed slowly, some choosing work, some death. But they had at least the advantage of human forms, while he knew himself for a monster his own mother had fled from. But then, the modern clothes were more concealing than the ancient ones.

Inside the house he found Emmet's other clothes, more or less presentable, and a hunting knife and soap. Men were partial to their own appearance, and horns were a stigma among them. Reluctantly, he brought the knife up against the base of one, cutting through it. Pain lanced through him at first, but enough of his godhead remained to make the stumps heal over almost instantly. Then the other one, followed by the long locks of his hair. He combed it out and hacked it into such form as he could.

As the beard came away he muttered ungodly phrases at the knife that took off skin with the hair. But even to his own eyes, the smooth-shaven face was less forbidding. The lips, as revealed, were firm and straight, and the chin was good, though a mark of different color showed where the beard had been.

He fingered his tail thoughtfully, touching it with the blade of the knife, then let it go; clothes could hide it, and Pan had no love for the barren spine that men regarded as a mark of superiority. The tail must stay. Shoes were another problem, but he solved it by carving wooden feet to fit them, and making holes for his hoofs. By lacing them on firmly, he found half an hour's practice enough to teach him to walk. The underclothes, that scratched against the hair on his thighs and itched savagely, were another factor he had no love for, but time might improve that.

Hobbling about in the rough walk his strange legs necessitated, he came on a few pieces of silver in another broken crock and pocketed them. From the scraps of conversation he had heard, work was hard enough for men to find, and he might need this small sum before he found occupation. Already hunger was creeping over him, or he guessed it was hunger. At least the vacuum in his stomach was as abhorrent to him as to nature. Heretofore, he had supped lightly on milk and honey as the moon suited him, but this was a man-sized craving.

Well, if work he must, work he would. The others had come to it, such as still lived. Ishtar, or Aphrodite, was working somewhere in the East as a nursemaid, though her old taste for men still cost her jobs as fast as she gained them. Pan's father, Hermes, had been working as a Postal Telegraph boy the last he'd seen of him. Even Zeus, proudest of all, was doing an electrician's work somewhere, leaving only Ares still thriving in full god-head. What his own talents might be, time alone would tell, but the rippling muscles of his body must be put to some good usage.

Satisfied that there was no more he could do, he trotted out and plowed his way through the underbrush that failed to make way for him as it should have. He jingled the money in one pocket thoughtfully as he hit the road, then drew out the syrinx and began a reedy tune of defiance on it. Work there must be, and he'd find it.

It was less than half an hour later, but the god's feet were already aching in the tight boxes he had made for them, and his legs threatened to buckle under the effort it took to ape man's walk. He moved past the ugly square house and toward the barn where the farmer was unhitching his team.

"Handout or work?" The man's voice was anything but enthusiastic.

"I'm looking for work."

"Uh-huh. Well, you do look strong enough. Living near the city the way I do, I get a lot of fellows in here, figuring they can always work in the country. But their arms wouldn't make toothpicks for a jaybird. Know anything about farming?"

"Something." It was more in Demeter's line, but he knew something about everything that grew. "I'm not asking more than room and board and a little on the side."

The farmer's eyes were appraising. "You do look as if you'd seen fresh air, at that. And you're homely enough to be honest. Grab a-holt here, and we'll talk it over. I don't rightly need a man, but—Hey! Whoa, there!"

Pan cursed silently. His god-head was still clinging to him, and the horses sensed the urge to wildness that was so intimately a part of him. As his hands fell on the tugs, they reared and bucked, lunging against their collars. He caught at the lines to steady them, but they flattened back their ears and whinnied wildly. That was enough; Pan moved back and let the farmer quiet them.

"Afraid I can't use you." The words were slow and decisive. "I use a right smart amount of horseflesh here, and some people just don't have the knack with them; animals are funny that way—temperamental, you might call it. Easy, there, Nelly. Tried any other places?''

"All the other farms along the road; they're not hiring hands.''

"Hm-m-m. Wouldn't be, of course. Bunch of city men. Think they can come out and live in the country and do a little farming on the side. If I had the money, I'd sell out and move somewhere where people knew what the earth was made for. You won't find any work around here." He slapped a horse on the withers and watched as it stretched out and rolled in the short grass. "Stay for lunch?''

"No.'' He wasn't hungry enough to need food yet, and the delay might cost him a job elsewhere. "Any sheepherding done around here?'' As the god of the shepherds, it should come natural to him, and it was work that would be more pleasant than the tight closeness of the city.

"Not around here. Out West they have, but the Mexicans do all that. If you're a sheep man, though, that's why the horses didn't take to you; they hate the smell of sheep.''

Again the limitations of a human life imposed themselves; instead of transporting himself to the sheepherding country in a night, he'd have to walk there slowly, or ride. "How much would it cost to go out West?''

"Blamed if I know. Seventy dollars, maybe more.''

So that was out. It would have to be the city, after all, where the fetid stench of close-packed humans tainted the air, and their meaningless yammering beat incessantly in one's ears. "I guess I'll have to go on into town,'' he said ruefully.

"Might be best. Nowadays, the country ain't what it used to be. Every fool that fails in town thinks he can fall back on the country, and every boy we have that amounts to anything goes to the city. Machinery's cutting down the number of men we need, and prices are shot haywire, even when a mortgage doesn't eat up all we make. You traveling on Shank's Mare?''

Pan nodded, and the other studied him again. "Uh-huh. Well, down the road a piece you'll see a brick house set away back from the road. Go in there and tell Hank Sherman I said you was a friend of mine. He's going into the city, and you might as well ride. Better hurry, though.''

Pan made his thanks hastily, and left. If memory served him right, the friendliness of the farmer was the last he'd see. In the cities, even in the old days, men were too busy with their own importance and superiority to bother with others. But beggars made ill choosers.

The god clumped down the hot sidewalk, avoiding the press of the one o'clock rush, and surveyed the signs thoughtfully. Food should come first, he guessed, but the prices were discouraging. One read:

BUSINESS MAN'S LUNCH

Blue plate special, 75¢

He cut away from the large street into an older part of the city, and found that the prices dropped steadily. Finally a sign that suited his pocketbook came into view, and he turned in, picking the only vacant booth. Now he was thankful for the time he'd believed wasted in studying men's ways.

The menu meant little to him. He studied it carefully, and decided that the safest course was to order one of their combinations. Fish—no, that was food for Poseidon. But the lamb plate looked better, and the price fell within his means. "Lamb," he ordered.

The waitress shifted her eyes from the man behind the counter and wrote it down in the manner of all waitresses who expect no tip from the customer. "Coffeetearmilk?" she asked. "Rollerwhiterrye?"

"Eh? Oh, milk and roll." Pan had a word for her type in several languages, and was tempted to use it. As a god—but he wasn't a god now, and men no longer respected their gods, anyway. The cashier eyed his clothes thoughtfully until he moved in irritation, jingling the few coins in his pocket. Then she went back to her tickets, flipping gum from one tooth to another in an abstract manner.

The food, when it came, was a soggy-looking mess, to him, but that was true of all human food, and he supposed it was good enough. At least the plate was better filled than those he had seen through the windows of the more expensive places, and Pan's appetite was immense. He stuffed half a roll in his mouth and chewed on it quickly.

Not bad; in fact, he might grow to like this business of eating. His stomach quieted down and made itself at home, while another half bun followed the first. As he started to pick up the cut of meat and swallow it, he caught the eyes of another diner, and rumbled unhappily. Should he know the sissies nipped off shavings with their knives and minced the food down? But he put the meat back on the plate and fell to as they did. It was best to ape them.

"Mind if I sit here, old-timer?" Pan looked up at a clean-cut young man. "The other booths are filled, you know."

Where the man sat was no business of his. The seat opposite him was vacant, and he motioned to it. "I didn't buy it, and your face isn't misshapen. Sit down."

The other grinned good-naturedly and inspected the menu. "Lamb any good?"

"Seems all right." He was no judge of food, naturally, but it wasn't burned, and he had seen no dirt on it. At least his stomach was satisfied. He cleaned the last of the gravy from his plate with a bun and transferred it to his mouth. "At least, it partly fills a man."

"O.K., lamb it is." This time the waitress showed more interest, and even brought water, a thing she'd neglected before. "Make it lamb, sugar. And a beer. How about you, stranger?"

"Eh?" Unless he was mistaken, that was an invitation, and a welcome one. It was long years since he'd had a chance to sample even the anemic brew of the modern world, but that had been none of his choosing.

"Have a beer?"

"Why not?" As an after-thought, he added an ungodlike thanks. The man was likable, he decided, though friendship among city men was not what he had expected. "You wouldn't know about work in this city, would you—uh?"

"Bob Bailey."

"Men call me Pan—or Faunus, sometimes."

"Pan Faunus, eh? Tried the want ads yet, or the employment agencies?" Bailey pulled a folded paper from his pocket and handed it over. "There might be a job in the back there. What kind of work?"

"Whatever I can do." He began at the bottom and skimmed up the list from xylophone players to bartenders. "But nothing they have here. I'm supposed to be good at herding and playing the syrinx, but that's about all."

"Syrinx?" He inspected the instrument Pan held out, and amusement danced in his eyes. "Oh, that. Afraid it wouldn't do, Mr. Faunus. You don't happen to play the clarinet?"

"Never tried it."

"Then you don't. I'm looking for someone who does, right now, for my band— Bob Bailey's Barnstormers. Ever heard of it? Well, you're not the only one. Since we lost the best darndest clarinetist in the business, we've slipped plenty. Playing the third-rate spots now with the substitute we had to hire. Corny? *Wheoo!* He used to be on the Lady Lee Lullaby hour, and never got over it."

"Why not get a good one then?" The talk made little sense to the god, but the solution seemed obvious.

"Where? We get plenty of applicants—there's an ad in there now. But they'd either soothe the jitterbugs to sleep or rattle the strings off the dog house. Not a good clear tone in the bunch. All the good guys are signed up, or starting their own outfits."

They finished the beers and Pan counted out the amount marked on his ticket, estimating the length of time what was left would last; two days maybe, by going half hungry. He grunted. "Where are these employment agencies you mentioned?"

"One just down the street. It's a United States' employment center, and won't try to rob you. Good luck, Faunus."

"And to you. My thanks for the beer." Then they separated, and Pan headed down the street toward the mecca of the jobless. The ads had all called for training of some sort, but there must be other work in this town that needed no previous experience. Perhaps meeting two friendly men in one day was a good omen. He hoped so.

The girl at the desk, when he finally found the right division, looked as bored as had the waitress. Looking over the collection of people waiting, Pan felt she had more reason. There were the coarsened red faces of professional sots, the lack-luster stares of men whose intelligence ranked slightly below the apes, and the dreary faces of people who struggle futilely for a life that brings nothing but death to break its monotony.

But there were others there who looked efficient and purposeful, and these were the ones Pan feared. They had at least some training, some experience, and their appearance was better than his. Surely the preference would go to them, and even as a minority, there were still many of that type there.

He studied the applicants and strained his ears to familiarize himself with the questions asked, holding down his impatience as best he could. But the machine ground slowly on, and his time finally came, just as the hot fetid air was becoming unbearable. "Your name," said the girl studying him impersonally.

"Pan—Pan Faunus."

Many strange names had passed over the desk to her, and her expression remained the same. "Middle name?"

"Uh . . . Sylvanus." The Romans had done him a good turn in doubling up on their names for him though he preferred the Greek.

"Address?"

For a moment, that stumped him. Then he gave the address of the restaurant, figuring that he might be able to arrange with the cashier to accept any mail that came there; he'd heard another man talking of that scheme while he waited, and it was as good as any.

"Age?"

"Seven thou— *Ulp!* Forty-five." Since a pack of lies were needed of him, they might as well be good ones. "Born June 5, 1894."

There were more questions, and at some of his answers the girl looked up sharply, but his wits had always been good, and he passed the test with some fair success. Then came what he had been dreading.

"Experience and type of work?"

"General work in the country," he decided. "No trade, and I can't give references, since my former foll—employer is dead."

"Social Security Number?"

"Eh?" He had been hearing that asked of the applicants, but it still meant nothing to him. "I don't have one."

"Sorry." She nodded. "Naturally you wouldn't, as a farmhand. You'll have to have a card, though. Get that as soon as you find work."

Finally it was done, and he was sent into a cubbyhole where a man asked more questions and made marks on a piece of paper. Some of his answers were true; Hermes was his father, at least. Even that questioning came to a final end that left him sweating and cursing the underclothes that itched again in the hot room. The man leaned back and surveyed him.

"We haven't much of a job for you, Mr. Faunus. As a matter of fact, you'd probably do much better in the country where you came from. But"—he searched through his records—"this call just came in for an office boy, and they want someone of your age, for some reason. It pays only $12.50 a week, but they didn't mention experience. Want to try it?"

Pan nodded emphatically and blessed the luck that had opened the job at precisely the right moment; he'd seen enough others turned away to know how small his chances were. He wasted no time in taking the little address slip and tracking the job to its lair.

Late afternoon found him less enthusiastic about the work. The air in the office was thick and stuffy, and there was an incessant thudding from the typewriters, jarring of the comptometer, and the general buzz that men think necessary to business. He leaned over on the table, taking some of the ache from his tired feet and cursing the endless piles of envelopes that needed sealing and stamping.

This was work for a fool or one of the machines men were so proud of. Pick up an envelope, draw one finger under the flap to lift it, roll the flap over the wet roller, and close it with the other hand as it came off. Lift, roll, seal, lift, roll, seal. No wonder men shut themselves in tight houses, away from the good, clean winds and light of the sun; they were ashamed of what served for life among them, and with good reason.

But if it had to be done, he was willing to try. At first, the exultation of getting the work had served to keep his mind from it. Lying and deceit were not his specialty, and only a driving urge to adapt himself had made him use them to the extent that had been necessary. Now the men had put him on work that shriveled the mind, and did the muscles no good.

The old office boy came up to inspect his work, and Pan understood, looking at him, why the manager no longer wanted boys. The kid didn't know as yet that his job was being taken over, but thought he was in line for promotion, and was cocky enough for two. He seized the envelope rudely and ran it over the roller with a flourish.

"Awful dumb help they're sending out these days," he told the air. "Now I told you these had to go out tonight, and I find you loafing. Keep moving. You don't catch me laying down on the job. Ain't you never had work before?"

Pan looked at him, a side-long glance that choked off the kid's words, and fell to on the envelopes again. The air was getting the best of him. His head felt numb and thick, and his whole body was logy and dull. With what was supposed to be a chummy air, the boy sat his overgrown body on the desk and opened up his reservoir of personal anecdotes.

"Boy, you should 'a' been with me last night. Good-looking babes— Hm-m-m! Maybe they didn't like me, too. One little baby'd seen me work on the football team last year, and that didn't do me any harm. Best high school team in the State we had. You like football, guy?"

Pan's lips twitched. "No!" He redid an envelope that hadn't been properly wetted and reviewed the reasons for not committing mayhem on the boy. They were good reasons, but their value was depreciating with the passage of time in the stinking office, and with each new visit from the boy. The direct bluntness he longed to use came out a little in his voice, and the kid bounced off the table, scowling.

"O.K., don't let it get you. Hey, whatda you think stamps are? Don't tear them that way. Some of you hicks are ignorant enough to eat them."

The god caught himself on the table again, throbbing pains running through his head. There was a conference around the manager's desk and cigar smoke was being added to the thickness of the room. He groped out behind him for a stool, and eased himself down on it. Something sharp cut into him, and brought him up with a wild bellow!

The boy giggled. "Dawgonne, I didn't think you'd fall for it. Oldest trick there is, and you still sat right down on that tack. Boy, you should 'a' seen yourself."

Pan wasn't seeing himself, but he was seeing red. Homeric Greek is probably the most expressive of all languages, and his command of it included a good deal

Homer had forgotten to mention. With a sharp leap, his head came down and his body jerked forward. He missed the horns, now, but his hard skull on the boy's midsection served well enough.

Sudden confusion ran through the office, and the manager rose quickly from his chair and headed toward the scene. Pan's senses were returning and he knew it was time to leave. The back door opened on an alley and he didn't wait to ask for directions.

The outer air removed the last traces of his temper and sobered him down, but there was no regret in his mind. What was done was done, and there was no room in his philosophy for regrets. Of course, word of it would get back to the employment agency, and he'd have no more jobs from them, but he wanted no more of such jobs. Maybe Apollo had the right idea in dying.

He made a slow meal in the restaurant, noting that Bailey was not there. He'd liked that young man. With a rush of extravagance, he bought a beer for himself and hung around, half waiting in hopes of Bailey's appearance and half planning for tomorrow; but nothing came of his plans.

Finally he got up and moved out into a little park across from the restaurant, just as darkness began to replace the twilight. Sleeping accommodations were the least of his worries. He found a large bush which concealed his body, and lay down on the ground under it. Sleep came quickly.

When he awoke, he found himself better for the sleep, though the same wasn't true of his clothes. He located his shoes and clamped his hoofs into them again, muttering dark thoughts about cobblers in general. If this kept up, he'd get bog spavins yet.

He made his way across to the restaurant again, where the waitress who was on at that hour regarded him with less approval than the other had. Out of the great pity of her heart, her actions said, she'd condescend to serve him, but she'd be the last to object to his disappearance. The sweet bun he got must have been well chosen for dryness.

"Hello there, old-timer." Bob Bailey's easy voice broke in on his gloom as the young man sat down opposite him. His eyes studied the god's clothes, and he nodded faintly to himself, but made no comment. "Have any luck yesterday?"

"Some, if you'd call it that." Pan related his fortunes shortly. Bailey grinned faintly.

"The trouble with you," Bailey said around a mouthful of eggs, "is that you're a man; employers don't want that. They want machines with self-starters and a high regard for so-called business ideals. Takes several years to inculcate a man with the proper reverence for all forms of knuckling under. You're supposed to lie down and take it, no matter how little you like it."

"Even empty fools who hold themselves better than gods?"

"That or worse; I know something about it myself. Stood all I could of a two-bit, white-collar job before I organized the Barnstormers."

Pan considered the prospect, and wondered how long it would take him to starve. "Slavery isn't what I'm looking for. Find your musician?"

"Not a chance. When they've got rhythm, they don't bother learning to play; and most of them don't have it. Smoke?"

Pan took the cigarette doubtfully, and mimicked the other's actions. He'd seen men smoking for centuries now, but the urge to try it had never come to him. He coughed over the first puff, letting out a bleat that startled the couple in the next booth, then set about mastering this smoke-sucking. Once the harsh sting of the tobacco was gone, there was something oddly soothing about it, and his vigorous good health threw off any toxic effect it might have had.

Bob finished his breakfast, and picked up the checks. "On me, Faunus," he said. "The shows should open in a few minutes. Want to take one in?"

Pan shook his head vigorously. The close-packed throng of humans in a dark theater was not his idea of a soothing atmosphere. "I'm going over to the park again. Maybe in the outdoor air, I can find some idea."

"O.K., we'll make it a twosome, if it's all right with you. Time to kill is about the only thing I have now." As he paid the checks, Pan noticed that the man's pocketbook was anything but overflowing, and guessed that one of Bailey's difficulties was inability to pay for a first-class musician.

They found a bench in the shade and sat down together, each thinking of his own troubles and mulling over the other's. It was the best way in the world of feeling miserable. Above them in a tree, a bird settled down to a high, bubbling little song and a squirrel came over to them with the faint hopes of peanuts clearly in its mind.

Pan clucked at it, making clicking sounds that brought its beady little eyes up at him quickly. It was a fat well-fed squirrel that had domesticated man nicely for its purposes, and there was no fear about it. When even the animals had learned to live with man and like it, surely a god could do as well.

He tapped his thighs slowly and felt the syrinx under his hand. The squirrel regarded him carefully as he drew it out, saw there was no bag of peanuts there, and started to withdraw. The first low notes blown from the reeds called it back, and it sat down on its tail, paws to its mouth in a rapt attitude that aped a critic listening to Bach.

Pan took courage, and the old bluff laughter fell from his lips. He lifted the syrinx again and began a wild quick air on the spur of the moment, letting the music roam through the notes as it would. There was no set tempo, but his feet tapped lightly on the graveled path, and the bird fell in step.

Bailey looked up quickly, his fingers twitching at the irregular rhythm. There was a wildness to it, a primitiveness that barely escaped savagery, and groped out toward man's first awareness of the fierce wild joy of living. Now the notes formed into a regular cadence that could be followed, and Bailey whistled an impromptu harmony. The squirrel swayed lightly from side to side, twitching his tail.

"Jitterbug, isn't he?" Bob asked, as Pan paused. "I've never seen music hit an animal that way before. Where'd you learn the piece?"

"Learn it?" Pan shook his head. "Music isn't learned—it's something that comes from inside."

"You mean you made that up as you went along? *Whew!* But you can play a regular tune, can't you?"

"I never tried."

"Uh. Well, here's one." He pursed his lips and began whistling one of the swingy popular things his orchestra played at, but never hit. Pan listened to it carefully, only half sure he liked it, then put the syrinx to his lips, beat his foot for time, and repeated it. But there were minor variations that somehow lifted it and set the rhythm bouncing along, reaching out to the squirrel and making its tail twitch frenziedly.

Bailey slapped him on the back, grinning. "Old-timer," he chuckled, "you've got the corniest instrument there is, but you can roll it down the groove. I'd like to have the boys hear what a real hepeat can do to a piece."

Pan's face was blank, though the voice seemed approving. "Can't you speak English?"

"Sure. I'm telling you you're hot. Give the jitterbugs an earful of that and top-billing would follow after. Come on!"

Pan followed him, uncertain. "Where?"

"Over to the boys. If you can wrap your lips around a clarinet the way you do that thing, our worries are over. And I'm betting you can."

It was their last night's engagement at the Grotto a month later, and Pan stood up, roaring out the doggerel words in a deep rich basso that caught and lifted the song. Strictly speaking, his voice was a little too true for swing, but the boisterous paganism in it was like a beat note from a tuba, something that refused to permit feet to be still. Then it ended, and the usual clamor followed. His singing was a recent experiment, but it went over.

Bob shook hands with himself and grinned. "Great, Pan! You're hot tonight." Then he stepped to the microphone. "And now, for our last number, folks, I'd like to present a new tune for the first time over played. It's called 'The Gods Got Rhythm,' and we think you'll like it. Words and music by Tin Pan Faunus, the Idol of the Jitterbugs. O.K., Tin Pan, take it!"

Pan cuddled the clarinet in his mouth and watched the crowd stampede out onto the floor. Bob winked at him, and he opened up, watching the dancers. This was like the rest, a wild ecstasy that refused to let them stay still. Primitive, vital, every nerve alive to the music. Even the nymphs of old had danced less savagely to his piping.

One of the boys passed a note over to his knee, and he glanced at it as he played. "Boys, we're set. Peterson just gave Bob the signal, and that means three months at the Crystal Palace. Good-by blues."

Pan opened up, letting the other instruments idle in the background, and went in for a private jam session of his own. Out on the floor were his worshipers, every step an act of homage to him. Homage that paid dividends, and was as real in its way as the sacrifices of old; but that was a minor detail. Right now he was hot.

He lifted the instrument higher, drawing out the last wild ecstasy from it. Under his clothes, his tail twitched sharply, but the dancers couldn't see that, and wouldn't have cared if they had. Tin Pan Faunus, Idol of the Jitterbugs, was playing, and that was enough.

THEODORE STURGEON

It

It walked in the woods.

It was never born. It existed. Under the pine needles the fires burn, deep and smokeless in the mold. In heat and in darkness and decay there is growth. There is life and there is growth. It grew, but it was not alive. It walked unbreathing through the woods, and thought and saw and was hideous and strong, and it was not born and it did not live. It grew and moved about without living.

It crawled out of the darkness and hot damp mold into the cool of a morning. It was huge. It was lumped and crusted with its own hateful substances, and pieces of it dropped off as it went its way, dropped off and lay writhing, and stilled, and sank putrescent into the forest loam.

It had no mercy, no laughter, no beauty. It had strength and great intelligence. And—perhaps it could not be destroyed. It crawled out of its mound in the wood and lay pulsing in the sunlight for a long moment. Patches of it shone wetly in the golden glow, parts of it were nubbled and flaked. And whose dead bones had given it the form of a man?

It scrabbled painfully with its half-formed hands, beating the ground and the bole of a tree. It rolled and lifted itself up on its crumbling elbows, and it tore up a great handful of herbs and shredded them against its chest, and it paused and gazed at the gray-green juices with intelligent calm. It wavered to its feet, and seized a young sapling and destroyed it, folding the slender trunk back on itself again and again, watching attentively the useless, fibered splinters. And it snatched up a fear-frozen field-creature, crushing it slowly, letting blood and pulpy flesh and fur ooze from between its fingers, run down and rot on the forearms.

It began searching.

Kimbo drifted through the tall grasses like a puff of dust, his bushy tail curled tightly over his back and his long jaws agape. He ran with an easy lope, loving his freedom and the power of his flanks and furry shoulders. His tongue lolled listlessly over his lips. His lips were black and serrated, and each tiny pointed liplet swayed with his doggy gallop. Kimbo was all dog, all healthy animal.

He leaped high over a boulder and landed with a startled yelp as a longeared cony shot from its hiding place under the rock. Kimbo hurtled after it, grunting with each great thrust of his legs. The rabbit bounced just ahead of him, keeping its distance, its ears flattened on its curving back and its little legs nibbling away at distance hungrily. It stopped, and Kimbo pounced, and the rabbit shot away at a tangent and popped into a hollow log. Kimbo yelped again and rushed snuffling at the log, and knowing his failure, curvetted but once around the stump and ran on into the forest. The thing that watched from the wood raised its crusted arms and waited for Kimbo.

Kimbo sensed it there, standing dead-still by the path. To him it was a bulk which smelled of carrion not fit to roll in, and he snuffled distastefully and ran to pass it.

The thing let him come abreast and dropped a heavy twisted fist on him. Kimbo saw it coming and curled up tight as he ran, and the hand clipped stunningly on his rump, sending him rolling and yipping down the slope. Kimbo straddled to his feet, shook his head, shook his body with a deep growl, came back to the silent thing with green murder in his eyes. He walked stiffly, straight-legged, his tail as low as his lowered head and a ruff of fury round his neck. The thing raised its arms again, waited.

Kimbo slowed, then flipped himself through the air at the monster's throat. His jaws closed on it; his teeth clicked together through a mass of filth, and he fell choking and snarling at its feet. The thing leaned down and struck twice, and after the dog's back was broken it sat beside him and began to tear him apart.

"Be back in an hour or so," said Alton Drew, picking up his rifle from the corner behind the wood box. His brother laughed.

"Old Kimbo 'bout runs your life, Alton," he said.

"Ah, I know the ol' devil," said Alton. "When I whistle for him for half an hour and he don't show up, he's in a jam or he's treed something wuth shootin' at. The ol' son of a gun calls me by not answerin'."

Cory Drew shoved a full glass of milk over to his nine-year-old daughter and smiled. "You think as much o' that houn' dog o' yours as I do of Babe here."

Babe slid off her chair and ran to her uncle. "Gonna catch me the bad fella, Uncle Alton?" she shrilled. The "bad fella" was Cory's invention—the one who lurked in corners ready to pounce on little girls who chased the chickens and played around mowing machines and hurled green apples with a powerful young arm at the sides of the hogs, to hear the synchronized thud and grunt; little girls who swore with an Austrian accent like an ex-hired man they had had; who dug caves in haystacks till they tipped over, and kept pet crawfish in tomorrow's milk cans, and rode work horses to a lather in the night pasture.

"Get back here and keep away from Uncle Alton's gun!" said Cory. "If you see the bad fella, Alton, chase him back here. He has a date with Babe here for that stunt of hers last night." The preceding evening, Babe had kind-heartedly poured pepper on the cows' salt block.

"Don't worry, kiddo," grinned her uncle, "I'll bring you the bad fella's hide if he don't get me first."

* * *

Alton Drew walked up the path toward the wood, thinking about Babe. She was a phenomenon—a pampered farm child. Ah well—she had to be. They'd both loved Clissa Drew, and she'd married Cory, and they had to love Clissa's child. Funny thing, love. Alton was a man's man, and thought things out that way; and his reaction to love was a strong and frightened one. He knew what love was because he felt it still for his brother's wife and would feel it as long as he lived for Babe. It led him through his life, and yet he embarrassed himself by thinking of it. Loving a dog was an easy thing, because you and the old devil could love one another completely without talking about it. The smell of gun smoke and wet fur in the rain were perfume enough for Alton Drew, a grunt of satisfaction and the scream of something hunted and hit were poetry enough. They weren't like love for a human, that choked his throat so he could not say words he could not have thought of anyway. So Alton loved his dog Kimbo and his Winchester for all to see, and let his love for his brother's women, Clissa and Babe, eat at him quietly and unmentioned.

His quick eyes saw the fresh indentations in the soft earth behind the boulder, which showed where Kimbo had turned and leaped with a single surge, chasing the rabbit. Ignoring the tracks, he looked for the nearest place where a rabbit might hide, and strolled over to the stump. Kimbo had been there, he saw, and had been there too late. "You're an ol' fool," muttered Alton. "Y' can't catch a cony by chasin' it. You want to cross him up some way." He gave a peculiar trilling whistle, sure that Kimbo was digging frantically under some nearby stump for a rabbit that was three counties away by now. No answer. A little puzzled, Alton went back to the path. "He never done this before," he said softly.

He cocked his .32-40 and cradled it. At the county fair someone had once said of Alton Drew that he could shoot at a handful of corn and peas thrown in the air and hit only the corn. Once he split a bullet on the blade of a knife and put two candles out. He had no need to fear anything that could be shot at. That's what he believed.

The thing in the woods looked curiously down at what it had done to Kimbo, and tried to moan the way Kimbo had before he died. It stood a minute storing away facts in its foul, unemotional mind. Blood was warm. The sunlight was warm. Things that moved and bore fur had a muscle to force the thick liquid through tiny tubes in their bodies. The liquid coagulated after a time. The liquid on rooted green things was thinner and the loss of a limb did not mean loss of life. It was very interesting, but the thing, the mold with a mind, was not pleased. Neither was it displeased. Its accidental urge was a thirst for knowledge, and it was only—interested.

It was growing late, and the sun reddened and rested awhile on the hilly horizon, teaching the clouds to be inverted flames. The thing threw up its head suddenly, noticing the dusk. Night was ever a strange thing, even for those of us who have known it in life. It would have been frightening for the monster had it been capable of fright, but it could only be curious; it could only reason from what it had observed.

What was happening? It was getting harder to see. Why? It threw its shapeless head from side to side. It was true—things were dim, and growing dimmer. Things were changing shape, taking on a new and darker color. What did the creatures it had crushed and torn apart see? How did they see? The larger one, the one that had attacked, had used two organs in its head. That must have been it, because after the thing had torn off two of the dog's legs it had struck at the hairy muzzle; and the dog, seeing the blow coming, had dropped folds of skin over the organs— closed its eyes. Ergo, the dog saw with its eyes. But then after the dog was dead, and its body still, repeated blows had had no effect on the eyes. They remained open and staring. The logical conclusion was, then, that a being that had ceased to live and breathe and move about lost the use of its eyes. It must be that to lose sight was, conversely, to die. Dead things did not walk about. They lay down and did not move. Therefore the thing in the wood concluded that it must be dead, and so it lay down by the path, not far away from Kimbo's scattered body, lay down and believed itself dead.

Alton Drew came up through the dusk to the wood. He was frankly worried. He whistled again, and then called, and there was still no response, and he said again, "The ol' flea-bus never done this before," and shook his heavy head. It was past milking time, and Cory would need him. "Kimbo!" he roared. The cry echoed through the shadows, and Alton flipped on the safety catch of his rifle and put the butt on the ground beside the path. Leaning on it, he took off his cap and scratched the back of his head, wondering. The rifle butt sank into what he thought was soft earth; he staggered and stepped into the chest of the thing that lay beside the path. His foot went up to the ankle in its yielding rottenness, and he swore and jumped back.

"*Whew!* Somp'n sure dead as hell there! Ugh!" He swabbed at his boot with a handful of leaves while the monster lay in the growing blackness with the edges of the deep footprint in its chest sliding into it, filling it up. It lay there regarding him dimly out of its muddy eyes, thinking it was dead because of the darkness, watching the articulation of Alton Drew's joints, wondering at this new uncautious creature.

Alton cleaned the butt of his gun with more leaves and went on up the path, whistling anxiously for Kimbo.

Clissa Drew stood in the door of the milk shed, very lovely in red-checked gingham and a blue apron. Her hair was clean yellow, parted in the middle and stretched tautly back to a heavy braided knot. "Cory! Alton!" she called a little sharply.

"Well?" Cory responded gruffly from the barn, where he was stripping off the Ayrshire. The dwindling streams of milk plopped pleasantly into the froth of a full pail.

"I've called and called," said Clissa. "Supper's cold, and Babe won't eat until you come. Why—where's Alton?"

Cory grunted, heaved the stool out of the way, threw over the stanchion lock and slapped the Ayrshire on the rump. The cow backed and filled like a towboat, clattered down the line and out into the barn-yard. ''Ain't back yet.''

''Not back?'' Clissa came in and stood beside him as he sat by the next cow, put his forehead against the warm flank. ''But, Cory, he said he'd—''

''Yeh, yeh, I know. He said he'd be back fer the milkin'. I heard him. Well, he ain't.''

''And you have to— Oh, Cory, I'll help you finish up. Alton would be back if he could. Maybe he's—''

''Maybe he's treed a blue jay,'' snapped her husband. ''Him an' that damn dog.'' He gestured hugely with one hand while the other went on milking. ''I got twenty-six head o' cows to milk. I got pigs to feed an' chickens to put to bed. I got to toss hay for the mare and turn the team out. I got harness to mend and a wire down in the night pasture. I got wood to split an' carry.'' He milked for a moment in silence, chewing on his lip. Clissa stood twisting her hands together, trying to think of something to stem the tide. It wasn't the first time Alton's hunting had interfered with the chores. ''So I got to go ahead with it. I can't interfere with Alton's spoorin.' Every damn time that hound o' his smells out a squirrel I go without my supper. I'm gettin' sick and—''

''Oh, I'll help you!'' said Clissa. She was thinking of the spring, when Kimbo had held four hundred pounds of raging black bear at bay until Alton could put a bullet in its brain, the time Babe had found a bearcub and started to carry it home, and had fallen into a freshet, cutting her head. You can't hate a dog that has saved your child for you, she thought.

''You'll do nothing' of the kind!'' Cory growled. ''Get back to the house. You'll find work enough there. I'll be along when I can. Dammit, Clissa, don't cry! I didn't mean to—Oh, shucks!'' He got up and put his arms around her. ''I'm wrought up,'' he said. ''Go on now. I'd no call to speak that way to you. I'm sorry. Go back to Babe. I'll put a stop to this for good tonight. I've had enough. There's work here for four farmers an' all we've got is me an' that . . . that huntsman.

Go on now, Clissa.''

''All right,'' she said into his shoulder. ''But, Cory, hear him out first when he comes back. He might be unable to come back. He might be unable to come back this time. Maybe he . . . he—''

''Ain't nothin' kin hurt my brother that a bullet will hit. He can take care of himself. He's got no excuse good enough this time. Go on, now. Make the kid eat.''

Clissa went back to the house, her young face furrowed. If Cory quarreled with Alton now and drove him away, what with the drought and the creamery about to close and all, they just couldn't manage. Hiring a man was out of the question. Cory'd have to work himself to death, and he just wouldn't be able to make it. No one man could. She sighed and went into the house. It was seven o'clock, and the milking not done yet. Oh, why did Alton have to—

Babe was in bed at nine when Clissa heard Cory in the shed, slinging the wire cutters into a corner. "Alton back yet?" they both said at once as Cory stepped into the kitchen; and as she shook her head he clumped over to the stove, and lifting a lid, spat into the coals. "Come to bed," he said.

She laid down her stitching and looked at his broad back. He was twenty-eight, and he walked and acted like a man ten years older, and looked like a man five years younger. "I'll be up in a while," Clissa said.

Cory glanced at the corner behind the wood box where Alton's rifle usually stood, then made an unspellable, disgusted sound and sat down to take off his heavy muddy shoes.

"It's after nine," Clissa volunteered timidly. Cory said nothing, reaching for house slippers.

"Cory, you're not going to—"

"Not going to what?"

"Oh, nothing. I just thought that maybe Alton—"

"Alton," Cory flared. "The dog goes hunting field mice. Alton goes hunting the dog. Now you want me to go hunting Alton. That's what you want?"

"I just—He was never this late before."

"I won't do it! Go out lookin' for him at nine o'clock in the night? I'll be damned! He has no call to use us so, Clissa."

Clissa said nothing. She went to the stove, peered into the wash boiler, set aside at the back of the range. When she turned around, Cory had his shoes and coat on again.

"I knew you'd go," she said. Her voice smiled though she did not.

"I'll be back durned soon," said Cory. "I don't reckon he's strayed far. It is late. I ain't feared for him, but—" He broke his 12-gauge shotgun, looked through the barrels, slipped two shells in the breech and a box of them into his pocket. "Don't wait up," he said over his shoulder as he went out.

"I won't," Clissa replied to the closed door, and went back to her stitching by the lamp.

The path up the slope to the wood was very dark when Cory went up it, peering and calling. The air was chill and quiet, and a fetid odor of mold hung in it. Cory blew the taste of it out through impatient nostrils, drew it in again with the next breath, and swore. "Nonsense," he muttered. "Houn' dawg. Huntin', at ten in th' night, too. Alton!" he bellowed. "Alton Drew!" Echoes answered him, and he entered the wood. The huddled thing he passed in the dark heard him and felt the vibrations of his foot-steps and did not move because it thought it was dead.

Cory strode on, looking around and ahead and not down since his feet knew the path.

"Alton!"

"That you, Cory?"

Cory Drew froze. That corner of the wood was thickly set and as dark as a burial vault. The voice he heard was choked, quiet, penetrating.

"Alton?"

"I found Kimbo, Cory."

"Where the hell have you been?" shouted Cory furiously. He disliked this pitch-darkness; he was afraid at the tense hopelessness of Alton's voice, and he mistrusted his ability to stay angry at his brother.

"I called him, Cory. I whistled at him, an' the ol' devil didn't answer."

"I can say the same for you, you . . . you louse. Why weren't you to milkin'? Where are you? You caught in a trap?"

"The houn' never missed answerin' me before, you know," said the tight, monotonous voice from the darkness.

"Alton! What the devil's the matter with you? What do I care if your mutt didn't answer? Where—"

"I guess because he ain't never died before," said Alton, refusing to be interrupted.

"You *what?*" Cory clicked his lips together twice and then said, "Alton, you turned crazy? What's that you say?"

"Kimbo's dead."

"Kim . . . oh! Oh!" Cory was seeing that picture again in his mind— Babe sprawled unconscious in the freshet, and Kimbo raging and snapping against a monster bear, holding her back until Alton could get there. "What happened, Alton?" he asked more quietly.

"I aim to find out. Someone tore him up."

"Tore him up?"

"There ain't a bit of him left tacked together, Cory. Every damn joint in his body tore apart. Guts out of him."

"Good God! Bear, you reckon?"

"No bear, nor nothin' on four legs. He's all here. None of him's been et. Whoever done it just killed him an'—tore him up."

"Good God!" Cory said again. "Who could've—" There was a long silence, then. "Come 'long home," he said almost gently "There's no call for you to set up by him all night."

"I'll set. I aim to be here at sunup, an' I'm going to start trackin', an' I'm goin' to keep trackin' till I find the one done this job on Kimbo."

"You're drunk or crazy, Alton."

"I ain't drunk. You can think what you like about the rest of it. I'm stickin' here."

"We got a farm back yonder. Remember? I ain't going to milk twenty-six head o' cows again in the mornin' like I did jest now, Alton."

"Sombody's got to. I can't be there. I guess you'll just have to, Cory."

"You dirty scum!" Cory screamed. "You'll come back with me now or I'll know why!"

Alton's voice was still tight, half-sleepy. "Don't you come no nearer, bud."

Cory kept moving toward Alton's voice.

"I said"—the voice was very quiet now—"*stop where you are.*" Cory kept coming. A sharp click told of the release of the .32–40's safety. Cory stopped.

"You got your gun on me, Alton?" Cory whispered.

"Thass right, bud. You ain't a-trompin' up these tracks for me. I need 'em at sunup."

A full minute passed, and the only sound in the blackness was that of Cory's pained breathing. Finally:

"I got my gun, too, Alton. Come home."

"You can't see to shoot me."

"We're even on that."

"We ain't. I know just where you stand, Cory. I been here four hours."

"My gun scatters."

"My gun kills."

Without another word Cory Drew turned on his heel and stamped back to the farm.

Black and liquidescent it lay in the blackness, not alive, not understanding death, believing itself dead. Things that were alive saw and moved about. Things that were not alive could do neither. It rested its muddy gaze on the line of trees at the crest of the rise, and deep within it thoughts trickled wetly. It lay huddled, dividing its new found facts, dissecting them as it had dissected live things when there was light, comparing, concluding, pigeonholing.

The trees at the top of the slope could just be seen, as their trunks were a fraction of a shade lighter than the dark sky behind them. At length they, too, disappeared, and for a moment sky and trees were a monotone. The thing knew it was dead now, and like many a being before it, it wondered how long it must stay like this. And then the sky beyond the trees grew a little lighter. That was a manifestly impossible occurrence, thought the thing, but it could see it and it must be so. Did dead things live again? That was curious. What about dismembered dead things? It would wait and see.

The sun came hand over hand up a beam of light. A bird somewhere made a high yawning peep, and as an owl killed a shrew, a skunk pounced on another, so that the night shift deaths and those of the day could go on without cessation. Two flowers nodded archly to each other, comparing their pretty clothes. A dragon fly nymph decided it was tired of looking serious and cracked its back open, to crawl out and dry gauzily. The first golden ray sheared down between the trees, through the grasses, passed over the mass in the shadowed bushes. "I am alive again," thought the thing that could not possibly live. "I am alive, for I see clearly." It stood up on its thick legs, up into the golden glow. In a little while the wet flakes that had grown during the night dried in the sun, and when it took its first steps, they cracked off and a small shower of them fell away. It walked up the slope to find Kimbo, to see if he, too, were alive again.

Babe let the sun come into her room by opening her eyes. Uncle Alton was gone—that was the first thing that ran through her head. Dad had come home last night and had shouted at mother for an hour. Alton was plumb crazy. He'd turned a gun on his own brother. If Alton ever came ten feet into Cory's land, Cory would fill him so full of holes, he'd look like a tumbleweed. Alton was lazy, shiftless, selfish, and one or two other things of questionable taste but undoubted vividness. Babe knew her father. Uncle Alton would never be safe in this county.

She bounced out of bed in the enviable way of the very young, and ran to the window. Cory was trudging down to the night pasture with two bridles over his arm, to get the team. There were kitchen noises from downstairs.

Babe ducked her head in the washbowl and shook off the water like a terrier before she toweled. Trailing clean shirt and dungarees, she went to the head of the stairs, slid into the shirt, and began her morning ritual with the trousers. One step down was a step through the right leg. One more, and she was into the left. Then, bouncing step by step on both feet, buttoning one button per step, she reached the bottom fully dressed and ran into the kitchen.

"Didn't Uncle Alton come back a-tall, Mum?"

"Morning, Babe. No, dear." Clissa was too quiet, smiling too much, Babe thought shrewdly. Wasn't happy.

"Where'd he go, Mum?"

"We don't know, Babe. Sit down and eat your breakfast."

"What's a misbegotten, Mum?" the Babe asked suddenly. Her mother nearly dropped the dish she was drying. "Babe! You must never say that again!"

"Oh. Well, why is Uncle Alton, then?"

"Why is he what?"

Babe's mouth muscled around an outsize spoonful of oatmeal. "A misbe—"

"Babe!"

"All right, Mum," said Babe with her mouth full. "Well, why?"

"I told Cory not to shout last night," Clissa said half to herself.

"Well, whatever it means, he isn't," said Babe with finality. "Did he go hunting again?"

"He went to look for Kimbo, darling."

"Kimbo? Oh Mummy, is Kimbo gone, too? Didn't he come back either?"

"No dear. Oh, please, Babe, stop asking questions!"

"All right. Where do you think they went?"

"Into the north woods. Be quiet."

Babe gulped away at her breakfast. An idea struck her; and as she thought of it she ate slower and slower, and cast more and more glances at her mother from under the lashes of her tilted eyes. It would be awful if daddy did anything to Uncle Alton. Someone ought to warn him.

Babe was halfway to the woods when Alton's .32–40 sent echoes giggling up and down the valley.

Cory was in the south thirty, riding a cultivator and cussing at the team of grays when he heard the gun. "Hoa," he called to the horses, and sat a moment to listen to the sound. "One-two-three. Four," he counted. "Saw someone, blasted away at him. Had a chance to take aim and give him another, careful. My God!" He threw up the cultivator points and steered the team into the shade of three oaks. He hobbled the gelding with swift tosses of a spare strap, and headed for the woods. "Alton a killer," he murmered, and doubled back to the house for his gun. Clissa was standing just outside the door.

"Get shells!" he snapped and flung into the house. Clissa followed him. He was strapping his hunting knife on before she could get a box off the shelf. "Cory—"

"Hear that gun, did you? Alton's off his nut. He don't waste lead. He shot at someone just then, and he wasn't fixin' to shoot pa'tridges when I saw him last. He was out to get a man. Gimme my gun."

"Cory, Babe—"

"You keep her here. Oh, God, this is a helluva mess. I can't stand much more." Cory ran out the door.

Clissa caught his arm: "Cory I'm trying to tell you. Babe isn't here. I've called, and she isn't here."

Cory's heavy, young-old face tautened. "Babe—Where did you last see her?"

"Breakfast." Clissa was crying now.

"She say where she was going?"

"No. She asked a lot of questions about Alton and where he'd gone."

"Did you say?"

Clissa's eyes widened, and she nodded, biting the back of her hand.

"You shouldn't ha' done that, Clissa," he gritted, and ran toward the woods, Clissa looking after him, and in that moment she could have killed herself.

Cory ran with his head up, straining with his legs and lungs and eyes at the long path. He puffed up the slope to the woods, agonized for breath after the forty-five minutes' heavy going. He couldn't even notice the damp smell of mold in the air.

He caught a movement in a thicket to his right, and dropped. Struggling to keep his breath, he crept forward until he could see clearly. There was something in there, all right. Something black, keeping still. Cory relaxed his legs and torso completely to make it easier for his heart to pump some strength back into them, and slowly raised the 12-gauge until it bore on the thing hidden in the thicket.

"Come out!" Cory said when he could speak.

Nothing happened.

"Come out or by God I'll shoot!" rasped Cory.

There was a long moment of silence, and his finger tightened on the trigger.

"You asked for it," he said, and as he fired, the thing leaped sideways into the open, screaming.

It was a thin little man dressed in sepulchral black, and bearing the rosiest baby-face Cory had ever seen. The face was twisted with fright and pain. The man scrambled to his feet and hopped up and down saying over and over, "Oh, my hand. Don't shoot again! Oh, my hand. Don't shoot again!" He stopped after a bit, when Cory had climbed to his feet, and he regarded the farmer out of sad china-blue eyes. "You shot me," he said reproachfully, holding up a little bloody hand. "Oh, my goodness."

Cory said, "Now, who the hell are you?"

The man immediately became hysterical, mouthing such a flood of broken sentences that Cory stepped back a pace and half-raised his gun in self-defense. It seemed to consist mostly of "I lost my papers," and "I didn't do it," and "It was horrible. Horrible. Horrible," and "The dead man," and "Oh, don't shoot again."

Cory tried twice to ask him a question, and then he stepped over and knocked the man down. He lay on the ground writhing and moaning and blubbering and putting his bloody hand to his mouth where Cory had hit him.

"Now what's going on around here?"

The man rolled over and sat up. "I didn't do it!" he sobbed. "I didn't. I was walking along and I heard the gun and I heard some swearing and an awful scream and I went over there and peeped and I saw the dead man and I ran away and you came and I hid and you shot me and—"

"Shut up!" The man did, as if a switch has been thrown. "Now," said Cory, pointing along the path, "you say there's a dead man up there?"

The man nodded and began crying in earnest. Cory helped him up. "Follow this path back to my farmhouse," he said. "Tell my wife to fix up your hand. Don't tell her anything else. And wait there until I come. Hear?"

"Yes. Thank you. Oh, thank you. Snff."

"Go on now." Cory gave him a gentle shove in the right direction and went alone, in cold fear, up the path to the spot where he had found Alton the night before.

He found him here now, too, and Kimbo. Kimbo and Alton had spent several years together in the deepest friendship; they had hunted and fought and slept together, and the lives they owed each other were finished now. They were dead together.

It was terrible that they died the same way. Cory Drew was a strong man, but he gasped and fainted dead away when he saw what the thing of the mold had done to his brother and his brother's dog.

The little man in black hurried down the path, whimpering and holding his injured hand as if he rather wished he could limp with it. After a while the whimper faded away, and the hurried stride changed to a walk as the gibbering terror of the last hour receded. He drew two deep breaths, said: "My goodness!" and felt almost normal. He bound a linen handkerchief around his wrist, but the hand kept bleeding. He tried the elbow, and that made it hurt. So he stuffed the handkerchief back in his pocket and simply waved the hand stupidly in the air until the blood clotted. He did not see the great moist horror that clumped along behind him, although his nostrils crinkled with its foulness.

The monster had three holes close together on its chest, and one hole in the middle of its slimy forehead. It had three close-set pits in its back and one on the back of its head. These marks were where Alton Drew's bullets had struck and passed through. Half of the monster's shapeless face was sloughed away, and there was a deep indentation on its shoulder. This was what Alton Drew's gun butt had done after he clubbed it and struck at the thing that would not lie down after he put his four bullets through it. When these things happened the monster was not hurt or angry. It only wondered why Alton Drew acted that way. Now it followed the little man without hurrying at all, matching his stride step by step and dropping little particles of muck behind it.

The little man went on out of the wood and stood with his back against a big tree at the forest's edge, and he thought. Enough had happened to him here. What good would it do to stay and face a horrible murder inquest, just to continue this silly, vague search? There was supposed to be the ruin of an old, old hunting lodge deep in this wood somewhere, and perhaps it would hold the evidence he wanted. But it was a vague report—vague enough to be forgotten without regret. It would be the height of foolishness to stay for all the hick-town red tape that would follow that ghastly affair back in the wood. Ergo, it would be ridiculous to follow that farmer's advice, to go to his house and wait for him. He would go back to town.

The monster was leaning against the other side of the big tree.

The little man snuffled disgustedly at a sudden overpowering odor of rot. He reached for his handkerchief, fumbled and dropped it. As he bent to pick it up, the monster's arm *whuffed* heavily in the air where his head had been—a blow that would certainly have removed that baby-face protuberance. The man stood up and would have put the handkerchief to his nose had it not been so bloody. The creature behind the tree lifted its arm again just as the little man tossed the handkerchief away and stepped out into the field, heading across country to the distant highway that would take him back to town. The monster pounced on the handkerchief, picked it up, studied it, tore it across several times and inspected the tattered edges. Then it gazed vacantly at the disappearing figure of the little man, and finding him no longer interesting, turned back into the woods.

Babe broke into a trot at the sound of the shots. It was important to warn Uncle Alton about what her father had said, but it was more interesting to find out what he had bagged. Oh, he'd bagged it, all right. Uncle Alton never fired without killing. This was about the first time she had ever heard him blast away like that. Must be a bear, she thought excitedly, tripping over a root, sprawling, rolling to her feet again, without noticing the tumble. She'd love to have another bearskin in her room. Where would she put it? Maybe they could line it and she could have it for a blanket. Uncle Alton could sit on it and read to her in the evening— Oh, no. No. Not with this trouble between him and dad. Oh, if she could only do something! She tried to run faster, worried and anticipating, but she was out of breath and went more slowly instead.

At the top of the rise by the edge of the woods she stopped and looked back. Far down in the valley lay the south thirty. She scanned it carefully, looking for her father. The new furrows and the old were sharply defined, and her keen eyes saw immediately that Cory had left the line with the cultivator and had angled the team over to the shade trees without finishing his row. That wasn't like him. She could see the team now, and Cory's pale-blue denim was nowhere in sight. She giggled lightly to herself as she thought of the way she would fool her father. And the little sound of laughter drowned out, for her, the sound of Alton's hoarse dying scream.

She reached and crossed the path and slid through the brush beside it. The shots came from up around here somewhere. She stopped and listened several times, and then suddenly heard something coming toward her, fast. She ducked under cover, terrified, and a little baby-faced man in black, his blue eyes wide with horror, crashed blindly past her, the leather case he carried catching on the branches. It spun a moment and then fell right in front of her. The man never missed it.

Babe lay there for a long moment and then picked up the case and faded into the woods. Things were happening too fast for her. She wanted Uncle Alton, but she dared not call. She stopped again and strained her ears. Back toward the edge of the wood she heard her father's voice, and another's—probably the man who had dropped the brief case. She dared not go over there. Filled with enjoyable terror, she thought hard, then snapped her fingers in triumph. She and Alton had played Injun many times up here; they had a whole repertoire of secret signals. She had practiced birdcalls until she knew them better than the birds themselves. What would it be? Ah—blue jay. She threw back her head and by some youthful alchemy produced a nerve-shattering screech that would have done justice to any jay that ever flew. She repeated it, and then twice more.

The response was immediate—the call of a blue jay, four times, spaced two and two. Babe nodded to herself happily. That was the signal that they were to meet immediately at The Place. The Place was a hide-out that he had discovered and shared with her, and not another soul knew of it; an angle of rock beside a stream not far away. It wasn't exactly a cave, but almost. Enough so to be entrancing. Babe trotted happily away toward the brook. She had just known that Uncle Alton would remember the call of the blue jay, and what it meant.

In the tree that arched over Alton's scattered body perched a large jay bird, preening itself and shining in the sun. Quite unconscious of the presence of death, hardly noticing the Babe's realistic cry, it screamed again four times, two and two.

It took Cory more than a moment to recover himself from what he had seen. He turned away from it and leaned weakly against a pine, panting. Alton. That was Alton lying there, in—parts.

"God! God, God, God—"

Gradually his strength returned, and he forced himself to turn again. Stepping carefully, he bent and picked up the .32–40. Its barrel was bright and clean, but the butt and stock were smeared with some kind of stinking rottenness. Where had he seen the stuff before? Somewhere—no matter. He cleaned it off absently, throwing the befouled bandanna away afterward. Through his mind ran Alton's words—was that only last night? — *"I'm goin' to start trackin'. An' I'm goin' to keep trackin' till I find the one done this job on Kimbo."*

Cory searched shrinkingly until he found Alton's box of shells. The box was wet and sticky. That made it—better, somehow. A bullet wet with Alton's blood was the right thing to use. He went away a short distance, circled around till he found heavy footprints, then came back.

"I'm a-trackin' for you, bud," he whispered thickly, and began. Through the brush he followed its wavering spoor, amazed at the amount of filthy mold about, gradually associating it with the thing that had killed his brother. There was nothing in the world for him any more but hate and doggedness. Cursing himself for not getting Alton home last night, he followed the tracks to the edge of the woods. They led him to a big tree there, and there he saw something else—the footprints of the little city man. Nearby lay some tattered scraps of linen, and—what was that?

Another set of prints—small ones. Small, stub-toed ones.

"Babe!"

No answer. The wind sighed. Somewhere a blue jay called.

Babe stopped and turned when she heard her father's voice, faint with distance, piercing.

"Listen at him holler," she crooned delightedly. "Gee, he sounds mad." She sent a jay bird's call disrespectfully back to him and hurried to The Place.

It consisted of a mammoth boulder beside the brook. Some upheaval in the glacial age had cleft it, cutting out a huge V-shaped chunk. The widest part of the cleft was at the water's edge, and the narrowest was hidden by bushes. It made a little ceilingless room, rough and uneven and full of pot-holes and cavelets inside, and yet with quite a level floor. The open end was at the water's edge.

Babe parted the bushes and peered down the cleft.

"Uncle Alton!" she called softly. There was no answer. Oh, well, he'd be along. She scrambled in and slid down to the floor.

She loved it here. It was shaded and cool, and the chattering stream filled it with shifting golden lights and laughing gurgles. She called again, on principle, and then perched on an outcropping to wait. It was only then she realized that she still carried the little man's brief case.

She turned it over a couple of times and then opened it. It was divided in the middle by a leather wall. On one side were a few papers in a large yellow envelope, and on the other some sandwiches, a candy bar, and an apple. With a youngster's complacent acceptance of manna from heaven, Babe fell to. She saved one sandwich for Alton, mainly because she didn't like its highly spiced bologna. The rest made quite a feast.

She was a little worried when Alton hadn't arrived, even after she had consumed the apple core. She got up and tried to skim some flat pebbles across the roiling brook, and she stood on her hands, and she tried to think of a story to tell herself, and she tried just waiting. Finally, in desperation, she turned again to the brief case, took out the papers, curled up by the rocky wall and began to read them. It was something to do, anyway.

There was an old newspaper clipping that told about strange wills that people had left. An old lady had once left a lot of money to whoever would make the trip from the Earth to the Moon and back. Another had financed a home for cats whose masters and mistresses had died. A man left thousands of dollars to the first person who could solve a certain mathematical problem and prove his solution. But one item was blue-penciled. It was:

> One of the strangest of wills still in force is that of Thaddeus M. Kirk, who died in 1920. It appears that he built an elaborate mausoleum with burial vaults for all the remains of his family. He collected and removed caskets from all over the country to fill the designated niches. Kirk was the last of his line; there were no relatives when he died. His will stated that the mausoleum was to be kept in repair permanently, and that a certain sum was to be set aside as a reward for whoever could produce the body of his grandfather, Roger Kirk, whose niche is still empty. Anyone finding his body is eligible to receive a substantial fortune.

Babe yawned vaguely over this, but kept on reading because there was nothing else to do. Next was a thick sheet of business correspondence, bearing the letterhead of a firm of lawyers. The body of it ran:

> In regard to your query regarding the will of Thaddeus Kirk, we are authorized to state that his grandfather was a man about five feet, five inches, whose left arm had been broken and who had a triangular silver plate set into his skull. There is no information as to the whereabouts of his death. He disappeared and was declared legally dead after the lapse of fourteen years.
>
> The amount of the reward as stated in the will, plus accrued interest, now amounts to a fraction over sixty-two thousand dollars. This will be paid to anyone who produces the remains, providing that said remains answer descriptions kept in our private files.

There was more, but Babe was bored. She went on to the little black notebook. There was nothing in it but penciled and highly abbreviated records of visits to libraries; quotations from books with titles like "History of Angelina and Tyler Counties" and "Kirk Family History." Babe threw that aside, too. Where could Uncle Alton be?

She began to sing tunelessly, "Tumalumalum tum, ta ta ta," pretending to dance a minuet with flowing skirts like a girl she had seen in the movies. A rustle of the bushes at the entrance to The Place stopped her. She peeped upward, saw them being thrust aside. Quickly she ran to a tiny cul-de-sac in the rock wall, just big enough for her to hide in. She giggled at the thought of how surprised Uncle Alton would be when she jumped out at him.

She heard the newcomer come shuffling down the steep slope of the crevice and land heavily on the floor. There was something about the sound—What was it? It occurred to her that though it was a hard job for a big man like Uncle Alton to get through the little opening in the bushes, she could hear no heavy breathing. She heard no breathing at all!

Babe peeped out into the main cave and squealed in utmost horror. Standing there was, not Uncle Alton, but a massive caricature of a man: a huge thing like an irregular mud doll, clumsily made. It quivered and parts of it glistened and parts of it were dried and crumbly. Half of the lower left part of its face was gone, giving it a lopsided look. It had no perceptible mouth or nose, and its eyes were crooked, one higher than the other, both a dingy brown with no whites at all. It stood quite still looking at her, its only movement a seady unalive quivering.

It wondered about the queer little noise Babe had made.

Babe crept far back against a little pocket of stone, her brain running round and round in tiny circles of agony. She opened her mouth to cry out, and could not. Her eyes bulged and her face flamed with the strangling effort, and the two golden ropes of her braided hair twitched and twitched as she hunted hopelessly for a way out. If only she were out in the open—or in the wedge-shaped half-cave where the thing was—or home in bed!

The thing clumped toward her, expressionless, moving with a slow inevitability that was the sheer crux of horror. Babe lay wide-eyed and frozen, mounting pressure of terror stilling her lungs, making her heart shake the whole world. The monster came to the mouth of the little pocket, tried to walk to her and was stopped by the sides. It was such a narrow little fissure, and it was all Babe could do to get in. The thing from the wood stood straining against the rock at its shoulders, pressing harder and harder to get to Babe. She sat up slowly, so near to the thing that its odor was almost thick enough to see, and a wild hope burst through her voiceless fear. It couldn't get in! It couldn't get in because it was too big!

The substance of its feet spread slowly under the tremendous strain and at its shoulder appeared a slight crack. It widened as the monster unfeelingly crushed itself against the rock, and suddenly a large piece of shoulder came away and the being twisted slushily three feet farther in. It lay quietly with its muddy eyes fixed on her, and then brought one thick arm up over its head and reached.

Babe scrambled in the inch farther she had believed impossible, and the filthy clubbed hand stroked down her back, leaving a trail of muck on the blue denim of the shirt she wore. The monster surged suddenly and, lying full length now, gained that last precious inch. A black hand seized one of her braids, and for Babe the lights went out.

When she came to, she was dangling by her hair from that same crusted paw. The thing held her high, so that her face and its featureless head were not more than a foot apart. It gazed at her with a mild curiosity in its eyes, and it swung her slowly back and forth. The agony of her pulled hair did what fear could not do—gave her a voice. She screamed. She opened her mouth and puffed up her powerful young lungs, and she sounded off. She held her throat in the position of the first scream, and her chest labored and pumped more air through the frozen throat. Shrill and monotonous and infinitely piercing, her screams.

The thing did not mind. It held her as she was, and watched. When it had learned all it could from this phenomenon, it dropped her jarringly, and looked around the half-cave, ignoring the stunned and huddled Babe. It reached over and picked up the leather briefcase and tore it twice across as if it were tissue. It saw the sandwich Babe had left, picked it up, crushed it, dropped it.

Babe opened her eyes, saw that she was free, and just as the thing turned back to her she dove between its legs and out into the shallow pool in front of the rock, paddled across and hit the other bank screaming. A vicious little light of fury burned in her; she picked up a grapefruit-sized stone and hurled it with all her frenzied might. It flew low and fast, and struck squashily on the monster's ankle. The thing was just taking a step toward the water; the stone caught it off balance, and its unpracticed equilibrium could not save it. It tottered for a long, silent moment at the edge and then splashed into the stream. Without a second look Babe ran shrieking away.

Cory Drew was following the little gobs of mold that somehow indicated the path of the murderer, and he was nearby when he first heard her scream. He broke into a run, dropping his shotgun and holding the .32-40 ready to fire. He ran with such deadly panic in his heart that he ran right past the huge cleft rock and was a hundred yards past it before she burst out through the pool and ran up the bank. He had to run hard and fast to catch her, because anything behind her was that faceless horror in the cave, and she was living for the one idea of getting away from there. He caught her in his arms and swung her to him, and she screamed on and on and on.

Babe didn't see Cory at all, even when he held her and quieted her.

The monster lay in the water. It neither liked nor disliked this new element. It rested on the bottom, its massive head a foot beneath the surface, and it curiously considered the facts that it had garnered. There was the little humming noise of Babe's voice that sent the monster questing into the cave. There was the black material of the brief case that resisted so much more than green things when he tore it. There was the little two-legged one who sang and brought him near, and who screamed when he came. There was this new cold moving thing he had fallen into. It was washing his body away. That had never happened before. That was interesting. The monster decided to stay and observe this new thing. It felt no urge to save itself; it could only be curious.

The brook came laughing down out of its spring, ran down from its source beckoning to the sunbeams and embracing freshets and helpful brooklets. It shouted and played with streaming little roots, and nudged the minnows and pollywogs about in its tiny backwaters. It was a happy brook. When it came to the pool by the cloven rock it found the monster there, and plucked at it. It soaked the foul substances and smoothed and melted the molds, and the waters below the thing eddied darkly with its diluted matter. It was a thorough brook. It washed all it touched, persistently. Where it found filth, it removed filth; and if there were layer on layer of foulness, then layer by foul layer it was removed. It was a good brook. It did not mind the poison of the monster, but took it up and thinned it and spread it in little rings round rocks downstream, and let it drift to the rootlets of water plants, that they might grow greener and lovelier. And the monster melted.

"I am smaller," the thing thought. "That is interesting. I could not move now. And now this part of me which thinks is going, too. It will stop in just a moment, and drift away with the rest of the body. It will stop thinking and I will stop being, and that, too, is a very interesting thing."

So the monster melted and dirtied the water, and the water was clean again, washing and washing the skeleton that the monster had left. It was not very big, and there was a badly-healed knot on the left arm. The sunlight flickered on the triangular silver plate set into the pale skull, and the skeleton was very clean now. The brook laughed about it for an age.

They found the skeleton, six grimlipped men who came to find a killer. No one had believed Babe, when she told her story days later. It had to be days later because Babe had screamed for seven hours without stopping, and had lain like a dead child for a day. No one believed her at all, because her story was all about the bad fella, and they knew that the bad fella was simply a thing that her father had made up to frighten her with. But it was through her that the skeleton was found, and so the men at the bank sent a check to the Drews for more money than they had ever dreamed about. It was old Roger Kirk, sure enough, that skeleton, though it was found five miles from where he had died and sank into the forest floor where the hot molds built around his skeleton and emerged—a monster.

So the Drews had a new barn and fine new livestock and they hired four men. But they didn't have Alton. And they didn't have Kimbo. And Babe screams at night and has grown very thin.

C. L. MOORE

Fruit of Knowledge

It was the first Sabbath. Down the open glades of Eden a breeze stirred softly. Nothing else in sight moved except a small winged head that fluttered, yawning, across the glade and vanished among leaves that drew back to receive it. The air quivered behind it like a wake left in water of incomparable clarity. From far away and far above a faint drift of singing echoed, "Hosannah . . . hosannah . . . hosannah—" The seraphim were singing about the Throne.

A pool at the edge of the glade gave back light and color like a great, dim jewel. It gave back reflections, too. The woman who bent over it had just discovered that. She was leaning above the water until her cloudy dark hair almost dipped into the surface. There was a curious shadow all about her, like a thin garment which did not quite conceal how lovely she was, and though no breeze stirred just now, that shadow garment moved uneasily upon her and her hair lifted a little as if upon a breeze that did not blow.

She was so quiet that a passing cherub-head paused above the water to look, too, hanging like a hummingbird motionless over its own reflection in the pool.

"Pretty!" approved the cherub in a small, piping voice. "New here, aren't you?"

The woman looked up with a slow smile, putting back the veil of her hair.

"Yes, I am," she answered softly. Her voice did not sound quite sure of itself. She had never spoken aloud before until this moment.

"You'll like the Garden," said the cherub in a slightly patronizing tone, giving his rainbow wings a shake. "Anything I can do for you? I'm not busy just now. Be glad to show you around."

"Thank you," smiled the woman, her voice sounding a little more confident. "I'll find my way."

The cherub shrugged his colored wings. "Just as you say. By the way, I suppose they warned you about the Tree?"

The woman glanced up at him rather quickly, her shadowy eyes narrowing.

"The Tree? Is there danger?"

"Oh, no. You mustn't touch it, that's all. It's the one in the middle of the Garden, the Tree of the Knowledge of Good and Evil—you can't miss it. I saw the Man looking at it yesterday for quite a while. That reminds me, have you met the Man?"

The woman bent her head so that the hair swung forward to veil her face. From behind it, in a voice that sounded as if she might be smiling, she said:

"He's waiting for me now."

"Oh?" said the cherub, impressed. "Well, you'll find him over by the orange grove east of the Tree. He's resting. It's the Day of Rest, you know." The cherub tilted an intimate eyebrow heavenward and added. "He's resting, too. Hear the singing? He made the Man only yesterday, right out of this very earth you're standing on. We were all watching. It was wonderful— Afterward, He called the man Adam, and then Adam named the animals— By the way, what's your name?"

The woman smiled down at her own veiled reflection in the water. After a moment—

"Lilith," she said.

The cherub stared, his eyes widening into two blue circles of surprise. He was speechless for an instance. Then he pursed his pink mouth to whistle softly.

"Why," he stammered, "you . . . you're the Queen of Air and Darkness!"

Smiling up at him from the corners of her eyes, the woman nodded. The cherub stared at her big-eyed for a moment longer, too overcome for speech. Then, suddenly, he beat his rainbow pinions together and darted off through the trees without another word, the translucent air rippling in a lazy, half-visible wake behind him. Lilith looked after him with a shadowy smile on her face. He was going to warn Adam. The smile deepened. Let him.

Lilith turned for one last glance into the mirror of the pool at the strange new shape she had just put on. It was the newest thing in creation—not even God knew about it. And rather surprisingly, she thought she was going to like it. She did not feel nearly as stifled and heavy as she had expected to feel, and there was something distinctly pleasant in the softness of the breeze pouring caressingly about her body, the fragrance of springtime sweet in her nostrils, the grass under her bare feet. The Garden was beautiful with a beauty she had not realized until she saw it through human eyes. Everything she saw through them, indeed, was curiously different now. Here in this flesh all her faculties seemed refocused, as if she, who had always seen with such crystal clarity, now looked through rainbows at everything she saw. But it was a pleasant refocusing. She wished she had longer to enjoy her tenancy in this five-sensed flesh she shared with Adam.

But she had very little time. She glanced up toward the bright, unchanging glory above the trees as if she could pierce the floor of heaven and see God resting on the unimaginable splendor of the Throne while the seraphim chanted in long, shining rows about him. At any moment he might stir and lean forward over Eden, looking down. Lilith instinctively shrugged her shadowy garment closer about her. If he did not look too closely, he might not pierce that shadow. But if he did— A little thrill of excitement, like forked lightning, went through the strange new flesh she wore. She liked danger.

She bent over the pool for one last look at herself, and the pool was a great dim eye looking back at her, almost sentient, almost aware of her. This was a living Garden. The translucent air quivered with a rhythmic pulsing through the trees; the ground was resilient under her feet; vines drew back to let her pass beneath them. Lilith, turning away through the swimming air after the cherub, puzzled a little as she walked through the parting trees. The relation was very close between flesh and earth—perhaps her body was so responsive to the beauty of the Garden because it aped so closely flesh that had been a part of the Garden yesterday. And if even she felt that kinship, what must Adam feel, who was himself earth only yesterday?

The Garden was like a vast, half-sentient entity all around her, pulsing subtly with the pulse of the lucent air. Had God drawn from this immense and throbbing fecundity all the life which peopled Eden? Was Adam merely an extension of it, a focus and intensification of the same life which pulsed through the Garden? Creation was too new; she could only guess.

She thought, too, of the Tree of Knowledge as she walked smoothly through the trees. That Tree, tempting and forbidden. Why? Was God testing Man somehow? Was Man then, not quite finished, after all? Was there any flaw in Eden? Suddenly she knew that there must be. Her very presence here was proof of it, for she, above all others, had no right to intrude into this magical closed sphere which was God's greatest work. Yet here she walked through the heart of it, and not even God knew, yet—

Lilith slanted a smile up through the leaves toward the choruses of the seraphim whose singing swelled and sank and swelled again, unutterably sweet high above the trees. The animals watched her pass with wide, bewildered eyes, somehow not quite at ease, although no such thing as fear had yet stirred through the Garden. Lilith glanced at them curiously as she passed. They were pretty things. She liked Eden.

Presently a swooning fragrance came drifting to her through the trees, almost too sweet to enjoy, and she heard a small voice piping excitedly: "Lilith . . . Air and Darkness— He won't like it! Michael ought to know—"

Lilith smiled and stepped clear of the trees into the full, soft glow of Eden's sun. It did not touch the shadow that dimly veiled the pale contours of this newest shape in Eden. Once or twice that intangible breeze lifted her hair in a great, dim cloud about her, though no leaves moved. She stood quiet, staring across the glade, and as she stared she felt the first small tremor of distrust in this new flesh she wore.

For on a grassy bank in the sunlight, under the blossoming orange trees, lay Adam. And the trees and the flowers of Eden had seemed beautiful to the eyes of this body Lilith wore, and the breezes and the perfumes had delighted it—but here was flawless perfection newly shaped out of the warm red earth of Eden into the image of its Maker, and the sight of him frightened Lilith because it pleased her so. She did not trust a beauty that brought her to a standstill under the trees, not quite certain why she had stopped.

He sprawled in long-limbed magnificence on the grass, laughing up at the cherub with his curly yellow head thrown back. Every line of him and every motion had a splendid male beauty as perfect as Omnipotence could make it. Though he wore no clothing he was no more naked than she, for there was a curious glow all about him, a garment of subtle glory that clothed him as if with an all-enveloping halo.

The cherub danced excitedly up and down in the air above him, shrilling:

"She shouldn't be here! You know she shouldn't! She's evil, that's what she is! God won't like it! She—" Then above Adam's head he caught Lilith's eye, gulped a time or two, piped one last admonishing, "Better watch out!" and fluttered away among the leaves, looking back over one wing as he flew.

Adam's gaze followed the cherub's. The laughter faded from his face and he got up slowly, the long, smooth muscles sliding beautifully under his garment of subtle glory as he moved. He was utter perfection in everything he did, flawless, new-made at the hands of God. He came toward her slowly, a shining wonder on his face.

Lilith stared at him distrustfully. The other glories of the Garden had pleased her abstractly, in a way that left her mistress of herself. But here was something she did not understand at all. The eternal Lilith looked out, bewildered, through the eyes of a body that found something strange and wonderful in Adam. She laid a hand on the upper part of that body which rose and fell with her breathing, and felt something beating strongly beneath the smooth, curved surface of the stuff called flesh.

Adam came toward her slowly. They met in the middle of the glade, and for a long moment neither spoke. Then Adam said in a marveling voice, resonant and deep:

"You . . . you're just as I knew you'd be— I knew you'd be somewhere, if I could only find you. Where were you hiding?"

With an effort Lilith mastered this odd, swimming warmth in her which she did not understand. After all, he was nothing but a certain limited awareness housed in newly shaped flesh, and it made no real difference at all what shape that flesh wore. Her business was too dangerous for her to linger here admiring him because by some accident he was pleasing to the eyes of her newly acquired body. She made her voice like honey in her throat and looked up at him under her lashes, crooning:

"I wasn't here at all, until you thought of me."

"Until I—" Adam's golden brows met.

"God made you in His image," said Lilith, fluttering the lashes. "There's so much of God in you still—didn't you know you could create, too, if you desired strongly enough?"

She remembered that deep need of his pulsing out and out in great, demanding waves from the Garden, and how it had seemed a call addressed to her alone. She had delighted as she yielded to it, deliberately subordinating her will to the will of the unseen caller in the Garden. She had let it draw her down out of the swimming void, let it mold flesh around her in the shape it chose, until all her being was incased in the strange, soft, yielding substance which was proving so treacherously responsive to the things she was encountering in Eden.

Adam shook his curly head uncomprehendingly. "You weren't here. I couldn't find you," he repeated, as if he had not heard her. "I watched all day among the animals, and they were all in twos but Man. I knew you must be somewhere. I knew just how you'd look. I thought I'd call you Eve when I found you—Eve, the Mother of All Living. Do you like it?''

"It's a good name," murmured Lilith, coming nearer to him, "but not for me. I'm Lilith, who came out of the dark because you needed me." She smiled a heady smile at him, and the shadowy garment drew thin across her shoulders as she lifted her arms. Adam seemed a little uncertain about what to do with his own arms as she clasped her hands behind his neck and tiptoed a little, lifting her face.

"Lilith?" he echoed in a bemused voice. "I like the sound. What does it mean?"

"Never mind," she crooned in her sweetest voice. "I came because you wanted me." And then, in a murmur: "Bend you head, Adam. I want to show you something—"

It was the first kiss in Eden. When it was over, Lilith opened her eyes and looked up at Adam aghast, so deeply moved by the pleasantness of that kiss that she could scarcely remember the purpose that had prompted it. Adam blinked dizzily down at her. He had found what to with his arms. He stammered, still in that bemused voice:

"Thank God, you did come! I wish He could have sent you sooner. We—"

Lilith recovered herself enough to murmur gently: "Don't you understand, dear? God didn't send me. It was you, yourself, waiting and wanting me, that let me take shape out of . . . never mind . . . and come to you in the body you pictured for me, because I knew what wonderful things we could accomplish here in Eden, together. You're God's own image, and you have greater powers than you know, Adam." The tremendous idea that had come to her in the ether when she first heard his soundless call glowed in her voice. "There's no limit to what we could do here, together! Greater things than even God ever dreamed—"

"You're so pretty," interrupted Adam, smiling down at her with his disarming, empty smile. "I'm so glad you came—"

Lilith let the rest of her eagerness run out in a long sigh. It was no use trying to talk to him now. He was too new. Powerful with a godlike power, yes, but unaware of it—unaware even of himself as an individual being. He had not tasted the Fruit of Knowledge and his innocence was as flawless as his beauty. Nothing was in his mind, or could be, that God had not put there at his shaping from the warm earth of Eden.

And perhaps it was best, after all. Adam was too close to godhood to see eye to eye with her in all she might want to do. If he never tasted knowledge, then he would ask no questions—and so he must never touch the Tree.

The Tree— It reminded her that Eden was still a testing ground, not a finished creation. She thought she knew now what the flaw in man had been which made it possible for Lilith, of all the creatures of ether, to stand here at the very focus of all the power and beauty and innocence in Eden. Lilith, who was evil incarnate and knew it very well. God had made Adam incomplete, and not, perhaps, realized the flaw. And out of Adam's need Adam himself had created woman—who was not complete either. Lilith realized it suddenly, and began to understand the depth of her reaction to this magnificent creature who still held her in his arms.

There was an idea somewhere of all this which was immensely important, but her mind would not pursue it. Her mind kept sliding off the question to dwell cloudily on the Man upon whose shoulder she was leaning. What curious stuff this flesh was! While she wore it, not even the absorbing question of God's purpose, not even her own peril here, could quite obliterate the knowledge of Adam's presence, his arm about her. Values had changed in a frightening way, and the most frightening thing of all was that she did not care. She laid her head back on his shoulder and inhaled the honeyed perfume of the orange blossoms, futilely reminding herself that she was dangerously wasting time. At any moment God might look down and see her, and there was so much to be done before that happened. She must master this delicious fogging of the senses whenever Adam's arm tightened about her. The Garden must be fortified, and she must begin now.

Sighing, she laced her fingers through Adam's and crooned in the softest voice: "I want to see the Garden. Won't you show it to me?"

His voice was warm as he answered:

"I want to! I hoped you'd ask me that. It's such a wonderful place."

A cherub fluttered across the valley as they strolled eastward, and paused on beating wings to frown down at them.

"Wait till *He* looks down," he piped. "Just wait, that's all!" Adam laughed, and the cherub clucked disapprovingly and fluttered off, shaking his head.

Lilith, leaning on Adam's shoulder, laughed, too. She was glad that he could not understand the cherub's warnings, deaf in the perfection of his innocence. So long as she could prevent it he would never taste that Fruit. The knowledge of evil was not in him and it must never be. For she was herself, as she realized well, the essence of abstract evil as opposed to abstract good—balancing it, making it possible. Her part was necessary as God's in the scheme of creation, for light cannot exist without dark, nor positive without negative, nor good without evil.

Yet she did not feel in the least evil just now. There was no antagonism at all between her negation and the strong positive innocence of the man beside her.

"Look," said Adam, sweeping a long-armed gesture. A low hillside lay before them, starry with flowers except for a scar in its side where the raw, bare earth of Eden showed through. The scar was already healing over with a faint mist of green. "That's where I was made," said Adam softly. "Right out of that hillside. Does it seem rather . . . rather wonderful to you, Lilith?"

"If it does to you," she crooned, and meant it. "Why?"

"The animals don't seem to understand. I hoped you would. It's as if the . . . the whole Garden were part of me. If there are other men, do you suppose they'll love the earth like this, Lilith, for its own sake? Do you think they'll have this same feeling about the place where they were born? Will one certain hill or valley be almost one flesh with theirs, so that they'd sicken away from it and fight and die if they had to, to keep it—as I think I would? Do you feel it, too?"

The air went pulsing past them, sweet with the music of the seraphim, while Lilith looked out over the valley that had brought Adam to birth. She was trying hard, but she could not quite grasp that passionate identification with the earth of Eden which beat like blood through Adam's veins.

"Eden *is* you," she murmured. "I can understand that. You mustn't ever leave it."

"Leave it?" laughed Adam. "Where else is there? Eden belongs to us forever—and you belong to me."

Lilith let herself relax delightfully against his shoulder, knowing suddenly that she loved this irresponsible, dangerous flesh even while she distrusted it. And—

Something was wrong. The sudden awareness of it chilled her and she glanced uneasily about, but it was several minutes before her fleshbound senses located the wrongness. Then she put her head back and stared up through the trees with puckered brows.

"What is it?" Adam smiled down at her. "Angels? They go over quite often, you know."

Lilith did not answer. She was listening hard. Until now all Eden had echoed faintly and sweetly with the chanting of seraphim about the Throne. But now the sounds that sifted down through the bright, translucent air were not carols of praise. There was trouble in heaven. She could hear faraway shouts in great, ringing, golden voices from infinitely high above, the clash and hiss of flaming swords, and now and again a crash as if part of the very walls of heaven had crumbled inward under some unimaginable onslaught.

It was hard to believe—but there was war in heaven.

A wave of relief went delightfully through Lilith. Good—let them fight. She smiled to herself and snuggled closer to Adam's side. The trouble, whatever it might be, would keep God's attention distracted a while longer from what went on in Eden, and she was devoutly grateful for that. She needed this respite. She had awhile longer, then, to accustom herself to the vagaries of this strange body, and to the strange reaction Adam was causing, before the war was over in heaven and war began in Eden between Lilith and God.

A shudder of terror and anticipation went over her again as she thought of that. She was not sure God could destroy her if He would, for she was a creature of the darkness beyond His light and her existence was necessary to the structure he was rearing in heaven and upon earth. Without the existence of such as Lilith, the balance of creation might tip over. No, God would not—perhaps could not—destroy her, but He could punish very terribly.

This flesh, for instance. It was so soft, so perishable. She was aware of a definite cleavage between the mind and the body that housed it. Perhaps God had been wise in choosing this fragile container instead of some imperishable substance into which to pour all the innocence, the power that was Adam. It was dangerous to trust such power in an independent body—as Lilith meant to prove to God if her plan went well. But it was no part of that plan—now—to have an angered God destroy His fleshy image.

She must think of some way to prevent it. Presently she would waken out of this warm, delightful fog that persisted so long as Adam's arm was about her, but there was no hurry yet. Not while war raged in heaven. She had never known a mood like this before, when cloudy emotions moved like smoke through her mind and nothing in creation had real significance except this magnificent male upon whose shoulder she leaned.

Then Adam looked down at her and smiled, and all the noises of war above blanked out as if they had never been. The Garden, half sentient, stirred uneasily from grass roots to treetops in response to those ringing battle shouts from above; but the Man and the woman did not even hear.

Time was nothing. Imperceptibly it passed, and presently a soft green twilight deepened over Eden. Adam and Lilith paused after a while on a mossy bank above a stream that tinkled over stones. Sitting with her head on Adam's shoulder and listening to the sound of the water, Lilith remembered how lightly life was rooted in this flesh of theirs.

"Adam," she murmured, "awhile ago you mentioned dying. Do you know about death?"

"Death?" said Adam comfortably. "I don't remember. I think I never heard of it."

"I hope," she said, "that you never will. It would mean leaving, Eden, you know."

His arm went rigid around her. "I couldn't! I wouldn't!"

"You're not immortal, dear. It could happen, unless—"

"Unless what? Tell me!"

"If there were a Tree of Life," she said slowly, measuring her words, "a Tree whose fruit would give you immortality as the fruit of that other Tree would give you knowledge, then I think not even God could drive you out of Eden."

"A Tree of Life—" he echoed softly. "What would it be like?"

Lilith closed her eyes. "A dark Tree, I think," she answered, almost in a whisper. "Dark limbs, dark leaves—pale, shining fruit hanging among them like lanterns. Can't you see it?"

Adam was silent. She glanced up at him. His eyes were shut and a look of intense longing was on his face in the twilight. There was silence about them for a long while. Presently she felt the tenseness of his body slacken beside her. He breathed out in a long sigh.

"I think there is a Tree of Life," he said. "I think it's in the center of the Garden near the other Tree. I'm sure it's there. The fruit are pale, just as you thought. They send out a light like moonlight in the dark. Tomorrow we'll taste them."

And Lilith relaxed against his shoulder with a sigh of her own. Tomorrow he would be immortal, like herself. She listened anxiously, and still heard the faraway battle cries of the seraphim echoing through the sky. War in heaven and peace on earth—

Through the deepening twilight of Eden no sound came except the music of the water and, somewhere off through the trees, a crooning lullaby in a tiny, piping voice as some cherub sang himself to sleep. Somewhere nearer other small voices squabbled drowsily a while, then fell silent. The most delightful lassitude was stealing over Lilith's body. She turned her cheek against Adam's shoulder and felt that cloudy fogging of the senses which she was coming to know so well—close like water above her head.

And the evening and the morning were the eighth day.

Lilith woke first. Birds were singing gloriously, and as she lay there on Adam's shoulder a cherub flashed across the stream on dazzling wings, caroling at the top of his piping voice. He did not see them. The pleasant delirium of a spring morning filled the whole wakening Garden, and Lilith sat up with a smile. Adam scarcely stirred. Lilith looked down at him with a glow of tenderness that alarmed her. She was coming to identify herself with Adam, as Adam was one with the Garden—this flesh was a treacherous thing.

Suddenly, blindingly, she knew that. Terror of what it was doing to the entity which was Lilith rolled over her in a great wave, and without thinking, almost without realizing what she did, she sprang up and out of the flesh that was betraying her. Up, up through the crystal morning she sprang, impalpable as the air around her. Up and up until the Adam that flesh had valued too highly was invisible, and the very treetops that hid him were a feathery green blur and she could see the walls that closed the Garden in, the rivers running out of it like four great blades of silver in the morning sun.

Beside the sleeping Adam nothing was left but the faintest blur of a woman shape, wrapped in shadow that made it almost invisible against the moss. The eye could scarcely have made it out there under the trees.

Lilith swam delightfully through the bright, still emptiness of the early morning. From here she could hear quite clearly the strong hosannahs of the seraphim pouring out in mighty golden choruses over the jasper walls. Whatever trouble had raged in heaven yesterday, today it was resolved. She scarcely troubled her mind about it.

She was free—free of the flesh and the terrifying weakness that had gone with it. She could see clearly now, no longer deluded by the distortions of value that had made life in the flesh so confusing. Her thoughts were not colored by it anymore. Adam was nothing but a superb vessel now, brimmed with the power of God. Her perspective had been too warped down there in Eden to realize how little that magnificent body of his mattered in comparison to the power inherent in it.

She let the cold, clear ether bathe her of illusions while the timeless time of the void swam motionless around her. She had been in greater danger than she knew; it had taken this morning dip in the luminous heights to cleanse her mind of Adam. Refreshed, fortified against that perilous weakness, she could return now and take up her mission again. And she must do it quickly, before God noticed her. *Or was he watching already?*

She swooped luxuriously in a long, airy curve and plummeted toward Eden.

Adam still slept timelessly upon the moss. Lilith dropped closer, shrugging herself together in anticipation of entering and filling out into life the body she had thrown off. And then—then a shock like the shock of lightning jolted her in midair until the Garden reeled beneath her. For where she had left only the faint, ephemeral husk of a woman beside Adam, a woman of firm, pale flesh lay now, asleep on the Man's shoulder. Golden hair spilled in a long skein across the moss, and the woman's head moved a little to the rhythm of Adam's breathing.

Lilith recovered herself and hovered near, incandescent with such jealousy and rage as she had never dreamed could touch her. The woman was clothed in a softly glowing halo as Adam was clothed. But it was Lilith's own shape she wore beneath that halo.

A sick dismay shook Lilith bodilessly in the air. God *had* been watching, then—waiting, perhaps, to strike. He had been here—it might have been no longer than a moment ago. She knew it by the very silence of the place. Everything was still hushed and awed by the recent Presence. God had passed by, and God had seen that tenantless garment of flesh she had cast off to swim in the ether, and God had known her whole scheme in one flash of His all-seeing eye.

He had taken the flesh she had worn, then, and used it for His own purposes—her precious, responsive flesh that had glowed at the touch of Adam's hand belonged now to another woman, slept in her place on Adam's shoulder. Lilith shook with intolerable emotion at the thought of it. She would not—

Adam was waking. Lilith hovered closer, watching jealously as he yawned, blinked, smiled, turned his curly head to look down at the woman beside him. Then he sat up so abruptly that the golden creature at his side cried out in a sweet, high voice and opened eyes bluer than a cherub's to stare at him reproachfully. Lilith, hating her, still saw that she had beauty of a sort comparable to Adam's, exquisite, brimming with the glorious emptiness of utter innocence. There was a roundness and an appealing softness to her that was new in Eden, but the shape she wore was Lilith's and none other.

Adam stared down at her in amazement.

"L-Lilith—" he stammered. "Who are you? Where's Lilith? I—"

"Who is Lilith?" demanded the golden girl in a soft, hurt voice, sitting up and pushing the glowing hair back with both hands in a lovely, smooth gesture. "I don't know. I can't remember—" She let the words die and stared about the Garden with a blue gaze luminous with wonder. Then the eyes came back to Adam and she smiled very sweetly.

Adam had put a hand to his side, a pucker of the first pain in Eden drawing his golden brows together. For no reason at all he was remembering the scarred bank from which the earth that shaped him had been taken. He opened his mouth to speak.

And then out of the glow of the morning a vast, bodiless Voice spoke quietly.

"I have taken a rib from your side, Man," said the Voice. The whole glade trembled at the sound; the brook ceased its tinkling, the leaves stood still upon the trees. Not a bird sang. Filling the whole morning, the whole Garden, the Voice went on: "Out of the flesh of your flesh I have made a helpmate and a wife for you. Forsaking all others, cleave unto her. *Forsaking all others*—"

The Voice ceased not suddenly, but by echoing degrees that made the leaves shiver upon the trees in rhythm to Its fading syllables, "Forsaking all others . . . all others . . . all others—"

And then it was as if a light ceased to glow in the Garden which, until it went out, no one had perceived. The air dimmed a little, and thickened and dulled, so that one blinked in the aftermath when the presence of God was withdrawn.

The woman drew closer to Adam's side, putting out uncertain hands to him, frightened by the quiet, tremendous Voice and the silence of the Garden. Adam dropped an arm automatically about her, stilling her fright against his shoulder. He bent his head as the Voice ceased to echo through the shaken air.

"Yes, Lord," he said obediently. There was an instant more of silence everywhere. Then timidly the brook sent a tentative ripple of sound into the air, a bird piped once, a breeze began to blow. God had withdrawn.

Bodiless, trembling with emotions she had no name for, Lilith watched the Man and the woman alone on the moss bank she had shared last night with Adam. He looked down at the frightened girl huddling against him.

"I suppose you're Eve," he said, a certain gentleness in his voice that made Lilith writhe.

"If you say so," murmured the girl, glancing up at him under a flutter of lashes. Lilith hated him. Over her fair head Adam looked out across the quiet glade.

"Lilith?" he said. "Lilith—"

A warm rush of answer focused all Lilith's being into one responding cry.

"Yes, Adam . . . yes! I'm here!"

He might have heard her bodiless reply, it was so passionate an answer to his call, but at that instant Eve said with childish petulance:

"Who is this Lilith, Adam? Why do you keep calling her? Won't I do?"

Adam looked down uncertainly. While he hesitated, Eve deliberately snuggled against him with a warm little wiggle that was Lilith's alone. By that, if by no other sign, Lilith knew it was her very flesh God had taken to mold this pale girl from Adam's rib, using the same pattern which Adam had designed for Lilith. Eve wore it now, and in that shape knew, without learning them, all the subtle tricks that Lilith's age-old wisdom had evolved during the brief while she dwelt in the body. Lilith's lost flesh, Lilith's delightful use of it, Lilith's Adam—all were Eve's now.

Fury and wild despair and an intolerable ache that made the world turn black around her blinded Lilith to the two beneath the tree. She could not bear to watch them any longer. With a soundless wail of despair she turned and flung herself up again into the limitless heights above Eden.

But this time the ether was no anodyne for her grief. It had been no true anodyne before, she knew now. For a disease was upon her that had its seed, perhaps, in the flesh she wore briefly—but too long. God had made Adam incomplete, and Adam to assuage his need had flung out a net to trap some unwary creature for his own. Shame burned in her. The Queen of Air and Darkness, like some mind-less elemental, had fallen into his trap; he had used her as she had meant to use him. She was a part of him, trapped in the flesh that was incomplete without him, and her need for him was so deep that she could not escape, even though that body was no longer hers. The roots of her disease had been in the flesh, but the virulence had spread into the very essence of the being which was Lilith and no bath in the deeps of space could cleanse her now. In the flesh or out of it, on earth or in ether, an insatiable need was upon her that could never be slaked.

And a dreadful suspicion was taking shape in her mind. Adam in his innocence could never have planned this. Had God known, all along? Had it been no error, after all, that Adam was created incomplete? And was this a punishment designed by God for tampering with his plan? Suddenly she thought that it must be. There would be no awe-inspiring struggle between light and dark such as she had half expected when God recognized her presence. There would be no struggle at all. She was vanquished, judged and punished all at a blow. No glory was in it, only this unbearable longing, a spiritual hunger more insatiable than any hunger the flesh could feel for the man she would never have again. She clove the airy heights above Eden for what might have been a thousand years, or a moment, had time existed in the void, knowing only that Adam was lost to her forever.

Forever? She writhed around in mid-ether, checking the wild, aimless upward flight. Forever? Adam still looked out across the Garden and called her name, even while he held that pale usurper in his arms. Perhaps God had not realized the strength of the strange unity between the man and the first woman in Eden. Perhaps God had not thought that she would fight. Perhaps there was a chance left, after all—

Downward through the luminous gulfs she plunged, down and down until Eden expanded like a bubble beneath her and the strong choruses of the seraphim were sweet again above the Garden. Adam and Eve were still beside the brook where she had left them. Eve on a rock was splashing her small feet and flashing blue-eyed glances over her shoulder that made Adam smile when he met them. Lilith hated her.

"Adam!" squealed Eve as the plunging Lilith came into hearing. "Look out—I'm slipping! Catch me! Quick!" It was the same croon Lilith had put into the throat of the body she had lost. Remembering how roundly and softly it had come swelling up in her throat, she writhed with a vitriolic helplessness that made the Garden dance in waves like heat around her.

"Catch me!" cried Eve again in the most appealing voice in the world. Adam sprang to clasp her as she slid. She threw both pale arms about his neck and crowed with laughter so infectious that two passing cherubs paused in midair to rock with answering mirth and beat each other over the shoulders with their wings.

"*Adam . . . Adam . . . Adam—*" wailed Lilith voicelessly. It was a silent wail, but all her heartbreak and despair and intolerable longing went into it, and above Eve's golden head Adam looked up, the laughter dying on his face. *"Adam!"* cried Lilith again. And this time he heard.

But he did not answer directly. Association with women was beginning to teach him tact. Instead he beckoned to the reeling cherubs. Rosy with mirth, they fluttered nearer. Eve looked up in big-eyed surprise as the plump little heads balanced on rainbow wings swooped laughing toward her and poised to await Adam's pleasure.

"These are a couple of our cherubs," said Adam. "Dan and Bethuel, from over toward the Tree. They have a nest there. Tell her about the Tree, will you, boys? Eve dear, I'll be getting you some fruit for breakfast. Wait for me here."

She obeyed with only a wistful glance after him as the cherubs burst into eager chatter, squabbling a little as they spoke.

"Well, there's this Tree in the middle of the Garden—"

"Tell her about the Fruit, Dan. You mustn't—"

"Yes, you mustn't touch—"

"No, that's not right, Dan. Michael says you can touch it, you just can't eat—"

"Don't interrupt me! Now it's like this. You see, there's a Tree—"

Adam went slowly off down to the brook. A lie had never yet been spoken in Eden. He was hunting fruit. But Lilith saw him searching the dappled spaces between the trees, too, a certain wistfulness on his face, and she came down with a rustle of invisibility through the leaves.

"Adam . . . Adam!"

"Lilith! Where are you?"

With a tremendous effort Lilith focused her whole being into an intensity so strong that although she remained bodiless, voiceless, intangible, yet the strength of her desire was enough to make Adam hear her dimly, see her remotely in a wavering outline against the leaves, in the shape he had created for her. She held it with difficulty, shimmering before his eyes.

"Lilith!" he cried, and reached her in two long strides, putting out his arms. She leaned into them. But the muscular, light-sheathed arms closed about her and through her and met in empty air.

She called his name miserably, quivering against him through all her bodiless body. But she could feel him no more than he could touch her, and the old ache she had known in mid-ether, came back with a rush. Even here in his arms, then, she was forbidden to touch the Man. She could never be more than a wraith of the air to him, while Eve—while Eve, in her stolen body—

"Adam!" cried Lilith again. "You were mine first! Can you hear me? Adam, you could bring me back if you tried! You did it once—you could again. Try, try!"

He stared down at her dim face, the flowers on the hillside beyond visible through it.

"What's wrong, Lilith? I can hardly see you!"

"You wanted me once badly enough to bring me out of nowhere into the flesh," she cried desperately. "Adam, Adam—want me again!"

He stared down at her. "I do," he said, his voice unexpectedly shaken. And then, more strongly, "Come back, Lilith! What's happened to you? Come back!"

Lilith closed her eyes, feeling reality pour marvelously along her bodiless limbs. Faintly now she could feel grass underfoot, Adam's chest against her anxious hands; his arms were around her and in his embrace she was taking shape out of nothingness, summoned into flesh again by the godhood in this image of God. And then—

"Adam . . . Adam!" Eve's sweet, clear voice rang lightly among the leaves. "Adam, where are you? I want to go look at the Tree, Adam. Where are you, dear?"

"Hurry!" urged Lilith desperately, beating her half-tangible hands against his chest.

Adam's arms loosed a little about her. He glanced across his shoulder, his handsome, empty face clouded. He was remembering.

"Forsaking all others—" he murmured, in a voice not entirely his own. Lilith shuddered a little against him, recognizing the timbre of that Voice which had spoken in the silence. *"Forsaking all others—"* God had said that. "Forsaking all others but Eve—"

His arms dropped from about Lilith. "I . . . I'll . . . will you wait for me?" he said hesitantly, stepping back from her half-real shape, lovely and shadow-veiled under the shadow of the trees. "I'll be back—"

"Adam!" called Eve again, nearer and very sweetly. "Adam, I'm lost! Adam! Adam, where are you?"

"Coming," said Adam. He looked once more at Lilith, a long look. Then he turned and ran lightly off through trees that parted to receive him, the glow of his half-divinity shining upon the leaves as he passed. Lilith watched the beautiful, light-glowing figure as far as she could see it.

Then she put her half-real hands to her face and her knees loosened beneath her and she doubled down in a heap upon the grass, her shadowy hair billowing out around her on a breeze that blew from nowhere, not touching the leaves. She was half-flesh now. She had tears. She found a certain relief in the discovery that she could weep.

The next sound she heard—it seemed a long while after—was a faint hiss. Cloaked in the tented shadow of her hair, she considered it a while, hiccuping now and then with receding sobs. Presently she looked up. Then she gasped and got to her feet with the effortless ease of the half-material.

The serpent looked at her sidewise out of slanted eyes, grinning. In the green gloom under the trees he was so handsome that even she, who had seen Adam, was aware of a little thrill of admiration. In those days the serpent went upright like a man, nor was he exactly non-human in shape, but his beauty was as different from man's as day is from night. He was lithe and gorgeously scaled and by any standards a supremely handsome, supremely male creature.

All about him in shadowy outline a radiance stood out that was vaguely an angel shape, winged, tremendous. It invested the serpent body with a glow that was not its own. Out of that celestial radiance the serpent said in a cool voice:

"The Queen of Air and Darkness! I didn't expect you here. What are you doing in that body?"

Lilith collected herself, hiccupped once more and stood up, the cloudy hair moving uneasily about her. She said with a grim composure:

"The same thing I suspect you're doing in that one, only you'll have to do better if you want to deceive anybody. What brings you to Eden—Lucifer?"

The serpent glanced down at himself and sent one or two long, sliding ripples gliding along his iridescent body. The angel shape that hung in the air about him gradually faded, and the beauty deepened as it focused itself more strongly in the flesh he wore. After a moment he glanced up.

"How's that—better? Oh, I came down for a purpose. I have—business with Adam." His cool voice took on a note of grimness. "You may have heard a little trouble in heaven yesterday. That was me."

"Trouble?" echoed Lilith. She had almost forgotten the sounds of combat and the great battle cries of the seraphim in the depths of her own grief.

"It was a fine fight while it lasted," Lucifer grinned. "Blood running like water down the golden streets! I tell you, it was a relief to hear something beside 'hosannah' in heaven for a change! Well"—he shrugged—"they won. Too many of them were fools and stood by Jehovah. But we gave them a good fight, and we took part of the jasper walls with us when they hurled us over." He gave her a satisfied nod. "God won, but he'll think twice before He insults me again."

"Insults you?" echoed Lilith. "How?"

Lucifer drew himself up to a magnificent height. Radiance glowed along his scaled and gleaming body. "God made me of fire! Shall I bow down before this . . . this lump of clay they call Adam? He may be good enough for the other angels to worship when God points a finger, but he isn't good enough for me!"

"Is that why you're here?"

"Isn't it reason enough? I have a quarrel with this Adam!"

"You couldn't touch him," said Lilith desperately. "He's God's image, and remember, you were no match for God."

Lucifer stretched his magnificent, gleaming height and glared down at her.

"The creature's made of clay. He must have a flaw somewhere. What is it? You know him."

Lilith looked up at him speechless, a great excitement beginning to swell so tremendously in her that her half-formed body could hardly contain it. There was a chance! God himself had put a weapon straight into her hands!

"Yes, there is a flaw," she said. "I'll tell you . . . if you'll give me a promise."

"All right, I give it," said Lucifer carelessly. "Tell me."

She hesitated, choosing her words. "Your feud isn't with Adam. He never asked you to worship him. God did that. Your quarrel is with God, not Adam. The Man himself you can't touch, but God had given him a . . . a wife," she choked when she said it. "I think there's a weakness in her, and through her you could spoil God's plan. But you must spare the Man—for me."

Lucifer whistled soundlessly, lifting his brows. "Oh—?"

"I saw him first," said Lilith defensively. "I want him."

The serpent looked at her narrowly. "Why? No . . . never mind. I won't quarrel with you. I may have an idea to suggest to you later, if a plan of mine works out. You and I together could make quite a thing of hell."

Lilith winced a little. She and Adam together had had great prospects, once, too. Perhaps they still had—if God were not listening.

"You promise not to touch him, then?"

"Yes, I won't hurt your precious clod. You're right—my quarrel's with God, not that animated lump of clay named Adam. What's the secret?"

"Eden," said Lilith slowly, "is a testing ground. There are flaws in it, there must be, or neither of us would be here. God planted a Tree in the middle of the Garden and forbade anyone to touch it. That's the test . . . I think I see it now. It's a test of obedience. God doesn't trust man—he made him too strong. The Tree is the knowledge of Good and Evil, and God doesn't dare let that knowledge exist in the Garden, because he controls Man only by Man's ignorance of his own power. If either of them eats, then God will have to destroy that one quickly. You tempt the woman to eat, Lucifer, and leave Adam and Eden to me!"

The serpent eyed her sidelong. He laughed.

"If either of them fails in this test you're talking about, then God will know neither can be trusted, won't he? He'll know their present form's imperfect, and he'll destroy them both and work out some other plan for the world."

Lilith drew a deep breath. Excitement was rising like a tide in her, and the wind from nowhere swirled the dark hair in a cloud about her shoulders.

"Let him try!" she cried exultantly. "I can save Adam. God made a mistake when he put such power in the Garden. He shouldn't have left it living, half-conscious of itself. He shouldn't have let Adam know how close he is to the earth he was taken from. Adam and the Garden are one flesh, and the power of God is in them both. God can't destroy one without the other, and together they are very strong—If they defied God together, and I helped them—"

Lucifer looked at her, a trace of compassion on his handsome, reptilian face.

"God defeated *me*," he reminded her. "Do you think He couldn't you?"

She gave him a proud glance. "I am the Queen of Air and Darkness. I have secrets of my own, and powers not even God can control. If I join them with Adam's, and the Gardens. . . . God made the Garden alive and powerful, and Adam is one flesh with it, each incomplete without the other as Man is without woman. Adam has Eve now—but when Eve's gone he'll remember Lilith. I'll see that he remembers! And I'll see that he understands his danger. With my help, perhaps he can avert it."

"If God destroys Eve," said Lucifer, "he'll destroy Adam, too. They're one pattern."

"But he may not destroy them at the same time. I'll gamble on that. I'd kill her myself if I could, but I can't touch anything in the Garden without its own consent. . . . No, I'll have to wait until Eve proves to God her unfitness to wear flesh, and while he punishes her I must seize that moment to rouse the Garden. It's almost aware of itself already. I think I could awaken it—through Adam, perhaps. Adam and Eden are almost one, as Adam and I will be again if we can get rid of Eve. None of us separately has the power to defy God, but Eden and Adam and I together might do it!'' She tossed back her head and the wild dark hair swirled like a fog around her. "Eden is an entity of its own—I think I could close a shell of space around us, and there are places in my Darkness where we could hide even from God!''

Lucifer narrowed his eyes at her. "It might work," he nodded slowly. "You're mad—but it might work, with my help. The woman is beautiful, in her way—'' He laughed. "And what a revenge on God!''

"The woman," mused Lilith, "is in my body, and I am evil. . . . I think enough evil remains there that Eve will find you—interesting. Good luck, Lucifer!''

In a hollow, velvety cup in the Garden's very center the two Trees stood. One at the edge of the clearing was a dark Tree, the leaves folded like a cloak about a pale glow from within where the Fruit of Life hung hidden. But in the center of the hollow the Tree of Knowledge flaunted its scarlet fruit that burned with a flame almost of their own among the green and glossy leaves. Here was the heart of the Garden. Out of the Tree of the Knowledge of Good and Evil the beat went pulsing that shook the air of Eden.

Eve set one small, bare foot upon the downward slope and looked back timidly over her shoulder. The serpent flicked a forked red tongue at her. His voice was cool and clear, and sweet as honey.

"Eva," he said softly. *"Eva—"*

She smiled and went on, he rippling after her with an unearthly beauty to his gait that is lost forever now. No one knows today how the serpent walked before the Fall. Of all human creatures only Eve knows that, and there were things Eve never told Adam.

They paused under the shadow of the tree. In long, slow rhythms the air went pulsing past them. Eve's fair hair stirred a little, so strong was the rhythm here. All the Fruit of the Tree pushed out among the leaves to see her, and the nearer branches bent caressingly toward this woman who was of the flesh of Adam.

The nearest branch stooped down enticingly. Eve reached for a scarlet apple that dipped into her hand. Almost of itself it snapped free of the twig that held it. Eve stared at the apple in her palm, and her hand began to shake. She drew back against the serpent, a little whimper of terror rising in her throat.

The serpent dropped a coiled embrace about the lovely, light-clothed pallor of her body and bent his handsome, slanted head to hers, whispering at her ear in a voice so cool and sweet that the terror faded from her face. She smiled a little, and her hand steadied.

She lifted the Fruit of Knowledge to her lips. There was a hush all through the

Garden as she hesitated for a long moment, the red fruit at her red mouth, her teeth denting the scarlet cheek of Knowledge. The last few timeless moments stood still while innocence yet reigned over Eden.

Then the serpent whispered again, urgently: *"Eva—"* he said.

Lilith stood shivering in Adam's arms.

"You were mine first," she was whispering fiercely. "You and I and the Garden—don't you remember? I was your wife before her, and you belong to me!"

Adam could see his own arms through the ephemeral stuff of Lilith's body. He was shaken by the violence in her voice, but his mind was too fogged with the unthinking blank of innocence to understand very clearly. He tried hard.

The rhythm that pulsed through Eden was curiously uneven now. Lilith knew what it meant, and excitement choked her. She cried more desperately:

"Adam . . . Adam! Don't let anything separate us, you and the Garden and I! You can hold us together if you try! I know you can! You—"

One great, annihilating throb shook through the air like thunder. The whole Garden reeled with it and every tree in Eden bowed as if before a tremendous wind. Adam looked up, aghast. But Lilith laughed a wild, excited laugh and cried, "This is it! Oh, hurry, Adam, hurry!"

She slipped through his arms that were still clasped about her and went fluttering effortlessly off through branches that did not impede her passage, Adam following half stunned with the stunned Garden. All Eden was still reeling from the violence of what had just happened beneath the Tree.

Lilith watched the sky as she ran. Would a great bolt of lightning come ravening down out of heaven to blast the woman out of being before they reached the Tree? "Wait, wait!" she panted voicelessly to God. "Give me a moment longer—" Would a bolt strike Adam, too, as he slipped through the parting trees beside her? "Hurry!" she gasped again.

Breathless, they paused at the edge of the hollow where the Tree stood. Looking down, they could see Eve just clear of the shadow of it, the fruit in her hand with one white bite flawing its scarlet cheek. She was staring about the Garden as if she had never seen it before. *Where was God? Why had He not blasted her as she stood there?*

Lilith in her first wild glance could not see the serpent except for a glitter of iridescence back in the shadow of the Tree. Even in her terrible excitement she smiled wryly. Lucifer was taking no chances with God.

But she had no time to waste now on Lucifer or on Eve. For some inexplicable reason God was staying His hand, and she must make the most of the respite. For when God was finished with Eve He would turn to Adam, and before that much had to be done. Adam was her business now, and the living Eden, and all eternity waited on what the next few moments held.

She stood out on the lip of the hollow and a great dark wind from nowhere swelled monstrously about her, tossing out her hair until it was a cloud that shut her from sight. Out of the cloud her voice came rolling in tremendous rhythms paced to the rhythm at which Eden breathed—and Adam.

"Garden!" she called. "Eden—hear me! I am Lilith, the wife of Adam—"

She could feel a vast, dim awareness stirring around her. All through Eden the wakening motion ran, drawing closer, welling up deeply from the earth underfoot, monstrously, wonderfully, a world coming alive at her call.

"Adam!" she cried. "Adam do you hear me? You and Eden are one flesh, and Eve has destroyed you both. She has just brought knowledge into Eden, where God dares not let it exist. God will destroy you all, because of Eve . . . unless you listen to me—"

She felt Adam's attention torn away from Eve and focusing upon herself in fear and wonder. She felt the Garden's wakening awareness draw around him with growing intensity, until it was as if the earth of Eden and the flesh of Man quickened into one, married by the same need for one another as the thought of parting and destruction shuddered through each.

Was this what God had planned as an ending for His divine scheme, as it was the beginning of Lilith's? She had no time to wonder, but the thought crossed her mind awesomely even as she wooed the Garden in a voice as sweet and coaxing as the voice she used to Adam.

And the whole great Garden shuddered ponderously around her, awareness thrilling down every tendril and branch and blade, pulsing up out of the very hill on which she stood. And all of it was Adam. The Garden heard and hung upon her words, and Adam heard, and they three together were all that existed. Success was in her hands. She could feel it. And then—

"Adam . . . Adam!" screamed Eve beneath the Tree.

Lilith's sonorous voice paused in its invocation; the Garden hesitated around her.

"Adam!" cried Eve again, terror flattening all the sweetness out of her voice.

And behind Lilith, in a drugged voice, Adam said: "Eve—?"

"God . . . God, destroy her now!" prayed Lilith soundlessly. And aloud, "Eve has no part in Eden! Don't listen to her, Adam! She'll destroy you and the Garden together!"

"Adam, Adam! Where are you?"

"Coming—" said Adam, still in that thick, drugged voice.

Lilith whirled in the mist of her cloudy hair. Where was God! Why had He stayed His hand? Now was the time to strike, if her hope were not to fail. Now, now! Surely the lightning would come ravening down from heaven if she could hold Adam a moment longer—

"Adam, wait!" she cried desperately. "Adam, you know you love me! If you leave—"

Her voice faltered as he peered at her as blindly as if he had never seen her before. The haloed light was like fire all around him, and her words had been a drug to him as they had been to the Garden, until the earth that loved and listened to her had been one with his own earth-formed flesh; a moment ago there had been nothing in creation for Adam or for Eden but this one woman speaking out of the dark. But now—

"Adam!" screamed Eve again in the flat, frightened voice.

"Don't listen!" cried Lilith frantically. "She doesn't belong here! You can't save her now! God will destroy her, and He'll destroy you, too, if you leave me! Stay here and let her die! You and I will be alone again, in the Garden . . . Adam, don't listen!"

"I . . . I have to listen," he stammered almost stupidly. "Get out of my way, Lilith. Don't you understand? She's my own flesh—I have to go."

Lilith stared at him dumbly. His own flesh! She had forgotten that. She had leaned too heavily on his oneness with the Garden—she had forgotten he was one with Eve, too. The prospect of defeat was suddenly like lead in her. If God would only strike now—She swayed forward in one last desperate effort to hold him back from Eve while the Garden stirred uneasily around them, frightened with Lilith's terror, torn with Adam's distress. She wavered between Adam and the valley as if her ephemeral body could hold him, but he went through her as if through a cloud and stumbled blindly downhill toward the terrified Eve beneath the Tree with the fruit in her hand and a dreadful knowledge on her face.

From here Lilith could see what Adam had not yet. She laughed suddenly, wildly, and cried:

"Look at her, Adam! Look!" And Adam blinked and looked.

Eve stood naked beneath the Tree. That burning beauty which had clothed her like a garment was gone with her divine innocence and she was no longer the flawless goddess who had wakened on Adam's shoulder that morning. She stood shivering a little, looking forlorn and somehow pinched and thin, almost a caricature of the perfect beauty that had gone down the hill with the serpent an hour ago. But she did not know that. She looked up at Adam as he hesitated above her, and smiled uncertainly with a sort of leer in her smile.

"Oh, there you are," she said, and even her voice was harsher now. "Everything looked so . . . so queer, for a minute. Look." She held up the fruit. "It's good. Better than anything *you* ever gave me. Try it."

Lilith stared at her from the hilltop with a horror that for a moment blanked out her growing terror because of God's delay. Was knowledge, then, as ugly as this? Why had it destroyed Eve's beauty as if it were some evil thing? Perfect knowledge should have increased her strength and loveliness in the instant before God struck her down, if— Suddenly Lilith understood. Perfect knowledge! But Eve had only tasted the fruit, and she had only a warped half-knowledge from that single taste. The beauty of her innocence was lost, but she had not yet gained the beauty of perfect knowledge. Was this why God delayed? So long as her knowledge was imperfect perhaps she was no menace to God's power in Eden. And yet she had disobeyed, she had proved herself unworthy of the trust of God— Then why did He hesitate? Why had He not blasted her as she stood there with the apple at her lips? A panic was rising in Lilith's throat. *Could it be that He was laughing, even now?* Was He giving her the respite she had prayed for, and watching her fail in spite of it?

"Taste the apple," said Eve again, holding it out.

"Adam!" cried Lilith despairingly from the edge of the hill. "Adam, look at me! You loved me first—don't you remember? Look at me, Adam!"

And Adam turned to look. The wind, which had clouded her from sight in the darkness of her hair, had calmed. She stood now, luminous on the hilltop, the darkness parted like a river by the whiteness of her shoulders. And she was beautiful with a beauty that no mortal woman will ever wear again.

"I was first!" cried Lilith. "You loved me before her—come back to me now, before God strikes you both! Come back, Adam!"

He stared up at her miserably. He looked back at the flawed, shivering creature at his side, knowledge curiously horrible in her eyes. He stared at Eve, too, a long stare. And then he reached for the apple.

"Adam—no!" shrieked Lilith. "See what knowledge did to Eve! You'll be ugly and naked, like her! Don't taste it, Adam! You don't know what you're doing!"

Over the poised red fruit he looked up at her. The light quivered gloriously all around him. He stood like a god beneath the Tree, radiant, perfect.

"Yes, I know," he said, in a clearer voice than she had ever heard him use before.

"God will destroy you!" wailed Lilith, and rolled her eyes up to look for the falling thunderbolt that might be hurtling downward even now.

"I know," said Adam again. And then, after a pause, "You don't understand, Lilith. Eve is my own flesh, closer than Eden—closer than you. Don't you remember what God said? *Forsaking all others—*"

"Eve!" screamed Lilith hopelessly. "Stop him! Your punishment's certain— are you going to drag him down, too?"

Eve looked up, knowledge dark in her blue eyes. She laughed a thin laugh and the last vestige of her beauty went with it.

"Leave him to you?" she sneered. "Oh no! He and I are one flesh—we'll go together. Taste the apple, Adam!"

He turned it obediently in his hand: his teeth crunched through scarlet skin into the sweet white flesh inside. There was a tremendous silence all through the Garden; nothing stirred in Eden while Adam chewed and swallowed the Fruit of Knowledge. And then turned to stare down into Eve's lifted eyes while awareness of himself as an individual, free-willed being dawned gradually across his awakening mind.

And then the burning glory that clothed him paled, shimmered, went out along his limbs. He, too, was naked. The queer, pinched look of humanity shivered over that magnificent body, and he was no longer magnificent, no longer Adam.

Lilith had forgotten to look for God. Sickness of the heart was swelling terribly in her, and for a moment she no longer cared about God, or Eden, or the future. This was not Adam any more— It would never be Adam again—

"Listen," said Eve in a small, intimate voice to Adam. "How quiet it is! Why, it's the music. The seraphim aren't singing any more around the Throne!"

Lilith glanced up apathetically. That meant, then, that God was coming— But even as she looked up a great golden chorus resounded serenely from high over Eden. Adam tipped his tarnished head to listen.

"You're right," he agreed. "They've stopped their song."

Lilith did not hear him. That dreadful sickness in her was swelling and changing, and she knew now what it was—hatred. Hatred of Adam and Eve and the thing they had done to her. Hatred of these naked caricatures, who had been the magnificent half-god she had loved and the shape she had put on to delight him. True, they might finish the eating of knowledge and grow perfect again, but it would be a perfection that shut her out. They were one flesh together, and even God had failed her now. Looking down, she loathed them both. Eve's very existence was an insult to the unflawed perfection which Lilith still wore, and Adam— Adam shivering beneath the Tree with a warped, imperfect knowledge leering in his eyes—

A sob swelled in her throat. He had been flawless once—she would never forget that. Almost she loved the memory still as it lingered about this shivering human creature beneath the Tree. So long as he was alive she knew now she would never be free of it; this weakness would torment her still for the flesh that had once been Adam. The prospect of an eternity of longing for him, who would never exist again, was suddenly unbearable to her.

She tipped her head back and looked up through the glory above Eden where golden voices chanted that neither Adam nor Eve would ever hear again.

"Jehovah!" she sobbed. "Jehovah! Come down and destroy us all! You were right—they are both too flawed to bring anything but misery to all who know them. God, come down and give us peace!"

Eve squealed in terror at Adam's side. "Listen!" she cried. "Adam, listen to her!"

Answering human terror dawned across the pinched features that had once been Adam's handsome, immortal face. "The Tree of Life!" he shouted. "No one can touch us if we eat that fruit!"

He whirled to scramble up the slope toward the dark Tree, and Lilith's heart ached to watch how heavily he moved. Yesterday's wonderful, easy litheness was gone with his beauty, and his body was a burden to him now.

But he was not to reach the Tree of Life. For suddenly glory brightened unbearably over the Garden. A silence was in the sky, and the breeze ceased to blow through Eden.

"Adam," said a Voice in the great silence of the Garden, "hast thou eaten of the Tree?"

Adam glanced up the slope at Lilith, standing despairingly against the sky. He looked at Eve beside him, a clumsy caricature of the loveliness he had dreamed of. There was bitterness in his voice.

"The woman thou gavest me—" he began reproachfully, and then hesitated, meeting Eve's eyes. The old godlike goodness was lost to him now, but he had not fallen low enough yet to let Eve know what he was thinking. He could not say, "The woman Thou gavest me has ruined us both—but I had a woman of my own before her and she never did me any harm." No, he could not hurt this flesh of his flesh so deeply, but he was human now and he could not let her go unrebuked. He went on sulkily, "—she gave me the apple, and I ate."

The Voice said awfully, "Eve—?"

Perhaps Eve was remembering that other voice, cool and sweet, murmuring, "Eva—" In the cool, green dimness of the Garden, the voice that had whispered secrets she would never share with Adam. Perhaps if he had been beside her now—but he was not, and her resentment bubbled to her lips in speech.

"The serpent beguiled me," she told God sullenly, "and I ate."

There was silence for a moment in the Garden. Then the Voice said, "Lucifer—" with a sorrow in the sound that had not stirred for the man's plight, or the woman's. "Lucifer, my enemy, come forth from the Tree." There was a divine compassion in the Voice even as It pronounced sentence. "Upon thy belly shalt thou go, and dust shalt thou eat all the days of thy life—"

Out from beneath the shadow of the Tree a flat and shining length came pouring through the grass. This was the hour for the shedding of beauty: the serpent had lost the fire-bright splendor that had been his while Lucifer dwelt in his flesh, but traces lingered yet in the unearthly fluidness of his motion, in his shining iridescence. He lifted a wedged head toward Eve, flickered his tongue at her once and then dropped back into the grass. Its ripple above him marked his course away. Eve drew one long, sobbing breath for that green twilight hour in the Garden, that Adam would never guess, as she watched him ripple away.

"Adam, Eve," went on the Voice quietly, "the Garden is not for you." There was a passionless pity in It as the Garden stood still to listen. "I made your flesh too weak, because your godhood was too strong to trust. You are not to blame for that—the fault was Mine. But Adam . . . Eve . . . what power did I put in you, that the very elements of fire and darkness find kinship with you? What flaw is in you, that though you are the only two human things alive, yet you cannot keep faith with one another?"

Adam glanced miserably up toward Lilith standing motionless on the hill's edge, clothed in the flawless beauty he had dreamed for her and would never see again. Eve's eyes followed the serpent through the grass that was blurred for her because of the first tears of Eden. Neither of them answered.

"You are not fit yet to put forth your hand to the Tree of Life, and eat, and live forever," went on the Voice after a moment.

"Man . . . woman . . . you are not yet fit for perfect knowledge or immortality. You are not yet fit for trust. But for Lilith the tale would have spun itself out here in the walls of Eden, but now you must go beyond temptation and work your own salvation out in the sweat of your brow, in the lands beyond the Garden. Adam, I dare not trust you any longer in your kinship with the earth I shaped you from. Cursed is the ground for your sake. Adam—it shall be one with you no longer. But I promise this . . . in the end you shall return to it—" The Voice fell silent, and there was far from above the flash of a flaming sword over the gate of Eden.

In the silence Lilith laughed. It was a clear, ringing sound from the hill's edge:

"Deal with me now," she said in an empty voice. "I have no desire to exist any longer in a world that has no Adam—destroy me, Jehovah."

The Voice said emotionlessly, "You are punished already, by the fruit of what you did."

"Punished enough!" wailed Lilith in sudden despair. "Make an end of it, Jehovah!"

"With man's end," said God quietly. "No sooner. You four among you have shattered a plan in Eden that you must shape anew before your travail ends. Let the four of you build a new plan with the elements of your being—Adam is Earth, Lucifer is Fire, Lilith is Air and Darkness, and Eve the Mother of All Living, the fertile seas from which all living springs. Earth, Air, Fire and Water—you thought your plan was better than Mine. Work it out for yourselves!"

"What is our part to be, Lord?" asked Adam in a small, humbled voice.

"Earth and water," said the Voice. "The kingdom of earth for you and the woman and your children after you."

"I was Adam's wife before her," wailed Lilith jealously. "What of me . . . and mine?"

The Voice fell silent for a while. Then it said quietly: "Make your own choice, Queen of Air and Darkness."

"Let my children and Adam's haunt hers to their graves, then!" decided Lilith instantly. "Mine are the disinherited—let them take vengeance! Let her and hers beware of my children who wail in the night, and know she deserves their wrath. Let them remind her always that Adam was mine before her!"

"So be it," said the Voice. And for an instant there was silence in Eden while the shadow of times to come brooded inscrutably in the mind of God. Lilith caught flashes of it in the glory so bright over Eden that every grass blade had a splendor which hurt the eyes. She saw man loving his birthplace upon earth with a deep-rooted love that made it as dear as his very flesh to him, so that dimly he might remember the hour when all earth was as close to him as his newly created body. She saw man cleaving to one woman as dear as the flesh of his flesh, yet remembering the unattainable and the lost—Lilith, perfect in Eden. She looked down from the hilltop and met Adam's eyes, and voicelessly between them a long farewell went flashing.

No one was watching Eve. She was blinking through tears, remembering a twilight hour and a fire-bright beauty that the dust had quenched a moment ago at God's command. And then . . . then there was the faintest rustling in the air around her, and a cool, clear voice was murmuring:

"Eva—" against her cheek.

She stared. There was nothing. But—

"Eva," said the voice again. "Give me my vengeance too—upon the Man. Pretty Eva, do you hear me? Call your first child Kayn . . . Eva, will you do as I say? Call him Kayn the Spear of my vengeance, for he shall set murder loose among Adam's sons. Remember, Eva—"

And Eve echoed in a small, obedient whisper, "Cain . . . Cain."

L. SPRAGUE DE CAMP

The Wheels of If

King Oswiu of Northumbria squirmed in his chair.

In the first place these synods bored him. In the second, his mathematics comprised the ability to add and subtract numbers under twenty on his fingers. Hence all this argument among the learned clerics, assembled in Whitby in the year of Our Lord 664, about the date of Easter and the phases of the moon and cycles of 84 and 532 years, went over the King's head completely.

What did the exact date of Easter matter, anyhow? If they wanted to, why couldn't the Latins celebrate their Easter when they wanted, and the Ionans celebrate theirs? The Ionans had been doing all right, as far as Oswiu could see. And then this Wilfrid of York had to bring in his swarms of Latin priests, objecting to this and that as schismatic, heretical, etc. They were abetted by Oswiu's queen, Eanfled, which put poor Oswiu in an awkward position. He not only wanted peace in the family, but also hoped to attain to Heaven some day. Moreover, he liked the Abbot Colman, leader of the Ionans. And he certainly didn't want any far-off Bishop of Rome sticking his nose into his affairs. On the other hand . . .

King Oswiu came to with a jerk. Father Wilfrid was speaking to him directly: ". . . the arguments of my learned friend—" *he indicated the Abbot Colman of Lindisfarne* "—are very ingenious, I admit. But that is not the fundamental question. The real decision is, shall we accept the authority of His Holiness of Rome, like good Christians, or—"

"Wait a minute, wait a minute," *interrupted Oswiu.* "Why must we accept Gregory's authority to be good Christians? I'm a good Christian, and I don't let any foreign—"

"The question, my lord, is whether one can be a good Christian and a rebel against—"

"I am too a good Christian!" *bristled Oswiu.*

Wilfrid of York smiled. "Perhaps you remember the statement of our Savior to Peter, the first Bishop of Rome? 'Thou art Peter; and upon this rock I will build my Church; and the gates of Hell shall not prevail against it. And I will give unto thee the keys of the Kingdom of Heaven; and whatsoever thou shalt bind on earth shall be bound in heaven; and whatsoever thou shalt loose on earth shall be loosed in Heaven.' You see?"

Oswiu thought. That put a different light on the matter. If this fellow Peter actually had the keys of Heaven . . .

He turned to the Abbot Colman and asked: "Is that a correct quotation?"

"It is, my lord. But—"

"Just a minute, just a minute. You'll get me all confused again if you start arguing. Now, can you quote a text showing that equivalent powers were granted to Saint Columba?"

The grave Irishman's face registered sudden dismay. He frowned in concentration so intense that one could almost hear the wheels.

"Well?" said Oswiu. "Speak up!"

Colman sighed. "No, my lord, I cannot. But I can show that it is the Latins, not we, who are departing from—"

"That's enough, Colman!" Oswiu's single-track mind, once made up, had no intention of being disturbed again. "I have decided that from this day forth the Kingdom of Northumbria shall follow the Latin practice concerning Easter. And that we shall declare our allegiance to the Roman Bishop Gregory, lest, when I come to the gates of Heaven, there would be none to open them for me—he being my adversary who has the keys. The synod is adjourned."

King Oswiu went out, avoiding the reproachful look that the Abbot sent after him. It was a dirty trick on Colman, who was a very decent chap. But after all, it wouldn't do to antagonize the heavenly doorman. And maybe now Eanfled would stop nagging him . . .

Allister Park rubbed his eyes and sat up in bed, as he usually did. He noticed nothing wrong until he looked at the sleeve of his pajamas.

He could not recall ever having had a pair of pajamas of that singularly repulsive green. He couldn't recall having changed to clean pajamas the night before. In short, he couldn't account for these pajamas at all.

Oh, well, probably, Eunice or Mary had given them to him, and he'd put them on without thinking. He yawned, brushing his mouth with the back of his hand.

He jerked his hand away. Then he cautiously felt his upper lip.

He got out of bed and made for the nearest mirror. There was no doubt about it. He had a mustache. He had not had a mustache when he went to bed the night before.

'Abd-ar-Rahman, Governor of Cordoba for the Khalifah Hisham ibn 'Abd-al-Malik, Lord of Damascus, Protector of the Faithful, etc., etc., paced his tent like a caged leopard with claustrophobia. He hated inactivity, and to him the last six days of tentative skirmishing had been just that.

He glowered over his pepper-and-salt beard and his chiefs, sitting cross-legged in an ellipse on the rugs. "Well?" he barked.

Yezid spoke up. "But a little longer, Commander-in-Chief, and the Franks will melt away. The infidels have little cavalry, save Gothic and Aquitanian refugees. Without cavalry, they cannot keep themselves fed. Our horse can range the coun-

try, supplying us and cutting off help from our enemies. There is no God but God."

Ya'qub snorted. "How long do you think our men will abide this fearful Frankish climate? The winter is almost upon us. I say strike now, while their spirits are still up. This rabble of Frankish farmers on foot will show some rare running. Have the armies of the Faithful come this far by sitting in front of their enemies and making grimaces at them?"

Yezid delivered an impressive snort of his own. "Just the advice one would expect from a dog of a Ma'ddite. This Karel, who commands the infidels, is no fool—"

"Who's a dog?" yelped Ya'qub, jumping up. "Pig of a Yemenite—"

'Abd-ar-Rahman yelled at them until they subsided. One major idea of this foray into Francia was to bury the animosity between members of the two parties. Yezid's starting a quarrel on political grounds put the Governor in an embarrassing position, as he was a Yemenite himself. He was still undecided. An intelligent man, he could see the sense to Yezid's Fabian advice. Emotionally, however, he burned to get to grips with the army of Charles, Mayor of Austrasia. And Yezid should be punished for his insulting remark.

"I have decided," said 'Abd-ar-Rahman, "that, while there is much to be said on both sides, Ya'qub's advice is the sounder. Nothing hurts an army's spirit like waiting. Besides, God has planned the outcome of the battle anyway. So why should we fear? If He decides that we shall win, we shall win.

"Therefore tomorrow, Saturday, we shall strike the Franks with all our force. God is God, and Mohammed is His prophet . . ."

But the next night 'Abd-ar-Rahman lay dead by the banks of the River Vienne, near Tours, with his handsome face waxy in the starlight and blood in his pepper-and-salt beard. The Austrasian line had held. Yezid, who had been right, was dead likewise, and so was Ya'qub, who had been wrong. And the surviving Arabs were fleeing back to Narbonne and Barcelona.

Allister Park opened the door of his apartment and grabbed up his *Times*. Sure enough, the date was Monday, April eleventh, just as it ought to have been. The year was right, too. That ruled out the possibility of amnesia.

He went back to the mirror. He was still a slightly stout man in his middle thirties, with pale-blue eyes and thinning sandy hair. But he wasn't the same man. The nose was different. So were the eyebrows. The scar under the chin was gone . . .

He gave up his self-inspection and got out his clothes. At that juncture he got another shock. The clothes weren't his. Or rather, they were clothes for a man of his size, and of the quality that a self-indulgent bachelor with an income of $12,000 a year would buy. Park didn't object to the clothes. It was just that they weren't *his* clothes.

Park gave up speculation about his sanity for the nonce; he had to get dressed. Breakfast? He was sick of the more cardboard-like cereals. To hell with it; he'd make himself some French toast. If it put another inch on his middle, he'd sweat it off Sunday at the New York Athletic Club.

The mail was thrust under his door. He finished knotting his necktie and picked it up. The letters were all addressed to a Mr. Arthur Vogel.

Then Allister Park, really awake, did look around. The apartment was built on the same plan as his own, but it wasn't the same. The furniture was different. Lots of little things were different, such as a nick in the wall that shouldn't be there.

Park sat down and smoked a cigarette while he thought. There was no evidence of kidnapping, which, considering his business, was not too unlikely a possibility. He'd gone to bed Sunday night sober, alone, and reasonably early. Why should he wake up in another man's apartment? He forgot for the moment that he had also awakened with another man's face. Before he had time to remember it, the sight of the clock jostled him into action. No time for French toast—it would have to be semi-edible cardboard after all.

But the real shock awaited him when he looked for his briefcase. There was none. Neither was there any sign of the sheaf of notes he had so carefully drawn up on the conduct of the forthcoming Antonini case. That was more than important. On his convicting the Antonini gang depended his nomination for District Attorney for the County of New York next fall. The present DA was due to get the bipartisan nomination to the Court of General Sessions at the same time.

He was planning, with thoroughly dishonorable motives, to invite Martha up for dinner. But he didn't want to have dinner with her until he'd cleared this matter up. The only trouble with calling her up was that the address-book didn't have her name in it—or indeed the name of anybody Park had ever heard of. Neither was he listed in the 'phone book.

He dialed CAnal 6-5700. Somebody said: "Department of Hospitals."

"Huh? Isn't this CAnal 6-5700?"

"Yes, this is the Department of Hospitals."

"Well what's the District Attorney's office then? Hell, I ought to know my own office 'phone."

"The District Attorney's office is WOrth 2-2200."

Park groggily called WOrth 2-2200. "Mr. Park's office please."

"What office did you ask for, please?"

"The office of Assistant District Attorney Park!" Park's voice took on the metallic rasp. "Racket Bureau to you, sister."

"I'm sorry, we have no such person."

"Listen, young lady, have you got a Deputy Assistant DA named Frenczko? John Frenczko? You spell it with a z."

Silence. "No, I'm sorry, we have no such person."

Allister Park hung up.

The old building at 137 Center was still there. The Racket Bureau was still there. But they had never heard of Allister Park. They already had an

Assistant DA of their own, a man named Hutchison, with whom they seemed quite well satisfied. There were no sign of Park's two deputies, Frenczko and Burt.

As a last hope, Park went over to the Criminal Courts Building. If he wasn't utterly mad, the case of *People* v. *Cassidy,* extortion, ought to come up as soon after ten as it would take Judge Segal to read his calendar. Frenczko and Burt would be in there, after Cassidy's hide.

But there was no Judge Segal, no Frenczko, no Burt, no Cassidy . . .

"Very interesting, Mr. Park," soothed the psychiatrist. "Very interesting indeed. The most hopeful feature is that you quite realize your difficulty, and come to me now—"

"What I want to know," interrupted Park, "is: was I sane up to yesterday, and crazy since then, or was I crazy up to then and sane now?"

"It seems hard to believe that one could suffer from a coherent set of illusions for thirty-six years," replied the psychiatrist. "Yet your present account of your perceptions seems rational enough. Perhaps your memory of what you saw and experienced today is at fault."

"But I want to get straightened out! My whole political future depends on it! At least—" he stopped. *Was* there such an Antonini gang? *Was* there a nomination awaiting an Allister Park if they were convicted?

"I know," said the psychiatrist gently. "But this case isn't like any I ever heard of. You go ahead and wire Denver for Allister Park's birth-certificate. We'll see if there is such a person. Then come back tomorrow . . ."

Park awoke, looked around, and groaned. The room had changed again. But he choked off his groan. He was occupying a twin bed. In its mate lay a fair-to-middling handsome woman of about his own age.

His groan had roused her. She asked: "How are you feeling, Wally?"

"I'm feeling fine," he mumbled. The significance of his position was soaking in. He had some trouble suppressing another groan. About marriage, he was an adherent of the why-buy-a-cow philosophy, as he had had occasion to make clear to many women by way of fair warning.

"I hope you are," said the woman anxiously. "You acted so queer yesterday. Do you remembe˙ your appointment with Dr. Kerr?"

"I certainly do," said Park. Kerr was not the name of the psychiatrist with whom he had made the appointment.

The woman prepared to dress. Park gulped a little. For years he'd managed to get along without being mixed up with other men's wives, ever since . . .

And he wished he knew her name. A well-mannered man, under those circumstances, wouldn't refer to the woman as "Hey, you."

"What are we having for breakfast, sweetie-pie?" he asked with a sickly grin. She told him, adding: "You never called me that before, dear." When she started toward him with an expectant smile, he jumped out of bed and dressed with frantic haste.

He ate silently. When the woman inquired why, he pointed to his mouth and mumbled: "Canker sore. It hurts to talk."

He fled as soon as he decently could, without learning his "wife's" name. His wallet told him his name was Wallace Heineman, but little else about himself. If he wanted to badly enough, he could no doubt find out whom he worked for, who his friends were, which if any bank he had money in, etc. But if these daily changes were going to continue, it hardly seemed worthwhile. The first thing was to get back to that psychiatrist.

Although the numbers of the streets were different, the general layout was the same. Half an hour's walking brought him to the block where the psychiatrist's office had been. The building had been on the southeast corner of Fifty-seventh and Eighth. Park could have sworn the building that now occupied that site was different.

However, he went up anyway. He had made a careful note of the office number. His notebook had been missing that morning, like all the rest of his (or rather Arthur Vogel's) things. Still, he remembered the number.

The number turned out to be that of a suite of offices occupied by Williamson, Ostendorff, Cohen, Burke, and Williamson, Attorneys. No, they had never heard of Park's brain-man. Yes, Williamson, Ostendorff, Cohen, Burke, and Williamson had occupied those offices for years.

Park came out into the street and stood a long time, thinking. A phenomenon that he had hitherto noticed only vaguely now puzzled him: the extraordinary number of Union Jacks in sight.

He asked the traffic cop about it. The cop looked at him. "King's birthday," he said.

"What king?"

"Why, *our* king of course. David the Fuist." The cop touched his finger to the peak of his cap.

Park settled himself on a park bench with a newspaper. The paper was full of things like references to the recent Anglo-Russian war, the launching of the *Queen Victoria,* His Majesty's visit to a soap factory ("where he displayed a keen interest in the technical problems involved in . . ."), the victory of Massachusetts over Quebec in the Inter-Colonial football matches (Massachusetts a colony? And football in April?), the trial of one Diedrichs for murdering a man with a cross-cut saw . . .

All this was very interesting, especially the Diedrichs case. But Allister Park was more concerned with the whereabouts and probable fate of the Antonini gang. He also thought with gentle melancholy of Mary and Eunice and Dorothy and Martha and Joan and. . . . But that was less important than the beautiful case he had dug up against such a slimy set of public enemies. Even Park, despite the cynical view of humanity that public prosecutors get, had felt a righteous glow when he tallied up the evidence and knew he had them.

And the nomination was not to be sneezed at either. It just happened that he was available when it was a Protestant's turn at that nomination. If he missed out, he'd have to wait while a Catholic and a Jew took theirs. Since you had to be one or the other to get nominated at all, Park had become perforce a church member and regular if slightly hypocritical goer.

His plan was, after a few terms as DA, to follow the incumbent DA onto the bench. You would never have guessed it, but inside Allister Park lingered enough of the idealism that as a young lawyer he had brought from Colorado to give the bench an attractiveness not entirely comprised of salary and social position.

He looked in his pockets. There was enough there for one good bender.

Of the rest of the day, he never could remember much afterwards. He did remember giving a pound note to an old woman selling shoe-laces, leading a group of drunks in a song about one Columbo who knew the world was round-o (unexpurgated), and trying to take a fireman's hose away from him on the ground that the city was having a water shortage.

He awoke in another strange room, without a trace of a hangover. A quick look-around assured him that he was alone.

It was time, he thought, that he worked out a system for the investigation of his identity on each successive morning. He learned that his name was Wadsworth Noe. The pants of all the suits in his closet were baggy knee-pants, plus-fours.

Something was going *ping, ping, ping,* like one of those tactful alarm clocks. Park located the source of the noise in a goose-necked gadget on the table, which he finally identified as a telephone. As the transmitter and receiver were built into a single unit on the end of the goose-neck, there was nothing to lift off the hook. He pressed a button in the base. A voice spoke: "Waddy?"

"Oh—yeah. Who's this?"

"This is your little bunnykins."

Park swore under his breath. The voice sounded female and young, and had a slight indefinable accent. He stalled: "How are you this morning?"

"Oh, I'm fine. How's my little butter-ball?"

Park winced. Wadsworth Noe had a figure even more portly than Allister Park's. Park, with effort, infused syrup into his voice: "Oh, I'm fine too, sweetie-pie. Only I'm lonesome as all hell."

"Oh, isn't that too bad! Oo poor little thing! Shall I come up and cook dinner for my precious?"

"I'd love it." A plan was forming in Park's mind. Hitherto all these changes had taken place while he was asleep. If he could get somebody to sit around and watch him while he stayed up . . .

The date was made. Park found he'd have to market.

On the street, aside from the fact that all the men wore plus-fours and wide-brimmed hats, the first thing that struck him was the sight of two dark men in uniform. They walked in step down the middle of the sidewalk. Their walk implied that they expected people to get out of their way. People got. As the soldiers passed him, Park caught a sentence in a foreign language, sounding like Spanish.

At the market everyone spoke with that accent Park had heard over the 'phone. They fell silent when another pair of soldiers entered. These loudly demanded certain articles of food. A clerk scurried around and got the order. The soldiers took the things and departed without paying.

Park thought of going to a library to learn about the world he was in. But if he were going to shift again, it would hardly be worth while. He bought a *New York Record,* noticing that the stand also carried a lot of papers in French and Spanish.

Back in his apartment he read of His Majesty Napoleon V, apparently emperor of New York City and God knew what else!

His little bunnykins turned out to be a smallish dark girl, not bad-looking, who kissed him soundly. She said: "Where have you been the last few days, Waddy? I haven't heard from you for simply *ages!* I was beginning to think you'd forgotten me. Oo hasn't forgotten, has oo?"

"Me forget? Why, sweetie-pie, I couldn't any more forget you than I could forget my own name." (And what the hell's that? he asked himself. Wordsworth—no, Wadsworth Noe. Thank God.) "Give us another kiss."

She looked at him. "What makes you talk so funny, Waddy?"

"Canker sore," said Allister Park.

"O-o-o, you poor angel. Let me see it."

"It's all right. How about that famous dinner?"

At least Wadsworth Noe kept a good cellar. After dinner Park applied himself cautiously to this. It gave an excuse for just sitting. Park asked the girl about herself. She chattered on happily for some hours.

Then the conversation began to run dry. There were long silences.

She looked at him quizzically. "Are you worrying about something, Waddy? Somehow you seem like a different man."

"No," he lied. "I'm not worrying."

She looked at the clock. "I suppose I ought to go," she said hesitantly.

Park sat up. "Oh, please don't!"

She relaxed and smiled. "I didn't *think* you'd let me. Just wait." She disappeared into the bedroom and presently emerged in a filmy nightgown.

Allister Park was not surprised. But he was concerned. Attractive as the girl was, the thought of solving his predicament was more so. Besides, he was already sleepy from the liquors he had drunk.

"How about making some coffee, sweetie-pie?" he asked.

She acquiesced. The making and drinking of the coffee took another hour. It was close to midnight. To keep the ball rolling, Park told some stories. Then the conversation died down again. The girl yawned. She seemed puzzled and a bit resentful.

She asked: "Are you going to sit up all night?"

That was just what Park intended to do. But while he cast about for a plausible reason to give, he stalled: "Ever tell you about that man Wugson I met last week? Funniest chap you ever saw. He has a big bunch of hairs growing out the end of his nose . . ."

He went on in detail about the oddities of the imaginary Mr. Wugson. The girl had an expression of what-did-I-do-to-deserve-this. She yawned again.

Click! Allister Park rubbed his eyes and sat up. He was on a hard knobby thing that might, by gross misuse of the language, be called a mattress. His eyes focused on a row of iron bars.

He was in jail.

Allister Park's day in jail proved neither interesting nor informative. He was marched out for meals and for an hour of exercise. Nobody spoke to him except a guard who asked: "Hey there, chief, who ja think you are today, huh? Julius Caesar?"

Park grinned. "Nope. I'm God, this time."

This was getting to be a bore. If one could do this flitting about from existence to existence voluntarily, it might be fun. As it was, one didn't stay put long enough to adjust oneself to any of these worlds of—illusion?

The next day he was a shabby fellow sleeping on a park bench. The city was still New York—no it wasn't; it was a different city built on the site of New York.

He had money for nothing more than a bottle of milk and a loaf of bread. These he bought and consumed slowly, while reading somebody's discarded newspaper. Reading was difficult because of the queer spelling. And the people had an accent that required the closest attention to understand.

He spent a couple of hours in an art museum. The guards looked at him as if he were something missed by the cleaners. When it closed he went back to his park bench and waited. Night came.

A car—at least, a four-wheeled vehicle—drew up and a couple of cops got out. Park guessed they were cops because of their rhinestone epaulets. One asked: "Are you John Gilby?" He pronounced it. "Air yew Zhawn Gilbü?"

But Allister Park caught his drift. "Damned if I know, brother. Am I?"

The cops looked at each other. "He's him, all right," said one. To Park: "Come along."

Park learned, little by little, that he was not wanted for anything more serious than disappearance. He kept his own counsel until they arrived at the stationhouse.

Inside was a fat woman. She jumped up and pointed at him, crying raucously: "That's him! That's the dirty deserter, running off and leaving his poor wife to starve! The back of me hand to you, you dirty—"

"Please, Mrs. Gilby!" said the desk sergeant.

The woman was not to be silenced. "Heaven curse the day I met you! Sergeant darlin', what can I do to put the dirty loafer in jail where he belongs?"

"Well," said the sergeant uncomfortably, "you can charge him with desertion, of course. But don't you think you'd better go home and talk it over? We don't want to—"

"Hey!" cried Park. They looked at him. "I'll take jail, if you don't mind—"

Click! Once again he was in bed. It was a real bed this time. He looked around. The place had the unmistakable air of a sanitarium or hospital.

Oh, well. Park rolled over and went to sleep.

The next day he was still in the same place. He began to have hopes. Then he remembered that, as the transitions happened at midnight, he had no reason for assuming that the next one would not happen the following midnight.

He spent a very boring day. A physician came in, asked him how he was, and was gone almost before Park could say "Fine." People brought him his meals. If he'd been sure he was going to linger, he'd have made vigorous efforts to orient himself and to get out. But as it was, there didn't' seem any point.

The next morning he was still in bed. But when he tried to rub his eyes and sit up, he found that his wrists and ankles were firmly tied to the four posts. This wasn't the same bed, nor the same room; it looked like a room in somebody's private house.

And at the foot of the bed sat the somebody; a small gray-haired man with piercing black eyes that gleamed over a sharp nose.

For a few seconds Allister Park and the man looked at each other. Then the man's expression underwent a sudden and alarming change, as if internal pain had gripped him. He stared at his own clothes as if he had never seen them before. He screamed, jumped up, and dashed out of the room. Park heard his feet clattering down stairs, and the slam of a front door; then nothing.

Allister Park tried pulling at his bonds, but the harder he pulled, the tighter they gripped. So he tried not pulling which brought no results either.

He listened. There was a faint hiss and purr of traffic outside. He must be still in a city, though, it seemed, a fairly quiet one.

A stair creaked. Park held his breath. Somebody was coming up, and without unnecessary noise. More than one man, Park thought, listening to the creaks.

Somebody stumbled. From far below a voice called up a question that Park couldn't catch. There was several quick steps and the smack of a fist.

The door of Park's room was ajar. Through the crack appeared a vertical strip of face, including an eye. The eye looked at Park and Park looked at the eye.

The door jerked open and three men pounced into the room. They wore floppy trousers and loose blouses that might have come out of a Russian ballet. They had large, flat, pentagonal faces, red-brown skins and straight black hair. They peered behind the door and under the bed.

"What the hell?" asked Allister Park.

The largest of the three men looked at him. "You're not hurt, Hallow?"

"No. But I'm damn sick of being tied up."

The largest man's face showed a flicker of surprise. The large man cut Park's lashings. Park sat up, rubbing his wrists, and learned that he was wearing a suit of coarse woolen underwear.

"Where's the rascally Noggle?" asked the large brown man. Although he rolled his r's like a Scot, he did not look like a Scot. Park thought he might be an Asiatic or an American Indian.

"You mean the little gray-haired bird?"

"Sure. You know, the scoundrel." He pronounced the "k" in "know."

"Suppose I do. When I woke up he was in that chair. He looked at me and beat it out of here as if all the bats of Hell were after him."

"Maybe he's gone daft. But the weighty thing is to get you out." One of the men got a suit out of the closet, resembling the three men's clothes, but somber gray.

Allister Park dressed. The tenseness of the men made him hurry, though he didn't take all this very seriously yet.

Working his feet into the elastic-sided shoes with the big metal buckles, Park asked: "How long have I been here?"

"You dropped from the ken of a man a week ago today," replied the large man with a keen look.

A week ago today he had been Allister Park, assistant district attorney. The next day he hadn't been. It was probably not a mere coincidence.

He started to take a look at his new self in the mirror. Before he could do more than glimpse a week's growth of beard, two of the men were gently pulling his arms toward the door. There was something deferential about their urgency. Park went along. He asked: "What do I do now?"

"That takes a bit of thinking on," said the large man. "It might not be safe for you to go home. Shh!" He stole dramatically down the stairs ahead of them. "Of course," he continued, "you could put in a warrant against Joseph Noggle."

"What good would that do?"

"Not much, I fear. If Noggle was put up to this by MacSvensson, you can be sure the lazy knicks wouldn't find him."

Park had more questions, but he didn't want to give himself away any sooner than he had to.

The house was old, decorated in a curious geometrical style, full of hexagons and spirals. On the ground floor sat another brown man in a rocking chair. In one hand he held a thing like an automobile grease-gun, with a pistol grip. Across the room sat another man, with a black eye, looking apprehensively at the gun-thing.

The one in the chair got up, took off his bonnet, and made a bow toward Park. He said: "Haw, Hallow. Were you hurt?"

"He'll live over it, glory be to Patrick," said the big one, whom the others addressed as "Sachem." This person now glowered at the man with the black eye. "Nay alarums, understand? Or—" he drew the tip of his forefinger in a quick circle on the crown of his head. It dawned on Park that he was outlining the part of the scalp that an Indian might remove as a trophy.

They went quickly out, glancing up and down the street. It was early morning; few people were visible. Park's four companions surrounded him in a way that suggested that, much as they respected him, he had better not make a break.

The sidewalk had a wood-block paving. At the curb stood a well-streamlined automobile. The engine seemed to be in the rear. From the size of the closed-in section, Park guessed it to be huge.

They got in. The instrument board had more knobs and dials than a transport plane. The Sachem started the car noiselessly. Another car blew a resonant whistle, and passed them wagging a huge tail of water-vapor. Park grasped the fact that the cars were steam-powered. Hence the smooth, silent operation; hence also the bulky engine and the complex controls.

The buildings were large but low; Park saw none over eight or ten stories. The traffic-signals had semaphore arms with "STAI" and "COM" on them.

"Where are you taking me?" asked Park.

"Outside the burg bounds, first," said the Sachem. "Then we'll think on the next."

Park wondered what was up; they were still respectful as all Hell, but there was something ominous about their haste to get outside the "burg bounds," which Park took to be the city limits. He said, experimentally, "I'm half starved."

A couple of brown men echoed these sentiments, so the Sachem presently stopped the car at a restaurant. Park looked around it; except for that odd geometric style of decoration, it was much like other restaurants the world over.

"What's the program?" he asked the Sachem. Park had known some heavy drinkers in his time, but never one who washed his breakfast pancakes down with whiskey, as the large brown man was now doing.

"That'll be seen," said the Sachem. "What did Noggle try to do to you?"

"Never did find out."

"There's been an under talk about the swapping of minds. I wonder if—where are you going?"

"Be right back," said Park, heading for the men's room. In another minute the Sachem would have cornered him on the question of identity. They watched him go. Once in the men's room, he climbed onto a sink, opened a window, and squirmed out into the adjacent alley. He put several blocks between himself and his convoyers before he slowed down.

His pockets failed to tell him whose body he had. His only mark of identification was a large gold ring with a Celtic cross. He had a few coins in one pocket, wherewith he bought a newspaper.

Careful searching disclosed the following item:

BISJAP STILL MISSING

At a laet aur jestrdai nee toocan had ben faund of yi mising Bisjap Ib Scoglund of yi Niu Belfast Bisjapric of yi Celtic Cristjan Tjortj, hwuuz vanisjing a wiik agoo haz sterd yi borg. Cnicts sai yai aar leeving nee steen ontornd in yaeir straif tu faind yi hwarabouts of yi mising preetjr, hwuuz losti swink on bihaaf of yi Screlingz haz bimikst him in a furs yingli scofal . . .

It looked to Park as though some German or Norwegian had tried to spell English—or what passed for English in this city—phonetically according to the rules of his own language, with a little Middle English or Anglo-Saxon thrown in. He made a tentative translation:

BISHOP STILL MISSING

At a late hour yesterday no token (sign?) had been found of the missing Bishop Ib Scoglund of the New Belfast Bishopric of the Celtic Christian Church, whose vanishing a week ago has stirred the burg (city?). Cnicts (police?) say they are leaving no stone unturned in their strife (effort?) to find the whereabouts of the missing preacher . . .

It sounded like him, all right. What a hell of a name, Ib Scoglund! The next step was to find where he lived. If they had telephones, they ought to have telephone directories . . .

Half an hour later Park approached the bishop's house. If he were going to change again at midnight, the thing to do would be to find some quiet place, relax, and await the change. However, he felt that the events of the week made a pattern, of which he thought he could see the beginnings of an outline. If his guesses were right, he had arrived at his destination.

The air was moderately warm and a bit sticky, as New York City air might well be in April. A woman passed him, leading a floppy-eared dog. She was stout and fiftyish. Although Park did not think that a skirt that cleared her knees by six inches became her, that was what was being worn.

As he turned the corner onto what ought to be his block, he sighted a knot of people in front of a house. Two men in funny steeple-crowned hats sat in an open car. They were dressed alike, and Park guessed they were policemen.

Park pulled his bonnet—a thing like a Breton peasant's hat—over one side of his face. He walked past on the opposite side of the street, looking unconcerned. The people were watching No. 64, his number.

There was an alley on one side of the house. Park walked to the next corner, crossed, and started back toward No. 64. He had almost reached the entrance to the alley when one of the men spotted him. With a cry of "There's the bishop himself!" the men on the sidewalk—there were four—ran toward him. The men in the funny hats got out of their vehicle and followed.

Park squared his shoulders. He had faced down wardheelers who invaded his apartment to tell him to lay off certain people, or else. However, far from being hostile, these shouted: "Wher-r-re ya been Halloy?" "Were you kidnapped?" "Ja lose your recall?" "How about a wording?" All produced pads and pencils.

Park felt at home. He asked: "Who's it for?"

One of the men said: "I'm from the *Sooth*."

"The what?"

"The *New Belfast Sooth*. We've been upholding you on the Skrelling question."

Park looked serious. "I've been investigating conditions."

The men looked puzzled. Park added: "You know, looking into things."

"Oh," said the man from the *Sooth*. "Peering the kilters, eh?"

The men in the funny hats arrived. One of the pair asked: "Any wrongdoings, Bishop? Want to mark in a slur?"

Park, fumbling through the mazes of this dialect, figured that he meant "file a complaint." He said: "No, I'm all right. Thanks anyway."

"But," cried the hat, "are you *sure* you don't want to mark in a slur? We'll take you to the lair if you do."

"No, thank you," said Park. The hats sidled up to him, one on either side. In the friendliest manner they took his arms and gently urged him toward the car, saying: "Sure you want to mark in a slur. We was sent special to get you so you could. If somebody kidnapped you, you must, or it's helping wrongdoing, you know. It's just a little way to the lair—"

Park had been doing some quick thinking. They had an ulterior reason for wanting to get him to the "lair" (presumably a police-station); but manhandling a bishop, especially in the presence of reporters, just wasn't done. He wrenched loose and jumped into the doorway of No. 64. He snapped: "I haven't got any slurs, and I'm not going to your lair, get me?"

"Aw, but Hallow, we wasn't going to hurt you. Only if you have a slur, you have to mark it in. That's the law, see?" The man, his voice a pleading whine, came closer and reached for Park's sleeve. Park cocked a fist, saying: "If you want me for anything, you can get a warrant. Otherwise the *Sooth*'ll have a story about how you tried to kidnap the bishop, and how he knocked the living bejesus out of you!" The reporters made encouraging noises.

The hats gave up and got back in their car. With some remark about ". . . he'll sure give us hell," they departed.

Park pulled the little handle on the door. Something went *bong, bong* inside. The reporters crowded around, asking questions. Park, trying to look the way a bishop should, held up a hand. "I'm very tired, gentlemen, but I'll have a statement for you in a few days."

They were still pestering him when the door opened. Inside, a small monkey-like fellow opened his mouth. "Hallow Colman keep us from harm!" he cried.

"I'm sure he will," said Park gravely, stepping in. "How about some food?"

"Surely, surely," said Monkey-face. "But—but what on earth has your hallowship been doing? I've been fair sick with worry."

"Peering the kilters, old boy, peering the kilters." Park followed Monkey-face upstairs, as if he had intended going that way of his own accord. Monkey-face doddered into a bedroom and busied himself with getting out clean clothes.

Park looked at a mirror. He was—as he had been throughout his metamorphoses—a stocky man with thinning light hair, in his middle thirties. While he was not Allister Park, neither was he very different from him.

The reddish stubble on his face would have to come off. In the bathroom Park found no razor. He stumbled on a contraption that might be an electric razor. He pushed the switch experimentally, and dropped the thing with a yell. It had bitten a piece out of his thumb. Holding the injured member, Park cut loose with the condemnatory vocabulary that ten years of work among New York City's criminal class had given him.

Monkey-face stood in the doorway, eyes big. Park stopped his swearing long enough to rasp: "Damn your lousy little soul, don't stand there! Get me a bandage!"

The little man obeyed. He applied the bandage as though he expected Park to begin the practice of cannibalism on him at any moment.

"What's the matter?" said Park. "I won't bite you!"

Monkey-face looked up. "Begging pardon, your hallowship, but I thock you wouldn't allow the swearing of aiths in your presence. And now such frickful aiths I never did hear."

"Oh," said Park. He remembered the penetrating look the Sachem had given his mild damns and hells. Naturally a bishop would not use such language—at least not where he could be overheard.

"You'd better finish my shave," he said.

Monkey-face still looked uneasy. "Begging your forgiveness again, Hallow, but what makes you talk such a queer speech?"

"Canker sore," growled Park.

Shaved, he felt better. He bent a kindly look on Monkey-face. "Listen," he said, "your bishop has been consorting with low uncouth persons for the past week. So don't mind it if I fall into their way of speaking. Only don't tell anybody, see? Sorry I jumped on you just now. D'you accept my apology?"

"Yes—yes, of course, Hallow."

"All right, then. How about that famous breakfast?"

After breakfast he took his newspaper and the pile of mail into the bishop's well-equipped library. He looked up "Screling" in the "Wörd-buk" or dictionary. A "Screling" was defined as one of the aboriginal inhabitants of Vinland.

"Vinland" stirred a faint chord; something he'd learned in school. The atlas contained a map of North America. A large area in the north and east thereof, bounded on the west and south by an irregular line running roughly from Charleston to Winnipeg, was labeled the Bretwaldate of Vinland. The remaining two-thirds of the continent comprised half a dozen political areas, with such names as Dacoosja, Tjeroogia, Aztecia. Park, referring back to the dictionary, derived these from Dakota, Cherokee, Aztec, etcetera.

In a couple of hours telephone calls began coming in. Monkey-face, according to his instructions, told one and all that the bishop was resting up and couldn't be disturbed. Park meanwhile located a pack of pipes in the library, and a can of tobacco. He got out several pads of paper and sharpened a dozen pencils.

Monkey-face announced lunch. Park told him to bring it in. He announced dinner. Park told him to bring it in. He announced bed-time. Park told him to go soak his head. He went, clucking. He had never seen a man work with such a fury of concentration for so long at a stretch, let alone his master. But then, he had never seen Allister Park reviewing the evidence for a big criminal case.

History, according to the encyclopedia, was much the same as Park remembered it down to the Dark Ages. Tracing down the point at which the divergence took place, he located the fact that King Oswiu of Northumbria had decided in favor of the Celtic Christian Church at the Synod of Whitby, 644 A.D. Park had never heard of the Synod or of King Oswiu. But the encyclopedia ascribed to this decision the rapid spread of the Celtic form of Christianity over Great Britain and Scandinavia. Hence it seemed to Park that probably, in the history of the world *he* had come from, the king had decided the other way.

The Roman Christian Church had held most of its ground in northern Europe for a century more. But the fate of its influence there had been sealed by the defeat of the Franks by the Arabs at Tours. The Arabs had occupied all southern Gaul before they were finally stopped, and according to the atlas they were still there. The Pope and the Lombard duchies of Italy had at once placed themselves under the protection of the Byzantine emperor Leo the Iconoclast. (A Greek-speaking "Roman" Empire still occupied Anatolia and the Balkans, under a Serbian dynasty.)

A Danish king of England named Gorm had brought both the British Isles and Scandinavia under his rule, as Knut had done in Park's world. But Gorm's kingdom proved more durable than Knut's; the connection between England and Scandinavia had survived, despite intervals of disunion and civil war, down to the present. North America was discovered by one Ketil Ingolfsson in 989 A.D. Enough Norse, English, and Irish colonists had migrated thither during the Eleventh Century to found a permanent colony, from which the Bretwaldate of Vinland had grown. Their language, while descended from Anglo-Saxon, naturally contained fewer words of Latin and French origin than Park's English.

The Indians—"Screlingz" or Skrellings—had not proved a pushover, as the colonists had neither the gunpowder nor the numbers that the whites of Park's history had had. By the time the whites had reached the present boundaries of Vinland, expelling or enslaving the Skrellings as they went, the remaining natives had acquired enough knowledge of ferrous metallurgy and organized warfare to hold their own. Those that remained in Vinland were no longer slaves, but were still a suppressed class suffering legal and economic disabilities. He, Bishop Ib Scoglund, was a crusader for the removal of these disabilities. ("Hallow" was simply a respectful epithet, meaning about the same as "Reverend.")

An Italian named Caravello had invented the steam engine about 1790, and the Industrial Revolution had followed as a matter of course . . .

It was the following morning, when Park, having caught the three hours of sleep that sufficed for him when necessary, was back at the books, that Monkey-face (right name: Eric Dunedin) came timidly in. He coughed deferentially. "The pigeon came with a writing from Thane Callahan."

Park frowned up from his mountain of printed matter. "Who? Never mind; let's see it." He took the note. It read (spelling conventionalized):

> Dear Hallow: Why in the name of the Blood Witnesses of Belfast did you run away from us yesterday? The papers say you have gone back home; isn't that risky? Must have a meeting with you forthwith; shall be at Bridget's Beach this noon, waiting. Respectfully, RC

Park asked Dunedin: "Tell me, is Callahan a tall heavy guy who looks like an In—a Skrelling?"

Dunedin looked at him oddly. By this time Park was getting pretty well used to being looked at oddly. Dunedin said: "But he *is* a Skrelling, Hallow; the Sachem of all the Skrellings of Vinland."

"Hm. So he'll meet me at this beach—why the devil can't he come here?"

"Ooooh, but Hallow, bethink what happened to him the last time the New Belfast knicks caught him!"

Whatever that was, Park reckoned he owed the Sachem something for the rescue from the clutches of the mysterious Mr. Noggle. The note didn't sound like one from a would-be abductor to his escaped prey. But just in case, Park went out to the modest episcopal automobile (Dunedin called it a "wain") and put a wrench in his pocket. He told Dunedin: "You'll have to drive this thing; my thumb's still sore."

It took a few minutes to get steam up. As they rolled out of the driveway, a car parked across the street started up too. Park got a glimpse of the men therein. While they were in civilian clothes, as he was, they had a grim plainclothesman look about them.

After three blocks the other car was still behind them. Park ordered Dunedin to go around the block. The other car followed.

Park asked: "Can you shake those guys?"

"I—I don't know, your hallowship. I'm not very good at fast driving."

"Slide over then. How in hell do you run this thing?"

"You mean you don't know—"

"Never mind!" roared Park. "Where's the accelerator or throttle or whatever you call it?"

"Oh, the strangle. There." Dunedin pointed a frankly terrified finger. "And the brake—"

The wain jumped ahead with a rush. Park spun it around a couple of corners, getting the feel of the wheel. The mirror showed the other car still following. Park opened the "strangle" and whisked around the next corner. No sooner had he straightened out than he threw the car into another dizzy turn. The tires screeched and Dunedin yelped as they shot into an alleyway. The pursuers whizzed by without seeing them.

An egg-bald man in shirtsleeves popped out of a door in the alley. "Hi," he said, "this ain't no hitching place." He looked at Park's left front fender, clucking. "Looks like you took off some paint."

Park smiled. "I was just looking for a room, and I saw your sign. How much are you asking?"

"Forty-five a month."

Park made a show of writing this down. He asked: "What's the address, please?"

"One twenty-five Isleif."

"Thanks. I'll be back, maybe." Park backed out, with a scrape of fender against stone, and asked Dunedin directions. Dunedin, gray of face, gave them. Park looked at him and chuckled. "Nothing to be scared of, old boy. I knew I had a good two inches clearance on both sides."

* * *

The Sachem awaited Park in the shade of the bathhouse. He swept off his bonnet with a theatrical flourish. "Haw, Hallow! A fair day for our tryst." Park reflected that on a dull day you could smell Rufus Callahan's breath almost as far as you could see Rufus Callahan. He continued: "The west end's best for talk. I have a local knick watching in case Greenfield sends a prowler. Did they follow you out?"

Park told him, meanwhile wondering how to handle the interview so as to make it yield the most information. They passed the end of the bath-house, and Allister Park checked his stride. The beach was covered with naked men and women. Not *quite* naked; each had a gaily colored belt of elastic webbing around his or her middle. Just that. Park resumed his walk with Callahan's amused look.

Callahan said: "If the head knick, Lewis, weren't a friend of mine, I shouldn't be here. If I ever did get pulled up—well, the judges are all MacSvensson's men, just as Greenfield is." Park remembered that Offa Greenfield was mayor of New Belfast. Callahan continued: "While MacSvensson's away, the pushing eases a little."

"When's he due back?" asked Park.

"In a week maybe." Callahan waved an arm toward distant New Belfast. "What a fair burg, and what a wretched wick to rule it! How do you like it?"

"Why, I live there, don't I?"

Callahan chuckled. "Wonderful, my dear Hallow, wonderful. In another week nobody'll know you aren't his hallowship at all."

"Meaning what?"

"Oh, you needn't look at me with that wooden face. You're nay mair Bishop Scoglund than I am."

"Yeah?" said Park noncommittally. He lit one of the bishop's pipes.

"How about a jinn?" asked Callahan.

Park looked at him, until the Sachem got out a cigarette.

Park lit it for him, silently conceding one to the opposition. How was he to know that a jinn was a match? He asked: "Suppose I was hit on the head?"

The big Skrelling grinned broadly. "That mick spoil your recall, in spots, but it wouldn't give you that frickful word-tone you were using when we befreed you. I see you've gotten rid of most of it, by the way. How did you do that in thirty-some hours?"

Park gave up. The man might be just a slightly drunken Indian with a conspiratorial manner, but he had the goods on Allister. He explained: "I found a bunch of records of some of my sermons, and played them over and over on the machine."

"My, my, you are a cool one! Joe Noggle mick have done worse when he picked your mind to swap with the bishop's. Who are you, in sooth? Or perhaps I should say who *were* you?"

Park puffed placidly. "I'll exchange information, but I won't give it away."

When Callahan agreed to tell Park all he wanted to know, Park told his story. Callahan looked thoughtful. He said: "I'm nay brain-wizard, but they do say there's a theory that every time the history of the world hinges on some decision, there are two worlds, one that which would happen if the card fell one way, the other that which would follow fro the other.''

"Which is the *real* one?''

"That I can't tell you. But they do say Noggle can swap minds with his thocks, and I don't doubt it's swapping between one of these possible worlds and another they mean.''

He went on to tell Park of the bishop's efforts to emancipate the Skrellings, in the teeth of the opposition of the ruling Diamond Party. This party's strength was mainly among the rural squirearchy of the west and south, but it also controlled New Belfast through the local boss, Ivor MacSvensson. If Scoglund's amendment to the Bretwaldate's constitution went through at the next session of the national Thing, as seemed likely if the Ruby Party ousted the Diamonds at the forthcoming election, the squirearchy might revolt. The independent Skrelling nations of the west and south had been threatening intervention on behalf of their abused minority. (That sounded familiar to Park, except that, if he took what he had read and heard at its face value, the minority really had something to kick about this time.) The Diamonds wouldn't mind a war, because in that case the elections, which they expected to lose, would be called off . . .

"You're not listening, Thane Park, or should I say Hallow Scoglund?''

"Nice little number,'' said Park, nodding toward a pretty blonde girl on the beach.

Callahan clucked. "Such a wording from a strict wedless!''

"What?''

"You're a pillar of the church, aren't you?''

"Oh, my Lord!'' Park hadn't thought of that angle. The Celtic Christian Church, despite its libertarian tradition, was strict on the one subject of sex.

"Anyhow,'' said Callahan, "what shall we do with you? For you're bound to arouse mistrust.''

Park felt the wrench in his pocket. *I* want to get *back.* Got a whole career going to smash in my own world.''

"Unless the fellow who's running your body knows what to do with it.''

"Not much chance.'' Park could visualize Frenczko or Burt frantically calling his apartment to learn why he didn't appear; the unintelligible answers they would get from the bewildered inhabitant of his body; the cops screaming up in the struggle-buggy to cart the said body off to Belleview; the headline: "PROSECUTOR BREAKS DOWN.'' So they yanked me here as a bit of dirty politics, eh? I'll get back, but meantime I'll show 'em some *real* politics!

Callahan continued: "The only man who could unswap you is Joseph Noggle, and he's in his own daffy-bin.''

"Huh?''

"They found him wandering about, clean daft. It's a good deed you didn't put in a slur against him; they'd have stripped you in court in nay time.''

"Maybe that's what they wanted to do.''

"That's an idea! That's why they were so anxious for you to go to the lair. I don't doubt they'll be watching for to pull you up on some little charge; it won't matter whether you're guilty or not. Once they get hold of you, you're headed for Noggle's inn. What a way to get rid of the awkward bishop without pipe or knife!''

When Callahan had departed with another flourish, Park looked for the girl. She had gone too. The day was blistering, and the water inviting. Since you didn't need a bathing-suit to swim in Vinland, why not try it?

Park returned to the bath-house and rented a locker. He stowed his clothes, and looked at himself in the nearest mirror. The bishop didn't take half enough exercise, he thought, looking at the waistline. He'd soon fix *that*. No excuse for a man's getting out of shape that way.

He strolled out, feeling a bit exposed with his white skin among all these bronzed people, but not showing it in his well-disciplined face. A few stared. Maybe it was his whiteness; maybe they thought they recognized the bishop. He plunged in and headed out. He swam like a porpoise, but shortness of breath soon reminded him that the bishop's body wasn't up to Allister Park's standards. He cut loose with a few casual curses, since there was nobody to overhear, and swam back.

As he dripped out onto the sand, a policeman approached, thundering: "You! You're under stoppage!"

"What for?"

"Shameful outputting!"

"But look at those!" protested Park, waving at the other bathers.

"That's just it! Come along, now!"

Park went, forgetting his anger in concern as to the best method of avoiding trouble. If the judges were MacSvensson men, and MacSvensson was out to expose him . . . He dressed under the cop's eagle eye, thanking his stars he'd had the foresight to wear nonclerical clothes.

The cop ordered: "Give your name and address to the bookholder."

"Allister Park, 125 Isleif Street, New Belfast."

The clerk filled out a blank; the cop added a few lines to it. Park and the cop went and sat down for a while, waiting. Park watched the legal procedure of this little court keenly.

The clerk called: "Thane Park!" and handed the form up to the judge. The cop went over and whispered to the judge. The judge said: "All women will kindly leave the courtroom!" There were only three; they went out.

"Allister Park," said the judge, "you are marked with shameful outputting. How do you plead?"

"I don't understand this, your honor—I mean your aerness," said Park. "I wasn't doing anything the other people on the beach weren't."

The judge frowned. "Knick Woodson says you afterthockly exposed—uh—" The judge looked embarrassed. "You afterthockly output your—uh—" He lowered his voice. "Your navel," he hissed. The judge blushed.

"Is that considered indecent?"

"Don't try to be funny. It's not in good taste. I ask you again, how do you plead?"

Park hesitated a second. "Do you recognize the plea of *non vult?*"

"What's that? Latin? We don't use Latin here."

"Well then—a plea that I didn't mean any harm, and am throwing myself on the mercy of the court."

"Oh, you mean a plea of good will. That's not usually used in a freerighter's court, but I don't see why you can't. What's your excuse?"

"You see, your honor, I've been living out in Dakotia for many years, and I've rather gotten out of civilized habits. But I'll catch on quickly enough. If you want a character reference, my friend Ivor MacSvensson will give me one."

The judge's eyebrows went up, like a buzzard hoisting its wings for the take-off. "You ken Thane MacSvensson?"

"Oh, sure?"

"Hrrrmph. Well. He's out of town. But—uh—if that's so, I'm sure you're a good burger. I hereby sentence you to ten days in jail, sentence withheld until I can check your mooding, and thereafter on your good acting. You are free."

Like a good thane's thane, Eric Dunedin kept his curiosity to himself. This became a really heroic task when he was sent out to buy a bottle of soluble hairdye, a false mustache, and a pair of phoney spectacles with flat glass panes in them.

There was no doubt about it; the boss was a changed man since his reappearance. He had raised Dunedin's salary, and except for occasional outbursts of choler treated him very considerately. The weird accent had largely disappeared; but this hard, inscrutable man wasn't the bishop Dunedin had known . . .

Park presented himself in his disguise to the renting agent at 125 Isleif. He said: "Remember me? I was here this morning asking about a room." The man said sure he remembered him; he never forgot a face. Park rented a small two-room apartment, calling himself Allister Park. Later in the evening he took some books, a folder of etchings, and a couple of suitcases full of clothes over. When he returned to the bishop's house he found another car with a couple of large watchful men waiting at the curb. Rather than risk contact with a hostile authority, he went back to his new apartment and read. Around midnight he dropped in at a small hash-house for a cup of coffee. In fifteen minutes he was calling the waitress "sweetie-pie." The etchings worked like a charm.

Dunedin looked out the window and announced: "Two wains and five knicks, Hallow. The twoth wain drew up just now. The men in it look as if they'd eat their own mothers without salt."

Park thought. He had to get out somehow. He had looked into the subject of search warrants, illegal entry, and so forth, as practiced in the Bretwaldate of Vinland, and was reasonably sure the detectives wouldn't invade his house. The laws of Vinland gave what Park thought was an impractically exaggerated sanctity to a man's home, but he was glad of that as things were. However, if he stepped out, the pack would be all over him with charges of drunken driving, conspiracy to violate the tobacco tax, and anything else they could think of.

He telephoned the "knicks' branch," or police department, and spoke falsetto: "Are you the knicks? Glory be to Patrick and Bridget! I'm Wife Caroline Chisholm, at 79 Mercia, and we have a crazy man running up and down the halls naked with an ax. Sure he's killed my poor husband already; spattered his brains all over the hall he did, and I'm locked in my room and looking for him to break in any time." Park stamped on the floor, and continued: "Eeek! That's the monster now, trying to break the door down. Oh, hurry, I pray. He's shouting that he's going to chop me in little bits and feed me to his cat! . . . Yes, 79 Mercia. Eeeee! Save me!"

He hung up and went back to the window. In five minutes, as he expected, the gongs of the police wains sounded, and three of the vehicles skidded around the corner and stopped in front of No. 79, down the block. Funny hats tumbled out like oranges from a burst paper bag, and raced up the front steps with guns and ropes enough to handle Gargantua. The five who had been watching the house got out of their cars too and ran down the block.

Allister Park lit his pipe, and strode briskly out the front door, down the street away from the disturbance, and around the corner.

Park was announced, as Bishop Scoglund, to Dr. Edwy Borup. The head of the Psychophysical Institute was a smallish, bald, snaggly-toothed man, who smiled with an uneasy cordiality.

Park smiled back. "Wonderful work you've been doing, Dr. Borup." After handing out a few more vague compliments, he got down to business. "I understand that poor Dr. Noggle is now one of your patients?"

"Umm—uh—yes, Reverend Hallow. He is. Uh—his lusty working seems to have brock on a brainly breakdown."

Park sighed. "The good Lord will see him through, let us hope. I wonder if I could see him? I had some small kenning of him before his trouble. He once told me he'd like my spiritual guidance, when he got around to it."

"Well—umm—I'm not sure it would be wise—in his kilter—"

"Oh, come now, Dr. Borup, surely thocks of hicker things would be good for him . . ."

The sharp-nosed, gray-haired man who had been Joseph Noggle sat morosely in his room, hardly bothering to look up when Park entered.

"Well, my friend," said Park, "what have they been doing to you?"

"Nothing," said the man. His voice had a nervous edge. "That's the trouble. Every day I'm a different man in a different sanitarium. Each day they tell me that two days previously I got violent and tried to poke somebody in the nose. *I* haven't poked *nobody* in the nose. Why in God's name don't they *do* something? Sure, I know I'm crazy. I'll cooperate, if they'll *do* something."

"There, there," said Park. "The good Lord watches over all of us. By the way, what were you before your trouble started?"

"I taught singing."

Park thought several "frickful aiths." If a singing-teacher, or somebody equally incompetent for his kind of work, were in his body now . . .

He lit a pipe and talked soothingly and inconsequentially to the man, who though not in a pleasant mood, was too grateful for a bit of company to discourage him. Finally he got what he was waiting for. A husky male nurse came in to take the patient's temperature and tell Park that his time was up.

Park hung around, on one excuse or another, until the nurse had finished. Then he followed the nurse out and grasped his arm.

"What is it, Hallow?" asked the nurse.

"Are you poor Noggle's regular attendant?"

"Yes."

"Got any kinfolk, or people you like specially, in the priesthood?"

"Yes, there's my Aunt Thyra. She's a nun at the New Lindisfarne Abbey."

"Like to see her advanced?"

"Why—I guess so; yes. She's always been pretty good to me."

"All right. Here's what you do. Can you get out, or send somebody out, to telephone Noggle's condition to me every morning before noon?"

The nurse guessed he could. "All right," snapped Park. "And it won't do anybody any good if anybody knows you're doing it, understand?" He realized that his public-prosecutor manner was creeping back on him. He smiled benignly. "The Lord will bless you, my son."

Park telephoned Dunedin; asked him to learn the name of somebody who dwelt on the top floor of the apartment-house next door, and to collect one ladder, thirty feet of rope, and one brick. He made him call back the name of the top-floor tenant. "But Hallow, what in the name of Patrick do you want a brick for . . ."

Park, chuckling, told him he'd learn. When he got off the folk-wain at Mercia Street, he didn't walk boldly up to his own house. He entered the apartment-house next door and said he was calling on Mrs. Figgis, his clericals constituting adequate credentials. When the elevator-man let him out on the top floor, he simply climbed to the roof and whistled for Monkey-face. He directed Dunedin in the tieing of the end of the rope to the brick, the heaving thereof to the roof of the apartment-house, and the planting of the ladder to bridge the ten-foot gap. After that it was a simple matter for Park to lower himself to his own roof, without being intercepted by the watch-dogs in front of his house.

As soon as he got in, the 'phone rang. A sweetness-and-light voice at the other end said: "This is Cooley, Hallow. Every time I've called your man has said you were out or else that you couldn't be bothered!"

"That's right," said Park. "I was."

"Yes? Anyway, we're all giving praises to the Lord that you were spared."

"That's fine," said Park.

"It surely is a wonderful case of how His love watches over us—"

"What's on your mind, Cooley?" said Park, sternly repressing a snarl of impatience.

"Oh—uh—what I meant was, will you give your usual sermon next Sunday?"

Park thought quickly. If he could give a sermon and get away with it, it ought to discourage the people who were trying to prove the bishop loony. "Sure I will. Where are you calling from?"

"Why—uh—the vestry." Some damned assistant, thought Park. "But, Hallow, won't you come up tonight? I'm getting some of the parishioners together in the chapel for a homish thanksgiving stint—with hymns of—"

"I'm afraid not," said Park. "Give 'em my love anyway. There goes my doorbell. 'Bye."

He marched into the library, muttering. Dunedin asked: "What is it, Hallow?"

"Gotta prepare a goddam sermon," said Park, taking some small pleasure at his thane's thane's expression of horror.

Fortunately the bishop was an orderly man. There were manuscripts of all his sermons for the past five years, and phonograph records (in the form of magnetized wire) of several. There was also plenty of information about the order of procedure in a Celtic Christian service. Park set about concocting a sermon out of fragments and paragraphs of those the bishop had delivered during the past year, playing the spools of wire over and over to learn the bishop's inflections. He wished he had some way of getting the bishop's gestures, too.

He was still at it next day when he dimly heard his doorbell. He thought nothing of it, trusting Dunedin to turn the visitor away, until Monkey-face came in and announced that a pair of knicks awaited without.

Park jumped up. "Did you let 'em in?"

"No, Hallow, I thought—"

"Good boy! I'll take care of 'em."

The larger of the two cops smiled disarmingly. "Can we come in, Hallow, to use your wiretalker?"

"Nope," said Park. "Sorry."

The knick frowned. "In that case we gotta come in anyway. Mistrust of unlawful owning of pipe." He put his foot in the door-crack.

A pipe, Park knew, was a gun. He turned and stamped on the toe of the shoe, hard; then slammed the door shut as the foot was jerked back. There were some seconds of "frickful aiths" wafting through the door, then the pounding of a fist against it.

"Get a warrant!" Park yelled through the door. The noise subsided. Park called Dunedin and told him to lock the other entrances. Presently the knicks departed. Park's inference, based upon what he had been able to learn of Vinland law, that they would not force an entrance without a warrant, had proved correct. However, they would be back, and there is nothing especially difficult about "finding" an illegal weapon in a man's house, whether he had one before or not.

So Park packed a suitcase, climbed to the roof of the adjoining apartment, and went down the elevator. The elevator man looked at him in a marked manner. Once in the street, he made sure nobody was looking, and slapped on his mustache and glasses. He pulled his bonnet well down to hide his undyed hair, and walked over to Allister Park's place. There he telephoned Dunedin, and directed him to call the city editors of all the pro-bishop newspapers and tip them off that an attempt to frame the bishop impended. He told Dunedin to let the reporters in when they came; the more the better. Preferably there should be at least one in every room. Now, he thought, let those flatfeet try to sneak a gun into one of my bureau drawers so they can "find" it and raise a stink.

He spent the night at the apartment, and the next day, having gotten his sermon in shape, he paid a visit to his church. He found a functionary of some sort in an office, and told him that he, Allister Park, was considering getting married in St. Columbanus', and would the functionary (a Th. Morgan) please show him around? Th. Morgan was pleased to; Dr. Cooley usually did that job, but he was out this afternoon. Park looked sharply through his phoney spectacles, memorizing the geography of the place. He wished now he'd passed up the sermon for one more week, and had instead attended next Sunday's service as Allister Park, so that he could see how the thing was done. But it was too late now. Morgan broke in on his thoughts: "There's Dr. Cooley now, Thane Park; wouldn't you like to meet him?"

"Ulp," said Park. "Sorry; got to see a man. Thanks a lot." Before the startled cleric could protest, Park was making for the door as fast as he could go without breaking into a run. The plump rosy young man in pince-nez, whom Park saw out of the corner of his eye, must be Cooley. Park had no intention of submitting his rather thin disguise to his assistant's inspection.

He telephoned the bishop's home. The other people in the lunch-room were startled by the roar of laughter that came through the glass of his telephone booth as Dunedin described the two unhappy cops trying to plant a gun in his house under the noses of a dozen hostile wise-cracking reporters. Monkey-face added: "I—I took the freedom, your hallowship, of finding out that two of the newsers live right near here. If the knicks try that again, and these newsers are at home, we could wirecall them over."

"You're learning fast, old boy," said Park. "Guess I can come home now."

It was Saturday when Dunedin answered a call from the Psychophysical Institute. He cocked an eye upward, whence came a series of irregular whams as if trunks were being tossed downstairs. "Yes," he said, "I'll get him." As he wheezed upstairs, the whams gave way to a quick, muffled drumming. If anything were needed to convince him that something drastic had happened to his master's mind, the installation and regular use of a horizontal bar and a punching-bag in a disused room was it.

Park, in a pair of sweat-soaked shorts, turned his pale eyes. Good old Monkey-face. Park, who treated subordinates with great consideration, never told Dunedin what he thought he looked like.

"It's the man at the Psychophysical Institute," announced Dunedin.

The male nurse announced that, for a change, Joseph Noggle was claiming to be Joseph Noggle.

Park grabbed his bonnet and drove the steamer over. Borup asked: "But, my dear, dear Hallow, why must you—uh—see this one patient? There are plenty mair who could use your ghostly guidance.''

Fool amateur, thought Park. If he doesn't want me to know why he wants to keep Noggle locked up, why doesn't he say he's violent or something? This way he's giving away his whole game. But aloud he gave a few smooth, pious excuses, and got in to see his man.

The original, authentic Noggle had a quick, nervous manner. It didn't take him more than a minute to catch on to who Park-Scoglund was.

"Look here," he said. "Look here. I've got to get out. I've got to get at my books and onmarkings. If I don't get out now, while I'm in my own body, I shan't be able to stop this damned merry-go-round for another six days!''

"You mean, my son, that you occupy your own body every six days? What happens the rest of the time?''

"The rest of the time I'm going around the wheel, indwelling ane after another of the bodies of the other men on my wheel. And the minds of these other men are following me around likewise. So every ane of the six bodies has each of our six minds in it in turn every six days.''

"I see." Park smiled benignly. "And what's this wheel you talk about?''

"I call it my wheel of if. Each of the other five men on it are the men I should most likely have been *if* certain things had been otherwise. For instance, the man in whose body my mind dwelt yesterday was the man I should most likely have been if King Egbert had fallen off his horse in 1781.''

Park didn't stop to inquire about King Egbert or the sad results of his poor equestrianism. He asked softly: "How did your wheel get started in the first place?''

"It was when I tried to stop yours! Law of keeping of psychic momentum, you know. I got careless, and the momentum of your wheel was overchanged to mine. So I've been going around ever since. Now look here, whatever your name is, I've got to get out of here, or I'll never get stopped. I ordered them to let me out this morning, but all they'd say was that they'd see about it tomorrow. Tomorrow my body'll be occupied by some other wheel-mate, and they'll say I'm crazy again. Borup won't let me go anyway if he can help it; he likes my job. But you've got to use your inflowing as bishop—''

"Oh," said Park silkily, "I've got to use my influence, eh? Just one more question. Are we all on wheels? And how many of these possible worlds are there?''

"Yes, we're all on wheels. The usual number of rooms on a wheel is fourteen—that's the number on yours—though it sometimes varies. The number of worlds is infinite, or almost, so that the chances that anybody on my wheel would be living in the same world as anybody on yours is pretty small. But that's not weightful. The weightful thing is to get me out so—''

"Ah yes, that's the weightful thing, isn't it? But suppose you tell me why you started my wheel in the first place?''

"It was just a forseeking in the mental control of wheels."

"You're lying," said Park softly.

"Oh, I'm lying, am I? Well then, reckon out your own reason."

"I'm sorry that you take this attitude, my son. How can I help you if you won't put your trust in me and in God?"

"Oh, come on, don't play-act. You're not the bishop, and you know it."

"Ah, but I *was* a churchman in my former being." Park fairly oozed holiness. "That's not odd, is it? Since I was the man the bishop would most likely have been if King Oswiu had chosen for the Romans, and the Arabs had lost the battle of Tours."

"You'd hold yourself bound by professional confidence?"

Park looked shocked. "What a thock! Of course I would."

"All right. I'm something of a sportsman, you know. About a month ago I got badly pinched by the ponies, and I—ah—borrowed a little heading on my pay from the Institute's funds. Of course I'd have paid it back; it was really quite an honest deed. But I had to make a few little—ah—rightings in the books, because otherwise one who didn't understand the conditions might have drawn the wrong thocks from them.

"Ivor MacSvensson somehow found out, and threatened to put me in jail if I didn't use my mental powers to start your wheel of if going until it had made a half-turn, and then stop it. With another man's mind in the bishop's body, it ought to be easy to prove the bishop daft; in any event his inflowing would be destroyed. But as you know, it didn't work out quite that way. You seemingly aren't in anybody's custody. So you'll have to do something to get me out."

Park leaned forward and fixed Noggle with the bishop's fish-pale eyes. He said harshly: "You know, Noggle, I admire you. For a guy who robs his hospital, and then to get out of it goes and starts fourteen men's minds spinning around, ruining their lives and maybe driving some of them crazy or to self-killing, you have more gall than a barn-rat. You sit there and tell me, one of your victims, that I'll have to do something to get you out. Why, damn your lousy little soul, if you ever *do* get out I'll give you a case of lumps that'll make you think somebody dropped a mountain on you!"

Noggle paled a bit. "Then—then you weren't a churchman in your own world?"

"Hell, no! My business was putting lice like you in jail. And I still ock to be able to do that here, with what you so kindly told me just now."

Noggle swallowed as this sank in. "But—you promised—"

Park laughed unpleasantly. "Sure I did. I never let a little thing like a promise to a crock keep me awake nights."

"But you want to get back, don't you? And I'm the only one who can send you back, and you'll have to get me out of here before I can do anything—"

"There is that," said Park thoughtfully. "But I don't know. Maybe I'll like it here when I get used to it. I can always have the fun of coming around here every sixth day and giving you the horse-laugh."

"You're—a devil!"

Park laughed again. "Thanks. You thought you'd get some poor bewildered dimwit in Scoglund's body, didn't you? Well, you'll learn just how wrong you were." He stood up. "I'll let you stay here a while more as Dr. Borup's prize looney. Maybe when you've been taken down a peg we can talk business. Meanwhile, you might form a club with those other five guys on your wheel. You could leave notes around for each other to find. So long, Dr. Svengali!"

Ten minutes later Park was in Borup's office, with a bland episcopal smile on his face. He asked Borup, apropos of nothing in particular, a lot of questions about the rules involving commitment and release of inmates.

"Nay," said Edwy Borup firmly. "We could—uh—parole a patient in your care only if he were rick most of the time. Those that are wrong most of the time, like poor Dr. Noggle, have to stay here."

It was all very definite. But Park had known lots of people who were just as definite until pressure was brought to bear on them from the right quarter.

The nearer the Sunday service came, the colder became Allister Park's feet. Which, for such an aggressive, self-confident man, was peculiar. But when he thought of all the little details, the kneeling and getting up again, the facing this way and that. . . . He telephoned Cooley at the cathedral. He had, he said, a cold, and would Cooley handle everything but the sermon? "Surely, Hallow, surely. The Lord will see to it that you're fully restored soon, I hope. I'll say a special prayer for you . . ."

It was also time, Park thought, to take Monkey-face into his confidence. He told him all, whereat Dunedin's eyes grew very large. "Now, old boy," said Park briskly, "if you ever want to get your master back into his own body, you'll have to help me out. For instance, here's that damned sermon. I'm going to read it, and you'll correct my pronunciation and gestures."

Sunday afternoon, Park returned wearily to the bishop's house. The sermon had gone off easily enough; but then he'd had to greet hundreds of people he didn't know, as if they were old friends. And he'd had to parry scores of questions about his absence. He had, he thought, earned a drink.

"A highball?" asked Dunedin. "What's that?"

Park explained. Dunedin looked positively shocked. "But Thane P—I mean Hallow, isn't it bad for your insides to drink such cold stuff?"

"Never mind my insides! I'll—hullo, who's that?"

Dunedin answered the doorbell, and reported that a Th. Figgis wanted to see the bishop. Park said to show him in. There was something familiar about that name. The man himself was tall, angular, and grim-looking. As soon as Dunedin had gone, he leaned forward and hissed dramatically: "I've got you now, Bishop Scoglund! What are you going to do about it?"

"What am I going to do about *what?*"

"My wife!"

"What about your wife?"

"You know well enough. You went up to my rooms last Tuesday, while I was away, and came down again Wednesday."

"Don't be an ass," said Park. "I've never been in your rooms in my life, and I've never met your wife."

"Oh, yes? Don't try to fool me, you wolf in priest's clothing! I've got witnesses. By God, I'll fix you, you seducer!"

"Oh, that!" Park grinned, and explained his ladder-and-rope procedure.

"Think I believe that?" sneered Figgis. "If you weren't a priest I'd challenge you and cut your liver out and eat it. As it is, I can make things so hot for you—"

"Now, now," interrupted Park. "Be reasonable. I'm sure we can come to an understanding—"

"Trying to bribe me, huh?"

"I wouldn't put it just that way."

"So you think you can buy my honor, do you? Well, what's your offer?"

Park sighed. "I thought so. Just another goddam blackmailer. Get out, louse!"

"But aren't you going to—"

Park jumped up, spun Figgis around, and marched him toward the door. "Out, I said! If you think you can get away with spreading your little scandal around, go to it. You'll learn that you aren't the only one who knows things about other people." Figgis tried to wriggle loose. Park kicked him into submission, and sent him staggering down the front steps with a final shove.

Dunedin looked awedly at this formidable creature into which his master had been metamorphosed. "Do you really know something to keep him quiet, Hallow?"

"Nope. But my experience is that most men of his age have something they'd rather not have known. Anyway, you've got to take a strong line with these blackmailers, or they'll raise no end of hell. Of course, my son, *we* hope the good Lord will show our erring brother the folly of his sinful ways, don't we?" Park winked.

Being a bishop entailed much more than putting on a one-hour performance at the cathedral every Sunday, as Park soon learned. But he transacted as much of his episcopal business as he could at home, and put the rest onto Cooley. He didn't yet feel that his impersonation was good enough to submit to close-range examination by his swarm of subordinates.

While he was planning his next step, an accident unexpectedly opened the way for him. He had just settled himself in the Isleif Street apartment the evening of Tuesday, April 26th, when a young man rang his doorbell. It took about six seconds to diagnose the young man as a fledgling lawyer getting a start on a political career as a precinct worker.

"No." said Park, "I won't sign your petition to nominate Thane Hammer, because I don't know him. I've just moved here from Dakotia. But I'd like to come around to the clubhouse and meet the boys."

The young man glowed. "Why don't you? There's a meeting of the precinct workers tomorrow night, and voters are always welcome . . ."

The clubhouse walls were covered with phoney Viking shields and weapons. "Who's he?" Park asked his young lawyer through the haze of smoke. "He" was a florid man to whom several were paying obsequious attention.

"That's Trigvy Darling, Brahtz's parasite." Park caught a note of dislike, and added it to the new card in his mental index file. Brahtz was a Diamond thingman from a western province, the leader of the squirearchy. In this somewhat naive culture, a gentleman had to demonstrate his financial standing by supporting a flock of idle friends, or deputy gentlemen. The name of the parasite was not merely accurate, but was accepted by these hangers-on without any feeling of derogation.

Through the haze wove an unpleasantly familiar angular figure. Park's grip on the edge of the table automatically tightened. "Haw, Morrow," said Figgis, and looked at Park. "Haven't I met you somewhere?"

"Maybe," said Park. "Ever live in Dakotia?"

Morrow, the young lawyer, introduced Park as Park. Park fervently hoped his disguise was thick enough. Figgis acknowledged the introduction, but continued to shoot uneasy little glances at Park. "I could swear—" he said. Just then the meeting was called. Although it would have driven a lot of people to suicide from boredom, Park enjoyed the interplay of personalities, the quick fencing with parliamentary rules by various factions. These rules differed from those he was used to, being derived from those of the ancient Icelandic Thing instead of the English Parliament. But the idea was the same. The local members wanted to throw a party for the voters of the hide (district). A well-knit minority led by the parasite Darling wanted to save the money for contribution to the national war-chest.

Park waited until the question was just about to be put to a vote, then snapped his fingers for the chairman's attention. The chairman, an elderly dodderer, recognized him.

"My friends," said Park, lurching to his feet, "of course I don't know that I really ock to say anything, being just a new incomer from the wilds of Dakotia. But I've always voted Diamond, and so did my father, and his father before him, and so on back as far as there *was* any Diamond Party. So I think I can claim as solid a party membership as some folks who live in New Belfast three months out of the year, and spend the rest of their time upholding the monetary repute of certain honorable country thanes." Park, with satisfaction, saw Darling jerk his tomato-colored face around, and heard a few snickers. "Though," he continued, "taking the healthy skin you get from country life, I don't know but what I envy such people." (More snickers.) "Now it seems to me that . . ."

Twenty minutes later the party had been voted: Park was the chairman (since he alone seemed really anxious to assume responsibility); and Trigvy Darling, at whose expense Park had acquired a frothy popularity by his jibes, had turned from vermillion to magenta.

After the meeting, Park found himself in a group of people including the chairman and Figgis. Figgis was saying something about that scoundrel Scoglund, when his eye caught Park's. He grinned his slightly sepulchral grin. "I know now why I thock I'd meet you! You remind me of the bishop!"

"Know him?"

"I met him once. Say, Dutt," (this was to the aged chairman) "what date's set for your withdrawal?"

"Next meeting," quavered the ancient one. "Ah, here is our crown prince, heh, heh!" Darling, his face back to normal tomato-color, advanced. "Do you ken Thane Park?"

"I ken him well enough," growled Darling with the look of one who has found a cockroach in his ice cream. "It seems to me, Thane Dutt, that part of a chairman's duty is to stop use of personalities on the part of speakers."

"You can always plead point of personal privilege, heh, heh."

Darling did something in his throat that was not quite articulate speech. Figgis murmured: "He knows the boys would laugh him down if he tried it."

"Yeah?" said Darling. "We'll see about that when I'm chairman." He stalked off.

Park wasted no time in exploiting his new job. Knowing that Ivor MacSvensson was due back in New Belfast the next day, he went around—as Allister Park—to the law office used by the boss as a front for his activities. The boss was already in, but the outer office was jammed with favor-seekers. Park, instead of preparing to spend the morning awaiting his turn, bribed the office boy to tell him when and where MacSvensson ate his lunch. Then he went to the nearby public library—movies not having been invented in this world—and took his ease until one o'clock.

Unfortunately, Ivor MacSvensson failed to show up at the restaurant indicated, though Park stretched one tunafish lunch out for half an hour. Park cursed the lying office-boy. Plain bribery he was hardened to, but he really became indignant when the bribee failed to deliver. So he set about it the hard way. A nearby knick gave him the locations of the five highest-priced restaurants in the neighborhood, and in the third he found his man. He recognized him from the pictures he had studied before starting his search—a big, good-looking fellow with cold blue eyes and prematurely white hair.

Park marched right up. "Haw, Thane MacSvensson. Bethink you me?"

MacSvensson looked puzzled for a fraction of a second, but he said smoothly: "Sure, of course I bethink me of you. Your name is—uh—"

"Allister Park, chairman of the amusement committee of the Tenth Hide," Park rattled off. "I only met you recently, just before you left."

"Sure, of course. I'd know you anywhere—let's see, Judge Vidolf of Bridget's Beach wirecalled me this morning; wanted to know if I kenned you. Told him I'd call him back." He gripped Park's hand. "Come on, sit down. Sure, of course, any good party worker is a friend of mine. What's the Tenth Hide doing?"

Park told of the party. MacSvensson whistled. "Saturday the thirtieth? That's the day after tomorrow."

"I can manage it," said Park. "Maybe you could tell me where I could pick up some sober bartenders."

"Sure, of course." Under Park's deferential prodding, the boss gave him all the information he needed. MacSvensson finished with the quick, vigorous handshake cultivated by people who have to shake thousands of hands and who don't want to develop a case of greeter's cramp. He urged Park to come around and see him again. "Especially after that fellow Darling gets the chairmanship of your committee."

Park went, grinning a little to himself. He knew just what sort of impression he had made, and could guess how the boss was reacting to it. He'd be glad to get a vigorous, aggressive worker in the organization; at the same time he'd want to keep a close watch on him to see that *his* power wasn't undermined.

Park congratulated himself on having arrived in a world where the political set-up had a recognizable likeness to that of his own. In an absolute monarchy, for instance, he'd have a hell of a time learning the particular brand of intrigue necessary to become a king's favorite. As it was . . .

The Bridget's Beach knicks stood glowering at a safe distance from the throng of picknickers. Although they were anti-MacSvensson, the judges were pro, so what could they do about it if the party violated the ordnances regarding use of the beach? Since Park's fellow-committeemen were by now too sodden with beer to do anything at all, Park was dashing around, clad in a pair of tennis-shoes and the absurd particolored belt that constituted the Vinland bathing-suit, running everything himself. Everybody seemed to be having a good time—party workers, the more influential of the voters and their families, everybody but a morose knot of Darling & followers at one end.

Near this knot a group of anti-Darlings was setting up a song:

"Trig Darling, he has a foul temper;
   "Trig Darling's as red as can be;
"Oh, nobody here loves Trig Darling,
   "Throw Trigvy out into the sea!
   "Throw—Trig.
   "Throw—Trig,
   "Throw Trigvy out into the sea!"

Park hurried up to shush them. Things were going fine, and he didn't want a fight—yet, at any rate. But his efforts were lost in the next stanza:

"Trig Darling, he has a pot-bellee;
   "Trig Darling's as mean as can be . . ."

At that moment, apparently, a giant hit Allister Park over the head with a *Sequoia sempervirens*. He reeled a few steps, shook the tears out of his eyes, and faced Trigvy Darling, advancing with large fists cocked.

"Hey," said Park, "this isn't—" He brought up his own fists. But Darling, instead of trying to hit him again, faced him for three seconds and then spat at him.

Park glanced at the drop of saliva trickling down his chest. So did everyone else. One of Darling's friends asked: "Do you make that a challenge, Trig?"

"Yes!" boomed the parasite.

Park didn't really catch on to what was coming until he was surrounded by his own party. He and Darling were pushed together until their bare chests were a foot apart. Somebody called the knicks over; these stationed themselves around the couple. Somebody else produced a long leather belt, which he fastened around the middles of both men at once, so they could not move farther apart. Darling, his red face expressionless, grabbed Park's right wrist with his left hand, and held out his own right forearm, evidently expecting Park to do the same.

It was not until a big sheath-knife was pressed into each man's right hand that Park knew he was in a duel. Somehow he had missed this phase of Vinland custom in his reading.

Park wondered frantically whether his mustache would come off in the struggle. One knick stepped up and said: "You know the rules: no kicking, biting, butting, or scratching. Penalty for a foul is one free stab. Ready?"

"Yes," said Darling. "Yes," said Park, with more confidence than he felt.

"Go," said the policeman.

Park felt an instant surge of his opponent's muscles. Darling had plenty of these under the fat. If he'd only had longer to train the bishop's body . . . Darling wrenched his wrist loose from Park's grip, threw a leg around one of Park's to trip him, and brought his fist down in a lightning overhand stab.

It was too successful. Park's leg went out from under him and he landed with a thump on his back, dragging Darling down on top of him. Darling drove his knife up to the hilt in the sand. When he jerked it up for another stab, Park miraculously caught his wrist again. A heave, and Darling toppled onto the sand beside him. For seconds they strained and panted, a tangle of limbs.

Park, his heart laboring and sand in his eyes, wrenched his own knife-arm free. But when he stabbed at Darling, the parasite parried with a curious twisting motion of his left arm, and gathered Park's arm into a bone-crushing grip. Park in agony heaved himself to his knees, pulling Darling up too. They faced each other on their knees, the belt still around them. Darling wrenched his knife-arm loose again, whipped it around as for a backhand stab, then back for an overhand. Park, trying to follow the darting blade, felt as if something had exploded in his own left arm. Darling's point was driven into it and into the bone. Before it had a chance to bleed, Darling tried to pull it out. It didn't yield the first pull. Park leaned forward suddenly. Darling unwound his left arm from Park's right to catch himself as he swayed backwards. Park stabbed at him. Darling blocked the stab with his forearm, making Park feel as if his wrist was broken. He played his last improvised trick: tossed up the knife, caught it the other way to, and brought it around in a quick up-and-out thrust. To his surprise, Darling failed to block it at all—the blade slid up under the parasite's ribs to the hilt. Park, warm blood running over his hand, twisted and sliced his way across Darling's abdomen . . .

Trigvy Darling lay on his back, mouth open and sand in his sightless eyeballs. The spectators looked in awe at the ten-inch wound. Park, feeling a bit shaken, stood while they bandaged his arm. The knicks gravely took down the vital information about the dead man, filling the last line in the blank with: "Killed in fair fight with Allister Park, 125 Isleif St., N.B."

Then people were shaking his hand, slapping his bare back, and babbling congratulations at him. "Had it coming to him . . ." ". . . never liked him anyway, only we had to take him on account of Brahtz . . ." "You'll make a better chairman . . ."

Park stole a hand to his upper lip. His mustache was a little loose on one side, but a quick press fixed that. He gradually became aware that the duel, so far from spoiling the party, had made a howling success of it.

Leading a double life is a strenuous business at best. It is particularly difficult when both one's identities are fairly prominent people. Nevertheless, Allister Park managed it, with single-minded determination to let nothing stop his getting the person of Joseph Noggle in such a position that he could make him give his, Park's, wheel of if another half-spin. It might not be too late, even if the Antonini case was washed up, to rehabilitate himself.

His next step was to cultivate Ivor MacSvensson, burg committee chairman for the Diamond Party of the Burg of New Belfast. This was easy enough, as the chairman of the hide committee was ex-officio a member of the burg committee.

They were dining in one of the small but expensive restaurants for which MacSvensson had a weakness. The burg chairman said: "We'll have to get Anlaff off, that's all there is to it. Those dim knicks should have known better than to pull him in it in the first place."

Park looked at the ceiling. "Even if it was Penda's daughter?"

"Even if it was Penda's daughter."

"After all, spoiling the morals of a ten-year-old—"

"I know, I know," said MacSvensson impatiently. "I know he's a dirty bastard. But what can I do? He's got the twenty-sixth hide in his fist, so I've got to play cards with him. Especially with the thingly choosing coming up in three months. It'll be close, even with Bishop Scoglund lying low the way he has been. I had a little plan for shushing the dear bishop; it didn't work, but it seems to have scared him into keeping quiet about the ricks of the Skrellings. And the Thing meeting next month . . . If that damned equal-ricks changelet goes through, it'll split the party wide open."

"If it doesn't?" asked Park.

"That'll be all right."

"How about the Dakotians and the rest?"

MacSvensson shrugged. "No trouble for fifty years. They talk a lot, but I never saw a Skrelling that would stand up and fick yet. And what if they did try a war?

New Belfast is a long way from the border; and the choosing would be called off. Maybe by the time it was over people would get some sense.''

Park had his own ideas. His researches had told him something about the unprepared state of the country. New Belfast had hundreds of miles between it and the independent Skrellings; in case of a sea attack, they could count on the friendly Northumbrian fleet, one of the world's largest, to come over and help out. Hence the New Belfast machine had consistently plugged for more money for harbor improvements and merchant-marine subsidies and less for military purposes. . . . However, if the Northumbrian fleet were immobilized by the threat of the navy of the Amirate of Cordova, and the Skrellings overran the hinterland of Vinland . . .

MacSvensson was speaking: ''. . . you know, the youngest daughter of mine, she wants to marry a *schoolteacher?* Craziest idea . . . And that boy of mine has the house full of his musical friends; at least that's what he calls 'em. They'll play their flugelhorns and yell and stamp all night.''

''Why not come up to my place?'' asked Park with the studied nonchalance of an experienced dry-fly fisherman making a cast.

''Sure, of course. Glad to. I've got three appointments, thinging, but hell with 'em.''

There was no doubt about it; Ivor MacSvensson was good company even if he did have a deplorable scale of moral values. Park, having made the necessary soundings, finally suggested getting some company. The chairman's blue eyes lit up a bit; there was some lechery in the old war-horse yet. Park telephoned his little waitress friend. Yes, she had a friend who was just *dying* to meet some big political pipes . . .

Many residents of New Belfast were wont to say of Ivor MacSvensson: ''He may be a serpent (crook), but at least leads a spotless home life.'' MacSvensson was at pains to encourage this legend, however insubstantial its basis. These people would have been pained to see the boss an hour later, smeared with lipstick, bouncing Park's friend's friend on his knee. The friend's friend was undressed to a degree that would have shocked Vinlanders anywhere but on a beach.

''Stuffy, isn't it?'' said Park, and got up to open a window. The unsuspecting MacSvensson was having too good a time to notice Park thrust his arm out the window and wag it briefly.

Five minutes later the doorbell rang. By the time MacSvensson had snapped out of his happy daze, Park had admitted a small, wrinkled man who pointed at the friend's friend and cried: ''Fleda!''

''Oswald!'' shrieked the girl.

''Sir!'' shouted Dunedin at the boss, ''what have you been doing with my wife? What have you been doing with my wife?''

''Oh,'' sobbed Fleda, ''I didn't mean to be unfaithful! Truly I didn't! If I'd only thought of you before it was too late . . .''

''Huh?'' mumbled MacSvensson. ''Too late? Unfaithful? Your wife?''

''Yes, you snake, you scoundrel, you bastard, my wife! You'll suffer for this, Boss MacSvensson! Just wait till I—''

"Here, here my man!" said Park, taking Dunedin by the arm and pulling him into the vestibule. For ten minutes the boss listened in sweaty apprehension to Park's and Dunedin's voices, rising and falling, the former soothing, the latter strained with rage. Finally the door slammed.

Park came back, and said: "I got him to promise not to put in any slurs or tell any newspapers for a while, until we talk things over again. I know who he is, and I *think* I can squelch him through the company he works for. I'm not sure that'll work, though. He's mad as a wet hen; won't believe that this was just an innocent get-together."

The imperturbable boss looked badly shaken. "You've got to stop him, Al! The story would raise merry hell. If you can do it, you can have just about anything I can give you."

"How about the secretaryship of the burg committee?" asked Park promptly.

"Surely, of course. I can find something else for Ethelbald to do. Only keep that man shut up!"

"All right, old boy. Right now you'd better get home as soon as you can."

When MacSvensson had been gone a few minutes, Eric Dunedin's ugly face appeared in the doorway. "All clear, Hal—I mean Thane Park?"

"Come on in, old boy. That was a neat piece of work. You did well, too, Fleda. Both you girls did. And now—" Park started to drive a corkscrew into another cork, "we can have a *real* party!"

"Damn it, Dunedin," said Park, "when I say put your breakfast down on the table and eat it, I mean it!"

"But Hallow, it simply isn't done for a thane's thane to eat with his master—"

"To hell with what's done and what isn't. I've got more for you to do than stand around and treat me as if I were God Almighty. We've got work, brother. Now get busy on that mail."

Dunedin sighed and gave up. When Park chose to, he could by now put on what Dunedin admitted was a nearly perfect imitation of Bishop Scoglund. But unless there were somebody present to be impressed thereby, he chose instead to be his profane and domineering self.

Dunedin frowned over one letter, and said: "Thane Callahan wants to know why you haven't been doing anything to push the glick-ricks changelet."

Park mentally translated the last to "equal-rights amendment." "Why should I? It isn't my baby. Oh, well, tell him I've been too busy, but I'll get around to it soon. That's always the stock excuse."

Dunedin whistled suddenly. "The kin of the late Trigvy Darling have filed a wergild claim of a hundred and fifty thousand crowns against you."

"What? What? Let's see that! . . . What's that all about? Have they got the right to sue me, when I killed him in self-defense?"

"Oh, but of course, Hallow. There's nay criminal penalty for killing a man in fair fight. But his heirs can claim two years' earnings from you. Didn't you know that when you took up his challenge?"

"Good lord, no! What can I do about it?"

"Oh, deary me, glory be to Patrick. You can try to prove the claim too big, as this one may be. I don't know, though; Darling got a big stipend from Brahtz as a parasite."

"I can always withdraw Allister Park from circulation and be just the bishop. Then let 'em try to collect!"

It would be wearisome to follow Allister Park's political activities in detail for the three weeks after his use of the badger-game on MacSvensson. But lest his extraordinary rise to power seem improbable, consider that it was not until the 1920's in Park's original world that a certain Josef Vissarianovitch Dzugashvili, better known as Joseph Stalin, discovered what could really be done with the executive secretaryship of a political committee. So it is not too surprising that, whereas Park knew what could be done with his office, the politicians of Vinland did not. They learned. Among other things, the secretary makes up the agenda of meetings. He puts motions in "proper" form, since a motion is seldom intelligible in the form in which it is presented from the floor. He prompts the chairman—the nominal head of the organization—on parliamentary procedure. He is the interim executive officer; wherefore all appointments go through his hands, and he has custody of all records. He is ex-officio member of all committees. Since a committee seldom has any clear idea of what it wants to do or how it wants to do it, an aggressive secretary can usually run as many committees as he has time for. Whereas the chairman can't speak at meetings, the secretary can not only speak but speak last. He gets the gavel when an appeal is made from the chair . . .

At least, that is how it is done in *this* world. In Vinland, the rules were not quite the same, but the similarity was close enough for Park's purpose—which was still to get back to good old New York and that judgeship, if there was still any chance of getting it.

It was after the burg committee meeting on the first of June that Park faced Ivor MacSvensson in the latter's office. Park intended to start needling the boss about the body of Joseph Noggle. But MacSvensson got there first, demanding: "What's all this about your making up to the committeemen?"

"What's that?" asked Park blandly. "I've being seeing them on routine duties only."

"Yeah? Not according to what I've been told. And I've found out that that girl you had up for me wasn't wedded at all. Trying to put one down on the boss, eh? Well, you can go back to hide-walking. You'll call a special committee-meeting for Friday night. Get those seeings out today without fail. That's all."

"Suits me," grinned Park. The chairman can demand special meetings, but the secretary's the man who sends out the notices.

When Friday evening arrived, two-thirds of the seats in the committee-room in Karlsefni Hall remained empty. MacSvensson, blue eyes glacial, fretted. Park, sending out thunder-heads of smoke from the bishop's largest pipe, lolled in a chair, glancing surreptitiously at his watch. If MacSvensson were down at the far end of the hall when the hand touched sixty, Park would simply arise and say:

"In the absence of the chairman, and of any other officers authorized to act as such, I, Allister Park, acting as chairman, hereby call this meeting to order . . ."

But MacSvensson, looking at him, divined his intention. He snatched out his own watch, and dashed to the chair. He made it by one and a half seconds.

Park was not disturbed. He took his place, hearing the boss's growl: "Did you send out all those seeings when I told you to, Park? There's just barely a quorum here."

"Absolutely. I can't help it if they go astray in the mail." Park neglected to add that, with the proper cooperation from a postal clerk, it is sometimes possible to make sure that certain of the notices, though duly postmarked as of the time they are received, are accidentally misplaced in the post office and completely overlooked until the day after the meeting.

"The meeting will kindly come to order," snapped MacSvensson. He did not like the look of the quorum at all; not one of his tried and true friends was in sight, except Sleepy Ethelbald.

He continued: "This is a special meeting called to hold in mind the good and welfare of the committee. As such there will be no reading of the minutes. The meeting will now consider items for the agenda."

MacSvensson caught the eye of Sleepy Ethelbald, who had been primed for just this occasion. Before Ethelbald could rouse himself, another committeeman popped up with: "I move that we take up the fitness of Chairman MacSvensson to last in his present office." "Twothed." "I move the agenda be closed." "Twothed."

MacSvensson sat up for a few seconds with his mouth open. He had had revolts before—plenty of them—but never one with the devastating speed and coordination of this. He finally mumbled: "All in favor—"

"Aye!" roared most of the quorum.

MacSvensson ran fingers through his hair, then squared his shoulders. He wasn't licked yet, by any means. There were more tricks . . . "The meeting will now consider the first item on the agenda."

"I move the impeachment of Chairman MacSvensson!" "Twothed!"

For the second time the chairman sat with his mouth open. Park said gently: "You take up the motion and give me the gravel."

"But—" wailed MacSvensson.

"No buts. A motion to impeach the chairman self-movingly shifts the gavel to the secretary. Come on, old boy."

An hour later Ivor MacSvensson stalked out, beaten. Park could have had the chairmanship himself, but he astutely preferred to keep the secretaryship and put the ancient of days, Magnus Dutt, in that exposed position.

Mayor Offa Greenfield knew his own mind, such as it was. He banged his fist on his desk, making all his chins quiver. "Nay!" he shouted. "I don't know what you're up to, Allister Park, but by the right ear of Hallow Gall, it's something! The freedom of a free people—"

"Now, now, we're not talking about the freedom of a free people. I'm sure we agree on that matter. It's just a question of the person of Joseph Noggle—"

"I won't be dictated to! I won't take orders from anybody!"

"Except Ivor MacSvensson?"

"Except Iv—nay! I said anybody! Go practice your snaky trick on somebody else, Allister Park; you'll get nothing from me! I won't interfere with Borup's running of his Institute. Unless, of course" (Greenfield lowered his voice to normal), "you can get MacSvensson to back you up."

Greenfield, it seemed, had the one virtue of loyalty. He intended to stick by the fallen boss to the bitter end, even though nearly all the rest of MacSvensson's staunch supporters had deserted him when the effectiveness of Park's coup had become patent.

But Greenfield was not elected, as were the members of the burg thing. He was appointed by a committee of the Althing, the national legislative body. So Park, for all his local power, could not displace Greenfield at the coming elections by putting up a rival candidate. He could only do it by acquiring sufficient power in the Althing. He set himself to study how to do this.

New Belfast elected six members to the Althing. As the city was firmly Diamond, nomination implied election. Therefore the six thing-men, however much they bragged about their independence in public, were careful to obey the whims of the boss of New Belfast.

The repeated efforts of Yon Brahtz to impose his control on the New Belfast Diamonds, by planting stooges like the late Trigvy Darling in their hide committees, had aroused some resentment. Park decided that he could trust his most active supporters, and the six thingmen, to back him in a gigantic double-cross: to desert the Diamond Party altogether and join the Rubies. The goats would be, not merely Brahtz and his squirearchy, but the local Ruby politicians of New Belfast. However, as these had never accomplished anything but draw some patronage from the Althing in the periods when the Rubies were in power there, Park thought he would not find much resistance to their sacrifice on the part of the Ruby leaders. And so it proved.

Twenty men, though, seldom keep a secret for long. The morning of June 9th, Park opened his paper to find the report of a defiant speech by Yon Brahtz, in which he announced bluntly that "the thanes of the Cherogian March of Vinland will defend the ricks they inherited from their heroic forebears, by any means needful, and moreover the means for such defense are ready and waiting!" Park translated this to mean that if the Scoglund amendment were passed by a coalition of Rubies and insurgent New Belfast Diamonds, the squirearchy would secede.

But that would mean civil war, which in turn would mean postponement of the elections. What was even more serious, the Diamond thingmen from the seceding provinces would automatically lose their seats, giving the Rubies a clear majority. Since the Rubies would no longer need the support of Park's insurgents, they would be disinclined to make a deal with him to appoint a mayor of his choice.

Park privately thought that, while in theory he supposed he believed in the Scoglund amendment, in practice both his and the Ruby leaders' interests would be better served by dropping it for the present, despite the growls of the Dakotians and Cherogians. However, the Ruby leaders were firm; that huge block of Skrelling votes they would get by emancipating the aborigines was worth almost any risk.

As for such questions as the rights of the Skrellings as human beings, or the unfortunate Vinlanders who would be killed or haggled up in a civil war, they were not considered at all.

Park, holed up in the Isleif Street apartment with a couple of bodyguards, answered a call from Dunedin. "Haw, Hallow? Thane Callahan is here to see you."

"Send him over here. Warn him ahead of time who I—" Park remembered the guards, and amended: "warn him about everything. You know."

Lord, he thought, all this just to get hold of Noggle, still shut up in the Psychophysical Institute! Maybe it would have been simpler to organize a private army like Brahtz's and storm that fortress-like structure. A long-distance call for the mobilization of his Sons of the Vikings, as he called his storm-troopers. Kedrick, the Bretwald of Vinland, had refused to mobilize the army because, he explained, such an action would be "provocative." . . . Maybe he secretly favored the squirearchy, whose man he was; maybe he was just a pacific civilian who found the whole subject of soldiers, guns, and such horrid things too repulsive to discuss; maybe he really believed what he said . . .

Callahan arrived with a flourish. Since MacSvensson was no longer boss of New Belfast, the Sachem went openly about the city without fear of arrest and beating-up by the police.

He told Park: "It would be worth my life if some of my fellow-Skrellings knew I'd told you. But the Dakotians have an army secretly assembled on the bounds. If the Vinlanders start fickting among themselves, the Dakotians'll jump in to grab the northwestern provinces."

Park whistled. "How about the Cherogians?"

"They're holding back, waiting to see how things are turning out. If the war seems to be fruitbearing, they'll try a little rickting of the bounds themselves."

"And what will your Skrellings do then?"

"That depends. If the Scotland changelet is lost, they'll join the foe to a man. If it goes through, I think I can hold most of them in line."

"Why do you tell me this, Callahan?"

The Sachem grinned his large disarming grin. "Two reasons. First, the bishop and I have been friends for years, and I'll stick to his body no matter where his soul may be. Twoth, I'm not fooled, as some of my Skrellings are, by talk of what fine things the Dakotians'll do for us if we help them overthrow the palefaces. The Dakotian realm is even less a folkish one than the Bretwaldate's. I know a thing or two about how they treat their ain folk. So if you'll stick to me, I'll stick to you."

Park would have liked to appear at the opening of the Althing as Bishop Scoglund. But, as too many people there knew him as Allister Park, he attended in his mustache, hair-dye, and spectacles.

The atmosphere was electric. Even Park, with all his acumen, had been unable to keep up with events. The risks were huge, whichever way he threw his insurgents' votes.

He kept them shut up in a committee-room with him until the last possible minute. He did not yet know himself whether he would order them to vote for or against the amendment.

The clock on the wall ticked around.

A boy came in with a message for Park. It said, in effect, that the Sons of the Vikings had received a report that the amendment had already been passed, had mobilized and seized the town of Olafsburg.

Who had sent that mistaken message and why, there was no way of finding out. But it was too late for anybody to back down. Park looked up and said, very seriously: "We're voting for the Scoglund Amendment." That was all; with his well-trained cogs no more was necessary.

The bell rang; they filed out. Park took his seat in the visitor's gallery. He said nothing but thought furiously as the session of the Althing was opened with the usual formalities. The chairman and the speaker and the chaplain took an interminable time about their business, as if afraid to come to grips with the fearful reality awaiting their attention.

When the first motions came up, a dead silence fell as Park's men got up and walked over to the Rubies' side of the house. Then the Rubies let out a yell of triumph. There was no more need of stalling or delicate angling for marginal votes. Motion after motion went through with a roar. Out went the Diamond chairman and speaker, and in went Rubies in their place.

In an hour the debate had been shut off, despite howls from Diamonds and their sympathizers about "gag law" and "high-handed procedure."

The amendment came up for its first vote. It fell short of the two-thirds required by eleven votes.

Park scribbled a note and had it delivered to the speaker. The speaker handed it to the chairman. Park watched the little white note drift around the Ruby side of the house. Then the Ruby leader got up and solemnly moved the suspension of thingmen Adamson, Arduser, Beurwulf, Dahl, Fessenden, Gilpatrick, Holmquist . . . all the thingmen from the seceding area.

Most of those named didn't wait; they rose and filed out, presumably to catch airwains for their home provinces.

The amendment passed on the second vote.

Park looked up the Ruby leader after the Althing adjourned. He said: "I hear Kedrick still won't order motion. Talks about 'Letting the erring brethren go in peace.' What's your party line on the matter?"

The Ruby leader, a thin cool man, blew smoke through his nose. "We're going to fight. If Kedrick won't go along, there are ways. The same applies to *you*, Thane Park."

Park suddenly realized that events had put him in a suspect position. If he didn't want himself and his cogs to be damned as copperheads, or the Vinland equivalent, he'd have to outshout the Rubies for unity, down with the rebels, etcetera.

Well, he might as well do a good job of it.

That afternoon the guards at the Psychophysical Institute were astonished to have their sanctuary invaded by a squad of uniformed knicks with the notorious Allister Park at their head flourishing a searchwarrant. The charge was violation of the fire-ordinances—in a building made almost entirely of tile, glass, and reinforced concrete.

"But, but, but!" stuttered Dr. Edwy Borup. Park merely whisked out another warrant, this time for the arrest of Joseph Noggle.

"But, but, you can't stop one of my patients! It's—uh—illegal! I'll call Mayor Greenfield!"

"Go ahead," grinned Park. "But don't be surprised if you get a busy signal." He had taken the precaution of seeing that all the lines to the mayor's office would be occupied at this time.

"Hello, Noggle," said Park.

"Haw. Who are you? I think I've met you—let me see—"

Park produced an air pistol. "I'm Allister Park. You'll figure out where you met me soon enough, but you won't talk about it. I'm glad to see my figuring came out right. Can you start a man's wheel today? Now?"

"I suppose I could. Oh, *I* know who you are now—"

"Nay comments, I said. You're coming along, brother, and doing just as you're told."

The next step was when Park walked arm in arm with Noggle into the imposing executive building. Park's standing as a powerful boss saw him through the guards and flunkeys that guarded the Bretwald's office on the top floor.

The Bretwald looked up from his desk. "Oh, haw, Thane Park. If you're going to nag me about that mobilization order, you're wasting your time. Who's—eee! Where am I? What's happened to me? Help! Help!"

In bounded the guards, guns ready. Park faced them sadly. "Our respected Bretwald seems to have had a mental seizure," he said.

The guards covered the two visitors and asked Kedrick what was the matter. All they could get out of Kedrick was: "Help! Get away from me! Let me out! I don't know who you're talking about. My name's not Kedrick, it's O'Shaughnessy!"

They took him away. The guards kept Park and Noggle until a message from the acting Bretwald said to let them go.

"By the brazen gates of Hell!" cried Park. "Is *that* all?"

"Yep," said the new Secretary of War. "Douglas was a Brahtz man; hence he saw to it that the army was made as harmless as possible before he skipped out."

Park laughed grimly. "The Secretary of War sabotages—"

"He does what?"

"Never mind. He raises hell with, if you want a more familiar expression. Raises hell with the army for the benefit of his party, with the Dakotians about to come whooping in. I suppose it oughtn't to surprise me, though. How many can we raise?"

"About twenty thousand in the burgish area, but we can arm only half of them rickly. Most of our quick-fire pipes and warwains have been hurt so it'll take a month to fix them."

"How about a force of Skrellings?"

The Secretary shrugged. "We can raise 'em, but we can't arm them."

"Go ahead and raise 'em anyway."

"All right, if you say so. But hadn't you better have a rank? It would look better."

"All right. You make me your assistant."

"Don't you want a commission?"

"Not on your life! Your generals would go on strike, and even if they didn't I'd be subject to military law."

The army was not an impressive one, even when its various contingents had all collected at what would have been Pittsburgh if its name hadn't been the lovely one of Guggenvik. The regulars were few and unimpressive; the militia were more numerous but even less prepossessing; the Skrelling levy was the most unmilitary of all. They stood around with silly grins on their flat brown faces, and chattered and scratched. Park though disgustedly, so these are the descendants of the noble red man and the heroic viking! Fifty years of peace had been a blessing to Vinland, but not an altogether unmitigated one.

The transport consisted of a vast fleet of private folkwains and goodwains (busses and trucks to you). It had been possible to put only six warwains in the field. These were a kind of steam-driven armored car carrying a compressor and a couple of pneumatic machine-guns. There was one portable liquid-air plant for charging shells and air-bombs.

The backwardness of Vinland chemistry compared with its physics caused a curious situation. The only practical military explosives were a rather low-grade black powder, and a carbon-liquid-oxygen-mixture. Since the former was less satisfactory as a propellant, considering smoke, flash, and barrel-fouling, than compressed air, and was less effective as a detonant than the liquid-air explosive, its military use was largely confined to land mines. Liquid oxygen, however, while as powerful as trinitrotoluol, had to be manufactured on the spot, as there was no way of preventing its evaporation. Hence it was a very awkward thing to use in mobile warfare.

Park walked into the intelligence tent, and asked the Secretary of War: "What do you think our chances are?"

The Secretary looked at him. "Against the squires, about even. Against the Dakotians, one to five. Against both, none." He held out a handful of dispatches. These told of the success of the Sons of the Vikings in extending their hold in the southwest, not surprising considering that the only division of regulars in that area were natives of the region and had gone over to the rebels. More dispatches described in brief fragments the attack of a powerful and fast-moving Dakotian army west of Lake Yanktonai (Michigan). The last of these was dated 6 P.M., June 26th, the preceding day.

"What's happened since then?" asked Park.

"Don't know," said the Secretary. Just then a message came in from the First Division. It told little, but the dateline told much. It had been sent from the city of Edgar, at the south of Lake Yanktonai.

Park looked at his map, and whistled. "But an army *can't* retreat fifty miles in one day!"

"The staff can," said the Secretary. "They ride."

Further speculation about the fate of the First Division seemed unnecessary. The one-eyed Colonel Montrose was dictating an announcement for the press to the effect that: "Our army has driven off severe Dakotian attacks in the Edgar area, with heavy losses to the foe. Nine Dakotian warwains were destroyed and five were captured. Other military booty included twenty-six machine-pipes. Two foeish airwains were shot down . . . ."

Park thought, this Montrose has a good imagination, which quality seems sadly lacking in most of the officers. Maybe we can do something with him—if we're still here long enough . . .

The Secretary pulled Park outside. "Looks as though they had us. We haven't anything to fick with. Not even brains. General Higgins is just an easygoing paradeground soldier who never expected to have to shoot at anybody in his life. For that matter neither did I. Got any ideas?"

"Still thinking, brother," said Park, studying his map. "I'm nay soldier either, you know; just a thingman. If I could give you any help it would be political."

"Well, if we can't win by fickting, politics would seem to be the only way left."

"Maybe." Park was still looking at the map. "I begin to have a thock. Let's see Higgins."

Fortunately for Park's idea, General Higgins was not merely easygoing; he was positively comatose. He sat in his tent with his blouse unbuttoned and a bottle of beer in front of him, serene in the midst of worry and confusion.

"Come in, thanes, come in," he said. "Have some beer. Pfff. Got any ideas? Blessed if I know where to turn next. Nay artillery, nay airwains to speak of, nay real soldiers. Pfff. Do you guess if we started fortifying New Belfast now, it'd be strong enough to hold when we were pushed back there? Nobody knows anything, pfff. I'm supposed to have a staff, but half of 'em have got lost or sneaked off to join the rebels. Blessed if I know what to do next."

Park thought General Higgins would make a splendid Salvation Army general. But there was no time for personalities. He sprang his plan.

"Goodness gracious!" said Higgins. "It sounds very risky—get Colonel Callahan."

The Sachem filled the tent-opening when he arrived, weaving lightly. "Somebody want me?" Belatedly he remembered to salute.

Higgins barked at him: "Colonel Callahan, do you ken you have your blouse on *backwards?*"

Callahan looked down. "So I have, ha-ha, sir."

"That's a very weighty matter. Very weighty. No, don't change it here. You're drunk, too."

"So are—" Callahan suppressed an appalling violation of discipline just in time. "Maybe I had a little, sir."

"That's very weighty, very weighty. Just think of it. I ought to have you shot."

Callahan grinned. "What would my regiment do then?"

"I don't know. What would they do?"

"Give you three guesses, sir. *Hic.*"

"Run away, I suppose."

"Right the first time, sir. Congratulations."

"Don't congratulate me, you fool! The Secretary has a plan."

"A plan, really? Haw, Thane Park; I didn't see you. How do you like our army?"

Park said: "I think it's the goddamndest thing I ever saw in my life. It's a galloping nightmare."

"Oh, come now," said Higgins. "Some of the brave boys are a little green, but it's not as bad as all that."

A very young captain entered, gave a heel-click that would have echoed if there had been anything for it to echo against, and said: "Sir, the service company, twentieth regiment, third division, has gone on strike."

"What?" said the general. "Why?"

"No food, sir. The goodwains arrived empty."

"Have them all shot. No, shoot one out of ten. No, wait a minute. Arrived empty, you say? Somebody stole the food to sell to the local grocers. Take a platoon and clean out all the goods shops in Guggenvik. Pay them in thingly IOU's."

The Secretary interjected: "The Althing will never pay those off, you know."

"I know they won't, ha-ha. Now let's get down to that plan of yours."

The names were all different; Allister Park gave up trying to remember those of the dozens of small towns through which they rolled. But the gently rolling stretches of southern Indiana were much the same, cut up into a checkerboard of fields with woodlots here and there, and an occasional snaky line of cottonwoods marking the course of a stream. The Vinlanders had not discovered the beauties of billboard advertising, which, to Park's mind, was something. Not having a businessman's point of view, he had no intention of introducing this charming feature of his own civilization into Vinland. The Vinlanders did have their diabolical habit of covering the landscape with smoke from faulty burners in their wains, and that was bad enough.

A rising whistle and a shattering bang from the rear made Park jump around in the seat of his wain. A mushroom of smoke and dust was rising from a hillside. The airwain that had dropped the bomb was banking slowly to turn away. The pneumatics clattered all along the column, but without visible effect. A couple of their own machines purred over and chased the bomber off.

Those steam-turbine planes were disconcertingly quiet things. On the other hand the weight of their power plants precluded them from carrying either a heavy bomb load or a lot of fuel, so they were far from a decisive arm. They rustled across the sky with the dignity of dowagers, seldom getting much over 150 miles an hour, and their battles had the deliberation of a duel between sailing ships-of-the-line.

They wound down to the sunny Ohio (they called it the Okeeyo, both derived from the same Iroquois word) in the region where the airwains had reported the rebel army. A rebel airwain—a converted transport ship—came to look them over, and was shot down. From across the river came faintly the rebel yells and the clatter of pneumatics, firing at targets far out of range. Park guessed that discipline in Brahtz's outfit was little if any better than in his own.

Now, if they wanted to, the stage was set for an interminable campaign of inaction. Either side could try to sneak its men across the river without being caught in the act by the other. Or it could adopt a defensive program, contenting itself with guarding all the likely crossings. That sort of warfare would have suited General Higgins fine, minimizing as it did the chance that most of his musical-comedy army would do a lightning advance to the rear as soon as they came under fire.

It would in fact have been sound tactics, if they could have counted on the rebels' remaining on the south bank of the Okeeyo in that region, instead of marching east toward Guggenvik, and if the Dakotians were not likely to descend on their rear at any moment.

The Secretary of War had gone back to New Belfast, leaving Park the highest-ranking civilian with Higgins's army. He had the good sense to keep out of sight as much as possible, taking into account the soldier's traditional dislike of the interfering politician.

General Etheling, commanding the rebel army, got a message asking if he would hold a parley with a civilian envoy of General Higgins's army. General Etheling, wearing a military blouse over a farmer's overalls and boots, pulled his long mustache and said no, if Higgins wants to parley with me he can come himself. Back came the answer: This is a *very* high-ranking civilian; in fact he out-ranks Higgins himself. Would that island in the middle of the Okeeyo do? Etheling pulled his mustache some more and decided it would do.

So, next morning General Etheling, wearing the purely ornamental battle-ax that formed part of the Vinland officer's dress uniform, presented himself off the island. As he climbed out of his rowboat, he saw his opposite number's boat pull away from the far side of the little island. He advanced a way among the cotton-woods and yelled: "Haw!"

"Haw." A stocky blond man appeared.

"You all alone, Thane?"

"Yes."

"Well, I'll be jiggered! You boys kin go along back; I'll holler when I need you. Now, Thane, who be you?"

"I'm Bishop Ib Scoglund, General."

"What? But ain't you the wick who started the whole rumpus with all that silly talk about ricks for the Skrellings?"

The bishop sighed. "I did what I believed right in the sight of the Lord. But now a greater danger threatens us. The Dakotians are sweeping across our fair land like the hosts of Midian, of old! Surely it were wise to sink our little bickerings in the face of this peril?"

"You say the lousy redskins is doing an invasion? Well, now, that's the first I heered of that. What proof you got?"

Park produced an assortment of papers: dispatches, a copy of the *Edgar Daily Tidings,* etcetera.

The general was at last convinced. He said: "Well, I'll be tarnally damned. Begging your pardon, Hallow; I forgot as how you were a preacher."

"That's all rick, my son. There are times when, even in a cleric like me, the baser passions rise, and it is all I can do to refrain from saying 'damn' myself."

"Well, now, that's rick handsome of you. But what does old Cottonhead Higgins want me to do? I got my orders, you know."

"I know, my son. But don't you see the Divine will in these events? When we His children fall out and desecrate the soil of Vinland with our brothers' blood, He chastises us with the scourge of invasion. Let us unite to hurl back the heathen before it is too late! General Higgins has a plan for joint doing all worked out. If you take it up, he will prove his good faith by letting you cross the Okeeyo unopposed."

"What kind of plan is it? I never knew Cottonhead had enough brains to plan a barn-dance, not to mention a campaign."

"I couldn't give you all the details; they're in this paper. But I know they call for your army to put itself in the path of the invaders, and when you are engaged with them for our army to attack their left flank. If we lose, our brotherly quarrel with be one with Sodom and Gomorrah. If we win, it will be surely possible to settle our strife without further bloodshed. You will be a great man in the sight of the people and a good one in the sight of Heaven, General."

"Well, I guess maybe as how you're right. Give me the rest of the day to study these here plans . . ."

They shook hands; the general made a fumbling salute, and went over to his side of the island to call his boat. Thus, he did not see the bishop hastily don his mustache and spectacles.

When General Etheling's rebels crossed the river next morning, they found no trace of Higgins's force except for the usual camp-litter. Following directions, they set out for Edgar.

General Higgins, goaded to hurry by Allister Park, sent his army rolling northward. People in dust-colored workclothes came out to hang over fences and stare at them.

Park asked one of these, a strapping youth with some Skrelling blood, if he had heard of the invasion.

"Sure," said the man. "Reckon they won't git this fur, though. So we ain't worrying.'' The young man laughed loudly at the suggestion of volunteering. ''Me go off and git shot up so some other wick can sit on his rump and get rich? Not me, Thane! If the folks in Edgar gets scalped, it serves 'em right for not paying us mair for our stuff.''

As the army moved farther and farther toward Edgar, the expressions of the civilians grew more anxious. Ass they approached the Piankishaw (Wabash) River, they passed wains parked by the roads, piled with household goods. However, when the army had passed, many of these reversed their direction and followed the army back north toward their homes. Park was tempted to tell some of these people what idiots they were, but that would hardly have been politic. The army had little enough self-confidence as it was.

Higgins's army spread out along the south bank of the Piankishaw. All those in the front line had, by order, stained their hands and faces brown. The genuine Skrellings were kept well back.

Park took an observation post overlooking the main crossing of the river. He had just settled himself when there was a tremendous purring hum from the other side of the bridge. An enemy warwain appeared. Its ten tires screeched in unison as it stopped at the barrier on the road. Pneumatics began to pop on all sides. The forward turret swung back and forth, its gun clattering. Then a tremendous bang sent earth, bridge, and wain into the air. The wain settled into the water on its side, half out. Some men crawled out and swam for the far shore, bullets kicking up little splashes around their bobbing heads.

Up the river, Park could see a pontoon boat putting out from the north shore. It moved slowly by poling, passed out of sight. In a few minutes it reappeared, drifting downstream. It came slowly past Park and stopped against a ruined bridge-abutment. Water gradually leaked through the bullet-holes in the canvas, until only one corner was above water. A few arms and faces bobbed lazily just below the surface.

The firing gradually died down. Park could imagine the Dakotians scanning the position with their field-glasses and planning their next move. If their reputation was not exaggerated, it would be something devastating.

He climbed down from his perch and trotted back to headquarters, where he found Rufus Callahan, sober for once.

Ten minutes later the two, preceded by an army piper, exposed themselves at the east end of the bridge. Park carried a white flag, and the piper squealed ''parlay'' on his instrument. Nobody shot at them, so they picked their way across the bridge, climbing along the twisted girders. Callahan got stuck.

''I'm scared of high places,'' he said through his teeth, clinging to the iron-work.

Park took out his air-pistol. ''You'll be worse scared of me,'' he growled. The huge man was finally gotten under way again.

At the far end, a Skrelling soldier jumped out of the bushes, rifle ready. He crackled something at them in Dakotian. Callahan answered in the same language, and the man took them in tow.

As the road curved out of sight of the river, Park began to see dozens of warwains pulled up to the side of the road. Some had their turrets open, and red men sat in them, smoking or eating sandwiches. There were other vehicles, service cars of various kinds, and horse cavalry with lances and short rifles. They stopped by one warwain. Their escort snapped to a salute that must have jarred his bones. An officer climbed out. He wore the usual mustard-colored Dakotian uniform, topped off with the feathered warbonnet of the Sioux Indian. After more chattering, Park and Callahan were motioned in.

It was crowded inside. Park burned the back of his hand against a steam-pipe, and cut loose with a string of curses that brought admiring grins to the red-brown faces of the crew. Everything was covered with coal-soot.

The engineer opened the throttle, and the reciprocating engine started to chug. Park could not see out. They stopped presently and got out and got into another warwain, a very large one.

Inside the big machine were a number of Dakotian officers in the red-white-and-black war-bonnets. A fat one with a little silver war-club hanging from his belt was introduced to Park and Callahan as General Tashunkanitko, governor of the Oglala and commander-in-chief of the present expedition.

"Well?" snapped this person in a high-pitched, metallic voice.

Callahan gave his sloppy salute—which at first glance looked alarmingly as though he were thumbing his nose—and said: "I'm representing the commander of the Skrelling Division—"

"The *what?*"

"The Skrelling Division. We've been ordered by the Althing to put down the uprising of the Diamonds in the southwest of Vinland. They have a big army, and are likely to win all Vinland if not stopped. We can't stop them, and on the other hand we can't let them take all the south while you take all the north of Vinland.

"My commander humbly suggests that it is hardly proper for two armies of men of the same race to fick each other while their joint foe takes over all Vinland, as Brahtz's army will do unless we join against it."

General Tashunkanitko crackled something to one of his men, who rattled back. The general said: "It *was* taled that your men looked like Skrellings, but we could not get close enough to be sure, and did not believe the tale. What do you offer?"

Callahan continued: "My commander will not try to push the Dakotians from the area west of the Piankishaw, if you will help him against the rebels."

"Does that offer bind your thing?"

"Nay. But, as our army is the only real one at present under their command, they will have nay way of enforcing their objections. To prove our good faith we will, if you agree, let you cross the Piankishaw without fickting."

The general thought for some seconds. He said: "That offer ock to be put up to my government."

"Nay time, sir. The rebels are moving north from the Okeeyo already. Anyway, if we make a truce aside from our thing, you should be willing to do the same. After we've overthrown the Brahtz army. I'm sure we can find some workable arrangement between our armies."

Tashunkanitko thought again. "I will do it. Have you a plan worked out?"

"Yes, sir. Right here . . ."

When the Dakotians crossed the Piankishaw the next day, there was no sign of the large and supposedly redskin army that had held the passage against them.

Across the rolling Indiana plain came the rattle of pneumatic rifles and the crack of air- and mortar-bombs. General Higgins told Park: "We just got a message from General Etheling; says he's hard pressed, and it's about time we did our flank attack on the Dakotians. And this General Tush—Tash—General Mad-Horse wants to know why we haven't attacked the flank of the rebels. Says he's still pushing 'em back, but they outnumber him twa to ane and he's had a lot of mechanical breakdowns. Says if we'll hit them now they'll run."

"We don't want to let either side win," said Park. "Guess it's time to start."

With considerable confusion—though perhaps less than was to be expected—the Army of New Belfast got under way. It was strung out on a five-mile front at right angles to the line of contact of the Dakotian and rebel armies. The right wing was the stronger, since it would meet stronger resistance from Tashunkanit-ko's hardened professionals than from Etheling's armed hayseeds.

Park squeezed into the observation turret of the headquarters wain beside Higgins. They went slowly so as not to outrun the infantry, lurching and canting as the huge rubber doughnut-shaped wheels pulled them over walls and fences. They crunched through one corner of a farmyard, and the countryside was at once inundated by fleeing pigs and chickens. Park had a glimpse of an overalled figure shaking a fist at the wain. He couldn't help laughing; it was too bad about the farmer's livestock, but there was something ultra-rural about the man's indignation over a minor private woe when a battle was going on next door.

Men began to appear ahead; horsemen leaping fences and ditches scattered scouts dodging from tree to fence, firing at unseen targets, then frantically working the pump-levers of their rifles to compress the air for the next shot. One of them was not a hundred yards away when he saw the advancing wains. He stared stupidly at them until the forward machine-gunner in the headquarters wain fired a burst that sent the gravel flying around the scout's feet. The scout jumped straight up and came down running. Others ran when they saw the wains looming out of the dust. A few who didn't see soon enough ran toward the advancing line with their hands up.

They met larger groups of redskins, crawling or running from right to left with faces set. Each time there would be one face the first to turn; then they would all turn. The group would lose its form and purpose, sublimating into its component human atoms. Some stood; some ran in almost any direction.

Then they were in a half-plowed field. The plow and the steam tractor stood deserted among the brown furrows. On the other side of the field crouched a hostile wain. Park felt the engine speed up as the two machines lumbered toward each other. Bullets pattered about his cupola. It gratified him to see the general wince when they struck on and around the glass.

The wains came straight at each other. Park gripped the hand-holds tight. The other wain stopped suddenly, backed swiftly, and tried to run in at them from the side. Their own jumped ahead with a roar. Its ram dug into the side of the other machine with a terrible crash. They backed away; Park could see lubricating oil running out of the wound in the other machine. It still crawled slowly. His own mechanical rhinoceros charged again. This time the other machine heaved up on its far wheels and fell over . . .

The fight went out of the Dakotians all of a sudden. They had made a terrific assault on twice their number; then had fought steadily for two days. Their wains were battered, their horses hungry, and their infantry exhausted from pumping up their rifles. And to have a horde of strangers roll up their flank, just when victory was in sight—no wonder General Tashunkanitko, and his officers, let a tear or two trickle when they were rounded up.

General Etheling's rebels fared no better, rather worse, in fact. The Skrelling regiment ran wild among the rural Vinlanders, doing what they had wanted to do for generations—scalp the palefaces. Having somewhat hazy ideas about that ancestral ritual, they usually made the mistake of trying to take off the whole top of a man's head instead of the neat little two-inch circle of scalp. When they started in on the prisoners, they had to be restrained by a few bursts of machine-gun fire from one of Higgins's wains.

The train back to New Belfast stopped at every crossroads so the people could come out and whoop. They cheered Allister Park well enough; they cheered Rufus Callahan; they yelled for Bishop Scoglund. The story had gone ahead, how Park and General Higgins had devised a scheme for the entrapment of both the rebel and Dakotian armies; how the brave bishop had talked Etheling into it; how Etheling had treacherously shot the brave bishop; how Callahan had swum the Okeeyo with Bishop Scoglund on his back. . . . It was rumored that the city politician Allister Park had had something to do with these developments, but you never want to believe anything good of these politicians. Since he was Assistant Secretary of War, though, it was only polite to give him a cheer too . . .

Park did not think it would be prudent to show himself to the same audience both as Park and as the bishop, so they were all informed that his hallowship was recuperating.

As they rolled into New Belfast, Park experienced the let-down feeling that comes at such moments. What next? By now Noggle would have been rescued from Park's knicks and returned to Edwy Borup's hatch. That was bound to happen anyway, which was why Park hadn't tried to use that method of getting Noggle into his power before. The whirling of the wheel of if was a delicate business, not to be interrupted, by people with warrants, and he would have to see to it that somebody were left behind to force Noggle to stop the wheel when the right point had been reached.

It ought not to be difficult now, though. If he couldn't use his present power and position to get hold of Noggle, he'd have enough after election—which would come off as scheduled after all. First he'd make Noggle stop poor old Kedrick's wheel. Then he'd have Callahan or somebody stand over Noggle with a gun while he spun his, Park's, wheel through another half-turn. Then, maybe, Noggle would be allowed to halt his own carousel.

For the first three days after his return he was too busy to give attention to this plan. Everybody in New Belfast seemingly had written him or telephoned him or called at one of his two homes to see him. Although Monkey-face was a lousy secretary, Park didn't dare hire another so long as he had his double identity to maintain.

But the Antonini trials were due in a week, back in that other world. And the heirs and assigns of Trigvy Darling had had a date set for a hearing on their damage claim. And, if Park knew his history, there would probably be a "reconstruction" period in the revolted territories, of which he wanted no part.

For the second time Edwy Borup had his sanctuary invaded by Allister Park and a lot of tough-looking official persons, including Rufus Callahan. Borup was getting resigned if not reconciled to this. If they didn't let his prize patient Noggle escape before, they weren't likely to this time.

"Haw, Noggle," said Park. "Feel a little more withdoing?"

"Nay," snapped Noggle. "But since you have me by the little finger, I suppose I'll have to do what you say."

"All right. You're honest, anyway. First you're going to stop Bretwald Kedrick's wheel. Bring him in, boys."

"But I daren't stop a wheel without my downwritings. You bethink last time—"

"That's all right; we brought your whole damn library over."

There was nothing to it. Noggle stared at the fidgety Bretwald—the period of whose cycle was fortunately just twice his, so that both were in their own bodies at the same time. Then he said: "Whew. Had a lot of psychic momentum, that ane; I just did stop him. He'll be all rick now. What next?"

Park told everybody but Callahan to go out. Then he explained that Noggle was to give his wheel another half turn.

"But," objected Noggle, "that'll take seven days. What's going to be done with your body in the meantime?"

"It'll be kept here, and so will you. When the half-cycle's done, you'll stop my wheel, and then we'll let you stop your own whenever you like. I've made sure that you'll stay here until you do the right thing by my wheel, whether you cure your own case or not."

Noggle sighed. "And MacSvensson thock he'd get some simple-minded idealist like the bishop! How is it that your pattern of acting is otherly from his, when by the laws of luck you started out with much the same forebearish make-up?"

Park shrugged. "Probably because I've had to fick every step of the way, while he was more or less born into his job. We're not so otherly, at that; his excess energy went into social crusading, while mine's gone into politics. I *have* an ideal or two kicking around somewhere. I'd like to meet Bishop Scoglund some time; think I'd like him."

"I'm afraid that's undoable," said Noggle. "Even sending you back is risky. I don't know what would happen if your body died while his mind indwelt it. You might land in still another doable world instead of in your ain. Or you mick not land anywhere."

"I'll take a chance," said Park. "Ready?"

"Yes." Dr. Joseph Noggle stared at Park . . .

"Hey, Thane Park," said a voice from the doorway. "A wick named Dunedin wants to see you. Says it's weighty."

"Tell him I'm busy—no, I'll see him."

Monkey-face appeared, panting. "Have you gone yet? Have you changed? Glory to Bridget! You—I mean his hallowship—what I mean is, the Althing signed a treaty with the Dakotians and Cherogians and such, setting up an International Court for the Continent of Skrelleland, and the bishop has been chosen one of the judges! I thock you ock to know before you did anything."

"Well, well," said Park. "That's interesting, but I don't know that it changes anything."

Callahan spoke up: "I think you'd make a better judge, Allister, than *he* would. He's a fine fellow, but he will believe that everybody else is as uprick as he. They'd pull the wool over his eyes all the time."

Park pondered. After all, what had he gone to all this trouble for—why had he helped turn the affairs of half the continent upside down—except to resume a career as public prosecutor which, he hoped, would some day land him on the bench? And here was a judgeship handed him on a platter.

"I'll stay," he said.

"But," objected Noggle, "how about those thirteen other men on your wheel? Are you going to leave them out of their rick rooms?"

Park grinned. "If they're like me, they're adaptable guys who've probably got started on new careers by now. If we shift 'em all again, it'll just make more trouble for them. Come along, Rufus."

The funeral of Allister Park, assistant Secretary of War, brought out thousands of people. Some were politicans who had been associated with Park; some came for the ride. A few came because they liked the man.

In an anteroom of the cathedral, Bishop Scoglund waited for that infernal music to end, whereupon he would go out and preach the swellest damn funeral oration New Belfast had ever heard. It isn't given to every man to conduct that touching ceremony for his own corpse, and the bishop intended to give his alter-ego a good send-off.

In a way he was sorry to bid Allister Park good-bye. Allister had a good deal more in common with his natural, authentic self than did the bishop. But he couldn't keep up the two identities forever, and with the judgeship on one hand and the damage-suit on the other there wasn't much question of which of the two would have to be sacrificed. The pose of piety would probably become natural in time. The judgeship would give him an excuse for resigning his bishopric. Luckily the Celtic Christian Church had a liberal attitude toward folk who wished to leave the church. Of course he'd still have to be careful—girlfriends and such. Maybe it would even be worth while getting married . . .

"What the devil—what do you wish, my son?" said the bishop, looking up into Figgis's unpleasant face.

"You know what I wish, you old goat! What are you going to do about my wife?"

"Why, friend, it seems that you have been subject to a monstrous fooling!"

"You bet I—"

"Please, do not shout in the house of God! What I was saying was that the guilty man was none other than the late Allister Park, may the good Lord forgive his sins. He has been impersonating me. As you know, we looked much alike. Allister Park upowned to me on his deathbed two days ago. No doubt his excesses brought him to his untimely end. Still, for all his human frailties, he was a man of many good qualities. You will forgive him, will you not?"

"But—but I—"

"Please, for my sake. You would not speak ill of the dead, would you?"

"Oh, hell. Your forgiveness, Bishop. I thock I had a good thing, that's all. G'bye. Sorry."

The music was coming to an end. The bishop stood up, straightened his vestments, and strode majestically out. If he could only count on that drunken nitwit Callahan not to forget himself and bust out laughing . . .

The coffin, smothered in flowers, was, like all coffins in Vinland, shaped like a Viking longboat. It was also filled with pine planks. Some people were weeping a bit. Even Callahan, in the front row, was appropriately solemn.

"Friends, we have gathered here to pay a last gild to one who has passed from among us . . ."

FRITZ LEIBER

The Bleak Shore

"So you think a man can cheat death and outwit doom?" said the small, pale man, whose bulging forehead was shadowed by a black cowl.

The Gray Mouser, holding the dice box ready for a throw, paused and quickly looked sideways at the questioner.

"I said that a cunning man can cheat death for a long time."

The Silver Eel bustled with pleasantly raucous excitement. Fighting men predominated and the clank of swordsmen's harness mingled with the thump of tankards, providing a deep obbligato to the shrill laughter of the women. Swaggering guardsmen elbowed the insolent bravos of the young lords. Grinning slaves bearing open wine jars dodged nimbly between. In one corner a slave girl was dancing, the jingle of her silver anklet bells inaudible in the din. Outside the small, tight-shuttered windows a dry, whistling wind from the south filled the air with dust that eddied between the cobblestones and hazed the stars. But here all was jovial confusion.

The Gray Mouser was one of a dozen at the gaming table. He was dressed all in gray—jerkin, silken shirt, and mouseskin cap—but his dark, flashing eyes and cryptic smile made him seem more alive than any of the others, save for the huge copper-haired barbarian next to him, who laughed immoderately and drank tankards of the sour wine of Lankhmar as if it were beer.

"They say you're a skilled swordsman and have come close to death many times," continued the small, pale man in the black robe, his thin lips barely parting as he spoke the words.

But the Mouser had made his throw, and the odd dice of Lankhmar had stopped with the matching symbols of the eel and serpent uppermost, and he was raking in triangular golden coins. The barbarian answered for him.

"Yes, the gray one handles a sword daintily enough—almost as well as myself. He's also a great cheat at dice."

"Are you, then, Fafhrd?" asked the other. "And do you, too, truly think a man can cheat death, be he ever so cunning a cheat at dice?"

The barbarian showed his white teeth in a grin and peered puzzledly at the small, pale man whose somber appearance and manner contrasted so strangely with the revelers thronging the low-ceilinged tavern fumy with wine.

"You guess right again," he said in a bantering tone. "I am Fafhrd, a North-

204

erner, ready to pit my wits against any doom." He nudged his companion. "Look, Mouser, what do you think of this little black-coated mouse who's sneaked in through a crack in the floor and wants to talk with you and me about death?"

The man in black did not seem to notice the jesting insult. Again his bloodless lips hardly moved, yet his words were unaffected by the surrounding clamor, and impinged on the ears of Fafhrd and the Gray Mouser with peculiar clarity.

"It is said you two came close to death in the Forbidden City of the Black Idols, and in the stone trap of Angarngi, and on the misty island in the Sea of Monsters. It is also said that you have walked with doom on the Cold Waste and through the Mazes of Klesh. But who may be sure of these things, and whether death and doom were truly near? Who knows but what you are both braggarts who have boasted once too often? Now I have heard tell that death sometimes calls to a man in a voice only he can hear. Then he must rise and leave his friends and go to whatever place death shall bid him, and there meet his doom. Has death ever called to you in such a fashion?"

Fafhrd might have laughed, but did not. The Mouser had a witty rejoinder on the tip of his tongue, but instead he heard himself saying: "In what words might death call?"

"That would depend," said the small man. "He might look at two such as you and say the Bleak Shore. Nothing more than that. The Bleak Shore. And when he said it three times you would have to go."

This time Fafhrd tried to laugh, but the laugh never came. Both of them could only meet the gaze of the small man with the white, bulging forehead, stare stupidly into his cold cavernous eyes. Around them the tavern roared with mirth at some jest. A drunken guardsman was bellowing a song. The gamblers called impatiently to the Mouser to stake his next wager. A giggling woman in red and gold stumbled past the small, pale man, almost brushing away the black cowl that covered his pate. But he did not move. And Fafhrd and the Gray Mouser continued to stare—fascinatedly, helplessly—into his chill, black eyes, which now seemed to them twin tunnels leading into a far and evil distance. Something deeper than fear gripped them in iron paralysis. The tavern became faint and soundless, as if viewed through many thicknesses of glass. They saw only the eyes and what lay beyond the eyes, something desolate, dreary, and deadly.

"The Bleak Shore," he repeated.

Then those in the tavern saw Fafhrd and the Gray Mouser rise and without sign or word of leave-taking walk together to the low oaken door. A guardsman cursed as the huge Northerner blindly shoved him out of the way. There were a few shouted questions and mocking comments—the Mouser had been winning—but these were quickly hushed, for all perceived something strange and alien in the manner of the two. Of the small, pale, black-robed man none took notice. They saw the door open. They heard the dry moaning of the wind and a hollow flapping that probably came from the awnings. They saw an eddy of dust swirl up from the threshold. Then the door was closed and Fafhrd and the Mouser were gone.

No one saw them on their way to the great stone docks that bank the east side of the River Hlal from one end of Lankhmar to the other. No one saw Fafhrd's north-rigged, red-sailed sloop cast off and slip out into the current that slides down to the squally Inner Sea. The night was dark and the dust kept men indoors. But the next day they were gone, and the ship with them, and its Mingol crew of four—these being slave prisoners, sworn to life service, whom Fafhrd and the Mouser had brought back from an otherwise unsuccessful foray against the Forbidden City of the Black Idols.

About a fortnight later a tale came back to Lankhmar from Earth's End, the little harbor town that lies farthest of all towns to the west, on the very margin of the shipless Outer Sea; a tale of how a north-rigged sloop had come into port to take on an unusually large amount of food and water—unusually large because there were only six in the crew; a sullen, white-skinned Northern barbarian; an unsmiling little man in gray; and four squat, stolid, black-haired Mingols. Afterward the sloop had sailed straight into the sunset. The people of Earth's End had watched the red sail until nightfall, shaking their heads at its audacious progress. When this tale was repeated in Lankhmar, there were others who shook their heads, and some who spoke significantly of the peculiar behavior of the two companions on the night of their departure. And as the weeks dragged on into months and the months slowly succeeded one another, there were many who talked of Fafhrd and the Gray Mouser as two dead men.

Then Ourph the Mingol appeared and told his curious story of the dockmen of Lankhmar. There was some difference of opinion as to the validity of the story, for although Ourph spoke the soft language of Lankhmar moderately well, he was an outsider, and, after he was gone, no one could prove that he was or was not one of the four Mingols who had sailed with the north-rigged sloop. Moreover, his story did not answer several puzzling questions, which is one of the reasons that many thought it untrue.

"They were mad," said Ourph, "or else under a curse, those two men, the great one and the small one. I suspected it when they spared our lives under the very walls of the Forbidden City. I knew it for certain when they sailed west and west and west, never reefing, never changing course, always keeping the star of the ice fields on our right hand. They talked little, they slept little, they laughed not at all. Ola, they were cursed! As for us four—Teevs, Larlt, Ouwenyis, and I—we were ignored but not abused. We had our amulets to keep off evil magics. We were sworn slaves to the death. We were men of the Forbidden City. We made no mutiny.

"For many days we sailed. The sea was stormless and empty around us, and small, very small; it looked as if it bent down out of sight to the north and the south and the awful west, as if the sea ended an hour's sail from where we were. And then it began to look that way to the east, too. But the great Northerner's hand rested on the steering oar like a curse, and the small gray one's hand was as firm. We four sat mostly in the bow, for there was little enough sail-tending, and diced our destinies at night and morning, and gambled for our amulets and clothes—we would have played for our hides and bones, were we not slaves.

"To keep track of the days, I tied a cord around my right thumb and moved it over a finger each day until it passed from right little finger to left little finger and came to my left thumb. Then I put it on Teev's right thumb. When it came to his left thumb he gave it to Larlt. So we numbered the days and knew them. And each day the sky became emptier and the sea smaller, until it seemed that the end of the sea was but a bowshot away from our stem and sides and stern. Teevs said that we were upon an enchanted patch of water that was being drawn through the air toward the red star that is Hell. Surely Teevs may have been right. There cannot be so much water to the west. I have crossed the Inner Sea and the Sea of Monsters—and I say so.

"It was when the cord was around Larlt's left ring finger that the great storm came at us from the southwest. For three days it blew stronger and stronger, smiting the water into great seething waves; crags and gullies piled mast-high with foam. No other men have seen such waves nor should see them; they are not churned for us or for our oceans. Then I had further proof that our masters were under a curse. They took no notice of the storm; they let it reef their sails for them. They took no notice when Teevs was washed overboard, when we were half swamped and filled to the gunwales with spume, or bailing buckets foaming like tankards of beer. They stood in the stern, both braced against the steering oar, both drenched by the following waves, staring straight ahead, seeming to hold converse with creatures that only the bewitched can hear. Ola! They were accursed! Some evil demon was preserving their lives for a dark reason of his own. How else came we safe through the storm?

"For when the cord was on Larlt's left thumb, the towering waves and briny foam gave way to a great black sea swell that the whistling wind rippled but did not whiten. When the dawn came and we first saw it, Ouwenyis cried out that we were riding by magics upon a sea of black sand; and Larlt averred that we were fallen during the storm into the ocean of sulphurous oil that some say lies under the earth—for Larlt has seen the black, bubbling lakes of the Far East; and I remembered what Teevs had said and wondered if our patch of water had not been carried through the thin air and plunged into a wholly different sea on a wholly different world. But the small gray one heard our talk and dipped a bucket over the side and soused us with it, so that we knew our hull was still in water and that the water was salt—wherever that water might be.

"And then he bid us patch the sails and make the sloop shipshape. By midday we were flying west at a speed even greater than we had made during the storm, but so long were the swells and so swift did they move with us that we could only climb five or six in a whole day. By the Black Idols, but they were long!

"And so the cord moved across Ouwenyis' fingers. But the clouds were as leaden dark above us as was the strange sea heavy around our hull, and we knew not if the light that came through them was that of the sun or of some wizard moon, and when we caught sight of the stars they seemed strange. And still the white hand of the Northerner lay heavy on the steering oar, and still he and the gray one stared straight ahead. But on the third day of our flight across that black expanse the Northerner broke silence. A mirthless, terrible smile twisted his lips, and I heard him mutter 'the Bleak Shore.' Nothing more than that. The gray one nodded, as if there were some portentous magic in the words. Four times I heard the words pass the Northerner's lips, so that they were imprinted on my memory.

"The days grew darker and colder, and the clouds slid lower and lower, threatening, like the roof of a great cavern. And when the cord was on Ouwenyis' pointing finger we saw a leaden and motionless extent ahead of us, looking like the swells, but rising above them, and we knew that we were come to the Bleak Shore.

"Higher and higher that shore rose, until we could distinguish the towering basalt crags, rounded like the sea swell, studded here and there with gray boulders, whitened in spots as if by the droppings of gigantic birds—yet we saw no birds, large or small. Above the cliffs were dark clouds, and below them was a strip of pale sand, nothing more. Then the Northerner bent the steering oar and sent us straight in, as though he intended our destruction; but at the last moment he passed us at mast length by a rounded reef that hardly rose above the crest of the swell and found us harbor room. We sent the anchor over and rode safe.

"Then the Northerner and the gray one, moving like men in a dream, accoutered themselves, a shirt of light chain mail and a rounded, uncrested helmet for each—both helmets and shirts white with salt from the foam and spray of the storm. And they bound their swords to their sides, and wrapped great cloaks about them, and took a little food and a little water, and bade us unship the small boat. And I rowed them ashore and they stepped out onto the beach and walked toward the cliffs. Then, although I was much frightened, I cried out after them, 'Where are you going? Shall we follow? What shall we do?' For several moments there was no reply. Then, without turning his head, the gray one answered, his voice a low, hoarse, yet far-carrying whisper. And he said. 'Do not follow. We are dead men. Go back if you can.'

"And I shuddered and bowed my head to his words and rowed out to the ship. Ouwenyis and Larlt and I watched them climb the high, rounded crags. The two figures grew smaller and smaller, until the Northerner was no more than a tiny, slim beetle and his gray companion almost invisible, save when they crossed a whitened space. Then a wind came down from the crags and blew the swell away from the shore, and we knew we could make sail. But we stayed—for were we not sworn slaves? And am I not a Mingol?

"As evening darkened, the wind blew stronger, and our desire to depart—if only to drown in the unknown sea—became greater. For we did not like the strangely rounded basalt crags of the Bleak Shore; we did not like it that we saw no gulls or hawks or birds of any kind in the leaden air, no seaweed on the beach. And we all three began to catch glimpses of something shimmering at the summit of the cliffs. Yet it was not until the third hour of night that we upped anchor and left the Bleak Shore behind.

"There was another great storm after we were out several days, and perhaps it hurled us back into the seas we know. Ouwenyis was washed overboard and Larlt went mad from thirst, and toward the end I knew not myself what was happening. Only I was cast up on the southern coast near Quarmall and, after many difficulties, am come here to Lankhmar. But my dreams are haunted by those black cliffs and by visions of the whitening bones of my masters, and their grinning skulls staring empty-eyed at something strange and deadly.''

Unconscious of the fatigue that stiffened his muscles, the Gray Mouser wormed his way past the last boulder, finding shallow handholds and footholds at the juncture of the granite and black basalt, and finally stood erect on the top of the rounded crags that walled the Bleak Shore. He was aware that Fafhrd stood at his side, a vague, hulking figure in whitened chain-mail vest and helmet. But he saw Fafhrd vaguely, as if through many thicknesses of glass. The only things he saw clearly—and it seemed he had been looking at them for an eternity—were two cavernous, tunnel-like black eyes, and beyond them something desolate and deadly, which had once been across the Outer Sea but was now close at hand. So it had been, ever since he had risen from the gaming table in the low-ceilinged tavern in Lankhmar. Vaguely he remembered the staring people of Earth's End, the foam, and fury of the storm, the curve of the black sea swell, and the look of terror on the face of Ourph the Mingol; these memories, too, came to him as if through many thicknesses of glass. Dimly he realized that he and his companion were under a curse, and that they were now come to the source of that curse.

For the flat landscape that spread out before them was without sign of life. In front of them the basalt dipped down to form a large hollow of black sand—tiny particles of iron ore. In the sand were half embedded more than two score of what seemed to the Gray Mouser to be inky-black, oval boulders of various sizes. But they were too perfectly rounded, too regular in form to be boulders, and slowly it was borne in on the Mouser's consciousness that they were not boulders, but monstrous black eggs, a few small, some so large that a man could not have clasped his arms around them, one big as a tent.

Scattered over the sand were bones, large and small. The Mouser recognized the tusked skull of a boar, and two smaller ones—wolves. There was the skeleton of some great predatory cat. Beside it lay the bones of a horse, and beyond them the rib case of a man or ape. The bones lay all around the huge black eggs—a whitely gleaming circle.

From somewhere a toneless voice sounded, thin but clear, in accents of command, saying: "For warriors, a warrior's doom."

The Mouser knew the voice, for it had been echoing in his ears for weeks, ever since it had first come from the lips of a pale little man with a bulging forehead, wearing a black robe and sitting near him in a tavern in Lankhmar. And a more whispering voice came to him from within, saying, *He seeks always to repeat past experience, which has always been in his favor.*

Then he saw that what lay before him was not utterly lifeless. Movement of a sort had come to the Bleak Shore. A crack had appeared in one of the great black eggs, and then in another, and the cracks were branching, widening as bits of shell fell to the black, sandy floor.

The Mouser knew that this was happening in answer to the first voice, the thin one. He knew this was the end to which the thin voice had called him across the

Outer Sea. Powerless to move farther, he dully watched the slow progress of this monstrous birth. Under the darkening leaden sky he watched twin deaths hatching out for him and his companion.

The first hint of their nature came in the form of a long, swordlike claw which struck out through a crack, widening it farther. Fragments of shell fell more swiftly.

The two creatures which emerged in the gathering dusk held enormity even for the Mouser's drugged mind. Shambling things, erect like men but taller, with reptilian heads boned and crested like helmets, feet clawed like a lizard's, shoulders topped with bony spikes, forelimbs each terminating in a single yard-long claw. In the semidarkness they seemed like hideous caricatures of fighting men, armored and bearing swords. Dusk did not hide the yellow of their blinking eyes.

Then the voice called again: "For warriors, a warrior's doom."

At those words the bonds of paralysis dropped from the Mouser. For an instant he thought he was waking from a dream. But then he saw the new-hatched creatures racing toward them, a shrill, eager screeching issuing from their long muzzles. From beside him he heard a quick, rasping sound as Fafhrd's sword whipped from its scabbard. Then the Mouser drew his own blade, and a moment later it crashed against a steel-like claw which thrust at his throat. Simultaneously, Fafhrd parried a like blow from the other monster.

What followed was nightmare. Claws that were swords slashed and stabbed. Not so swiftly that they could not be parried, though there were four against two. Counter-thrusts glanced off impenetrable bony armor. Both creatures suddenly wheeled, striking at the Mouser. Fafhrd drove in from the side, saving him. Slowly the two companions were driven back toward where the crag sheered off. The beasts seemed tireless, creatures of bone and metal rather than flesh. The Mouser foresaw the end. He and Fafhrd might hold them off for a while longer, but eventually fatigue would supervene; their parries would become slower, weaker; the beasts would have them.

As if in anticipation of this, the Mouser felt a claw nick his wrist. It was then that he remembered the dark, cavernous eyes that had drawn them across the Outer Sea, the voice that had loosed doom upon them. He was gripped with a strange, mad rage—not against the beasts but their master. He seemed to see the black, dead eyes staring at him from the black sand. Then he lost control of his actions. When the two monsters next attempted a double attack on Fafhrd he did not turn to help, but instead dodged past and dashed down into the hollow, toward the embedded eggs.

Left to face the monsters alone, Fafhrd fought like a madman himself, his great sword whistling as his last resources of energy jolted his muscles. He hardly noticed when one of the beasts turned back to pursue his comrade.

The Mouser stood among the eggs, facing one of a glossier hue and smaller than most. Vindictively he brought his sword crashing down upon it. The blow numbed his hand, but the egg shattered.

Then the Mouser knew the source of the evil of the Bleak Shore, lying here and sending its spirit abroad, lying here and calling men to doom. Behind him he heard the scrabbling steps and eager screeching of the monster chosen for his destruction. But he did not turn. Instead, he raised his sword and brought it down whirring on the half-embryonic creature gloating in secret over the creatures he had called to death, down on the bulging forehead of the small pale man with the thin lips.

Then he waited for the finishing blow of the claw. It did not come. Turning, he saw the monster sprawled on the black sand. Around him, the deadly eggs were crumbling to dust. Silhouetted against the lesser darkness of the sky, he saw Fafhrd stumbling toward him, sobbing out vague words of relief and wonder in a deep, throaty voice. Death was gone from the Bleak Shore, the curse cut off at the root. From out of the night sounded the exultant cry of a sea bird, and Fafhrd and the Mouser thought of the long, trackless road leading back to Lankhmar.

They

They would not let him alone.

They never would let him alone. He realized that that was part of the plot against him—never to leave him in peace, never to give him a chance to mull over the lies they had told him, time enough to pick out the flaws, and to figure out the truth for himself.

That damned attendant this morning! He had come busting in with his breakfast tray, waking him, and causing him to forget his dream. If only he could remember that dream—

Someone was unlocking the door. He ignored it.

"Howdy, old boy. They tell me you refused your breakfast?" Dr. Hayward's professionally kindly mask hung over his bed.

"I wasn't hungry."

"But we can't have that. You'll get weak, and then I won't be able to get you well completely. Now get up and get your clothes on and I'll order an eggnog for you. Come on, that's a good fellow!"

Unwilling, but still willing at that moment to enter into any conflict of wills, he got out of bed and slipped on his bathrobe. "That's better," Hayward approved. "Have a cigarette?"

"No, thank you."

The doctor shook his head in a puzzled fashion. "Darned if I can figure you out. Loss of interest in physical pleasure does not fit your type of case."

"What is my type of case?" he inquired in flat tones.

"Tut! Tut!" Hayward tried to appear roguish. "If medicos told their profes-sional secrets, they might have to work for a living."

"What is my type of case?"

"Well—the label doesn't matter, does it? Suppose you tell me. I really know nothing about your case as yet. Don't you think it is about time you talked?"

"I'll play chess with you."

"All right, all right." Hayward made a gesture of impatient concession. "We've played chess every day for a week. If you will talk, I'll play chess."

What could it matter? If he was right, they already understood perfectly that he had discovered their plot; there was nothing to be gained by concealing the obvious. Let them try to argue him out of it. Let the tail go with the hide! To hell with it!

He got out the chessmen and commenced setting them up. "What do you know of my case so far?"

"Very little. Physical examination, negative. Past history, negative. High intelligence, as shown by your record in school and your success in your profession. Occasional fits of moodiness, but nothing exceptional. The only positive information was the incident that caused you to come here for treatment."

"To be brought here, you mean. Why should it cause comment?"

"Well, good gracious, man—if you barricade yourself in your room and insist that your wife is plotting against you, don't you expect people to notice?"

"But she was plotting against me—and so are you. White, or black?"

"Black—it's your turn to attack. Why do you think we are plotting against you?"

"It's an involved story, and goes way back into my early childhood. There was an immediate incident, however—" He opened by advancing the white king's knight to KB3. Hayward's eyebrows raised.

"You make a piano attack?"

"Why not? You know that it is not safe for me to risk a gambit with you."

The doctor shrugged his shoulders and answered the opening. "Suppose we start with your early childhood. It may shed more light than more recent incidents. Did you feel that you were being persecuted as a child?"

"No!" He half rose from his chair. "When I was a child I was sure of myself. I knew then, I tell you; I knew! Life was worthwhile, and I knew it. I was at peace with myself and my surroundings. Life was good and I was good and I assumed that the creatures around me were like myself."

"And weren't they?"

"Not at all! Particularly the children. I didn't know what viciousness was until I was turned loose with other children. The little devils! And I was expected to be like them and play with them."

The doctor nodded. "I know. The herd compulsion. Children can be pretty savage at times."

"You've missed the point. This wasn't any healthy roughness; these creatures were different—not like myself at all. They looked like me, but they were not like me. If I tried to say anything to one of them about anything that mattered to me, all I could get was a stare and a scornful laugh. Then they would find some way to punish me for having said it."

Hayward nodded. "I see what you mean. How about grownups?"

"That is somewhat different. Adults don't matter to children at first—or, rather they did not matter to me. They were too big, and they did not bother me, and they were busy with things that did not enter into my considerations. It was only when I noticed that my presence affected them that I began to wonder about them."

"How do you mean?"

"Well, they never did the things when I was around that they did when I was not around."

Hayward looked at him carefully. "Won't that statement take quite a lot of justifying? How do you know what they did when you weren't around?"

He acknowledged the point. "But I used to catch them just stopping. If I came into a room, the conversation would stop suddenly, and then it would pick up about the weather or something equally inane. Then I took to hiding and listening and looking. Adults did not behave the same way in my presence as out of it."

"Your move, I believe. But see here, old man—that was when you were a child. Every child passes through that phase. Now that you are a man, you must see the adult point of view. Children are strange creatures and have to be protected—at least, we do protect them—from many adult interests. There is a whole code of conventions in the matter that—"

"Yes, yes," he interrupted impatiently, "I know all that. Nevertheless, I noticed enough and remembered enough that was never clear to me later. And it put me on my guard to notice the next thing."

"Which was?" He noticed that the doctor's eyes were averted as he adjusted a castle's position.

"The things I saw people doing and heard them talking about were never of any importance. They must be doing something else."

"I don't follow you."

"You don't choose to follow me. I'm telling this to you in exchange for a game of chess."

"Why do you like to play chess so well?"

"Because it is the only thing in the world where I can see all the factors and understand all the rules. Never mind—I saw all around me this enormous plant, cities, farms, factories, churches, schools, homes, railroads, luggage, roller coaster, trees, saxophones, libraries, people, and animals. People that looked like me and who should have felt very much like me, if what I was told was the truth. But what did they appear to be doing? 'They went to work to earn the money to buy the food to get the strength to go to work to earn the money to buy the food to get the strength to go to work to get the strength to buy the food to earn the money to go to—' until they fell over dead. Any slight variation in the basic pattern did not matter, for they always fell over dead. And everybody tried to tell me that I should be doing the same thing. I knew better!"

The doctor gave him a look apparently intended to denote helpless surrender and laughed. "I can't argue with you. Life does look like that, and maybe it is just that futile. But it is the only life we have. Why not make up your mind to enjoy it as much as possible?"

"Oh, no!" He looked both sulky and stubborn. "You can't peddle nonsense to me by claiming to be fresh out of sense. How do I know? Because all this complex stage setting, all these swarms of actors, could not have been put here just to make idiot noises at each other. Some other explanation, but not that one. An insanity as enormous, as complex, as the one around me had to be planned. I've found the plan!"

"Which is?"

He noticed that the doctor's eyes again averted.

"It is a play intended to divert me, to occupy my mind and confuse me, to keep me so busy with details that I will not have time to think about the meaning. You are all in it, every one of you." He shook his finger in the doctor's face. "Most of them may be helpless automatons, but you're not. You are one of the conspirators. You've been sent in as a troubleshooter to try to force me to go back to playing the role assigned to me!"

He saw that the doctor was waiting for him to quiet down.

"Take it easy," Hayward finally managed to say. "Maybe it is all a conspiracy, but why do you think that you have been singled out for special attention? Maybe it is a joke on all of us. Why couldn't I be one of the victims as well as yourself?"

"Got you!" He pointed a long finger at Hayward. "That is the essence of the plot. All of these creatures have been set up to look like me in order to prevent me from realizing that I was the center of the arrangements. But I have noticed the key fact, the mathematically inescapable fact, that I am unique. Here am I, sitting on the inside. The world extends outward from me. I am the center—"

"Easy, man, easy! Don't you realize that the world looks that way to me, too. We are each the center of the universe—"

"Not so! That is what you have tried to make me believe, that I am just one of millions more just like me. Wrong! If they were like me, then I could get into communication with them. I can't. I have tried and tried and I can't. I've sent out my inner thoughts, seeking some one other being who has them, too. What have I gotten back? Wrong answers, jarring incongruities, meaningless obscenity. I've tried, I tell you. God!—how I've tried! But there is nothing out there to speak to me—nothing but emptiness and otherness!"

"Wait a minute. Do you mean to say that you think there is nobody home at my end of the line? Don't you believe that I am alive and conscious?"

He regarded the doctor soberly. "Yes, I think you are probably alive, but you are one of the others—my antagonists. But you have set thousands of others around me whose faces are blank, not lived in, and whose speech is a meaningless reflex of noise."

"Well, then, if you concede that I am an ego, why do you insist that I am so very different from yourself?"

"Why? Wait!" He pushed back from the chess table and strode over to the wardrobe, from which he took out a violin case.

While he was playing, the lines of suffering smoothed out of his face and his expression took on a relaxed beatitude. For a while he recaptured the emotions, but not the knowledge, which he had possessed in dreams. The melody proceeded easily from proposition to proposition with inescapable, unforced logic. He finished with a triumphant statement of the essential thesis and turned to the doctor. "Well?"

"Hmmm." He seemed to detect an even greater degree of caution in the doctor's manner. "It's an odd bit, but remarkable. 'S pity you didn't take up the violin seriously. You could have made quite a reputation. You could even now. Why don't you do it? You could afford to, I believe."

He stood and stared at the doctor for a long moment, then shook his head as if trying to clear it. "It's no use," he said slowly, "no use at all. There is no possibility of communication. I am alone." He replaced the instrument in its case and returned to the chess table. "My move, I believe?"

"Yes. Guard your queen."

He studied the board. "Not necessary. I no longer need my queen. Check."

The doctor interposed a pawn to parry the attack.

He nodded. "You use your pawns well, but I have learned to anticipate your play. Check again—and mate, I think."

The doctor examined the new situation. "No," he decided, "no—not quite." He retreated from the square under attack. "Not checkmate—stalemate at the worst. Yes, another stalemate."

He was upset by the doctor's visit. He couldn't be wrong, basically, yet the doctor had certainly pointed out logical holes in his position. From a logical standpoint the whole world might be a fraud perpetrated on everybody. But logic meant nothing—logic itself was a fraud, starting with unproved assumptions and capable of proving anything. The world is what it is!—and carries its own evidence of trickery.

But does it? What did he have to go on? Could he lay down a line between known facts and everything else and then make a reasonable interpretation of the world, based on facts alone—an interpretation free from complexities of logic and no hidden assumptions of points not certain. Very well—

First fact, himself. He knew himself directly. He existed.

Second facts, the evidence of his "five senses," everything that he himself saw and heard and smelled and tasted with his physical senses. Subject to their limitations, he must believe his senses. Without them he was entirely solitary, shut up in a locker of bone, blind, deaf, cut off, the only being in the world.

And that was not the case. He knew that he did not invent the information brought to him by his senses. There had to be something else out there, some otherness that produced the things his senses recorded. All philosophies that claimed that the physical world around him did not exist except in his imagination were sheer nonsense.

But beyond that, what? Were there any third facts on which he could rely? No, not at this point. He could not afford to believe anything that he was told, or that he read, or that was implicitly assumed to be true about the world around him. No, he could not believe any of it, for the sum total of what he had been told and read and been taught in school was so contradictory, so senseless, so wildly insane that none of it could be believed unless he personally confirmed it.

Wait a minute—The very telling of these lies, these senseless contradictions, was a fact in itself, known to him directly. To that extent they were data, probably very important data.

The world as it had been shown to him was a piece of unreason, an idiot's dream. Yet it was on too mammoth a scale to be without some reason. He came wearily back to his original point: Since the world could not be as crazy as it appeared to be, it must necessarily have been arranged to appear crazy in order to deceive him as to the truth.

Why had they done it to him? And what was the truth behind the sham? There must be some clue in the deception itself. What thread ran through it all? Well, in the first place he had been given a superabundance of explanations of the world around him, philosophies, religions, "commonsense" explanations. Most of them were so clumsy, so obviously inadequate, or meaningless, that they could hardly have expected him to take them seriously. They must have intended them simply as misdirection.

But there were certain basic assumptions running through all the hundreds of explanations of the craziness around him. It must be these basic assumptions that he was expected to believe. For example, there was the deep-seated assumption that he was a "human being," essentially like millions of others around him and billions more in the past and the future.

That was nonsense! He had never once managed to get into real communication with all those things that looked so much like him but were so different. In the agony of his loneliness, he had deceived himself that Alice understood him and was a being like him. He knew now that he had suppressed and refused to examine thousands of little discrepancies because he could not bear the thought of returning to complete loneliness. He had needed to believe that his wife was a living, breathing being of his own kind who understood his inner thoughts. He had refused to consider the possibility that she was simply a mirror, an echo—or something unthinkably worse.

He had found a mate, and the world was tolerable, even though dull, stupid, and full of petty annoyance. He was moderately happy and had put away his suspicions. He had accepted, quite docilely, the treadmill he was expected to use, until a slight mischance had momentarily cut through the fraud—then his suspicions had returned with impounded force; the bitter knowledge of his childhood had been confirmed.

He supposed that he had been a fool to make a fuss about it. If he had kept his mouth shut they would not have locked him up. He should have been as subtle and as shrewd as they, kept his eyes and ears open and learned the details of and the reasons for the plot against him. He might have learned how to circumvent it.

But what if they had locked him up—the whole world was an asylum and all of them his keepers.

A key scraped in the lock, and he looked up to see an attendant entering with a tray. "Here's your dinner, sir."

"Thanks, Joe," he said gently. "Just put it down."

"Movies tonight, sir," the attendant went on. "Wouldn't you like to go? Dr. Hayward said you could—"

"No, thank you. I prefer not to."

"I wish you would, sir." He noticed with amusement the persuasive intentness of the attendant's manner. "I think the doctor wants you to. It's a good movie. There's a Mickey Mouse cartoon—"

"You almost persuade me, Joe," he answered with passive agreeableness. "Mickey's trouble is the same as mine, essentially. However, I'm not going. They need not bother to hold movies tonight."

"Oh, there will be movies in any case, sir. Lots of our other guests will attend."

"Really? Is that an example of thoroughness, or are you simply keeping up the pretense in talking to me? It isn't necessary, Joe, if it's any strain on you. I know the game. If I don't attend, there is no point in holding movies."

He liked the grin with which the attendant answered this thrust. Was it possible that this being was created just as he appeared to be—big muscles, phlegmatic disposition, tolerant, doglike? Or was there nothing going on behind those kind eyes, nothing but robot reflex? No, it was more likely that he was one of them, since he was so closely in attendance on him.

The attendant left and he busied himself at his supper tray, scooping up the already-cut bites of meat with a spoon, the only implement provided. He smiled again at their caution and thoroughness. No danger of that—he would not destroy this body as long as it served him in investigating the truth of the matter. There were still many different avenues of research available before taking that possibly irrevocable step.

After supper he decided to put his thoughts in better order by writing them; obtained paper. He should start with a general statement of some underlying postulate of the credos that had been drummed into him all his "life." Life? Yes, that was a good one. He wrote:

"I am told that I was born a certain number of years ago and that I will die a similar number of years hence. Various clumsy stories have been offered me to explain to me where I was before birth and what becomes of me after death, but they are rough lies, not intended to deceive, except as misdirection. In every other possible way the world around me assures me that I am mortal, here but a few years, and a few years hence gone completely—nonexistent.

"WRONG—I am immortal. I transcend this little time axis; a seventy-year span on it is but a casual phase in my experience. Second only to the prime datum of my own existence is the emotionally convincing certainty of my own continuity. I may be a closed curve, but closed or open, I neither have a beginning nor an end. Self-awareness is not relational; it is absolute, and cannot be reached to be destroyed, or created. Memory, however, being a relational aspect of consciousness, may be tampered with and possibly destroyed.

"It is true that most religions which have been offered me teach immortality, but note the fashion in which they teach it. The surest way to lie convincingly is to tell the truth unconvincingly. They did not wish me to believe.

"Caution: Why have they tried so hard to convince me that I am going to die in a few years? There must be a very important reason. I infer that they are preparing me for some sort of a major change. It may be crucially important for me to figure out their intentions about this—probably I have several years in which to reach a decision. Note: Avoid using the types of reasoning they have taught me.''

The attendant was back. ''Your wife is here, sir.''

''Tell her to go away.''

''Please, sir—Dr. Hayward is most anxious that you should see her.''

''Tell Dr. Hayward that I said that he is an excellent chess player.''

''Yes, sir.'' The attendant waited for a moment. ''Then you won't see her, sir?''

''No, I won't see her.''

He wandered around the room for some minutes after the attendant had left, too distrait to return to his recapitulation. By and large they had played very decently with him since they had brought him here. He was glad that they had allowed him to have a room alone, and he certainly had more time free for contemplation than had ever been possible on the outside. To be sure, continuous effort to keep him busy and to distract him was made, but, by being stubborn, he was able to circumvent the rules and gain some hours each day for introspection.

But, damnation!—he did wish they would not persist in using Alice in their attempts to divert his thoughts. Although the intense terror and revulsion which she had inspired in him when he had first rediscovered the truth had now aged into a simple feeling of repugnance and distaste for her company, nevertheless it was emotionally upsetting to be reminded of her, to be forced into making decisions about her.

After all, she had been his wife for many years. Wife? What was a wife? Another soul like one's own, a complement, the other necessary pole to the couple, a sanctuary of understanding and sympathy in the boundless depths of aloneness. That was what he had thought, what he had needed to believe and had believed fiercely for years. The yearning need for companionship of his own kind had caused him to see himself reflected in those beautiful eyes and had made him quite uncritical of occasional incongruities in her responses.

He sighed. He felt that he had sloughed off most of the typed emotional reactions which they had taught him by precept and example, but Alice had gotten under his skin, way under, and it still hurt. He had been happy—what if it had been a dope dream? They had given him an excellent, a beautiful mirror to play with—the more fool he to have looked behind it!

Wearily he turned back to his summing up:

''The world is explained in either one of two ways; the commonsense way which says that the world is pretty much as it appears to be and that ordinary human conduct and motivations are reasonable, and the religio-mystic solution which states that the world is dream stuff, unreal, insubstantial, with reality somewhere beyond.

''WRONG—both of them. The commonsense scheme has no sense to it of any sort. Life is short and full of trouble. Man born of woman is born to trouble as the sparks fly upward. His days are few and they are numbered. All is vanity and vexation. Those quotations may be jumbled and incorrect, but that is a fair statement of the commonsense world-is-as-it-seems in its only possible evaluation. In such a world, human striving is about as rational as the blind dartings of a moth against a light bulb. The commonsense world is a blind insanity, out of nowhere, going nowhere, to no purpose.

"As for the other solution, it appears more rational on the surface, in that it rejects the utterly irrational world of common sense. But it is not a rational solution, it is simply a flight from reality of any sort, for it refuses to believe the results of the only available direct communication between the ego and the Outside. Certainly the 'five senses' are poor enough channels of communication, but they are the only channels."

He crumpled up the paper and flung himself from the chair. Order and logic were no good—his answer was right because it smelled right. But he still did not know all the answer. Why the grand scale to the deception, countless creatures, whole continents, an enormously involved and minutely detailed matrix of insane history, insane tradition, insane culture? Why bother with more than a cell and a straitjacket?

It must be, it had to be, because it was supremely important to deceive him completely, because a lesser deception would not do. Could it be that they dare not let him suspect his real identity no matter how difficult and involved the fraud?

He had to know. In some fashion he must get behind the deception and see what went on when he was not looking. He had had one glimpse; this time he must see the actual workings, catch the puppet masters in their manipulations.

Obviously the first step must be to escape from this asylum, but to do it so craftily that they would never see him, never catch up with him, not have a chance to set the stage before him. That would be hard to do. He must excel them in shrewdness and subtlety.

Once decided, he spent the rest of the evening in considering the means by which he might accomplish his purpose. It seemed almost impossible—he must get away without once being seen and remain in strict hiding. They must lose track of him completely in order that they would not know where to center their deceptions. That would mean going without food for several days. Very well—he could do it. He must not give them any warning by unusual action or manner.

The lights blinked twice. Docilely he got up and commenced preparations for bed. When the attendant looked through the peephole he was already in bed, with his face turned to the wall.

Gladness! Gladness everywhere! It was good to be with his own kind, to hear the music swelling out of every living thing, as it always had and always would—good to know that everything was living and aware of him, participating in him, as he participated in them. It was good to be, good to know the unity of many and the diversity of one. There had been one bad thought—the details escaped him—but it was gone—it had never been; there was no place for it.

The early-morning sounds from the adjacent ward penetrated the sleep-laden body which served him here and gradually recalled him to awareness of the hospital room. The transition was so gentle that he carried over full recollection of what he had been doing and why. He lay still, a gentle smile on his face, and savored the uncouth but not unpleasant languor of the body he wore. Strange that he had ever forgotten despite their tricks and stratagems. Well, now that he had recalled the key, he would quickly set things right in this odd place. He would call them in at once and announce the new order. It would be amusing to see old Glaroon's expression when he realized that the cycle had ended—

The click of the peephole and the rasp of the door being unlocked guillotined his line of thought. The morning attendant pushed briskly in with the breakfast tray and placed it on the tip table. "Morning, sir. Nice, bright day—want it in bed, or will you get up?"

Don't answer! Don't listen! Suppress this distraction! This is part of their plan— But it was too late, too late. He felt himself slipping, falling, wrenched from reality back into the fraud world in which they had kept him. It was gone, gone completely, with no single association around him to which to anchor memory. There was nothing left but the sense of heartbreaking loss and the acute ache of unsatisfied catharsis.

"Leave it where it is. I'll take care of it."

"Okey-doke." The attendant bustled out, slamming the door, and noisily locked it.

He lay quite still for a long time, every nerve end in his body screaming for relief.

At last he got out of bed, still miserably unhappy, and attempted to concentrate on his plans for escape. But the psychic wrench he had received in being recalled so suddenly from his plane of reality had left him bruised and emotionally disturbed. His mind insisted on rechewing its doubts, rather than engage in constructive thought. Was it possible that the doctor was right, that he was not alone in his miserable dilemma? Was he really simply suffering from paranoia, delusions of self-importance?

Could it be that each unit in this yeasty swarm around him was the prison of another lonely ego—helpless, blind, and speechless—condemned to an eternity of miserable loneliness? Was the look of suffering which he had brought to Alice's face a true reflection of inner torment and not simply a piece of play-acting intended to maneuver him into compliance with their plans?

A knock sounded at the door. He said "Come in," without looking up. Their comings and goings did not matter to him.

"Dearest—" A well-known voice spoke slowly and hesitantly.

"Alice!" He was on his feet at once, and facing her. "Who let you in here?"

"Please, dear, please—I had to see you."

"It isn't fair. It isn't fair." He spoke more to himself than to her. Then: "Why did you come?"

She stood up to him with a dignity he had hardly expected. The beauty of her childlike face had been marred by line and shadow, but it shone with an unexpected courage. "I love you," she answered quietly. "You can tell me to go away, but you can't make me stop loving you and trying to help you."

He turned away from her in an agony of indecision. Could it be possible that he had misjudged her? Was there, behind that barrier of flesh and sound symbols, a spirit that truly yearned toward his? Lovers whispering in the dark—*"You do understand, don't you?"*

"Yes, dear heart, I understand."

"Then nothing that happens to us can matter, as long as we are together and understand—" Words, words, rebounding hollowly from an unbroken wall—

No, he couldn't be wrong! Test her again—"Why did you keep me on that job in Omaha?"

"But I didn't make you keep that job. I simply pointed out that we should think twice before—"

"Never mind. Never mind." Soft hands and a sweet face preventing him with mild stubbornness from ever doing the thing that his heart told him to do. Always with the best of intentions, the best of intentions, but always so that he had never quite managed to do the silly, unreasonable things that he knew were worthwhile. Hurry, hurry, hurry, and strive, with an angelfaced jockey to see that you don't stop long enough to think for yourself—

"Why did you try to stop me from going back upstairs that day?"

She managed to smile, although her eyes were already spilling over with tears. "I didn't know it really mattered to you. I didn't want us to miss the train."

It had been a small thing, an unimportant thing. For some reason not clear to him he had insisted on going back upstairs to his study when they were about to leave the house for a short vacation. It was raining, and she had pointed out that there was barely enough time to get to the station. He had surprised himself and her, too, by insisting on his own way in circumstances in which he had never been known to be stubborn.

He had actually pushed her to one side and forced his way up the stairs. Even then nothing might have come of it had he not—quite unnecessarily—raised the shade of the window that faced toward the rear of the house.

It was a very small matter. It had been raining, hard, out in front. From this window the weather was clear and sunny, with no sign of rain.

He had stood there quite a long while, gazing out at the impossible sunshine and rearranging his cosmos in his mind. He re-examined long-suppressed doubts in the light of this one small but totally unexplainable discrepancy. Then he had turned and had found that she was standing behind him.

He had been trying ever since to forget the expression that he had surprised on her face.

"What about the rain?"

"The rain?" she repeated in a small, puzzled voice. "Why, it was raining, of course. What about it?"

"But it was not raining out my study window."

"What? But of course it was. I did notice the sun break through the clouds for a moment, but that was all."

"Nonsense!"

"But darling, what has the weather to do with you and me? What difference does it make whether it rains or not—to us?" She approached him timidly and slid a small hand between his arm and side. "Am I responsible for the weather?"

"I think you are. Now please go."

She withdrew from him, brushed blindly at her eyes, gulped once, then said in a voice held steady: "All right. I'll go. But remember—you can come home if you want to. And I'll be there, if you want me." She waited a moment, then added hesitantly: "Would you . . . would you kiss me good-bye?"

He made no answer of any sort, neither with voice nor eyes. She looked at him, then turned, fumbled blindly for the door, and rushed through it.

The creature he knew as Alice went to the place of assembly without stopping to change form. "It is necessary to adjourn this sequence. I am no longer able to influence his decisions."

They had expected it, nevertheless they stirred with dismay.

The Glaroon addressed the First for Manipulation. "Prepare to graft the selected memory track at once."

Then, turning to the First for Operations, the Glaroon said: "The extrapolation shows that he will tend to escape within two of his days. This sequence degenerated primarily through your failure to extend that rainfall all around him. Be advised."

"It would be simpler if we understood his motives."

"In my capacity as Dr. Hayward, I have often thought so," commented the Glaroon acidly, "but it we understood his motives, we would be part of him. Bear in mind the Treaty! He almost remembered."

The creature known as Alice spoke up. "Could he not have the Taj Mahal next sequence? For some reason he values it."

"You are becoming assimilated!"

"Perhaps. I am not in fear. Will he receive it?"

"It will be considered."

The Glaroon continued with orders: "Leave structures standing until adjournment. New York City and Harvard University are now dismantled. Divert him from those sectors.

"Move!"

FREDRIC BROWN

Armageddon

It happened—of all places—in Cincinnati. Not that there is anything wrong with Cincinnati, save that it is not the center of the Universe, nor even of the State of Ohio. It's a nice old town and, in its way, second to none. But even its Chamber of Commerce would admit that it lacks cosmic significance. It must have been mere coincidence that Gerber the Great—what a name!—was playing Cincinnati when things slipped elsewhere.

Of course, if the episode had become known, Cincinnati would be the most famous city of the world, and little Herbie would be hailed as a modern St. George and get more acclaim than a quiz kid. But no member of that audience in the Bijou Theater remembers a thing about it. Not even little Herbie Westerman, although he had the water pistol to show for it.

He wasn't thinking about the water pistol in his pocket as he sat looking up at the prestidigitator on the other side of the footlights. It was a new water pistol, bought en route to the theater when he'd inveigled his parents into a side trip into the five-and-dime on Vine Street, but at the moment, Herbie was much more interested in what went on upon the stage.

His expression registered qualified approval. The front-and-back palm was no mystery to Herbie. He could do it himself. True, he had to use pony-sized cards that came with his magic set and were just right for his nine-year-old hands. And true, anyone watching could see the card flutter from the front-palm position to the back as he turned his hand. But that was a detail.

He knew, though, that front-and-back palming seven cards at a time required great finger strength as well as dexterity, and that was what Gerber the Great was doing. There wasn't a telltale click in the shift, either, and Herbie nodded approbation. Then he remembered what was coming next.

He nudged his mother and said, "Ma, ask Pop if he's gotta extra handkerchief."

Out of the corner of his eyes, Herbie saw his mother turn her head and in less time than it would take to say, "Presto," Herbie was out of his seat and skinning down the aisle. It had been, he felt, a beautiful piece of misdirection and his timing had been perfect.

It was at this stage of the performance—which Herbie had seen before, alone—

that Gerber the Great asked if some little boy from the audience would step to the stage. He was asking it now.

Herbie Westerman had jumped the gun. He was well in motion before the magician had asked the question. At the previous performance, he'd been a bad tenth in reaching the steps from aisle to stage. This time he'd been ready, and he hadn't taken any chances with parental restraint. Perhaps his mother would have let him go and perhaps not; it had seemed wiser to see that she was looking the other way. You couldn't trust parents on things like that. They had funny ideas sometimes.

"—will please step up on the stage?" And Herbie's foot touched the first of the steps upward right smack on the interrogation point of that sentence. He heard the disappointed scuffle of other feet behind him, and grinned smugly as he went on up across the footlights.

It was the three-pigeon trick, Herbie knew from the previous performance, that required an assistant from the audience. It was almost the only trick he hadn't been able to figure out. There *must,* he knew, have been a concealed compartment somewhere in that box, but where it could be he couldn't even guess. But this time he'd be holding the box himself. If from that range he couldn't spot the gimmick, he'd better go back to stamp collecting.

He grinned confidently up at the magician. Not that he, Herbie, would give him away. He was a magician, too, and he understood that there was a freemasonry among magicians and that one never gave away the tricks of another.

He felt a little chilled, though, and the grin faded as he caught the magician's eyes. Gerber the Great, at close range, seemed much older than he had seemed from the other side of the footlights. And somehow different. Much taller, for one thing.

Anyway, here came the box for the pigeon trick. Gerber's regular assistant was bringing it in on a tray. Herbie looked away from the magician's eyes and he felt better. He remembered, even, his reason for being on the stage. The servant limped. Herbie ducked his head to catch a glimpse of the under side of the tray, just in case. Nothing there.

Gerber took the box. The servant limped away and Herbie's eyes followed him suspiciously. Was the limp genuine or was it a piece of misdirection?

The box folded out flat as the proverbial pancake. All four sides hinged to the bottom, the top hinged to one of the sides. There were little brass catches.

Herbie took a quick step back so he could see behind it while the front was displayed to the audience. Yes, he saw it now. A triangular compartment built against one side of the lid, mirror-covered, angles calculated to achieve invisibility. Old stuff. Herbie felt a little disappointed.

The prestidigitator folded the box, mirror-concealed compartment inside. He turned slightly. "Now, my fine young man—"

What happened in Tibet wasn't the only factor; it was merely the final link of a chain.

The Tibetan weather had been unusual that week, highly unusual. It had been warm. More snow succumbed to the gentle warmth than had melted in more years than man could count. The streams ran high, they ran wide and fast.

Along the streams some prayer wheels whirled faster than they had ever whirled. Others, submerged, stopped altogether. The priests, knee-deep in the cold water, worked frantically, moving the wheels nearer to shore where again the rushing torrent would turn them.

There was one small wheel, a very old one that had revolved without cease for longer than any man knew. So long had it been there that no living lama recalled what had been inscribed upon its prayer plate, nor what had been the purpose of that prayer.

The rushing water had neared its axle when the lama Klarath reached for it to move it to safety. Just too late. His foot slid in the slippery mud and the back of his hand touched the wheel as he fell. Knocked loose from its moorings, it swirled down with the flood, rolling along the bottom of the stream, into deeper and deeper waters.

While it rolled, all was well.

The lama rose, shivering from his momentary immersion, and went after other of the spinning wheels. What, he thought, could one small wheel matter? He didn't know that—now that other links had broken—only that tiny thing stood between Earth and Armageddon.

The prayer wheel of Wangur Ul rolled on, and on, until—a mile farther down— it struck a ledge, and stopped. That was the moment.

"And now, my fine young man—"

Herbie Westerman—we're back in Cincinnati now—looked up, wondering why the prestidigitator had stopped in midsentence. He saw the face of Gerber the Great contorted as though by a great shock. Without moving, without changing, his face began to change. Without appearing different, it became different.

Quietly, then, the magician began to chuckle. In the overtones of that soft laughter was all of evil. No one who heard it could have doubted who he was. No one did doubt. The audience, every member of it, knew in that awful moment who stood before them, knew it—even the most skeptical among them—beyond shadow of doubt.

No one moved, no one spoke, none drew a shuddering breath. There are things beyond fear. Only uncertainty causes fear, and the Bijou Theater was filled, then, with a dreadful certainty.

The laughter grew. Crescendo, it reverberated into the far dusty corners of the gallery. Nothing—not a fly on the ceiling—moved.

Satan spoke.

"I thank you for your kind attention to a poor magician." He bowed, ironically low. "The performance is ended."

He smiled. "All performances are ended."

Somehow the theater seemed to darken, although the electric lights still burned. In dead silence, there seemed to be the sound of wings, leathery wings, as though invisible. Things were gathering.

On the stage was a dim red radiance. From the head and from each shoulder of the tall figure of the magician there sprang a tiny flame. A naked flame.

There were other flames. They flickered along the proscenium of the stage, along the footlights. One sprang from the lid of the folded box little Herbie Westerman still held in his hands.

Herbie dropped the box.

Did I mention that Herbie Westerman was a Safety Cadet? It was purely a reflex action. A boy of nine doesn't know much about things like Armageddon, but Herbie Westerman should have known that water would never have put out that fire.

But, as I said, it was purely a reflex action. He yanked out his new water pistol and squirted it at the box of the pigeon trick. And the fire *did* vanish, even as a spray from the stream of water ricocheted and dampened the trouser leg of Gerber the Great, who had been facing the other way.

There was a sudden, brief hissing sound. The lights were growing bright again, and all the other flames were dying, and the sound of wings faded, blended into another sound—the rustling of the audience.

The eyes of the prestidigitator were closed. His voice sounded strangely strained as he said: "This much power I retain. None of you will remember this."

Then, slowly, he turned and picked up the fallen box. He held it out to Herbie Westerman. "You must be more careful, boy," he said. "Now hold it so."

He tapped the top lightly with his wand. The door fell open. Three white pigeons flew out of the box. The rustle of their wings was not leathery.

Herbie Westerman's father came down the stairs and, with a purposeful air, took his razor strop off the hook on the kitchen wall.

Mrs. Westerman looked up from stirring the soup on the stove. "Why, Henry," she asked, "are you really going to punish him with that—just for squirting a little water out of the window of the car on the way home?"

Her husband shook his head grimly. "Not for that, Marge. But don't you remember we bought him that water gun on the way downtown, and that he wasn't near a water faucet after that? Where do you think he filled it?"

He didn't wait for an answer. "When we stopped in at the cathedral to talk to Father Ryan about his confirmation, that's when the little brat filled it. Out of the baptismal font! Holy water he uses in his water pistol!"

He clumped heavily up the stairs, strop in hand.

Rhythmic thwacks and wails of pain floated down the staircase. Herbie—who had saved the world—was having his reward.

ROBERT ARTHUR

Mr. Jinx

The impact upon a certain section of the New York social stratum of the lean, mahogany-complexioned, knife-faced gentleman in the black turban for a time promised to be terrific—like the concussion of a Joe Louis jab on the jaw of a third-rate contender from Upper Yawkey Falls, Idaho, or the caress of a Florida hurricane on a new bungalow development.

If only he had never crossed Millie Duane's path—

And if Millie hadn't been trying to get fifty grand belonging to Jimmy Donegan out of Roscoe Wentworth, so she and Jimmy could get married and go to Texas to raise blooded livestock and a family—

And—

But heck, that's the story! It also includes the truth about what happened to Little Pitty, the jet-eyed killer who vanished from human view in broad daylight on Eight Avenue while waiting for a convenient opportunity to put the slug on Roscoe Wentworth. As well as how Maxie Mullion came to disappear from a running bath in a locked bathroom in his penthouse thirty-one stories in the air. Both here revealed for the first time.

So to begin. With Millie, of course—

Millie Duane was a red-headed little wren three sizes bigger than a minute and twice as energetic as a thimbleful of molecules, which are the stuff science says a thimbleful of would run a battleship from New York to London—providing, of course, it didn't hit a mine on the way.

Millie had as many attractive curves as a scenic railway, and she knew more about the manly art of modified murder than Roscoe Wentworth himself, who, though he didn't invent it, patented a lot of new improvements on it. Her dad had been Miltie Duane, a fight manager and an honest one. He died when she was fifteen. Millie hated crookedness of any kind, especially in fighting, but she worked for Roscoe Wentworth because a girl had to live.

Had to live because some day a guy like Jimmy Donegan was going to come along.

Now, strictly speaking, Jimmy Donegan doesn't come into this tale at all. He's distinctly offstage motivation. Except that if you looked into Millie's blue eyes you might have seen his reflection there even when he wasn't present. If you had—or if, more prosaically, you saw his mug on the sporting page the night he won the light-heavy crown—you saw a clean-cut face, a squarish jaw, a grin, nice teeth, laughing eyes, and brown hair with something of a curl in it.

Too nice a face—anyway, Millie thought so—to be scrambled around by the impact of countless fists. Especially when Jimmy didn't particularly like fighting and only had gone into it, after getting out of agricultural college, so he could collect a stake with which to buy a farm in Texas—a ranch he could turn into a show-place breeding farm.

So that when Roscoe signed him up, and Millie saw him for the first time, right down deep inside her she knew it had happened. She was in love. And she was determined that she, with her superior knowledge of the fight business—and of Roscoe Wentworth, whose private secretary she was—was going to look out for Jimmy's interests.

Which she did, so effectively that inside a year and a half—most of the time over Roscoe Wentworth's pitiful protests—she maneuvered Jimmy into the championship before a capacity crowd at the Garden. Roscoe hadn't been ready for Jimmy to be champ yet—figuring lots of cash-bearing angles in holding him off— but Millie willed otherwise.

If it had been love at first sight for Millie, it had been ditto and double that for Jimmy. The only thing they had waited for was the championship. With that to retire on, and fifty grand—that was what they figured his savings ought to be by then—to buy the farm with, they'd get married and shake the soot of Manhattan off their shoes faster than Roscoe Wentworth could chisel a dollar from a fighter's purse. Jimmy described Texas so vividly that Millie could hear the cattle bawling, and she knew she was going to love it.

So now Jimmy was champ. And they were all ready to take up the serious business of matrimony. Except that there was a fly, a short, plump, pink-faced fly named Roscoe Wentworth, in the well-known ointment.

"Roscoe," Millie said, her voice cool and crisp, a little green glow altering the blue of her eyes, "you're a louse."

"Please, Millie," Roscoe Wentworth begged, lifting a plump hand in half-hearted protest, "you mustn't bother me now. I got troubles on my mind."

It was a June day, with a benign sun gilding the pavements of Manhattan. Roscoe, seated behind a desk big enough for a fast game of tennis, was smoking a Havana stogie with nervous puffs. In the flat safe behind him were the receipts from the previous night's bout between Bombardier Benson, the Swedish Blitzkrieg, and Neverdown Nevens, the Granite Giant. Deducing expenses and taxes, there remained fifty grand clear for Roscoe Wentworth. But this morning Roscoe could not quite summon up the *joie de vivre* the figures called for.

Ever and again, all morning long, he had found himself glancing out the broad, plate glass windows at the figure stalking back and forth across the street. Of course, Johnny Pitty—better known as "Little" Pitty—probably wouldn't really shoot him. After all, even Roscoe had thought that Neverdown was going to win last night. It had been pure accident that the Bombardier, ducking to avoid a looping right, had somehow managed to bang his frontal bone against the Granite Giant's chin.

The damage to the Swedish Blitzkrieg's skull had been negligible. But no one could dispute that Neverdown Nevens had a fractured jaw. If Little Pitty had dropped ten Gs, still, hadn't Roscoe himself lost?

But Mr. Wentworth could not put his doubts at rest. There was something feline about Little Pitty's back-and-forth stalk. Roscoe found his head swiveling first one way then the other, like a spectator at a tennis match.

Perhaps it would be best to make good to the fellow his ten thousand dollars, even though—

"Roscoe!" Millie's voice interrupted his troubled thoughts. "Stop waggling your head back and forth and listen if you don't want me to get annoyed. I'm not here as your secretary any more. I've resigned. I'm here as Mrs. Jimmy Donegan to-be, about Jimmy's contract—and a little matter of fifty thousand dollars in lawful United States currency, legal tender for the payment of all debts, public or private."

"Now, Millie," Roscoe began placatingly, with an effort taking his eyes off Little Pitty, "I don't know what you mean. All Jimmy's contract says is that he is gonna fight three more fights for me before he retires. Or else he forfeits fifty thousand, the amount of his last purse, which I am withholding persuant to article five, paragraph B, as security for the performance of the agreed upon—"

"Yes, Roscoe"—honey dripped from Millie's curved and kissable lips—"I have had a lawyer look at the contract, and he has already told me what it says. But Roscoe, you and Jimmy had a verbal agreement that after he won the championship, he would be released from all contracts without obligation, providing he didn't fight again for somebody else."

Roscoe Wentworth mopped his brow.

"Yeah, Millie," he conceded. "But that was only a gentleman's agreement. This other contract is *signed*. Look at it like this, Millie. I, personally, spent a lot of money building Jimmy up. No, don't snort like that. It don't become a pretty girl to curl her lips so. He's a valuable propitty. Now am I gonna lose all my investment because he wants to go back to Texas an' raise hogs?"

Millie snorted again, shaking her red-gold curls in a menacing manner.

"It would be fair, *if* you had spent any money on Jimmy, which you haven't, and *if* that was all the contract said," she declared. "But the contract specifies *three fights in defense of his championship!* And I know you, Roscoe Wentworth! For every fight in defense of his title, you'd book him for three others that weren't. And suppose he lost the crown! Then he'd have to fight for you until he won it again so he could defend it, so he wouldn't lose the fifty thousand you're holding out, and that we've been planning all along to buy a stock farm with. It might take years!

"No, Roscoe, I won't stand for it. I want that contract torn up, and I want that fifty thousand of Jimmy's, right now!"

She stamped a small foot and glared at Roscoe Wentworth. Roscoe, secure in the knowledge that if she manhandled him in any way she could to go jail for it, glared back, unyieldingly.

It was an impasse, will meeting will in a contest of strength, and how it would have turned out no one knows. For it was at that moment the tall gentleman with the beady eyes and the black turban entered, unannounced.

Mr. Jinx had arrived in town.

He came in through the door, but to Millie and Roscoe it was as if he had materialized on Roscoe's Bokhara rug. Not until he coughed did they turn and realize anyone was there.

Roscoe's eyes bugged. Even Millie stared in open-mouthed astonishment as the intruder favored them with a calm, narrow-lidded scrutiny.

The arrival of the sinister, turbaned one in New York was quite unobserved, and so far as can be determined, no one can recall noticing him before his arrival that morning in the office of the Fair-Square Sporting Club. Which is odd, for if ever there was an observable figure, it was him. It was he? Thanks. Six feet two he stood, dressed in a drape-cut suit of coffee-colored silk of a special weave that would wear till doomsday. In a way, fortunate. Otherwise his clothing was conventional, save that topping off the outfit—literally—a jet-black turban was wrapped about his high-domed head. And beneath the turban, eyes like black glass marbles gazed unwinkingly at Millie and Roscoe from either side of a hawk-beaked nose.

The curious caller carried a cane with a golden head, unpleasantly carved to look like a cobra, and on his ring finger, Millie noticed, being more observant than Roscoe Wentworth, a ring of beaten gold which held, not a jewel, but a tiny crystal globe half an inch across.

With a flourish, their visitor held out a parchment card.

"Permit me," he said, his voice deep, with a curious muted quality, like the throbbing of a temple gong in the distance. Then, as Roscoe took the proffered card, the turbaned one let his eyes rest on Millie, traveling over her from head to feet in a leisurely journey that brought a crimson flush of embarrassment to her cheeks.

His gaze only left her, after having apparently appraised—and approved of—every charm she possessed, concealed or revealed, when Roscoe Wentworth looked up from the card, on which flowing characters spelled out *The Prince Agah Shan y Pasha Rehab Neroc d'Ghengs.*

"Pronounced *Jinx*," the caller informed Roscoe somberly. "We will dispense with formality. You may call me simply—Mr. Jinx."

"Uh . . . how-do, Mr. . . . um, Jinx," Roscoe gulped. "Uh—"

"Of course. You wish to know my business here. I am in the accident . . . ah, profession."

"Uh, insurance?" Roscoe mumbled. "Sorry. Can't use any." Then his eyes swiveled toward that pacing figure in the street, momentarily forgotten. "Although, maybe—"

"Ah, no," Mr. Jinx purred, clasping both hands over the top of his cobra cane. "You misunderstand. I *cause* accidents."

"Cause accidents!" Breathing heavily, Roscoe found himself on his feet. The old protection racket! As if he hadn't just bought off the Mahoney mob by promising them inside dope on all his fights, so they could place their money right. Now this faker—

"Not faker." The deep voice was resonant in the room. "Fakir. You must not confuse the two. Now sit down. Mr. Wentworth"—and under the unwinking, snakelike gaze Roscoe found himself sitting again—"and let me explain. Briefly. I do not enjoy conversation. Although —"

The black eyes flicked for an instant to Millie. Then the turbaned one resumed.

"My profession," he went on, "is that of a causer of accidents. For a consideration I will refrain from employing my somewhat peculiar and unique talents to your disadvantage. If you do not care to retain my services—well, odd things may happen to your hirelings in their combats, and it is even possible that you yourself may suffer some unfortunate experiences. Do I make myself clear?"

"You're darn tootin' you do!" Roscoe declared, inelegantly. "Protection, huh! Well, I got protection awready. An' you're gonna get th' gate."

He pressed a buzzer. The door opened. Two large bruisers, retired from active service in the wrestling wracket—pardon me, racket—but still plenty good enough for bouncers, lumbered in. They were Murderous Mordred, the Minnesota Mauler, once champion of Mexico, and Ivan Yousapouf, the Russian Massacre, once Champion of Champions—the only title he could win.

"Throw him out!" Roscoe hollered. "Toss him on his ear so hard he bounces!"

With fire in their eyes and garlic on their breath, Wentworth's two behemoths charged. Mr. Jinx, however, made no move to avoid them. He threw himself up, folded his arms so that the hand bearing his ring was uppermost, and stared down into the transparent depth of its tiny crystal ball.

What he saw there is unknown. But what happened was immediate. The Mauler stepped on one of his own feet and fell heavily, banging his head against the desk and chipping the corner. From there he thundered to the floor and lay prone, smiling in unconsciousness—probably dreamed he was back on the mat again in the careless days of his youth.

The Massacre, continuing on, swung on Mr. Jinx. He missed and whirled around, getting in a solid blow at the base of his own skull. Like a poled ox he fell on top of the Mauler, and after a moment began to snore.

"You see?" the turbaned one asked. "It is but a minor example of my powers."

"Powers!" Millie snorted. "Those poor, punch-drunk palookas could knock themselves silly in a feather bed. Why, Ivan had a bad dream one night and bit himself in the small of the back. And got blood poisoning, too!"

"Sure!" Roscoe chimed in. "You ain't proved nothing."

Mr. Jinx did not smile. He stared at Roscoe, and his unwinking gaze probed the fat little man like a knife. Finally he nodded, the black turban moving in a slow, ominous arc.

"You have an enemy," he told Roscoe in resonant tones. "The one outside now. He wishes to kill you. You fear him. Upon him I will demonstrate my greatest power. It will not be an accident that he suffers. I will make the proof of my talents plain. I will dispose of him, once and for all, beyond the art of man to recall. He will go into limbo.''

"Limbo?" Roscoe repeated doubtfully. "That's in Russia some place, ain't it?''

"Limbo," Mr. Jinx assured him, teeth flashing briefly in a cruel smile, "lies in a land between life and death. It is not a nice place.''

"It still sounds like Russia to me," Roscoe murmured, uneasily, but he turned to the window to watch. Millie turned too, skepticism and doubt struggling on her countenance.

Mr. Jinx folded his arms and gazed into the crystal of his ring with such concentration that perspiration sprang out on his forehead. His lips moved, and they heard words, strange and harsh and ringing, like the muted clash of brass.

Across the street Little Pitty was staring up at the window. He saw Roscoe Wentworth and made a motion toward his pocket. The fat man would have ducked back, except for a sight that held him in a species of paralysis.

Eighth Avenue was tolerably empty, except for the little gunman. So there was no one in the way of the mustard-colored haze that began to collect at the corner of Forty-ninth Street, and swirling gently, drifted northward toward Little Pitty.

The killer did not see it. It came up from behind him, vague of outline, like a top spinning at terrific speed. And then it swirled into him. The gunman staggered backward, as if some great force had seized him, and was engulfed in the heart of the mist. For a second or so the shadowy mass whirled there, then it began to drift north again, dissolving as it moved, so that by the time it reached Fiftieth Street it was gone.

And so was Little Pitty!

"He's gone," Millie whispered, her voice queer. "Gone!"

Mr. Roscoe Wentworth stumbled backward to his swivel chair and collapsed into it.

"Ulp!" he gurgled. "What ha-happened to him?"

"He has been removed," Mr. Jinx murmured. "The doorway has been opened for him, and he has been drawn through into limbo. Which is a most unpleasant place where one is neither dead nor alive, but wanders homeless until doomsday.''

"You can bring him back, though?" Roscoe asked.

The tall, turbaned one shook his head. "That is beyond my power. The forces I control do not extend to that. I offer one-way passage only."

And he smiled, his lips drawing back in a curious curl that made Roscoe Wentworth shudder, though the day was hot.

But disbelief still was mirrored on Millie's features.

"Just what *are* these 'powers' of yours, Mr. Jinx?" she demanded. "And who are you anyway?''

The man in the black turban breathed on the gold head of his cobra cane and polished it gently with his palm. His lips smiled, but his eyes held no mirth.

"I am from the East," he answered, directing his whole attention upon Millie. "In my boyhood I was destined to be a priest, but found the studies boring. I took up others, less well known. My master was a magician of rather sinister repute. From him I learned the control of certain powers, such as you have seen demonstrated. In seeking to turn these to my profit, it occurred to me that here in the Western world is to be found much wealth. I have come to obtain a share of it, by placing my abilities at the service of those who may have use for them.''

There was mockery in his voice now.

''It has occurred to me that what is known as the sporting world is a good place to begin. In it men are—less scrupulous. In time I shall extend my services to higher levels of society. For the present I shall deal in simple accidents and re-movals—such as you have witnessed. In time, when I have a sufficiency of worldly goods, I shall return to my own land. Until then''—a curious reddish flame leaped in the black eyes—''until then I shall take what I want of this Western land to which I have come, and ill will befall the man who tries to balk my purpose.''

He smiled again, and again Roscoe shivered.

''You are unconvinced,'' the turbaned man told Millie. ''In your mind lurks the suspicion that the one who vanished was my cohort, acting under my orders to deceive and frighten you.''

Millie stiffened, for that was the exact suspicion in her mind.

''I shall give you further proof, then.''

The tall man whirled, took up the daily paper on Roscoe's desk, opened to a picture on the sporting page of the previous night's bout. A pointed nail touched a bald head in the foreground of the news photo.

''This man,'' Mr. Jinx said deeply. ''I do not know his name. His face I can not see. I judge him to be important—''

''Important!'' Roscoe choked. ''That's Maxie Mullion. Why, he's the boss of the whole East Side. He has a finger in more crooked—''

''A politician!'' There was distant thunder in Mr. Jinx's voice.

''But look!'' Roscoe began, worriedly. ''You ain't—''

''Silence!''

Quivering like a nervous jellyfish, Roscoe gulped and subsided. Placing the picture upon the desk, Mr. Jinx folded his arms and concentrated as before upon his crystal ring. For a long moment he stood so, murmuring strange words. Then he looked up.

''It is done,'' he announced. ''You will read about it presently. For the moment I shall bid you adieu. There are other calls to be made, and I must find a suitable office. I shall have many clients. Later I shall return, for the first payment of my fees.''

Black eyes rested briefly on the locked safe behind Roscoe.

''Fifty thousand dollars will be the figure,'' Mr. Jinx announced, as though divining the exact amount in safekeeping there.

''You won't get it!'' Millie stated crisply, as Roscoe Wentworth turned a pale green with despair. ''We don't like crooks or chiselers around here, and you come under those headings whether you're a yogi, a swami, a fakir, or a faker. Besides, that fifty grand is mine—Jimmy's, I mean. And if Roscoe lets you have it, we never will be able to collect it from him. So—anyway, don't come back, unless you're looking for trouble. You may be able to buffalo poor Roscoe, but I'm not a man, and I'm not buffaloed.''

"It is true you are not a man." The turbaned one's voice was bland. "And the master who taught me gave urgent warning that women should be avoided, for they have no souls, and so many of my spells are impotent against them. But there are other minor powers that are effective, and I think I can make you believe in me. And at a later date, perhaps—more. If you will but look—''

He glanced at her shapely legs. Millie followed the direction of his gaze, and saw two long runs suddenly appear in the new, off-shade silk stockings that set off her legs so well. It was as though a sharp instrument had been drawn lightly down the threads, though she had felt nothing.

While Millie still stared in speechless horror at her stockings, Mr. Jinx turned to Roscoe Wentworth.

"Remember, I shall return," he warned, as he backed to the door.

"Why, you—" Millie spluttered, choked with wrath. "You—"

But the door closed and Mr. Jinx was gone before she could express herself.

For a time after the gentleman from the Orient vanished, relative silence held the office. Relative, because it was broken by the sharp click of Millie's high heels as she strode back and forth, sparks flashing from her eyes and electricity fairly crackling from her red curls. It was broken also by the asthmatic breathing of the Mauler and the Massacre, who still encumbered the floor, and by a low moaning, as of an animal dying in extreme agony somewhere distant, coming from Roscoe.

And presently it was broken additionally by shouts from the street of newsboys proclaiming an extra.

Ivan, the Massacre, groaned and got to his feet. The Mauler opened his eyes and also hoisted himself upright.

"Geez," the Massacre groaned, blinking about him, "I feel terrible. Did he t'row me outa th' ring?"

"Was we wrasslin'?" the Mauler inquired. "I dunno—I thought—"

"Get out!" Roscoe screamed, in high passion. "Bouncers, phooey! Bring me one of them extras, an' don't come back for a week!"

The two stampeded for the door. Millie turned away from the window and faced the fight promoter, whose cigar was a frayed stub.

"He went into a restaurant," she announced. "I watched. Well?"

"Well, what?" Roscoe groaned, all three chins quivering.

"Well, what do you intend to do?" Millie stamped her foot. "Pay, I suppose!"

Roscoe stabbed at his mouth with the cigar, and missed by two inches.

"But what can I do, Millie?" he groaned. "Against a guy like him? Mr. Jinx! If he was to get mad—" Roscoe shuddered, and swallowed hard. Then his gaze fell on his safe. That recalled to mind the fifty grand Mr. Jinx was demanding. Roscoe Wentworth stiffened. There was nothing like the impending loss of a dollar to put starch in his spine.

"I got it!" he exclaimed, with relief. "It didn't any of it happen. He hypnotized us! Sure. He hypnotized me an' you an' Butch an' Ivan. Certainly I ain't
gonna pay him anything. He— Well, what is it?"

The Russian Massacre, edging in, dropped a pink-sheet paper on the desk and
scrambled out again.

"Just th' extra," he mumbled, and was gone, fleeing Roscoe's possible wrath.
But Roscoe was paying him no more attention. His gaze was riveted upon the
extra's headlines. His mouth opened. His cigar plopped to the floor.

"*Glug!*" he choked. "*Blup!*"

Millie looked over his shoulder at the headlines.

PROMINENT POLITICIAN VANISHES FROM BATH
*Secretary Hears Scream, Rushes to Aid. Finds Bathroom Door Locked, Water Run-
ning, Max J. Mullion Gone.*

"Then it wasn't hypnotism after all," Millie remarked, in a cool voice. "He
said he could do it just from a picture, too, and he did."

Roscoe sat down with a thud.

"Wh-what," he quavered, "can we d-do, Millie?"

"Do!" Millie snorted. "Fight back at him. If you don't, you'll be practically
his slave. I suppose you realize that?"

"Y-yes," Roscoe gulped. "But fight him *h-how?*"

"When you're fighting fire, fight it with more fire," Millie said obscurely, a
strange, cold gleam in her blue eyes. "Set a thief to catch a thief. You men! But
if you think you're going to pay Jimmy's fifty thousand dollars to that . . . that
swami, you've got three more thinks coming. Now I'm going out. I'll be back.
You stay here."

But Roscoe Wentworth had no intention of leaving. Even as, with unexplained
determination, Millie marched out, he was reaching for the bottle in his lower
left-hand drawer. When he got it, he raised the neck to his lips and held it there.
For he desperately wanted to erase the mental image that had come to him, of
rapacious old Maxie Mullion wandering through eternity, waiting for the crack of
doom, without even a bath towel to hide behind.

When Millie returned, two hours later, Mr. Roscoe Wentworth had consumed
the bottle, without apparent effect. His features were flushed and perspiration
spangled his brow and triplex chin, but he still was unable to forget how Little
Pitty had vanished into a mustard-colored cloud, or to put away from himself the
vision of Maxie Mullion—

"Well," Millie stared briskly, "after he ate, he went to call on Bennie Barber,
Nat Miller, and Colonel Worth. I expect he'll be coming back here soon."

"I know." Roscoe's voice was the plaintive moan of a beaten man. "They
called me up. Said he was there. Said he'd showed a few . . . tricks. Wanted to
know if I was going to pay. I said 'yes.' He wants fifty Gs from them, too. And
it's just a beginning. He let drop he was going to contact the mobs—like the

Schwartz mob and the Dougal boys—about removals! Ten grand apiece. In a year he'll own this town. All of it. And anybody who holds out will go to that . . . that place. Oh, what did I ever do to deserve this, Millie?''

"Plenty,'' Millie stated, unfeelingly. "But that's not the point. You men! Sometimes I think all of you put together haven't as much brains or courage as just one woman. You'll let him walk all over you. You'll pay him what he wants, and be glad of the chance.''

"Yeah,'' moaned Roscoe.

"You'll be afraid all the time.''

"Yeah,'' Roscoe groaned.

"Your life won't be worth living.''

"I know it, Millie,'' Roscoe said piteously. Then he looked up. Millie was gazing in a reflective manner down at the ugly runs in her stockings, and her lips were pursed.

"Millie!'' Roscoe Wentworth exclaimed, clutching at a straw of hope. "You're thinking of something?''

Millie raised her eyes, so large, so blue, so innocent.

"Maybe I *could* think of something,'' she suggested, "if only I wasn't so upset. About Jimmy's contract, and the fifty thousand dollars.''

She sighed. Roscoe sighed, too.

"You mean''—his tone was hollow—"if I was to say I'd tear up the contract and pay over the fifty thousand, you might be able to shoo off this Mr. Jinx?''

"I might,'' Millie answered. "I just barely might, Roscoe.''

The plump little man expelled his breath gustily.

"If you would say twenty-five grand, Millie,'' he began, and then the opening of the office door broke off his words.

"Good afternoon,'' Mr. Jinx said, and his smile was catlike. "I have returned, as I promised. Shall we now discuss the business we left unfinished?''

The words were addressed to Roscoe, but his eyes were on Millie. Millie stared back for a moment, then dropped her gaze. The cat smile broadened. The black turbaned man advanced into the office, and indicated the pink sheet on Roscoe's desk.

"You have read. You are convinced?''

Roscoe gulped, but Millie spoke before he could answer.

"Of course not,'' she said stoutly. "I still think it's a trick. So does he. I'm not convinced you're not a phony one little bit.''

"Ah.'' The dark eyes rested on her with a curious expression. "You are stubborn. What proof, then, will convince you?''

"To make somebody *I* pick out disappear,'' Millie answered.

Mr. Jinx leaned on his cobra cane, and seemed not displeased.

"You are a practical woman,'' he said, almost pleasantly. "And *why* not? Name the one, and limbo shall open for him. My powers are inexhaustible. One man more or less''—and the black eyes rested fleetingly on Roscoe, with so chill a menace that that plump gentleman shivered violently—"means to me as little as the life or death of a fly.''

"Well"—Millie hesitated now—"I . . . I don't, really—"

"You have chosen the test! Now name the one you wish the world relieved of!"

"All . . . all right," Millie gulped and opened her handbag. From it she took a picture, frayed at the edges, with a crease down the middle, the corners bent with soiled spots on the back. It was a blurred street scene with half a dozen figures in it.

"Th-this one," Millie stated, indicating a white splotch that was barely identifiable as the shoulder of a man in a summer suit, all the rest of him being hidden by the surrounding crowds. "I don't know his right name, or where he lives, or anything. I tried to get a picture of him once, and this was all I could get. But he's a b-blackmailer, and very ruthless and—"

"It is enough." Mr. Jinx took the picture, letting his fingers touch her hand as he did so, and a cold electric shock tingled up Millie's arm. "It will suffice. In a moment he will be no more."

Millie licked her lips.

"It's . . . sort of drastic," she said. "But . . . well, he deserves it."

"I am glad"—and Mr. Jinx's eyes held hers—"you have not a woman's usual squeamishness about such matters. And I think that when I have set your doubts at rest, we may become—better acquainted. Much, much better acquainted. You will—appreciate me more. Now—"

"Roscoe," Millie directed, her voice crisp again, "you'd better get out that fifty thousand dollars you have."

"Well—" Roscoe began, then catching the look in her eye, hurriedly swung around. "All right," he muttered, and spun the combination. "Here it is."

He laid five packets of bills on the desk, and prepared to close the steel door again, but Millie was too quick.

"Isn't that Jimmy Donegan's contract?" she cooed, snatching out a white, legal-looking document. "Jimmy wants to read it over later. All right, Roscoe, you can close it now."

Roscoe slammed the safe shut, angrily. Millie tucked the contract in her purse and faced Mr. Jinx.

The tall man in the black turban let his eyes traverse her visible charms again, lingeringly, then he took up the blurred photo.

"In a moment," he said vibrantly, "your enemy will leave this life for another, endless and unpleasant. Please be silent now."

Millie backed away toward the window, eyes wide. The turbaned one bowed his head, and concentrated upon the tiny globe of crystal in his ring. Roscoe Wentworth, baffled and bewildered, caught Millie's urgent gestures and tiptoed toward her.

Mr. Jinx, head bowed, was murmuring unknown words as, staring into the transparent depths of the bit of crystal, he summoned up the forces which blindly obeyed his orders.

Behind the turbaned man, in the corner of the big office, something stirred. Dust whirled, and Roscoe Wentworth almost let out a squeal of terror. Millie clapped her hand over his mouth just in time, and he was silent as that dark, shadowy mass in the corner, began to take form, began to spin, faster and faster, and spinning, swept down upon the motionless Mr. Jinx.

The one from the Orient had just time to wrench his mind from its task of directing terrible forces toward the unknown one and become aware of what was happening. But it was too late to stop the powers he had loosed. The spinning shadow touched him. Something like a terrific suction pulled at him and engulfed him. He had only time to know he had been tricked, and by a woman, and then he was hurtling through invisible portals into a world whose horrors he had never fully cared to think about—

Roscoe Wentworth stared at the spot where Mr. Jinx had been only a moment before, and still seemed to hear that last cry, coming as if from a land an immeasurable distance away. Then, still strangling as he tried to get air into his lungs, he started forward. Millie was ahead of him, though, and reached the five packets of bills still lying on the desk first.

She tucked them into her purse as Roscoe drew up, baffled, and shook her head.

"You men!" her voice dripped scorn. "If it wasn't for me, he *would* have owned this city. And it was so simple, too. I just bought a camera when I left, and waited for him outside the restaurant. Then I followed him until he was in a crowd, and took a picture of his back. For five dollars the drugstore downstairs rushed me a print. I rubbed it and folded it to make it look old."

"A picture of himself!" Roscoe croaked. "You mean . . . you made him put the finger on himself, Millie?"

"Of course," Millie cooed. "He said his powers would work, even from a picture he couldn't recognize, didn't he? And proved it by that old Maxie Mullion. Any woman would have thought of that right away—especially when she saw he was sort of stuck on her. Only a man would think of giving him fifty thousand dollars when it was so easy to get rid of him forever. And another person's fifty thousand, at that!" Millie finished accusingly.

"But—" Roscoe Wentworth stammered. "But—"

"Oh, he won't come back," Millie assured him, heading for the door. "You heard him say himself it's a one-way passage. So you don't have to worry. Of course, in a way I'm sorry for him, because he did have interesting eyes. But wherever he is"—and Millie's eyes flashed fire for a moment—"he deserves it! Maybe he'll know better next time than to say a girl hasn't got a soul, and to put runs in the last pair of silk stockings she's got!"

Then the door slammed, and she was gone. To Jimmy. And shortly thereafter, to Texas.

After a time, Roscoe Wentworth's mouth stopped opening and closing like a fish's. He looked at his ravished safe and winced. Then, into his eyes came a gleam of the native guile which always enabled him to emerge triumphant from any situation.

For a moment Roscoe stared hard at the emptiness that a moment before had been Mr. Jinx. Then cautiously skirting the spot, he gained his desk and his telephone, and dialed.

"Hello," he caroled. "Hello, Benny Barber? Is Nat Miller and Colonel Worth there? Lissen, about this Jinx fella. Yeah"—Roscoe looked quickly at the emptiness again, and decided to stretch matters a bit—"he's here now. I been talking him into a proposition. To go away and never bother us any more. For a hundred an' fifty grand he'll do it. I already put up fifty. If you fellas are interested, an' can raise th' other hundred, send it over to my office before five. An' I'll promise you'll never see him again. I'll take th' full responsibility. You think it's worth it? I think so, too! O. K. I'll be looking for your boy."

He put down the phone, elevated his feet, and reached for the cigar box. Then, lighting it, he deliberately blew strong smoke toward the spot where the gentleman in the black turban had last been seen and began to hum a glad little tune as he pondered on what he could give Millie and Jimmy as a wedding present, for which he was willing to spend as high as five dollars even.

HENRY KUTTNER

A Gnome There Was

Tim Crockett should never have snaked into the mine on Dornsef Mountain. What is winked at in California may have disastrous results in the coal mines of Pennsylvania. Especially when gnomes are involved.

Not that Tim Crockett knew about the gnomes. He was just investigating conditions among the lower classes, to use his own rather ill-chosen words. He was one of a group of southern Californians who had decided that labor needed them. They were wrong. They needed labor—at least eight hours of it a day.

Crockett, like his colleagues, considered the laborer a combination of a gorilla and The Man with the Hoe, probably numbering the Kallikaks among his ancestors. He spoke fierily of down-trodden minorities, wrote incendiary articles for the group's organ, *Earth,* and deftly maneuvered himself out of entering his father's law office as a clerk. He had, he said, a mission. Unfortunately, he got little sympathy from either the workers or their oppressors.

A psychologist could have analyzed Crockett easily enough. He was a tall, thin, intense-looking young man, with rather beady little eyes, and a nice taste in neckties. All he needed was a vigorous kick in the pants.

But definitely not administered by a gnome!

He was junketing through the country, on his father's money, investigating labor conditions, to the profound annoyance of such laborers as he encountered. It was with this idea in mind that he surreptitiously got into the Ajax coal mine— or, at least, one shaft of it—after disguising himself as a miner and rubbing his face well with black dust. Going down in the lift, he looked singularly untidy in the midst of a group of well-scrubbed faces. Miners look dirty only after a day's work.

Dornsef Mountain is honeycombed, but not with the shafts of the Ajax Company. The gnomes have ways of blocking their tunnels when humans dig too close. The whole place was complete confusion to Crockett. He let himself drift along with the others, till they began to work. A filled car rumbled past on its tracks. Crockett hesitated, and then sidled over to a husky specimen who seemed to have the marks of a great sorrow stamped on his face.

"Look," he said, "I want to talk to you."

"Inglis?" asked the other inquiringly. "Viskey. Chin. Vine. Hell."

Having thus demonstrated his somewhat incomplete command of English, he

241

bellowed hoarsely with laughter and returned to work, ignoring the baffled Crockett, who turned away to find another victim. But this section of the mine seemed deserted. Another loaded car rumbled past, and Crockett decided to see where it came from. He found out, after banging his head painfully and falling flat at least five times.

It came from a hole in the wall. Crockett entered it, and simultaneously heard a hoarse cry from behind him. The unknown requested Crockett to come back.

"So I can break your slab-sided neck," he promised, adding a stream of sizzling profanity. "Come outa there!"

Crockett cast one glance back, saw a gorillalike shadow lurching after him, and instantly decided that his stratagem had been discovered. The owners of the Ajax mine had sent a strong-arm man to murder him—or, at least, to beat him to a senseless pulp. Terror lent wings to Crockett's flying feet. He rushed on, frantically searching for a side tunnel in which he might lose himself. The bellowing from behind re-echoed against the walls. Abruptly Crockett caught a significant sentence clearly.

"—before that dynamite goes off!"

It was at that exact moment that the dynamite went off.

Crockett, however, did not know it. He discovered, quite briefly, that he was flying. Then he was halted, with painful suddenness, by the roof. After that he knew nothing at all, till he recovered to find a head regarding him steadfastly.

It was not a comforting sort of head—not one at which you would instinctively clutch for companionship. It was, in fact, a singularly odd, if not actually revolting, head. Crockett was too much engrossed with staring at it to realize that he was actually seeing in the dark.

How long had he been unconscious? For some obscure reason Crockett felt that it had been quite a while. The explosion had—what?

Buried him here behind a fallen roof of rock? Crockett would have felt little better had he known that he was in a used-up shaft, valueless now, which had been abandoned long since. The miners, blasting to open a new shaft, had realized that the old one would be collapsed, but that didn't matter.

Except to Tim Crockett.

He blinked, and when he reopened his eyes, the head had vanished. This was a relief. Crockett immediately decided the unpleasant thing had been a delusion. Indeed, it was difficult to remember what it had looked like. There was only a vague impression of a turnip-shaped outline, large, luminous eyes, and an incredibly broad slit of a mouth.

Crockett sat up, groaning. Where was this curious silvery radiance coming from? It was like daylight on a foggy afternoon, coming from nowhere in particular, and throwing no shadows. "Radium," thought Crockett, who knew very little of mineralogy.

He was in a shaft that stretched ahead into dimness till it made a sharp turn perhaps fifty feet away. Behind him—behind him the roof had fallen. Instantly Crockett began to experience difficulty in breathing. He flung himself upon the rubbly mound, tossing rocks frantically here and there, gasping and making hoarse, inarticulate noises.

He became aware, presently, of his hands. His movements slowed till he remained perfectly motionless, in a half-crouching posture, glaring at the large, knobbly, and surprising objects that grew from his wrists. Could he, during his period of unconsciousness, have acquired mittens? Even as the thought came to him, Crockett realized that no mittens ever knitted resembled in the slightest degree what he had a right to believe to be his hands. They twitched slightly.

Possibly they were caked with mud—no. It wasn't that. His hands had—altered. They were huge, gnarled, brown objects, like knotted oak roots. Sparse black hairs sprouted on their backs. The nails were definitely in need of a manicure—preferably with a chisel.

Crockett looked down at himself. He made soft cheeping noises, indicative of disbelief. He had squat bow legs, thick and strong, and no more than two feet long—less, if anything. Uncertain with disbelief, Crockett explored his body. It had changed—certainly not for the better.

He was slightly more than four feet high, and about three feet wide, with a barrel chest, enormous splay feet, stubby thick legs, and no neck whatsoever. He was wearing red sandals, blue shorts, and a red tunic which left his lean but sinewy arms bare. His head—

Turnip-shaped. The mouth—*Yipe!* Crockett had inadvertently put his fist clear into it. He withdrew the offending hand instantly, stared around in a dazed fashion, and collapsed on the ground. It couldn't be happening. It was quite impossible. Hallucinations. He was dying of asphyxiation, and delusions were preceding his death.

Crockett shut his eyes, again convinced that his lungs were laboring for breath. "I'm dying," he said. "I c-can't breathe."

A contemptuous voice said, "I hope you don't think you're breathing *air!*"

"I'm n-not—" Crockett didn't finish the sentence. His eyes popped again. He was hearing things.

He heard it again. "You're a singularly lousy specimen of gnome," the voice said. "But under Nid's law we can't pick and choose. Still, you won't be put to digging hard metals, I can see that. Anthracite's about your speed. What're you staring at? You're *very* much uglier than I am."

Crockett, endeavoring to lick his dry lips, was horrified to discover the end of his moist tongue dragging limply over his eyes. He whipped it back, with a loud smacking noise, and managed to sit up. Then he remained perfectly motionless, staring.

The head had reappeared. This time there was a body under it.

"I'm Gru Magru," said the head chattily. "You'll be given a gnomic name, of course, unless your own is guttural enough. What is it?"

"Crockett," the man responded, in a stunned, automatic manner.

"Hey?"

"Crockett."

"Stop making noises like a frog and—oh, I see. Crockett. Fair enough. Now get up and follow me or I'll kick the pants off you."

But Crockett did not immediately rise. He was watching Gru Magru—obviously a gnome. Short, squat and stunted, the being's figure resembled a bulging little barrel, topped by an inverted turnip. The hair grew up thickly to a peak—the root, as it were. In the turnip face was a loose, immense slit of a mouth, a button of a nose, and two very large eyes.

"Get *up!*" Gru Magru said.

This time Crockett obeyed, but the effort exhausted him completely. If he moved again, he thought, he would go mad. It would be just as well. Gnomes—

Gru Magru planted a large splay foot where it would do the most good, and Crockett described an arc which ended at a jagged boulder fallen from the roof. "Get up," the gnome said, with gratuitous bad temper, "or I'll kick you again. It's bad enough to have an outlying prospect patrol, where I might run into a man any time, without, *Up!* Or—"

Crockett got up. Gru Magru took his arm and impelled him into the depths of the tunnel.

"Well, you're a gnome now," he said. "It's the Nid law. Sometimes I wonder if it's worth the trouble. But I suppose it is—since gnomes can't propagate, and the average population has to be kept up somehow."

"I want to die," Crockett said wildly.

Gru Magru laughed. "Gnomes *can't* die. They're immortal, till the Day. Judgment Day, I mean."

"You're not logical," Crockett pointed out, as though by disproving one factor he could automatically disprove the whole fantastic business. "You're either flesh and blood and have to die eventually, or you're not, and then you're not real."

"Oh, we're flesh and blood, right enough," Gru Magru said. "But we're not mortal. There's a distinction. Not that I've anything against some mortals," he hastened to explain. "Bats, now—and owls—they're fine. But men!" He shuddered. "No gnome can stand the sight of a man."

Crockett clutched at a straw. "I'm a man."

"You were, you mean," Gru said. "Not a very good specimen, either, for my ore. But you're a gnome now. It's the Nid law."

"You keep talking about the Nid law," Crockett complained.

"Of course you don't understand," said Gru Magru, in a patronizing fashion. "It's this way. Back in ancient times, it was decreed that if any humans got lost in underearth, a tithe of them would be transformed into gnomes. The first gnome emperor, Podrang the Third, arranged that. He saw that fairies could kidnap human children and keep them, and spoke to the authorities about it. Said it was unfair. So when miners and such-like are lost underneath, a tithe of them are transformed into gnomes and join us. That's what happened to you. See?"

"No," Crockett said weakly. "Look. You said Podrang was the first gnome emperor. Why was he called Podrang the Third?"

"No time for questions," Gru Magru snapped. "Hurry!"

He was almost running now, dragging the wretched Crockett after him. The new gnome had not yet mastered his rather unusual limbs, and, due to the extreme wideness of his sandals, he trod heavily on his right hand, but after that learned to keep his arms bent and close to his sides. The walls, illuminated with that queer silvery radiance, spun past dizzily.

"W-what's that light?" Crockett managed to gasp. "Where's it coming from?"

"Light?" Gru Magru inquired. "It isn't light."

"Well, it isn't dark—"

"Of course it's dark," the gnome snapped. "How could we see if it wasn't dark?"

There was no possible answer to this, except, Crockett thought wildly, a frantic shriek. And he needed all his breath for running. They were in a labyrinth now, turning and twisting and doubling through innumerable tunnels, and Crockett knew he could never retrace his steps. He regretted having left the scene of the cave-in. But how could he have helped doing so?

"Hurry!" Gru Magru urged. "Hurry!"

"Why?" Crockett got out breathlessly.

"There's a fight going on!" the gnome said.

Just then they rounded a corner and almost blundered into the fight. A seething mass of gnomes filled the tunnel, battling with frantic fury. Red and blue pants and tunics moved in swift patchwork frenzy; turnip heads popped up and down vigorously. It was apparently a free-for-all.

"See!" Gru gloated. "A fight! I could smell it six tunnels away. Oh, a beauty!" He ducked as a malicious-looking little gnome sprang out of the huddle to seize a rock and hurl it with vicious accuracy. The missile missed its mark, and Gru, neglecting his captive, immediately hurled himself upon the little gnome, bore him down on the cave floor, and began to beat his head against it. Both parties shrieked at the tops of their voices, which were lost in the deafening din that resounded through the tunnel.

"Oh—my," Crockett said weakly. He stood staring, which was a mistake. A very large gnome emerged from the pile, seized Crockett by the feet, and threw him away. The terrified inadvertent projectile sailed through the tunnel to crash heavily into something which said, "*Whoo-doof!*" There was a tangle of malformed arms and legs.

Crockett arose to find that he had downed a vicious-looking gnome with flaming red hair and four large diamond buttons on his tunic. This repulsive creature lay motionless, out for the count. Crockett took stock of his injuries—there were none. His new body was hardy, anyway.

"You saved me!" said a new voice. It belonged to a—lady gnome. Crockett decided that if there was anything uglier than a gnome, it was the female of the species. The creature stood crouching just behind him, clutching a large rock in one capable hand.

Crockett ducked.

"I won't hurt you," the other howled above the din that filled the passage. "You saved me! Mugza was trying to pull my ears off—oh! He's waking up!"

The red-haired gnome was indeed recovering consciousness. His first act was to draw up his feet and, without rising, kick Crockett clear across the tunnel. The feminine gnome immediately sat on Mugza's chest and pounded his head with the rock till he subsided.

Then she arose. "You're not hurt? Good! I'm Brockle Buhn . . . Oh, look! He'll have his head off in a minute!"

Crockett turned to see that his erstwhile guide, Gru Magru, was gnomefully tugging at the head of an unidentified opponent, attempting, apparently, to twist it clear off. "What's it all about?" Crockett howled. "Uh-Brockle Buhn! *Brockle Buhn!*"

She turned unwillingly. "What?"

"The fight! What started it!"

"I did," she explained. "I said, 'Let's have a fight.' "

"Oh, that was all?"

"Then we started." Brockle Buhn nodded. "What's your name?"

"Crockett."

"You're new here, aren't you? Oh—I know. You were a human being!" Suddenly a new light appeared in her bulging eyes. "Crockett, maybe you can tell me something. What's a kiss?"

"A—kiss?" Crockett repeated, in a baffled manner.

"Yes. I was listening inside a knoll once, and heard two human beings talking—male and female, by their voices. I didn't dare look at them, of course, but the man asked the woman for a kiss."

"Oh," Crockett said, rather blankly. "He asked for a kiss, eh?"

"And then there was a smacking noise and the woman said it was wonderful. I've wondered ever since. Because if any gnome asked me for a kiss, I wouldn't know what he meant."

"Gnomes don't kiss?" Crockett asked in a perfunctory way.

"Gnomes dig," said Brockle Buhn. "And we eat. I like to eat. Is a kiss like mud soup?"

"Well, not exactly." Somehow Crockett managed to explain the mechanics of osculation.

The gnome remained silent, pondering deeply. At last she said, with the air of one bestowing mud soup upon a hungry applicant, "I'll give you a kiss."

Crockett had a nightmare picture of his whole head being engulfed in that enormous maw. He backed away. "N-no," he got out. "I-I'd rather not."

"Then let's fight," said Brockle Buhn, without rancor, and swung a knotted fist which smacked painfully athwart Crockett's ear. "Oh, no," she said regretfully, turning away. "The fight's over. It wasn't very long, was it?"

Crockett, rubbing his mangled ear, saw that in every direction gnomes were picking themselves up and hurrying off about their business. They seemed to have forgotten all about the recent conflict. The tunnel was once more silent, save for the pad-padding of gnomes' feet on the rock. Gru Magru came over, grinning happily.

"Hello, Brockle Buhn," he greeted. "A good fight. Who's this?" He looked down at the prostrate body of Mugza, the red-haired gnome.

"Mugza," said Brockle Buhn. "He's still out. Let's kick him."

They proceeded to do it with vast enthusiasm, while Crockett watched and decided never to allow himself to be knocked unconscious. It definitely wasn't safe. At last, however, Gru Magru tired of the sport and took Crockett by the arm again. "Come along," he said, and they sauntered along the tunnel, leaving Brockle Buhn jumping up and down on the senseless Mugza's stomach.

"You don't seem to mind hitting people when they're knocked out," Crockett hazarded.

"It's *much* more fun," Gru said happily. "That way you can tell just where you want to hit 'em. Come along. You'll have to be inducted. Another day, another gnome. Keeps the population stable," he explained, and fell to humming a little song.

"Look," Crockett said. "I just thought of something. You say human beings are turned into gnomes to keep the population stable. But if gnomes don't die, doesn't that mean that there are more gnomes now than ever? The population keeps rising, doesn't it?"

"Be still," Gru Magru commanded. "I'm singing."

It was a singularly tuneless song. Crockett, his thoughts veering madly, wondered if the gnomes had a national anthem. Probably "Rock Me to Sleep." Oh, well.

"We're going to see the Emperor," Gru said at last. "He always sees the new gnomes. You'd better make a good impression, or he'll put you to placer-mining lava."

"Uh—" Crockett glanced down at his grimy tunic. "Hadn't I better clean up a bit? That fight made me a mess."

"It wasn't the fight," Gru said insultingly. "What's wrong with you, anyway? I don't see anything amiss."

"My clothes—they're dirty."

"Don't worry about that," said the other. "It's good filthy dirt, isn't it? Here!" He halted, and, stooping, seized a handful of dust, which he rubbed into Crockett's face and hair. "That'll fix you up."

"I—*pffht!* . . . Thanks . . . *pffh!*" said the newest gnome. "I hope I'm dreaming. Because if I'm not—" He didn't finish. Crockett was feeling unwell.

They went through a labyrinth, far under Dornsef Mountain, and emerged at last in a bare, huge chamber with a throne of rock at one end of it. A small gnome was sitting on the throne paring his toenails. "Bottom of the day to you," Gru said. "Where's the Emperor?"

"Taking a bath," said the other. "I hope he drowns. Mud, mud, mud—morning, noon and night. First it's too hot. Then it's too cold. Then it's too thick. I work my fingers to the bone mixing his mud baths, and all I get is a kick," the small gnome continued plaintively. "There's such a thing as being too dirty. Three mud baths a day—that's carrying it too far. And never a thought for me! Oh, no.

I'm a mud puppy, that's what I am. He called me that today. Said there were lumps in the mud. Well, why not? That damned loam we've been getting is enough to turn a worm's stomach. You'll find His Majesty in there," the little gnome finished, jerking his foot toward an archway in the wall.

Crockett was dragged into the next room, where, in a sunken bath filled with steaming, brown mud, a very fat gnome sat, only his eyes discernible through the oozy coating that covered him. He was filling his hands with mud and letting it drip over his head, chuckling in a senile sort of way as he did so.

"Mud," he remarked pleasantly to Gru Magru, in a voice like a lion's bellow. "Nothing like it. Good rich mud. *Ah!*"

Gru was bumping his head on the floor, his large, capable hand around Crockett's neck forcing the other to follow suit.

"Oh, get up," said the Emperor. "What's this? What's this gnome been up to? Out with it."

"He's new," Gru explained. "I found him topside. The Nid law, you know."

"Yes, of course. Let's have a look at you. Ugh! I'm Podrang the Second, Emperor of the Gnomes. What have you to say to that?"

All Crockett could think of was: "How—how can you be Podrang the Second? I thought Podrang the Third was the first emperor."

"A chatterbox," said Podrang II, disappearing beneath the surface of the mud and spouting as he rose again. "Take care of him, Gru. Easy work at first. Digging anthracite. Mind you don't eat any while you're on the job," he cautioned the dazed Crockett. "After you've been here a century, you're allowed one mud bath a day. Nothing like 'em," he added, bringing up a gluey handful to smear over his face.

Abruptly he stiffened. His lion's bellow rang out.

"Drook! *Drook!*"

The little gnome Crockett had seen in the throne room scurried in, wringing his hands. "Your Majesty! Isn't the mud warm enough?"

"You crawling blob!" roared Podrang II. "You slobbering, offspring of six thousand individual offensive stenches! You mica-eyed, incompetent, draggle-eared, writhing blot on the good name of gnomes! You geological mistake! You—you—"

Drook took advantage of his master's temporary inarticulacy. "It's the best mud, Your Majesty! I refined it myself. Oh, Your Majesty, what's wrong?"

"There's a worm in it!" His Majesty bellowed, and launched into a stream of profanity so horrendous that it practically made the mud boil. Clutching his singed ears, Crockett allowed Gru Magru to drag him away.

"I'd like to get the old boy in a fight," Gru remarked, when they were safely in the depths of a tunnel, "but he'd use magic, of course. That's the way he is. Best emperor we've ever had. Not a scrap of fair play in his bloated body."

"Oh," Crockett said blankly. "Well, what next?"

"You heard Podrang, didn't you? You dig anthracite. And if you eat any, I'll kick your teeth in."

* * *

Brooding over the apparent bad tempers of gnomes, Crockett allowed himself to be conducted to a gallery where dozens of gnomes, both male and female, were using picks and mattocks with furious vigor. "This is it," Gru said. "Now! You dig anthracite. You work twenty hours, and then sleep six."

"Then what?"

"Then you start digging again," Gru explained. "You have a brief rest once every ten hours. You mustn't stop digging in between, unless it's for a fight. Now, here's the way you locate coal. Just think of it."

"Eh?"

"How do you think I found you?" Gru asked impatiently. "Gnomes have—certain senses. There's a legend that fairy folk can locate water by using a forked stick. Well, we're attracted to metals. Think of anthracite," he finished, and Crockett obeyed. Instantly he found himself turning to the wall of the tunnel nearest him.

"See how it works?" Gru grinned. "It's a natural evolution, I suppose. Functional. We have to know where the underneath deposits are, so the authorities gave us this sense when we were created. Think of ore—or any deposit in the ground—and you'll be attracted to it. Just as there's a repulsion in all gnomes against daylight."

"Eh?" Crockett started slightly. "What was that?"

"Negative and positive. We need ores, so we're attracted to them. Daylight is harmful to us, so if we think we're getting too close to the surface, we think of light, and it repels us. Try it!"

Crockett obeyed. Something seemed to be pressing down the top of his head.

"Straight up," Gru nodded. "But it's a long way. I saw daylight once. And—a man, too." He stared at the other. "I forgot to explain. Gnomes can't stand the sight of human beings. They—well, there's a limit to how much ugliness a gnome can look at. Now you're one of us, you'll feel the same way. Keep away from daylight, and never look at a man. It's as much as your sanity is worth."

There was a thought stirring in Crockett's mind. He could, then, find his way out of this maze of tunnels, simply by employing his new sense to lead him to daylight. After that—well, at least he would be above ground.

Gru Magru shoved Crockett into a place between two busy gnomes and thrust a pick into his hands. "There. Get to work."

"Thanks for—" Crockett began, when Gru suddenly kicked him and then took his departure, humming happily to himself. Another gnome came up, saw Crockett standing motionless, and told him to get busy, accompanying the command with a blow on his already tender ear. Perforce Crockett seized the pick and began to chop anthracite out of the wall.

"Crockett!" said a familiar voice. "It's you! I thought they'd send you here."

It was Brockle Buhn, the feminine gnome Crockett had already encountered. She was swinging a pick with the others, but dropped it now to grin at her companion.

"You won't be here long," she consoled. "Ten years or so. Unless you run into trouble, and then you'll be put at really hard work."

Crockett's arms were already aching. "*Hard* work! My arms are going to fall off in a minute."

He leaned on his pick. "Is this your regular job?"

"Yes—but I'm seldom here. Usually I'm being punished. I'm a troublemaker, I am. I eat anthracite."

She demonstrated, and Crockett shuddered at the audible crunching sound. Just then the overseer came up. Brockle Buhn swallowed hastily.

"What's this?" he snarled. "Why aren't you at work?"

"We were just going to fight," Brockle Buhn explained.

"Oh—just the two of you? Or can I join in?"

"Free for all," the unladylike gnome offered, and struck the unsuspecting Crockett over the head with her pick. He went out like a light.

Awakening some time later, he investigated bruised ribs and decided Brockle Buhn must have kicked him after he'd lost consciousness. What a gnome! Crockett sat up, finding himself in the same tunnel, dozens of gnomes busily digging anthracite.

The overseer came toward him. "Awake, eh? Get to work!"

Dazedly Crockett obeyed. Brockle Buhn flashed him a delighted grin. "You missed it. I got an ear—see?" She exhibited it. Crockett hastily lifted an exploring hand. It wasn't his.

Dig . . . dig . . . dig . . . the hours dragged past. Crockett had never worked so hard in his life. But, he noticed, not a gnome complained. Twenty hours of toil, with one brief rest period—he'd slept through that. Dig . . . dig . . . dig . . .

Without ceasing her work, Brockle Buhn said, "I think you'll make a good gnome, Crockett. You're toughening up already. Nobody'd ever believe you were once a man."

"Oh—no?"

"No. What were you, a miner?"

"I was—" Crockett paused suddenly. A curious light came into his eyes.

"I was a labor organizer," he finished.

"What's that?"

"Ever heard of a union?" Crockett asked, his gaze intent.

"Is it an ore?" Brockle Buhn shook her head. "No, I've never heard of it. What's a union?"

Crockett explained. No genuine labor organizer would have accepted that explanation. It was, to say the least, biased.

Brockle Buhn seemed puzzled. "I don't see what you mean, exactly, but I suppose it's all right."

"Try another tack," Crockett said. "Don't you ever get tired of working twenty hours a day?"

"Sure. Who wouldn't?"

"Then why do it?"

"We always have," Brockle Buhn said indulgently. "We can't stop."

"Suppose you did?"

"I'd be punished—beaten with stalactites, or something."

"Suppose you did," Crockett insisted. "Every damn gnome. Suppose you had a sit-down strike."

"You're crazy," Brockle Buhn said. "Such a thing's never happened. It—it's *human*."

"Kisses never happened underground, either," said Crockett. "No, I don't want one! And I don't want to fight either. Good heavens, let me get the set-up here. Most of the gnomes work to support the privileged classes."

"No. We just work."

"But why?"

"We always have. And the Emperor wants us to."

"Has the Emperor ever worked?" Crockett demanded, with an air of triumph. "No! He just takes mud baths! Why shouldn't every gnome have the same privilege? Why—"

He talked on, at great length, as he worked. Brockle Buhn listened with increasing interest. And eventually she swallowed the bait—hook, line and sinker.

An hour later she was nodding agreeably. "I'll pass the word along. Tonight. In the Roaring Cave. Right after work."

"Wait a minute," Crockett objected. "How many gnomes can we get?"

"Well—not very many. Thirty?"

"We'll have to organize first. We'll need a definite plan."

Brockle Buhn went off at a tangent. "Let's fight."

"No! Will you listen? We need a—a council. Who's the worst trouble-maker here?"

"Mugza, I think," she said. "The red-haired gnome you knocked out when he hit me."

Crockett frowned slightly. Would Mugza hold a grudge? Probably not, he decided. Or, rather, he'd be no more ill tempered than other gnomes. Mugza might attempt to throttle Crockett on sight, but he'd no doubt do the same to any gnome. Besides, as Brockle Buhn went on to explain, Mugza was the gnomic equivalent of a duke. His support would be valuable.

"And Gru Magru," she suggested. "He loves new things, especially if they make trouble."

"Yeah." These were not the two Crockett would have chosen, but at least he could think of no other candidates. "If we could get somebody who's close to the Emperor . . . What about Drook—the guy who gives Podrang his mud baths?"

"Why not? I'll fix it." Brockle Buhn lost interest and surreptitiously began to eat anthracite. Since the overseer was watching, this resulted in a violent quarrel, from which Crockett emerged with a black eye. Whispering profanity under his breath, he went back to digging.

But he had time for a few more words with Brockle Buhn. She'd arrange it. That night there would be a secret meeting of the conspirators.

Crockett had been looking forward to exhausted slumber, but this chance was too good to miss. He had no wish to continue his unpleasant job digging anthracite. His body ached fearfully. Besides, if he could induce the gnomes to strike, he might be able to put the squeeze on Podrang II. Gru Magru had said the Emperor was a magician. Couldn't he, then, transform Crockett back into a man?

"He's never done that," Brockle Buhn said, and Crockett realized he had spoken his thought aloud.

"Couldn't he, though—if he wanted?"

Brockle Buhn merely shuddered, but Crockett had a little gleam of hope. To be human again!

Dig . . . dig . . . dig . . . dig . . . with monotonous, deadening regularity. Crockett sank into a stupor. Unless he got the gnomes to strike, he was faced with an eternity of arduous toil. He was scarcely conscious of knocking off, of feeling Brockle Buhn's gnarled hand under his arm, of being led through passages to a tiny cubicle, which was his new home. The gnome left him there, and he crawled into a stony bunk and went to sleep.

Presently a casual kick aroused him. Blinking, Crockett sat up, instinctively dodging the blow Gru Magru was aiming at his head. He had four guests—Gru, Brockle Buhn, Drook and the red-haired Mugza.

"Sorry I woke up too soon," Crockett said bitterly. "If I hadn't, you could have got in another kick."

"There's lots of time," Gru said. "Now, what's this all about? I wanted to sleep, but Brockle Buhn here said there was going to be a fight. A *big* one, huh?"

"Eat first," Brockle Buhn said firmly. "I'll fix mud soup for everybody." She bustled away, and presently was busy in a corner, preparing refreshments. The other gnomes squatted on their haunches, and Crockett sat on the edge of his bunk, still dazed with sleep.

But he managed to explain his idea of the union. It was received with interest—chiefly, he felt, because it involved the possibility of a tremendous scrap.

"You mean every Dornsef gnome jumps the Emperor?" Gru asked.

"No, no! Peaceful arbitration. We just refuse to work. All of us."

"*I* can't," Drook said. "Podrang's got to have his mud baths, the bloated old slug. He'd send me to the fumaroles till I was roasted."

"Who'd take you there?" Crockett asked.

"Oh—the guards, I suppose."

"But they'd be on strike, too. *Nobody'd* obey Podrang, till he gave in."

"Then he'd enchant me," Drook said.

"He can't enchant us all," Crockett countered.

"But he could enchant *me*," Drook said with great firmness. "Besides, he *could* put a spell on every gnome in Dornsef. Turn us into stalactites or something."

"Then what? He wouldn't have any gnomes at all. Half a loaf is better than none. We'll just use logic on him. Wouldn't he rather have a little less work done than none at all?"

"Not him," Gru put in. "He'd rather enchant us. Oh, he's a bad one, he is," the gnome finished approvingly.

* * *

But Crockett couldn't quite believe this. It was too alien to his understanding of psychology—human psychology, of course. He turned to Mugza, who was glowering furiously.

"What do you think about it?"

"I want to fight," the other said rancorously. "I want to kick somebody."

"Wouldn't you rather have mud baths three times a day?"

Mugza grunted. "Sure. But the Emperor won't let me."

"Why not?"

"Because I want 'em."

"You can't be contented," Crockett said desperately. "There's more to life than—than digging."

"Sure. There's fighting. Podrang lets us fight whenever we want."

Crockett had a sudden inspiration. "But that's just it. He's going to stop all fighting! He's going to pass a new law forbidding fighting except to himself."

It was an effective shot in the dark. Every gnome jumped.

"Stop—*fighting!*" That was Gru, angry and disbelieving. "Why, we've always fought."

"Well, you'll have to stop," Crockett insisted.

"Won't!"

"Exactly! Why should you? Every gnome's entitled to life, liberty and the pursuit of pugilism."

"Let's go and beat up Podrang," Mugza offered, accepting a steaming bowl of mud soup from Brockle Buhn.

"No, that's not the way—no thanks, Brockle Buhn—not the way at all. A strike's the thing. We'll peaceably force Podrang to give us what we want."

He turned to Drook. "Just what can Podrang do about it if we all sit down and refuse to work?"

The little gnome considered. "He'd swear. And kick me."

"Yeah—and then what?"

"Then he'd go off and enchant everybody, tunnel by tunnel."

"Uh-huh." Crockett nodded. "A good point. Solidarity is what we need. If Podrang finds a few gnomes together, he can scare the hell out of them. But if we're all together—that's it! When the strike's called, we'll all meet in the biggest cave in the joint."

"That's the Council Chamber," Gru said. "Next to Podrang's throne room."

"O.K. We'll meet there. How many gnomes will join us?"

"All of 'em," Mugza grunted, throwing his soup bowl at Drook's head. "The Emperor can't stop us fighting."

"And what weapons can Podrang use, Drook?"

"He might use the Cockatrice Eggs," the other said doubtfully.

"What are those?"

"They're not really eggs," Gru broke in. "They're magic jewels for wholesale enchantments. Different spells in each one. The green ones, I think, are for turning people into earthworms. Podrang just breaks one, and the spell spreads out for twenty feet or so. The red ones are—let's see. Transforming gnomes into human beings—though that's a bit *too* tough. No . . . yes. The blue ones—''

''Into *human beings!*'' Crockett's eyes widened. ''Where are the eggs kept?''

''Let's fight,'' Mugza offered, and hurled himself bodily on Drook, who squeaked frantically and beat his attacker over the head with his soup bowl, which broke. Brockle Buhn added to the excitement by kicking both battlers impartially, till felled by Gru Magru. Within a few moments the room resounded with the excited screams of gnomic battle. Inevitably Crockett was sucked in . . .

Of all the perverted, incredible forms of life that had ever existed, gnomes were about the oddest. It was impossible to understand their philosophy. Their minds worked along different paths from human intelligences. Self-preservation and survival of the race—these two vital human instincts were lacking in gnomes. They neither died nor propagated. They just worked and fought. Bad-tempered little monsters, Crockett thought irritably. Yet they had existed for—ages. Since the beginning, maybe. Their social organism was the result of evolution far older than man's. It might be well suited to gnomes. Crockett might be throwing the unnecessary monkey wrench in the machinery.

So what? He wasn't going to spend eternity digging anthracite, even though, in retrospect, he remembered feeling a curious thrill of obscure pleasure as he worked. Digging might be fun for gnomes. Certainly it was their *raison d'être*. In time Crockett himself might lose his human affiliations, and be metamorphosed completely into a gnome. What had happened to other humans who had undergone such an—alteration as he had done? All gnomes look alike. But maybe Gru Magru had once been human—or Drook—or Brockle Buhn.

They were gnomes now, at any rate, thinking and existing completely as gnomes. And in time he himself would be exactly like them. Already he had acquired the strange tropism that attracted him to metals and repelled him from daylight. But he didn't *like* to dig!

He tried to recall the little he knew about gnomes—miners, metalsmiths, living underground. There was something about the Picts—dwarfish men who hid underground when invaders came to England, centuries ago. That seemed to tie in vaguely with the gnomes' dread of human beings. But the gnomes themselves were certainly not descended from Picts. Very likely the two separate races and species had become identified through occupying the same habitat.

Well, that was no help. What about the Emperor? He wasn't, apparently, a gnome with a high I.Q., but he *was* a magician. Those jewels—Cockatrice Eggs— were significant. If he could get hold of the ones that transformed gnomes into men . . .

But obviously he couldn't, at present. Better wait. Till the strike had been called. The strike . . .

Crockett went to sleep.

He was roused, painfully, by Brockle Buhn, who seemed to have adopted him. Very likely it was her curiosity about the matter of a kiss. From time to time she offered to give Crockett one, but he steadfastly refused. In lieu of it, she supplied

him with breakfast. At least, he thought grimly, he'd get plenty of iron in his
system, even though the rusty chips rather resembled corn flakes. As a special
inducement Brockle Buhn sprinkled coat dust over the mess.

Well, no doubt his digestive system had also altered. Crockett wished he could
get an X-ray picture of his insides. Then he decided it would be much too dis-
turbing. Better not to know. But he could not help wondering. Gears in his stomach? Small millstones? What would happen if he inadvertently swallowed some
emery dust? Maybe he could sabotage the Emperor that way.

Perceiving that his thoughts were beginning to veer wildly, Crockett gulped the
last of his meal and followed Brockle Buhn to the anthracite tunnel.

"How about the strike? How's it coming?"

"Fine, Crockett." She smiled, and Crockett winced at the sight. "Tonight all
the gnomes will meet in the Roaring Cave. Just after work."

There was no time for more conversation. The overseer appeared, and the gnomes
snatched up their picks. Dig . . . dig . . . dig . . . It kept up at the same pace.
Crockett sweated and toiled. It wouldn't be for long. His mind slipped a cog, so
that he relapsed into a waking slumber, his muscles responding automatically to
the need. Dig, dig, dig. Sometimes a fight. Once a rest period. Then dig again.

Five centuries later the day ended. It was time to sleep.

But there was something much more important. The union meeting in the Roaring Cave. Brockle Buhn conducted Crockett there, a huge cavern hung with glittering green stalactites. Gnomes came pouring into it. Gnomes and more gnomes.
The turnip heads were everywhere. A dozen fights started. Gru Magru, Mugza
and Drook found places near Crockett. During a lull Brockle Buhn urged him to
a platform of rock jutting from the floor.

"Now," she whispered. "They all know about it. Tell them what you want."

Crockett was looking out over the bobbing heads, the red and blue garments,
all lit by that eerie silver glow. "Fellow gnomes," he began weakly.

"*Fellow gnomes!*" The words roared out, magnified by the acoustics of the
cavern. That bull bellow gave Crockett courage. He plunged on.

"Why should you work twenty hours a day? Why should you be forbidden
to eat the anthracite you dig, while Podrang squats in his bath and laughs at
you? Fellow gnomes, the Emperor is only one; you are many! He can't make
you work. How would you like mud soup three times a day? The Emperor can't
fight you all. If you refuse to work—all of you—he'll have to give in! He'll
have to!"

"Tell 'em about the non-fighting edict," Gru Magru called.

Crockett obeyed. That got 'em. Fighting was dear to every gnomic heart. And
Crockett kept on talking.

"Podrang will try to back down, you know. He'll pretend he never intended to
forbid fighting. That'll show he's afraid of you! We hold the whip hand! We'll
strike—and the Emperor can't do a damn thing about it. When he runs out of
mud for his baths, he'll capitulate soon enough."

"He'll enchant us all," Drook muttered sadly.

"He won't dare! What good would that do? He knows which side his—ugh—which side his mud is buttered on. Podrang is unfair to gnomes! That's our watchword!"

It ended, of course, in a brawl. But Crockett was satisfied. The gnomes would not go to work tomorrow. They would, instead, meet in the Council Chamber, adjoining Podrang's throne room—and sit down.

That night he slept well.

In the morning Crockett went, with Brockle Buhn, to the Council Chamber, a cavern gigantic enough to hold the thousands of gnomes who thronged it. In the silver light their red and blue garments had a curiously elfin quality. Or, perhaps, naturally enough, Crockett thought. Were gnomes, strictly speaking, elves?

Drook came up. "I didn't draw Podrang's mud bath," he confided hoarsely. "Oh, but he'll be furious. Listen to him."

And, indeed, a distant crackling of profanity was coming through an archway in one wall of the cavern.

Mugza and Gru Magru joined them. "He'll be along directly," the latter said. "What a fight there'll be!"

"Let's fight now," Mugza suggested. "I want to kick somebody. Hard."

"There's a gnome who's asleep," Crockett said. "If you sneak up on him, you can land a good one right in his face."

Mugza, drooling slightly, departed on his errand, and simultaneously Podrang II, Emperor of the Dornsef Gnomes, stumped into the cavern. It was the first time Gru Magru had seen the ruler without a coating of mud, and he could not help gulping at the sight. Podrang was *very* ugly. He combined in himself the most repulsive qualities of every gnome Crockett had previously seen. The result was perfectly indescribable.

"Ah," said Podrang, halting and swaying on his short bow legs. "I have guests. Drook! Where in the name of the nine steaming hells is my bath?" But Drook had ducked from sight.

The Emperor nodded. "I see. Well, I won't lose my temper, *I won't lose my temper!* I WON'T—"

He paused as a stalactite was dislodged from the roof and crashed down. In the momentary silence, Crockett stepped forward, cringing slightly.

"W-we're on strike," he announced. "It's a sit-down strike. We won't work till—"

"*Yaah!*" screamed the infuriated Emperor. "You won't work, eh? Why, you boggle-eyed, flap-tongued, drag-bellied offspring of unmentionable algae! You seething little leprous blotch of bat-nibbled fungus! You cringing parasite on the underside of a dwarfish and ignoble worm! *Yaaah!*"

"Fight!" the irrepressible Mugza yelled, and flung himself on Podrang, only to be felled by a well-placed foul blow.

Crockett's throat felt dry. He raised his voice, trying to keep it steady.

"Your Majesty! If you'll just wait a minute—"

"You mushroom-nosed spawn of degenerate black bats," the enraged Emperor shrieked at the top of his voice. "I'll enchant you all! I'll turn you into naiads!

Strike, will you! Stop me from having my mud bath, will you? By Kronos, Nid, Ymir and Loki, you'll have cause to regret this! *Yah!*" he finished, inarticulate with fury.

"Quick!" Crockett whispered to Gru and Brockle Buhn. "Get between them and the door, so he can't get hold of the Cockatrice Eggs."

"They're not in the throne room," Gru Magru explained unhelpfully. "Podrang just grabs them out of the air."

"Oh!" the harassed Crockett groaned. At that strategic moment Brockle Buhn's worst instincts overcame her. With a loud shriek of delight she knocked Crockett down, kicked him twice and sprang for the Emperor.

She got in one good blow before Podrang hammered her atop the head with one gnarled fist, and instantly her turnip-shaped skull seemed to prolapse into her torso. The Emperor, bright purple with fury, reached out—and a yellow crystal appeared in his hand.

It was one of the Cockatrice Eggs.

Bellowing like a *musth* elephant, Podrang hurled it. A circle of twenty feet was instantly cleared among the massed gnomes. But it wasn't vacant. Dozens of bats rose and fluttered about, adding to the confusion.

Confusion became chaos. With yells of delighted fury, the gnomes rolled forward toward their ruler. "Fight!" the cry thundered out, reverberating from the roof. "*Fight!*"

Podrang snatched another crystal from nothingness—a green one, this time. Thirty-seven gnomes were instantly transformed into earthworms, and were trampled. The Emperor went down under an avalanche of attackers, who abruptly disappeared, turned into mice by another of the Cockatrice Eggs.

Crockett saw one of the crystals sailing toward him, and ran like hell. He found a hiding place behind a stalagmite, and from there watched the carnage. It was definitely a sight worth seeing, though it could not be recommended to a nervous man.

The Cockatrice Eggs exploded in an incessant stream. Whenever that happened, the spell spread out for twenty feet or more before losing its efficacy. Those caught on the fringes of the circle were only partially transformed. Crockett saw one gnome with a mole's head. Another was a worm from the waist down. Another was—*ulp!* Some of the spell patterns were not, apparently, drawn even from known mythology.

The fury of noise that filled the cavern brought stalactites crashing down incessantly from the roof. Every so often Podrang's battered head would reappear, only to go down again as more gnomes sprang to the attack—to be enchanted. Mice, moles, bats and other things filled the Council Chamber. Crockett shut his eyes and prayed.

He opened them in time to see Podrang snatch a red crystal out of the air, pause and then deposit it gently behind him. A purple Cockatrice Egg came next. This crashed against the floor, and thirty gnomes turned into tree toads.

Apparently only Podrang was immune to his own magic. The thousands who had filled the cavern were rapidly thinning, for the Cockatrice Eggs seemed to come from an inexhaustible source of supply. How long would it be before Crockett's own turn came? He couldn't hide here forever.

His gaze riveted to the red crystal Podrang had so carefully put down. He was remembering something—the Cockatrice Egg that would transform gnomes into human beings. Of course! Podrang wouldn't use *that*, since the very sight of men was so distressing to gnomes. If Crockett could get his hands on that red crystal . . .

He tried it, sneaking through the confusion, sticking close to the wall of the cavern, till he neared Podrang. The Emperor was swept away by another onrush of gnomes, who abruptly changed into dormice, and Crockett got the red jewel. It felt abnormally cold.

He almost broke it at his feet before a thought stopped and chilled him. He was far under Dornsef Mountain, in a labyrinth of caverns. No human being could find his way out. But a gnome could, with the aid of his strange tropism to daylight.

A bat flew against Crockett's face. He was almost certain it squeaked, "What a fight!" in a parody of Brockle Buhn's voice, but he couldn't be sure. He cast one glance over the cavern before turning to flee.

It was a complete and utter chaos. Bats, moles, worms, ducks, eels and a dozen other species crawled, flew, ran, bit, shrieked, snarled, grunted, whooped and croaked all over the place. From all directions the remaining gnomes—only about a thousand now—were converging on a surging mound of gnomes that marked where the Emperor was. As Crockett stared the mound dissolved, and a number of gecko lizards ran to safety.

"*Strike, will you!*" Podrang bellowed. "*I'll show you!*"

Crockett turned and fled. The throne was deserted, and he ducked into the first tunnel. There, he concentrated on thinking of daylight. His left ear felt compressed. He sped on till he saw a side passage on the left, slanting up, and turned into it at top speed. The muffled noise of combat died behind him.

He clutched the red Cockatrice Egg tightly. What had gone wrong? Podrang should have stopped to parley. Only—only he hadn't. A singularly bad-tempered and short-sighted gnome. He probably wouldn't stop till he'd depopulated his entire kingdom. At the thought Crockett hurried along faster.

The tropism guided him. Sometimes he took the wrong tunnel, but always, whenever he thought of daylight, he would *feel* the nearest daylight pressing against him. His short, bowed legs were surprisingly hardy.

Then he heard someone running after him.

He didn't turn. The sizzling blast of profanity that curled his ears told him the identity of the pursuer. Podrang had no doubt cleared the Council Chamber, to the last gnome, and was now intending to tear Crockett apart pinch by pinch. That was only one of the things he promised.

Crockett ran. He shot along the tunnel like a bullet. The tropism guided him, but he was terrified lest he reach a dead end. The clamor from behind grew louder. If Crockett hadn't known better, he would have imagined that an army of gnomes pursued him.

Faster! Faster! But now Podrang was in sight. His roars shook the very walls. Crockett sprinted, rounded a corner, and saw a wall of flaming light—a circle of it, in the distance. It was daylight, as it appeared to gnomic eyes.

He could not reach it in time. Podrang was too close. A few more seconds, and those gnarled, terrible hands would close on Crockett's throat.

Then Crockett remembered the Cockatrice Egg. If he transformed himself into a man now, Podrang would not dare touch him. And he was almost at the tunnel's mouth.

He stopped, whirling and lifted the jewel. Simultaneously the Emperor, seeing his intention, reached out with both hands, and snatched six or seven of the crystals out of the air. He threw them directly at Crockett, a fusillade of rainbow colors.

But Crockett had already slammed the red gem down on the rock at his feet. There was an ear-splitting crash. Jewels seemed to burst all around Crockett—but the red one had been broken first.

The roof fell in.

A short while later, Crockett dragged himself painfully from the debris. A glance showed him that the way to the outer world was still open. And—thank heaven!— daylight looked normal again, not that flaming blaze of eye-searing white.

He looked toward the depths of the tunnel, and froze. Podrang was emerging, with some difficulty, from a mound of rubble. His low curses had lost none of their fire.

Crockett turned to run, stumbled over a rock, and fell flat. As he sprang up, he saw that Podrang had seen him.

The gnome stood transfixed for a moment. Then he yelled, spun on his heel, and fled into the darkness. He was gone. The sound of his rapid footfalls died.

Crockett swallowed with difficulty. *Gnomes are afraid of men—whew!* That had been a close squeak. But now . . .

He was more relieved than he had thought. Subconsciously he must have been wondering whether the spell would work, since Podrang had flung six or seven Cockatrice Eggs at him. But he had smashed the red one first. Even the strange, silvery gnome-light was gone. The depths of the cave were utterly black—and silent.

Crockett headed for the entrance. He pulled himself out, luxuriating in the warmth of the afternoon sun. He was near the foot of Dornsef Mountain, in a patch of brambles. A hundred feet away a farmer was plowing one terrace of a field.

Crockett stumbled toward him. As he approached, the man turned.

He stood transfixed for a moment. Then he yelled, spun on his heel, and fled.

His shrieks drifted back up the mountain as Crockett, remembering the Cockatrice Eggs, forced himself to look down at his own body.

Then he screamed too. But the sound was not one that could ever have emerged from a human throat.

Still, that was natural enough—under the circumstances.

Hereafter, Inc.

Phineas Theophilus Potts, who would have been the last to admit and the first to believe he was a godly man, creaked over in bed and stuck out one scrawny arm wrathfully. The raucous jangling of the alarm was an unusually painful cancer in his soul that morning. Then his waking mind took over and he checked his hand, bringing it down on the alarm button with precise, but gentle, firmness. Would he never learn to control these little angers? In this world one should bear all troubles with uncomplaining meekness, not rebel against them; otherwise——
But it was too early in the morning to think of that.

He wriggled out of bed and gave his thoughts over to the ritual of remembering yesterday's sins, checking to make sure all had been covered and wiped out the night before. That's when he got his first shock; he couldn't remember anything about the day before—bad, very bad. Well, no doubt it was another trap of the forces conspiring to secure Potts' soul. Tch, tch. Terrible, but he could circumvent even that snare.

There was no mere mumbling by habit to his confession; word after word rolled off his tongue carefully with full knowledge and unctuous shame until he reached the concluding lines. "For the manifold sins which I have committed and for this greater sin which now afflicts me, forgive and guide me to sin no more, but preserve me in righteousness all the days of my life. Amen." Thus having avoided the pitfall and saved himself again from eternal combustion, he scrubbed hands with himself and began climbing into his scratchy underclothes and cheap black suit. Then he indulged in a breakfast of dry toast and buttermilk flavored with self-denial and was ready to fare forth into the world of temptation around him.

The telephone jangled against his nerves and he jumped, grabbing for it impatiently before he remembered; he addressed the mouthpiece contritely. "Phineas Potts speaking."

It was Mr. Sloane, his lusty animal voice barking out from the receiver. " 'Lo, Phin, they told me you're ready to come down to work today. Business is booming and we can use you. How about it?"

"Certainly, Mr. Sloane. I'm not one to shirk my duty." There was no reason for the call that Potts could see; he hadn't missed a day in twelve years. "You know——"

"Sure, okay, That's fine. Just wanted to warn you that we've moved. You'll see the name plate right across the street when you come out—swell place, too. Sure you can make it all right?"

"I shall be there in ten minutes, Mr. Sloane," Phineas assured him, and remembered in time to hang up without displaying taste. Tch, poor Sloane, wallowing in sin and ignorant of the doom that awaited him. Why, the last time Phineas had chided his employer—mildly, too—Sloane had actually laughed at him! Dear. Well, no doubt he incurred grace by trying to save the poor lost soul, even though his efforts seemed futile. Of course, there was danger in consorting with such people, but no doubt his sacrifices would be duly recorded.

There was a new elevator boy, apparently, when he came out of his room. He sniffed pointedly at the smoke from the boy's cigarette; the boy twitched his lips, but did not throw it away.

"Okay, bub," he grunted as the doors clanked shut, grating across Phineas' nerves, "I don't like it no better'n you will, but here we are."

Bub! Phineas glared at the shoulders turned to him and shuddered. He'd see Mrs. Biddle about this later.

Suppressing his feelings with some effort, he headed across the lobby, scarcely noting it, and stepped out onto the street. Then he stopped. That was the second jolt. He swallowed twice, opened his eyes and lifted them for the first time in weeks, and looked again. It hadn't changed. Where there should have been a little twisted side street near the tenements, he saw instead a broad gleaming thoroughfare, busy with people and bright in warm golden sunshine. Opposite, the ugly stores were replaced with bright, new office buildings, and the elevated tracks were completely missing. He swung slowly about, clutching his umbrella for support as he faced the hotel; it was still a hotel—but not his—definitely not his. Nor was the lobby the same. He fumbled back into it, shaken and bewildered.

The girl at the desk smiled up at him out of dancing eyes, and she certainly wasn't the manager. Nor would prim Mrs. Biddle, who went to his church, have hired this brazen little thing; both her lips and fingernails were bright crimson, to begin with, and beyond that he preferred not to go.

The brazen little thing smiled again, as if glorying in her obvious idolatry. "Forget something, Mr. Potts?"

"I . . . uh . . . no. That is . . . you know who I am?"

She nodded brightly. "Yes indeed, Mr. Potts. You moved in yesterday. Room 408. Is everything satisfactory?"

Phineas half nodded, gulped, and stumbled out again. Moved in? He couldn't recall it. Why should he leave Mrs. Biddle's? And 408 was his old room number; the room was identical with the one he had lived in, even to the gray streak on the wallpaper that had bothered his eyes for years. Something was horribly wrong— first the lack of memory, then Sloane's peculiar call, now this. He was too upset even to realize that this was probably another temptation set before him.

Mechanically, Phineas spied Sloane's name plate on one of the new buildings and crossed over into it. "Morning, Mr. Potts," said the elevator boy, and Phineas jumped. He'd never seen this person before, either. "Fourth floor, Mr. Potts. Mr. Sloane's office is just two doors down."

Phineas followed the directions automatically, found the door marked "G. R. Sloane—Architect," and pushed into a huge room filled with the almost unbearable clatter of typewriters and Comptometers, the buzz of voices, and the jarring thump of an addressing machine. But this morning the familiarity of the sound seemed like a haven out of the wilderness until he looked around. Not only had Sloane moved, but he'd apparently also expanded and changed most of his office force. Only old Callahan was left, and Callahan——Strange, he felt sure Callahan had retired or something the year before. Oh, well, that was the least of his puzzles.

Callahan seemed to sense his stare, for he jumped up and brought a hamlike fist down on Phineas' back, almost knocking out the ill-fitting false teeth. "Phin Potts, you old doom-monger! Welcome back!" He thumped again and Potts coughed, trying to reach the spot and rub out the sting. Not only did Callahan have to be an atheist—an argumentative one—but he had to indulge in this gross horseplay. Why hadn't the man stayed properly retired?

"Mr. Sloane?" he managed to gurgle.

Sloane himself answered, his rugged face split in a grin. "Hi, Phin. Let him alone, Callahan. Another thump like that and I'll have to hire a new draftsman. Come on, Phin, there's the devil's own amount of work piled up for you now that you're back from your little illness." He led around a bunch of tables where bright-painted hussies were busily typing, down a hall, and into the drafting room, exchanging words with others that made Phineas wince. Really, his language seemed to grow worse each day.

"Mr. Sloane, would you please——"

"Mind not using such language," Sloane finished, and grinned. "Phin, I can't help it. I feel too good. Business is terrific and I've got the world by the tail. How do you feel?"

"Very well, thank you." Phineas fumbled and caught the thread of former conversation that had been bothering him. "You said something about—illness?"

"Think nothing of it. After working for me twelve years, I'm not going to dock your pay for a mere month's absence. Kind of a shame you had to be off just when I needed you, but such things will happen, so we'll just forget it, eh?" He brushed aside the other's muttered attempt at questioning and dug into the plans. "Here, better start on this—you'll notice some changes, but it's a lot like what we used to do; something like the Oswego we built in '37. Only thing that'll give you trouble is the new steel they put out now, but you can follow specifications on that."

Phineas picked up the specifications, ran them over, and blinked. This would never do; much as he loathed the work, he was an excellent draftsman, and he knew enough of general structural design to know this would never do. "But, two-inch I-beams here——"

" 'Sall right, Phin, structural strength is about twelve times what you're used to. Makes some really nice designing possible, too. Just follow the things like I said, and I'll go over it all later. Things changed a little while you were delirious. But I'm in a devil of a rush right now. See you." He stuck his body through the door, thrust his head back inside and cocked an eyebrow. "Lunch? Need somebody to show you around, I guess."

"As you wish, Mr. Sloane," agreed Phineas. "But would you please mind——"

"Not swearing. Sure, okay. And no religious arguments this time; if I'm damned, I like it." Then he was gone, leaving Phineas alone—he didn't work with the distraction of others, and always had a room to himself.

So he'd been sick, had he, even delirious? Well, that might explain things. Phineas had heard that such things sometimes produced a hiatus in the memory, and it was a better explanation than nothing. With some relief, he put it out of his mind, remembering only to confess how sinfully he'd lost his trust in divine guidance this morning, shook his head mournfully, and began work with dutiful resignation. Since it had obviously been ordained that he should make his simple living at drafting, draft he would, with no complaints, and there would be no fault to be found with him there.

Then the pen began to scratch. He cleaned and adjusted it, finding nothing wrong, but still it made little grating sounds on the paper, lifting up the raw edges of his nerves. Had Phineas believed in evolution, he'd have said the hair his ancestors had once grown was trying to stand on end, but he had no use for such heretical ideas. Well, he was not one to complain. He unclenched his teeth and sought forbearance and peace within.

Then, outside, the addressograph began to thump again, and he had to force himself not to ruin the lines as his body tried to flinch. Be patient, all these trials would be rewarded. Finally, he turned to the only anodyne he knew, contemplation of the fate of heretics and sinners. Of course, he was sorry for them roasting eternally and crying for water which they would never get—very sorry for the poor deluded creatures, as any righteous man should be. Yet still they had been given their chance and not made proper use of it, so it was only just. Picturing morbidly the hell of his most dour Puritan ancestors—something very real to him— he almost failed to notice the ache of his bunion where the cheap shoes pinched. But not quite.

Callahan was humming out in the office, and Phineas could just recognize the tune. Once the atheist had come in roaring drunk, and before they'd sent him home, he'd cornered Phineas and sung it through, unexpurgated. Now, in time with the humming, the words insisted in trickling through the suffering little man's mind, and try as he would, they refused to leave. Prayer did no good. Then he added Callahan to the tortured sinners, and that worked better.

"Pencils, shoestrings, razor blades?" The words behind him startled him, and he regained his balance on the stool with difficulty. Standing just inside the door was a one-legged hunch-back with a handful of cheap articles. "Pencils?" he repeated. "Only a nickel. Help a poor cripple?" But the grin on his face belied the words.

"Indeed, no, no pencils." Phineas shuddered as the fellow hobbled over to a window and rid himself of a chew of tobacco. "Why don't you try the charities? Furthermore, we don't allow beggars here."

"Ain't none," the fellow answered with ambiguous cheerfulness, stuffing in a new bite.

"Then have faith in the Lord and He will provide." Naturally, man had been destined to toil through the days of his life in this mortal sphere, and toil he must to achieve salvation. He had no intention of running this uncouth person's small chance to be saved by keeping him in idleness.

The beggar nodded and touched his cap. "One of them, eh? Too bad. Well, keep your chin up, maybe it'll be better later." Then he went off down the hall, whistling, leaving Phineas to puzzle over his words and give it up as a bad job.

Potts rubbed his bunion tenderly, then desisted, realizing that pain was only a test, and should be borne meekly. The pen still scratched, the addressing machine thumped, and a bee had buzzed in somehow and went zipping about. It was a large and active bee.

Phineas cowered down and made himself work, sweating a little as the bee lighted on his drafting board. Then, mercifully, it flew away and for a few minutes he couldn't hear it. When it began again, it was behind him. He started to turn his head, then decided against it; the bee might take the motion as an act of aggression, and declare war. His hands on the pen were moist and clammy, and his fingers ached from gripping it too tightly, but somehow, he forced himself to go on working.

The bee was evidently in no hurry to leave. It flashed by his nose, buzzing, making him jerk back and spatter a blob of ink into the plans, then went zooming around his head and settled on his bald spot. Phineas held his breath and the bee stood pat. Ten, twenty, thirty seconds. His breath went out suddenly with a rush, the insect gave a brief buzz, evidently deciding the noise was harmless, and began strolling down over his forehead and out onto his nose. It tickled; the inside of his nose tickled, sympathetically.

"No, no," Phineas whispered desperately. "N—*Achee*OO! EEOW!" He grabbed for his nose and jerked violently, bumping his shins against the desk and splashing more ink on the plans. "Damn, oh, da——"

It was unbelievable; it couldn't be true! His own mouth had betrayed him! With shocked and leaden fingers he released the pen and bowed his head, but no sense of saving grace would come. Too well he could remember that even the smallest sin deserves just damnation. Now he was really sweating, and the visions of eternal torment came trooping back; but this time he was in Callahan's place, and try as he would, he couldn't switch. He was doomed!

Callahan found him in that position a minute later, and his rough, mocking laugh cut into Phineas' wounded soul. "Sure, an angel as I live and breathe." He dumped some papers onto the desk and gave another back-breaking thump. "Got the first sheets done, Phin?"

Miserably, Phineas shook his head, glancing at the clock. They should have been ready an hour ago. Another sin was piled upon his burden, beyond all hope of redemption, and of all people, Callahan had caught him not working when he was already behind. But the old Irishman didn't seem to be gloating.

"There now, don't take it so hard, Phin. Nobody expects you to work like a horse when you've been sick. Mr. Sloane wants you to come out to lunch with him now."

"I——uh——" Words wouldn't come.

Callahan thumped him on the back again, this time lightly enough to rattle only two ribs. "Go along with you. What's left is beginner's stuff and I'll finish it while you're eating. I'm ahead and got nothing to do, anyhow. Go on." He pratically picked the smaller man off the stool and shoved him through the door. "Sloane's waiting. Heck, I'll be glad to do it. Feel so good I can't find enough to keep me busy."

Sloane was flirting with one of the typists as Phineas plogged up, but he wound up that business with a wink and grabbed for his hat. " 'Smatter, Phin? You look all in. Bad bruise on your nose, too. Well, a good lunch'll fix up the first part, at least. Best damned food you ever ate, and right around the corner."

"Yes, Mr. Sloane, but would you . . . uh!" He couldn't ask that now. He himself was a sinner, given to violent language. Glumly he followed the other out and into the corner restaurant. Then, as he settled into the seat, he realized he couldn't eat; first among his penances should be giving up lunches.

"I . . . uh . . . don't feel very hungry, Mr. Sloane. I'll just have a cup of tea, I think." The odors of the food in the clean little restaurant that brought twinges to his stomach would only make his penance that much greater.

But Sloane was ordering for two. "Same as usual, honey, and you might as well bring a second for my friend here." He turned to Phineas. "Trouble with you, Phin, is that you don't eat enough. Wait'll you get a whiff of the ham they serve here—and the pie! Starting now, you're eating right if I have to stuff it down you. Ah!"

Service was prompt, and the plates began to appear before the little man's eyes. He could feel his mouth watering, and had to swallow to protest. Then the look in Sloane's eye made him decide not to. Well, at least he could fast morning and night instead. He nodded to himself glumly, wishing his craven appetite wouldn't insist on deriving so much pleasure from the food.

"And so," Sloane's voice broke in on his consciousness again, "after this, you're either going to promise me you'll eat three good meals a day or I'll come around and stuff it down you. Hear?"

"Yes, Mr. Sloane, but——"

"Good. I'm taking that as a promise."

Phineas cringed. He hadn't meant it that way; it couldn't go through as a promise. "But——"

"No buts about it. Down there I figured you had as good a chance of being right as I did, so I didn't open my mouth on the subject. But up here, that's done with. No reason why you can't enjoy life now."

That was too much. "Life," said Phineas, laying down his knife and preparing for siege, "was meant to give us a chance to prepare for the life to come, not to be squandered in wanton pleasure. Surely it's better to suffer through a few brief years, resisting temptations, than to be forever damned to perdition. And would you sacrifice heaven for mere mundane cravings, transient and worthless?"

"Stow it, Phin. Doesn't seem to me I sacrificed much to get here." Then, at Phineas' bewildered look. "Don't tell me you don't realize where you are? They told me they were sending a boy with the message; well, I guess he just missed you. You're dead, Phin! *This* is heaven! We don't talk much about it, but that's the way it is!"

"No!" The world was rolling in circles under Phineas' seat. He stared uncomprehendingly at Sloane, finding no slightest sign of mockery on the man's face. And there was the hole in the memory of sins, and the changes, and—Callahan! Why, Callahan had died and been buried the year before; and here he was, looking ten years younger, and hearty as ever. But it was all illusion; of course, it was all illusion. Callahan wouldn't be in heaven. "No, it can't be."

"But it is, Phin. Remember? I was down your way to get you for overtime work, and yelled at you just as you came out of your house. Then you started to cross, I yelled again——Come back now?"

There'd been a screeching of tires, Sloane running toward him suddenly waving frantically, and—blackout! "Then it hit? And this . . . is——"

"Uh-huh. Seems they picked me up with a shovel, but it took a month to finish you off." Sloane dug into the pie, rolling it on his tongue and grinning. "And this is Hereafter. A darned good one, too, even if nobody meets you at the gate to say 'Welcome to Heaven'."

Phineas clutched at the straw. "They didn't tell you it was heaven, then? Oh." That explained everything. Of course, he should have known. This wasn't heaven after all; it couldn't be. And though it differed from his conceptions, it most certainly could be the other place; there'd been that bee! Tch, it was just like Callahan and Sloane to enjoy perdition, misguided sinners, glorying in their unholiness.

Slowly the world righted itself, and Phineas Potts regained his normal state. To be sure, he'd used an ugly word, but what could be expected of him in this vile place? They'd never hold it against him under the circumstances. He lowered his eyes thankfully, paying no attention to Sloane's idle remarks about unfortunates. Now if he could just find the authorities of this place and get the mistake straightened out, all might yet be well. He had always done his best to be righteous. Perhaps a slight delay, but not long; and then—no Callahan, no Sloane, no drafting, or bees, or grating noises!

He drew himself up and looked across at Sloane, sadly, but justly doomed to this strange Gehenna. "Mr. Sloane," he asked firmly, "is there some place here where I can find . . . uh . . . authorities to . . . umm——"

"You mean you want to register a complaint? Why sure, a big white building about six blocks down; Adjustment and Appointment office." Sloane studied him thoroughly. "Darned if you don't look like you had a raw deal about something, at that. Look, Phin, they made mistakes sometimes, of course, but if they've handed you the little end, we'll go right down there and get it put right."

Phineas shook his head quickly. The proper attitude, no doubt was to leave Sloane in ignorance of the truth as long as possible, and that meant he'd have to go alone. "Thank you, Mr. Sloane, but I'll go by myself, if you don't mind. And . . . uh . . . if I don't come back . . . uh——"

"Sure, take the whole afternoon off. Hey, wait, aren't you gonna finish lunch?"

But Phineas Potts was gone, his creaking legs carrying him out into the mellow noon sunlight and toward the towering white building that must be his destination. The fate of a man's soul is nothing to dally over, and he wasn't dallying. He tucked his umbrella close under his arm to avoid contact with the host of the damned, shuddering at the thought of mingling with them. Still, undoubtedly this torture would be added to the list of others, and his reward be made that much greater. Then he was at the "Office of Administration, Appointments and Adjustments."

There was another painted Jezebel at the desk marked *Information*, and he headed there, barely collecting his thoughts in time to avoid disgraceful excitement. She grinned at him and actually winked! "Mr. Potts, isn't it? Oh, I'm so sorry you left before our messenger arrived. But if there's something we can do now——"

"There is," he told her firmly, though not too unkindly; after all, her punishment was ample without his anger. "I wish to see an authority here. I have a complaint; a most grievous complaint."

"Oh, that's too bad, Mr. Potts. But if you'll see Mr. Alexander, down the hall, third door left, I'm sure he can adjust it."

He waited no longer, but hurried where she pointed. As he approached, the third door opened and a dignified-looking man in a gray business suit stepped to it. The man held out a hand instantly. "I'm Mr. Alexander. Come in, won't you? Katy said you had a complaint. Sit right over there, Mr. Potts. Ah, so. Now, if you'll tell me about it, I think we can straighten it all out."

Phineas told him—in detail. "And so," he concluded firmly—quite firmly, "I feel I've been done a grave injustice, Mr. Alexander. I'm positive my destination should have been the other place."

"The other place?" Alexander seemed surprised.

"Exactly so. Heaven, to be more precise."

Alexander nodded thoughtfully. "Quite so, Mr. Potts, Only I'm afraid there's been a little misunderstanding. You see . . . ah . . . this is heaven. Still, I can see you don't believe me yet, so we've failed to place you properly. We really want to make people happy here, you know. So, if you'll just tell me what you find wrong, we'll do what we can to rectify it."

"Oh." Phineas considered. This might be a trick, of course, but still, if they could make him happy here, give him his due reward for the years filled with temptation resisted and noble suffering in meekness and humility, there seemed nothing wrong with it. Possibly, it came to him, there were varying degrees of blessedness, and even such creatures as Callahan and his ilk were granted the lower ones—though it didn't seem quite just. But certainly his level wasn't Callahan's.

"Very well," he decided. "First, I find myself living in that room with the gray streak on the wallpaper, sir, and for years I've loathed it; and the alarm and telephone; and——"

Alexander smiled. "One at a time please. Now, about the room. I really felt we'd done a masterly job on that, you know. Isn't it exactly like your room on the former level of life? Ah, I see it is. And didn't you choose and furnish that room yourself?"

"Yes, but——"

"Ah, then we were right. Naturally, Mr. Potts, we assumed that since it was of your own former creation, it was best suited to you. And besides, you need the alarm and telephone to keep you on time and in contact with your work, you know."

"But I loathe drafting!" Phineas glanced at this demon who was trying to trap him, expecting it to wilt to its true form. It didn't. Instead, the thing that was Mr. Alexander shook its head slowly and sighed.

"Now that is a pity; and we were so pleased to find we could even give you the same employer as before. Really, we felt you'd be happier under him than a stranger. However, if you don't like it, I suppose we could change. What other kind of work would you like?"

Now that was more like it, and perhaps he had even misjudged Alexander. Work was something Phineas hadn't expected, but—yes, that would be nice, if it could be arranged here. "I felt once I was *called*," he suggested.

"Minister, you mean? Now that's fine. Never get too many of them, Mr. Potts. Wonderful men, do wonderful work here. They really add enormously to the happiness of our Hereafter, you know. Let me see, what experience have you had?" He beamed at Potts, who thawed under it; then he turned to a bookshelf, selected a heavy volume and consulted it. Slowly the beam vanished, and worry took its place.

"Ah, yes, Phineas Theophilus Potts. Yes, entered training 1903. Hmmm. Dismissed after two years of study, due to a feeling he might . . . might not be quite temperamentally suited to the work and that he was somewhat too fana . . . ahem! . . . overly zealous in his criticism of others. Then transferred to his uncle's shop and took up drafting, which was thereafter his life's work. Umm. Really, that's too bad." Alexander turned back to Phineas. "Then, Mr. Potts, I take it you never had any actual experience at this sort of work?"

Phineas squirmed. "No, but——"

"Too bad." Alexander sighed. "Really, I'd like to make things more to your satisfaction, but after all, no experience—afraid it wouldn't do. Tell you what, we don't like to be hasty in our judgements; if you'll just picture exactly the life you want—no need to describe it, I'll get it if you merely think it—maybe we can adjust things. Try hard now.''

With faint hope, Phineas tried. Alexander's voice droned out at him. ''A little harder. No, that's only a negative picture of what you'd like not to do. Ah . . . um, no. I thought for a minute you had something, but it's gone. I think you're trying to picture abstractions, Mr. Potts, and you know one can't do that; I get something very vague, but it makes no sense. There! That's better.''

He seemed to listen for a few seconds longer, and Phineas was convinced now it was all sham; he'd given up trying. What was the use? Vague jumbled thoughts were all he had left, and now Alexander's voice broke in on them.

''Really, Mr. Potts, I'm afraid there's nothing we can do for you. I get a very clear picture now, but it's exactly the life we'd arranged for you, you see. Same room, same work. Apparently that's the only life you know. Of course, if you want to improve we have a great many very fine schools located throughout the city.''

Phineas jerked upright, the control over his temper barely on. ''You mean— you mean, I've got to go on like that?''

''Afraid so.''

''But you distinctly said this was heaven.''

''It is.''

''And I tell you,'' Phineas cried, forgetting all about controlling his temper, ''that this is hell!''

''Quite so, I never denied it. Now, Mr. Potts, I'd like to discuss this further, but others are waiting, so I'm afraid I'll have to ask you to leave.''

Alexander looked up from his papers, and as he looked, Phineas found himself outside the door, shaken and sick. The door remained open as the girl called Katy came up, looked at him in surprise, and went in. Then it closed, but still he stood there, unable to move, leaning against the wooden frame for support.

There was a mutter of voices within, and his whirling thoughts seized on them for anchor. Katy's voice first. ''—seems to take it terribly hard, Mr. Alexander. Isn't there something we can do?''

Then the low voice of Alexander. ''Nothing, Katy. It's up to him now. I suggested the schools, but I'm afraid he's another unfortunate. Probably even now he's out there convincing himself that all this is merely illusion, made to try his soul and test his ability to remain unchanged. If that's the case, well, poor devil, there isn't much we can do, you know.''

But Phineas wasn't listening then. He clutched the words he'd heard savagely to his bosom and went stiffly out and back toward the office of G. R. Sloane across from the little room, No. 408. Of course he should have known. All this was merely illusion, made to try his soul. Illusion and test, no more.

Let them try him, they would find him humble in his sufferings as always, not complaining, resisting firmly their temptations. Even though Sloane denied him the right to fast, still he would find some other way to do proper penance for his sins; though Callahan broke his back, though a thousand bees attacked him at once, still he would prevail.

"Forgive and guide me to sin no more, but preserve me in righteousness all the days of my life," he repeated, and turned into the building where there was more work and misery waiting for him. Sometime he'd be rewarded. Sometime.

Back in his head a small shred of doubt sniggered gleefully.

ANTHONY BOUCHER

Snulbug

"That's a hell of a spell you're using," said the demon, "if I'm the best you can call up."

He wasn't much. Bill Hitchens had to admit. He looked lost in the center of that pentacle. His basic design was impressive enough—snakes for hair, curling tusks, a sharp-tipped tail, all the works—but he was something under an inch tall.

Bill had chanted the words and lit the powder with the highest hopes. Even after the feeble flickering flash and the damp fizzling *zzzt* which had replaced the expected thunder and lightning, he had still had hopes. He had stared up at the space above the pentacle waiting to be awe-struck until he had heard that plaintive little voice from the floor wailing, "Here I am."

"Nobody's wasted time and powder on a misfit like me for years," the demon went on. "Where'd you get the spell?"

"Just a little something I whipped up," said Bill modestly.

The demon grunted and muttered something about people that thought they were magicians.

"But I'm not a magician," Bill explained. "I'm a biochemist."

The demon shuddered. "I land the damnedest cases," he mourned. "Working for that psychiatrist wasn't bad enough, I should draw a biochemist. Whatever that is."

Bill couldn't check his curiosity. "And what did you do for a psychiatrist?"

"He showed me to people who were followed by little men and told them I'd chase the little men away." The demon pantomimed shooting motions.

"And did they go away?"

"Sure. Only then the people decided they'd sooner have little men than me. It didn't work so good. Nothing ever does," he added woefully. "Yours won't, either."

Bill sat down and filled his pipe. Calling up demons wasn't so terrifying, after all. Something quiet and homey about it. "Oh, yes, it will," he said. "This is foolproof."

"That's what they all think. People—" The demon wistfully eyed the match as Bill lit his pipe. "But we might as well get it over with. What do you want?"

"I want a laboratory for my embolism experiments. If this method works, it's going to mean that a doctor can spot an embolus in the bloodstream long before

271

it's dangerous and remove it safely. My ex-boss, that screwball old occultist Reuben Choatsby, said it wasn't practical—meaning there wasn't a fortune in it for him—and fired me. Everybody else thinks I'm wacky, too, and I can't get any backing. So I need $10,000.''

"There" the demon sighed with satisfaction. "I told you it wouldn't work. That's out for me. They can't start fetching money on demand till three grades higher than me. I told you."

"But you don't," Bill insisted, "appreciate all my fiendish subtlety. Look—Say, what is your name?"

The demon hesitated. "You haven't got another of those things?"

"What things?"

"Matches."

"Sure."

"Light me one, please?"

Bill tossed the burning match into the center of the pentacle. The demon scrambled eagerly out of the now cold ashes of the powder and dived into the flame, rubbing himself with the brisk vigor of a man under a needle shower. "There!" he gasped joyously. "That's more like it."

"And now what's your name?"

The demon's face fell again. "My name? You really want to know?"

"I've got to call you something."

"Oh no you don't. I'm going home. No money games for me."

"But I haven't explained yet what you are to do. What's your name?"

"Snulbug." The demon's voice dropped almost too low to be heard.

"Snulbug?" Bill laughed.

"Uh-huh. I've got a cavity in one tusk, my snakes are falling out, I haven't got troubles enough, I should be named Snulbug."

"All right. Now listen, Snulbug, can you travel into the future?"

"A little. I don't like it much, though. It makes you itch in the memory."

"Look, my fine snake-haired friend. It isn't a question of what you like. How would you like to be left there in that pentacle with nobody to throw matches at you?" Snulbug shuddered. "I thought so. Now, you can travel into the future?"

"I said a little."

"And," Bill leaned forward and puffed hard at his corncob as he asked the vital question, "can you bring back material objects?" If the answer was no, all the fine febrile fertility of his spellmaking was useless. And if that was useless, Heaven alone knew how the Hitchens Embolism Diagnosis would ever succeed in ringing down the halls of history, and incidentally saving a few thousand lives annually.

Snulbug seemed more interested in the warm clouds of pipe smoke than in the question. "Sure," he said. "Within reason I can—" He broke off and stared up piteously. "You don't mean—You can't be going to pull that old gag again?"

"Look, baby. You do what I tell you and leave the worrying to me. You can bring back material objects?"

"Sure. But I warn you—"

Bill cut him off short. "Then as soon as I release you from that pentacle, you're to bring me tomorrow's newspaper."

Snulbug sat down on the burned match and tapped his forehead sorrowfully with his tail tip. "I knew it," he wailed. "I knew it. Three times already this happens to me. I've got limited powers, I'm a runt, I've got a funny name, so I should run foolish errands."

"Foolish errands?" Bill rose and began to pace about the bare attic. "Sir, if I may call you that, I resent such an imputation. I've spent weeks on this idea. Think of the limitless power in knowing the future. Think of what could be done with it: swaying the course of empire, dominating mankind. All I want is to take this stream of unlimited power, turn it into the simple channel of humanitarian research, and get me $10,000; and you call that a foolish errand!"

"That Spaniard," Snulbug moaned. "He was a nice guy, even if his spell was lousy. Had a solid, comfortable brazier where an imp could keep warm. Fine fellow. And he had to go ask to see tomorrow's newspaper—I'm warning you—"

"I know," said Bill hastily. "I've been over in my mind all the things that can go wrong. And that's why I'm laying three conditions on you before you get out of that pentacle. I'm not falling for the easy snares."

"All right." Snulbug sounded almost resigned. "Let's hear 'em. Not that they'll do any good."

"First: This newspaper must not contain a notice of my own death or of any other disaster that would frustrate what I can do with it."

"But shucks," Snulbug protested. "I can't guarantee that. If you're slated to die between now and tomorrow, what can I do about it? Not that I guess you're important enough to crash the paper."

"Courtesy, Snulbug. Courtesy to your master. But I tell you what: When you go into the future, you'll know then if I'm going to die? Right. Well, if I am, come back and tell me and we'll work out other plans. This errand will be off."

"People," Snulbug observed, "make such an effort to make trouble for themselves. Go on."

"Second: The newspaper must be of this city and in English. I can just imagine you and your little friends presenting some dope with the Omsk and Tomsk *Daily Vuskutsukt*."

"We should take so much trouble," said Snulbug.

"And third: The newspaper must belong to this space-time continuum, to this spiral of the serial universe, to this Wheel of If. However you want to put it. It must be a newspaper of the tomorrow which I myself shall experience, not of some other, to me hypothetical tomorrow."

"Throw me another match," said Snulbug.

"Those three conditions should cover it, I think. There's not a loophole there, and the Hitchens Laboratory is guaranteed."

Snulbug grunted. "You'll find out."

Bill took a sharp blade and duly cut a line of the pentacle with cold steel. But Snulbug simply dived in and out of the flame of his second match, twitching his tail happily, and seemed not to give a rap that the way to freedom was now open.

"Come on!" Bill snapped impatiently. "Or I'll take the match away."

Snulbug got as far as the opening and hesitated. "Twenty-four hours is a long way."

"You can make it."

"I don't know. Look." He shook his head, and a microscopic dead snake fell to the floor. "I'm not at my best. I'm shot to pieces lately, I am. Tap my tail."

"Do what?"

"Go on. Tap it with your fingernail right there where it joins on."

Bill grinned and obeyed. "Nothing happens."

"Sure nothing happens. My reflexes are all haywire. I don't know as I can make twenty-four hours." He brooded, and his snakes curled up into a concentrated clump. "Look. All you want is tomorrow's newspaper, huh? Just tomorrow's, not the edition that'll be out exactly twenty-four hours from now?"

"It's noon now—" Bill reflected. "Sure, I guess tomorrow morning's paper'll do."

"O.K. What's the date today?"

"August 21."

"Fine. I'll bring you a paper for August 22. Only I'm warning you: It won't do any good. But here goes nothing. Good-by now. Hello again. Here you are." There was a string in Snulbug's horny hand, and on the end of the string was a newspaper.

"But hey!" Bill protested. "You haven't been gone."

"People," said Snulbug feelingly, "are dopes. Why should it take any time out of the present to go into the future? I leave this point, I come back to this point. I spent two hours hunting for this damned paper, but that doesn't mean two hours out of your time. People—" he snorted.

Bill scratched his head. "I guess it's all right. Let's see the paper. And I know: You're warning me." He turned quickly to the obituaries to check. No Hitchens. "And I wasn't dead in the time you were in?"

"No," Snulbug admitted. "Not *dead*," he added, with the most pessimistic implications possible.

"What was I then? Was I—"

"I had salamander blood," Snulbug complained. "They thought I was an undine like my mother and they put me in the cold-water incubator when any dope knows salamandry is a dominant. So I'm a runt and good for nothing but to run errands, and now I should make prophecies! You read your paper and see how much good it does you."

Bill laid down his pipe and folded the paper back from the obituaries to the front page. He had not expected to find anything useful there—what advantage could he gain from knowing who won the next naval engagement or which cities were bombed?—but he was scientifically methodical. And this time method was rewarded. There it was, streaming across the front page in vast black blocks:

MAYOR ASSASSINATED
FIFTH COLUMN KILLS CRUSADER

Bill snapped his fingers. This was it. This was his chance. He jammed his pipe in his mouth, hastily pulled a coat on his shoulders, crammed the priceless paper into a pocket, and started out of the attic. Then he paused and looked around. He'd forgotten Snulbug. Shouldn't there be some sort of formal discharge?

The dismal demon was nowhere in sight. Not in the pentacle or out of it. Not a sign or a trace of him. Bill frowned. This was definitely not methodical. He struck a match and held it over the bowl of his pipe.

A warm sigh of pleasure came from inside the corncob.

Bill took the pipe from his mouth and stared at it. "So that's where you are?" he said musingly.

"I told you salamandry was a dominant," said Snulbug, peering out of the bowl. "I want to go along. I want to see just what kind of a fool you make of yourself." He withdrew his head into the glowing tobacco, muttering about newspapers, spells, and, with a wealth of unhappy scorn, people.

The crusading mayor of Granton was a national figure of splendid proportions. Without hysteria, red-baiting, or strike-breaking, he had launched a quietly purposeful and well-directed program against subversive elements which had rapidly converted Granton into the safest and most American city in the country. He was also a persistent advocate of national, state, and municipal subsidy of the arts and sciences—the ideal man to wangle an endowment for the Hitchens Laboratory, if he were not so surrounded by overly skeptical assistants that Bill had never been able to lay the program before him.

This would do it. Rescue him from assassination in the very nick of time—in itself an act worth calling up demons to perform—and then when he asks, "And how, Mr. Hitchens, can I possibly repay you?" come forth with the whole great plan of research. It couldn't miss.

No sound came from the pipe bowl, but Bill clearly heard the words, "Couldn't it just?" ringing in his mind.

He braked his car to a fast stop in the red zone before the city hall, jumped out without even slamming the door, and dashed up the marble steps so rapidly, so purposefully, that pure momentum carried him up three flights and through four suites of offices before anybody had the courage to stop him and say, "What goes?"

The man with the courage was a huge bull-necked plainclothes man, whose bulk made Bill feel relatively about the size of Snulbug. "All right there," this hulk rumbled. "All right. Where's the fire?"

"In an assassin's gun," said Bill. "And it had better stay there."

Bullneck had not expected a literal answer. He hesitated long enough for Bill to push him to the door marked MAYOR—PRIVATE. But though the husky's brain might move slowly, his muscles made up for the lag. Just as Bill started to shove the door open, a five-pronged mound of flesh lit on his neck and jerked.

Bill crawled from under a desk, ducked Bullneck's left, reached the door, executed a second backward flip, climbed down from the table, ducked a right, reached the door, sailed in reverse, and lowered himself nimbly from the chandelier.

Bullneck took up a stand in front of the door, spread his legs in ready balance, and drew a service automatic from its holster. "You ain't going in there," he said, to make the situation perfectly clear.

Bill spat out a tooth, wiped the blood from his eyes, picked up the shattered remains of his pipe, and said, "Look. It's now 12:30. At 12:32 a red-headed hunchback is going to come out on that balcony across the street and aim through the open window into the mayor's office. At 12:33 His Honor is going to be slumped over his desk, dead. Unless you help me get him out of range."

"Yeah?" said Bullneck. "And who says so?"

"It says so here. Look. In the paper."

Bullneck guffawed. "How can a paper say what ain't even happened yet? You're nuts, brother, if you ain't something worse. Now go on. Scram. Go peddle your paper."

Bill's glance darted out the window. There was the balcony facing the mayor's office. And there coming out on it—

"Look!" he cried. "If you won't believe me, look out the window. See on that balcony? The red-headed hunchback? Just like I told you. Quick!"

Bullneck stared despite himself. He saw the hunchback peer across into the office. He saw the sudden glint of metal in the hunchback's hand. "Brother," he said to Bill, "I'll tend to you later."

The hunchback had his rifle halfway to his shoulder when Bullneck's automatic spat and Bill braked his car in the red zone, jumped out, and dashed through four suites of offices before anybody had the courage to stop him.

The man with the courage was a huge bull-necked plainclothes man, who rumbled, "Where's the fire?"

"In an assassin's gun," said Bill, and took advantage of Bullneck's confusion to reach the door marked MAYOR—PRIVATE. But just as he started to push it open, a vast hand lit on his neck and jerked.

As Bill descended from the chandelier after his third try, Bullneck took up a stand in front of the door, with straddled legs and drawn gun. "You ain't going in," he said clarifyingly.

Bill spat out a tooth and outlined the situation. "—at 12:33," he ended, "His Honor is going to be slumped over his desk dead. Unless you help me get him out of range. See. It says so here. In the paper."

"How can it? Gwan. Go peddle your paper."

Bill's glance darted to the balcony. "Look, if you won't believe me. See the red-headed hunchback? Just like I told you. Quick! We've got to—"

Bullneck stared. He saw the sudden glint of metal in the hunchback's hand. "Brother," he said. "I'll tend to you later."

The hunchback had his rifle halfway to his shoulder when Bullneck's automatic spat and Bill braked his car in the red zone, jumped out, and—dashed through four suites before anybody stopped him.

The man who did was a bull-necked plain-clothes man, who rumbled—

"Don't you think," said Snulbug, "you've had about enough of this?"

Bill agreed mentally, and there he was sitting in his roadster in front of the city hall. His clothes were unrumpled, his eyes were bloodless, his teeth were all there, and his corncob was still intact. "And just what," he demanded of his pipe bowl, "has been going on?"

Snulbug popped his snaky head out. "Light this again, will you? It's getting cold. Thanks."

"What happened?" Bill insisted.

"People!" Snulbug moaned. "No sense. Don't you see? So long as that newspaper was in the future, it was only a possibility. If you had, say, a hunch that the mayor was in danger, maybe you could have saved him. But when I brought it into now, it became a fact. You can't possibly make it untrue."

"But how about man's free will? Can't I do whatever I want to do?"

"Sure. It was your precious free will that brought the paper into now. You can't undo your own will. And, anyway, your will's still free. You're free to go getting thrown around chandeliers as often as you want. You probably like it. You can do anything up to the point where it would change what's in that paper. Then you have to start in again and again and again until you make up your mind to be sensible."

"But that—" Bill fumbled for words, "that's just as bad as . . . as fate or predestination. If my soul wills to—"

"Newspapers aren't enough. Time theory isn't enough. So I should tell him about his soul! People—" And Snulbug withdrew into the bowl.

Bill looked up at the city hall regretfully and shrugged his resignation. Then he folded his paper to the sports page and studied it carefully.

Snulbug thrust his head out again as they stopped in the many-acred parking lot. "Where is it this time?" he wanted to know. "Not that it matters."

"The racetrack."

"Oh—" Snulbug groaned. "I might have known it. You're all alike. No sense in the whole caboodle. I suppose you found a long shot?"

"Darned tooting I did. Alhazred at twenty to one in the fourth. I've got $500, the only money I've got left on earth. Plunk on Alhazred's nose it goes, and there's our $10,000."

Snulbug grunted. "I hear his lousy spell, I watch him get caught on a merry-go-round, it isn't enough, I should see him lay a bet on a long shot."

"But there isn't a loophole in this. I'm not interfering with the future; I'm just taking advantage of it. Alhazred'll win this race whether I bet on him or not. Five pretty $100 parimutuel tickets, and behold: The Hitchens Laboratory!" Bill jumped spryly out of his car and strutted along joyously. Suddenly he paused and addressed his pipe: "Hey! Why do I feel so good?"

Snulbug sighed dismally. "Why should anybody?"

"No, but I mean: I took a hell of a shellacking from that plug-ugly in the office. And I haven't got a pain or an ache."

"Of course not. It never happened."

"But I felt it then."

"Sure. In a future that never was. You changed your mind, didn't you? You decided not to go up there?"

"O.K., but that was after I'd already been beaten up twice."

"Uh-uh," said Snulbug firmly. "It was before you hadn't been." And he withdrew again into the pipe.

There was a band somewhere in the distance and the raucous burble of an announcer's voice. Crowds clustered around the $2 windows, and the five weren't doing bad business. But the $500 window, where the five beautiful pasteboards lived that were to create an embolism laboratory, was almost deserted.

Bill buttonholed a stranger with a purple nose. "What's the next race?"

"Second, Mac."

Swell, Bill thought. Lots of time. And from now on—He hastened to the $100 window and shoved across the five bills which he had drawn from the bank that morning. "Alhazred, on the nose," he said.

The clerk frowned with surprise, but took the money and turned to get the tickets.

Bill buttonholed a stranger with a purple nose. "What's the next race?"

"Second, Mac."

Swell, Bill thought. And then he yelled, "Hey!"

A stranger with a purple nose paused and said, " 'Smatter, Mac?"

"Nothing," Bill groaned. "Just everything."

The stranger hesitated. "Ain't I seen you some place before?"

"No," said Bill hurriedly. "You were going to, but you haven't. I changed my mind."

The stranger walked away shaking his head and muttering how the ponies could get a guy.

Not till Bill was back in his roadster did he take the corncob from his mouth and glare at it. "All right!" he barked. "What was wrong this time? Why did I get on a merry-go-round again? I didn't try to change the future!"

Snulbug popped his head out and yawned a tuskful yawn. "I warn him, I explain it, I warn him again, now he wants I should explain it all over."

"But what did I do?"

"What did he do? You changed the odds, you dope. That much folding money on a long shot at a parimutuel track, and the odds change. It wouldn't have paid off at twenty to one the way it said in the paper."

"Nuts," Bill muttered. "And I suppose that applies to anything? If I study the stock market in this paper and try to invest my $500 according to tomorrow's market—"

"Same thing. The quotations wouldn't be quite the same if you started in playing. I warned you. You're stuck," said Snulbug. "You're stymied. It's no use." He sounded almost cheerful.

"Isn't it?" Bill mused. "Now look, Snulbug. Me, I'm a great believer in Man. This universe doesn't hold a problem that Man can't eventually solve. And I'm no dumber than the average."

"That's saying a lot, that is," Snulbug sneered. "People—"

"I've got a responsibility now. It's more than just my $10,000. I've got to redeem the honor of Man. You say this is the insoluble problem. I say there *is* no insoluble problem."

"I say you talk a lot."

Bill's mind was racing furiously. How can a man take advantage of the future without in any smallest way altering that future? There must be an answer somewhere, and a man who devised the Hitchens Embolus Diagnosis could certainly crack a little nut like this. Man cannot refuse a challenge.

Unthinking, he reached for his tobacco pouch and tapped out his pipe on the sole of his foot. There was a microscopic thud as Snulbug crashed onto the floor of the car.

Bill looked down half-smiling. The tiny demon's tail was lashing madly, and every separate snake stood on end. "This is too much!" Snulbug screamed. "Dumb gags aren't enough, insults aren't enough, I should get thrown around like a damned soul. This is the last straw. Give me my dismissal!"

Bill snapped his fingers gleefully. "Dismissal!" he cried. "I've got it, Snully. We're all set."

Snulbug looked up puzzled and slowly let his snakes droop more amicably. "It won't work," he said, with an omnisciently sad shake of his serpentine head.

It was the dashing act again that carried Bill through the Choatsby Laboratories, where he had been employed so recently, and on up to the very anteroom of old R. C.'s office.

But where you can do battle with a bull-necked guard, there is not a thing you can oppose against the brisk competence of a young lady who says, "I shall find out if Mr. Choatsby will see you." There was nothing to do but wait.

"And what's the brilliant idea this time?" Snulbug obviously feared the worst.

"R. C.'s nuts," said Bill. "He's an astrologer and a pyramidologist and a British Israelite—American Branch Reformed—and Heaven knows what else. He . . . why, he'll even believe in you."

"That's more than I do," said Snulbug. "It's a waste of energy."

"He'll buy this paper. He'll pay anything for it. There's nothing he loves more than futzing around with the occult. He'll never be able to resist a good solid slice of the future, with illusions of a fortune thrown in."

"You better hurry then."

"Why such a rush? It's only 2:30 now. Lots of time. And while that girl's gone there's nothing for us to do but cool our heels."

"You might at least," said Snulbug, "warm the heel of your pipe."

The girl returned at last. "Mr. Choatsby will see you."

Reuben Choatsby overflowed the outsize chair behind his desk. His little face, like a baby's head balanced on a giant suet pudding, beamed as Bill entered. "Changed your mind, eh?" His words came in sudden soft blobs, like the abrupt glugs of pouring sirup. "Good. Need you in K-39. Lab's not the same since you left."

Bill groped for the exactly right words. "That's not it, R. C. I'm on my own now and I'm doing all right."

The baby-face soured. "Damned cheek. Competitor of mine, eh? What you want now? Waste my time?"

"Not at all." With a pretty shaky assumption of confidence, Bill perched on the edge of the desk. "R. C.," he said, slowly and impressively, "what would you give for a glimpse into the future?"

Mr. Choatsby glugged vigorously. "Ribbing me? Get out of here! Have you thrown out—Hold on! You're the one—Used to read queer books. Had a grimoire here once." The baby-face grew earnest. "What you mean?"

"Just what I said, R. C. What would you give for a glimpse into the future?"

Mr. Choatsby hesitated. "How? Time travel? Pyramid? You figured out the King's Chamber?"

"Much simpler than that. I have here"—he took it out of his pocket and folded it so that only the name and the date line were visible—"tomorrow's newspaper."

Mr. Choatsby grabbed. "Let me see."

"Uh-uh. Naughty. You'll see after we discuss terms. But there it is."

"Trick. Had some printer fake it. Don't believe it."

"All right. I never expected you. R. C., to descend to such unenlightened skepticism. But if that's all the faith you have—" Bill stuffed the paper back in his pocket and started for the door.

"Wait!" Mr. Choatsby lowered his voice. "How'd you do it? Sell your soul?"

"That wasn't necessary."

"How? Spells? Cantrips? Incantations? Prove it to me. Show me it's real. Then we'll talk terms."

Bill walked casually to the desk and emptied his pipe into the ash tray.

"I'm underdeveloped. I run errands. I'm named Snulbug. It isn't enough—now I should be a testimonial!"

Mr. Choatsby stared rapt at the furious little demon raging in his ash tray. He watched reverently as Bill held out the pipe for its inmate, filled it with tobacco, and lit it. He listened awe-struck as Snulbug moaned with delight at the flame.

"No more questions," he said. "What terms?"

"Fifteen thousand dollars." Bill was ready for bargaining.

"Don't put it too high," Snulbug warned. "You better hurry."

But Mr. Choatsby had pulled out his check book and was scribbling hastily. He blotted the check and handed it over. "It's a deal." He grabbed up the paper. "You're a fool, young man. Fifteen thousand! *Hmf!*" He had it open already at the financial page. "With what I make on the market tomorrow, never notice $15,000. Pennies."

"Hurry up," Snulbug urged.

"Good-by, sir," Bill began politely, "and thank you for—" But Reuben Choatsby wasn't even listening.

"What's all this hurry?" Bill demanded as he reached the elevator.

"People!" Snulbug sighed. "Never you mind what's the hurry. You get to your bank and deposit that check."

So Bill, with Snulbug's incessant prodding, made a dash to the bank worthy of his descents on the city hall and on the Choatsby Laboratories. He just made it, by stop-watch fractions of a second. The door was already closing as he shoved his way through at 3 o'clock sharp.

He made his deposit, watched the teller's eyes bug out at the size of the check, and delayed long enough to enjoy the incomparable thrill of changing the account from William Hitchens to The Hitchens Research Laboratory.

Then he climbed once more into his car, where he could talk with his pipe in peace. "Now," he asked as he drove home, "what was the rush?"

"He'd stop payment."

"You mean when he found out about the merry-go-round? But I didn't promise anything. I just sold him tomorrow's paper. I didn't guarantee he'd make a fortune off it."

"That's all right. But—"

"Sure, you warned me. But where's the hitch? R. C.'s a bandit, but he's honest. He wouldn't stop payment."

"Wouldn't he?"

The car was waiting for a stop signal. The newsboy in the intersection was yelling "Uxtruh!" Bill glanced casually at the headline, did a double take, and instantly thrust out a nickel and seized a paper.

He turned into a side street, stopped the car, and went through this paper. Front page: MAYOR ASSASSINATED. Sports page: Alhazred at twenty to one. Obituaries: The same list he'd read at noon. He turned back to the date line. August 22. Tomorrow.

"I warned you," Snulbug was explaining. "I told you I wasn't strong enough to go far into the future. I'm not a well demon, I'm not. And an itch in the memory is something fierce. I just went far enough ahead to get a paper with tomorrow's date on it. And any dope knows that a Tuesday paper comes out Monday afternoon."

For a moment Bill was dazed. His magic paper, his $15,000 paper, was being hawked by newsies on every corner. Small wonder R. C. might have stopped payment! And then he saw the other side. He started to laugh. He couldn't stop.

"Look out!" Snulbug shrilled. "You'll drop my pipe. And what's so funny?"

Bill wiped tears from his eyes. "I was right. Don't you see, Snulbug? Man can't be licked. My magic was lousy. All it could call up was you. You brought me what was practically a fake, and I got caught on the merry-go-round of time trying to use it. You were right enough there; no good could come of that magic.

"But without the magic, just using human psychology, knowing a man's weaknesses, playing on them, I made a sirup-voiced old bandit endow the very research he'd tabooed, and do more good for humanity than he's done in all the rest of his life. I was right, Snulbug. You can't lick Man.''

Snulbug's snakes writhed into knots of scorn. ''People!'' he snorted. ''You'll find out.'' And he shook his head with dismal satisfaction.

FRANK BELKNAP LONG

The Refugees

PROLOGUE

"Michael," the girl called. *"Michael Harragan."*

A shadow fell on the wet pavement and One-eared Harragan appeared in the doorway of his tavern, his pale blue eyes mother-mournful. The air reeked of beer and sauerkraut.

"And what would you be wanting of me at this hour, Miss Kelly?" he asked.

"Michael, they've come. The house is entirely full of them, whispering together. Refugees, Michael—from the Old Country. And me not knowing what to say or think."

Into One-eared Harragan's eyes came a look of resignation. "Aye, aye, it was to be expected," he muttered.

"Michael, I have need of you. Does the tavern mean more to you than I? Sure, you know myself when I was a wee bratling, as red as a lobster."

"Aye, that I did, Miss Kelly. But I have my own beautiful business now, and the old ways—"

"Michael!"

"This is America, Miss Kelly. I am not a servant now."

"Michael, you were never a servant. You ought to know that."

"But did you not hear me say I am a busy man?"

"So is the Devil, Mike Harragan. Is a tavern beautiful? Is spreading drunkenness beautiful?"

One-eared Harragan flushed scarlet and glanced back into the tavern. "It is no fault of mine if men abuse the good things, Miss Kelly."

"You knew they were coming, Michael. Why didn't you answer my note?"

"Sure, and why should I have done that? Me that has always loved them. Sure, it would be a sin."

"To call them away? Oh, Michael, you must. I'll lose Roger if you don't. He cannot abide the whisperings."

"Miss Kelly, why do you want to wed a man like that? It's stony-hearted he is."

Miss Kelly's eyes misted. "He is not Irish, Michael. You and I know it was the bombings brought them. They could not abide the horrible, horrible bombings. But sure, in America they could be happy anywhere.''

"Not anywhere, Miss Kelly. Only with us of the Old Country with eyes to see and hearts to feel. It's a good Irish home they'll be needing.''

"But you can see them, Michael. All the others could only hear them, scurrying around the eaves of the big houses. They love you, Michael. You can make them sing and dance.''

"Aye, that I can.''

"Come home with me, Michael. Call them away. I'll lose Roger if you don't.''

When Roger Prindle ascended the stoop of the Kelly mansion smoke was swirling from the bowl of his pipe and his face was darker than a ripe thundercloud.

Helen Kelly was the sweetest girl in the world, but there was a strain of mysticism in her nature which disturbed and frightened him. She just didn't realize that it wasn't normal for a young, sensitive girl to live all alone in a memory-haunted house.

Since the death of her father the house had become a mausoleum. The house had acquired a moldy, sepulchral taint. Massive oak chairs and Victorian sofas and heavy hangings all combined to create an atmosphere of mustiness and decay.

Even worse were the whisperings. Roger Prindle didn't believe in the supernatural, but he had to admit that the whisperings were damned queer. Everywhere in the big house his ears were assailed by mysterious, tiny whisperings.

Up and down the great central stairway, behind the draperies in the halls, in the guest room on the third floor, and even down in the cellar. Whisperings! Following him wherever he went, chilling him to the core of his being.

It was pretty late to be returning to the big house, but he had reached the end of his tether. Up on Cape Cod he owned a pleasant little cottage fanned by sea breezes, brightened by copper ware and marine paintings—a paradise for two.

He felt confident that the whisperings would not follow them there. His only problem was to get her to see it his way. The matter would have to be thrashed out between them tonight.

He had very foolishly departed at ten without delivering an ultimatum. She had her heart set on remaining in the big house, and a dread of hurting her had restrained him. At the last moment he had become so panicky that he had left without a word to her about it.

But now he was fortified by three whisky and sodas and a determination which could not be overthrown. He'd take her by the shoulders and speak his mind freely.

"Darling, we're getting married and leaving Elfland on the eight-fifteen. We're putting all those cobwebs behind us, you hear?"

It disturbed him to discover that she had left the door unlatched. Living without servants in the big house was risky enough, neglecting to lock the front door inexcusable.

He had a scalp-tingly feeling as he passed into the darkened entrance hall, as though he were being followed. He always had that feeling in the big house. It was one of the penalties of falling in love with a "Killarney" colleen.

He wasn't being followed, of course. It was all nonsense. A fellow like him, a certified public accountant, had too firm a grip on reality to believe in anything he couldn't see and touch.

The darkness was very dense in the entrance hall. He had foolishly closed the front door behind him, shutting out the street light. Gropingly he advanced toward the central staircase, feeling his way to keep from bumping into tables, urns and statuary.

He was still advancing when a tiny, tinkling voice whispered close to his ear. "You are taller than you think, Roger Prindle."

There was an instant of silence and then from all sides came a strident hum. "He is taller than he thinks. He is taller than he dreams."

Roger Prindle turned pale. He ceased to advance in the darkness, ceased to breathe. Something bad had grown worse, had become suddenly a menace to his sanity. For the first time the whisperings coalesced into actual speech. It was as though a gulf had abruptly opened beneath his feet.

He didn't realize how tall he had become until his head bumped against the ceiling. He nearly screamed when he discovered that he was at least thirty feet tall.

He was up above the banisters looking down. At least, his head was. And the long length of himself beneath was indisputably growing. He could see most of himself dimly because it wasn't so dark up where his head was. There was a light halfway down the passage at the top of the staircase.

He could see as far down on his knees, although not very clearly. His feet were still planted firmly on the rug at the base of the stairs.

"It would be a sin if he stopped growing. He isn't nearly tall enough."

"Don't you want to stoop low, Roger Prindle? Don't you want to grow out over the ceiling?"

"He is taller than he thinks. He is taller than he dreams," came a mocking chorus of tiny voices close to his ears.

His shoulders were spreading out over the ceiling now. Bent nearly double, he stared down in consternation at his swollen knees. Obscurely visible beneath his expanding waistline were great, knobbly pads of flesh supported by ebon pillars which rose in jerks toward the top of the stairs.

Horror and sick revulsion came into him as he stared. It was all he could do to keep his back from breaking. He had to stoop lower and lower and the lower he stooped the more monstrously deformed his body became.

Then all at once he began to shrink. His shoulders ceased to press upon the ceiling and his legs shortened beneath him.

"You are smaller than you think, Roger Prindle," whispered the tinkling voice.

"He is smaller than he thinks. He is smaller than he dreams," came the chorus from above.

Unbelievably rapid was Prindle's diminishment. He shrivelled in spurts, like a child's punctured balloon. Now his head was lower than the staircase, now six inches from the floor.

"How small would you *like* to get, Roger Prindle?" asked the tinkling voice.

"Don't make Roger Prindle *too* small. A mouse will eat him. A mouse will eat poor Roger Prindle up."

"Oh, crunchy crunch, how delightful!"

"You don't mean that, blue spriteling. When you grow up you'll have nothing but compassion for poor, suffering mortals."

"You've pampered and spoiled him, Mother Ululee. He should be turned over and spanked."

The darkness was dissolving now. A faint, spectral radiance was creeping into the house. Roger Prindle stared up at the dimly glowing staircase, and his brain spun.

It wasn't a staircase any longer. It was a vast, glimmering mountain with mile-wide ledges traversing its sloping face.

Prindle clapped his hands to his ears and swayed dizzily. The voices were thunderous now—deafening.

"You don't want to be as small as that, Roger Prindle. You're less than one inch tall."

"He doesn't *want* to be as small as that. He's smaller than he thinks. He's smaller than he dreams."

"There's no reason for it. He could be as big and strong as King O'Loch-lainn."

"But Roger Prindle is *not* kingly, Anululu. Shining bright were my eyes when O'Lochlainn came through the Norman spears. A man o' men was he, with red hair on his chest."

"You do not think that Roger Prindle could be a fine, strong man?"

"I did not say that, Mother Ululee. He is stronger than he thinks. He is larger than he dreams."

Prindle glanced down and saw the floor descending. It fell away and ran out from under him like a dissolving plain. He grew by leaps and bounds. Now he was two feet tall, now four, and then—

He was a normal-sized man again. He stood trembling at the foot of the stair-case, his throat as dry as death. The voices had ceased to reverberate thunderously from caverns measureless to man.

"Did you know, Raspit, that there is evil in Roger Prindle's mind?"

"There is evil in the minds of all mortals, Kinnipigi. Think of the horrible bombings!"

"I did not mean to imply that Roger Prindle was as bad as all that. He is a good, kind gentleman. But his thoughts are very unruly at times."

"I think I know what you mean, Kinnipigi. The call of the flesh. At times Roger Prindle is more of a satyr than he dreams."

"He is more of a satyr than he thinks. He is more of a satyr than he dreams."

There was something wrong with Roger Prindle's hands. They felt queer, scratchy.

He had been rubbing them together unconsciously, as was his wont when anxiety beset him. Now he suddenly stopped doing that. His teeth came together with a little click.

His hands—his hands felt *very* queer. They seemed to be all bristly and damp. He was afraid to raise them and look at them. Prindle wasn't a physical coward, but there were some things—

"Mama Ululee, Roger Prindle looks just like a goat," shrilled the tiniest of voicelings. "Mama Ululee, does he eat tin cans, and *everything?*"

"Roger Prindle, look at yourself now. You are a satyr, and you should be ashamed."

Prindle stared down at himself. Coarse, red hair covered him from his waist to his shining—*hoofs*. His ankles were shaggy and his toenails had coalesced into horny black sheaths which clattered on the floor as he bounded backward in sick revulsion.

"Roger Prindle, you should be ashamed. You're nothing but a coarse, shaggy satyr. You're not deceiving anybody, Roger Prindle. Why don't you be honest with yourself? What do you dream about most? How many times have you crouched in the bracken, and watched the white nymphs bathing?"

"You mean, in his dreams, Kinnipigi?"

"Of course."

"You are being unfair to Roger Prindle. He is not responsible for his dreams. Did you ever know a poor, weak mortal who did not hearken to the call of the flesh in his dreams?"

"I have, Kinnipigi. In 1037 there was an idiot who—"

"There, you see."

"But Roger Prindle is not dreaming now. There never was a mortal so awake and shameless. Just look at his eyes!"

Prindle's eyes *were* glistening. He couldn't help it. Coming down the central staircase was the whitest, most beautiful nymph he had ever seen. Her expression was so lascivious that it sickened him, and yet he couldn't tear his gaze from her face.

"What strong, hairy hands you have, Roger Prindle. King O'Lochlainn was scarcely more of a man."

"He is more tuppish than he thinks. He is more tuppish than he dreams."

In all his life Roger Prindle had never felt so primitive, so masterful. The nymph had flashed him a challenging glance and was racing back up the staircase, her raven-dark tresses streaming out behind her like a wind-wafted cloak.

There was nothing modest about her; quite the contrary. She was the exact opposite of everything he would have wanted in a wife. She was as brazen as a harridan, and yet—

Up the stairs Roger Prindle clattered in furious pursuit, his hairy arms out-thrust.

"Do you think Roger Prindle will catch her, Mama Ululee?"

"You may be sure he'll not be forever trying, blue spriteling. Just look at him go."

"He'll not be forever trying. He's more fleet-footed than he dreams."

"Oh, look, Mama Ululee. He's caught her. He's caught her, oh."

"By her long, black hair! Roger Prindle, you're a lucky man. We congratulate you, and wish you every happiness."

"No, no, no, he mustn't do that! He's dragging her downstairs by the hair. Doesn't he realize how disgraceful that looks?"

Roger Prindle didn't realize. His senses were reeling now. He had only the vaguest conception of what he was doing. He was grasping the nymph's long, dark tresses, and tugging, and she seemed to be floating on her back in the air.

He was halfway down the stairs when a ghastly thing happened. The nymph's beautiful, pale face shrivelled and darkened and rotted away before his very eyes. The horror impinged on all his senses simultaneously.

While an odor of putrefaction assailed his nostrils her hair hissed like a nest of snakes, and dried out between his fingers. He was no longer grasping silken tresses but a stringy mass of cobwebs. He was no longer staring at a beautiful white nymph with curvate limbs, but a gleaming skeleton with maggoty eye-sockets which writhed and twisted gruesomely in the dim light.

He recoiled shrieking. His hoofs flew out from under him and he went hurtling backward, his hairy arms outflung.

"Mother Ululee, he'll break his neck! He'll fracture his spine!"

"Raspit, Raspit, throw a spell. Quickly, or he'll be hurt."

A dull concussion shook the staircase as Roger Prindle crashed to the floor on his spine, and rolled over groaning.

"Oh, I'm sorry, Mother Ululee. I was a second too late."

"You always are, Raspit."

"He isn't hurt badly, Mother Ululee. See, he's trying to get up."

"Why, so he is, so he is. He's a good, kind gentleman again. His natural self!"

Bruised and shaken, Roger Prindle got swayingly to his feet. His head seemed to be bursting. He couldn't stand any more of this. He was going mad. His head was bursting, and——

"I'm sorry you fell, Roger Prindle," shrilled the tinkling voice. "If I wasn't so small, I'd bend over and let you kick me upstairs. It's just that—well, nobody has paid any attention to us, and we've become very morbid. We were miserable on the big ship, and lonely since we've been here."

"We're lonelier than he thinks. We're lonelier than he dreams."

"We had to let off steam, Prindle. We were all pent up inside. We are the Kellys' own little people. Their very, very own. We stood it as long as we could before we trooped into the big ship, and hid ourselves away. We knew that Miss Kelly would give us a home. She was six when she sailed away, and big for her age, and sad we were to see her go. But we knew she would always be loving us, and when the bombings began we thought of her."

Roger Prindle's face was twitching. "I can't see you," he gasped. "Where are you?"

"I'm standing right here in your left ear, Roger Prindle. And very hot and tired

I am, too. Your ear is all choked with dust right back to the wall at the end of it.''

Prindle turned pale. He could feel it now. Unmistakably something was moving about just inside his left ear, tickling him. Terrified, he crooked his finger and jabbed at the auricle, cold sweat breaking out all over him.

"Take care, Roger Prindle," the voice shrilled. "You'll crush me if you probe. Just raise your palm, if you want to see me.''

Tremulously Prindle obeyed. The instant he did so, something ticklish and fly-like alighted on his palm and ran swiftly across it.

"Careful now, Prindle," it shrilled. "Don't jar me. Lower your palm slowly and keep it raised. There, that's it. Easy does it.''

An instant later Prindle's handsome, mobile face, with its melancholy eyes and expressive mouth stiffened to a rigidly staring mask.

The elf was sitting cross-legged in the center of his palm staring up at him. A tiny, mottled elf the color of an October salamander, its webbed hands locked on its knees.

"Now don't be alarmed, Prindle," it said. "You wouldn't be seeing me if I didn't like you. It's part Irish you are, or I wouldn't be sitting here talking to you.''

"My great-grandmother on my mother's side was Irish," stammered Prindle. "So *that's* why—''

"Of course that's why," said the elf, as though aware of his thoughts. "We knew you could not be angry with *us,* Roger Prindle. There never was an Irishman who did not love the elves. We will all die when one such Irishman is born.''

"So that's why you played all those pranks on me?''

"Roger Prindle, don't let her send us away. We came to this big, new country to be with the last of *our* Kellys. The bombings were horrible, but more horrible would be leaving her to go to that tavern. It's not that we don't love Michael Harragan. A fine man he is, but he is not a Kelly.''

Prindle wiped sweat from his forehead. "You gave me the worst half-hour I ever experienced," he muttered. "Making me a giant and a midget, and bringing out all the dark, hidden thoughts in the depths of my mind.''

"We ensorcelled you because we liked you, Roger Prindle. It does a mortal no harm to get a good scare now and then. And you ought to walk in the daylight with your hidden self more often.''

Roger Prindle stood up. He closed his palm slowly.

"I'm holding you captive until she gets back here," he said. "I'm not taking any more chances with you. I've a suspicion you're the ring-leader, and I've heard that an elf can't play around with magic when he's locked up in the dark.''

He smiled wryly, ignoring a furious squirming inside his hand.

"Listen, all of you," he said. "I'm taking her away with me tomorrow. We're leaving this big, gloomy house. We're going to live by the sea, and there won't be any dark corners for elves to hide in on a wind-swept bluff in Massachusetts. Nothing but sun and wind and water—and plenty of headaches for any elf who thinks he can buck an environment like that.''

Instantly there was a despairing murmur all about him. "He's taking her away. Roger Prindle is crueller than he thinks. He is crueller than he dreams."

"A fine bunch of hoodlums! Listen, all of you. If I take you all along, will you promise to behave and lay off the spell-casting monkey business? Will you help me trim the sails of my sloop, and keep the brass polished, and collect sandworms for me so that I can go fishing now and then?"

"Oh, yes, yes, yes, yes. Roger Prindle, you are more of an Irishman than you think. You are more of an Irishman than you dream."

Roger Prindle sighed and fumbled in his pocket for his pipe. It was true, of course. No man on Earth could escape from his heritage or evade the obligations of his birth.

Smoke was swirling from the bowl of Roger Prindle's pipe again when Helen Kelly opened the front door and stood as though entranced, a breeze from the street ruffling her bobbed, auburn hair. Beside her stood Michael Harragan, wonder and gratification in his gaze.

"Bless my soul, Miss Kelly, just look at that. It's entirely visible they are to him, or he wouldn't be standing here so calm and contented-like. Not with them perched all over him and whispering like a swarm of Connemara bees."

ALFRED BESTER

Hell is Forever

Round and round the shutter'd Square
I strolled with the Devil's arm in mine.
No sound but the scrape of his hoofs was there
And the ring of his laughter and mine.
We had drunk black wine.

I screamed, "I will race you, Master!"
"What matter," he shriek'd, "tonight
Which of us runs the faster?
There is nothing to fear tonight
In the foul moon's light!"

Then I look'd him in the eyes,
And I laughed full shrill at the lie he told
And the gnawing fear he would fain disguise.
It was true, what I'd time and again been told
He was old—old.

From "Fungoids," by Enoch Soames

There were six of them and they had tried everything.

They began with drinking and drank until they had exhausted the sense of taste. Wines—Amontillado, Beaune, Kirschwasser, Bordeaux, Hock, Burgundy, Medoc and Chambertin; whiskey, Scotch, Irish, usquebaugh and Schnapps; brandy, gin and rum. They drank them separately and together; they mixed the tart alcohols and flavors into stupendous punches, into a thousand symphonies of taste; they experimented, created, invented, destroyed—and finally they were bored.

Drugs followed. The milder first, then the more potent. Crisp brown licoricelike opium, toasted and rolled into pellets for smoking in long ivory pipes; thick green absinthe sipped bitter and strong, without sugar or water; heroin and cocaine in rustling snow crystals; marijuana rolled loosely in brown-paper cigarettes; hashish in milk-white curds to be eaten or tarry plugs of Bhang that were chewed and stained the lips deep tan—and again they were bored.

Their search for sensation became frantic with so much of their senses already dissipated. They enlarged their parties and turned them into festivals of horror. Exotic dancers and esoteric half-human creatures crowded the broad low room and filled it with their incredible performances. Pain, fear, desire, love and hatred were torn apart and exhibited to the least quivering detail like so many laboratory specimens.

The cloying odor of perfume mingled with the knife-sharp sweat of excited bodies; the anguished screams of tortured creatures merely interrupted their swift, never-ceasing talk—and so in time this, too, palled. They reduced their parties to the original six and returned each week to sit, bored and still hungry for new sensations. Now, languidly and without enthusiasm, they were toying with the occult; turning the party room into a necromancer's studio.

Offhand you would not have thought it was a bomb shelter. The room was large and square, the walls paneled with imitation-grained soundproofing, the ceiling low-beamed. To the right was an inset door, heavy and bolted with an enormous wrought-iron lock. There were no windows, but the air-conditioning inlets were shaped like the arched slits of a Gothic monastery. Lady Sutton had paned them with stained glass and set small electric bulbs behind them. They threw showers of sullen color across the room.

The flooring was of ancient walnut, high polished and gleaming like metal. Across it were spread a score of lustrous Oriental scatter rugs. One enormous divan, covered with Indian Batik, ran the width of the shelter against a wall. Above, were tiers of book shelves, and before it was a long trestle table piled with banquet remains. The rest of the shelter was furnished with deep, seductive chairs, soft, quilted and inviting.

Centuries ago this had been the deepest dungeon of Sutton Castle, hundreds of feet beneath the earth. Now—drained, warmed, air-conditioned and refurnished, it was the scene of Lady Sutton's sensation parties. More—it was the official meeting place of the Society of Six. The Six Decadents, they called themselves.

"We are the last spiritual descendants of Nero—the last of the gloriously evil aristocrats," Lady Sutton would say. "We were born centuries too late, my friends. In a world that is no longer ours we have nothing to live for but ourselves. We are a race apart—we six."

And when unprecedented bombings shook England so catastrophically that the shudders even penetrated to the Sutton shelter, she would glance up and laugh: "Let them slaughter each other, those pigs. This is no war of ours. We go our own way, always, eh? Think, my friends, what a joy it would be to emerge from our shelter one bright morning and find all London dead—all the world dead—" And then she laughed again with her deep hoarse bellow.

She was bellowing now, her enormous fat body sprawled half across the divan like a decorated toad, laughing at the program that Digby Finchley had just handed her. It had been etched by Finchley himself—an exquisite design of devils and angels in grotesque amorous combat encircling the cabalistic lettering that read:

THE SIX PRESENT
ASTAROTH WAS A LADY
By Christian Braugh
Cast:
(In order of appearance)

A Necromancer .... Christian Braugh
A Black Cat .... Merlin
(By courtesy of Lady Sutton)
Astaroth .... Theone Dubedat
Nebiros, an Assistant Demon .... Digby Finchley
    Costumes .... Digby Finchley
    Special Effects .... Robert Peel
    Music .... Sidra Peel

Finchley said: "A little comedy *is* a change, isn't it?"

Lady Sutton shuddered with uncontrolled laughter. "Astaroth was a lady! Are you sure you wrote it, Chris?"

There was no answer from Braugh, only the buzz of preparations from the far end of the room, where a small stage had been erected and curtained off.

She bellowed in her broken bass: "Hey, Chris! Hey, there—"

The curtain split and Christian Braugh thrust his albino head through. His face was partially made up with red eyebrows and beard and dark-blue shadows around the eyes. He said: "Beg pardon, Lady Sutton?"

At the sight of his face she rolled over the divan like a mountain of jelly. Across her helpless body, Finchley smiled to Braugh, his lips unfolding in a cat's grin. Braugh moved his white head in imperceptible answer.

"I said, did you really write this, Chris . . . or have you hired a ghost again?"

Braugh looked angry, then suddenly disappeared behind the curtain.

"Oh my hat!" gurgled Lady Sutton. "This is better than a gallon of champagne. And, speaking of the same . . . who's nearest the bubbly? Bob? Pour some more. Bob! Bob Peel!"

The man slumped in the chair alongside the ice buckets never moved. He was lying on the nape of his neck, feet thrust out in a V before him, his dress shirt buckled under his bearded chin. Finchley went across the room and looked down at him.

"Passed out," he said.

"So early? Well, no matter. Fetch me a glass, Dig, there's a good lad."

Finchley filled a prismed champagne glass and brought it to Lady Sutton. From a small, cameo-faced vial she added three drops of laudanum, swirled the sparkling mixture once and then sipped while she read the program.

"A Necromancer . . . that's you, eh, Dig?"

He nodded.

"And what's a Necromancer?"

"A kind of magician, Lady Sutton."

"Magician? Oh, that's good . . . that's very good!" She spilled champagne on her vast, blotchy bosom and dabbed ineffectually with the program.

Finchley lifted a hand to restrain her and said: "You ought to be careful with that program, Lady Sutton. I made only one print and then destroyed the plate. It's unique and liable to be valuable."

"Collector's item, eh? Your work, of course, Dig?"

"Yes."

"Not much of a change from the usual pornography, hey?" She burst into another thunder of laughter that degenerated into a fit of hacking coughs. She dropped the glass altogether. Finchley flushed, then retrieved the glass and returned it to the buffet, stepping carefully over Peel's legs. "And who's this Astaroth?" Lady Sutton went on.

From behind the curtain, Theone Dubedat called: "Me! I! *Ich! Moi!*" her voice was husky. It had a quality of gray smoke.

"Darling, I know it's you, but *what* are you?"

"A devil, I think."

Finchley said: "Astaroth is some sort of legendary arch-demon—a top-ranking devil, so to speak."

"Theone a devil? No doubt of it—" Exhausted with rapture, Lady Sutton lay quiescent and musing on the patterned divan. At last she raised an enormous arm and examined her watch. The flesh hung from her elbows in elephantine creases, and at the gesture it shook and a little shower of torn sequins glittered down from her sleeve.

"You'd best get on with it, Dig. I've got to leave at midnight."

"Leave?"

"You heard me."

Finchley's face contorted. He bent over her, tense with suppressed emotions, his bleak eyes examining her. "What's up? What's wrong?"

"Nothing."

"Then—"

"A few things have changed, that's all."

"What's changed?"

Her face turned harsh as she returned his stare. The bulging features seemed to stiffen into obsidian. "Too soon to tell you . . . but you'll find out quick enough. Now I don't want any more pestering from you, Dig, m'lad!"

Finchley's scarecrow features regained some measure of control. He started to speak, but before he could utter a word Sidra Peel suddenly popped her head out of the alcove alongside the stage, where the organ had been placed. She called: "Ro-bert!"

In a constricted voice Finchley said: "Bob's passed out again, Sidra."

She emerged from the alcove, walked jerkily across the room and stood looking down in her husband's face. Sidra Peel was short, slender and dark. Her body was like an electric high-tension wire, alive with too much current, yet coruscated, stained and rusted from too much exposure to passion. The deep black sockets of her eyes were frigid coals with gleaming white points. As she gazed at her husband, her long fingers writhed; then, suddenly, her hand lashed out and struck the inert face.

"Swine!" she hissed.

Lady Sutton laughed and coughed all at once. Sidra Peel shot her a venomous glance and stepped toward the divan, the sharp crack of her heel on the walnut sounding like a pistol shot. Finchley gestured a quick warning that stopped her. She hesitated, then returned to the alcove, and said: "The music's ready."

"And so am I," said Lady Sutton. "On with the show and all that, eh?" She spread herself across the divan like a crawling tumor the while Finchley propped scarlet pillows under her head. "It's really nice of you to play this little comedy for me, Dig. Too bad there're only six of us here tonight. Ought to have an audience, eh?"

"You're the only audience we want, Lady Sutton."

"Ah! Keep it all in the family?"

"So to speak."

"The Six—Happy Family of Hatred."

"That's not so, Lady Sutton."

"Don't be an ass, Dig. We're all hateful. We glory in it. I ought to know. I'm the Bookkeeper of Disgust. Some day I'll let you see all the entries. Some day soon."

"What sort of entries?"

"Curious already, eh? Oh, nothing spectacular. Just the way Sidra's been trying to kill her husband—and Bob's been torturing her by holding on. And you making a fortune out of filthy pictures and eating your rotten heart out for that frigid devil, Theone—"

"Please, Lady Sutton!"

"And Theone," she went on with relish, "using that icy body of hers like an executioner's scalpel to torture and . . . and Chris . . . How many of his books d'you think he's stolen from those poor Grub Street devils?"

"I couldn't say."

"I know. All of them. A fortune on other men's brains. Oh, we're a beautifully loathsome lot, Dig. It's the only thing we have to be proud of—the only thing that sets us off from the billion blundering moralistic idiots that have inherited our earth. That's why we've got to stay a happy family of mutual hatred."

"I should call it mutual admiration," Finchley murmured. He bowed courteously and went to the curtains, looking more like a scarecrow than ever in the black dinner clothes. He was extremely tall—three inches over six feet—and extremely thin. The pipestem arms and legs looked like warped dowel sticks, and his horsy flat features seemed to have been painted on a pasty pillow.

Finchley pulled the curtains together behind him. A moment after he disappeared there was a whispered cue and the lights dimmed. In the vast room there was no sound except Lady Sutton's croupy breathing. Peel, still slumped in his deep chair, was motionless and invisible except for the limp angle of his legs.

From infinite distances came a slight vibration—almost a shudder. It seemed at first to be a sinister reminder of the hell that was bursting across England, hundreds of feet over their heads. Then the shuddering quickened and by imperceptible stages swelled into the deepest tones of the organ. Above the background of the throbbing diapasons, a weird tremolo of fourths, empty and spine-chilling, cascaded down the keyboard in chromatic steps.

Lady Sutton chuckled faintly. "My word," she said, "that's really horrid, Sidra. Ghastly."

The grim background music choked her. It filled the shelter with chilling tendrils of sound that were more moan than tone. The curtains slipped apart slowly, revealing Christian Braugh garbed in black, his face a hideous, twisted mass of red and purple-blue that contrasted starkly to the near-albino white hair. Braugh stood at the center of the stage surrounded by spider-legged tables piled high with Necromancer's apparatus. Prominent was Merlin, Lady Sutton's black cat, majestically poised atop an iron-bound volume.

Braugh lifted a piece of black chalk from a table and drew a circle on the floor twelve feet around himself. He inscribed the circumference with cabalistic characters and pentacles. Then he lifted a wafer and exhibited it with a flirt of his wrist.

"This," he declaimed in sepulchral tones, "is a sacred wafer stolen from a church at midnight."

Lady Sutton applauded satirically, but stopped almost at once. The music seemed to upset her. She moved uneasily on the divan and looked about her with little uncertain glances.

Muttering blasphemous imprecations, Braugh raised an iron dagger and plunged it through the center of the wafer. Then he arranged a copper chafing dish over a blue alcohol flame and began to stir in powders and crystals of bright colors. He lifted a crystal vial filled with purple liquid and poured the contents into a porcelain bowl. There was a faint detonation and a thick cloud of vapor lifted to the ceiling.

The organ surged. Braugh muttered incantations under his breath and performed oddly suggestive gestures. The shelter swam with scents and mists, violet clouds and deep fogs. Lady Sutton glanced toward the chair across from her. "Splendid, Bob," she called. "Wonderful effects—really." She tried to make her voice cheerful, but it came out in a sickly croak. Peel never moved.

With a savage motion, Braugh pulled three black hairs from the cat's tail. Merlin uttered a yowl of rage, and sprang at the same time from the table to the top of an inlaid cabinet in the background. Through the mists and vapors his giant yellow eyes gleamed balefully. The hairs went into the chafing dish and a new aroma filled the room. In quick succession the claws of an owl, the powder of vipers, and a human-shaped mandrake root followed.

"Now!" cried Braugh.

He cast the wafer, transfixed by the dagger, into the porcelain bowl containing the purple fluid, and then poured the whole mixture into the copper chafing dish.

There was a violent explosion.

A jet-black cloud enfolded the stage and swirled out into the shelter. Slowly it cleared away, faintly revealing the tall form of a naked devil; the body exquisitely formed, the head a frightful mask. Braugh had disappeared.

Through the drifting clouds, in the husky tones of Theone Dubedat, the devil spoke: "Greetings, Lady Sutton—"

She stepped forward out of the vapor. In the pulsating light that shot down to the stage her body shone with a shimmering nacreous glow of its own. The toes and fingers were long and graceful. Color slashed across the rounded torso. Yet that whole perfect body was cold and lifeless—as unreal as the grotesque papier-mâché that covered her head.

Theone repeated: "Greetings—"

"Hi, old thing!" Lady Sutton interrupted. "How's everything in hell?"

There was a giggle from the alcove where Sidra Peel was playing softly. Theone posed statuesquely and lifted her head a little higher to speak. "I bring you—"

"Darling!" shrieked Lady Sutton, "why didn't you let me know it was going to be like this. I'd have sold tickets!"

Theone raised a gleaming arm imperiously. Again she began: "I bring you the thanks of the five who—" And then abruptly she stopped.

For the space of five heartbeats there was a gasping pause while the organ murmured and the last of the black smoke filtered away, mushrooming against the ceiling. In the silence Theone's rapid, choked breathing mounted hysterically—then came a ghastly, piercing scream.

The others darted from behind the stage, exclaiming in astonishment—Braugh, Necromancer's costume thrown over his arm, his make-up removed; Finchley like a pair of animated scissors in black habit and cowl, a script in his hand. The organ stuttered, then stopped with a crash, and Sidra Peel burst out of the alcove.

Theone tried to scream again, but her voice caught and broke. In the appalled silence Lady Sutton cried: "What is it? Something wrong?"

Theone uttered a moaning sound and pointed to the center of the stage. "Look—There—" The words came off the top of her throat like the squeal of nails on slate. She cowered back against a table upsetting the apparatus. It clashed and tinkled.

"What is it? For the love of—"

"It worked—" Theone moaned. "The r-ritual—It worked!"

They stared through the gloom, then started. An enormous sable Thing was slowly rising in the center of the Necromancer's circle—a vague, morphous form towering high, emitting a dull, hissing sound like the whisper of a caldron.

"Who is that?" Lady Sutton shouted.

The Thing pushed forward like some sickly extrusion. When it reached the edge of the black circle it halted. The seething sounds swelled ominously.

"It is one of us?" Lady Sutton cried. "Is this a stupid trick? Finchley . . . Braugh—"

They shot her startled glances, bleak with terror.

"Sidra . . . Robert . . . Theone . . . No, you're all here. Then who is that? How did it get in here?"

"It's impossible," Braugh whispered, backing away. His legs knocked against the edge of the divan and he sprawled clumsily.

Lady Sutton beat at him with helpless hands and cried: "Do something! Do something—"

Finchley tried to control his voice. He stuttered: "W-we're safe so long as the circle isn't broken. It can't get out—"

On the stage, Theone was sobbing, making pushing motions with her hands. Suddenly she crumpled to the floor. One outflung arm rubbed away a segment of the black chalk circle. The Thing moved swiftly, stepped through the break in the circle and descended from the platform like a black fluid. Finchley and Sidra Peel reeled back with terrified shrieks. There was a growing thickness pervading the shelter atmosphere. Little gusts of vapor twisted around the head of the Thing as it moved slowly toward the divan.

"You're all joking!" Lady Sutton screamed. "This isn't real. It can't be!" She heaved up from the divan and tottered to her feet. Her face blanched as she counted the tale of her guests again. One—two—and four made six—and the shape made seven. But there should only be six—

She backed away, then began to run. The Thing was following her when she reached the door. Lady Sutton pulled at the door handle, but the iron bolt was locked. Quickly, for all her vast bulk, she ran around the edge of the shelter, smashing over the tables. As the Thing expanded in the darkness and filled the room with its sibilant hissing, she snatched at her purse and tore it open, groping for the key. Her shaking hands scattered the purse's contents over the room.

A deep bellow pierced the blackness. Lady Sutton jerked and stared around desperately, making little animal noises. As the Thing threatened to engulf her in its infinite black depths, a cry tore up through her body and she sank heavily to the floor.

Silence.

Smoke drifted in shaded clouds.

The china clock ticked off a sequence of delicate periods.

"Well—" Finchley said in conversational tones. "That's that."

He went to the inert figure on the floor. He knelt over it for a moment, probing and testing, his face flickering with savage hunger. Then he looked up and grinned. "She's dead, all right. Just the way we figured. Heart failure. She was too fat."

He remained on his knees, drinking in the moment of death. The others clustered around the toadlike body, staring with distended nostrils. The moment hardly lasted, then the languor of infinite boredom again shaded across their features.

The black Thing waved its arms a few times. The costume split at last to reveal a complicated framework and the sweating, bearded face of Robert Peel. He dropped the costume around him, stepped out of it, and went to the figure in the chair.

"The dummy idea was perfect," he said. His bright little eyes glittered momentarily. He looked like a sadistic miniature of Edward VII. "She'd never have believed it if we hadn't arranged for a seventh unknown to enter the scene." He glanced at his wife. "That slap was a stroke of genius, Sidra. Wonderful realism—"

"I meant it."

"I know you did, dearly beloved, but thanks nevertheless."

Theone Dubedat had risen and gotten into a white dressing gown. She stepped down and walked over to the body, removing the hideous devil's mask. It revealed a beautifully chiseled face, frigid and lovely. Her blond hair gleamed in the darkness.

Braugh said: "Your acting was superb, Theone—" He bobbed his white albino head appreciatively.

For a time she didn't answer. She stood staring down at the shapeless mound of flesh, an expression of hopeless longing on her face; but there was nothing more to her gazing than the impersonal curiosity of a bystander watching a window chef. Less.

At last Theone sighed. She said: "So it wasn't worth it, after all."

"What?" Braugh groped for a cigarette.

"The acting—the whole performance. We've been let down again, Chris."

Braugh scratched a match. The orange flame flared, flickering across their disappointed faces. He lit his cigarette, then held the flame high and looked at them. The illumination twisted their features into caricatures, emphasizing their weariness, their infinite boredom. Braugh said: "My-my—"

"It's no use, Chris. This whole murder was a bust. It was about as exciting as a glass of water."

Finchley hunched his shoulders and paced up and back of the shelter like a bundle of stilts. He said: "I got a bit of a kick when I thought she suspected. It didn't last long, though."

"You ought to be grateful for even that."

"I am."

Peel clucked his tongue in exasperation, then knelt like a bearded humpty-dumpty, his bald head gleaming, and raked in the contents of Lady Sutton's scattered purse. The banknotes he folded and put in his pocket. He took the fat dead hand and lifted it slightly toward Theone. "You always admired her sapphire, Theone. Want it?"

"You couldn't get it off, Bob."

"I think I could," he said, pulling strenuously.

"Oh, to hell with the sapphire."

"No—it's coming."

The ring slipped forward, then caught in the folds of flesh at the knuckle. Peel took a fresh grip and tugged and twisted. There was a sucking, yielding sound and the entire finger tore away from the hand. The dull odor of putrefaction struck their nostrils as they looked on with vague curiosity.

Peel shrugged and dropped the finger. He arose, dusting his hands slightly. "She rots fast," he said. "Peculiar—"

Braugh wrinkled his nose and said: "She was too fat."

Theone turned away in sudden frantic desperation, her hands clasping her elbows. "What are we going to do?" she cried. "What? Isn't there a sensation left on earth we haven't tried?"

With a dry whir the china clock began quick chimes. Midnight.

Finchley said: "We might go back to drugs."

"They're as futile as this paltry murder."

"But there are other sensations. New ones."

"Name one!" Theone said in exasperation. "Only one!"

"I could name several—if you'll have a seat and permit me—"

Suddenly Theone interrupted: "That's you speaking, isn't it, Dig?"

In a peculiar voice Finchley answered: "N-no. I thought it was Chris."

Braugh said: "Wasn't me."

"You, Bob?"

"No."

"Th-then—"

The small voice said: "If the ladies and gentlemen would be kind enough to—"

It came from the stage. There was something there—something that spoke in that quiet, gentle voice; for Merlin was stalking back and forth, arching his high black back against an invisible leg.

"—to sit down," the voice continued persuasively.

Braugh had the most courage. He moved to the stage with slow, steady steps, the cigarette hanging firmly from his lips. He leaned across the apron and peered. For a while his eyes examined the stage, then he let a spume of smoke jet from his nostrils and called: "There's nothing here."

And at that moment the blue smoke swirled under the lights and swept around a figure of emptiness. It was no more than a glimpse of an outline—of a negative, but it was enough to make Braugh cry out and leap back. The others turned sick, too, and staggered to chairs.

"So sorry," said the quiet voice. "It won't happen again."

Peel gathered himself and said: "Merely for the sake of—"

"Yes?"

He tried to freeze his jerking features. "Merely for the sake of s-scientific curiosity it—"

"Calm yourself, my friend."

"The ritual . . . it did w-work?"

"Of course not. My friends, there is no need to call us with such fantastic ceremony. If you really want us, we come."

"And you?"

"I? Oh . . . I know you have been thinking of me for some time. Tonight you wanted me—really wanted me, and I came."

The last of the cigarette smoke convulsed violently as that terrible figure of emptiness seemed to stoop and at last seat itself casually at the edge of the stage. The cat hesitated and then began rolling its head with little mews of pleasure as something fondled it.

Still striving desperately to control himself, Peel said: "But all those ceremonies and rituals that have been handed down—"

"Merely symbolic, Mr. Peel." Peel started at the sound of his name. "You have read, no doubt, that we do not appear unless a certain ritual is performed, and only if it is letter-perfect. That is not true, of course. We appear if the invitation is sincere—and only then—with or without ceremony."

Sick and verging on hysteria, Sidra whispered: "I'm getting out of here." She tried to rise.

The gentle voice said: "One moment, please—"

"No!"

"I will help you get rid of your husband, Mrs. Peel."

Sidra blinked, then sank back into her chair. Peel clenched his fists and opened his mouth to speak. Before he could begin, the gentle voice continued: "And yet you will not lose your wife, if you really want to keep her, Mr. Peel. I guarantee that."

The cat was suddenly lifted into the air and then settled comfortably in space a few feet from the floor. They could see the thick fur on the back smooth and resmooth from the gentle petting.

At length Braugh asked: "What do you offer us?"

"I offer each of you his own heart's desire."

"And that is?"

"A new sensation—all new sensations—"

"What new sensation?"

"The sensation of reality."

Braugh laughed. "Hardly anyone's heart's desire."

"This will be, for I offer you five different realities—realities which you may fashion, each for himself. I offer you worlds of your own making wherein Mrs. Peel may happily murder her husband in hers—and yet Mr. Peel may keep his wife in his own. To Mr. Braugh I offer the dreamworld of the writer, and to Mr. Finchley the creation of the artist—"

Theone said: "Those are dreams, and dreams are cheap. We all possess them."

"But you all awaken from your dreams and you pay the bitter price of that realization. I offer you an awakening from the present into a future reality which you may shape to your own desires—a reality which will never end."

Peel said: "Five simultaneous realities is a contradiction in terms. It's a paradox—impossible."

"Then I offer you the impossible."

"And the price?"

"I beg pardon?"

"The price," Peel repeated with growing courage. "We're not altogether naïve. We know there's always a price."

There was a long pause, then the voice said reproachfully: "I'm afraid there are many misconceptions and many things you fail to understand. Just now I cannot explain, but believe me when I say there is no price."

"Ridiculous. Nothing is ever given for nothing."

"Very well, Mr. Peel, if we must use the terminology of the market place, let me say that we never appear unless the price for our service is paid in advance. Yours has already been paid."

"Paid?" They shot involuntary glances at the rotting body on the shelter floor.

"In full."

"Then?"

"You're willing, I see. Very well—"

The cat was again lifted high in the air and deposited on the floor with a last gentle pat. The remnants of mist clinging to the shelter ceiling weaved and churned as the invisible donor advanced. Instinctively the five arose and waited, tense and fearful, yet with a mounting sense of fulfillment.

A key darted up from the floor and sailed through midair toward the door. It paused before the lock an instant, then inserted itself and turned. The heavy wrought-iron bolt lifted and the door swung wide. Beyond should have been the dungeon passage leading to the upper levels of Sutton Castle—a low, narrow corridor, paved with flags and lined with limestone blocks. Now, a few inches beyond the door jamb, there hung a veil of flame.

Pale, incredibly beautiful, it was a tapestry of flickering fire, the warp and weft an intermesh of rainbow colors. Those pastel strands of color locked and interlocked, swam, threaded and spun like so many individual life lines. They were an infinity of beads, emotions, the silken countenance of time, the swirling skin of space— They were all things to all men, and above all else, they were beautiful.

"For you," that quiet voice said, "your old reality ends in this room—"

"As simply as this?"

"Quite."

"But—"

"Here you stand," interrupted the voice, "in the last kernel, the last nucleus so to speak, of what once was real for you. Pass the door—pass through the veil, and you enter the reality I promised."

"What will we find beyond the veil?"

"What each of you desires. Nothing lies beyond that veil now. There is nothing there—nothing but time and space waiting for the molding. There is nothing and the potential of everything."

Peel, in a low voice, said: "One time and one space? Will that be enough for all different realities?"

"All time, all space, my friend," the quiet voice answered. "Pass through and you will find the matrix of dreams."

They had been clustered together, standing close to each other in a kind of strained companionship. Now, in the silence that followed, they separated slightly as though each had marked out for himself a reality all his own—a life entirely divorced from the past and the companions of old times. It was a gesture of utter isolation.

Mutually impulsed, yet independently motivated, they moved toward the glittering veil—

II

I am an artist, Digby Finchley thought, and an artist is a creator. To create is to be godlike, and so shall I be. I shall be god of my world, and from nothing I shall create all—and my all will be beauty.

He was the first to reach the veil and the first to pass through. Across his face the riot of color flicked like a cool spray. He blinked his eyes momentarily as the brilliant scarlets and purples blinded him. When he opened them again he had left the veil a step behind and stood in the darkness.

But not darkness.

It was the blank jet-black of infinite emptiness. It smote his eyes like a heavy hand and seemed to press the eyeballs back into his skull like leaden weights. He was terrified and jerked his head about, staring into the impenetrable nothingness, mistaking the ephemeral flashes of retinal light for reality.

Nor was he standing.

For he took one hasty stride and it was as though he were suspended out of all contact with mass and matter. His terror was tinged with horror as he became aware that he was utterly alone; that there was nothing to see, nothing to hear, nothing to touch. A bitter loneliness assailed him and in that instant he understood how truthfully the voice in the shelter had spoken, and how terribly real his new reality was.

That instant, too, was his salvation. "For," Finchley murmured with a wry smile to the blankness, "it is of the essence of godhood to be alone—to be unique."

Then he was quite calm and hung quiescent in time and space while he mustered his thoughts for the creation.

"First," Finchley said at length, "I must have a heavenly throne that befits a god. Too, I must have a heavenly kingdom and angelic retainers; for no god is altogether complete without an entourage."

He hesitated while his mind rapidly sorted over the various heavenly kingdoms he had known. There was no need, he thought, to be especially original with this sort of thing. Originality would play an important role in the creation of his universe. Just now the only essential thing was to insure himself a reasonable degree of dignity and luxury—and for that the secondhand furnishings of ancient Yahweh would do.

Raising one hand in a self-conscious gesture, he commanded. Instantly the blackness was riven with light, and before him a flight of gold-veined marble steps rose to a glittering throne. The throne was high and cushioned. Arms, legs and back were of glowing silver, and the cushions were imperial purple. And yet— the whole was incredibly hideous. The legs were too long and thin, the arms were rachety, the back narrow and sickly.

Finchley said: "Ow-w-w-w!" and tried to remodel. Yet no matter how he altered the proportions, the throne remained horrible. And for that matter, the steps, too, were disgusting, for by some freak of creation the gold veins twisted and curved through the marble to form obscene designs too reminiscent of the pictures Finchley had drawn in his past existence.

He gave it up at last, mounted the crooked steps and settled himself uneasily on the throne. It felt as though he was sitting on the lap of a corpse with dead arms poised to infold him in ghastly embrace. He shuddered slightly and said: "Oh, hell, I was never a furniture designer—"

Finchley glanced around, then raised his hand again. The jet clouds that had crowded around the throne rolled back to reveal high columns of crystal and a soaring roof arched and paved with smooth blocks. The hall stretched back for thousands of yards like some never-ending cathedral, and all that length was filled with rank on rank of his retainers.

Foremost were the angels: slender, winged creatures, white-robed, with blond, shining heads, sapphire-blue eyes, and scarlet, smiling mouths. Behind the angels knelt the order of Cherubin: giant winged bulls with tawny hides and hoofs of beaten metal. Their Assyrian heads were heavily bearded with gleaming jet curls. Third were the Seraphim: ranks of huge six-winged serpents whose jeweled scales glittered with a startling silent flame.

As Finchley sat and stared at them with admiration for his handiwork, they chanted in soft unison: "Glory to god. Glory to the Lord Finchley, the All Highest. . . . Glory to the Lord Finchley—"

He sat and stared and it was as though his eyes were slowly acquiring the distortion of astigmatism, for he realized that this was more a cathedral of evil than of heaven. The columns were carved with revolting grotesques at the capitals and bases, and as the hall stretched into dimness it seemed peopled with cavorting shadows that grimaced and danced.

And in the far reaches of those twisting lengths, covert little scenes were playing that sickened him. Even as they chanted, the angels gazed sidelong with their glistening blue eyes at the Cherubin; and behind a column he saw one winged creature reach out and seize a lovely blond angel of lust to crush her to him.

In sheer desperation Finchley raised his hand again, and once more the blackness swirled around him—

"So much," he said, "for a Heavenly Kingdom—"

He pondered for another ineffable period as he drifted in emptiness, grappling with the most stupendous artistic problem he had ever attacked.

Up to now, Finchley thought with a shudder for the horror he had recently wrought, I have been merely playing—feeling my strength—warming up, so to speak, the way an artist will toy with pastel and a block of grained paper. Now it's time for me to go to work.

Solemnly, as he thought would befit a god, he conducted a laborious conference with himself in space.

What, he asked himself, has creation been in the past?

One might call it nature.

Very well, we shall call it nature. Now, what are the objections to nature's creation?

Why—nature was never an artist. Nature merely blundered into things in an experimental sort of way. Whatever beauty existed was merely a byproduct. The difference be—

The difference, he interrupted himself, between the old nature and the new God Finchley shall be order. Mine will be an ordered cosmos devoid of waste and devoted to beauty. There will be nothing haphazard. There will be no blundering.

First, the canvas.

"There shall be infinite space!" Finchley cried.

In the nothingness, his voice roared through the bony structure of his skull and echoed in his ears with a flat, sour sound; but on the instant of command, the opaque blackness was filtered into a limpid jet. Finchley could still see nothing, but he felt the change.

He thought: Now, in the old cosmos there were simply stars and nebulae and vast fiery bodies scattered through the realms of the sky. No one knew their purpose—no one knew their origin or destination.

In mine there shall be purpose, for each body shall serve to support a race of creatures whose sole function shall be to serve me—

He cried: "Let there be universes to the number of one hundred, filling space. One thousand galaxies shall make up each universe, and one million suns shall be the sum of each galaxy. Ten planets shall circle each sun, and two moons each planet. Let all revolve around their creator! Let all this come to pass. Now!"

Finchley screamed in terror as light burst in a soundless cataclysm around him. Stars, close and hot as suns, distant and cold as pinpricks— Separately, by twos and in vast smudgy clouds— Blazing crimson—yellow—deep green and violet— The sum of their brilliance was a welter of light that constricted his heart and filled him with a devouring fear of the latent power within him.

"This," Finchley whimpered, "is enough cosmic creation for the time being—"

He closed his eyes determinedly and exerted his will once more. There was a sensation of solidity under his feet and when he opened his eyes cautiously he was standing on one of his earths with blue sky and a blue-white sun lowering swiftly toward the western horizon.

It was a bare, brown earth—Finchley had seen to that—it was a vast sphere of inchoate matter waiting for his molding, for he had decided that first above all other creation he would form a good green earth for himself—a planet of beauty where Finchley, God of all Creation, would reside in his Eden.

All through that waning afternoon he worked, swiftly and with artistic finesse. A vast ocean, green and with sparkling white foam, swept over half the globe; alternating hundreds of miles of watery space with clusters of warm islands. The single continent he divided in half with a backbone of jagged mountains that stretched from pole to snowy pole.

With infinite care he worked. Using oils, water colors, charcoal and plumbago sketches, he planned and executed his entire world. Mountains, valleys, plains; crags, precipices and mere boulders were all designed into a fluent congruence of beautifully balanced masses.

All his spirit of artistry went into the clever scattering of lakes like so many sparkling jewels; and into the cunning arabesques of winding rivers that traced intricate glistening designs over the face of the planet. He devoted himself to the selection of colors: gray gravels; pink, white and black sands; good earths, brown, umber and sepia; mottled shales, glistening micas and silica stones— And when the sun at last vanished on the first day of his labor, his Eden was a shining jewel of stone, earth and metal, ready for life.

As the sky darkened overhead, a pale, gibbous moon with a face of death was revealed riding in the vault of the sky; and even as Finchley gazed at it uneasily, a second moon with a blood-red disk lifted its ravaged countenance above the eastern horizon and began a ghastly march across the heavens. Finchley tore his eyes away from them and stared out at the twinkling stars.

There was much satisfaction to be gained from their contemplation. "I know exactly how many there are," he thought complacently. "You multiply one hundred by a thousand by a million and there's your answer— And that happens to be my idea of order!"

He lay back on a patch of warm, soft soil and placed palms under the back of his head, staring up. "And I know exactly what all of them are there for—to support human lives—the countless billions upon billions of lives which I shall design and create solely to serve and worship the Lord Finchley— That's purpose for you!"

And he knew where each of those blue and red and indigo sparks were going, for even in the vasty reaches of space they were thundering a circular course, the pivot of which was that point in the skies he had just left. Some day he would return to that place and there build his heavenly castle. Then he would sit through all eternity watching the wheeling flight of his worlds.

There was a peculiar splotch of red in the zenith of the sky. Finchley watched it absently at first, then with guarded attention as it seemed to burgeon. It spread slowly like an ink stain, and as the curious moments fled by, became tinged with orange and then the purest white. And for the first time Finchley was uncomfortably aware of a sensation of heat.

An hour passed and then two and three. The fist of red-white spread across the sky until it was a fiery nebulous cloud. A thin, tenuous edge approached a star gently, then touched. Instantly there was a blinding blaze of radiance and Finchley was flooded with gleaming, glittering light that illuminated the landscape with the eerie glow of flaring magnesium. The sensation of heat grew in intensity and tiny beads of perspiration prickled across his skin.

With midnight, the incredible inferno filled half the sky, and the gleaming stars, one after another, were bursting into silent explosions. The light was blinding white and the heat suffocating. Finchley tottered to his feet and began to run, searching vainly for shade or water. It was only then that he realized his universe was running amuck.

"No!" he cried desperately. "No!"

Heat bludgeoned him. He fell and rolled across cutting rocks that tore at him and anchored him back down with his face upthrust. Past his shielding hands, past his tight-shut eyelids, the intolerable light and heat pressed.

"Why should it go wrong?" Finchley screamed. "There was plenty of room for everything! Why should it—"

In heat-borne delirium he felt a thunderous rocking as though his Eden were beginning to split asunder.

He cried: "Stop! Stop! Everything stop!" He beat at his temples with futile fists and at last whispered: "All right . . . if I've made another mistake then— All right—" He waved his hand feebly.

And instantly the skies were black and blank. Only the two scabrous moons rode overhead, beginning the long downward journey to the west. And in the east a faint glow hinted at the rising sun.

"So," Finchley murmured, "one must be more a mathematician and physicist to run a cosmos. Very well, I can learn all that later. I'm an artist and I never pretended to know all that. But . . . I *am* an artist, and there is still my good green earth to people— Tomorrow— We shall see . . . tomorrow—"

And so presently he slept.

The scarlet sun was high when he awoke, and its evil solitary eye filled him with unrest. Glancing at the landscape he had fashioned the day previous, he was even more uncertain; for there was some subtle distortion in everything. Valley floors looked unclean with the pale sheen of lepers scales. The mountain crags formed nebulous shapes suggestive only of terror. Even the lakes contained the hint of horror under their smooth, innocent surfaces.

Not, he noticed, when he stared directly at these creations, but only when his glance was sidelong. Viewed full-eyed and steadfastly, everything seemed to be right. Proportion was good, line was excellent, coloring perfection. And yet— He shrugged and decided he would have to put in some practice at drafting. No doubt there was some subtle error of distortion in his work.

He walked to a tiny stream and from the bank scooped out a mass of moist red clay. He kneaded it smooth, wet it down to a thin mud and strained it. After it had dried under the sun slightly he arranged a heavy block of stone as a pedestal and set to work.

His hands were still practiced and certain. With sure fingers he shaped his concept of a large, furred rabbit. Body, legs and head; exquisitely etched features—it crouched on the stone ready, it seemed, to leap off at a moment's notice. Finchley smiled affectionately at his work, his confidence at last restored. He tapped it once on the rounded head and said: "Live, my friend—"

There was a second's indecision while life invaded the clay form, then it arched its back with an incredibly clumsy motion and attempted to leap. It moved forward to the edge of the pedestal where it hung crazily for an instant before it dropped heavily to the ground. As it lumbered along on a crazy course, it uttered horrible little grunting sounds and turned once to gaze at Finchley. On that animal face was an evil expression of malevolence.

Finchley's smile froze. He frowned, hesitated, then scooped up another chunk of clay and set it on the stone. For the space of an hour he worked, shaping a graceful Irish setter. At last he tapped this, too, on the narrow skull and said: "Live—"

Instantly the dog collapsed. It mewled helplessly and then struggled to shaking feet like some enormous spider, eyes distended and glassy. It tottered to the edge of the pedestal, leaped off and collided with Finchley's leg. There was a low growl and the beast tore sharp fangs into Finchley's skin. He leaped back with a cry and kicked the animal furiously. Mewling and howling, the setter went gangling across the fields like a crippled monster.

* * *

With furious intent, Finchley returned to his work. Shape after shape he modeled and endowed with life; and each: ape, monkey, fox, weasel, rat, lizard and toad—fish; long and short, stout and slender—birds by the score—each was a grotesque monstrosity that swam, shambled or fluttered off like some feverish nightmare. Finchley was horrified and exhausted. He sat himself down on the pedestal and began to sob while his tired fingers still twitched and prodded at a lump of clay.

He thought: "I'm still an artist—What's gone wrong? What turns everything I do into horrible nonsense?"

His fingers turned and twisted, and without his realizing it, a head began to form in the clay.

He thought: "I made a fortune with my art once. Everyone couldn't have been crazy. They bought my work for many reasons—but an important one was that it was beautiful."

He stared at the lump of clay in his hands. It had been partially formed into a woman's head. He examined it closely and for the first time in many hours, he smiled.

"Why, of course!" he exclaimed. "I'm no shaper of animals. Let's see how well I do with a human figure—"

Swiftly, with heavy chunks of clay, he built up the understructure of his figure. Legs, arms, torso and head were formed. He hummed slightly under his breath as he worked, and he thought: She'll be the loveliest Eve ever created—and more— her children shall truly be the children of a god!

With loving hands he turned the full swelling calves and thighs, and cunningly joined slender ankles to graceful feet. The hips were rounded and girdled a flat slightly mounded belly. As he set the strong shoulders, he suddenly stopped and stepped back a pace.

Is it possible? He wondered.

He walked slowly around the half-completed figure.

Yes—

Force of habit, perhaps?

Perhaps that—and maybe the love he had borne for so many empty years.

He returned to the figure and redoubled his efforts. With a sense of growing elation, he completed arms, neck and head. There was a certainty within him that told him it was impossible to fail. He had modeled this figure too often not to know it down to the finest detail. And when he was finished, Theone Dubedat, magnificently sculpted in clay, stood atop the stone pedestal.

Finchley was content, Wearily he sat down with his back to a jagged boulder, produced a cigarette from space and lit it. For perhaps a minute he sat, dragging in the smoke to quiet his jerking nerves. At last with a sense of chaotic anticipation he said: "Woman—"

He choked and stopped. Then he began again.

"Be alive—Theone!"

The second of life came and passed. The nude figure moved slightly, then began to tremble. Magnetically drawn, Finchley arose and stepped toward her, arms outstretched in mute appeal. There was a hoarse gasp of indrawn breath and slowly the great eyes opened and examined him.

The living girl straightened and screamed. Before Finchley could touch her she beat at his face, her long nails ripping his skin. She fell backward off the pedestal, leaped to her feet and began running off across the fields like all the others—running like a crazy, crippled creature while she screamed and howled. The low sun dappled her body and the shadow she cast was monstrous.

Long after she disappeared, Finchley continued to gaze in her direction while within him all that futile, bitter love surged and burned with an acid tide. At length he turned again to the pedestal and with icy impassivity set once more to work. Nor did he stop until the fifth in a succession of lurid creatures ran screaming out into the night—Then and only then did he stop and stand for a long time gazing alternately at his hands and the crazy, careening moons that sailed overhead.

There was a tap on his shoulder and he was not too surprised to see Lady Sutton standing beside him. She still wore the sequined evening gown, and in the lurid moonlight her face was as course and masculine as ever.

Finchley said: "Oh . . . it's you."

"How are you, Dig, m'lad?"

He thought it over, trying to bring some reason to the dumb despair and yet ludicrous insanity that pervaded his cosmos. At last he said: "Not so good, Lady Sutton."

"Trouble?"

"Yes—" He broke off and stared at her. "I say, Lady Sutton, how the devil did you get here?"

She laughed. "I'm dead, Dig. You ought to know."

"Dead? Oh . . . I—" He floundered in a horror of embarrassment.

"No hard feelings, though. I'd have done the same m'self, y'know."

"You would?"

"Anything for a new sensation. That was always our motto, eh?" She nodded complacently and grinned at him. It was that same old grin of pure deviltry.

Finchley said: "What are you doing here? I mean, how did—"

"I said I was dead," Lady Sutton interrupted. "There's lots you don't understand about this business of dying."

"But this is my own personal private reality. I own it."

"And I'm still dead, Dig. I can get into any bloody damned reality I choose. Wait—you'll find out."

He said: "I won't—ever—That is, I can't. Because I won't ever die."

"Oh-ho?"

"No, I won't. I'm a god."

"You are, eh? How d'you like it?"

"I . . . I don't." He faltered for words. "I . . . that is, someone promised me a reality I could shape for myself, but I can't, Lady Sutton, I can't."

"And why not?"

"I don't know. I'm a god, and yet every time I try to shape something beautiful it turns out disgusting and loathsome."

"As how, for instance?"

He showed her the twisted mountains and plains, the evil lakes and rivers, the distorted grunting creatures he had created. All this Lady Sutton examined carefully and with close attention. At last she pursed her lips and thought for a moment; then she gazed keenly at Finchley and said: "Odd that you've never made a mirror, Dig."

"A mirror?" he echoed. "No, I haven't—I never needed one—"

"Go ahead. Make one now."

He gave her a perplexed look, and still staring at her, waved a hand in the air. A square of silvered glass appeared in his hand and he held it toward her.

"No," Lady Sutton said, "it's for you. Look in it."

Wondering, he raised the mirror and gazed in it. He uttered a hoarse cry and peered closer. Leering back at him out of the dim night was the distorted, evil face of a gargoyle. In the small slant-set eyes, the splayed nose, the broken yellow teeth, the twisted ruin of a face he saw everything he had seen in his ugly cosmos.

He saw the distorted cathedral of heaven and all its unholy hierarchy of ribald retainers; the spinning chaos of crashing stars and suns; the lurid landscape of his Eden; each mewling, ghastly creature he had created; every individual horror that his brain had spawned.

Violently he hurled the mirror spinning and turned to confront Lady Sutton.

"What?" he demanded hoarsely, "what is this?"

"Why, you're a god, Dig," Lady Sutton laughed, "and you ought to know that a god can create only in his own image. Yes—the answer's as simple as that. It's a grand joke, ain't it?"

"Joke?" The import of all the eons to come thundered down over his head. An eternity of living with his hideous self, upon himself, inside himself—over and over, re-repeated in every sun and star, every living and dead thing, every creature, every everlasting moment. A monstrous god feeding upon himself and slowly, inexorably going mad.

"Joke!" he screamed.

He flung out his hand and instantly he floated once more, suspended out of all contact with mass and matter. Once more he was utterly alone, with nothing to see, nothing to hear, nothing to touch. And as he pondered for another ineffable period on the inevitable futility of his next attempt, he heard quite distinctly, the deep bellow of familiar laughter.

Of such was the Kingdom of Finchley's Heaven.

III

"Give me the strength! Oh, give me the strength!"

She went through the veil sharp on Finchley's heels, that short, slender, dark woman; and she found herself in the dungeon passage of Sutton Castle. For a moment she was startled out of her prayer, half disappointed at not finding a land of mists and dreams. Then, with a bitter smile, she recalled the reality she wanted.

Before her stood a suit of armor; a strong, graceful figure of polished metal edged with sweeping flutings. She went to it and stared. Dully from the gleaming steel cuirass, a slightly distorted reflection stared back. It showed the drawn, high-strung face, the coal-black eyes, the coal-black hair dipping down over the brow in a sharp widow's peak. It said: "This is Sidra Peel. This is a woman whose past has been fettered to a dull-witted creature that called itself her husband. She will break that chain this day if only she finds the strength—"

"Break the chain!" she murmured fiercely, "and this day repay him for a life's worth of agony. God—if there be a god in my world—help me balance the account in full! Help me—"

Sidra stared, then froze while her pulse jerked wildly. Someone had come soundlessly down the lonesome passage and stood behind her. She could feel the heat—the aura of a presence—the almost imperceptible pressure of a body against hers. Mistily in the mirror of the armor she made out a face peering over her shoulder.

She spun around, crying: "Ahhhh!"

"So sorry," he said. "Thought you were expecting me."

Her eyes riveted to his face. He was smiling slightly in an affable manner, and yet the streaked blond hair, the hollows and mounds, the pulsing veins and shadows of his features were a lurid landscape of raw emotions.

"Calm yourself," he said while she teetered crazily and fought down the screams that were tearing through her.

"But wh-who—" she broke off and tried to swallow.

"I thought you were expecting me," he repeated.

"I . . . expecting you?"

He nodded and took her hands. Against his, her palms felt chilled and moist. "We had an engagement."

She opened her mouth slightly and shook her head.

"At twelve forty—" He released one of her hands to look at his watch. "And here I am, on the dot."

"No," she said, yanking herself away. "No, this is impossible. We have no engagement. I don't know you."

"You don't recognize me, Sidra? Well—that's odd; but I think you'll recollect who I am before long."

"But who are you?"

"I shan't tell you. You'll have to remember yourself."

A little calmer, she inspected his features closely. Suddenly, with the rush of a waterfall, a blended sensation of attraction and repulsion surged over her. This man alarmed and fascinated her. She was filled with horror at his mere presence, yet intrigued and drawn.

At last she shook her head and said: "I still don't understand. I never called for you, Mr. Whoever-you-are, and we had no engagement."

"You most certainly did."

"I most certainly did not!" she flared, outraged by his insolent assurance. "I wanted my old world. The same old world I'd always known—"

"But with one exception?"

"Y-yes—" Her furious glance faltered and the rage drained out of her. "Yes, with one exception."

"And you prayed for the strength to make that exception?"

She nodded.

He grinned and took her arm. "Well, Sidra, then you did call for me and we did have an engagement. I'm the answer to your prayer."

She suffered herself to be led through the narrow, steep-mounting passages, unable to break free of that magnetic leash. His touch on her arm was a frightening thing. Everything in you cried out against the misery and disgust—and yet another something in you welcomed it eagerly.

As they passed through the cloudy light of infrequent lamps, she watched him covertly. He was tall and magnificently built. Thick cords strained in his muscular neck at the slightest turn of his arrogant head. He was dressed in tweeds that had the texture of sandstone and gave off a pungent, peaty scent. His shirt was open at the collar, and where his chest showed it was thickly matted.

There were no servants about on the street floor of the castle. The man escorted her quietly through the graceful rooms to the foyer where he removed her coat from the closet and placed it around her shoulders. Suddenly he pressed his hard hands against her arms.

She tore herself away at last, one of the old rages sweeping over her. In the quiet gloom of the foyer she could see that he was still smiling, and it added fuel to her fury.

"Ah," she cried, "what a fool I am . . . to take you so for granted. 'I prayed for you—' you say. 'I know you—' what kind of booby do you think I am? Keep your hands off me!"

She glared at him, breathing heavily, and he made no answer. His expression remained unchanged. It's like those snakes, she thought, those snakes with the jeweled eyes. They coil in their impassive beauty and you can't escape the deadly fascination. It's like soaring towers that make you want to leap to earth—like keen, glittering razors that invite the tender flesh of your throat. You can't escape!

"Go on!" she screamed in a last desperate effort. "Get out of here! This is my world. It's all mine to do with as I choose. I want no part of your kind of rotten, arrogant swine!"

Swiftly, silently, he gripped her shoulders and brought her close to him. While he kissed her she struggled against the hard talons of his fingers and tried to force her mouth away from his. And yet she knew that if he had released her she could not have torn herself away from that savage kiss.

She was sobbing when he relaxed his grip and let her head drop back. Still in the affable tones of a casual conversation he said: "You want one thing in this world of yours, Sidra, and you must have me to help you."

"In Heaven's name, who are you?"

"I'm that strength you prayed for. Now come along."

Outside the night was pitch black, and after they had gotten into Sidra's roadster and started for London, the road was impossible to follow. As she edged the car cautiously along, Sidra was able at last to make out the limed white line that bisected the road, and the lighter velvet of the sky against the jet of the horizon. Overhead the Milky Way was a long smudge of powder.

The wind on her face was good to feel. Passionate, reckless and headstrong as ever, she pressed her foot on the accelerator and sent the car roaring down the dangerous dark road, eager for more of the cool breeze against her cheeks and brow. The wind tugged at her hair and sent it streaming back. The wind gusted over the top of the glass shield and around it like a solid stream of cold water. It whipped up her courage and confidence. Best of all, it recalled her sense of humor.

Without turning, she called: "What's you name?"

And dimly through the chattering breeze came his answer: "Does it matter?"

"It certainly does. Am I supposed to call you: 'Hey!' or 'I say there—' or 'Dear sir—' "

"Very well, Sidra. Call me Ardis."

"Ardis? That's not English, is it?"

"Does it matter?"

"Don't be so mysterious. Of course it matters. I'm trying to place you."

"I see."

"D'you know Lady Sutton?"

Receiving no answer she glanced at him and received a slight chill. He did look mysterious with his head silhouetted against the star-filled sky. He looked out of place in an open roadster.

"D'you know Lady Sutton?" she repeated.

He nodded and she turned her attention back to the road. They had left the open country and were boring through the London suburbs. The little squat houses, all alike, all flat-faced and muddy-colored, whisked past with a muffled *whump-whump-whump,* echoing back the drone of the engine.

Still gay, she asked: "Where are you stopping?"

"In London."

"Where, in London."

"Chelsea Square."

"The Square? That's odd. What number?"

"One hundred and forty-nine."

She burst into laughter. "Your impudence is too wonderful," she gasped, glancing at him again. "That happens to be my address."

He nodded. "I know that, Sidra."

Her laughter froze—not at the words, for she had hardly heard them. Barely suppressing another scream, she turned and stared through the windshield, her hands trembling violently on the wheel. For the man sat there in the midst of that howling turmoil of wind and not a hair of his head was moving.

"Merciful Heaven!" she cried in her heart, "what kind of mess did I—Who is this monster, this—Our Father who art in heaven, hallowed be thy—Get rid of him! I don't want him. If I've asked for him, consciously or not, I don't want him now. I want my world changed. Right now! I want him out of it!''

"It's no use, Sidra," he said.

Her lips twitched and still she prayed: "Get him out of here! Change anything—everything, only take him away. Let him vanish. Let the darkness and the void devour him. Let him dwindle, fade—''

"Sidra," he shouted, "stop that!" He poked her violently. "You can't get rid of me that way—it's too late!"

She stopped as a final panic overtook her and congealed her brain.

"Once you've decided on your world," Ardis explained carefully as though to a child, "you're committed to it. There's no changing your mind and making minor alterations. Weren't you told?"

"No," she whispered, "we weren't told."

"Well, now you know."

She was mute, numb and wooden. Not so much wooden as putty. She followed his directions without a word; drove carefully to the little park of trees that was behind her house, and parked there. Very carefully, Ardis explained that they would have to enter the house through the servants' door.

"You don't," he said, "walk openly to murder. Only clever criminals in storybooks do that. We, in real life, find it best to be cautious."

Real life! she thought hysterically as they got out of the car. Reality! That Thing in the shelter—

Aloud, she said: "You sound experienced."

"Through the park," he answered, touching her lightly on the arm. "We shan't be seen."

The path through the trees was narrow and the grass and prickly shrubs on either side were high. Ardis stepped aside and then followed her as she passed the iron gate and entered. He strode a few paces behind her.

"As to the experience," he said, "yes—I've had plenty. But then, you ought to know, Sidra."

She didn't know. She didn't answer. Trees, brush and grass were thick around her, and although she had traversed this park a hundred times, they were alien and distorted. They were not alive—no, thank God for that—she was not yet imagining things; but for the first time she realized how skeletal and haunted they looked. Almost as if each had participated in some sordid murder or suicide through the years.

Deeper into the park, a dank mist made her cough, and behind her, Ardis patted her back sympathetically. She quivered like a length of supple steel under his touch, and when she had stopped coughing and the hand still remained on her shoulder, she knew in another burst of terror what he would attempt here in the darkness.

She quickened her stride. The hand left her shoulder and hooked at her arm. She yanked her arm free and ran crazily down the path, stumbling on her stilt heels. There was a muffled exclamation from Ardis and she heard the swift pound of his feet as he pursued her.

The path led down a slight depression and past a marshy little pond. The earth turned moist and sucked at her feet with hollow grunts. In the warmth of the night her skin began to prickle and perspire, but the sound of his panting was close behind her.

Her breath was coming in gasps and when the path veered and began to mount, she felt her lungs would burst. Her legs were aching and it seemed that at the next instant she would flounder to the ground. Dimly through the trees, she made out the iron gate at the other side of the park, and with the little strength left to her she redoubled her efforts to reach it.

But what, she wondered dizzily, what after that? He'll overtake me in the street— Perhaps before the street—I should have turned for the car—I could have driven— I—

He clutched at her shoulder as she passed the gate and she would have surrendered at that moment. Then she heard voices and saw figures on the street across from her. She cried: "Hello, there!" and ran to them, her shoes clattering on the pavement. As she came close, still free for the moment, they turned.

"So sorry," she babbled crazily, "thought I recognized you . . . was walking through the par—"

She stopped short. Staring at her were Finchley, Braugh and Lady Sutton.

"Sidra darling! What the devil are you doing here?" Lady Sutton demanded. She cocked her gross head forward to examine Sidra's face, then nudged at Braugh and Finchley with her elbows. "The girl's been running through the park. Mark my words, Chris, she's touched."

"Looks like she's been chevied," Braugh answered. He stepped to one side and peered past Sidra's shoulder, his white head gleaming in the starlight.

Sidra caught her breath at last and looked about uneasily. Ardis stood alongside her, calm and affable as ever. There was, she thought helplessly, no use trying to explain. No one would believe her. No one would help.

She said: "Just a bit of exercise. It was such a lovely night."

"Exercise!" Lady Sutton snorted. "Now I know you're cracked!"

Finchley said: "Why'd you pop off like that, Sidra? Bob was furious. We've just been driving him home."

"I—" It was too insane. She'd seen Finchley vanish through the veil of fire less than an hour ago—vanish into the world of his own choosing. Yet here he was, asking questions.

Ardis murmured: "Finchley was in your world, too. He's still here."

"But that's impossible!" Sidra exclaimed. "There can't be two Finchleys."

"Two Finchleys?" Lady Sutton echoed. "Now I know where you've been and gone, my girl! You're drunk. Reeling, stinking drunk. Running through the park! Exercise! Two Finchleys!"

And Lady Sutton? But she was dead. She had to be! They'd murdered her less than—

Again Ardis murmured: "That was another world ago, Sidra. This is your new world, and Lady Sutton belongs in it. Everyone belongs in it—except your husband."

"But . . . even though she's dead?"

Finchley started and asked: "Who's dead?"

"I think," Braugh said, "we'd better get her upstairs and put her to bed."

"No," Sidra said, "no—there's no need—really! I'm quite all right."

"Oh, let her be!" Lady Sutton grunted. She gathered her coat around her tub of a waist and moved off. "You know our motto, m'lads. 'Never Interfere.' See you and Bob at the shelter next week, Sidra. 'Night—"

"Good night."

Finchley and Braugh moved off, too—the three figures merging with the shadows with the delicate shadings of a misty fade-out. And as they vanished, Sidra heard Braugh murmur: "The motto ought to be 'Unashamed'!"

"Nonsense," Finchley answered. "Shame is a sensation we seek like all others, it redu—"

Then they were gone.

And with a return of that horrible chill, Sidra realized that they had not seen Ardis—nor heard him—nor been aware even of his—

"Naturally," Ardis interrupted.

"But how, naturally?"

"You'll understand later. Just now we've a murder before us."

"No!" she cried, hanging back. "No!"

"How's this, Sidra? And after you've looked forward to this moment for so many years. Planned it. Feasted on it—"

"I'm . . . too upset . . . unnerved."

"You'll be calmer. Come along."

Together they walked a few steps down the narrow street, turned up the gravel path and passed the gate that led to the back court. As Ardis reached out for the knob of the servants' door, he hesitated and turned a suffused face to her.

"This," he said, "is your moment, Sidra. It begins now. This is the time when you break that chain and make payment for a life's worth of agony. This is the day when you balance the account. Love is good—hate is better. Forgiveness is a trifling virtue—passion is all-consuming and the end-all of living!"

He pushed open the door, grasped her elbow and dragged her after him into the pantry. It was dark and filled with odd corners. They eased through the darkness cautiously, reached the swinging door that led to the kitchen, and pushed past it. Sidra stared and gagged. She uttered a faint moan and sagged against Ardis.

It *had* been a kitchen at one time. Now the stoves and sinks, cupboards and tables, chairs, closets and all loomed high and twisted like the distorted scenery of a nightmare jungle. A dull-blue spark glittered on the floor, and around it cavorted a score of silent shadows.

They were solidified smoke—semiliquid gas. Their translucent depths writhed and interplayed with the nauseating surge of living muck. Like looking through a microscope, Sidra thought in sick horror, at those creatures that foul corpse-blood; that scum a slack-water stream; that fill a swamp with noisome vapors—And most hideous of all, they were all in the wavering gusty image of her husband. Twenty Robert Peels, gesticulating obscenely and singing a whispered chorus:

"Quis multa gracilis te puer in rosa
Perfusus liquidis urget odoribus
Grato, Sidra, sub antro?"

"Ardis! What is this?"

"Don't know yet, Sidra."

"But these shapes!"

"We'll find out."

Twenty leaping vapors crowded around them, still chanting. Sidra and Ardis were driven forward and stood at the brink of that sapphire spark that burned in the air a few inches above the floor. Gaseous fingers pushed and probed at Sidra, pinched and prodded while the blue figures cavorted with hissing laughter, slapping their naked rumps in weird ecstasies.

A slash on Sidra's arm made her start and cry out, and when she looked down, unaccountable beads of blood stood out on the white skin of her wrist. And even as she stared in disembodied enchantment, her wrist was raised to Ardis' lips. Then his wrist was raised to her mouth and she felt the stinging salt of his blood on her lips.

"No!" she screamed. "I don't believe this. You're making me see this—"

She turned and ran from the kitchen toward the serving pantry. Ardis was close behind her. And the blue shapes still hissed a droning chorus:

"Qui nunc te fruitur credulus aurea:
Qui semper vacuam, semper amabilem,
Sperat, nescius aurae
Fallacis—"

When they reached the foot of the winding stairs that led to the upper floors, Sidra clutched at the balustrade for support. With her free hand she dabbed at her mouth to erase the salt taste that made her stomach crawl.

"I think I've an idea what all that was," Ardis said.

She stared at him.

"A sort of betrothal ceremony," he went on casually. "You've read of something like that before, haven't you? Odd, wasn't it—Some powerful influences in this house. Recognize those phantoms?"

She shook her head insanely. What was the use of thinking—talking?

"Didn't, eh? We'll have to see about this. I never cared for unsolicited haunting. We shan't have any more of this tomfoolery in the future—" He mused for a moment, then pointed up the stairs. "Your husband's up there, I think. Let's continue."

They trudged up the sweeping gloomy stairs, and the last vestiges of Sidra's sanity struggled up, step by step, with her.

One—You go up the stairs. Stairs leading up to what? More madness? That damned Thing in the shelter!

Two—this is hell, not reality.

Three—Or nightmare. Yes! Nightmare. Lobster last night. Where were we last night, Bob and I?

Four—Dear Bob. Why did I ever—And this Ardis. I know why he's so familiar. Why he almost speaks my thoughts. He's probably some—

Five—Nice young man who plays tennis in real life. Distorted by a dream. Yes.

Six—

Seven—

"Don't run into it!" Ardis cautioned.

She halted in her tracks, and simply stared. There were no more screams or shudders left in her. She simply stared at the thing that hung with a twisted head from the beam over the stair landing. It was her husband, limp and slack, dangling at the end of a length of laundry rope.

The limp figure swayed ever so slightly, like the gentle swing of a massive pendulum. The mouth was wrinkled into a sardonic grin and the eyes popped from their sockets and glanced down at her with impudent humor. Vaguely, Sidra was aware that ascending steps behind it showed through the twisted form.

"Join hands," the corpse said in sacrosanct tones.

"Bob!"

"Your husband?" Ardis exclaimed.

"Dearly beloved," the corpse began, "we are gathered together in the sight of God and in the face of this company to join together this man and this woman in holy matrimony; which is commanded to be honorable among all men and therefore is not by any to be entered into unadvisedly or lightly—" The voice boomed on and on and on.

"Bob!" Sidra croaked.

"Kneel!" the corpse commanded.

Sidra flung her body to one side and ran stumbling up the stairs. She faltered for a gasping instant, then Ardis' strong hands grasped her. Behind them the shadowy corpse intoned: "I pronounce you man and wife—"

Ardis whispered: "We must be quick, now! Very quick!"

But at the head of the stairs Sidra made a last bid for liberty. She abandoned all hope of sanity, of understanding. All she wanted was freedom—and a place where she could sit in solitude, free of the passions that were hedging her in, gutting her soul. There was no word spoken, no gesture made. She drew herself up and faced Ardis squarely. This was one of the times, she understood, when you fought motionlessly.

For minutes they stood, facing each other in the dark hall. To their right was the descending well of the stairs; to the left, Sidra's bedroom; behind them, the short hallway that led to Peel's study—to the room where he was so unconsciously awaiting slaughter. Their eyes met, clashed and battled silently. And even as Sidra met that deep, gleaming glance, she knew with an agonizing sense of desperation that she would lose.

There was no longer any will, any strength, any courage left in her. Worse, by some spectral osmosis it seemed to have drained out of her into the man that faced her. While she fought she realized that her rebellion was like that of a hand or a finger rebelling against its guiding brain.

Only one sentence she spoke: "For Heaven's sake! *Who are you?*"

And again he answered: "You'll find out—soon. But I think you know already. I think you know!"

Helpless, she turned and entered her bedroom. There was a revolver there and she understood she was to get it. But when she pulled open the drawer and yanked aside the piles of silk clothes to pick it up, the clothes felt thick and moist. As she shuddered, Ardis reached past her and picked up the gun. Clinging to the butt, a finger tight-clenched around the trigger, was a hand, the stump of a wrist clotted and torn.

Ardis clucked his lips impatiently and tried to pry the hand loose. It would not give. He pressed and twisted a finger at a time and still the sickening corpse-hand clenched the gun stubbornly. Sidra sat at the edge of the bed like a child, watching the spectacle with naïve interest, noting the way the broken muscles and tendons on the stump flexed as Ardis tugged.

There was a crimson snake oozing from under the closed bathroom door. It writhed across the hardwood floor, thickening to a small river as it touched her skirt so gently. As Ardis tossed the gun down angrily, he noted the stream. Quickly he stepped to the bathroom and thrust open the door, then slammed it a second later. He jerked his head at Sidra and said: "Come on!"

She nodded mechanically and arose, careless of the sopping skirt that smacked against her calves. At Peel's study she turned the doorknob carefully until a faint click warned her that the latch was open, then she pushed the door in. The leaf opened to reveal her husband's study in semi-darkness. The desk was before the high window curtains and Peel sat at it, his back to them. He was hunched over a candle or a lamp or some rosy light that enhaloed his body and sent streams of light flickering out. He never moved.

Sidra tiptoed forward, then hesitated. Ardis touched finger to lips and moved like a swift cat to the cold fireplace where he picked up the heavy bronze poker. He brought it to Sidra and held it out urgently. Her hand reached out of its own accord and took the cool metal handle. Her fingers gripped it as though they had been born for murder.

Against all that impelled her to advance and raise the poker over Peel's head, something weak and sick inside her cried out and prayed. Cried, prayed and moaned with the mewlings of a fevered child. Like spilt water, the last few drops of her self-possessions trembled before they disappeared altogether.

Then Ardis touched her. His fingers pressed against the small of her back and a charge of bestiality shocked along her spine with cruel, jagged edges. Surging with hatred, rage and livid vindictiveness, she raised the poker high and crashed it down over the still-motionless head of her husband.

The entire room burst into a silent explosion. Lights flared and shadows whirled. Remorselessly, she beat and pounded at the falling body that toppled out of the chair to the floor. She struck again and again, her breath whistling hysterically, until the head was a mashed, bloodied pulp. Only then did she let the poker drop and reel back.

Ardis knelt beside the body and turned it over.

"He's dead all right. This is the moment you prayed for, Sidra. You're free!"

She looked down in horror. Dully, from the crimsoned carpet, a slightly distorted corpse face stared back. It showed the drawn, high-strung features, the coal-black eyes, the coal-black hair dipping over the brow in a sharp widow's peak.

She moaned as understanding touched her.

The face said: "This is Sidra Peel. In this man whom you have slaughtered you have killed yourself—killed the only part of yourself worth saving."

She cried: "Aieeee—" and clasped arms about herself, rocking in agony.

"Look well on me," the face said. "By my death you have broken a chain—only to find another!"

And she knew. She understood. For though she still rocked and moaned in the agony that would be never-ending, she saw Ardis arise and advance on her with arms outstretched. His eyes gleamed and were pools of horror; and his reaching arms were tendrils of her own unslaked passion eager to infold her. And once infolded, she knew there would be no escape—no escape from this sickening marriage to her own lusts that would forever caress her.

So it would be forevermore in Sidra's brave new world.

IV

After the others had passed the veil, Christian Braugh still lingered in the shelter. He lit another cigarette with a simulation of perfect aplomb, blew out the match, then called: "Er . . . Mr. Thing?"

"What is it, Mr. Braugh?"

Braugh could not restrain a slight start at that voice sounding from nowhere. "I—well, the fact is, I stayed for a chat."

"I thought you would, Mr. Braugh."

"You did, eh?"

"Your insatiable hunger for fresh material is no mystery to me."

"Oh!" Braugh looked around nervously. "I see."

"Nor is there any cause for alarm. No one will overhear us. Your masquerade will remain undetected."

"Masquerade!"

"You're not a really bad man, Mr. Braugh. You've never belonged in the Sutton shelter clique."

Braugh laughed sardonically.

"And there's no need to continue your sham before me," the voice continued in the friendliest manner. "I know the story of your many plagiarisms was merely another concoction from the fertile imagination of Christian Braugh."

"You know?"

"Of course. You created that legend to obtain entree to the shelter. For years you've been playing the role of a lying scoundrel, even though your blood ran cold at times."

"And do you know why I did that?"

"Naturally. As a matter of fact, Mr. Braugh, I know almost everything; but I do confess that one thing still confuses me."

"What's that?"

"Why, in that devouring appetite for fresh material, were you not content to work as other authors do? Why this almost insane desire for unique material—for absolutely untrodden fields? Why were you willing to pay such a bitter and often exorbitant price for a few ounces of novelty?"

"Why—" Braugh sucked in smoke and gushed it out past clenched teeth. "I'll tell you why. It's something that's been torturing me all my life. A man is born with imagination."

"Ah . . . imagination."

"If his imagination is slight, a man will always find the world a source of deep and infinite wonder, a place of many delights. But if his imagination is strong, vivid, restless, he finds the world a sorry place indeed—a drab jade beside the wonders of his own creations!"

"These are wonders past all imagining."

"For whom? Not for me, my invisible friend. Nor for any earth-bound, flesh-bound creature. Man is a pitiful thing. Born with the imagination of gods and forever pasted to a round lump of spittle and clay. I have within me the uniqueness, the ego, the fertile loam of a timeless spirit . . . and all that richness is wrapped in a parcel of quickly rotting skin!"

"Ego—" mused the voice. "That is something which, alas, none of us can understand. Nowhere in all the knowable cosmos is it to be found but on your planet, Mr. Braugh. It is a frightening thing that convinces me at times that yours is the race that will—" The voice broke off abruptly.

"That will—" Braugh prompted.

"Come," said the Thing briskly, "there is less owing you than the others and I shall give you the benefit of my experience. Let me help you select a reality."

Braugh pounced on the word: "Less?"

And again he was brushed aside. "Will you have another reality in your own cosmos? I can offer you vast worlds, tiny worlds; great creatures that shake space and fill the voids with their thunders, little creatures of charm and perfection that barely touch the ear with the sensitive timbre of their tinkling. Will you care for terror? I can give you a reality of shudders. Beauty? I can show you realities of infinite ecstasy. Pain. Torture. Any sensation. Name one, several, all. I will shape you a reality to outdo even the giant intellect that is assuredly yours."

"No—" Braugh answered at length. "The senses are only senses at best—and in time they tire of anything. You cannot satisfy the imagination with whipped cream in new forms and flavors."

"Then I can take you to worlds of extra dimensions that will stun your imagination. There is a region I know that will entertain you forever with incongruity—

where, if you sorrow, you scratch your ear; where, if you love, you eat a potato; where, if you die, you burst out laughing—

"There is a dimension I have seen where one can assuredly perform the impossible—where creatures daily compete in the composition of paradox and where the mere feat of turning oneself mentally inside out is known as *'chrythna,'* which is to say, *'corny'* in the American jargon.

"Do you want to probe the emotions in classical order? I can take you to a dimension of twenty-seven planes where one by one, *seriatim et privatim,* you may exhaust the intricate nuances of the twenty-seven primary emotions—and thence go on to infinite combinations and permutations. Come, which will you take?"

"None," Braugh said impatiently. "It is obvious, my friend, that you do not understand the ego of man. The ego is not a childish thing to be satisfied with toys; and yet it is a childish thing in that it yearns after the unattainable—"

"Yours seems to be a childish thing in that it does not laugh. You have no sense of humor, Mr. Braugh."

"The ego," Braugh continued abstractedly, "desires only what it cannot hope to attain. Once a thing is attainable, it is no longer desired. Can you grant me a reality where I may possess something which I desire because I cannot possibly possess it; and by that same possession not break the qualifications of my desire? Can you do this?"

"I'm afraid," the voice answered hesitantly, "that your imagination reasons too deviously for me."

"Ah," Braugh murmured, half to himself. "I was afraid of that. Why does the universe seem to be run by second-rate individuals not half so clever as myself? Why this mediocrity in the appointed authorities?"

"You seek to attain the unattainable," the voice said in reasonable tones, "and by that act not to attain it. The limitations are within yourself. Would you be changed?"

"No . . . no, not changed." Braugh shook his head. He stood for a moment deep in thought, then sighed and tamped out his cigarette. "There's only one solution for my problem."

"And that is?"

"Erasure. If you cannot satisfy a desire, you must explain it away. If a man cannot find love, he must write a psychological treatise on passion. I shall do much the same thing—"

He shrugged and moved toward the veil. There was a slight motion behind him and the voice asked: "Where does that ego of yours take you, O man?"

"To the truth of things," Braugh called. "If I cannot slake my yearning, at least I shall find out why I yearn."

"You'll find the truth only in hell, my friend."

"How so?"

"Because truth is always hell."

"Nevertheless I'm going there—to hell or wherever truth is to be found."

"May you find the answers pleasant, O man."

"Thank you."

"And may you learn to laugh."

But Braugh no longer heard, for he had passed the veil.

And he found himself standing before a high desk—a bench, almost—as high as the top of his head. Around him was nothing else. It looked as though a sulphurous fog had filled the room, concealing everything but this clerkly bench. Braugh tilted his head back and looked up. Staring down at him from the other side was a tiny little face, ancient as sin, whiskered and cockeyed. It was on a shriveled little head that was covered with a high-pointed hat. Like a sorcerer's cap. Or a dunce cap, Braugh thought.

Dimly, behind the head, he made out towering shelves of books and files labeled: A—AB, AC—AD, and so on. There was also a gleaming black pot of ink and a rack of quill pens. An enormous hourglass completed the picture. Inside the hourglass a spider had spun a web and was crawling shakily across sand-clotted strands.

The little man croaked: "A-mazing! A-stonishing! Incredible!"

Braugh still stared.

The little man hunched forward like Richard Crookback in an amateur play and got his seamed, comical face as close as possible to Braugh's. He reached down a knobby finger and poked Braugh gingerly. Abruptly he tumbled backward and bawled: "THAMM—UZ! DA—GON! RIMM—ON!"

There was a busy bustle and three more little men bounced up behind the desk and gaped at Braugh. The staring went on for minutes.

"All right," Braugh said at last. "That's enough gawping. Say something. Do something!"

"It speaks!" they shouted in unison. "Its alive!" They pressed four noses together and began to gabble swiftly. It went: "MostastonishingthingDagonthat IeverhespeaksRimmoncoulditbehumanheardwhatitsaidBelialyou'dthinktheremust besomeexplanationd'youthinksoThammuzIcan'tsay!"

Then it stopped.

One said: "First thing is to find out how it got here."

"Not at all. Find out what it is."

The third said: "Find out where it's from."

"I don't know about that, Belial. Cart before the horse, you know."

They raved and again turned noses together. The gabble was very loud: "THE IMPORTANTTHING'SWHERENOTATALLIT'SWHEREFROMYOU'RECRAZY YOU'REBOTHCRAZYLISTENTOMEHOWCANYOUOHALLRIGHTALLRIGHT ALLRIGHT!"

Then apparently they came to a decision. The number one sorcerer pointed an accusing finger at Braugh and said: "What are you doing here?"

"The point is," Braugh countered, "where am I?"

The little man turned to brothers Thammuz, Dagon and Rimmon. He smirked and said: "It wants to know where it is."

Dagon said: "Silly animal, ain't he, Belial?"

Rimmon said: "Oh, get on with it, Belial. Can't hold up business all day."

"You!" Belial swiveled on Braugh. "Listen carefully. This is General Administration, Universal Control Center. Belial, Rimmon, Dagon and Thammuz, acting for Satan."

"Tuts," said Braugh, "I came here to see Satan."

"It wants to see Satan!" They were utterly appalled. Then Dagon jabbed the others with his sharp little elbows and placed a finger alongside his nose with a shrewd look.

"Spy!" he said. To elaborate, he jabbed one finger significantly toward the ceiling, then gave a shrewd look.

"Could be . . . could be," Belial said, flipping the pages of a giant ledger. "It certainly don't belong here. No deliveries scheduled today. It's not dead because it don't smell. It's not alive because only the dead ones come here. Question still is: What is it? What do we do with it?"

Thammuz said: "Divination. Only answer."

"Right!"

"Great mind, that Thammuz!"

Belial glared at Braugh and snapped: "Name?"

"Christian Braugh."

"Ha!" cried Dagon. "Onomancy—C, third letter—H, eighth letter—and so on. Take total sum. Double it and add ten. Divide by two, then subtract original total—"

They added and divided. Quills scratched on parchment and a bumbling, muttering noise droned. At last Belial held up the scrap and scrutinized it carefully. They all scrutinized it. As one man they shrugged and tore the parchment up.

"I can't understand it," Dagon complained. "We always get five for an answer."

"Never mind!" Belial glared at Braugh. "When born?"

"December eighteenth, nineteen thirteen."

"Time?"

"Twelve fifteen, a.m."

"Star Charts!" screamed Thammuz. "We'll try Genethliacs."

They tore at the books behind them and took out huge sheets that unrolled like window shades. This time it took them fifteen minutes to produce a scrap of parchment which they again examined carefully and again tore up.

Rimmon said: "It *is* odd."

Belial said: "It gets odder and odder."

Thammuz said: "We better take it into the laboratory for a check. The old boy will be plenty peeved if we muff this one."

They leaned over the bench and beckoned imperatively. Braugh followed their directions, walked around the side of the bench and found himself before a small door set in the books. The four little sorcerers bounced down from the desk and crowded him through. They just about came up to his waist.

Braugh entered the so-called laboratory. It was a circular room with a low ceiling, tile floors and walls covered with cupboards, shelves, glass gimmicks, alchemists' gadgets, books, bones and bottles. In the center was a large flat rock, the shape of a millstone. There was a slight depression in the center that had a charred look. But there wasn't any chimney over it.

Belial rooted around in a corner and came out with an armful of dry sticks.

"Altar fire," he said and tripped. The sticks went flying. Braugh solemnly bent to pick up the pieces of wood.

"Sortilege!" Rimmon squawked. He yanked a lizard out of a box and began writing on its back with a piece of charcoal, noting the order in which Braugh picked up the scattered bits of wood.

"Which way is east?" Rimmon demanded, crawling after the lizard. Thammuz pointed directly overhead. Rimmon nodded curt thanks and began to figure rapidly on the lizard's back. Gradually his hand moved slower. By the time Braugh had helpfully placed the bundle of wood on the altar, Rimmon was holding the lizard by the tail, gawping at his notations with a look of sickly wonder. Finally he shoved the lizard under the wood pile. Instantly it caught fire.

Rimmon said: "Salamander. Not bad, eh?" and swaggered off.

Dagon screamed: "Pyromancy!" and ran to the flames. He stuck his nose within an inch of the fire and mumbled rapidly in a long, droning whisper. Belial fidgeted uneasily and muttered to Thammuz: "Last time he tried that he fell asleep."

The droning faded out and Dagon, eyes blissfully closed, fell forward into the crackling flames.

"Did it again!" Belial snapped irritably.

They ran up and dragged Dagon out of the flames. After they had slapped his face awhile, his whiskers stopped burning. Thammuz sniffed the stench of burned hair, then pointed overhead to the drifting smoke.

"Capnomancy!' he said. "It can't fail. We'll find out what this thing is yet!"

All four joined hands and danced around the rising smoke cloud, puffing at it with little pursed lips. Eventually the smoke disappeared. Thammuz gave a sour look and said: "It failed."

There was a dead silence and all glared angrily at Braugh. He endured it about as long as he could, then he said: "What's up, lads? Anything wrong?"

"It wants to know if anything's wrong," Belial sneered.

"Deceitful thing!" said Dagon.

"Not at all," Braugh said. "I'm not hiding anything. Of course I don't believe a particle of what's happening here, but that don't matter."

"Don't matter! What d'you mean, you don't believe?"

"Why," Braugh said, "you can't make me believe that you charlatans have anything to do with truth—much less His Black Majesty, Father Satan."

"Anything to do with— Why, you blasted booby, *we're Satan*—"

A second later they looked scared, lowered their voices and added: "So to speak."

Belial glanced around uneasily and said to unseen ears; "No offense—"

"Merely referring to power of attorney," Dagon trembled.

"I see," Braugh said. "And how, exactly, am I deceiving you?"

"How? We'll tell you how! You've got a devil with you that obstructs official divination. You're a cacodaemon or maybe a barghest or an ouphe or an incubus. But we'll get to the heart of the matter. We'll ferret you out. We'll track you down. We'll make you talk. Bring on the iron!"

Well, Braugh thought, what's all this? Bring on the iron. Sounds like dancing girls.

Dagon trundled out a little wheelbarrow filled with lumps of iron. To Braugh he said: "Take one—any one." Braugh picked up a heavy lump of blue-gray metal and handed it to Dagon, who snatched it from him irritably and plunked it into a small vat. He placed the vat over the fire and got a pair of bellows which he pumped energetically into the flames. The iron heated white-hot. They nipped it out with pincers and waved it over Braugh's head, chanting: "Sideromancy! Sideromancy! Sideromancy!"

After a while, Dagon said: "No soap."

"Let's try Molybdomancy," Belial suggested.

They dropped the iron into a pot of solid lead. It hissed and fumed as though it had been dropped into cold water. Presently the lead melted. Belial tipped the pot over and the silvery liquid streamed slowly across the floor.

"Lead, lead, beautiful lead!" chanted Rimmon. "Tell us the story of this creature. Is it a man? Is it a—"

A crack, loud and sharp as a pistol shot, answered him. One of the floor tiles shattered to pieces, the lead dropped with a gurgle, and the next instant a fountain of water hissed and spurted up through the hole.

Belial said: "We busted the pipes again."

"Pegomancy!" Dagon cried eagerly. He approached the fountain with a reverent look, knelt before it and began to drone. In thirty seconds his eyes closed rapturously and he fell forward into the water. They dragged him back and wrung out his beard.

"Got to get him dry," Thammuz said hastily. "He'll catch his death. Get him over to the fire."

Taking Dagon by each arm, Thammuz and Belial ran him over to the altar fire. They circled the bright blaze once, and as they were about to stop, Dagon choked: "Keep me moving. We'll try Gyromancy. There's got to be some answer to what that thing is!"

They made another circle while Dagon muttered: "Hubbble-ka-bubble-ka-hubble-ka-bubble—"

Suddenly Rimmon, who was squatting over the broken tile, paddling ineffectually at the food, stopped and said: "Oi!"

The others stopped, too, and said: "Oi!"

Braugh turned.

A girl had just entered the door. She was short, red-headed, and delightfully the right side of plump. Her copper hair was done up on top of her head. She was breathing with indignant short breaths that made her look as though she would shake to pieces. She wore an expression of utter exasperation and nothing else.

"So!" she rapped out. "At it again!"

No answer. Much quartet trembling.

"How many times—" she began, then stopped and bit her lip. Abruptly she ran to the wall, seized a prodigious glass retort and hurled it straight and true. When the pieces stopped falling, she said: "How many times have I told you to cut out this nonsense or I'd report you!"

"N-nonsense?" quavered Belial. He tried to stanch his bleeding cuts and attempted an innocent smile. "Why Astarte, wh-what d'you m-mean?"

"You know damned well what I mean! I will not have you smashing my ceiling, dripping things down on my office. First molten lead—then water. Four weeks work ruined. My new Sheraton desk ruined!" She hitched around and exhibited a long red sear that ran straight down from shoulder to hip. "Twelve inches of skin—ruined!"

Belial went: *"Tsk-tsk!"*

Braugh went: "My-my!"

The red-headed Astarte turned on him and lanced him with level green eyes. "Who's this?"

"We don't know," Belial began eagerly in an effort to change the subject. "That's why we were . . . er—Well, it just walked up to my desk, and . . . and that's all."

As Braugh stepped forward he heard Rimmon whisper: "Might try Parthenomancy . . . that is, if Astarte is—"

Then he took the girl's hand and said: "The name is Braugh. Christian Braugh."

Her hand was cool and firm. She said: "The name is Astarte. I, too, am a Christian."

"Satan's crew Christians?"

"Why not?"

There was no answer to that. He said: "Is there some place where we can get away from these Zanies?"

"There's always my office."

"I like offices."

And he also liked Astarte. She ushered him into her place, on the floor below, swept a pile of papers and books off a chair, and casually invited him to sit down. Then she sprawled before the ruin of her desk and after one malevolent glance at the ceiling, listened to his story.

"As I get this," she said, "you're looking for Satan. Evil Lord of the Universe. Well, this is the only hell there is, and ours is the only Satan there is. You're in the right place."

Braugh was perplexed. "Hell?" he inquired. "Fire, brimstone, and so forth?"

"There are the business offices," she explained. "If you're looking for torments—"

"No," Braugh interrupted hastily. "I thank you. No torments."

She smiled at his solemn face and went on: "All this brings us to something rather vital. Just how did you get here? Dead?"

Braugh shook his head.

"Hm-m-m—" She made an interested survey. "You'll bear more looking into. I've never had anything to do with the live ones. You *are* alive, aren't you?"

"Very much so."

"And what business have you with Father Satan?"

"The truth," Braugh said. "I was granted a wish. I wished to discover the truth of all. I was sent here. Why Father Satan, as you call him, should be official purveyor of truth rather than—" He hesitated, then delicately indicated heaven. "I don't know. But to me the truth is worth any price, so I should like very much to have an interview."

Astarte rapped glittering nails on the desk and smiled broadly. "This," she said, "is going to be delicious!" She arose, flung open the door of her office and pointed down the corridor. "Straight ahead," said Astarte, "then turn to the left. Keep on and you can't miss."

"I'll see you again?" Braugh asked as he set off.

"You'll see me again," Astarte laughed.

This, Braugh thought as he trudged along the corridor, is all too ridiculous. You pass a veil intending to seek the Citadel of Truth. You are entertained by four ridiculous creatures and by a red-head goddess. You ask to see the Knower of All Things and discover Him to be Satan rather than God. Then off you go down a musty corridor, turn left and then straight ahead.

What of this yearning of mine? What of these truths I seek? Is there no solemnity, no dignity anywhere? Is not Satan a fearful, thunderous deity? Why all this low comedy—this saturnalian air of slapstick that pervades the Underworld Offices of Satan?

He turned the corner to the left and kept on. The short hall ended abruptly in a pair of green baize doors. Almost timidly Braugh pushed them open and to his great relief found himself merely entering an open stone bridge—rather like the Bridge of Sighs, he thought. Around him was nothing but that same sulphurous mist. Behind him was the giant façade of the building he had just left—a wall of brimstone blocks. Before him was a smallish building shaped like a globe.

He stepped quickly across the bridge, for those misty depths on either side of him made him queasy. He paused only a moment before a second pair of baize doors to gather his courage, then tried to smile and pushed them in. You do not, he muttered to himself, come before Satan with a smirk in your heart; but there is an air of general insanity in hell that has touched me.

It was a large office—a kind of file room, and for the second time Braugh was relieved at having put the awesome moment a little further into the future. The office was round as a planetarium and was filled with the largest and most complicated adding machine Braugh had ever seen in his life. The thing was all keyboard. A long platform before the banks of keys buckled and creaked like a painter's scaffolding as a dried-out little clerk wearing glasses the size of binoculars rushed up and back, punching keys with lightning speed.

More as an excuse to put off the meeting than anything else, Braugh watched the little old man scurry before those keys, punching them so rapidly they chattered like a dozen stuttering motors. This little old chap, Braugh thought, has probably put in an eternity figuring out sin totals and death totals and all sorts of statistical totals. He looks like a total himself.

Aloud, Braugh called: "Hello, there!"

Without wavering, the clerk said: "What is it?" His voice was drier than his skin.

Braugh said: "Those figures can wait a moment, can't they?"

"Sorry," said the little old man. He bustled down the scaffolding on a mad run.

"Will you stop a moment!" Braugh shouted.

The clerk paused and turned, removing the enormous binoculars very slowly.

"Now—that's better," Braugh said. "See here, my man, I'd like to get in to see Satan. His Black Majesty, Satan—"

"That's me," said the little man.

"Braugh said: "G-Gug—"

For a fleeting instant the dried-out face flickered into a smile. "Yes, that's me, son. I'm Satan."

And, despite all his imagination, Braugh had to believe.

He slumped down on the lowermost tread of the steps that led up to the scaffold. Satan chuckled faintly and touched a clutch on the gigantic adding machine. Instantly there was a click of gears and with the sound of free-wheeling the machine began to cluck softly like a contented hen.

His Diabolic Majesty came creaking down the stairs and seated himself alongside Braugh. He took out an old silk handkerchief and began polishing his glasses. He was just a nice little old man sitting friendly like alongside Braugh. At last he said: "What's on your mind, son?"

"W-well, Satan—" Braugh began.

"You can call me Father, son."

"B-but why should I? I mean—" Braugh broke off in embarrassment.

"Well now, son, I guess you're a little worried about that heaven-and-hell business, eh?"

Braugh nodded.

Satan clicked his tongue and shook his head dubiously. "Don't know what to do about that," he said. "Fact is, son, it's all the same thing. Naturally I let it get around in certain quarters that there's two places. Got to, to keep certain folks on their toes. But the fact is, it's not really so. I'm all there is, son. God or Satan or Siva or Official Co-ordinator or Nature—or whatever you want to call it."

With a sudden rush of good feeling toward this friendly old man, Braugh said: "I call you a fine old man!"

"Well—that's nice of you, son. Glad you feel that way. You understand, of course, that we couldn't let everyone see me that way. Might instill disrespect."

"Y-yes, sir, I see."

"Got to have efficiency." The little old man went: *Tsk!* and shook his head. "Got to frighten folks now and then. Got to have respect, you understand. Can't run things without respect."

"Yes, sir."

"Got to have efficiency. Can't be running things all day long, all year long, all eternity long, without efficiency. Can't have efficiency without respect."

Again Braugh said: "Yes, sir—" While within him a hideous uncertainty grew. This was a nice old man—but this was also a maudlin old man. His Satanic Majesty was a tired creature much duller and not nearly so clever as Christian Braugh.

"What I always say," the old man went on, rubbing his knee reflectively, "is that love and all that—you can have 'em. They're nice, of course, but I'll take efficiency any time. Yes, indeed . . . any time . . . leastways, for a body in my position. Now then, son, what was on your mind?"

Mediocrity, Braugh thought grimly. He said: "The Truth, Father Satan. I came seeking the truth."

"And what do you want with the truth, Christian?"

"I just want to know it, Father Satan. I came seeking it. Want to know why we are, why we live, why we yearn—I want to know all that."

"Well, now"—the old man chuckled—"that's quite an order, son. Yes, sir, quite an order indeed."

"Can you tell me, Father Satan?"

"A little, son, just a little. What was it you wanted to know mostly?"

"What there is inside of us that makes us seek the unattainable!" Braugh cried with passion. "What are those forces that pull and tug and surge within us? What is this ego of mine that gives me no rest, that seeks no rest, that frets at turbulence and yet seeks nothing but turbulence. What is all this?"

"Why," the old man said, pointing to his adding machine. "It's that gadget over there. It runs everything."

"That!"

"Yes. That."

"It runs everything?"

"Everything that I run—and I run everything there is." The old man chuckled again, then held out the binoculars. "You're an unusual boy, Christian. First person that ever said a kind word for old Father Satan. First person that ever had the decency to pay the old man a visit. I'll return the favor. Here!"

Wondering, Braugh accepted the glasses.

"Put 'em on." said the old man.

And then the wonder began, for as Braugh slipped the glasses over his head he found himself peering with the eyes of the universe at all the universe. And the adding machine was no longer a machine, but a vastly complex marionetteers crossbar from which an infinity of shimmering silver threads descended.

And with his all-seeing eyes, with the spectacles of Satan, Braugh perceived how each thread attached itself to the nape of the neck of a creature and how each living entity danced the dance of life to the tune of Father Satan's efficient machine.

Wondering, he stumbled up to the scaffold and reached toward the banks of keys. One key he pressed and on a pale planet a creature hungered and killed. A second key and it felt remorse. A third, and it forgot. A fourth, and a half a continent away another entity arose five minutes early and so began a chain of events that culminated in discovery and hideous punishment for the murderer.

Slowly Braugh backed away from the adding machine and in a kind of horror slipped the glasses up to his brow. The machine went on clucking, and only vaguely did he note that the meticulous chronometer on the wall had ticked away a space of three months' time.

"This," he thought, "is ghastliest of all. We were puppets. We danced the dance of death in life, for we were little better than dead things hung from a string. Up here an old man, not overly intelligent, clicks a few keys, and down there we dance on our strings and take it for a thousand things—for fate, for free will, for Karma, for evolution, for nature, for a thousand false things.

"And none of us knew or knows or will care to know the truth—that there is neither reason, nor beauty, nor sanity to life. That all our mysterious yearning is the push of a decrepit finger on a tab. Oh—it's a bitter thing, this sour discovery. It's a bitter thing always to yearn after truth and find it to be shoddy!"

He glanced down. Old Father Satan was still seated on the steps, but his head slumped a little to one side, his eyes were half closed and he murmured indistinctly about work and rest and not enough of it.

"You're a good boy, Christian," the old man mumbled, "a good boy—"

And revolt stirred in Braugh. "This isn't fair!" he cried. "Father Satan!"

"Yes, my boy?" The old man roused himself slightly.

"This is true? We all dance to your key-tapping?"

"All of you, my boy. All of you."

"And although we think we are free, yet we dance to your tune?"

"You all think yourselves free, Christian, and yet you all dance to Father Satan's playing."

"Then, Father, grant me one thing—one very small thing. There is in a small corner of your mighty kingdom a very tiny planet . . . a very insignificant speck called the Earth—"

"Earth? Earth? Can't say I recollect it off-hand, son, but I could look it up."

"No, don't bother, Father Satan. It's there. Only grant me this favor—break the cords that bind it. Let it go free!"

"Now, son, don't be foolish. I can't do that."

"In all your kingdom," Braugh pleaded, "there are souls too numerous to count. There are suns and planets too vast to measure. Surely this one tiny bit of dust with its paltry few people—You who own so much can surely part with so little!"

"No, my boy, couldn't do it. Sorry—"

"You who alone knows freedom," Braugh cried. "Would you deny it to others?"

But the Co-ordinator of All slumbered.

"This, then, is His Satanic Majesty," Braugh thought. "This likable, simple old man is the one free agent in an entire cosmos. This is the answer to my seeking, and behold, the answer sleeps!"

Braugh grimly slipped the glasses back over his eyes. Let him slumber then, while Braugh, Satan pro tem, takes over. Oh, we shall be repaid for this disappointment. We shall have a giddy time writing novels in flesh and blood! And perhaps, if we can find the cord that leads to my neck and search out the proper key in all these billions, we may do something to free Christian Braugh!

He turned from the keyboard and craned his head over his shoulder, and even as his eyes searched, he stopped short, stunned, transfixed. His eyes ran up, then down, then up again. His hands began to tremble, then his arms, and finally his whole body shuddered uncontrollably. For the first time in his life he began to laugh, and the hysterical peals rang through the vast-domed room.

And Father Satan awoke and cried anxiously: "Christian! What is it? What is this laughter?"

Laughter of frustration? Laughter of relief? Laughter of promise? He could not tell as he shook at the sight of that slender tendril that stretched from the nape of Satan's neck and turned him, too, into a capering puppet. A silver thread that stretched upward into the infinite heights toward some other vaster machine hidden in the still unknowable reaches of the cosmos—

The blessedly unknowable cosmos.

V

Now in the beginning all was darkness. There was neither land nor sea nor sky nor the circling stars. There was nothing. Then came Yaldabaoth and rent the light from the darkness. And the darkness He gathered up and formed into the night and the skies. And the light He gathered up and formed into the Sun and the stars. Then from the flesh and the blood of His blood did Yaldabaoth form the earth and all things upon it.

But the children of Yaldabaoth were new and green to living and unlearned, and the race did not bear fruit. And as the children of Yaldabaoth diminished in numbers they cried out unto their Lord: "Grant us a sign, Great God, that we may know how to increase and multiply! Grant us a sign, O Lord, that Thy good and mighty race may not perish from Thine earth!"

And Lo, Yaldabaoth withdrew himself from the face of his importunate people and they were sore at heart and sinful, thinking their Lord had forsaken them. And their paths were the paths of evil until a prophet arose whose name was Maart. Then did Maart gather the children of Yaldabaoth around him and spoke to them, saying: "Evil are thy ways, O people of Yaldabaoth, to doubt thy God. For He has given a sign of faith unto you."

Then gave they answer, saying: "Where is this sign?"

And Maart went into the high mountains and with him was a vast concourse of people. Nine days and nine nights did they travel even unto the peak of Mount Sinar. And at the crest of Mount Sinar all were struck with wonder and fell to their knees, crying: "Great is God! Great are His works!"

For Lo, before them blazed a mighty curtain of fire.

Book of Maart; XIII:29–37.

Pass the veil toward what reality? There's no sense trying to make up my mind. I cannot. God knows, that's been the agony of living for me—trying to make up my mind. How can I when I've felt nothing . . . when nothing's touched me— ever! Take this or take that. Take coffee or tea. Buy the black gown or the silver. Marry Lord Buckley or live with Freddy Witherton. Let Finchley make love to me or stop posing for him. No—there's no sense even trying.

How it glitters in the doorway. Like silk moiré or rainbow lamé. There goes Sidra. Passed through as though nothing was there. Doesn't seem to hurt. That's good. God knows I could stand anything except being hurt. No one left but Bob and myself—and he doesn't seem to be in any hurry. My turn now, I suppose. But where to?

To nowhere?

Yes—that's it. To nowhere!

In this world I'm leaving there's never been any place for me. There was nothing I could do; nothing I ever wanted to do. The world wanted nothing from me but my beauty. It had no need of me. Nothing but to pose naked while nearsighted little men smudged pictures on canvas.

I want to be useful. I want to belong. Perhaps if I belonged—if living had some purpose for me, this lump of ice in my heart might melt. I could learn to feel things—enjoy things. Even learn to fall in love.

Yes—that's it. To nowhere!

Let the reality that needs me, that wants me, that can use me . . . let that reality have me and call me to itself. For if I must choose, I know I shall choose wrong again. And if I am not wanted . . . anywhere; if I go through to wander forever in blank time and space . . . still am I better off.

Take me, you who want me and need me!

How cool the veil . . . like scented sprays caressing the skin.

And even as the multitude knelt in prayer, Maart cried aloud: "Rise, ye children of Yaldabaoth, and behold!"
Then did all arise and were struck dumb and trembled. For through the curtain of fire stepped a beast that chilled the hearts of all. To the height of eight cubits it stood and its skin was pink and white as nacre. The hair of its head was yellow and its body was long and curving like unto a sickly tree. And all was covered with slack folds of white fur.

Book of Maart; XIII: 38–39

God in Heaven!

Is this the reality that called me? This the reality that needs me?

That scarlet sun . . . so high . . . with its blood-red evil eye. Mountaintops . . . like pain-racked titans. Towering mounds of gray slime—The scabrous sheen of valley floors—The pervading sickroom stench of fetid ruination—

And those monstrous creatures crowding around me—like gorillas made of black, rotting coal. Not animal, not human. As though man had fashioned beasts not too

well—or beasts had fashioned men still worse. They have a familiar look to them, these monstrosities. The landscape has a familiar look. Somewhere I have seen all this before. Somehow I have been here before. In dreams of death—Yes—
This is a reality of death and twisted shadows.

Again the multitude cried out: "Glory to Yaldabaoth!" and at the sound of the sacred name, the beast turned toward the curtain of flames whence it had come. And Behold! The curtain was gone.

Book of Maart; XIII: 40.

No retreat?
No way out?
No way back to sanity?
But it was behind me a second ago, the veil! No escape—Listen to the sounds they make. The swilling of swine in muck. This can't be real. No reality was ever so horrible. This is all a ghastly trick. Like the one we played on Lady Sutton. I'm in the shelter now. Bob Peel's given us a new kind of hashish or opium—I'm lying on the couch dreaming and groaning. Presently I'll be awake—Before they come any closer—
I must awaken!

With a loud and piercing cry, the beast of the fire ran through the multitude. Through all the gathered thousands it ran and thundered down the mountainside. And the shrill sound of its cries was as the brazen clangor of beaten shields.

And as it passed under the low boughs of the mountain trees, the children of Yaldabaoth cried out in new alarm; for the beast shed its white furred hide in a manner horrible to behold. And the skin remained clinging to the trees. And the beast ran farther, a hideous pink-and-white thing.

Book of Maart; XIII: 41–43.

Quick! Quick! Run through them before they clutch me. Down the mountainside! If this is a nightmare, running will awaken me. If this is reality—But it can't be. That so cruel a thing should happen to me—Were the gods jealous of my beauty? Jealous of the pride I took in my beauty? No. The gods are never jealous.
My dressing gown!
Gone.
No time to go back for it. Run naked, then—Listen to them howl at me—Raven at me. Down! Down! Quickly and down. This rotten soft offal earth sucks my feet like a leech's mouth. Like the pulsating tendrils of an octopus.
They're following.
Why can't I wake up?
My breath—like knives in my chest that dance quickstep of cutting torture.
Why can't I wake up?

Close! I hear them. Close!
WHY CAN'T I WAKE UP?

And Maart cried aloud: "Take you this beast for an offering to our Lord Yaldabaoth!"

Then did the multitude raise stout courage and gird its loins. With clubs and stones all pursued the beast down the jagged slopes of Mount Sinar, chanting the name of the Lord.

And on a small plateau stout warriors pursued it until a shrewdly thrown stone brought the beast to its knees, still screaming in a manner horrible to hear. Then did the warriors smite it many times with strong clubs until at last the cries ceased and the beast was still. And out of the pink-and-white carcass oozed a fetid red matter that sickened all who beheld it.

But when the beast was brought to the High Temple of Yaldabaoth and placed in a cage before the altar, the cries once more resounded, desecrating the sacred halls. And the High Priests were troubled, saying: "What foul offering is this to place before Yaldabaoth, Lord of Gods?"

Book of Maart; XIII: 44–47.

Pain.

Like burning and scalding.

Can't move.

No dream was ever so long—so real. This, then, is real, all real. And I, too, am real. A stranger in a reality of filth and horror and torture. My beauty—But why? Why? Why?

My head—still ringing. It feels twisted. It itches inside. I want to scratch it.

This is torture, and somewhere . . . some place—I have heard that word before. Torture. It has a pleasant sound. Torture. The sound of a madrigal; the name of a boat; the title of a prince. Prince Torture.

So light in my head. Great lights and blinding sounds that come and go and have no meaning.

Once upon a time I torture a man—they say.

His name was?

Finchley? Yes. Digby Finchley.

Digby Finchley, they say, loved a pink ice goddess named Theone Dubedat—they say.

The pink ice goddess.

Where is she now?

And while the beast did moan malicious spells upon the altar steps, the Sanhedrin of Priests held council, and to the council came Maart, saying: "O ye priests of Yaldabaoth, raise up your hearts and voices in praise of our Lord. For He was displeased with us and turned His face away. And Lo, a sacrifice has been vouchsafed unto us that we may make our peace with Him."

Then spoke the High Priest, saying: "How now, Maart? Do ye say that this is a sacrifice for our Lord?"

And Maart spoke: "Yea. For it is a beast of fire. It was born of the fire and through fire it shall return whence it came."

And the High Priest said: "Is this offering seemingly in the sight of Yaldabaoth?"

And Maart spoke, saying: "All things are from Yaldabaoth. Therefore are all things good in His sight. Perchance through this strange offering Yaldabaoth will grant us a sign that His people may not vanish from the earth. Let the beast be offered."

Then did the priests agree, for they, too, were sore afraid lest the children of the Lord be no more.

Book of Maart; XIII: 48–54.

See the pretty monkeys dance.

They dance around and around and around.

And they snort.

Almost like speaking.

Almost like—I must stop the singing in my head. The ring-ring-singing. Like the days when Dig was working hard and I would take those difficult poses and hold them for hour after hour with maybe five minutes' time out and I would get dizzy sometimes and reel off the dais and Dig would drop his palette in fright and come running with those big solemn eyes of his ready to cry.

And I knew he loved me and I wanted to love him, but I had no need then. I had no need of anything but finding myself. Now I'm found. This is me. Now I have a need and an ache and a loneliness deep, deep inside for Dig and his love. To see him all eyes and fright at the fainting spells and dancing around me with a cup of tea.

Dancing—dancing—dancing—

And thumping their chests and grunting and thumping.

And when they grunt the spittle drools and gleams on their yellow fangs. And those seven with the rotting shreds of cloth across their chests.

See the pretty monkeys dance.

They dance around and around and around—

So it came to pass that the high holiday of Yaldabaoth was nigh. And on that day did the priests throw wide the portals of the temple and the hosts of children of Yaldabaoth did enter. Then did the priests remove the beast from the cage and drag it to the altar. Each of four priests held a limb and spread the beast wide across the altar stone, and the beast screamed again with evil, blasphemous sounds.

Then cried Maart: "Rend this thing to pieces that the smell of its evil death may rise to please the nostrils of Yaldabaoth!"

And the four priests, strong and holy, put powerful hands to the limbs of the beast so that its struggles were wondrous to behold; and the light of evil on its hideous hide struck terror into all.

And as Maart lit the altar fires, a great trembling shook the earth.

Book of Maart; XIII: 55–59.

Digby, come to me!
Digby—wherever you are—come to me!
Digby, I need you.
This is Theone.
Theone.
The pink ice goddess.
No longer pink ice, Digby.
Digby, I can't stay sane much longer.
Wheels whirl faster in my head.
Faster and faster.
Digby, come to me.
I need you.
Torture—

Then did the vaults of the temple split asunder with a thunderous roar, and all that were gathered there quailed and their bowels were as water. And all beheld the glittering image of the Lord, Yaldabaoth, descend from pitch-black skies to the temple. Yea, to the very altar itself.

For the space of an eternity did the Lord God Yaldabaoth gaze at the beast of the fire and the beast snarled and writhed, helpless in its evil.

Book of Maart; XIII: 59–60.

It is the final horror—the torture.
This monstrosity that floats down from the heavens.
This hideous apelike, manlike, bestial thing.
It is the final jest that it should float down like the ephemera, like a thing of fluff, a thing of lightness and joy. A monster on wings of light. A monster that stands like a rotting corpse with its twisted legs and twisted arms and the shaggy, loathsome body. A monster with the head of a man that looks torn and broken, smashed and ravaged. With those great saucer eyes—
Eyes? Where have I—
THOSE EYES!
This isn't madness. No. I know those eyes—those great, solemn eyes. I've seen them before. Years ago. Minutes ago. Great, solemn eyes filled with hopeless love and adoration.
No—let me be wrong.
Those big, solemn eyes of his ready to cry.
No, not Digby. It can't be. Please—

That's where I've seen this scene before, seen these creatures and the landscape—Digby's drawings. Those monstrous pictures he drew.

But why does he look like that? Why is he rotten and loathsome like the others—like his pictures?

This is your reality, Digby? Did you call me? Need me? Want me?

Digby!

Why don't you listen to me? Why do you look at me that way, like a mad thing when only a minute ago you walked up and back the length of the shelter and finally darted through the veil toward—

And with a voice like unto shattering mountains, the Lord Yaldabaoth spoke to His people, saying: "Now praise ye the Lord, my children, for one has been sent unto you to be thy queen and consort to thy God."

With one voice the multitude cried out: "Praise the Lord, Yaldabaoth!"

And Maart groveled before the Lord and spoke, saying: "A sign to Thy children, O Lord, that they may increase and multiply!"

Then the Lord God reached out to the beast and touched it, raising it with both hands from the altar fires. And behold! The evil cried out for the last time and fled the body of the beast, leaving only a pleasant song in its place. And the Lord spoke unto Maart, saying: "Lo, I will give you a sign."

Book of Maart; XIII: 60–63.

Let me die.

Let me die.

Let me not see and not hear and not feel the—

The?

Pretty monkeys that dance around and around and around while the great, solemn eyes stare into my soul, and Digby, the darling, touches me with hands so strangely changed.

Changed by the turpentine, perhaps, or the ochre or the bice green or Vandyke brown or burnt umber or sepia or chrome yellow which always seemed to stain his fingers each time he put down the brush.

How good to be loved by Digby. How warm and comforting to be loved and to be needed to want one alone in all the millions and to find him so strangely walking in a reality like that of when Sutton Castle can't see and I really knew that the cliffs down which I ran so funny so funny so funny so funny so funny—

Then did the children of Yaldabaoth take the sign of the Lord to their hearts, and Lo, thenceforward did they increase and multiply, forever chanting the praise of their Lord and His Consort on high.

Thus ends the Book of Maart.

VI

Exactly at the moment when he entered the veil, Peel paused in astonishment. He had not yet made up his mind. To him, a man of utter objectivity and absolute logic, this was an amazing thing. It was the first time in all his life that he had not made a decision with trigger speed. It was the final proof of how violently the Thing in the shelter had socked him.

He stood where he was and took stock. He was sheathed in a mist of fire that flamed like an opal and was far thicker than any veil should be. It was not beautiful to Peel, but it was interesting. The color dispersion was wide and embraced hundreds of fine gradations of the visible spectrum. He could identify more than a score by name.

With the little data he had at hand he judged that he was standing somewhere either outside time and space or between dimensions. Evidently the Thing in the shelter had placed all of them en rapport with the matrix of existence so that the mere intent as they entered the veil could govern the direction they would take on emergence. In other words—would direct the time and space into which they would step. The veil was more or less a pivot that could spin them into any desired existence.

Which brought Peel to the matter of his own choice. Carefully he considered, weighed and balanced accounts. So far he was satisfied with the life he led. He had plenty of money, a remunerative profession as consultant engineer, a lovely house, an attractive wife. To give all this up in reliance on the vague promises of an invisible donor would be sheer idiocy. Peel had learned never to make a change without good and sufficient reason. There was neither good nor sufficient reason now.

"I am not," Peel thought coldly, "adventurous by nature. It is not my business to be so. Romance does not attract me, nor does the unknown. I know that I like to keep what I have. Perhaps I am overly fond of keeping. The acquisitive instinct is strong in me and I am not ashamed to be a possessive man. Acquisitiveness has brought me wealth and success. Now I want to keep what I have. There can be no other decision for me. Let the others have their romance—I keep my world precisely as it is."

He strode forward firmly, a punctilious, bald, bearded martinet, and emerged into the dungeon corridor of Sutton Castle.

A few feet before him, a little scullery maid in blue and gray was scurrying directly toward him, a tray in her hands. There was a bottle of beer and an enormous sandwich on the tray. At the sound of his step she looked up, stopped short, her eyes widening, then dropped the tray with a crash.

"What the devil—" Peel began, confounded at the sight of her.

"M-Mr. P-Peel!" she squawked. She began to scream: "Help! Murder! Help!"

Peel slapped her sharply. "Will you shut up and tell me what in blazes you're doing down here this time of night—carrying on like this?"

The girl squawked and sputtered. Exactly, Peel noted, like a decapitated hen.

Before he could slap her again he felt the hand on his shoulder. He turned sharply and received another shock to find himself staring into the red, beefy face of a policeman. The man was in uniform and there was a rather eager expression on his heavy face. Peel gaped, then subsided. He realized quite suddenly that he was in the vortex of phenomena. No sense struggling until he understood the tides.

"Na then, sir," the policeman said. "No call ter strike the gel, sir."

Peel made no answer. The sharp needles of his mind plucked at the facts. A maid and a policeman. What were they doing down here?

"If I recollect a'right, sir, I heard the gel call yer by name. Would yer give it again, sir?"

"I'm Robert Peel, you blasted idiot. I'm a guest of Lady Sutton's. What is all this?"

"Mr. Peel!" the policeman cried. "What a piece er luck. I got to take yer into custody, Mr. Peel. Yer under arrest."

"Arrest? You're out of your mind, my man!" Peel stepped back and glanced over the policeman's shoulder. The veil was gone and in its place the door to the shelter yawned wide. The entire place was turned upside down. It looked as though it had just been subjected to a spring cleaning. There was no one inside.

"I must warn yer not ta resist, Mr. Peel."

The girl emitted a wail that verged on another scream.

"See here," Peel snapped irritably, "who the deuce are you? What right do you have to break into a private home and prance around making arrests?"

The policeman waved his hand indignantly. "Name of Jenkins, sir. Sutton Township Force. And I ain't prancin', sir."

"Then you're serious?"

The policeman pointed a majestic finger up the corridor. "Come along, sir."

"Answer me, you blithering idiot! Are you serious?"

"*You* oughter, know, sir," replied the policeman with considerable dignity. "Now come along."

Peel gave it up helplessly and went. He had learned long ago that when one is faced with an incomprehensible situation it is folly to take any action until sufficient data comes to hand. He preceded the policeman up the winding stairs and heard the whimpering scullery maid come after them. So far he still only knew two things. One: Something, somewhere, had happened. Two: The police had taken over. All this was upsetting to say the least, but he would keep his head. He prided himself that no situation ever took him at a loss.

When they emerged from the cellars, Peel received his second surprise. It was broad daylight outside—bright daylight. He glanced at his watch. It read exactly twelve forty. He dropped his wrist and blinked. The unexpected sunlight made him a little ill. The policeman touched his arm and directed him toward the library. Peel immediately marched to the high, sliding doors and pulled them open.

The library was high, long and narrow, with a small balcony running around it just under the ceiling. There was a long trestle table filling the length of the room, and at the far end three figures were seated, silhouetted against the light that streamed through the narrow window. Peel stepped in, vaguely conscious of a second policeman on guard beside the door. His eyes narrowed as he tried to distinguish faces.

While he peered, he listened carefully to the tremendous hubbub of surprise and exclamations that greeted him. He judged that: One: People had been looking for him. Two: He had been missing for some time. Three: No one had ever expected to find him here in Sutton Castle. Four: How did he get back in, anyway? All this from the astonished voices. Then his eyes accommodated to the light.

One of the three was a lanky, angular man with a narrow, graying head and deep-furrowed features. He looked familiar to Peel. The second was short and stout with ridiculously fragile glasses perched on a bulbous nose. The third was a woman, and again Peel was shocked to see that it was his wife. She wore a plaid suit and held a crumpled green felt hat in her lap.

Before he could analyze the data further, the angular man quieted the others and then turned. He said: "Mr. Peel?"

Peel advanced quietly and said: "Yes?"

"I'm Inspector Hoss."

"I thought I recognized you, inspector. We've met before, I believe?"

"We have." Hoss nodded curtly, then indicated the fat man. "This is Dr. Richards."

"How d'you do, doctor—" Peel turned toward Sidra and bowed with a faint air of irony. "Sidra?"

In flat tones she said: "Hello, Robert."

"I'm afraid I'm a little confused by all this," Peel went on amiably. "Things seem to be happening—" This, he knew, was the right talk. Be cautious. Commit yourself to nothing.

"They are," Hoss said grimly.

"Before we go any further, might I inquire the time?"

Hoss was a little taken aback. He said: "It's two o'clock."

"Thank you." Peel held his watch to his ear, then adjusted the hands. "My watch seems to be running, but somewhere it's lost a little time—" While he apparently devoted himself to his wrist watch he examined their expressions minutely. He would have to navigate with exquisite care purely by the light of their countenances until he learned much more.

Then, quite abruptly, Peel forgot his watch and stared at the desk calendar before Hoss. This was like a punch in the ribs. He swallowed and said: "Is that date quite right, inspector?"

Hoss glanced at the calendar, then back at Peel, his eyes widening. "It is, Mr. Peel. Sunday the twenty-third."

His mind screamed: Three days! Impossible.

Easy—Easy—Peel stiffened and controlled himself. Very well. Somewhere he had lost three days—for he had entered the veil Thursday just past midnight. He felt himself beginning to perspire and reached out blindly for a chair. "You'll have to excuse me," he said faintly, and sat down.

Keep cool, you confounded idiot. There's more at stake than three lost days. He lectured to himself in swift silence to give his nerves time to calm. You know you're a match for anyone. People don't know how to think. A man with a logical mind can cope with anything. Wait for more data.

After a moment of silence, Hoss said: "The fact is, Mr. Peel, we've been looking for you these past three days. You disappeared quite suddenly and we thought we knew why. We're rather surprised to find you in the castle. Rather surprised, indeed—"

"Ah? Why?" Careful now. Be careful!

"I should have thought you'd stay as far away from Sutton Castle as possible."

"Again why?" What's happened? Why the police—the suspicion—the guarded tone? What's Sidra doing here sitting like an avenging fury?

"Because, Mr. Peel, you're charged with the willful and intended murder of Lady Sutton."

Shock! Shock! Shock! They piled on one after the other, and still Peel kept hold of himself. The data was coming in a little too explicitly now. He had hesitated in the veil for a few seconds, and those seconds amounted to three days. Lady Sutton was found dead—evidently. He was charged with murder. Still he needed more facts before he spoke. Now, more than ever, he had to steer carefully.

Peel said: "I don't understand. You had better explain."

"Early Friday morning," Hoss began without preamble, "the death of Lady Sutton was reported. Immediate medical examination proved she died of shock. Witnesses' evidence revealed that you had deliberately frightened her with full knowledge of her weak heart and with the express intent so to kill her. That is murder, Mr. Peel."

'It certainly is," Peel answered coldly, "if you can prove it. May I ask whom your witnesses are?"

"Digby Finchley. Christian Braugh. Theone Dubedat, and—" Hoss broke off, coughed and laid the paper aside.

"And Sidra Peel," Peel finished dryly. Again he met his wife's eye and read the venomous expression clearly. "How very choice!"

But the light broke and he understood at last. They had lost their nerve, those quaking swine, and selected him for the scapegoat. Perhaps because of the golden opportunity of his disappearance. Perhaps—and this was more likely—under the malicious aegis of his wife. This would be Sidra's move to get rid of him, humiliate him, drag him through the courts and up to the executioner's dock. This would be Sidra's perfect revenge.

He got to his feet and before Hoss or Richards could interfere, he grasped Sidra by the arm and dragged her to a corner of the library. Over his shoulder he said: "Don't be alarmed, inspector, I only want a word with my wife."

Hoss coughed and called: "It's all right, officer—" and the menacing blue shadow retreated from Peel's elbow and returned to its post at the door.

Sidra tore her arm free and glared up at Peel, her face suffused with passion; her lips drawn back slightly, showing the sharp white edges of her teeth.

Peel snapped: "You arranged this."

"I don't know what you're talking about."

"Don't stall, Sidra. This was your idea."

"It was your murder," she countered.

"Ah?"

"It was. We saw you do it. We tried to stop you, but we couldn't. We've sworn to it—the four of us."

"And it was all your idea?"

Her eyes flashed: "Yes!"

"Hoss will be interested to hear that."

"He won't."

"What if I tell him—"

"He won't believe you. We're four to one."

"I can pick holes in your story."

"Try!"

"You're well prepared, eh?"

"Braugh is a good writer," she said. "You won't find any flaws in our story."

"So you're getting rid of me, eh? I hang for the murder on your trumped-up evidence. You get the house, my fortune and, best of all, you get rid of me."

She smiled like a cat. "You catch on fast, Robert."

"And this is the reality you asked for? This is what you planned when you went through the veil?"

"What veil?"

"You know what I mean."

"You're mad." She was confused.

"You're lying."

She smashed her knuckles into his face.

"Never mind," Peel said quite loudly, a plan taking shape in his mind, "never mind, Sidra. But if you think you're going to turn me into a scapegoat you're quite mistaken. Yes—quite mistaken."

"Here," Hoss called sharply, "What's all this?"

"He wanted me to bribe the witnesses," Sidra said in a clear voice, walking back to her seat. "I was to offer them ten thousand pounds each."

The doctor grunted: "Cad!"

Hoss said: "Now see here, Peel, we've been—"

"Please, inspector," Peel interrupted. He sauntered up to the desk, his mind clicking rapidly. The best defense was a startling offensive. The best time to begin was now. "My wife has just told you a fantastic lie."

"Ha?"

"More than that, inspector, your other witnesses have lied, too. I wish to charge Braugh, Finchley, Miss Dubedat and my wife with the willful murder of Lady Sutton!"

Hoss gasped and started forward, slapping the papers off the table. As the doctor bent to pick them up, Hoss stuttered: "My-my d-dear Peel! Really . . . you know!"

"Don't believe him!" Sidra screamed. "He's lying. He's trying to lie out of it!"

He let her scream, grateful for more time to whip his story into shape. It must be convincing—flawless. The truth was impossible. And who would believe the truth, anyway? What was truth for him was plainly unknown to the others.

"The murder of Lady Sutton," Peel went on smoothly, "was planned and executed by those four persons. I was the only member of the party to demur. You will grant me, inspector, that it sounds far more logical for four persons to commit a murder against the will of one, than one against four. Four could stop one. One could not possibly stand in the way of four."

Hoss nodded, fascinated by Peel's cold logic.

"Moreover, it is far easier for four persons to trump up a false account and swear to it, than for one to outweigh the evidence of four."

Again Hoss nodded.

Sidra beat at Hoss' shoulder and cried shrilly: "He's lying, inspector. If he's telling the truth ask him why he ran away! Ask him where he's been these last three days! Ask him—"

"Unfortunately there's little love lost between my wife and myself," Peel commented dryly. "Her evidence is entirely wishful thinking."

Hoss freed himself and said: "Please . . . Mrs. Peel. I beg you—"

With a graceful gesture, Peel ran sensitive fingers across his crisp beard and mustache. "My story is this, " he continued, "the four whom I accuse desired to murder Lady Sutton. Motive? A craving for the ultimate in emotional sensation. They were utterly depraved and degenerate. The only reason I was part of their devilish clique was to protect my wife as much as possible. On Thursday night I learned of their plans for the first time. I refused to permit them to continue and threatened to reveal all to Lady Sutton. Evidently they were prepared for this. My wine was drugged and I was rendered unconscious. I have a faint recollection of being lifted and carried somewhere by the two men and—that's all I know of the murder."

"My word!" Hoss gasped. The doctor leaned over to him and whispered. Hoss nodded and murmured: "Yes, yes—the tests can come later." He turned to Peel and said: "Please, go on."

So far, Peel thought, so good. Add a little truth to a lie and it makes the whole seem truthful. Now for the rest, he would have to add just enough color to gloss over the rough edges.

"I came to in pitch darkness. I was lying on a stone floor. I heard no sounds, nothing but the ticking of my watch. These dungeon walls are fifteen and twenty feet thick in places so I could not possibly hear anything. When I got to my feet I found I was in a small cavity about ten feet square.

"I realized that I was in some secret cell that was as yet unknown to any but the members of the clique. After an hour's shouting vainly for help and pounding on the wall, an accidental blow of my fist must have touched the proper spring or lever. One section, vastly thick, swung open quite abruptly and I found myself in the passage were I was picked up—''

''He's lying!'' Sidra screamed again.

While Hoss calmed her, Peel coolly considered his position. His story was excellent so far. The evidence at hand was sufficiently strong. Sutton Castle was known for its secret passages. His clothes were still rumpled from the framework he had worn to frighten Lady Sutton. There was no known saliva or blood test to show that he had been drugged seventy-two hours previous. His beard and mustache would eliminate the shaving line of attack. So far his logic was excellent.

''That,'' Peel said quietly, ''is my story.''

''We note that you plead not guilty, Mr. Peel,'' Hoss said, ''and we note your story and accusation. I confess that your three-day disappearance seemed to incriminate you, but now—'' He shrugged. ''All we need do is locate this mysterious cell in which you were confined.''

Peel was even prepared for this. He said: ''You may, and then again you may not. I'm an engineer, you know. I warn you that the only way we may be able to locate the cell is by blasting through the stone, which may only serve to wipe out all traces.''

''We'll take that chance.''

''That chance may not have to be taken,'' the little round doctor said.

Hoss turned slowly and gave the doctor a curious glance. Sidra exclaimed. Peel shot a sharp look toward the man. Experience warned him that fat men were always dangerous.

''It was a perfect story, Mr. Peel,'' the fat doctor said pleasantly, ''quite a perfect story. Most entertaining. But really, my dear sir, for an engineer you slipped up quite badly.''

''I beg your pardon?'' Peel said stiffly, every nerve on guard.

''When you awoke in your cell,'' the doctor went on with a childish smile, ''you mentioned that you were in complete darkness and silence. The walls were so thick all you heard was the ticking of your watch. Very colorful. But, alas, proof of a lie. You awoke seventy hours later—*No watch will run seventy hours without rewinding!*''

He was right. Peel realized that at once. He had made a mistake, and there was no going back for alterations. The entire story depended on the wholeness of the fabric. Tear away one threat and the whole thing would ravel. The fat doctor was right—and he was trapped.

One glance at Sidra's malevolent, triumphant face was enough for him. He decided that now was the time for action, and very quick action indeed. He arose from his chair, laughing in obvious defeat. Hoss was gaping again; the doctor chuckling like a pleased puzzle-solver; Sidra gloating. Peel sprinted to the window like a shot, crossed arms before his face, and smashed through the glass pane.

The shattering of the glass and the excited shouts behind him were only vague sounds. Peel limbered his legs as the soft earth came up at him and landed with a jarring shock. It was a fifteen-foot drop, but he took it well. He was on his feet in a trice and running toward the rear of the castle where the cars were parked. Five seconds later he was vaulting into Sidra's roadster. Ten seconds later he was speeding past the high iron gates to the highway outside.

Even in this crisis, Peel thought swiftly and with precision. He had driven out of the grounds too quickly for anyone to note which direction he would take. He turned toward London and sent the car roaring down the road until he came to an abrupt curve. Here he stopped and snatched a hammer from the tool kit.

He smashed every window in the car and the windshield, too. The broken glass he spread evenly across the road. It might not cause a puncture, and then again it might. The loss of time was worth the gamble. He leaped back into the car and started off again toward London. A man could lose himself in a metropolis.

But he was not a man to flee blindly, nor was there panic in his heart. Even as his eyes mechanically followed the road, his mind was sorting through facts, accurately and methodically, and inevitably drawing closer to a stern conclusion. He knew that he could never prove his innocence. The three-day hiatus was the bar to that. He knew he would be pursued as Lady Sutton's murderer.

In war time it would be impossible to get out of the country. It would even be impossible to hide very long. What remained then was an outlaw living in miserable hiding for a few brief months only to be taken and brought to trial. Peel had no intention of giving his wife the satisfaction of watching him dragged through a murder trial.

Still cool, still in full possession of himself, Peel planned as he drove. The audacious thing would be to go straight to his home. They would never think of looking for him there—for a while. At home he would have time enough to do what had to be done. He set his mouth in a thin, straight line.

Rapidly he drove deep into London toward Chelsea Square, a frigid, bearded, bald man at the wheel of the car looking like some icy buccaneer from the past.

He approached the square from the rear, watching for the police. There were none about and the house looked quite calm and inauspicious. But, as he drove into the square and saw the front façade of his home, he was grimly amused to see that an entire wing had been demolished in a bombardment. Evidently the catastrophe had taken place some days previous, for all the rubble was neatly piled and the broken side of the building was fenced off.

So much the better, Peel decided. No doubt the house would be empty. He parked the car, unnoticed by the few people in the street, leaped out and walked briskly to the front door. Now that he had made his decision and formed his plans he was absolutely impassive.

There was no one inside. Peel went to the library, took pen and ink and seated himself at the desk. Carefully, with lawyerlike acumen, he made out a new will cutting his wife off beyond legal impeachment. While the ink was drying, he went to the front door and waited until a couple of laborers trudged by with shovels on their shoulders.

"You there!" Peel called.

They turned weary faces toward him. "Yes, sir?"

"Want to earn a fiver?"

Their faces glowed.

"Step in a moment."

With many apologies for their muddied boots, they edged into the library, glancing around curiously. Peel sat them down and read the will to them. They listened with open mouths, then witnessed his signature. Laboriously, with much protrusion of tongues, they signed their names and received the bank note. Peel ushered them out and locked the door.

He paused grimly and took a breath. So much for Sidra. It was the old possessive instinct, he knew, that forced him to act this way. He wanted to keep his fortune, even after death. He wanted to keep his honor and dignity, even after death. He had made sure of the first. He would have to perform the second—quickly!

He thought for another moment, then nodded his head decisively and marched back to the kitchen. From the linen closet he took down an armful of sheets and towels and with them padded the windows and edges of the doors. As an afterthought, he took a large square of cardboard and on it, with shoe-blacking, printed: DANGER! GAS! He placed it outside the kitchen door.

When the room was sealed tight, Peel went to the stove, opened the oven door and turned the gas cock over. The gas hissed out of the jets, rank and yet cooling. Peel knelt and thrust his head into the oven, breathing with deep, even breaths. It would not, he knew, take very long. It would not be painful.

For the first time in hours, some of the tension left him, and he relaxed almost gratefully, calmly awaiting his death. Although he had lived a hard, geometrically patterned life; and traveled a rigidly realistic road—now his mind reached back toward more tender moments. He regretted nothing; he apologized for nothing; he was ashamed of nothing—and yet he thought of the days when he first met Sidra with a sense of sorrow.

> What slender youth, bedewed with liquid odors,
> Courts thee on roses in some pleasant cave,
> Sidra—

He almost smiled. Those were the lines he wrote to her when, in the romantic beginning, he worshiped her as a goddess of youth, of beauty and goodness. Those had been great days—the days when he had finished at Manchester College and had come to London to build a reputation, a fortune, a life. A thin-haired boy with precise habits and precise thoughts. Dreamily he sauntered through the backwash of memory as though he were recalling an entertaining play.

He came to with a start and realized that he had been kneeling before the oven for twenty minutes. There was something very much awry. He had not forgotten his chemistry and he knew that twenty minutes of illuminating gas should have been sufficient to make him lose consciousness. Perplexed, he got to his feet, rubbing his stiff knees. There was no time for analysis now. The pursuit would be on his neck at any moment.

Neck! That was an idea. Almost as painless as gas. Much quicker!

Peel shut off the oven, took a length of laundry rope from a cupboard and left the kitchen, picking up the sign en route. As he tore up the cardboard, his alert little eyes pried through the house, looking for the proper spot. Yes, there. In the stairwell. He could throw the rope over that beam and stand on the balcony above the stairs. When he leaped, he would have a ten-foot drop to the landing.

He ran up the stairs to the balcony, straddled the railing and carefully threw the rope over the beam. He caught the flying end as it whipped around the beam and swung toward him. He tied it into a loose knot and ran it up the length of the rope until it snuggled tight. After he had yanked twice to tighten the knot, he put his full weight on the rope and swung himself clear of the balcony. The rope supported his weight admirably. There was no chance of its snapping.

When he had climbed back to the railing, he shaped a hangman's noose and slipped it over his head, tightening the knot under his right ear. There was enough slack to give him a six-foot drop. He weighed one hundred fifty pounds. It was just about right to snap his neck clean and painlessly at the end of the drop. Peel poised, took a deep breath, and leaped—

His only thought as he fell was a chaotic attempt to figure how much time he had left to live. Thirty-two feet per second square divided by six gave him almost a fifth of a second. Then there was a blinding jerk that racked his entire body, a dull *crack* that sounded large and blunt in his ears, and a sensation of intolerable pain in his neck.

And for the first time, Peel's iron control was broken.

It took him fully five seconds to realize that he was still alive. He hung by his neck in a kind of horror and slowly understood that he was not dead. The horror crawled over his skin like a wave of chill ants, and for a long time he hung and shuddered, refusing to believe that the impossible had happened. He shuddered while his arms flailed helplessly and the chill reached his mind numbing it with terrible trepidation.

At last he reached into his pocket and withdrew a penknife. He opened it with difficulty, for his body was slowly turning palsied and unmanageable. After much sawing he at last severed the rope and dropped the last few feet to the landing. While he still crouched, he reached up fingers and felt his neck. It was broken. His head was tilted at an angle that made everything seem topsy-turvy. He could feel the jagged edges of the broken cervical vertibrae. He shuddered again.

As Peel dragged himself up the stairs, he realized that something too ghastly to understand was taking place. There was no attempting a cool appraisal of this; there was no data to be taken, no logic to apply. He reached the top of the stairs and lurched through the bedroom to the bath. In the mirror he examined his twisted neck.

With fumbling hands he groped in the medicine cabinet until he grasped his razor. He closed the cabinet door, then opened the blade, faintly admiring the six inches of gleaming steel. There was promise in the hair-fine, hollow-ground edge. He gripped the handle firmly, tilted his chin back as far as the twisted neck would allow, and with a firm, steady stroke sliced the steel across his throat.

Instantly he was deluged with a great gout of blood, and, as he drew breath, his windpipe was choked. He doubled over, coughing, and his throat was lathered with red foam. Still coughing and gasping, with the wind whistling madly through the ragged slit in his neck, Peel slowly crumpled to the tile floor and lay there while the blood gushed with every heartbeat and soaked him through. Yet as he lay there, gasping with little hacking, foaming coughs, he did not lose consciousness.

For the first time in all his life, Peel was afraid—desperately afraid. The agony of his twisted neck was nothing to the agony in his mind. He floundered on the bathroom floor and realized vaguely that life was clinging to him with all the possessiveness with which he had clung to life and the things he owned.

He crawled upright at last, not daring to look at his wax-white, bloodless face in the mirror, nor at the yawning red slash in his throat. The blood—what remained of it—had clotted slightly. He still could breathe normally at times. Gasping and almost completely paralyzed, Peel stumbled back into the bedroom and searched through Sidra's dresser until he found her revolver.

It took all his presence of mind to steady the muzzle at his chest and still his shaking hands. Deliberately, he pumped three shots into his heart. And when the echo of the reports died away and the sharp powder tang lifted, he was still alive, with a great ghastly hole torn in him.

It's the body, he thought crazily. Life clings to the body. So long as there's a body—the merest shell to contain a spark—then life will remain. It possesses me, this life, but there's yet a solution. I'm still enough of an engineer to work out a solution.

That solution, he knew, would have to be absolute disintegration. Let him shatter this body of his to particles—to bits—to a thousand pieces—and there would no longer be the cup of flesh to contain that persistent life. For that he needed explosives, and there was nothing in the house. Nor could he drag himself to his laboratory.

He lurched into his study and removed a deck of washable plastic playing cards from his drawer. For long minutes he cut them to pieces with his desk scissors, until he had a bowlful of minute pieces. He carried them to the bathroom and with the little strength that was left in his shattered body he removed a section of brass pipe from the tap inlet and carried it to his study.

There was a small spirit lamp on his desk, used to keep pots of coffee hot. Peel lit the lamp, placed a dry pot over it on the gimbals and dropped a lead paper weight in. After hours, it seemed, the lead melted. He used half the molten metal to plug one end of the pipe tight.

It took all his remaining energy to return to the bathroom for the forgotten bits of playing cards, but he knew it would be the last trip he would have to make. He rammed the frayed shreds of nitrocellulose into the brass pipe, using a heavy pencil as a ramrod. When the pipe was packed solid, he put in the heads of three matches and sealed the open end with the remaining lead and then placed the end of the pipe directly in the spirit flame.

With a sigh, he drew his desk chair close and hunched before the heating bomb. Nitrocellulose—a powerful-enough explosive when ignited under pressure. It was

only a question of time, he knew, before the pipe would burst into violent explosion and scatter him around the room—scatter him in blessed death.

The agony in his chest and neck made him rock gently and sway from side to
side. He began to whimper like a child as each individual nerve took up the
screaming chorus of pain. The red froth at his throat burst forth anew, while the
blood on his clothes caked and hardened.

Slowly the bomb heated.

Slowly the minutes passed.

Slowly the agony increased.

Peel rocked and whimpered, and when he reached out a palsied hand to push
the bomb a little closer into the flame, his fingers could not feel the heat. He
could see the red-caked flesh scorch and blister but he felt nothing. All the pain
writhed inside him—none outside.

It made noises in his ears, that pain, but even above the blunt sounds he heard
the dull tread of footsteps far out in the house. They were coming toward him,
slowly and almost with the inexorable tread of fate. Panic struck him at the thought
of the police and Sidra's triumph. He tried to coax the spirit flame higher.

The steps passed through the downstairs hall and then began to mount the steps
of the stairway. Each steady thud sounded louder and more terrifying. Peel hunched
lower and in the dim recesses of his mind began to pray. The steps reached the
top of the stairs, turned and advanced on his study. There was a faint whisper as
the study door was thrust open. Running hot and cold with pain and fear, Peel
refused to turn.

So abruptly that it jarred him, a voice said: "Now then, Bob, what's all this?"

He neither turned nor answered.

"Bob!" the voice called hoarsely, "don't be a fool!"

Vaguely he understood that he had heard that voice somewhere.

Steps sounded again, then a figure stood at his elbow. With bloodless eyes he
flicked a frightened glance up. It was Lady Sutton. She still wore the sequined
evening gown.

"My hat!" she gasped, her tiny eyes goggling in their casement of flesh, "you've
gone and messed yourself up, haven't you!"

"Go away—" His words were cracked and whistling as half his breath hissed
through the slit in his throat. "I will not be haunted."

"Haunted?" Lady Sutton laughed shrilly. "That's a good one, that is."

"'Go away," Peel muttered. "You're dead."

"What've you got there?" Lady Sutton inquired in brassy tone. She hesitated for a moment. "Oh, I see; a bomb. Going to blow yourself to bits, eh,
Bob?"

His lips formed soundless words. Still he hunched over the heating bomb.

"Here," Lady Sutton said. "Let me—" She reached forward to knock the
brass tube off the gimbals. With a convulsive effort Peel struggled to his feet and
grasped her arm with clawing hands. She was solid for a ghost. Nevertheless he
flung her back.

"Let be!" he wheezed.

"Now stop this, Bob!" Lady Sutton ordered. "I never intended this much misery for you."

Without bothering to puzzle at her words, he struck at her feebly as she tried to get past him to the bomb. She was far too strong for him. He turned quickly and flung himself forward toward the spirit lamp, arms outstretched to infold it and protect it from interference.

Lady Sutton cried: "Bob! You damned fool!"

There was a blinding explosion. It smashed into Peel's face with a flaring white light and a burst of shattering sound. The entire study rocked and a portion of the wall fell away. A heavy shower of books rained down from the jolted shelves. Smoke and dust filled space with a dense cloud.

As the cloud cleared, Lady Sutton still stood alongside the place where the desk had been. For the first time in many years—in many eternities, perhaps, her face wore an expression of sadness. For a long time she stood in silence. At last she shrugged and began to speak.

"Don't you realize, Bob," she said in a low voice, "that you can't kill yourself? The dead only die once, my boy, and you're dead already. You've all been dead for days. How is it that none of you could realize that? Perhaps it was that ego that Braugh spoke of— Perhaps— But you were all dead before you reached the shelter that night. You should have known when you saw your bombed house. That was a heavy raid last Thursday—very heavy."

Slowly she raised her hands and began to unpeel the gown that covered her. In the dead, unnatural silence, the little sequins rustled and tinkled. They glittered as the gown dropped from her body to reveal—nothing. Mere empty space.

"I enjoyed that little murder," she said. "It was amusing—quite amusing to see the dead attempt to kill. That's why I let you go on with it. It was amusing—"

She removed her shoes and stockings. She was now nothing more than arms, shoulders and a gross head in space. Nothing more. The face was still heavy and still wore the slightly sorrowful expression.

"But it was ridiculous trying to murder me," she went on, "seeing who I was. It was even a little ridiculous producing that play. Because, Bob, Astaroth does happen to be a lady—so to speak—and I happen to be Astaroth."

With a sudden motion, the head and arms jerked into the air and then dropped to the floor alongside the heaped-up dress. They clattered dully like waxen figures, and yet the voice continued from the smoke-filled space. Where the dusty mist swirled, it revealed a figure of emptiness—a mere outline in space—a bubble— and yet a figure horrible to behold.

"Yes," the voice went on, softening slightly to a quiet tone, "I am Astaroth, Bob—Astaroth, as old as the ages—as old and bored as eternity itself." It took on a pleading note. "That's why I had to play my little joke on you back in the shelter. I had to turn the tables and have a bit of a laugh. Satan knows, you cry out for a bit of novelty and entertainment after an eternity of arranging hells for the damned! And Satan knows, there's no hell like the hell of boredom—"

The passionate, pleading voice broke off.

And a thousand scattered bloody fragments of Robert Peel heard and understood. A thousand particles, each containing a tortured spark of life, heard the voice of Astaroth and understood.

"Of life I know nothing," Astaroth cried out, "but death I do know—death and justice. I know that each living creature creates its own hell forevermore. What you are now, you have wrought with your own hands. Hear ye all, before I depart—if any of ye can deny this—if any one of you would argue this—if any one of you would cavil at the Justice of Astaroth—let him speak! Speak now!"

Through all the far reaches the voice echoed, and there was no answer.

A thousand pain-thorned particles of Robert Peel heard and made no answer.

Theone Dubedat heard and made no answer.

A questing doubt-crazed Christian Braugh heard and made no answer.

A rotting, self-devouring Digby Finchley heard and made no answer.

All the damned of all eternity in an infinity of self-made hells heard and understood and made no answer.

For the Justice of Astaroth is unanswerable.

THEODORE STURGEON

The Hag Séleen

It was while we were fishing one afternoon, Patty and I, that we first met our friend the River Spider. Patty was my daughter and Anjy's. Tacitly, that is. Figuratively she had originated in some hot corner of hell and had left there with such incredible violence that she had taken half of heaven with her along her trajectory and brought it with her.

I was sprawled in the canoe with the nape of my neck on the conveniently curved cedar stern piece of the canoe, with a book of short stories in my hands and my fish pole tucked under my armpit. The only muscular energy required to fish that way is in moving the eyes from the page to the float and back again, and I'd have been magnificently annoyed if I'd had a bite. Patty was far more honest about it; she was fast asleep in the bilges. The gentlest of currents kept my mooring line just less than taut between the canoe and a half-sunken snag in the middle of the bayou. Louisiana heat and swampland mosquitoes tried casually to annoy me, and casually I ignored them both.

There was a sudden thump on the canoe and I sat upright just as a slimy black something rose out of the muddy depths. It came swiftly until the bow of the canoe rested on it, and then more slowly. My end of the slender craft sank and a small cascade of blood-warm water rushed on, and down, my neck. Patty raised her head with a whimper; if she moved suddenly I knew the canoe would roll over and dump us into the bayou. "Don't move!" I gasped.

She turned puzzled young eyes on me, astonished to find herself looking downward. "Why, daddy?" she asked, and sat up. So the canoe did roll over and it did dump us into the bayou.

I came up strangling, hysterical revulsion numbing my feet and legs where they had plunged into the soft ooze at the bottom. "Patty!" I screamed hoarsely.

She popped up beside me, trod water while she knuckled her eyes. "I thought we wasn't allowed to swim in the bayou, daddy," she said.

I cast about me. Both banks presented gnarled roots buried in rich green swamp growth, and I knew that the mud there was deep and sticky and soft. I knew that that kind of mud clutches and smothers. I knew that wherever we could find a handhold we could also find cottonmouth moccasins. So I knew that we had to get into our canoe again, but fast!

Turning, I saw it, one end sunken, the other high in the air, one thwart fouled in the black tentacles of the thing that had risen under us. It was black and knotted and it dripped slime down on us, and for one freezing second I thought it was alive. It bobbed ever so slowly, sluggishly, in the disturbed water. It was like breathing. But it made no further passes at us. I told Patty to stay where she was and swam over to what I could reach of the canoe and tugged. The spur that held it came away rottenly and the canoe splashed down, gunwale first, and slowly righted itself half full of water. I heard a shriek of insane laughter from somewhere in the swamp but paid no attention. I could attend to that later.

We clung to the gunwales while I tried to think of a way out. Patty kept looking up and down the bayou as if she thought she hadn't enough eyes. "What are you looking for, Patty?"

"Alligators," she said.

Yeah, I mused, that's a thought. We've got to get out of here! I felt as if I were being watched and looked quickly over my shoulder. Before my eyes could focus on it, something ducked behind a bush on the bank. The bush waved its fronds at me in the still air. I looked back at Patty—

"Patty! Look out!"

The twisted black thing that had upset us was coming down, moving faster as it came, and as I shrieked my warning its tangled mass came down on the child. She yelped and went under, fighting the slippery fingers.

I lunged toward her. "Patty!" I screamed. "Pat—"

The bayou bubbled where she had been. I dived, wrenching at the filthy thing that had caught her. Later—it seemed like minutes later, but it couldn't have been more than five seconds—my frantic hand closed on her arm. I thrust the imprisoning filth back, hauled her free, and we broke surface. Patty, thank Heaven, remained perfectly still with her arms as far around me as they would go. Lord knows what might have happened if she had struggled.

We heard the roar of a bull alligator and that was about all we needed. We struck out for the bank, clawed at it. Fortunately Patty's hands fell on a root, and she scuttled up it like a little wet ape. I wasn't so lucky—it was fetid black mud that I floundered through. We lay gasping, at last on solid ground.

"Mother's gonna be mad," said Patty after a time.

"Mother's going to gnash her teeth and froth at the mouth," I said with a good deal more accuracy. We looked at each other and one of the child's eyes closed in an eloquent wink. "Oh, yeah," I said, "and how did we lose the canoe?"

Patty thought hard. "We were paddling along an' a big fella scared you with a gun and stoled our canoe."

"How you talk! I wouldn't be scared!"

"Oh, *yes* you would," she said with conviction.

I repressed an unpaternal impulse to throw her back into the bayou. "That won't do. Mother would be afraid to have a man with a gun stompin' around the bayou. Here it is. We saw some flowers and got out to pick them for mother. When we came back we found the canoe had drifted out into the bayou, and we knew she wouldn't want us to swim after it, so we walked home."

She entered into it with a will. "Silly of us, wasn't it?" she asked.

"Sure was," I said. "Now get those dungarees off so's I can wash the mud out of 'em."

A sun suit for Patty and bathing trunks for me were our household garb; when we went out for the afternoon we pulled on blue denim shirts and slacks over them to ward off the venomous mosquitoes. We stripped off the dungarees and I searched the bank and found a root broad enough for me to squat on while I rinsed off the worst of the filth we had picked up in our scramble up the bank. Patty made herself comfortable on a bed of dry Spanish moss that she tore out of the trees. As I worked, a movement in midstream caught my eye. A black tentacle poked up out of the water, and, steadily then, the slimy branches of the thing that had foundered us came sloshing into the mottled sunlight. It was a horrible sight, the horror of which was completely dispelled by the sight of the sleek green flank of the canoe which bobbed up beside it.

I ran back up my root, tossed the wet clothes on a convenient branch, broke a long stick off a dead tree and reached out over the water. I could just reach one end of the canoe. Slowly I maneuvered it away from its black captor and pulled it to me. I went into mud up to my knees in the process but managed to reach it; and then it was but the work of a moment to beach it, empty out the water and set it safely with its stern on the bank. Then I pegged out our clothes in a patch of hot sunlight and went back to Patty.

She was lying on her back with her hands on her eyes, shielding them from the light. Apparently she had not seen me rescue the canoe. I glanced at it and just then saw the slimy mass in mid-bayou start sinking again.

"Daddy," she said drowsily, "what was that awful thing that sinked us?"

"What they call a sawyer," I said. "It's the waterlogged butt of a cypress tree. The bottom is heavy and the top is light, and when the roots catch in something on the bottom the current pushes the top under. Then one of the branches rots and falls off, and the top end gets light again and floats up. Then the current will push it down again. It'll keep that up for weeks."

"Oh," she said. After a long, thoughtful pause she said, "Daddy—"

"What?"

"Cover me up." I grinned and tore down masses of moss with which I buried her. Her sleepy sigh sounded from under the pile. I lay down in the shade close by, switching lazily at mosquitoes.

I must have dozed for a while. I woke with a start, fumbling through my mind for the thing that had disturbed me. My first glance was at the pile of moss; all seemed well there. I turned my head. About eight inches from my face was a pair of feet.

I stared at them. They were bare and horny and incredibly scarred. Flat, too— splayed. The third toe of each foot was ever so much longer than any of the others. They were filthy. Attached to the feet was a scrawny pair of ankles; the rest was out of my range of vision. I debated sleepily whether or not I had seen enough, suddenly realized that there was something not quite right about this, and bounced to my feet.

I found myself staring into the blazing eye of the most disgusting old hag that ever surpassed imagination. She looked like a Cartier illustration. Her one good eye was jaundiced and mad; long, slanted—feline. It wasn't until long afterward that I realized that her pupil was not round but slitted—not vertically like a cat's eyes, but horizontally. Her other eye looked like—well, I'd rather not say. It couldn't possibly have been of any use to her. Her nose would have been hooked if the tip were still on it. She was snaggle-toothed, and her fangs were orange. One shoulder was higher than the other, and the jagged lump on it spoke of a permanent dislocation. She had enough skin to adequately cover a sideshow fat lady, but she couldn't have weighed more than eighty pounds or so. I never saw great swinging wattles on a person's upper arms before. She was clad in a feathered jigsaw of bird and small animal skins. She was diseased and filthy and—and evil.

And she spoke to me in the most beautiful contralto voice I have ever heard.

"How you get away from River Spider?" she demanded.

"River Spider?"

She pointed, and I saw the sawyer rising slowly from the bayou. "Oh—that." I found that if I avoided that baleful eye I got my speech back. I controlled an impulse to yell at her, chase her away. If Patty woke up and saw that face—

"What's it to you?" I asked quietly, just managing to keep my voice steady.

"I send River Spider for you," she said in her Cajun accent.

"Why?" If I could mollify her—she was manifestly furious at something, and it seemed to be me—perhaps she'd go her way without waking the child.

"Because you mus' go!" she said. "This my countree. This swamp belong Séleen. Séleen belong this swamp. Wan man make *p'tit cabane* in bayou, Séleen *l'enchante*. Man die far away, smash."

"You mean you haunted the man who had my cabin built and he died?" I grinned. "Don't be silly."

"Man is dead, no?"

I nodded. "That don't cut ice with me, old lady. Now look—we aren't hurting your old swamp. We'll get out of it, sure; but we'll go when we're good and ready. You leave us alone and we'll sure as hell"—I shuddered, looking at her—"leave you alone."

"You weel go *now—ce jour!*" She screamed the last words, and the pile of moss behind me rustled suddenly.

"I won't go today or tomorrow or next week," I snapped. I stepped toward her threateningly. "Now beat it!"

She crouched like an animal, her long crooked hands half raised. From behind me the moss moved briskly, and Patty's voice said, "Daddy, what . . . oh. *Ohh!*"

That does it, I said to myself, and lunged at the old woman with some crazy idea of shoving her out of the clearing. She leaped aside like a jackrabbit and I tripped and fell on my two fists, which dug into my solar plexus agonizingly. I lay there mooing "uh! uh! u-u-uh!" trying to get some wind into my lungs, and finally managed to get an elbow down and heave myself over on my side. I looked, and saw Séleen crouched beside Patty. The kid sat there, white as a corpse, rigid with terror, while the old nightmare crooned to her in her lovely voice.

"*Ah! C'est une jolie jeune fille, ça! Ah, ma petite, ma fleur douce, Séleen t'aime, trop, trop—*" and she put out her hand and stroked Patty's neck and shoulder.

When I saw the track of filth her hand left on the child's flesh, a white flame exploded in my head and dazzled me from inside. When I could see again I was standing beside Patty, the back of one hand aching and stinging; and Séleen was sprawled eight feet away, spitting out blood and yellow teeth and frightful curses.

"Go away." I whispered it because my throat was all choked up. "Get—out—of—here—before—I—kill you!"

She scrambled to her knees, her blazing eyes filled with hate and terror, shook her fist and tottered swearing away into the heavy swamp growth.

When she had gone I slumped to the ground, drenched with sweat, cold outside, hot inside, weak as a newborn babe from reaction. Patty crawled to me, dropped her head in my lap, pressed the back of my hand to her face and sobbed so violently that I was afraid she would hurt herself. I lifted my hand and stroked her hair. "It's all right, now. Patty—don't be a little dope, now—come on," I said more firmly, lifting her face by its pointed chin and holding it until she opened her eyes. "Who's Yehudi?"

She gulped bravely. "Wh-who?" she gasped.

"The little man who turns on the light in the refrigerator when you open the door," I said. "Let's go find out what's for dinner."

"I . . . I—" She puckered all up the way she used to do when she slept in a bassinet—what I used to call "baby's slow burn." And then she wailed the same way. "I don' want dinno-o-o!"

I thumped her on the back, picked her up and dropped her on top of her dungarees. "Put them pants on," I said, "and be a man." She did, but she cried quietly until I shook her and said gently, "Stop it now. I didn't carry on like that when I was a little girl." I got into my clothes and dumped her into the bow of the canoe and shoved off.

All the way back to the cabin I forced her to play one of our pet games. I would say something—anything—and she would try to say something that rhymed with it. Then it would be her turn. She had an extraordinary rhythmic sense, and an excellent ear.

I started off with "We'll go home and eat our dinners."

"An' Lord have mercy on us sinners," she cried. Then, "Let's see you find a rhyme for 'month'!"

"I bet I'll do it . . . jutht thith onth," I replied. "I guess I did it then, by cracky."

"Course you did, but then you're wacky. Top that, mister funny-lookin'!"

I pretended I couldn't, mainly because I couldn't, and she soundly kicked my shin as a penance. By the time we reached the cabin she was her usual self, and I found myself envying the resilience of youth. And she earned my undying respect by saying nothing to Anjy about the afternoon's events, even when Anjy looked us over and said, "Just look at you two filthy kids! What have you been doing—swimming in the bayou?"

"Daddy splashed me," said Patty promptly.

"And you had to splash him back. Why did he splash you?"

"'Cause I spit mud through my teeth at him to make him mad," said my outrageous child.

"Patty!"

"Mea culpa," I said, hanging my head. "'Twas I who spit the mud."

Anjy threw up her hands. "Heaven knows what sort of a woman Patty's going to grow up to be," she said, half angrily.

"A broad-minded and forgiving one like her lovely mother," I said quickly.

"Nice work, bud," said Patty.

Anjy laughed. "Outnumbered again. Come in and feed the face."

On my next trip into Minette I bought a sweet little S. & W. .38 and told Anjy it was for alligators. She was relieved.

I might have forgotten about the hag Séleen if it were not for the peculiar chain of incidents which had led to our being here. We had started with some vague idea of spending a couple of months in Natchez or New Orleans, but a gas station attendant had mentioned that there was a cabin in the swamps for rent very cheap down here. On investigation we found it not only unbelievably cheap, but deep in real taboo country. Not one of the natives, hardened swamp runners all, would go within a mile of it. It had been built on order for a very wealthy Northern gentleman who had never had a chance to use it, due to a swift argument he and his car had had one day when he turned out to pass a bridge. A drunken rice farmer told me that it was all the doing of the Witch of Minette, a semimythological local character who claimed possession of that corner of the country. I had my doubts, being a writer of voodoo stories and knowing therefore that witches and sech are nonsense.

After my encounter with Séleen I no longer doubted her authenticity as a horrid old nightmare responsible for the taboo. But she could rant, chant, and ha'nt from now till a week come Michaelmas—when *is* Michaelmas, anyway?—and never pry me loose from that cabin until I was ready to go. She'd have to fall back on enchantment to do it, too—of that I was quite, quite sure. I remembered her blazing eye as it had looked when I struck her, and I knew that she would never dare to come within my reach again. If she as much as came within my sight with her magics I had a little hocus-pocus of my own that I was sure was more powerful than anything she could dream up. I carried it strapped to my waist, in a holster, and while it couldn't call up any ghosts, it was pretty good at manufacturing 'em.

As for Patty, she bounced resiliently away from the episode. Séleen she dubbed the Witch of Endor, and used her in her long and involved games as an archvillain in place of Frankenstein's monster, Adolf Hitler, or Miss McCauley, her schoolteacher. Many an afternoon I watched her from the hammock on the porch, cooking up dark plots in the witch's behalf and then foiling them in her own coldbloodedly childish way. Once or twice I had to put a stop to it, like the time I caught her hanging the Witch of Endor in effigy, the effigy being a rag doll, its poor throat cut with benefit of much red paint. Aside from these games she never mentioned Séleen, and I respected her for it. I saw to it that she didn't stray alone into the swamp and relaxed placidly into my role of watchful skeptic. It's nice to feel oneself superior to a credulous child.

Foolish, too. I didn't suspect a thing when Patty crept up behind me and hacked off a lock of my hair with my hunting knife. She startled me and I tumbled out of the hammock onto my ear as she scuttled off. I muttered imprecations at the little demon as I got back into the hammock, and then comforted myself by the reflection that I was lucky to have an ear to fall on—that knife was sharp.

A few minutes later Anjy came out to the porch. Anjy got herself that name because she likes to wear dresses with masses of tiny pleats and things high on her throat, and great big picture hats. So *ingenue* just naturally became Anjy. She is a beautiful woman with infinite faith and infinite patience, the proof of which being that: a—she married me and, b—she stayed married to me.

"Jon, what sort of crazy game is your child playing?" She always said "your child" when she was referring to something about Patty she didn't like.

"S'matter?"

"Why, she just whipped out that hog-sticker of yours and made off with a hank of my hair."

"No! Son of a gun! What's she doing—taking up barbering? She just did the same thing to me. Thought she was trying to scalp me and miscalculated, but I must have been wrong—she wouldn't miss twice in a row."

"Well, I want you to take that knife away from her," said Anjy. "It's dangerous."

I got out of the hammock and stretched. "Got to catch her first. Which way'd she go?"

After a protracted hunt I found Patty engaged in some childish ritual of her own devising. She pushed something into a cleft at the foot of a tree, backed off a few feet, and spoke earnestly. Neither of us could hear a word she said. Then she backed still farther away and squatted down on her haunches, watching the hole at the foot of the tree carefully.

Anjy clasped her hands together nervously, opened her mouth. I put my hands over it. "Let me take care of it," I whispered, and went out.

"Whatcha doin', bud?" I called to Patty as I came up. She started violently and raised one finger to her lips. "Catchin' rabbits?" I asked as loudly as I could without shouting. She gestured me furiously away. I went and sat beside her.

"Please, daddy," she said, "I'm making a magic. It won't work if you stay here. Just this once—please!"

"Nuts," I said bluntly. "I chased all the magic away when I moved here."

She tried to be patient. "Will you *please* go away? Oh, daddy. Daddy, PLEASE!"

It was rough but I felt I had to do it. I lunged for her, swept her up, and carried her kicking and squalling back to the cabin. "Sorry, kiddo, but I don't like the sort of game you're playing. You ought to trust your dad."

I meant to leave her with Anjy while I went out to confiscate that bundle of hair. Not that I believe in such nonsense. But I'm the kind of unsuperstitious apple that won't walk under a ladder *just in case* there's something in the silly idea. But Patty really began to throw a whingding, and there was nothing for me to do but to stand by until it had run its course. Patty was a good-natured child, and only good-natured children can work themselves up into that kind of froth. She screamed and she bit, and she accused us of spoiling everything and we didn't love her and she wished she was dead and why couldn't we leave her alone—"Let me alone," she shrieked, diving under the double bed and far beyond our reach. "Take your *hands* off me!" she sobbed when she was ten feet away from us and moving fast. And then her screams became wordless and agonized when we cornered her in the kitchen. We had to be rough to hold her, and her hysteria was agony to us. It took more than an hour for her fury to run its course and leave her weeping weak apologies and protestations of love into her mother's arms. Me, I was bruised outside and in, but inside it hurt the worst. I felt like a heel.

I went out then to the tree. I reached in the cleft for the hair but it was gone. My hand closed on something far larger, and I drew it out and stood up to look at it.

It was a toy canoe, perhaps nine inches long. It was an exquisite piece of work. It had apparently been carved painstakingly from a solid piece of cedar, so carefully that nowhere was the wood any more than an eighth of an inch thick. It was symmetrical and beautifully finished in brilliant colors. They looked to me like vegetable stains—dyes from the swamp plants that grew so riotously all around us. From stem to stern the gunwales were pierced, and three strips of brilliant bark had been laced and woven into the close-set holes. Inside the canoe were four wooden spurs projecting from the hull, the end of each having a hole drilled through it, apparently for the purpose of lashing something inside.

I puzzled over it for some minutes, turning it over and over in my hands, feeling its velvet smoothness, amazed by its metrical delicacy. Then I laid it carefully on the ground and regarded the mysterious tree.

Leafless branches told me it was dead. I got down on my knees and rummaged deep into the hole between the roots. I couldn't begin to touch the inside wall. I got up again, circled the tree. A low branch projected, growing sharply upward close to the trunk before it turned and spread outward. And around it were tiny scuff marks in the bark. I pulled myself up onto the branch, cast about for a handhold to go higher. There was none. Puzzled, I looked down—and there, completely hidden from the ground, was a gaping hole leading into the hollow trunk!

I thrust my head into it and then clutched the limb with both arms to keep from tottering out of the tree. For that hole reeked with the most sickly, noisome smell I had encountered since . . . since Patty and I—

Séleen!

I dropped to the ground and backed away from the tree. The whole world seemed in tune with my revulsion. What little breeze there had been had stopped, and the swampland was an impossible painting in which only I moved.

Never taking my eyes off the tree, I went back step by step, feeling behind me until my hand touched the wall of the cabin. My gaze still riveted to the dead hole of the tree, I felt along the wall until I came to the kitchen door. Reaching inside, I found my ax and raced back. The blade was keen and heavy, and the haft of it felt good to me. The wood was rotten, honeycombed, and the clean blade bit almost noiselessly into it. *Thunk!* How dare she, I thought. What does she mean by coming so near us! *Thunk!* I prayed that the frightful old hag would try to fight, to flee, so that I could cut her down with many strokes. It was my first experience with the killer instinct and I found it good.

The sunlight faded out of the still air and left it hotter.

At the uppermost range of my vision I could see the trunk trembling with each stroke of the ax. Soon, now—soon! I grinned and my lips cracked; every other inch of my body was soaking wet. She who would fill Patty's clean young heart with her filthy doings! Four more strokes would do it; and then I remembered that skinny hand reaching out, touching Patty's flesh; and I went cold all over. I raised the ax and heard it hiss through the thick air; and my four strokes were one. Almost without resistance that mighty stroke swished into and through the shattered trunk. The hurtling ax head swung me around as the severed tree settled onto its stump. It fell, crushing its weight into the moist earth, levering itself over on its projecting root; and the thick bole slid toward me, turned from it as I was, off balance. It caught me on the thigh, kicking out at me like a sentient, vicious thing. I turned over and over in the air and landed squashily at the edge of the bayou. But I landed with my eyes on the tree, ready to crawl, if need be, after whatever left it.

Nothing left it. Nothing. There had been nothing there, then, but the stink of her foul body. I lay there weakly, weeping with pain and reaction. And when I looked up again I saw Séleen again—or perhaps it was a crazed vision. She stood on a knoll far up the bayou, and as I watched she doubled up with silent laughter. Then she straightened and lifted her arm; and, dangling from her fingers, I saw the tiny bundle of hair. She laughed again though I heard not a sound. I knew then that she had seen every bit of it—had stood there grinning at my frantic destruction of her accursed tree. I lunged toward her, but she was far away, and across the water; and at my movement she vanished into the swamp.

I dragged myself to my feet and limped toward the cabin. I had to pass the tree, and as I did the little canoe caught my eye. I tucked it under my arm and crept back to the cabin. I tripped on the top step of the porch and fell sprawling, and I hadn't strength to rise. My leg was an agony, and my head spun and spun.

Then I was inside and Anjy was sponging off my head, and she laughed half hysterically when I opened my eyes. "Jon, Jon, beloved, what have you done? Who did this to you?"

"Who . . . heh!" I said weakly. "A damn fool, sweetheart. Me!" I got up and stood rockily. "How's Pat?"

"Sleeping," said Anjy. "Jon, what on earth is happening?"

"I don't know," I said slowly, and looked out through the window at the fallen tree. "Anjy, the kid took that hair she swiped and probably some of her own and poked it all into that tree I just cut down. It—seems important for me to get it back. Dunno why. It . . . anyway, I got out there as soon as we had Pat quieted, but the hair had disappeared in the meantime. All I found was this." I handed her the canoe.

She took it absently. "Pat told me her story. Of course it's just silly, but she says that for the past three days that tree has been talking to her. She says it sang to her and played with her. She's convinced it's a magic tree. She says it promised her a lovely present if she would poke three kinds of hair into a hole at the roots, but if she told anyone the magic wouldn't work." Anjy looked down at the little canoe and her forehead puckered. "Apparently it worked," she whispered.

I couldn't comment without saying something about Séleen, and I didn't want that on Anjy's mind, so I turned my back on her and stood looking out into the thick wet heat of the swamp.

Behind me I heard Patty stir, shriek with delight as she saw the canoe. "My present . . . my pretty present! It was a *real* magic!" And Anjy gave it to her.

I pushed down an impulse to stop her. As long as Séleen had the hair the harm was done.

Funny, how suddenly I stopped being a skeptic.

The silence of the swamp was shattered by a great cloud of birds—birds of every imaginable hue and size, screaming and cawing and chuckling and whirring frantically. They startled me and I watched them for many minutes before it dawned on me that they were all flying one way. The air grew heavier after they had gone. Anjy came and stood beside me.

I have never seen such rain, never dreamed of it. It thundered on the shingles, buckshotted the leaves of the trees, lashed the mirrored bayou and the ground alike, so that the swamp was but one vast brown steam of puckered mud.

Anjy clutched my arm. "Jon, I'm frightened!" I looked at her and knew that it wasn't the rain that had whitened her lips, lit the fires of terror in her great eyes. "Something out there—*hates* us," she said simply.

I shook her off, threw a poncho over me. "Jon—you're not—"

"I got to," I gritted. I went to the door, hesitated, turned back and pressed the revolver into her hand. "I'll be all right," I said, and flung out into the storm. Anjy didn't try to stop me.

I knew I'd find the hag Séleen. I knew I'd find her unharmed by the storm, for was it not a thing of her own devising? And I knew I must reach her—quickly, before she used that bundle of hair. Why, and how did I know? Ask away, I'm still asking myself, and I have yet to find an answer.

I stumbled and floundered, keeping to the high ground, guided, I think, by my hate. After a screaming eternity I reached a freakish rocky knoll that thrust itself out of the swamp. It was cloven and cracked, full of passages and potholes; and from an opening high on one side I saw the guttering glare of firelight. I crept up the rough slope and peered within.

She crouched over the flames, holding something to her withered breast and crooning to it. The rock walls gathered her lovely, hateful voice and threw it to me clear and strong—to me and to the turgid bayou that seethed past the cleft's lower edge.

She froze as my eyes fell upon her, sensing my presence; but like many another animal she hadn't wit enough to look upward. In a moment she visibly shrugged off the idea, and she turned and slid and shambled down toward the bayou. Above her, concealed by the split rock, I followed her until we were both at the water's edge with only a four-foot stone rampart between us. I could have reached her easily then, but I didn't dare attack until I knew where she had hidden that bundle of hair.

The wind moaned, rose an octave. The rain came in knives instead of sheets. I flattened myself against the rock while Séleen shrank back into the shelter of the crevice. I will never know how long we were there, Séleen and I, separated by a few boulders, hate a tangible thing between us. I remember only a shrieking hell of wind and rubble, and then the impact of something wet and writhing and whimpering against me. It had come rolling and tumbling down the rocky slope and it lodged against me. I was filled with horror until I realized that it sheltered me a little against the blast. I found the strength to turn and look at it finally. It was Patty.

I got her a little under me and stuck it out till the wind had done its work and was gone, and with it all the deafening noise—all but the rush of the bayou and Séleen's low chuckle.

"Daddy—" She was cut and battered. "I brought my little boat!" She held it up weakly.

"Yes, butch. Sure. That's dandy. Patty—what happened to mother?"

"She's back there," whimpered Patty. "The cabin sagged, like, an' began m-movin', an' then it just fell apart an' the bits all flew away. I couldn' find her so I came after you."

I lay still, not breathing. I think even my heart stopped for a little while.

Patty's whisper sounded almost happy. "Daddy—I—hurt—all—over—"

Anjy was gone then, I took my hatred instead, embraced it and let it warm me and give me life and hope and strength the way she used to. I crawled up the rock and looked over. I could barely see the hag, but she was there. Something out in the bayou was following the rhythmic movement of her arms. Something evil, tentacled, black. Her twisted claws clutched a tiny canoe like the one she had left in the tree for Patty. And she sang:

> "River Spider, black and strong,
> Folks 'bout here have done me wrong.
> Here's a gif' I send to you,
> Got some work for you to do.

> "If Anjy-woman miss the flood,
> River Spider, drink her blood.

> Little one was good to me,
> Drown her quick and let her be.

> "River Spider, Jon you know,
> Kill that man, and—kill—him—slow!"

And Séleen bent and set the canoe on the foaming brown water. Our hair was tied inside it.

Everything happened fast then. I dived from my hiding place behind and above her, and as I did so I sensed that Patty had crept up beside me, and that she had seen and heard it all. And some strange sense warned Séleen, for she looked over her crooked shoulder, saw me in midair, and leaped into the bayou. I had the terrified, malevolent gleam of her single eye full in my face, but I struck only hard rock, and for me even that baleful glow went out.

Patty sat cross-legged with my poor old head in her lap. It was such a gray morning that the wounds on her face and head looked black to me. I wasn't comfortable, because the dear child was rolling my head back and forth frantically in an effort to rouse me. The bones in my neck creaked as she did it and I knew they could hear it in Scranton, Pennsylvania. I transmitted a cautionary syllable but what she received was a regular houn'-dawg howl.

"Owoo! Pat—"

"Daddy! Oh, you're awake!" She mercifully stopped gyrating the world about my tattered ears.

"What happened?" I moaned, half sitting up. She was so delighted to see my head move that she scrambled out from under so that when the ache inside it pounded it back down, it landed stunningly on the rock.

"Daddy darling, I'm sorry. But you got to stop layin' around like that. It's time to get up!"

"Uh. How you know?"

"I'm hungry, that's how, so there."

I managed to sit up this time. I began to remember things and they hurt so much that the physical pain didn't matter any more. "Patty! We've got to get back to the cabin!"

She puckered up. I tried to grin at her and she tried to grin back, and there is no more tragedy left in the world for me after having seen that. I did a sort of upward totter and got what was left of my feet and legs under me. Both of us were a mess, but we could navigate.

We threaded our way back over a new, wrecked landscape. It was mostly climbing and crawling and once when Patty slipped and I reached for her I knocked the little canoe out of her hand. She actually broke and ran to pick it up. "Daddy! You got to be careful of this!"

I groaned. It was the last thing in the world I ever wanted to see. But then— Anjy had said that she should have it. And when she next dropped it I picked it up and handed it back to her. And then snatched it again.

"Patty! What's this?" I pointed to the little craft's cargo: a tiny bundle of hair.

"That's the little bag from the tree, silly."

"But how . . . where . . . I thought—"

"I made a magic," she said with finality. "Now please, daddy, don't stand here and talk. We have to get back to . . . y-you know."

If you don't mind, I won't go into detail about how we dragged trees and rubbish away to find what was left of our cabin, and how we came upon the pathetic little heap of shingles and screening and furniture and how, wedged in the firm angle of two mortised two-by-fours, we found Anjy. What I felt when I lifted her limp body away from the rubble, when I kissed her pale lips—that is mine to remember. And what I felt when those lips returned my kiss—oh, so faintly and so tenderly—that, too, is mine.

We rested, the three of us, for five days. I found part of our store of canned goods and a fishing line, though I'm sorry now that we ate any of the fish, after what happened. And when the delirium was over, I got Patty's part of the story. I got it piecemeal, out of sequence, and only after the most profound cross-questioning. But the general drift was this:

She had indeed seen that strange performance in the rocky cleft by the bayou; but what is more, by her childish mysticism, she understood it. At least, her explanation is better than anything I could give. Patty was sure that the River Spider that had attacked us that time in the bayou was sent by Séleen, to whom she always referred as the Witch of Endor. "She did it before, daddy, I jus' betcha. But she didn't have anythin' strong enough for to put on the canoe." I have no idea what she did use—flies, perhaps, or frogs or cray-fish. "She hadda have some part of us to make the magic, an' she made me get it for her. She was goin' to put that li'l' ol' hair ball in a canoe, an' if a River Spider caught it then the Spider would get us, too."

When I made that crazed leap for the old woman she had nowhere to go but into the bayou. Pat watched neither of us. She watched the canoe. She always claimed that she hooked it to shore with a stick, but I have a hunch that the little idiot plunged in after it. "They was one o' those big black sawyer things right there," she said, "an' it almos' catched the canoe. I had a lot of trouble." I'll bet she did.

"You know," she said pensively, "I was mad at that ol' Witch of Endor. That was a mean thing she tried to do to us. So I did the same thing to her. I catched the ugliest thing I could find—all crawly and nasty an' bad like the Witch of Endor. I found a nice horrid one, too, you betcha. An' I tied him into my canoe with your shoelaces, daddy. You di'n' say not to. An' I singed to it:

"Ol' Witch of Endor is your name,
An' you an' Witchie is the same;
Don't think it's a game."

She showed me later what sort of creature she had caught for her little voodoo boat. Some call it a mud puppy and some call it a hellbender, but it is without doubt the homeliest thing ever created. It is a sort of aquatic salamander, any-where from three inches to a foot and a half in length. It has a porous, tubercular skin with two lateral streamers of skin on each side; and these are always ragged and torn. The creature always looks as if it is badly hurt. It has almost infinitesi-mal fingered legs, and its black shoe-button eyes are smaller than the head of a hatpin. For the hag Séleen there could be no better substitute.

"Then," said Patty complacently, "I singed that song the way the Witch of Endor did:

> "River Spider, black an' strong,.
> Folks 'bout here have done me wrong.
> Here's a gif' I send to you,
> Got some work for you to do."

"The rest of the verse was silly," said Pat, "but I had to think real fast for a rhyme for 'Witch of Endor' an' I used the first thing that I could think of quick-like. It was somepin I read on your letters, daddy, an' it was silly."

And that's all she would say for the time being. But I do remember the time she called me quietly down to the bayou and pointed out a sawyer to me, because it was the day before Carson came in a power launch from Minette to see if we had survived the hurricane; and Carson came six days after the big blow. Patty made absolutely sure that her mother was out of hearing, and then drew me by the hand down to the water's edge. "Daddy," she said, "we got to keep this from mother on account of it would upset her," and she pointed.

Three or four black twisted branches showed on the water, and as I watched they began to rise. A huge sawyer, the biggest I'd ever seen, reared up and up—and tangled in its coils was a . . . a *something*.

Séleen had not fared well, tangled in the whips of the River Spider under water for five days, in the company of all those little minnows and crawfish.

Patty regarded it critically while my stomach looped itself around violently and finally lodged between my spine and the skin of my back. "She ain't pretty a-*tall!*" said my darling daughter. "She's even homelier'n a mud puppy, I betcha."

As we walked back toward the lean-to we had built, she prattled on in this fashion: "Y'know, daddy, that was a real magic. I thought my verse was a silly one but I guess it worked out right after all. Will you laugh if I tell you what it was?"

I said I did not feel like laughing.

"Well," said Patty shyly, "I said:

> "Spider, kill the Witch of Endor.
> If five days lapse, return to sender."

That's my daughter.

A. E. VAN VOGT

The Witch

From where he sat, half hidden by the scraggly line of bushes, Marson watched the old woman. It was minutes now since he had stopped reading. The afternoon air hung breathless around him. Even here, a cliff's depth away from the sparkling tongue of sea that curled among the rocks below, the heat was a material thing, crushing at his strength.

But it was the letter in his pocket, not the blazing sunlight, that weighed on Marson's mind. Two days now since that startling letter had arrived; and he still hadn't the beginning of the courage necessary to ask for an explanation.

Frowning uncertainly—unsuspected—unsuspecting—he watched.

The old woman basked in the sun. Her long, thin, pale head drooped in sleep. On and on she sat, moveless, an almost shapeless form in her black sack of a dress.

The strain of looking hurt his eyes; his gaze wandered; embraced the long, low, tree-protected cottage with its neat, white garage and its aloneness there on that high, green hill overlooking the great spread of city. Marson had a brief, cozy sense of privacy—then he turned back to the old woman.

For a long moment, he stared unshaken at the spot where she had been. He was conscious of a dim, intellectual surprise, but there was not a real thought in his head. After a brief period, he grew aware of the blank, and he thought:

Thirty feet to the front door from where she had been sitting; and she would have had to cross his line of vision to get there.

An old woman, perhaps ninety, perhaps a hundred or more, an incredibly old woman, capable of moving—well thirty feet a minute.

Marson stood up. There was a searing pain where an edge of the sun had cut into his shoulders. But that passed. From his upright position, he saw that not a solitary figure was visible on the steeply mounting sidewalk. And only the sound of the sea on the rocks below broke the silence of that hot Saturday afternoon.

Where had the old wretch disappeared to?

The front door opened; and Joanna came out. She called to him:

"Oh, there you are, Craig. Mother Quigley was just asking where you were."

Marson came silently down from the cliff's edge. Almost meticulously, he took his wife's words, figuratively rolled them over in his mind, and found them utterly inadequate. The old woman couldn't have been *just* asking for him, because the old woman had NOT gone through that door and therefore hadn't asked anyone anything for the last twenty minutes.

At last an idea came. He said: "Where's Mother Quigley now?"

"Inside." He saw that Joanna was intent on the flower box of the window beside the door. "She's been knitting in the living room for the last half hour."

Amazement in him yielded to sharp annoyance. There was too damn much old woman in his mind since that letter had come less than forty-eight hours before. He drew it out, and stared bleakly at the scrawl of his name on the envelope.

It was simple enough, really, that this incredible letter had come to him. After the old woman's arrival nearly a year before, an unexpected nightmare, he had mentally explored all the possible reverberations that might accrue from her presence in his home. And the thought had come that, if she had left any debts in the small village where she had lived, he'd better pay them.

A young man, whose appointment to the technical school principalship had been severely criticized on the grounds of his youth, couldn't afford to have *anything* come back on him. And so a month before he had leisurely written the letter to which this was the answer.

Slowly, he drew the note from its envelope and once more reread the mind-staggering words in it:

Dear Mr. Marson:

As I am the only debtor, the postmaster handed me your letter; and I wish to state that, when your great grandmother died last year, I buried her myself and in my capacity as gravestone maker, I carved a stone for her grave. I did this at my own expense, being a God-fearing man, but if there is a relative, I feel you should bear cost of same, which is eighteen (18) dollars. I hope to hear from you, as I need the money just now.

Pete Cole.

Marson stood for a long moment; then he turned to speak to Joanna—just in time to see her disappearing into the house. Once more undecided, he climbed to the cliff's edge, thinking:

The old scoundrel! The nerve of a perfect stranger of an old woman walking into a private home and pulling a deception like that.

His public situation being what it was, his only solution was to pay her way into an institution; and even that would require careful thought—

Frowning blackly, he hunched himself deeper into his chair there on the cliff's edge, and deliberately buried himself in his book. It was not until much later that memory came of the way the old woman had disappeared from the lawn. Funny, he thought then, it really was damned funny.

The memory faded—

Blankly sat the old woman.

Supper was over; and, because for years there had been no reserves of strength in that ancient body, digestion was an almost incredible process, an all-out affair.

She sat as one dead, without visible body movement, without thought in her brain; even the grim creature purpose that had brought her here to this house lay like a stone at the bottom of the black pool that was her mind.

It was as if she had always sat there in that chair by the window overlooking the sea, like an inanimate object, like some horrible mummy, like a wheel that, having settled into position, seemed now immovable.

After an hour, awareness began to creep into her bones. The creature mind of her, the strange, inhuman creature mind behind the parchmentlike, sharp-nosed mask of human flesh, stirred into life.

It studied Marson at the living room table, his head bent thoughtfully over the next term curriculum he was preparing. Toothless lips curled finally into a contemptuous sneer.

The sneer faded, as Joanna slipped softly into the room. Half-closed, letching eyes peered then, with an abruptly ravenous, beastlike lust at the slim, lithe, strong body. Pretty, pretty body, soon now to be taken over.

In the three-day period of the first new moon after the summer solstice . . . in nine days exactly—

Nine days! The ancient carcass shuddered and wriggled ecstatically with the glee of the creature. Nine short days, and once again the age-long cycle of dynamic existence would begin. Such a pretty young body, too, capable of vibrant, world-ranging life—

Thought faded, as Joanna went back into the kitchen. Slowly, for the first time, awareness came of the sea.

Contentedly sat the old woman. Soon now, the sea would hold no terrors, and the blinds wouldn't have to be down, nor the windows shut; she would even be able to walk along the shore at midnight as of old; and *they,* whom she had deserted so long ago, would once more shrink from the irresistible energy aura of her new, young body.

The sound of the sea came to her, where she sat so quietly; calm sound at first, almost gentle in the soft sibilation of each wave thrust. Farther out, the voices of the water were louder, more raucous, blatantly confident, but the meaning of what they said was blurred by the distance, a dim, clamorous confusion that rustled discordantly out of the gathering night.

Night!

She shouldn't be aware of night falling, when the blinds were drawn.

With a little gasp, she twisted toward the window beside which she sat. Instantly, a blare of hideous fear exploded from her lips.

The ugly sound bellowed into Marson's ears, and brought him lurching to his feet. It raged through the door into the kitchen, and Joanna came running as if it was a rope pulling at her.

The old woman screeched on; and it was Marson who finally penetrated to the desire behind that mad terror.

"Good Lord!" he shrugged. "It's the windows and the blinds. I forgot to put them down when dusk fell."

He stopped, irritated, then: "Damned nonsense! I've a good mind to—"

"For Heaven's sake!" his wife urged. "We've got to stop that noise. I'll take this side of the room; you take the windows next to her."

Marson shrugged again, acquiescently. But he was thinking: They wouldn't have this to put up with much longer. As soon as the summer holidays arrived, he'd make arrangements to put her in the Old Folks Home. And that would be that. Less than two weeks now.

His wife's voice broke almost sharply across the silence that came, as Mother Quigley settled back into her chair: "I'm surprised at you forgetting a thing like that. You're usually so thoughtful."

"It was so damned hot!" Marson complained.

Joanna said no more; and he went back to his chair. But he was thinking suddenly: Old woman who fears the sea and the night, why did you come to this house by the sea, where the street lamps are far apart and the nights are almost primevally dark?

The gray thought passed; his mind returned with conscientious intentness to the preparation of the curriculum.

Startled sat the old woman!

All the swift rage of the creature burned within her. That wretched man, daring to forget. And yet—"You're usually so thoughtful!" his wife had said.

It was true. Not once in eleven months had he forgotten to look after the blinds—until today.

Was it possible that he suspected? That somehow, now that the time for the change was so near, an inkling of her purpose had dripped from her straining brain?

It had happened before. In the past, she had had to fight for her bodies against terrible, hostile men who had nothing but dreadful suspicion.

Jet-black eyes narrowed to pin points. With this man, there would have to be more than suspicion. Being what he was, practical, skeptical, cold-brained, not all the telepathic vibrations, nor the queer mind storms with their abnormal implications—if he had yet had any—would touch him or remain with him of themselves. Nothing but facts would rouse this man.

What facts? Was it possible that, in her intense concentrations of thought, she had unwittingly permitted images to show? Or had he made inquiries?

Her body shook, and then slowly purpose formed: She must take no chances.

Tomorrow was Sunday, and the man would be home. So nothing was possible. But Monday—

That was it. Monday morning while Joanna slept—and Joanna always went back to bed for an hour's nap after her husband had gone to work—on Monday morning she would slip in and prepare the sleeping body so that, seven days later, entry would be easy.

No more wasting time trying to persuade Joanna to take the stuff voluntarily. The silly fool with her refusal of home remedies, her prating of taking only doctors' prescriptions.

Forcible feeding would be risky—but not half so risky as expecting this wretched, doting wreck of a body to survive another year.

Implacable sat the old woman.

In spite of herself, she felt the toll of the hours of anticipation. At Monday breakfast, she drooled with the inner excitement of her purpose. The cereal fell from her misshaped mouth, milk and saliva splattered over the tablecloth—and she couldn't help it. Old hands shook, mouth quivered; in everything her being yielded to that dreadful anility of body. Better get to her room before—

With a terrible start, she saw that the man was pushing clear of the table, and there was such a white look on his face that she scarcely needed his words, as he said:

"There's something I've been intending to say to Mother Quigley"—his voice took on a rasping note—"and right now, when I'm feeling thoroughly disgusted, is a darned good time to say it."

"For Heaven's sake, Craig"—Joanna cut in, sharply; and the old woman snatched at the interruption, and began queasily to get to her feet—"what's made you so irritable these last few days? Now, be a good lover and go to school. Personally, I'm not going to clean up this mess till I've had my nap, and I'm certainly not going to let it get me down. 'By."

A kiss; and she was gone into the hallway that led to the bedrooms. Almost instantly, she vanished into the master bedroom; and then, even as the old woman struggled desperately to get farther out of her chair, Marson was turning to her, eyes bleak and determined.

Cornered, she stared up at him like a trapped animal, dismayed by the way this devilish body had betrayed her in an emergency, distorted her will. Marson said:

"Mother Quigley—I shall continue to call you that yet for the moment—I have received a letter from a man who claims to have carved a stone for the body he himself buried in your grave. What I would like to know is this: Who is occupying that grave? I—"

It was his own phrasing that brought Marson to startled silence. He stood strangely taut, struck rigid by a curious, alien horror, unlike anything he had ever known. For a long, terrible moment, his mind seemed to lie naked and exposed to the blast of an icy inner wind that whirled at him out of some nether darkness.

Thoughts came, a blare of obscene mental vaporings, unwholesome, black with ancient, incredibly ancient evil, a very seething mass of unsuspected horrors.

With a start he came out of that grisly world of his own imagination, and grew aware that the old crone was pouring forth harsh, almost eager words:

"It wasn't me that was buried. There were two of us old ones in the village; and when she died, I made her face to look like mine, and mine to look like hers, and I took her money and . . . I used to be an actress, you know, and I could use make-up. That's how it was, yes, yes, make-up; that's the whole explanation, and I'm not what you think at all, but just an old woman who was poor. That's all, just an old woman to be pitied—"

She would have gone on endlessly if the creature-logic in her had not, with dreadful effort, forced her quiet. She stood, then, breathing heavily, conscious that her voice had been too swift, too excited, her tongue loose with the looseness of old age, and her words had damned her at every syllable.

It was the man who brought surcease to her desperate fear; the man saying explosively:

"Good heavens, woman, do you mean to stand there and tell me you did a thing like that—"

Marson stopped, overwhelmed. Every word the old woman had spoken had drawn him further back from the strange, unsettling morass of thoughts that had briefly flooded his mind, back into the practical world of his own reason—and his own ethics. He felt almost physically shocked, and it was only after a long moment that he was able to go on. He said finally, slowly:

"You actually confess to the ghoulish deed of disfiguring a dead body for the purpose of stealing its money. Why that's—"

His voice collapsed before that abyss of unsuspected moral degradation. Here was a crime of the baser sort, an unclean, revolting thing that, if it was ever found out, would draw the censure of an entire nation, and ruin any school principal alive.

He shuddered; he said hastily: "I haven't the time to go into this now but—"

With a start, he saw that she was heading toward the hallway that led to her bedroom. More firmly, he called: "And there's another thing. Saturday afternoon, you were sitting out on the lawn—"

A door closed softly. Behind it, the old woman stood, gasping from her exertions, but with a growing conviction of triumph. The silly stupid man still didn't suspect. What did she care what he thought of her. Only seven days remained; and if she could last them, nothing else mattered.

The danger was that her position would become more difficult every day. That meant—when the time came, a quick entry would be absolutely necessary. That meant—the woman's body must be prepared *now!*

Joanna, healthy Joanna, would already be asleep. So it was only a matter of waiting for that miserable husband to get out. She waited—

The sweet sound came at last from the near distance—the front door opening and then shutting. Like a stag at bay, the old woman quivered; her very bones shook with the sudden, sickish thrill of imminent action. If she failed, if she was discovered—

Some preparation she had made to offset such a disaster but—

The spasm of fear passed. With a final, reassuring fumble into the flat, black bosom of her dress, where the little bag of powder hung open, she glided forth.

For the tiniest instant, she paused in the open doorway of Joanna's bedroom. Her gimlet eyes dwelt with a glitter of satisfaction on the sleeping figure. And then—

Then she was into the room.

* * *

The morning wind from the sea struck Marson like a blow, as he opened the door. He shut it with a swift burst of strength, and stood in the dully lighted hallway, indecisive.

It wasn't that he wasn't going out—there were too many things to do before the end of the school year; it was just that the abrupt resistance of the wind had crystallized a thought:

Ought he to go out without telling Joanna about the letter from the gravestone maker?

After all, the old woman now knew that he knew. In her cunning eagerness to defend herself and the security she must consider threatened, she might mention the subject to Joanna—and Joanna would know nothing.

Still undecided, Marson took several slow steps, then paused again just inside the living room. Damn it, the thing could probably wait till noon, especially as Joanna would be asleep by now. Even as it was, he'd have to go by car or streetcar if he hoped to reach the school at his usual early hour.

His thought twisted crazily, as the black form of the old woman glided ghost-like across the bedroom hallway straight into Joanna's room.

Senselessly, a yell quivered on Marson's lips—senselessly, because there was in him no reasoned realization of alienness. The sound froze unuttered because abruptly that icy, unnatural wind out of blackness was blowing again in his mind. Abnormal, primordial things echoed and raged—

He had no consciousness of running, but, suddenly, there was the open bed-room door, and there was the old woman—and at that last instant, though he had come with noiseless speed, the creature woman sensed him.

She jumped with a sheer physical dismay that was horrible to see. Her fingers that had been hovering over Joanna's mouth jerked spasmodically, and a green-ish powder in them sprayed partly on the bed, mostly on the little rug beside the bed.

And then, Marson was on top of her. That loathsome mindwind was blowing stronger, colder; and in him was an utter, deadly conviction that demonic muscles would resist his strength to the limit. For a moment, that certainly prevailed even over reality.

For there was nothing.

Thin, bony arms yielded instantly to his devastatingly hard thrust; a body that was like old, rotten paper crumbled to the floor from his murderous rush.

For the barest moment, the incredibly easy victory gave Marson pause. But no astonishment could genuinely restrain the violence of his purpose or cancel that unnatural sense of unhuman things; no totality of doubt at this instant could begin to counterbalance his fury at what he had seen.

The old woman lay at his feet in a shapeless, curled-up blob. With a pitiless ferocity, a savage intent beyond any emotion he had ever known, Marson snatched her from the floor.

Light as long-decayed wood, she came up in his fingers, a dangling, inhuman, black-clothed thing. He shook it, as he would have shaken a monster; and it was then, when his destroying purpose was a very blaze of unreasoning intensity that the incredible thing happened.

Images of the old woman flooded the room. Seven old women, all in a row, complete in every detail, from black, sack-like dress to semi-bald head, raced for the door. Three exact duplicates of the old woman were clawing frantically at the nearest window. The eleventh replica was on her knees desperately trying to squeeze under the bed.

With an astounded gasp, brain whirling madly, Marson dropped the thing in his hands. It fell squalling, and abruptly the eleven images of the old woman vanished like figments out of a nightmare.

"Craig!"

In a dim way, he recognized Joanna's voice. But still he stood, like a log of wood, unheeding. He was thinking piercingly: That was what had happened Saturday on the lawn—an image of the old woman unwittingly projected by her furiously working mind, as she sat in the living room knitting.

Unwitting images had they been now, of a certainty. The old woman's desperately fearful mind seeking ways of escape.

God, what was he thinking? There was—there *could* be nothing here but his own disordered imagination.

The thing was impossible.

"Craig, what is all this anyway? What's happened?"

He scarcely heard; for suddenly, quite clearly, almost calmly, his mind was co-ordinating around a single thought, simple, basic and terrible:

What did a man do with a witch in A. D. 1942?

The hard thought collapsed as he saw, for the first time, that Joanna was half-sitting, half-kneeling in the taut position she had jerked herself into when she wakened. She was swaying the slightest bit, as if her muscle control was incomplete. Her face was creased with the shock of her rude awakening.

Her eyes, he saw, were wide and almost blank; and they were staring at the old woman. With one swift glance, he followed that rigid gaze—and alarm struck through him.

Joanna had not wakened till the old woman screamed. She *hadn't* seen the images at all.

She would have only the picture of a powerful, brutal young man standing menacingly over the moaning form of an old woman—and by Heaven he'd have to act fast.

"Look!" Marson began curtly. "I caught her putting a green powder on your lips and—"

It was putting the thing in words that struck him dumb. His mind reeled before the tremendous fact that a witch had tried to feed dope to Joanna—*his* Joanna! In some incomprehensible way, Joanna was to be a victim—and he must convince her now of the action they must take.

Before that purpose, rage fled. Hastily, he sank down on the bed beside Joanna.

Swiftly, he launched into his story. He made no mention of the images or of his own monstrous suspicions. Joanna was even more practical than he. It would only confuse the issue to let her get the impression that he was mad. He finished finally:

"I don't want any arguments. The facts speak for themselves. The powder alone damns her; the letter serves to throw enough doubt on her identity to relieve us of any further sense of obligation.

"Here's what we're going to do. First, I shall phone my secretary that I may not be in till late. Then I'll ring up the Old Folks Home. I have no doubt under normal conditions there are preliminaries to entry, but money ought to eliminate all red tape. We're getting rid of her today and—"

Amazingly, Joanna's laughter interrupted him, a wave of laughter that ended in a sharp, unnormal, hysterical note. Marson shook her.

"Darling," he began anxiously.

She pushed him away, scrambled off the bed, and knelt with a curious excitement beside the old woman.

"Mother Quigley," she started, and her voice was so high-pitched that Marson half-climbed to his feet. He sank down again, as she went on: "Mother Quigley, answer one question: That powder you were placing in my mouth—was it that ground seaweed remedy of yours that you've been trying to feed me for my headaches?"

The flare of hope that came to the old woman nearly wrecked her brain. How could she have forgotten her long efforts to make Joanna take the powder voluntarily? She whispered:

"Help me to my bed, dearie. I don't think anything is broken, but I'll have to lie down . . . yes, yes, my dear, that was the powder. I was so sure it would help you. We women, you know, with our headaches, have to stick together. I shouldn't have done it of course but—"

A thought, a blaze of anxiety, struck her. She whimpered: "You won't let him send me away, will you? I know I've been a lot of trouble and—"

She stopped, because there was a queer look on Joanna's face; and enough was enough. Victory could be overplayed. She listened with ill-suppressed content as Joanna said swiftly:

"Craig, hadn't you better go? You'll be late."

Marson said sharply: "I want the rest of that weed powder. I'm going to have that stuff analyzed."

But he evaded his wife's gaze; and he was thinking, stunned: "I'm crazy. I was so dizzy with rage that I had a nightmare of hallucinations."

Wasn't it Dr. Lycoming who had said that the human mind must have racial memory that extended back to the nameless seas that spawned man's ancestors? And that under proper and violent stress, these memories of terror would return?

His shame grew, as the old woman's shaking fingers produced a little canvas bag. Without a word, he took the container, and left the room.

Minutes later, with the soft purr of his car throbbing in his ears, eyes intent on the traffic, the whole affair seemed as remote and unreal as any dream.

He thought: "Well, what next? I still don't want her around but—"

It struck him with a curious, sharp dismay that there was not a plan in his head.

Tuesday—the old woman wakened with a start, and lay very still. Hunger came, but her mind was made up. She would not dress or eat till after the man was gone to work, and she would not come out at noon, or after school hours, but would remain in this room, with the door shut whenever he was around.

Six days before she could act, six days of dragging minutes, of doubts and fears.

Wednesday at 4:30 p.m., Marson's fingers relaxed on the shining knob of the front door, as the laughter of women tinkled from inside; and memory came that he had been warned of an impending tea.

Like an unwelcome intruder, he slipped off down the street, and it was seven o'clock before he emerged from the "talkie" and headed silently homewards.

He was thinking for the hundredth time: "I saw those old woman images. I know I saw them. It's my civilized instinct that makes me want to doubt, and so keeps me inactive."

The evening paper was lying on the doorstep. He picked it up; and later, after a supper of left-over sandwiches and hot coffee, at least two hours later, a paragraph from a war editorial caught first his eyes, and then his mind.

> The enemy has not really fooled us. We know that all his acts, directly or indirectly, have been anti-*us*. The incredible and fantastic thing is this knowing all we know and doing nothing.
>
> If an individual had as much suspicion, as much evidence, that someone was going to murder him at the first opportunity, he would try to prevent the act from being committed; he would not wait for the full, bloody consummation.
>
> The greater fact is that there will come a time when everything possible is too little, even all-out effort too late.

With a start, Marson allowed the paper to fall. The war angle was already out of his mind. Twice he had voted "no opinion" on public-opinion war polls, and that had been strictly true. A young man in the first throes of the responsibility of running a great school had no time for war or politics. Later perhaps—

But the theme, the inmost meaning of that editorial, was for him, for his problem. *Knowing what he knew and doing nothing.*

Uneasily, but with sudden determination, he climbed to his feet. "Joanna," he began—and realized he was talking to an empty room.

He peered into the bedroom. Joanna lay on the bed, fully dressed, sound asleep. Marson's grimness faded into an understanding smile. Preparing that afternoon tea had taken its toll.

After an hour, she was still asleep, and so very quietly, very gently, he undressed her and put her to bed. She did not waken even when he kissed her good night.

* * *

Thursday: By noon, his mind was involved with a petty-larceny case, a sordid, miserable affair of a pretty girl caught stealing. He saw Kemp, the chemistry assistant, come in; and then withdraw quietly.

In abrupt fever of excitement, he postponed the unwelcome case, and hastened after Kemp. He found the man putting on his hat to go to lunch.

The young chemistry instructor's eyes lighted as they saw Marson, then he frowned.

"That green powder you gave me to analyze, Mr. Marson, it's been a tough assignment. I like to be thorough, you know."

Marson nodded. He knew the mettle of this man, which was why he had chosen him rather than his equally obliging chief. Kemp was young, eager; and he knew his subject.

"Go on," said Marson.

"As you suggested," Kemp continued, "it was ground weed. I took it up to Biology Bill . . . pardon me, I mean Mr. Grainger."

In spite of himself, Marson smiled. There was a time when he had said "Biology Bill" as a matter of course.

"Go on," was all he said now.

"Grainger identified it as a species of seaweed, known as *Hydrodendon Barelia*."

"Any special effects if taken into the human system?" Marson was all casualness.

"No-o! It's not dangerous, if that's what you mean. Naturally, I tried it on the dog, meaning myself, and it's rather unpleasant, not exactly bitter but sharp."

Marson was silent. He wondered whether he ought to feel disappointed or relieved. Or what? Kemp was speaking again:

"I looked up its history, and, surprisingly, it has quite a history. You know how in Europe they make you study a lot of stuff about the old alchemists and all that kind of stuff, to give you an historical grounding."

"Yes?"

Kemp laughed. "You haven't got a witch around your place by any chance?"

"Eh!" The exclamation almost burned Marson's lips. He fought hard to hide the tremendousness of that shock.

Kamp laughed again. "According to *'Die Geschichte der Zauberinnen'* by the Austrian, Karl Gloeck, *Hydrodendon Barelia* is the modern name for the sinister witch's weed of antiquity. I'm not talking about the special witches of our Christian lore, with their childish attributes, but the old tribe of devil's creatures that came out of prehistory, regular full-blooded sea witches. It seems when each successive body gets old, they choose a young woman's body, attune themselves to it by living with the victim, and take possession any time after midnight of the first full moon period following the 21st of June. Witch's weed is supposed to make the entry easier. Gloeck says . . . why, what's the matter, sir?"

His impulse, his wild and terrible impulse, was to babble the whole story to Kemp. With a gigantic effort, he stopped himself; for Kemp, though he might talk easily of witches, was a scientist to the depths of his soul.

And what he—Marson—might have to do, must not be endangered by the knowledge that some practical, doubting person—anyone—suspected the truth. The mere existence of suspicion would corrode his will, and, in the final issue, undermine his decision to act.

He heard himself muttering words of thanks; minutes later, on his way, he was thinking miserably: What could he say, how could he convince Joanna that the old woman must be gotten rid of?

And there was one more thing that he *had* to clear up before he would dare risk everything in the only, unilateral action that remained. One more thing—

All Saturday morning, the sun shone brilliantly, but by afternoon black clouds rode above his racing car. At six in the evening it rained bitterly for ten minutes; and then, slowly, the sky cleared.

His first view of the village was from the hill, and that, he thought, relieved, should make it easier. From a group of trees, he surveyed the little sprawl of houses and buildings. It was the church that confused him at first.

He kept searching in its vicinity with his field glasses. And it was nearly half an hour before he was convinced that what he sought was not there. Twilight was thick over the world now, and that brought surging panic. He couldn't possibly dare to go down to the village, and inquire where the graveyard was. Yet—hurry, hurry!

Genuinely unsettled physically, he walked deeper into the woods along the edge of the hill. There was a jutting point of ground farther along, from where he would be able to sweep the countryside. These villages sometimes had their grave-yards a considerable distance away and—

The little roadway burst upon him abruptly, as he emerged from the brush; and there a few scant feet away was a trellised gate. Beyond it, in the gathering shadows, simple crosses gleamed; an angel stood whitely, stiffly, poised for flight; and several great, shining granite stones reared rigidly from a dark, quiet earth.

Night lay black and still on the graveyard when his cautiously used flashlight at last picked out the headstone he craved. The inscription was simple:

Mrs. Quigley
Died July 7, 1941
Over 90 years old

He went back to the car, and got the shovel; and then he began to dig. The earth was strong; and he was not accustomed to digging. After an hour, he had penetrated about a foot and a half.

Breathless, he sank down on the ground, and for a while he lay there under the night sky with its shifting panoply of clouds. A queer, intellectual remembrance came that the average weight of university presidents and high school principals was around one hundred eighty pounds, according to Young.

But the devil of it was, he thought grimly, it was all weight and no endurance. Nevertheless, he had to go on, if it took all night.

At least, he was sure of one thing—Joanna wasn't home. It had been a tough job persuading her to accept that week-end invitation alone, tougher still to lie about the duties that would take him out of the city until Sunday morning; and he had had to promise faithfully that he would drive out Sunday to get her.

The simplest thing of all had been getting the young girl to look after the old woman over the week end and—

The sound of a car passing brought him to his feet in one jerky movement. He frowned. It wasn't that he was worried, or even basically alarmed. His mind felt rock-steady; his determination was an unshaken thing. Here in this dark, peaceful setting, disturbance was as unlikely as his own ghoullike incursion. People simply didn't come to graveyards at night.

The night sped, as he dug on and on, deeper, nearer to that secret he must have before he could take the deadly action that logic dictated even now. And he didn't feel like a ghoul—

There was no feeling at all, only his purpose, his grim unalterable purpose; and there was the dark night, and the quietness, broken only by the swish of dirt flung upward and outward. His life, his strength flowed on here in this little, tree-grown field of death; and his watch showed twenty-five minutes to two when at last the spade struck wood.

It was after two when his flashlight peered eerily into the empty wooden box.

For long seconds, he stared; and now that the reality was here, he didn't know what he had expected. Obviously, only too obviously, an image had been buried here—and vanished gleefully as the dirt began to thud in the filling of the grave.

But why a burial at all? Who was she trying to fool? What?

His mind grew taut. Reasons didn't matter now. He *knew;* that was what counted. And his actions must be as cold and deadly, as was the purpose of the creature that had fastened itself on his household.

His car glided onto the deserted early morning highway. The gray dawn came out of the east to meet him, as he drove; and only his dark purpose, firmer, icier each minute, an intellectualized thing as unquenchable as sun fire, kept him companion.

It was deep into the afternoon when his machine, in its iron-throated second gear, whirred up the steep hill, and twisted into the runway that led to the garage.

He went into the house, and for a while he sat down. The girl whom Joanna had left in charge was a pretty, red-haired thing named Helen. She was quite fragilely built, he noted with grim approval; he had suggested her for the week end with that very smallness in mind. And yes, she wouldn't mind staying another night, if they didn't come home. And when was he leaving to get his wife?

"Oh, I'm going to have a nap first," Marson replied. "Had rather a hard drive. And you . . . what are you going to do while I sleep?"

"I've found some magazines," the girl said. "I'm going to sit here and read. I'll keep very quiet, I assure you."

"Thank you," Marson said. "It's just for a couple of hours, you know."

He smiled bleakly to himself, as he went into the bedroom, and closed the door.

Men with desperate plans had to be bold, had to rely on the simplest, most straightforward realities of life—such as the fact that people normally stayed away from cemeteries at night. And that young women didn't make a nuisance of themselves by prowling around when they had promised not to.

He took off his shoes, put on his slippers, and then—

Five long minutes he waited to give her time to settle down. Finally, softly, he went through the bathroom door that led to the hallway that connected the kitchen and the bedrooms. The kitchen door creaked as he went out, but he allowed himself no qualms; not a trace of fear entered into the ice-cold region that was his brain.

Why should a girl, comfortably seated, reading an absorbing story, tied by a promise to be silent—why should such a girl investigate an ordinary sound? Even new houses were notoriously full of special noises.

The car was parked at the side of the house, where there was ony one window. He took the five gallon tin of gasoline out of the back seat, carried it through the kitchen, down into the basement. He covered it swiftly with some old cloth, then he was up again, through the kitchen—

He reached the bedroom, thinking tensely: It was these details that must paralyze most people planning murder. Tonight when he came back, he wouldn't be able to drive the car up the hill, because it was to be a very special, unseen, ghostly trip. The car would be parked at least a mile away; and, obviously, it would be fantastically risky, and tiring, to lug a five gallon tin of gas a whole mile through back alleys.

And what a nightmare it would be to blunder with such a tin through the kitchen and into the basement at midnight. Impossible too, he had found, to get it past Joanna without her seeing.

Murder had its difficulties; and quite simply of course, murder it must be. And by fire. All that he ever remembered about witches showed the overwhelming importance of fire. And just let lightly built Helen try to break down the old woman's door after the fire had started and he had locked that door from the outside—

He lay for a while quietly on the bed; and the thought came that no man would seem a greater scoundrel than he if all that he had done and all that he intended was ever found out.

For a moment, then, a fear came black as pitch; and as if the picture was there before his eyes, he saw the great school slipping from him, the greater college beyond fading like the dream it was, fading into the mists that surrounded a prison cell.

He thought: It would be so easy to take half measures that would rid him and Joanna of the terrible problem. All he needed to do next day was to take her to the Old Folks Home, while Joanna was still away—and ruthlessly face down all subsequent objections.

She would escape perhaps, but never back to them.

He could retreat, then, into his world of school and Joanna; existence would flow on in its immense American way—and somewhere soon there would be a young woman witch, glowing with the strength of ancient, evil life renewed; and somewhere too there would be a human soul shattered out of its lawful body, a home where an old woman had blatantly, skillfully, intruded.

Knowing what he did, and doing nothing short of—everything!

He must have slept on that thought, the demanding sleep of utterly weary nerves, unaccustomed to being denied their rest. He wakened with a shock. It was pitch dark, he saw, and—

The bedroom door opened softly. Joanna came tiptoeing in. She saw him by the light that streamed from the hall. She stopped and smiled. Then she came over and kissed him.

"Darling," she said, "I'm so glad you hadn't started out to get me. A delightful couple offered to drive me home, and I thought, if we met you on the way, at least it would have saved you that much anyway, after your long, tiring week end. I've sent Helen home; it's after eleven, so just undress and go straight to bed. I'm going to have a cup of tea myself; perhaps you'd like one too."

Her voice barely penetrated through the great sounds that clanged in his brain, the pure agony of realization.

After eleven—less than an hour to the midnight that, once a year, began the fatal period of the witch's moon. The whole world of his plans was crashing about his ears.

He hovered about her, while she put the kettle on. It was half past eleven when they finished the tea; and still he couldn't speak, couldn't begin to find the beginning that would cover all the things that had to be said. Wretchedly, he grew aware of her eyes watching him, as she puffed at her cigarette.

He got up, and started to pace the floor; and now there was dark puzzlement in her fine brown eyes. Twice, she started to speak, but each time cut herself off.

And waited. He could almost feel her waiting in that quiet, earnest way of hers, waiting for him to speak first.

The impossibility, he thought then, the utter impossibility of convincing this calm, practical, tender-hearted wife of his. And yet, it *had* to be done, now before it was too late, before even all-out effort would be too little.

The recurrence of that phrase from the editorial started a streak of cold perspiration down his face. He stopped short, stopped in front of her; and his eyes must have been glaring pools, his rigid posture terrifying; for she shrank the faintest bit.

"Craig—"

"Joanna, I want you to take your hat and coat and go to a hotel."

It needed no imagination to realize that his words must sound insane. He plunged on with the volubility of a child telling an exciting story. And that was the way he felt—like a child talking to a tolerant grownup. But he couldn't stop. He omitted only his grim murder purpose. She would have to absorb the shock of that later when it was all over. When he had finished, he saw that her gaze was tender.

"You poor darling," she said, "so that's what's been bothering you. You were worried about me. I can just see how everything would work on your mind. I'd have felt the same, if it was you apparently in danger.''

Marson groaned. So that was the angle she was taking—sweet understanding; humoring his natural alarm; believing not a word. He caught his mind into a measure of calm; he said in a queer, shaky voice:

"Joanna, think of Kemp's definite analysis of it as witch's weed, and the fact the body is not in the grave—"

Still there was no fire in her eyes, no flame of basic fear. She was frowning; she said:

"But why would she have to go to all that trouble of burying one of her images, when all she had to do was get on the train and come here? Physically, that is what she did; why that enormous farce of a burial?''

Marson flared: "Why the lie she told me about having put make-up on someone else, who was buried there? Oh, darling, don't you see—"

Slowly, reasonably, Joanna spoke again: "There may have been some connivance, Craig, perhaps between the man, Pete Cole, who wrote you the letter, and Mother Quigley. Have you thought of that?''

If she had been with him, he thought, when he opened that dark grave. If she had seen the incredible image—If, if, if—

He stole a glance at the clock on the wall. It was seventeen minutes to twelve, and that nearly twisted his brain. He shuddered—and fought for control of his voice. There were arguments he could think of, but the time for talk was past— far past. Only one thing mattered.

"Joanna," he said, and his voice was so intense that it shocked him, "you'll go to the hotel for three days, for my sake?''

"Why, of course, darling.'' She looked serene, as she stood up. "My night bag is still packed. I'll just take the car and—"

A thought seemed to strike her. Her fine, clear brow creased. "What about you?''

"I'll stay here of course," he said, "to see that she stays here. You can phone me up at the school tomorrow. Hurry, for Heaven's sake.''

He felt chilled by the way her gaze was appraising him. "Just a minute," she said, and her voice was slow, taut. "Originally, you planned to have me out of the way only till tomorrow. What—are you—planning to do—tonight?''

His mind was abruptly sullen, rebellious; his mouth awkward, as if only the truth could come easily from it. Lies had always been hard for him. But he tried now, pitifully:

"All I wanted was to get you out of the way, while I visited the grave. I didn't really figure beyond that.''

Her eyes didn't believe him; her voice said so, but just what words she used somehow didn't penetrate; for an odd steadiness was coming to him, realization that the time must be only minutes away, and that all this talk was worthless. Only his relentless purpose mattered. He said simply, almost as if he were talking to himself:

"I intended to lock her door from the outside, and burn the house, but I can see now that isn't necessary. You'd better get going, darling, because this is going to be messy; and you mustn't see it. You see, I'm going to take her out to the cliff's edge, and throw her to the night sea she fears so violently."

He stopped because the clock, incredibly, said eight minutes to twelve. Without a sound, without waiting for the words that seemed to quiver on her lips, he whirled and raced into the bedroom corridor. He tried the old woman's door. It was locked. A very fury of frustation caught at his throat.

"Open up!" he roared.

There was silence within; he felt Joanna's fingers tugging futilely at his sleeve. And then he was flinging the full weight of his one hundred eighty pounds at that door. Two bone wrenching thrusts—and it went down with an ear-splitting crash.

His fingers fumbled for the light switch. There was a click, and then—

He stopped, chilled, half paralyzed by what the light revealed: Twelve old women, twelve creatures snarling at him from every part of the room.

The witch was out in the open—and ready.

The queerest thing of all in that tremendous moment was the sheer, genuine glow of triumph that swept him—the triumph of a man who has indisputably won an argument with his wife. He felt a crazy, incredible joy; he wanted to shout: "See! see! wasn't I right? Wasn't it exactly as I told you?"

With an effort, he caught his whirling mind; and the shaky realization came that actually he was on the verge of madness. He said unsteadily:

"This is going to take a little time. I'll have to carry them one by one to the cliff; and the law of averages says that I'll strike the right one sooner or later. We won't have to worry about her slipping away in between, because we know her horrible fear of the night. It's only a matter of perseverance—"

His voice faltered the faintest bit; for suddenly the ghastly reality of what was here struck his inner consciousness. Some of the creatures sat on the bed, some on the floor; two stood, their arms around each other; and half of them were gibbering now in a fantastic caricature of terror. With a start, he grew aware of Joanna behind him.

She was pale, incredibly pale, for Joanna; and her voice, when she spoke, quavered; she said:

"The trouble with you, Craig, is that you're not practical. You want to do physical things like throwing her onto the rocks at the bottom of the cliff, or burning her. It proves that even yet your basic intellect doesn't believe in her. Or you'd know what to do."

She had been pressing against him, staring wide-eyed over his shoulder at that whimpering, terrified crew. Now, before he could realize her intention, she slipped under his arm, and was into the room.

Her shoulder bumped him slightly as she passed, and threw him off balance. It was only for a moment, but when he could look again, eight squalling crones had Joanna surrounded.

He had a brief glimpse of her distorted face. Six gnarled hands were clawing to open her mouth; a tangle of desperate old women's hands were clutching at her arms and her legs, trying to hold her flailing, furious body.

And they were succeeding! That was the terrifying reality that drove him into the midst of that brew of old women with battering fists—and pulled Joanna clear.

Immense anger grew out of his fear. "You silly fool!" he raged. "Don't you realize it must be after midnight?"

Then, with an abrupt, fuller realization that she had actually been attacked, piercingly:

"Are you all right?"

"Yes." Shakily. "Yes."

But *she* would have said that too. He glared at her with mad eyes, as if by the sheer intensity of his gaze, he would see through her face into her brain. She must have seen his terrible thought in his straining countenance, for she cried:

"Don't you see, darling? The blinds, the windows—pull them up. That's what I intended to do. Let in the night; let in the things she fears. If she exists, then so must they. Don't you see?"

He took Joanna with him, kicking at the creatures with his fists and his feet, with a grim, merciless ferocity. He tore the blind from its hooks; one thrust of his foot smashed the whole lower pane of the window. And then, back at the door, they waited.

Waited!

There was a whisper of water splattering on the window sill. A shape without shape silhoutted abnormally against the blue-black sky beyond the window. And then, the water was on the floor, trickling from a misty shape that seemed to walk. A voice sighed, or was it a thought:

"You nearly fooled us, Niyasha, with that false burial. We lost sight of you for months. But we knew that only by the sea and from the sea could your old body draw the strength for the change. We watched, as we have so long for so many of the traitors; and so at last you answer the justice of the ancient waters."

There was no sound but the sibilation of water trickling. The old women were silent as stones; and they sat like birds fascinated by snakes. And suddenly, the images were gone, snuffed out. One fragile, lonely-looking old woman sat on the floor directly in the path of the mist-thing. Almost primly, she gathered her skirts about her.

The mist enveloped her form. She was lifted into it, then instantly dropped. Swiftly, the mist retreated to the window. It was gone. The old woman lay flat on her back, eyes open and staring; her mouth open, too, unprettily.

That was the over-all effect—the utter lack of anything beautiful.

THE END.

JACK WILLIAMSON

Conscience, Ltd.

Nobody saw Murray Staples come into the crowded district courtroom. A trim, worried man in gray, he walked under the unseeing eyes of Sheriff Dixon, and glanced at the wall clock above Judge Prendick's head. With a puzzled expression, he hurried on down the aisle, through the breathless hush of a tense legal battle. He set his heavy brief case on the end of the long table cluttered with the papers of the prosecution, and frowned again at the clock.

Nobody noticed him. He caught the elbow of District Attorney William Platt, who was just rising to address the court. But Platt shook him off, with a little shuddery gesture, and turned to sum up his case for the jury. Hurriedly, with thin nervous fingers, Staples opened the bulging brief case. He fumbled for a thin gray card, and read again:

OFFICE MEMO

TO: Murray Staples, Deputy Advocate
SUBJECT: Call for William Platt
PLACE: District courtroom, Clifton
TIME: Expires November 14, 5:19 p. m.

The clock above Judge Prendick's habitual sleepy snarl already said five twenty. But Staples looked at the accurate watch on his wrist, and found that the courtroom clock was three minutes fast. Still unnoticed, although he was drumming nervously on the edge of the table, he waited impatiently.

District Attorney Platt was a tall, gaunt man, lean as a bloodhound. Inflexible justice flashed a glacial blue in his deep-set eyes. His thin-lipped mouth was stern with rigid self-restraint, his iron jaw square with rectitude. The pallor of an exhausted but triumphant crusader was gray on his hawk-nosed face.

This had been a trying day. Honoria had called him early, to keep an appointment with Dr. Venwick. Platt protested that he had no time to be ill. But Honoria was always right—that was why she had become the second Mrs. Platt. He went to see the doctor.

When the examination was done, Dr. Venwick laid his stethoscope aside, and fussed needlessly with the sac and tubes of the blood-pressure manometer. Something gave Platt a chill of icy alarm. There was a sudden hush, so that he could hear the loud, uneven beat of his own hurrying pulse; and the stabbing glitter of cold white light on bright steel instruments became acutely painful. At last the doctor turned.

"We had better face the facts, Bill." He put on a careful professional frown, over his best poker face. "We've got a heart condition, here. Not too serious, yet. But we'd better ease the strain. I'd suggest you take a long vacation."

Dr. Venwick's best poker face wasn't very good. Platt's ability to read it had earned him several fifty-dollar pots—before he married Honoria and joined the church and quit playing stud in the locker room at the Clifton Country Club. He knew what the doctor was thinking.

"You can't give me a death sentence, doc." His fine voice was brittle with urgency. "I haven't got time to let go. The Pickens case goes to the jury today. It's in the bag—and it's the best break I've ever had. The city papers are covering it. It will give me a chance to accomplish some of the things I was elected to do."

Controlled again, his voice dropped confidentially.

"Listen, doc. Keep this quiet, but the grand jury is going to give me an indictment against Tanner. He has had the city hall in his vest pocket long enough. I've been working on the case for months, and I've got the evidence to turn him out. Can't you fix me up, doc, so I can go on?"

"Not much that I can do," Venwick said gravely. "I'm afraid you'll have to slow up, Bill—or pay the penalty."

"Then I'll pay it, if I must." Platt's gray hawk face was stern with righteous determination. "But I'm going to hang that gun moll, first, and put Tanner and his grafting gang where they belong."

Dr. Venwick's warning was the first jolt, and Stella administered the second. On his way to the courtroom, Platt found her waiting in his office. Stella had been the first Mrs. Platt. But it was six years since he had seen her, now, and at first he scarcely knew her.

Stella was the only daughter of his former law partner, old Murray Staples. She had been only a slim, dark-haired girl, when they were married. They didn't get on. She was extravagant and irresponsible, from the very first, and she soon took up with a fast crowd. Finally he discovered that she had made a week-end trip to Kansas City with Arthur Tanner, when she was supposed to be visiting her invalid aunt. Tanner was already an enemy of Platt's, and this transgression was beyond forgiveness. He divorced her, and he hadn't seen her since. Now she was waiting in a chair by his desk; a blond, hard-enameled, artificial stranger. Her eyebrows were penciled sharply, her lashes dark with mascara, her lips a hard perfect bow. She lazily crushed a red-stained cigarette, and gave him a cold languid hand.

"Why, Bill dear, you look almost ill." Her suave husky voice was as artificial as the color of her hair. "Aren't you glad to see your little darling Stellabel?"

Platt winced from the deliberate mockery of that old pet name, and frowned at the reek of gin on her breath. He closed his mind against the aching memories the name recalled. It was impossible to believe he had ever called this cold stranger by such a name.

"I'm already late for court, Stella." He remained standing. "If you want to see me, you'll have to come back later."

Her throaty voice turned hard.

"Better give me a few minutes, Bill."

"What do you want?"

She inhaled deliberately through another long cigarette.

"You're sitting pretty, Billy," she drawled through blue smoke. "I read all about you in the paper. You're going to hang Ysobel Pickens, and then you're going after my old pal Tanner." Platt winced again, from her hard-mouthed smile. "I want you to cut me into your little game. Willie—for a thousand dollars."

Platt blinked from the smoke in his eyes, and uttered an outraged gasp.

"So you've sunk to blackmail?" Just anger rang in his voice. "I might have given you something, Stella, for charity's sake, if you had explained your need. But I won't shake down. I've got a clean record, and you know it."

"Cool off, Billy." With calm insolence, she crossed mesh-stockinged legs. "I don't give a damn about your record. But I know all about the Claypool bonds. I can tell the newspapers a story that will upset your pretty little playhouse."

Platt sat down heavily, his face turning dark.

"You wouldn't dare," he protested hotly. "It was your own father who embezzled the Claypool bonds. I didn't find out till after I was in the partnership. Then I helped him pay back the money and hush the thing up. My conscience is clear."

"Damn your conscience and your record," she drawled. "I was your wife and the old man's daughter. I can tell a story that plenty of dumb but honest voters will believe."

Platt's gray face turned hard.

"Go ahead," he said harshly. "If you want to smear your own father's name, for spite. but you won't get one penny out of me. You'll find out that honest men don't pay blackmail." Something throbbed painfully in his temple. "You're playing with fire, Stella. You ought to know that I've made a career out of smashing evil." He stalked to open the door.

She put down the cigarette and slowly rose. Something had melted a little of her artificial hardness. Her crimson lip trembled. He saw the glint of a tear under her lashes.

"I guess you've done a pretty good job of smashing me already." Holding the door, Platt felt a momentary twinge of pity. But her drawling, insolent voice turned hard again. "Better think it over, Willie. You've got a lot to lose."

Platt shut the door and tried to quiet his fluttering pulse. Dr. Venwick had warned him not to get upset. Now his anger had turned him cold and ill. But he was in the right. He had settled generously with Stella, before he put her out of his life. Surely she wouldn't dare try anything. If she did, he grimly assured himself, she would go to prison.

Yet conscience nagged at him, faintly. Once he had loved slim, dark-eyed, little Stella Staples—though it was hard to see anything of her left in this cold, brittle, made-in-Hollywood product. He wondered just why she needed a thousand dollars. He felt a momentary impulse to call her back and try to talk things over in a more friendly way.

But he was already almost late for court.

The case was sensational. The stuffy, overheated courtroom was packed to the walls when Platt arrived, with spectators who had crowded in to see Ysobel Pickens on trial for her life. Most of them, he knew, expected him to get the death sentence he was fighting for.

Yet, many a citizen of Clifton felt a kind of pride in Ysobel Pickens, because her audacious exploits had put the little city on the map. The tellers in the Clifton National still proudly pointed out the bullet marks she had made when tipped-off officers trapped her gang there. Her last shot killed a deputy, and she was on trial for murder.

Her attorney was Arthur Tanner, Platt's old enemy. That was one cause of his determination to win a dramatic victory—it would make a good background for the coming indictment of Tanner himself.

Tanner was a big man, and still handsome in his rugged way, in spite of a paunch and thinning hair. Red from good living, his wide face was furrowed into a perpetual jolly smile, to which his shrewdly squinted eyes gave a cold contradiction. He was an affable speaker and a clever lawyer. Platt had had a long experience with his unscrupulous methods, and he had been a little worried by Tanner's seeming laxness in the defense of this case. He was still uneasily watchful for some unprincipled trick.

Late that afternoon, however, when Tanner rested for the defense, he had failed to score an important point. Platt was sure his case was won. This was a high point of his career, and he wanted to make the most of it. He was pleasantly aware of the big-city reporters at the tables arranged for them opposite the jury box, and he had got used to smiling into blinding flash guns.

It was five twenty when Platt rose to make his triumphant summation for the jury. His gray face was flushed with victory—yet something made him shiver as he addressed the court. The breathless tension of the moment made him cold and ill. The painful throb was back in his temple, his hands and feet felt clammy, and he wished he had a dose of bicarbonate. For a moment he stood dazed and voiceless.

"Gentlemen of the jury—" His voice came back. It was a mellifluous instrument, trained to carry sweet persuasion or tears of regret or gentle admonition or a storm of righteous wrath. "Gentlemen—look at this woman."

Ysobel Pickens, on Tanner's shrewd advice, was clothed in modest and becoming black. But her long fingernails were still defiantly red; and perhaps out of sheer panic she had used so much lipstick that her sullen, pouting lips were a scarlet wound in her terror-whitened face.

As she cringed beneath the jury's staring eyes, Platt had a vague disturbed sense that he had known her somewhere before. Conscience whispered uneasily. He wished for a moment that he had made a sympathetic effort to understand how she had become what she was. Suddenly he wondered if she had really earned the penalty of death.

Her dark, hollow eyes flashed him a look of trapped and helpless hate. But Tanner, beside her, appeared alarmingly unconcerned. Platt felt the stir of excitement that swept through the crowded room, and that doubtful whisper was forgotten. Once more he was the crusader, and Tanner was the champion of all wickedness.

"Look at her." His pliant voice held a practiced scorn. "Look through the rags and tatters of her soiled beauty, and you will see the ugly stain of evil on her sordid soul."

That touched the opening note he wanted. It woke the weather-beaten farmers and pink-scrubbed mechanics and oily-haired merchants in the jury box, and touched their complacent faces with just the right mixture of lust and disgust. His voice turned piously moderate again.

"Gentlemen, I would not be harsh or vengeful, and I know that you would not. But I believe in a Creator, gentlemen, as you do. I believe in Heaven, for good must be rewarded and the soul can never die. And I am old-fashioned enough to believe in Hell, for evil must be punished."

He saw the fat little smiles of self-righteous agreement. Ysobel Pickens dropped her head and started to whimper. But Tanner whispered some word of encouragement—Platt wondered uneasily what it might be—and she blew her nose and sat up straight and painted her lips defiantly. Platt waited a moment, to let the jurors see, and he noted their stiff disapproval.

"That is the law." Now his voice had a ring of iron. "And the law must be upheld for the preservation of society. Yes, gentlemen, for the protection of your homes and your dear ones."

On the wall, above Judge Prendick's sleepy snarl, the hands of the courtroom clock crept toward five twenty-two. Ysobel Pickens was shredding her sodden handkerchief, with terror-stiffened red-nailed fingers. But Tanner still kept his shrewd rugged smile.

"You have heard the evidence," Platt went on. "But let me recite to you once more the long catalogue of crimes, for which this unfortunate creature is doomed to pay. Let me paint the ugly picture—"

A disturbance interrupted him, in the rear of the courtroom. A newsboy was swiftly passing out papers. Judge Prendick woke and banged indignantly for order, and the sheriff started angrily after the intruding urchin. But then there was a sudden whispering stir among the newspapermen behind Platt, and flash bulbs blazed as he turned bewilderedly. Tanner came heavily to him, with a mocking challenge in his red perpetual smile, and thrust a damp extra into his hands. Platt read the screaming banner:

EX-WIFE ACCUSES D. A.

Mrs. Stella Flanders of Hollywood, former wife of District Attorney Platt, today filed suit in civil court for an accounting of the estate of her deceased father, Murray Staples, who was Platt's law partner before his death ten years ago. Platt was executor of the estate, and Mrs. Flanders alleges that certain bonds, left in trust for her, were never accounted for. She is represented in this action by Tanner & Higgens. Tanner told reporters, this afternoon, that criminal charges against the district attorney are expected to develop from the civil case.

Platt crumpled the paper, in hands turned suddenly numb. Now he understood Tanner's expectant smile. This paper was the *Chronicle,* controlled by the city hall gang. Tanner had seized upon Stella's desperate story and fashioned it into a conscienceless trick to save his client and damage Platt's reputation.

It was a lie. Platt wanted to shout out the truth. But the clock on the wall was only three minutes fast. Its crawling hands came to five twenty-two, and Platt felt a band of agony close around his chest. His protesting voice was choked. He swayed and fell sprawling toward the empty witness box.

Platt knew that he was dying.

Faintly, as he fell, he was aware of mounting confusion in the courtroom. People surged about him, but their excited voices faded swiftly into empty distance. Flash bulbs burned dimly through a gray, thickening haze. Judge Prendick was hammering with an angry gavel, but the sound was somewhere far away. Even Platt's own chill and agony receded. A warm, numbing darkness blotted out all sensation.

But the crisis passed.

Platt could breathe again, and the clammy weakness was gone from his limbs. His head swiftly cleared. Somebody was helping him back to his feet—a trim, worried-looking stranger in gray. They pushed out of the noisy mob in front of the witness box, and the stranger guided him through the open door into the quiet of the empty jury room.

"Why . . . why, thanks," Platt gasped uncertainly. "Must have had a little stroke." He still felt confused and uneasy, and he clung to the gray stranger's arm. "But now I think . . . I feel all right, now."

"Then let's go."

The stranger made a hurried check mark on a little gray card, and put it back in his bulging brief case. He raked lean fingers through his thick dark hair, in a harassed combing gesture that seemed queerly familiar to Platt.

"Your call has come at a rather unfortunate time." Now the worried voice was oddly familiar, too. "We're working under a terrific load." The stranger smiled a quick, one-sided smile—a smile that Platt had known. "But don't be alarmed, William. Of course, the organization will do everything possible for you."

Platt backed against the wall and stared bewilderedly. In spite of the troubled frown, this man looked young and fit. He wore a freshly pressed gray business suit. In the lapel was a curious pin: a tiny broom, made of yellow gold. Platt tried desperately to place him.

"Come, William." He picked up the brief case and jerked his head in a confusing urgent gesture. "What's the matter—don't you know me?"

"I'm sorry." Platt shook his head. "I don't seem able—"

Then his searching eyes found the gold letters stamped on the side of the bulging brief case, *Murray Staples, Deputy Advocate.* He blinked, unbelievingly. He had been a pallbearer at Murray's funeral ten years ago. And the old man had been bald as an onion—but Platt had seen him make that worried gesture to comb back imaginary hair, a thousand times.

"Yes, I was once your partner," Staples told him. "I've been your advocate since I was called." He made an irritated frown. "Now it's time for us to go. I'm afraid your case is going to be a little difficult. You are to appear before Inspector Ballantine, and he is inclined to be severe."

Staples tugged impatiently at his sleeve, but Platt braced his sweat-chilled palms against the wall behind him and continued to stare unbelievingly.

"You've been called, that's all." Staples urged fretfully. "Come along. I'll explain as we go. The organization allows no dawdling."

"But I'm not dead." Platt's voice rose in baffled anger. "I don't *feel* dead." He discovered, in fact, that all the slowly gathering unease and depression of the last several months had lifted. "I feel remarkably well."

"That's the rule," Staples said. "Our organization demands efficiency, and efficiency demands physical vigor. Come."

"But I can't come now," Platt protested. "Just when Tanner's trying to pull another crooked stunt, to save the Pickens woman. I'll hang her yet. I'll smash Tanner's gang—and his rotten yellow paper. I'll give Stella a lesson she needs."

"I think you've been too harsh with my daughter, William," Staples said sadly. "I tried to persuade you to call her back, today at noon—for both your sakes. But you didn't hear me."

Platt gulped at his astonishment.

"But I did," he whispered. "I mean, I wanted to call her back—I thought it was just a whim of conscience."

"That's what conscience is," Staples told him. "The influence of our organization. You've been my client for ten years, William. I've done my best to guide you. But you were often very deaf."

He looked at the watch on his wrist with an anxious frown.

"Come, or we'll be late at the Station," he urged sharply. "Inspector Ballantine will be annoyed with any delay, and he already has an unfortunate bias against the legal profession."

"I'm not dead," Platt repeated. "I can't believe it."

Staples gestured impatiently toward the open courtroom door. Platt saw uneasily that photographers and jurors and the sheriff were still crowded in front of the witness box. There was something on the floor. He heard somebody calling an ambulance. Then a newspaper reporter snatched the telephone.

"The Call?" His excited words blurred into Platt's mind. "Gimme the desk.
. . . Mack, the D. A.'s dead! A darb of a story. He keeled over when he saw

the *Chronicle* extra—maybe it ain't all Tanner's imagination. Fuller's got the pix—a honey of Platt falling, with the rag in his hands. Juries being human, this ought to save the Pickens gal her neck. . . . O. K., I'll call back.''

Leaning weakly against the wall, Platt caught his breath and tried to get used to the idea. He didn't know what to expect. Actually, he had regarded his church membership as nothing more than a speculative investment, a sort of insurance against an uncertain contingency. Several urgent questions crossed his mind, but he wasn't sure just how to phrase them.

"You see?'' Staples' voice was growing sharp with vexation. "Now are you willing to come?''

"I guess I'm dead, all right," Platt admitted heavily.

He peered sharply at his old partner. There was no evidence of any angelic transfiguration. Murray Staples looked as grimly preoccupied as he had always been when an important case was about to go to an unfriendly jury. Faintly apprehensive, Platt inquired:

"What . . . what do you want with me?''

Staples made his hurried, one-sided smile.

"Should have explained," he said hastily. "I had forgotten how confusing this experience was for me. And I heard you affirming your belief in the existence of Heaven and our organization, just a few minutes ago. I suppose I was taking too much for granted.''

He frowned at his watch again and swung the heavy brief case nervously as he talked.

"You see, we are no longer in competition. The old rivalry was, no doubt, the natural outcome of a primitive culture; but any such arrangement must be too illogical and inefficient to survive in the modern world. The only practical solution, along the lines of efficient business co-operation, was a merger.''

"Merger?'' Platt blinked. "Between Heaven and . . . and your organization?''

"Exactly.'' Staples made a jerky nod. "Under the new arrangement, we have taken over a great many of the local activities that used to be handled directly from Above. In particular, we have charge of the functions of conscience and securing clearances—the old phrase for these activities was the salvation of souls.''

Platt gasped.

"You seem astonished," Staples said. "Yet the arrangement is logical and efficient. We get a higher percentage of first clearances than our competitors ever did—no doubt because our organization had had a great deal of experience in handling the gravest cases.

"Also, our own working conditions are very much improved, under the terms of the merger—especially since the modern labor organizers began to be called, and our organization was forced to accept the union shop. Terms of service are shorter. In fact, our employees have been earning their clearances so rapidly, under the new contract, that the organization is very much understaffed.''

Platt nodded slowly, and made an uneasy little chuckle.

"Honoria's going to be surprised!''

"I'm afraid she is," Staples agreed. "Unfortunately, some excellent people are rather upset to discover that our organization is responsible for getting them into Heaven.''

''And you, Murray—'' Platt hesitated, suddenly afraid that the question would appear in bad taste.

''Yes, my clearance was suspended,'' Staples told him. ''But I hope to earn it, eventually, by securing clearances for my clients. Your case is my first to be called.''

''You mean—'' Platt gulped. ''You're my attorney?''

''The modern term is deputy advocate,'' Staples said. ''I've worked faithfully on your case. I believe it is largely through my influence that you quit playing poker and joined the church.'' He swung the brief case impatiently. ''Now are you willing to come with me?''

''Of course.'' But Platt licked his dry lips, and swallowed uneasily. ''Do you think—'' He peered anxiously at Staples: ''I mean . . . do you think—''

''Frankly, I wish you hadn't been so deaf to my advice.'' That harassed combing gesture showed that Staples was worried. ''But I haven't had much experience, and it's hard to tell how a case will come out. You see, they're always changing the conditions of admission. Not long ago, for instance, it was practically impossible to clear a woman with bobbed hair; but now, since Veronica Lake, they see you can't clear one who lets it grow. Ready?''

Platt turned back to the jury room door, for a final hasty look across the courtroom. Judge Prendick had recessed the court. Platt had a glimpse of Tanner helping Ysobel Pickens to her feet—and he wished uncomfortably that they had looked a little more sorrowful. Sheriff Dixon was escorting Dr. Venwick down the crowded aisle, followed by two men with a rolled stretcher.

''All right,'' Platt agreed nervously. ''Let's go.''

With a hurried nod, Staples touched the little golden broom on his gray lapel. He gripped the brief case, and caught Platt's arm.

''Better watch your step before Ballantine,'' he warned. ''The inspectors are a peculiar type. Mostly former policemen and judges. They've all earned their own clearances—that was stipulated in the contract—but they prefer not to use them. They've found paradise, right here on the job.''

Platt felt a sudden nightmarish certainty that his clothing had been left behind, on the courtroom floor. He shivered at the thought of appearing before Inspector Ballantine in nothing at all.

Looking down at himself, however, he was reassured as well as surprised to discover that he had on a crisp gray business suit, of the same cut and color as Staples'. It struck him, too, that his figure seemed trimmer than it had been for a good many years—the old double-breasted serge would hardly have fitted him now, anyhow.

''A small example of our efficiency,'' Staples commented. ''No doubt you will find customs very different Above. But our organization has adopted a uniform business suit, to be worn by every individual until clearance is secured.''

Platt was scarcely aware that they had left the jury room. But now he saw that they were on a wide flight of marble steps, before an impressive building. He supposed that it must stand on the summit of a high mountain, for the steps dropped into cottonlike mist, and white clouds stretched away in a bright, mysterious plain, under a sky turning gloomy with the dusk.

The building might have been designed by Norman Bel Geddes, for some super-colossal Hollywood production. Concealed floodlights painted its facade with garish color, and immense shining letters marched across the central tower, spelling: ETERNITY STATION.

A good many people were hurrying eagerly up the broad, golden-lit stair, and almost as many were hastening feverishly down again. Nearly all the men wore neat gray suits. The women had on uniform dark skirts, but he noticed that femininity had managed to express itself in a variety of bright-colored blouses.

"Come along." Staples urged. "The inspector is inclined to be nasty about any delay."

Platt followed him up the steps, into an immense waiting room. Hurried people were gathering into impatient queues. Many of them, both men and women, were burdened with heavy brief cases, and he supposed that they were devil's advocates—no, the modern term was "deputy"—looking after the interests of their clients.

"There's the ship." Staples made an offhand gesture, but his dry voice held a note of frustrated longing. He took a quick look at his watch. "There's still time for you to catch it—if we get your clearance through."

Platt gasped when he saw the ship, lying immense beyond a long row of guarded turnstiles. It was shaped somewhat like a blimp, but larger and much more substantial. It had a painful silvery shimmer; and some golden emblem on the side of the hull, was so blindingly brilliant that Platt could not distinguish it. People were filing into the vessel, up long, gaily draped gangways.

Walking briskly, Staples made a wide, hurried gesture.

"All this is new," he said. "Our design. Streamlined for service. Our contract covers everything at this end of the line."

Platt followed him across the vast crowded floor. His whole life since babyhood—at least in theory—had been planned to fit him for this supreme approaching moment. Yet, as it drew nearer, he felt a shudder of reluctant dread. He squared his shoulders, and tried to quiet his hammering pulse.

Staples stopped outside a frosted glass door which bore a neat brass plate:

Petitions for Clearance
N to R
J. A. Ballantine, Inspector

In a moment the door swung open. Two young men in identical gray emerged hastily, one carrying the brief case of an advocate. He appeared crestfallen, and his client looked pale and shaken.

"Next case," a deep voice boomed. "Eternity *vs*. William Platt."

* * *

Staples led the way nervously into a small square office. Inspector Ballantine sat behind a formidable desk, with a telephone at his elbow. He was an immense, bull-necked man, with an ugly genial face and steel-colored eyes. He took a blue card out of a wire basket, and asked in a too-soft interrogative voice:

"William Platt, attorney of Clifton? You want a clearance?"

Platt had been expecting to be asked some such question, since he was five years old. Even in early childhood, it had occurred to him that he would like to be a lawyer, so that he might be amply prepared to make his reply as fluent and convincing as possible. Yet now, when the awful question had been put to him at last, he was suddenly unable to utter any sound at all. He was mutely grateful for the presence of his advocate.

"Yes, inspector, this is Mr. Platt." Staples stepped briskly forward, set his bulging brief case on the end of the desk, and took out a thick mass of papers in a blue folder. "Perhaps you remember me, inspector?"

The steel eyes shifted to Staples, and the genial mouth smiled.

"Staples," the inspector recalled briefly. "Ten years ago. Clearance suspended—matter of bonds in trust. What progress are you making?"

Staples fumbled with his papers, visibly nervous.

"My first case, inspector."

"Good luck," Ballantine said curtly. "Proceed."

"My client's record." Staples pushed the blue folder across the table. "In full for the ten years that I have been his advocate, with a summary of his previous record from the files of our organization."

The inspector riffled hastily through the onion-skin pages. Staples caught his breath, and went on in a voice slightly too loud:

"You will see that Mr. Platt was a useful and respected citizen, a church member in good standing and a frequent contributor to worthy charities. He proved an enemy of evil in every guise. He was elected to the office of district attorney on a reform ticket, and only his calling prevented him from carrying out his campaign promise of a general clean-up."

The inspector nodded and referred to his blue card again.

"Our own records show that the petitioner was exceptionally zealous in his attacks upon what he regarded as evil," he said softly. "Yet I find that we have three very grave charges against him."

Staples raked a worried hand through his hair. He started to say something, thought better of it, and began nervously snapping and opening the catch of his brief case. The inspector paralyzed him with an annoyed steel glance.

Platt suddenly wanted to sit down. He looked uneasily about for a chair, and found none. Above the desk he discovered a sign which exhorted, *Don't Delay Eternity*. He waited uncomfortably. Ballantine read from the blue card, in his restrained velvet voice:

"The first charge dates from nearly twenty years ago, when the petitioner had just begun his law practice in Clifton. In one of his first cases—a civil action involving the ownership of forty rods of fence—he was opposed by another young attorney. He lost the case, through perjury. But he was later able to prove that his legal opponent had suborned the witnesses in the case, and he caused him to be suspended from the bar.

"The other lawyer was a young and able man. He might otherwise have enjoyed a distinguished and useful career. That suspension, however, denied to him for several years his right to the honorable practice of his chosen profession, and he was driven into crooked politics. Arthur Tanner is now a man whose clearance will be difficult."

"Tanner?" Platt suddenly found an indignant voice. "Why, inspector, that man's a worthless and conscienceless crook. I've fought him for twenty years. Why, he broke up my first marriage. And it was another dirty dishonest trick that caused my . . . er, calling."

The steel eyes were ruthless.

"Nevertheless, the petitioner is responsible."

"My client is overwrought." Staples was hovering uneasily. "Please overlook his outburst."

"Here is a second damaging act." Ballantine consulted his blue card again. "Ten years ago, the petitioner employed an office girl. He soon discovered that she had taken a small sum of money from the office cash. He discharged her, and reported her error to a business bureau in the city.

"This girl was attractive and intelligent and she might otherwise have found a successful business career. Because of the petitioner's act, however, she was unable to obtain other honest employment and she became a criminal. At our latest report, Ysobel Pickens was on trial for murder. She will be very hard to clear."

"I remember—I thought she looked familiar." Platt caught his breath. "Her name was Ann Pickens, then. She took seven dollars to buy a party dress. She was frightened when I accused her. She cried and promised to put the money back on pay day." He looked into Ballantine's steel eyes and his voice rose protestingly. "But that was such a small thing, inspector—and it happened so long ago."

"The consequences were not small," Ballantine said softly. "The petitioner is responsible."

He picked up the blue card again.

"The third charge is still more grave," he went on ominously. "Some nine years ago, the petitioner married. His wife was younger than he. She had tastes and whims of which he disapproved. Eventually—and that as a result of his severe and uncompromising attitude—she was guilty of an act for which he divorced her.

"This woman was beautiful and gifted and she might otherwise have been a loyal wife and a noble mother. As a consequence of the petitioner's acts, however, Stella Flanders has by now accumulated charges against her record which make her clearance very doubtful."

"Stella?" Platt swallowed an angry breath. "She tried to blackmail me out of a thousand dollars, just today. And she cooked up a malicious libel about me for Tanner's yellow newspaper."

"But you are responsible." Inspector Ballantine's velvet voice had become inexorable. "Now you have heard the charges against you. You have the right to speak. William Platt, is there any reason why you should not be remanded to Hell, so that you may atone for these acts?''

Platt started. Cold sweat sprang out on his forehead. His voice was gone again and he could find no answer. He looked to his advocate in mute appeal. But Staples made a nervous shrug, as if to show that he could do nothing, and began to gather up his papers. Ballantine cleared his throat and said heavily:

''The petitioner fails to answer. Clearance suspended.''

Platt wasn't sure just what the words implied, but their ominous ring made him feel a little ill. He clutched the edge of the desk, with weak, clammy fingers, and helplessly watched Staples replace the papers in his brief case.

Inspector Ballantine banged a rubber stamp down on the blue card and tossed it into another tray. He nodded impatiently at the sign over his head and picked up another card and boomed at the door:

''Next case. Eternity *vs*. Martha Potts.''

Numb and shaken, Platt followed his advocate out of the inspector's tiny office as Martha Potts came in. She was a large colored woman, still smelling faintly of laundry soap, accompanied by a dapper Negro advocate in gray. Her chocolate face was beaming, and she greeted him with a joyous:

''Hallelujah, brother!''

Platt looked despondently across the immense waiting room. Beyond the guarded gates, the elect were still streaming up into that mighty refulgent ship. He caught a distant, haunting chord of celestial music. Slowly, with a cold, sick feeling in his middle, he turned to follow Staples back toward the stair.

''What happens to me now?'' he inquired uneasily.

Staples made a sympathetic clucking sound.

''I know how you feel, William. It's depressing to be turned back, I know. But you'll soon find your niche in our organization. Clients will be assigned to you. If you manage to clear them, your own clearance will be issued at once. If you fail, the contract provides for earning credit by office work, but that's a rather tedious process.'' He chuckled with a hollow cheer. ''They say the first thousand years are the longest.''

As a joke, that was not successful.

''Of course''—Staples tried to be encouraging—''it is possible to appeal, if you aren't satisfied with the ruling. But you must consider that the motion might be denied. Then some of your own clients might come up before Ballantine in the future—and he is inclined to be nasty about appeals.''

Platt couldn't think of anything worth saying. He turned back for a final hopeless look at the long shining ship beyond the gates. Staples waited impatiently and at last he came on with dragging feet.

''I'm sorry,'' he said after a moment. ''I mean . . . I suppose it would have counted toward your own clearance, if I had gone through?''

''Never mind.'' Staples made a wry, one-sided grin. ''You did very well, for a lawyer.'' He looked at his watch, and raked worried fingers through his hair. ''Come along—we're already overdue at the office.''

They had come back upon the broad marble steps, golden under the floodlights, that dropped into that bright mysterious ocean of moonlit cloud. Staples touched the little golden broom on his lapel, and once more took Platt's arm.

Then they were standing on a sharp volcanic spur in the midst of a bleak landscape that fitted Platt's idea of Death Valley. The high moon shimmered on white lakes of salt. Dark eroded mountains rose jagged and treeless beyond. Grotesque lava shapes were black with the stain of fire, but Platt shivered a little from a penetrating chill in the air.

"I'll take a moment to show you our new office building." Staples pointed, and his voice had a ring of pride. "Just completed. You'll find it the last word in modern business efficiency."

Platt turned to look, and his mouth fell slack. A tremendous gray skyscraper towered startingly out of a black lava flow. Lighted windows drew his eyes up, floor on floor, to a red torch that burned luridly on a lofty tower. Tall crimson letters, along the cornice, flashed, SATAN SAVES.

Staples touched the golden broom again, and they were upon a wide, crowded sidewalk outside the building—only now, strangely enough, the skyscraper was somehow squeezed into the heart of Clifton. For he recognized the *Chronicle* office, across the dusky street; and he could read a familiar sign in flaking gold letters on a second-story window:

Staples & Platt
Attorneys of Law

Staples was already tugging at his sleeve. But he paused again, for a glimpse of the deep-carved inscription on the tower's massive cornerstone:

Erected, 1941
Central Office, American Division,
HADES
(High Administration of
Development, Education, and
Salvation)
A. Lucifer, Manager

Staples pulled him into a torrent of worried, hurried men and women, all burdened with heavy brief cases, and they were swept into a foyer of cold-looking chromium and glass, surrounding a huge illuminated terrestrial globe. They were fighting toward the elevators, when Staples stopped with a gasp of awe.

"There's the manager!" he whispered. "I heard that he was coming today, but I didn't hope to see him. He is going to address a convention of vice presidents."

A tall man in black hurried across the lobby in front of them, flanked by two or three nervous subordinates in identical gray. His sleek-combed hair was gray at the temples, and thinning. He wore the overconfident, extravert smile of a good bond salesman or a successful evangelist. Platt heard one of the subordinates murmur, too heartily:

"Yes, Mr. Lucifer. Yes, sir!"

The party went by. Staples broke out of his awed paralysis, and dragged Platt into a crowded automatic elevator. It shot them to the ninety-eighth floor. Staples pushed through a door lettered

District V-913

and stopped to punch a time clock.

They came into a long immense room, flooded with a merciless glare from fluorescent bulbs. An endless corridor separated two rows of fenced-in desks. Gray-clad men and uniformed girls were furiously busy, and the din of their activities made Platt want to cover his ears.

Typewriters clattered and telephones jangled. Teletypes, card sorters, dictographs, bookkeeping machines, all added their bit to the general pandemonium. Tense-faced men in gray shouted at flustered stenographers. Office boys darted here and there.

Platt bravely tried to grin, and called at Staples:

"Well, this isn't Heaven!"

But Staples didn't hear. He ran to touch the elbow of a hastening man with a white carnation in his buttonhole. Platt recognized him: Justice Bonafax, a former member of the State supreme bench, notorious for the undeviating uprighteousness of his decisions.

"Chief, Mr. Platt," Staples gasped hastily. "He's with us, from today. Mr. Bonafax is nine-hundred-and-thirteenth vice president, in charge of our district office."

"Glad to have you, Mr. Platt." Bonafax hastily pumped his hand. "Hades needs more men like you. I want you to feel that our whole organization is just one big, happy family, Mr. Platt. The staff will make you feel at home. And don't forget our district slogan, *Service First.*"

He turned quickly to Staples.

"Oh, Mr. Staples. I have good news for you. I understand that you are going to continue with the organization indefinitely, now. Or course, that means that you will be transferred to office work—although you will be allowed time to carry on the necessary field work in behalf of your remaining clients. You will be glad to know that we have an unusual opening ready for you. Mr. Bishop got his clearance today, and you will take his place as manager of Section R. Mr. Platt will begin under you."

"Thank you, Mr. Bonafax." Staples' voice was too warmly grateful. "This is a splendid opportunity, and I'm going to try to make the most of it."

Bonafax slapped his back.

"You see, Mr. Platt," he beamed, "we're all just one great big happy family. Mr. Staples, see that you don't neglect our service slogan." He jerked out a watch. "Now I've got to run, to catch the convention. The manager's here, himself, to give us a pep talk."

He hurried on toward the elevators and Staples guided Platt down the busy aisle, through the pandemonium of strained voices and clattering machines. Near the end of the immense room, a low barrier surrounded Section R—which was one large desk, facing a dozen smaller ones.

Two or three girls were typing furiously, at the smaller desks. A teletype machine clanked and whirred. A man in gray was frowning in baffled concentration over a bulky mimeographed document, which looked to Platt as if it might have been compiled for the regulation of something or other by one of the alphabetical agencies in Washington.

"Here we are, William."

Staples pointed to one of the smaller desks. A little bronze plaque on it was already neatly lettered:

WILLIAM PLATT
DEPUTY ADVOCATE

Paper, pencils, clips, and erasers were arranged in neat little stacks. The letter tray held a new brief case, with his name stamped on it.

"That's efficiency." Staples had seen his surprise. "Our employees have no time to waste." He pinned a little golden broom into Platt's gray lapel. "This is your badge of 'Service First' and your means of transportation about your strictly business duties—you are not permitted to use it for joyriding."

Against the endless rush of sound, he shouted at the nearest busy girl, a thin peroxide blonde abstractedly chewing gum.

"Miss Hamlett! This is our new Mr. Platt." She looked up briefly, with a vague dreamy nod—as if her inner mind still dwelt upon the robust charms of Clark Gable. "Miss Hamlett will take your reports."

"Call me Mabel." Her voice was a listless nasal drawl. She looked back at her propped-up notebook, and her red-nailed fingers never paused or faltered in their furious tattoo upon her keyboard.

"Your assignment should be here, William," Staples said, "I'll check the teletype."

Platt sat down at the neat new desk, and began to chew the eraser off a freshly sharpened pencil. He felt bewildered and despondent. The noise and hurry and tension of these vast offices gave him a bitter nostalgia for the small-town quiet of Clifton.

"I know it ain't Heaven, Mr. Platt." The nasal blonde laid a small yellow card on his desk. "But keep your chin up. You ain't the only one. Look at me—a five-strike, all over a no-good palooka that didn't care two cents about me."

"Thanks, Miss . . . Mabel."

Platt tried to smile. After all, the activities of a deputy advocate might prove to have a certain interest. And, if he had good luck with his clients, he might soon be out of this altogether. He remembered that bright mysterious ship, with a dull ache of longing.

"Here's your assignment, Mr. Platt, just off the teletype."

Platt took up the card, and read the names of his new clients. He shivered. The yellow oblong blurred. He couldn't breathe. The office din broke over him, in overwhelming waves of sound.

"What's the matter?" Hovering sympathetically, Mabel forgot her gum. "D'they hand you tough ones?"

"I'm afraid they did." Platt's voice came shaken and husky. "I couldn't get these people past Inspector Ballantine, in a thousand years." He looked hopefully toward the section manager's desk, where Staples was now surrounded with madly clamoring telephones. "Is there . . . can I get the assignments changed?"

"Not a chance." Mabel shook her thin peroxide locks. "They hand you a line about efficiency and office discipline. No, Mr. Platt, you just gotta take what they give you." She shrugged her narrow shoulders, philosophically. "After all, this ain't Heaven."

"I see it isn't," Platt said heavily. He read the yellow card again:

OFFICE MEMO

TO: William Platt, Deputy Advocate
CLIENTS ASSIGNED: Ysobel Pickens, Stella Flanders, and Arthur Tanner.

THE END.

JAMES H. SCHMITZ

Greenface

"What I don't like," the fat sport said firmly—his name was Freddie Something—"is snakes! That was a whopping, mean-looking snake that went across the path there, and I ain't going another step nearer the icehouse!"

Hogan Masters, boss and owner of Masters Fishing Camp on Thursday Lake, made no effort to conceal his indignation.

"What you don't like," he said, his voice a trifle thick, "is work! That li'l garter snake wasn't more than six inches long. What you want is for me to carry all the fish up there alone while you go off to the cabin and take it easy—"

Freddie was already on his way to the cabin. "I'm on vacation!" he bellowed back happily. "Gotta save my strength! Gotta 'cuperate!"

Hogan glared after him, opened his mouth and shut it again. Then he picked up the day's catch of bass and walleyes and swayed on toward the icehouse. Usually a sober young man, he'd been guiding a party of fishermen from one of his light-housekeeping cabins over the lake's trolling grounds since early morning. It was hot work in June weather and now, at three in the afternoon, Hogan was tanked to the gills with iced beer.

He dropped the fish between chunks of ice under the sawdust, covered them up and started back to what he called the lodge—an old, two-story log structure taken over from the previous owners and at present reserved for himself and a few campers too lazy even to do their own cooking.

When he came to the spot where the garter snake had given Freddie his excuse to quit, he saw it wriggling about spasmodically at the edge of a clump of weeds, as if something hidden in there had caught hold of it.

Hogan watched the tiny reptile's struggles for a moment, then squatted down carefully and spread the weeds apart. There was a sharp buzzing like the ghost of a rattler's challenge, and something slapped moistly across the back of his hand, leaving a stinging sensation as if he had reached into a cluster of nettles. At the same moment, the snake disappeared with a jerk under the plants.

The buzzing continued. It was hardly a real sound at all—more like a thin, quivering vibration inside his head and decidedly unpleasant! Hogan shut his eyes tight and shook his head to drive it away. He opened his eyes again, and found himself looking at Greenface.

Nothing even faintly resembling Greenface had ever appeared before in any of Hogan's weed patches, but at the moment he wasn't greatly surprised. It hadn't, he decided at once, any real face. It was a shiny, dark-green lump, the size and shape of a goose egg, standing on end among the weeds; it was pulsing regularly like a human heart; and across it ran a network of thin, dark lines that seemed to form two tightly shut eyes and a closed, faintly smiling mouth.

Like a fat little smiling idol in green jade—Greenface it became for Hogan then and there! With alcoholic detachment, he made a mental note of the cluster of fuzzy strands like hair roots about and below the thing. Then—somewhere underneath and blurred as though seen through milky glass—he discovered the snake, coiled up in a spiral and still turning with labored, writhing motions as if trying to swim in a mass of gelatin.

Hogan put his hand out to investigate this phenomenon, and one of the rootlets lifted as if to ward off his touch. He hesitated, and it flicked down, withdrawing immediately and leaving another red line of nettle-burn across the back of his hand.

In a moment, Hogan was on his feet, several yards away. A belated sense of horrified outrage overcame him—he scooped up a handful of stones and hurled them wildly at the impossible little monstrosity. One thumped down near it; and with that, the buzzing sensation in his brain stopped.

Greenface began to slide slowly away through the weeds, all its rootlets wriggling about it, with an air of moving sideways and watching Hogan over a nonexistent shoulder. He found a chunk of wood in his hand and leaped in pursuit—and it promptly vanished.

Hogan spent another minute or two poking around in the vegetation with his club raised, ready to finish it off wherever he found it lurking. Instead, he discovered the snake among the weeds and picked it up.

It was still moving, though quite dead; the scales peeling away from the wrinkled flabby body. Hogan stared at it, wondering. He held it by the head, and the pressure of his finger and thumb, the skull within gave softly, like leather. It became suddenly horrible to feel—and then the complete inexplicability of the grotesque affair broke in on him.

Hogan flung the dead snake away with a wide sweep of his arm. He went back of the icehouse and was briefly, but thoroughly, sick.

Julia Allison leaned on her elbows over the kitchen table, studying a mail-order catalogue, when Hogan walked unsteadily into the lodge. Julia had dark-brown hair, calm gray eyes, and a wicked figure. She and Hogan had been engaged for half a year; Hogan didn't want to get married until he was sure he could make a success out of Masters Fishing Camp, which was still in its first season.

Julia glanced up smiling. The smile became a stare. She closed the catalogue.

"Hogan!" she stated, in the exact tone of her pa, Whitey Allison, refusing a last one to a customer in Whitey's liquor store in town, "you're plain drunk! Don't shake your head—it'll slop out your ears!"

"Julia—" Hogan began excitedly.

She stepped up to him and sniffed, wrinkling her nose. *"Pfaah!* Beer! Yes, darling?"

"Julia, I just saw something—a sort of crazy little green spook—"

Julia blinked twice.

"Look, infant," she said soothingly, "that's how people get talked about! Sit down and relax while I make up coffee, black. There's a couple came in this morning, and I stuck them in the end cabin. They want the stove tanked with kerosene, ice in the icebox, and wood for a barbecue—I fixed them up with linen."

"Julia," Hogan inquired hoarsely, "are you going to listen to me or not?"

Her smile vanished. "Now you're yelling!"

"I'm *not* yelling. And I don't need coffee. I'm trying to tell you—"

"Then do it without shouting!" Julia replaced the cover on the coffee can with a whack that showed her true state of mind, and gave Hogan an abused look which left him speechless.

"If you want to stand there and sulk," she continued immediately, "I might as well run along—I got to help pa in the store tonight." That meant he wasn't to call her up.

She was gone before Hogan, struggling with a sudden desire to shake his Julia up and down for some time, like a cocktail, could come to a decision. So he went instead to see to the couple in the end cabin. Afterward he lay down bitterly and slept it off.

When he woke up, Greenface seemed no more than a vague and very uncertain memory, an unaccountable scrap of afternoon nightmare—due to the heat, no doubt! *Not* to the beer: on that point Hogan and Julia remained in disagreement, however completely they became reconciled otherwise. Since neither was willing to bring the subject up again, it didn't really matter.

The next time Greenface was seen, it wasn't Hogan who saw it.

In mid-season, on the twenty-fifth of June, the success of Masters Fishing Camp looked pretty well assured. Whitey Allison was hinting he'd be willing to advance money to have the old lodge rebuilt, as a wedding present. When Hogan came into camp for lunch everything was nice and peaceful, but before he got to the lodge steps, a series of piercing feminine shrieks from the direction of the north end cabin swung him around, running.

Charging up to the cabin with a number of startled camp guests strung out behind him, Hogan heard a babble of excited talk shushed suddenly and emphatically within. The man who was vacationing there with his wife appeared at the door.

"Old lady thinks she's seen a ghost, or something!" he apologized with an embarrassed laugh. "Nothing you can do. I . . . . I'll quiet her down, I guess—"

Waving the others away, Hogan ducked around behind the cabin and listened shamelessly. Suddenly the babbling began again. He could hear every word of it.

"I did so see it! It was sort of blue and green and wet—and it had a green face and it s-s-smiled at me! It fl-floated up a tree and disappeared! Oh—G-G-Georgie!''

Georgie continued to make soothing sounds. But before nightfall, he came into the lodge to pay his bill.

"Sorry, old man," he said—he still seemed more embarrassed than upset—"I can't imagine what the little woman saw but she's got her mind made up, and we gotta go home. You know how it is. I sure hate to leave, myself!''

Hogan saw them off with a sickly smile. Uppermost among his own feelings was a sort of numbed, horrified vindication. A ghost that was blue and green and wet and floated up trees and disappeared, was a far from exact description of the little monstrosity he'd persuaded himself he *hadn't* seen—but still too near it to be a coincidence. Julia, driving out from town to see him next day, didn't think it was a coincidence, either.

"You couldn't possibly have told that hysterical old goose about the funny little green thing you thought you saw? She got confidential in the liquor store last night, and her hubby couldn't hush her. Everybody was listening. That sort of stuff won't do the camp any good, Hogan!''

Hogan looked helpless. If he told her about the camp haunt, she wouldn't believe him anyhow. And if she did, it would scare her silly.

"Well?" she urged suspiciously.

Hogan sighed. "Never spoke more than a dozen words with the woman—"

Julia seemed miffed but puzzled. There was a peculiar oily hothouse smell in the air when Hogan walked up to the road with her and watched her start back to town in her ancient car, but with a nearly sleepless night behind him, he wasn't as alert as he might have been. He was recrossing the long, narrow meadow between the road and the camp before the extraordinary quality of that odor struck him. And then, for the second time, he found himself looking at Greenface—at a bigger Greenface and not a better one.

About sixty feet away, up in the birches on the other side of the meadow, it was almost completely concealed: an indefinable oval of darker vegetable green in the thick foliage. Its markings were obscured by the leaf shadows among which it lay motionless except for that sluggish pulsing.

Hogan stared at it for long seconds while his scalp crawled and his heart hammered a thudding alarm into every fiber of his body. What scared him was its size—that oval was as big as a football; it had been growing at a crazy rate since he saw it last!

Swallowing hard, he mopped off the sweat that was starting out on his forehead while he walked on stiffly toward the lodge. Whatever it was, he didn't want to scare it off! He had an automatic shotgun slung above the kitchen door, for emergencies; and a dose of No. 2 shot would turn this particular emergency into a museum specimen—

Around the corner of the lodge, he went up the entrance steps four at a time. A few seconds later, with the gun in his hands and reaching for a handful of shells, he shook his head to drive a queer soundless buzzing out of his ears. Instantly, he remembered when he'd experienced that sensation before and wheeled toward the screened kitchen window.

The big birch trembled slightly as if horrified to see a huge spider with jade-green body and blurred cluster of threadlike legs flow down along its trunk. Twelve feet from the ground, it let go of the tree and dropped with the long bunched threads stretched straight down before it. Hogan grunted and blinked.

It happened before his eyes: at the instant the bunched tips hit the ground, Greenface was jarred into what could only be called a higher stage of visibility. There was no change in the head, but the legs abruptly became flat, faintly green-ish ribbons, flexible and semitransparent. Each about six inches wide and perhaps six feet long, they seemed attached in a thick fringe all around the lower part of the head, like a Hawaiian dancer's grass skirt. They showed a bluish gloss wher-ever the sun struck them, but Greenface didn't wait for closer inspection.

Off it went, swaying and gliding swiftly on the ends of these foot ribbons into the woods beyond the meadow. For all the world, it *did* look like a conventional ghost, the ribbons glistening in a luxurious winding sheet around the area where a body should have been, but wasn't! No wonder that poor woman—

He found himself giggling helplessly. Forcing himself to stop, he laid the gun upon the kitchen table. Then he tried to control the shaking of his hands long enough to get a cigarette going.

Long before the middle of July, every last tourist had left Masters Fishing Camp in a more or less perturbed condition. Vaguely, Hogan sensed it was un-fortunate that two of his attempts to dispose of Greenface had been observed while his quarry remained unseen. It wasn't, of course, his fault if the creature chose to exercise an uncanny ability to become almost completely invisible at will—noth-ing more than a tall, glassy blur which flickered off through the woods and was gone. And it wasn't until he drove into town one evening that he realized just how unfortunate that little trick was, nevertheless, for him.

Whitey Allison's greeting seemed brief and chilly, while Julia delayed putting in an appearance for almost half an hour. Hogan waited patiently enough.

"You might pour me a Scotch," he suggested at last.

Whitey passed him a significant look.

"Better lay off the stuff," he advised heavily. Hogan flushed red.

"What you mean by that?"

"There's plenty of funny stories going around about you right now!" Whitey told him, blinking belligerently. Then he looked past Hogan, and Hogan knew Julia had come into the store behind him; but he was too angry to drop the matter there.

"What do you expect me to do about them?" he demanded.

"That's no way to talk to pa!"

Julia's voice was sharper than Hogan had ever heard it—he swallowed hard and tramped out of the liquor store without looking at her. Down the street he had a couple of drinks; and coming past the store again on the way to his car, he saw Julia behind the counter laughing and chatting with a group of summer residents. She seemed to be having a grand time; her gray eyes sparkled and there was a fine high color in her cheeks.

Hogan snarled out the worst word he knew and went on home. It was true he'd grown accustomed to an impressive dose of whiskey at night, to put him to sleep. At night, Greenface wasn't abroad and there was no sense in lying awake to wonder and worry about it. On warm, clear days around noon was the time to be on the alert; twice Hogan caught it basking in the treetops in full sunlight and each time took a long shot at it, which had no effect beyond scaring it into complete visibility. It dropped out of the tree like a rotten fruit and scudded off into the bushes, its foot ribbons weaving and flapping all about it.

Well, it all added up. Was it surprising if he seemed constantly on the watch for something nobody else could see? When the camp cabins grew empty one by one and stayed empty, Hogan told himself that he preferred it that way. Now he could devote all his time to tracking down that smiling haunt and finishing it off! Afterward would have to be early enough to repair the damage it had done his good name and bank balance.

He tried to keep Julia out of these calculations. Julia hadn't been out to the camp for weeks; and under the circumstances he didn't see how he could do anything now to patch up their misunderstanding.

After being shot at the second time, Greenface remained out of sight for so many days that Hogan almost gave up hunting for it. He tramped morosely down into the lodge cellar one afternoon and pulled a banana from a cluster he'd got from the wholesale grocer in town. Wedged in under the fruit he found the tiny mummified body of a hummingbird, some tropical species with a long curved beak and long ornamental tail feathers.

Except for beak and feathers, it would have been unrecognizable: bones, flesh and skin were shriveled together into a small lump of doubtful consistency, like dried gum. Hogan, reminded of the dead snake from which he had driven Greenface near the icehouse, handled it with fingers that shook a little. In part, at least, the hummingbird seemed to explain the origin of the camp spook.

Greenface was, of course, carnivorous, in some weird, out-of-the-ordinary fashion. The snake had been an indication, and since then birds of every type were growing shy around the camp, while red squirrels and chipmunks disappeared without trace. When that banana cluster was shipped from Brazil or some island in the Caribbean, Greenface—a seedling Greenface, very much smaller even than when Hogan first saw it—had come along with it, clinging to its hummingbird prey!

But during the transition, something—perhaps merely the touch of the colder North—must have removed some internal check on its growth which still seemed to be progressing in a jerky and unpredictable fashion. For though it appeared to lack any solid parts that might resist decomposition after death, creatures of such size and conforming to no recognizable pattern of either the vegetable or the animal kingdoms, couldn't very well be in existence anywhere without finally attract-ing human attention. Whereas, if they grew normally to be only a foot or two high in those luxuriant tropical places, they seemed intelligent and alert enough to escape observation—even discounting that inexplicable knack of turning transpar-ent from one second to the next!

HIs problem, meanwhile, was a purely practical one; and the next time he grew aware of the elusive hothouse smell near the lodge, he had a plan ready laid. His nearest neighbor, Peter Jeffries, who provided Hogan with most of his provisions from a farm two miles down the road to town, owned a hound by the name of Old Battler—a large, surly brute with a strain of Airedale in its make-up, and reputedly the best trailing nose in the county.

Hogan's excuse for borrowing Old Battler was a fat buck who'd made his head-quarters in the marshy ground across the bay. Pete had no objection to that sort of business. He whistled the hound in and handed him over to Hogan with a parting admonition to "keep an eye peeled for them damn game wardens!" Pete and Old Battler were the slickest pair of poachers for a hundred miles around.

The oily fragrance under the birches was so distinct that Hogan could almost have followed it himself. Unfortunately, it didn't mean a thing to the dog. Panting and growling as Hogan, cradling the shotgun, brought him up on a leash, Old Battler was ready for any type of quarry from rabbits to a pig-stealing bear; but he simply wouldn't or couldn't understand that he was to track down the bloodless vegetable odor to its source!

He walked off a few yards in the direction the thing had gone, nosing the grass; then, ignoring Hogan's commands, he returned to the birch, smelled carefully around its base and paused to demonstrate in unmistakable fashion what he thought of the scent. Finally he sat on his haunches and regarded Hogan with a baleful, puzzled eye.

There was nothing to do but take him back and tell Pete Jeffries the poaching excursion was off because the warden had put in an appearance. When Hogan got back to the lodge, he heard the telephone jingling above the cellar stairs and started for it with an eagerness that surprised himself.

"Hello!" he shouted into the mouthpiece. "Hello? Julia? That you?"

There was no answer from the other end. Hogan, listening, heard voices, sev-eral of them: people were laughing and talking. Then a door slammed faintly and someone called out: "Hi, Whitey! How's the old man?" She had called up from the liquor store all right, perhaps just to see what he was doing. He thought he could even hear the faint flutter of her breath.

"Julia," Hogan said softly, scared by the silence. "What's the matter, darling? Why don't you say something?"

Now he did hear her take a quick, deep breath. Then the receiver clicked down, and the line went dead.

The rest of the afternoon, he managed to keep busy cleaning out the cabins that had been occupied. Counting back to the day the last of them was vacated, he decided the reason nobody had arrived since was that a hostile Whitey Allison, in his strategic position at the town bus stop, was directing all tourist traffic to other camps. Not—Hogan assured himself again—that he wanted anyone around until he had solved his problem; it would only make matters worse.

But why had Julia called up? What did it mean?

That night the moon was full. Near ten o'clock, with no more work to do, Hogan settled down wearily on the lodge steps. Presently he lit a cigarette. His intention was to think matters out to some conclusion in the quiet night air, but all he seemed able to do was to tell himself uselessly, over and over again, that there *must* be some way of trapping that elusive green horror!

He pulled the sides of his face down slowly with his fingertips. "I gotta *do* something!"—the futile whisper seemed to have been running through his head all day: "Gotta *do* something! Gotta—" He'd be having a nervous collapse if he didn't watch out!

The rumbling barks of Jeffries' Old Battler began to churn up the night to the eastward—and suddenly Hogan caught the characteristic tinny stutter of Julia's little car as it turned down the road beyond the Jeffries farm and came rattling on in the direction of the camp.

The thrill that swung him to his feet was quenched at once by fresh doubts. Even if Julia was coming to tell him she'd forgiven him, he'd be expected to explain what was making him act like this. And he couldn't explain it! If she actually believed him, it might affect her mind. If she didn't, she'd think he was crazy or lying—he couldn't do it, Hogan decided despairingly. He'd have to send her away again!

He took the big flashlight down from its hook beside the door and started off forlornly to meet her when she would bring the car bumping along the path from the road. Then he realized that the car, past Jeffries' place but still a half mile or so away, had stopped.

He waited, puzzled. From a distance he heard the creaky shift of gears, a brief puttering of the motor—another shift and putter. Then silence. Old Battler was also quiet, probably listening suspiciously; though he, too, knew the sound of Julia's car. There was no one else to hear it; Jeffries had gone to the city with his wife that afternoon, and they wouldn't be back till late next morning.

Hogan frowned, flashing the light off and on against the moonlit side of the lodge. In the quiet, three or four whippoorwills were crying to each other with insane rapidity up and down the lake front. There was a subdued shrilling of crickets everywhere, and occasionally the threefold soft call of an owl dropped across the bay. He started reluctantly up the path toward the road.

The headlights were out, or he would have been able to see them from here. But the full moon sailed high, and the road was a narrow silver ribbon running straight down through the pines toward Jeffries' farmhouse.

Quite suddenly he discovered the car, drawn up beside the road and turned back toward town. It was Julia's car all right; and it was empty. Hogan walked slowly toward it, peering right and left, then jerked around with a start to a sudden crashing noise among the pines a hundred yards or so down off the road—a scrambling animal rush that seemed to be moving toward the lake. An instant later, Old Battler's angry roar told him the hound was running loose and had prowled into something it disapproved of down there.

He was still listening, trying to analyze the commotion, when a girl in a dark sweater and skirt stepped out quietly from the shadow of the roadside pines beyond him. Hogan didn't see her; he heard her cross the ditch to the road in a beautiful reaching leap. When he looked around, she was running like a rabbit for the car.

He yelped breathlessly: "Julia!"

For just an instant, Julia looked back at him, her face a pale, scared blur in the moonlight. Then the car door slammed shut behind her, and with a shiver and groan the old machine lurched into action. Hogan made no further attempt to stop her. Confused and unhappy, he watched the headlights sweep down the road until they swung out of sight around the corner behind Jeffries' farm.

"Now what the devil was *she* poking around here for?"

He sighed, shook his head and started back to the camp. There was a cool draft of air flowing up from the lake across the road, but Old Battler's vicious snarls were no longer audible on it. Hogan sniffed idly at the breeze, wondered at a faint, peculiar odor that tainted it, and sniffed again. Then, in a flash of apprehensive rage, he realized what had happened. Greenface was down in the pines somewhere—the hound had stirred it up, discovered it was alive and worth worrying, but lost it again and was now casting about silently to find its hiding place!

Hogan crossed the ditch in a jump that bettered Julia's, blundered into the wood and ducked just in time to avoid being speared in the eye by a jagged branch of asp. More cautiously he worked his way in among the trees, went sliding down a moldy incline, swore in exasperation as he tripped over a rotten trunk and was reminded thereby of the flashlight in his hand. He walked slowly across a moonlit clearing, listening, then found himself confronted by a dense cluster of evergreens and switched on the light.

It stabbed into a dark-green oval, bigger than a man's head, eight feet away.

He stared fascinated at the thing, expecting it to vanish. But Greenface made no move beyond a slow writhing among the velvety foot ribbons that supported it. It seemed to have grown again in its jack-in-the-box fashion; it was taller than Hogan and stooping slightly toward him. The lines on its pulsing head formed two tightly shut eyes and a wide, thin-lipped, insanely smiling mouth.

Gradually it was borne in upon Hogan that the thing was asleep! Or had been asleep—for in that moment, he became aware of a change in the situation through something like the buzzing escape of steam, a sound just too high to be audible, that throbbed through his head. Then he noticed that Greenface, swaying slowly, quietly, had come a foot or two closer, and he saw the tips of the foot ribbons grow dim and transparent as they slid over the moss toward him. A sudden horror of this stealthy approach seized him, draining the strength out of his body. Without thinking of what he did he switched off the light.

Almost instantly the buzzing sensation died away, and before Hogan had backed off to the edge of the moonlit clearing, he realized that Greenface had stopped its advance. Suddenly he understood.

Unsteadily he threw the beam on again and directed it full on the smiling face. For a moment there was no result; then the faint buzzing began once more in his brain, and the foot ribbons writhed and dimmed as Greenface came sliding forward. He snapped it off, and the thing grew still, solidifying.

Hogan began to laugh in silent hysteria. He had caught it now! Light brought Greenface alive, let it act, move—enabled it to pull its unearthly vanishing stunt. At high noon it was as vital as a cat or hawk. Lack of light made it still, pulled, though perhaps able to react automatically.

Greenface was trapped!

He began to play with it, savagely enjoying his power over the horror, switching the light off and on. Presently, Greenface would die; but first—he seemed to sense a growing dim anger in that soundless buzzing—and suddenly the thing did not stop!

In a flash, Hogan realized he had permitted it to reach the edge of the little moonlit clearing, and under the full glare of the moon, Greenface was still advancing upon him, though slowly. Its outlines grew altogether blurred—even the head started to fade.

Hogan leaped back, with a new rush of the helpless horror with which he had first sensed it coming toward him. But he retreated only into the shadows on the other side of the clearing.

The ghostly outline of Greenface came rolling on, its nebulous leering head swaying slowly from side to side like the head of a hanged and half-rotted thing. It reached the fringe of shadows and stopped, while the foot ribbons darkened as they touched the darkness and writhed back. Dimly it seemed to be debating this new situation.

Hogan swallowed hard. He had noticed a blurred, shapeless something which churned about slowly within the jellylike shroud beneath the head; and he had a sudden conviction that he knew the reason for Old Battler's silence. Greenface had become as dangerous as a tiger!

Meanwhile, he had no intention of leaving it in the moonlight's liberty. He threw the beam on the dim oval mask again, and slowly, stupidly, moving along that rope of light, Greenface entered the darkness; and the light flicked out, and it was trapped once more.

Trembling and breathless after his half-mile run, Hogan reached the lodge and began stuffing his pockets with as many shells as they would take. Then he picked up the shotgun and started back toward the spot where he had left the thing, forcing himself not to hurry. If he didn't blunder now, his troubles would be over. But if he did—Hogan shivered. He hadn't quite realized before that a time was bound to come when Greenface would be big enough to lose its fear of him.

Pushing down through the ditch and into the woods, he flashed the light ahead of him. In a few more minutes he reached the place where he had left Greenface. And it was not there!

Hogan glared about, wondering wildly whether he had missed the right spot and knowing he hadn't. He looked up and saw the tops of the jack pines swaying against the pale blur of the sky; and as he stared at them, a ray of moonlight flickered through that canopy and touched him and was gone again, and then he understood. Greenface had crept up along such intermittent threads of light into the trees.

One of the pine tops appeared blurred and top-heavy. Hogan watched it a few minutes; then he depressed the safety button on the automatic, cradled the gun, and put the flashlight beam dead-center on that blur. In a moment he felt the fine mental irritation as the blur began to flow downward through the tree toward him. Remembering that Greenface did not mind a long drop to the ground, he switched off the light and watched it take shape among the shadows, and then begin a slow retreat toward the treetops and the moon.

Hogan took a deep breath and raised the gun.

The five reports came one on top of the other in a rolling roar, while the pine top jerked and splintered and flew. Greenface was plainly visible now, still clinging, twisting and lashing in spasms like a broken snake. Big branches, torn loose in those furious convulsions, crashed ponderously down toward Hogan. He backed off hurriedly, flicked in five new shells and raised the gun again.

And again!

And again!

The whole top of the tree seemed to be coming down with it! Dropping the gun, Hogan covered his head with his arms and shut his eyes. He heard the sodden, splashy thump with which it landed on the forest mold a half dozen yards away. Then something hard and solid slammed down across his shoulders and the back of his skull.

There was a brief sensation of plunging headlong through a fire-streaked darkness. For many hours thereafter, no sort of sensation reached Hogan's mind at all.

"Haven't seen you around in a long time," bellowed Pete Jeffries across the fifty feet of water between his boat and Hogan's. The farmer pulled a fat flapping whitefish out of the illegal gill net he was emptying and plunked it down on the pile before him. "What you do with yourself—sleep up in the woods?"

"Times I do," Hogan admitted.

"Used to myself when I was your age. Out with a gun alla time," Pete said mournfully. "It ain't no real fun any more—'specially since them game wardens got Old Battler."

Hogan shivered imperceptibly, remembering the ghastly thing he'd buried that July morning, six weeks back, when he awoke, thinking his skull was caved in and found Greenface somehow had dragged itself away, with enough shot in it to lay out a township. At least it felt sick enough to disgorge what was left of Old Battler, and to refrain from harming Hogan. Maybe he'd killed it, at that—though he couldn't quite believe it.

"Think the storm will hit before evening?" he asked out of his thoughts, not caring much either way. Pete glanced at the sky.

"Yes!" he agreed matter-of-factly. "Hit the lake in half an hour maybe. I know two guys," he added, "who are going to get awful wet. Not meaning us—"

"That so?"

"Yeah. Know that little bay back where the Indian outfit used to live? There's two of the drunkest buggers I seen on Thursday Lake this summer—fishing there off from a little duck boat! They come across the lake somewheres."

"Think we ought to warn 'em?"

"Not me!" said Jeffries. "They made some kinda crack when I passed there. I like to have rammed 'em." He looked at Hogan with puzzled benevolence. "Seems there was something I was gonna tell you . . . well, guess it was a lie!" He sighed. "How's the walleyes hitting?"

"Pretty good." Hogan had picked up a stringful trolling along the lake bars.

"I got it now!" Pete spluttered excitedly. "Whitey told me last night: Julia's got herself engaged up with a guy in the city—place she's working at! They're going to get married real quick."

Hogan bent over the side of his boat and began to unknot the fish-stringer. He hadn't seen Julia since the night he last met Greenface. A week or so later he heard she'd left town and taken a job in the city.

"Seemed to me I oughta tell you," Pete continued with remorseless neighborliness. "Didn't you and she used to go around some?"

"Yeah, some," Hogan agreed desperately. He held up the walleyes. "Want to take these home for the missis, Pete? I was just fishing for the fun of it."

"Sure will!" Pete was delighted. "If you don't want 'em. Nothing beats walleyes for eatin', 'less it's whitefish. But I'm going to smoke these. Say, how about me bringing you a ham of buck, smoked, for the walleyes?"

"O. K.," Hogan smiled.

"Have to be next week," Pete admitted regretfully, "I went shooting the north side of the lake three nights back, and there wasn't a deer around. Something's scared 'em all out over there."

"O. K.," Hogan said again, not listening at all. He got the motor going and cut away from Pete with a wave of his hand. "Be seeing you, Pete!"

Two miles down the lake he got his mind off Julia long enough to find a possible unpleasant significance in Pete's last words.

He cut the motor to idling speed and then shut it off entirely, trying to get his thoughts into some kind of order. Since that chunk of pine rapped him over the head and robbed him of his chance of finishing off Greenface, he'd seen no more of the thing and heard nothing to justify his suspicion that it was still alive somewhere, maybe still growing. But from Thursday Lake northward to the border of Canada stretched two hundred miles of bush, tree and water, with only the barest scattering of towns and tiny farms. Hogan often pictured Greenface prowling about back there, safe from human detection and a ghastly new enemy for the harried small life of the bush, while it nourished its hatred for the man who had so nearly killed it.

It wasn't a pretty picture. It made him take the signs indicating MASTERS FISHING CAMP from the roads, and made him turn away the occasional would-be guest who still found his way to the camp in spite of Whitey Allison's unrelenting vigilance in town. It also made it possible for him even to try to get in touch with Julia and explain what couldn't have been explained anyhow.

A rumble of thunder broke through Hogan's thoughts. The sky in the east hung black with clouds; and the boat was beating in steadily toward shore with the wind and waves behind it. Hogan started the motor and came around a curve to take a direct line toward camp. As he did so, a white object rose sluggishly on the waves not a hundred yards ahead of him and sank again. With a start of dismay he realized it was the upturned bottom of a small flat boat, and remembered the two fishermen he'd intended warning against the approach of the storm.

The little bay Jeffries had mentioned, lay a half-mile in back of him; he'd come past it without being aware of the fact. There was no immediate reason to think the drunks had met with an accident; more likely they'd simply landed and neglected to draw the boat high enough out of the water, so that it drifted off into the lake on the first puff of wind.

Circling the derelict to make sure it was really empty, Hogan turned back to pick up the two sportsmen and take them to his camp until the storm was over.

On reaching the comparatively smooth water of the tree-ringed bay, Hogan throttled the motor and came in slowly because the bay was shallow and choked with pickerel grass and reeds. There was little breeze here; the air seemed even oppressively hot and still after the free race of wind on the outer lake. It was also darkening rapidly.

He stood up in the boat and stared along the shoreline over the tops of the reeds, wondering where the two had gone—and whether they mightn't have been in the boat anyway when it overturned.

"Hey, there!" he yelled uncertainly.

His voice echoed back out of the creaking shore pines. From somewhere near the end of the bay sounded a series of loud splashes—probably a big fish flopping about in the reeds. When that stopped, the stillness became almost tangible; and Hogan drew a quick, deep breath as if he found breathing difficult.

Again the splashing in the shallows, much closer now. Hogan faced the sound frowning; his frown became a puzzled stare. That was certainly no fish but some big animal, a deer, a bear, possibly a moose—the odd thing was that it should be coming toward him. Craning his neck, he saw the reed tops bend and shake about a hundred yards away, as if a slow, heavy wave of air were passing through them in his direction. There was nothing else to be seen.

Then the truth flashed on him—a rush of horrified comprehension.

Hogan tumbled back into the stern and threw the motor on full power. As the boat drove forward, he swung it around to avoid an impenetrable wall of reeds ahead, and straightened out toward the mouth of the bay. Over the roar of the motor and the splash and hissing of water, he was aware of one other sensation: that shrilling vibration of the nerves, too high to be a sound, that had haunted his dreams all summer! How near the thing came to catching him as he raced the boat through the weedy traps of the bay, he never knew; but once past the first broad patch of open water he risked darting a glance back over his shoulder—

And then, through a daze of incredulous shock, Hogan heard himself scream—raw, hoarse yells of sheer animal terror.

He wasn't in any immediate danger for Greenface had given up the pursuit. It stood, fully visible among the reeds, a hundred yards or so back. The smiling, jade-green face was turned toward Hogan, lit up by strange reflections from the stormy sky and mottled with red streaks and patches he didn't remember having seen there before. The glistening, flowing mass beneath it writhed like a cloak of translucent pythons. It towered in the bay, dwarfing even the trees behind it in its unearthly menace. It *had* grown again! It was all of thirty feet high.

The storm, breaking before Hogan reached camp, raged on through the night and throughout the next day. Since he would never be able to find the thing in that torrential downpour, he didn't have to decide whether he must try to hunt Greenface down or not. In any case, he wouldn't have to go looking for it, Hogan told himself, staring out of the lodge windows at the tormented chaos of water and wind without—it had come back for him, and presently it would find its way to the familiar neighborhood of the camp!

There was a certain justice in that. He'd been the nemesis of the monster as much as it had been his. It was simply time to bring the matter to an end before anyone else got killed.

Someone had told him—now he thought of it, it must have been Pete Jeffries, plodding up faithfully through the endless storm one morning with supplies for Hogan—that the two lost sportsmen were considered drowned; their boat had been discovered, and as soon as the weather made it possible, the lake would be searched for their bodies. Hogan nodded, saying nothing and keeping his face expressionless. Pete was looking at him in a worried way.

"You shouldn't drink so much, Hogan!" Pete blurted out suddenly. "It ain't doing you no good. The missis was telling me you was really keen on that Julia—maybe I shoulda kept my trap shut. But you'd have found out anyhow."

"Sure I would," Hogan said quickly. It hadn't dawned on him before that Pete believed he'd shut himself up here to mourn for Julia.

"Me," Pete told him confidentially, "I didn't marry the girl I was after, neither. But don't you never tell that to the missis, Hogan! Well, anyhow, it got me just like it got you . . . you gotta snap outta it, see?"

Something was moving, off in the grass back of the machine shed. Hogan watched it from the corner of his eye till he made sure it was only a bush shaking itself in the sleety wind.

"Eh?" he said. "Oh, sure. I'll snap out of it, Pete. Don't you worry."

"That's right." Pete sounded hearty but not quite convinced. "Come around see us some evening, Hogan. It don't do a guy no good to be sittin' off here by himself alla time."

Hogan gave his promise. Maybe he was thinking of Julia a good deal; but mostly, it seemed to him, he was thinking of Greenface. As for drinking too much, he was certainly far too smart even to look at the whiskey. There was no telling when the crisis would come, and he intended to be ready for it. At night he slept well enough.

Meanwhile, the storm continued, day and night. Hogan couldn't quite remember finally how long it had been going on, but it was as bad a wet blow as he'd ever got stuck in. The lake water rolled over the dock with every wave, and the little dock down near the end cabins had been taken clean away. At least three trees were down within the confines of the camp, the ground littered with branches. There were times when Hogan got to wondering why Greenface didn't come— and whether he hadn't possibly made the whole thing up.

But then he would always remember that on cold wet days it didn't like to move about. It was hiding up, waiting for the storm to subside. It would be hard for so huge a thing to find shelter anywhere, of course; but after a little thinking, he knew exactly where it must be—at the cut-off above the lake, about three miles west of the camp and a mile or so from the bay where he had seen it last.

On the eighth morning the storm ebbed out. In mid-afternoon the wind veered around to the south; shortly before sunset the cloud banks began to dissolve while mists steamed from the lake surface. Hogan went out with a hand ax and brought in a few dead birches from a windfall over the hill to the south of the lodge. His firewood was running low; he felt chilled and heavy all through, unwilling to exert himself. He had left the gun in the lodge, and as he came downhill dragging the last of the birches, he was frightened into a sweat by a pale, featureless face that stared at him out of the evening sky between the trees. The moon had grown nearly full in the week it was hidden from sight; and Hogan remembered that Greenface was able to walk in the light of the full moon.

He cast an anxious look overhead. The clouds were melting toward the horizon in every direction; it threatened to be an exceptionally clear night. He stacked the birch logs beside the fireplace in the lodge's main room. Then he brewed up the last of his coffee and drank it black. A degree of alertness returned to him.

Afterward he went about, closing the shutters over every window except those facing the south meadow. The tall cottonwoods on the other three sides of the house should afford a protective screen, but the meadow would be flooded with moonlight. He tried to remember at what time the moonset came—no matter, he'd watch till then and afterward sleep! The effect of the coffee was wearing off, and he had no more.

He pulled an armchair up to an open window from where, across the still, he controlled the whole expanse of open ground over which Greenface could approach. Since a rifle couldn't have much effect on a creature that lacked both vital parts and sufficient solidity to stop a bullet, he had the loaded shotgun across his knees. The flashlight and the contents of five more shell boxes lay on the small table beside him.

With the coming of night, all but the brightest of stars were dimmed in the gray gleaming sky. The moon itself stood out of Hogan's sight above the lodge roof, but he could look across the meadows as far as the machine shed and the ice-house.

He got up twice to replenish the fire which made a warm, heartening glow on his left side; and the second time he considered replacing the armchair with something less comfortable. He was becoming thoroughly drowsy. Occasionally a ripple of apprehension brought him bolt upright, pulse hammering; but the meadow always appeared quiet and unchanged, and the night alive only with familiar, heartening sounds: the crickets, a single whippoorwill, and the occasional dark wail of a loon from the outer lake.

Each time fear wore itself out again, and then, even thinking of Julia, it was hard to keep awake. But she remained in his mind tonight with almost physical clearness—sitting opposite him at the kitchen table, raking back her unruly hair while she leafed slowly through the mail-order catalogues; or diving off the float he'd anchored beyond the dock, a bathing cap tight around her head and the chin strap framing her beautiful, stubborn little face like a picture.

Beautiful but terribly stubborn, Hogan thought, frowning drowsily. Like one evening, when they'd quarreled again and she hid among the empty cabins at the north end of the camp. She wouldn't answer when Hogan began looking for her, and by the time he discovered her, he was worried and angry. So he came walking slowly toward her through the half-dark, without a word—and that was one time Julia did get a little scared of him. "Hogan!" she cried breathlessly. "Now wait! Listen, Hogan—"

He sat up with a jerky start, her voice still ringing in his mind.

The empty moonlit meadow lay like a vast silver carpet below him, infinitely peaceful; even the shrilling of the tireless crickets was withdrawn in the distance. He must have slept for some while, for the shadow of the house formed an inky black square on the ground immediately below the window. The moon was sinking.

Hogan sighed, shifted the gun on his knees, and immediately grew still again. There'd been something—and then he heard it clearly: a faint scratching on the outside of the bolted door behind him, and afterward a long breathless whimper like the gasp of a creature that has no strength to cry out.

Hogan moistened his lips and sat very quiet. In the next instant, the hair at the back of his neck rose hideously of its own accord.

"Hogan . . . Hogan . . . oh, please! . . . Hogan!"

The toneless cry might have come out of the shadowy room behind him, or over miles of space, but there was no mistaking that voice. Hogan tried to say something, and his lips wouldn't move. His hands lay cold and paralyzed on the shotgun.

"Hogan . . . please! Listen . . . Hogan—"

He heard the chair go over with a dim crash behind him. He was moving toward the door in a blundering, dreamlike rush, and then struggling with numb fingers against the stubborn resistance of the bolt.

"That awful thing! That awful thing! Standing there in the meadow! I thought it was a . . . a TREE! I . . . I'm not CRAZY, am I, Hogan?"

The jerky, panicky whispering went on and on, until he stopped it with his mouth on hers and felt her relax in his arms. He'd bolted the door behind them before carrying her to the fireplace couch—Greenface must be standing somewhere around the edge of the cottonwood patch if she'd seen it coming across the meadow from the road. Her hand tightened on his shoulder, and he looked down. Julia's eyes were wide and dark, but incredibly she was smiling—well, he'd always known Julia was wonderful!

"I came back, Hogan. I had to find out—was that it, Hogan? Was that what—"

He nodded hastily; there was no time to wonder, hardly any time left to explain. Now she was here, he realized he'd never have stopped Greenface with any amount of buckshot—but they could get away if only they kept to the shadows.

The look of nightmare came back into Julia's eyes as she listened; her fingers dug painfully into his shoulder. "But, Hogan," she whispered, "it's so big . . . big as the trees, a lot of them!"

Hogan frowned at her uncomprehendingly until, watching him, Julia's expression began to change. He knew it mirrored the change in his own face, but he couldn't do anything about that.

"It could come right through them—" she whispered.

Hogan still wasn't able to talk.

"It could be right outside the house!" Julia's voice wasn't a whisper any more, and he put his hand over her mouth, gently enough, until her breathing steadied.

"Don't you *smell* it?" he murmured, close to her ear.

It was Greenface all right; the familiar oily odor was seeping into the air they breathed, growing stronger moment by moment until it became the smell of some foul tropical swamp, a wet, rank rottenness. Hogan was amazed to find he'd stopped shaking. He felt quick and strong and reckless—he knew he couldn't afford to be reckless. He thought frantically.

"Look, Julia," he whispered, "it's dark in the cellar. No moonlight; nothing. Make it there alone?"

She nodded doubtfully.

"I'll put the fire out first," he explained in hasty answer to her look. "Be down right after you!"

"I'll help you," she gasped. All Julia's stubbornness was concentrated in the three words.

Hogan fought down an urgent impulse to slap her face hard, right and left. Like a magnified echo of that impulse was the vast soggy blow that smashed immediately against the outer lodge wall, above the door.

They stared stupidly. The whole house was shaking. The wall logs were strong, but a prolonged tinkling of broken glass announced that each of the shuttered windows on that side had been broken simultaneously. "The damn thing!" Hogan thought. "The damn thing! It's really come for me! If it hits the door—"

The ability to move returned to them together. They left the couch in a clumsy, frenzied scramble and reached the head of the cellar stairs not a step apart. With the second shattering crash, the telephone leaped from the wall beside Hogan. His hand on the stair railing, he stared back.

He couldn't see the door from there. The fire roared and danced in the hearth, as if it enjoyed being shaken up so roughly. The head of the eight-point buck had dropped off the cabinet and lay on the floor beside the fire, its glass eyes fixed in a red baleful glare on Hogan. Nothing else seemed changed.

"HOGAN!" Julia wailed aloud from the shadows at the foot of the stairs. He heard her start up again and turned to tell her to wait there.

Then Greenface hit the door.

Glass, wood and metal flew inward together with an indescribable explosive sound. Hogan slid down four steps and stopped again, his head on a level with the top of the stairs. Below him he heard Julia's choked breathing. Nothing else stirred.

A cool draft of air began to flow past his face. Then came a heavy scraping noise and the renewed clatter of glass.

"Hogan!" Julia sobbed recklessly. "Come down! IT'LL GET IN!"

"It can't!" Hogan breathed.

As if in answer, the stairs began to tremble under his feet. Wood splintered ponderously; the shaking continued and seemed to spread through the house. Then something smacked against the wall, just around the corner of the room that shut off Hogan's view of the door. Laboriously, like a floundering whale, Greenface was coming into the lodge.

At the foot of the stairs, Hogan caught his foot in a mess of telephone wires and nearly went headlong over Julia. She clung to him, trembling.

"Did you see it?"

"Just its head!" Hogan gasped. He was steering her by the arm through the dark cellar. "We gotta keep away from the stairs, out of the light. Stay there, will you? And, Julia, kid"—he was fumbling with the lock of the side entrance door—"keep awful quiet, please!"

"I will," she whispered scornfully. The timbers groaned overhead, and for a moment they stared up in tranced expectation, each sensing the other's thought. Julia gave a low, nervous giggle.

"Good thing that floor's double strength!"

"That's the fireplace, right over us," he said frowning. He opened the door an inch or so and peered out. "Look here, Julia!"

The shifting light of the fire streamed through the shattered frame of the main lodge door. The steps leading up to it had been crushed to kindling wood. As they stared, a shadow, huge and formless, dropped soundlessly across the lighted area. They shrank back.

"Oh, Hogan!" Julia whimpered. "It's horrible!"

"All of that," he said, with dry lips. "Do you feel anything—funny?"

She peered at him through the gloom. "Feel anything, Hogan?"

"Up here!" He put his fingertips to her temples. "Sort of buzzing?"

"Oh," she said; "yes, I do!" She was getting panicky again, and he squeezed her arm reassuringly. "What is it, Hogan?"

"A sort of sound our friend makes," he explained, "when he's feeling good. but it should be much louder. Julia, that thing's been out in the cold and rain all week. No sun at all. I should have remembered! I bet it *likes* that fire up there. It's getting friskier now, and that's why we hear it."

There was a moment's silence.

"Let's run for it, Hogan! The car's right up on the road."

"Uh-uh!" He shook his head. "We might make it all right, but Greenface can come along like a horse when it wants to . . . and the fire's pepping it up—it *might* know perfectly well that we're ducking around down here!"

"Oh, no!" she said, shocked.

"Anyway, it wouldn't settle anything. I got an idea—Julia, honey, promise just once you'll stay right here and not yell after me, or anything? I'll be right back."

"What you going to do?"

"I won't go out of the cellar," Hogan said soothingly. "Look, darling, there's no time to argue—do you promise, or do I lay you out cold?"

"I promise," she said after a sort of frosty gasp.

"What were you doing?"

"Letting out the kerosene tank." He was breathing hard. "Is *it* still there?"

"HOGAN!"

"All right!" he whispered excitedly. "I'm going to fix that devil's whistling. Now then, I'll put a match to it. But we won't leave just yet. Wait here as long as we can—and then slip over into the nearest cabin. No running around in the moonlight!"

He ducked off again. After a minute, she saw a pale flare light up the chalked brick wall at the end of the cellar, and realized he was holding the match to a wad of paper. The kerosene fumes went off suddenly with a faint *BOOM!* and the glare of yellow light drove the shadows back with a rush toward Julia.

She heard Hogan move around in the passageway behind the door to her left. There were two more muffled explosions; then he came out and closed the door softly behind him.

"Going up like pine shavings!" he muttered gleefully. "Well, we wanted a new lodge anyhow. Now, Julia—"

"It looks almost like a man, doesn't it, Hogan? Like a sick old man!"

Hogan hushed her nervously. The buzzing in his brain was louder now, rising and falling as if the strength of the thing were gathering and ebbing in waves. And Julia unconsciously had spoken too loud.

"Keep under the ledge of the window," he told her. "It hasn't any real eyes, but it sees things somehow just as well as you and I."

Julia subsided reproachfully, and he gave her arm a quick squeeze. "If it'll just stay put for another two minutes, the fire ought to catch it—"

From the corner of the cabin window he could see half of the main room of the lodge through the door Greenface had shattered. Greenface itself filled most of that space. It was hunched up before the fireplace, its great, red-splotched head bending and nodding toward the flames; in that attitude there was something vaguely human about it. But its foot ribbons sprawled over all the rest of the floor space like the tentacles of an octopus, and Hogan noticed they, too, were now splotched with red.

Most of his attention was directed toward the cellar windows of the lodge. Every one of them was alight with the flickering glare of the fires he had spread, and that glare was deepening while smoke poured out through the open door. The gathering roar of the fire mingled in his mind with the soundless, nervous rasp that meant Greenface's strength was returning.

It was like a race between the two: whether the fire would trap the thing before the heat which the fire kindled made it alert enough to perceive its danger and escape. It wasn't just a question of its escaping, either! Hogan hadn't told Julia how convinced he was that Greenface knew the two of them were there, to be caught at leisure as soon as it recovered enough to make the exertion. But it would make the exertion anyhow the instant it sensed they were trying to get away.

WOULDN'T THAT FIRE EVER BREAK THROUGH?

Then it happened—with blinding suddenness.

The thing swung its head around from the fireplace and lunged hugely backward. In a flash it turned nearly transparent, and Hogan heard Julia cry out beside him—he hadn't told her about that particularly ghastly little trick. In the same moment, the vibration in his mind became like a ragged, piercing shriek, like pain, brief and intolerable.

Hogan reeled away from the window, dragging Julia with him. There was a sudden series of muffled explosions—it wasn't till afterward he remembered the shells left lying on the table—then the lodge floor broke through into a cellar with a thundering crash, and the released flames leaped bellowing upward.

They were out of the cabin by then, running down toward the lake.

"Your Pa isn't going to like the idea," Hogan pointed out thoughtfully.

"He better like it!" Julia sounded a trifle grim. "But God bless the forest rangers—though they *were* kind of nasty!"

"They put the fire out anyhow," he said. "How would you care to mop up after a half-wit who lights a match to see how much kerosene he'd spilled in the dark?"

"Poor Hogan. . . . I got to tell you, too: I did get myself engaged in the city! I just couldn't go through with it without coming back first—"

"To find out if I really was batty? Can't blame you, honey! Well, it's all over with, anyhow," he said cheerily and put his arm around her.

"Hogan," Julia murmured after a suitably lengthy interval, "you think there might be anything left of it?"

He shook his head decisively. "Not after that bonfire. We can go have a look."

They walked up from the dock together toward the blackened, watersoaked mess that had been the lodge building. It was still an hour before dawn. They stood staring at it in silence. Greenface's funeral pyre had been worthy of a titan.

"We won't build here again till spring." Hogan told her at last. "We can winter in town, if you like. There won't be anything left of it then, for sure. There was nothing very solid about it, you know—just a big poisonous mass of jelly from the tropics. Winter would have killed it, anyhow.

"Those red spots; it was rotting last week—it never really had a chance."

"You aren't feeling sorry for it, are you?"

"Well, in a way." Hogan admitted. He kicked his foot and stood there frowning. "It was just a big crazy freak shooting up all alone in a world where it didn't fit in, and where it could only blunder around and do a lot of damage and die. I wonder how smart it really was and whether it ever understood the fix it was in."

"Quit worrying about it!" Julia commanded.

Hogan grinned down at her. "O. K.," he said.

"And kiss me," said Julia.

THE END.

CLEVE CARTMILL

Hell Hath Fury

ONE

The switchboard operator thought her eyes were tired; that was as near as she came to the truth. When she looked into the hospital waiting room at the father of the forthcoming child, he seemed faintly out of focus. And so did the old lecher who followed the father with amused yellow eyes. Therefore, her eyes must be tired.

The father acted like any father in a hospital waiting room. He sat down. He looked at his watch. He got up. He walked. He sat down. Looked at his watch.

Handsome devil, she thought, with his thin face, his floppy grey hat, his pin-stripe serge, his . . . his ears. That's all they were, ears. You look close and see it, as soon as you get him in focus. Handsome devil. Quiet, but with fire underneath. It would be wonderful to be loved the way he obviously loved his wife.

It would be wonderful to be loved. Period.

Not by the old goat, though, who yawned on the divan and shot an occasional leer across the counter at her.

She rubbed her eyes. Women, she thought wearily, keeping hospitals up all night, wearing out the help. She'd never had trouble with her eyes, but what with no sleep, routing doctors out of bed, soothing hysterical fathers, running down to Delivery to get the news, it was no wonder—

A light flashed on the board. Delivery. She plugged in, listened, then hurried down the corridor and through the swinging doors. She came back, and she had that old feeling.

She went to the counter between her office and the waiting room, wishing that it was her baby she was reporting on.

'You have a boy, Mr. Roberts,' she said mistily. 'My congratulations.'

He turned with the grace of a healthy cat. 'How is he?' he snapped.

The operator misunderstood. 'Oh, she's fine. You can see her in a few minutes.'

'The child!' he said harshly. 'Is he all right?'

'You fathers,' she chided. 'Listen for yourself.'

Thin, indignant wails penetrated the hospital walls, rising to a high pitch of anger.

The father's face relaxed. It didn't exactly soften, but it shone with dark joy.

The operator went back to her board, and the father turned to the old lecher on the divan.

'Chief! He has human form!'

A shaggy white eyebrow widened the distance between itself and the stiff white beard. 'Human form,' the Chief mused. 'What did you expect—butterflies?'

'Think what it means, Chief! He'll influence thousands.'

'I suppose he will,' the Chief said. 'It should be entertaining to watch.'

'And if he turns out right,' the father persisted eagerly, 'we can do it again, and again, and again.'

The Chief sort of flowed to his feet. 'You have my permission to experiment all you like. Not that it matters. Let me caution you against expecting too much. One's children are never exactly like one's self. I am living proof. But go ahead. It's interesting work.' He started away, smoothly, effortlessly, paused and smiled again. 'Fun, too,' he added.

His eye touched the telephone operator, became speculative. He went to the counter and twinkled at her. She approached expectantly.

'Breakfast?' he suggested.

She almost agreed. There was something compelling about the old goat, and he *was* distinguished, kind of. But she hesitated. There was something repelling, too.

He seemed to reconsider. 'Never mind.' He patted her cheek, and her skin crawled—voluptuously. 'You've probably got a mother or a mortgage.' He moved away. 'Or both,' he added pleasantly, and was gone.

The operator stared after him dreamily. He was a funny one. He had a wolfish smile and insulting speech, but these probably covered a butter heart. You couldn't get angry at him. She wondered if she'd ever see him again.

With a light shock, she saw that the waiting room was empty. Now how had Mr. Roberts managed to leave without her seeing him? Oh, well. He'd probably just stepped out for a breath of fresh air. New fathers needed it, sometimes.

The father went up through pre-dawn blackness away from the hospital to a place of his own making. There Jim Roberts waited, unknowing of events, unconscious of time, of anything.

The father spoke the necessary words and transferred into Jim Roberts' mind a complete memory pattern. Then he placed Jim Roberts outside the hospital door, where Jim drew in great gasps of air and exulted over the fact that he had a son. He recast in his mind the hours of jittery waiting, the telephoning from his job, the rushing out here.

A son. His and Lucille's. How was she, anyway?

He went inside the waiting room. 'When can I see my wife?' he asked the operator.

She smiled at him. He certainly was a handsome devil. The thin face, the pin-stripe serge, the floppy hat. Her eyes seemed to be all right now, too. He was sharply in focus.

'You can go up to the second floor, Mr. Roberts. But she won't know you for a while. She's still under the anæsthetic.'

* * *

She lay on the bed, lashes of her closed eyes spilling down over waxen cheeks. He felt for her pulse. It was strong and steady, and he sighed with relief. She was all right. He put a tender hand on her forehead.

Presently she opened her eyes, recognized him. A tired smile moved her full mouth. 'I'm going to have a baby,' she murmured weakly.

Jim grinned down at her. 'You've had it, kid. Hello, mamma.'

'It was a boy?'

'It was . . . is, a boy.'

She gripped his hand. 'Is it all right, Jim? Is it?'

'Sure,' he said easily. 'Sure.'

'Have you seen it?'

'No, but I'm going to, in just a minute.'

'Go look at him, Jim!' she urged in a tense whisper. 'I've got to know, I've just got to.'

He patted her tolerantly and loped out into the corridor where he snagged a nurse. 'Can I see my baby?'

'Name?' she asked with a large smile.

'Roberts. Just born.'

He thought she gave him a queer look as she went into the nursery. He stood at the big plate of glass, frowning through it as she went into a dim annex and searched through a series of cribs. Presently she brought a bundle to the other side of the window and unwrapped it.

So small, Jim Roberts thought, so small, so red. The little legs, with feet, churning the air. The little hands, waving. The angry face. He blinked, shook his head and looked again. The—face. He smiled, vaguely uncomfortable for a second time, then began waving his hand idiotically. The nurse beamed. Jim Roberts beamed. The baby glowered.

He forgot the strange feeling of momentary discomfort, and galloped back to Lucille's room. She watched him, wide-eyed.

'He's wonderful, kid. He's terrific.'

'Honest, Jim? There's nothing wrong with him?'

He smiled with vast, fatherly tolerance. 'He hasn't got two heads, or six legs. You can dismiss *that* worry, right now. It's all over. All you have to do is get well and bring him home."

She closed her blue eyes and Jim Roberts fixed the picture in his mind. Gold hair against the pillow, black lashes against pale cheeks, pale lips curved in a grave, satisfied smile. 'So sleepy,' she whispered.

He held one of her hands in both of his until the nurse came and told him to go away, promising that he could see his wife tomorrow.

They named him William Jerome, called him Billy, and he was six weeks old when the bearded visitor called. Billy could hear the self-introductions through the bedroom door.

Billy comprehended then the dark destiny which awaited the development of this clumsy body which enveloped him. He was cast in a strange, exciting role, and he thought of his puny human shell with impatient contempt. This mess of arms and legs, he knew, was subject to certain natural laws, and he must abide by them always.

But he, with his hybrid make-up, was subject to no law at all, and he was anxious to make that fact known. He listened to conversation in the 'parlour.'

'My name is Nicholas,' the visitor said in his crisp, harsh voice. 'Everyone calls me Nick to my face. Old Nick when I'm gone. I knew your uncle Bob in Kansas City. He mentioned once that his nephew lived in this dowdy little town, that he had married a beautiful girl. I see that he was correct. As I had some business matters here. I decided to call. Like St. Nick, whose namesake I am certainly not, I bring presents. For you, Jim, and for you, Lucille.'

'Gee!' Jim Roberts breathed. 'I've always wanted a rifle like this. Look, honey, it's automatic.'

'It's wonderful,' Billy Roberts' mother said abstractedly, 'but look at this dress. They've never seen one like it in this town. Thank you, Mr. Nicholas.'

'Please, Lucille. Nick, if you please. It makes your eyes bluer, and a trifle wicked, my dear. Jim, you may need that gun to ward off suitors when your exciting wife wears her new dress. I sincerely hope so,' he added with just the right touch of humour, and the young Roberts couple laughed gaily.

Jim Roberts came back to a social point. 'How is Uncle Bob, anyway? Haven't heard from him in years.'

'Oh, he's dead,' Old Nick replied. 'Been roasting over a fire for four years now.' He added sardonically, 'May he roast in peace.'

There was a little shocked silence. The shock was not concerned with the fact of Uncle Bob's death, but with Old Nick's method of announcing it and his comment. Then they chuckled a little. He was such an ingenuous old codger. He probably didn't mean half the things he said; witness his splendid gifts in memory of his friendship with Uncle Bob. It was likely that he made such remarks to cover up an excess of sentimentality, for nearly all old people were sentimental at heart, really.

'Now,' he said briskly, 'if there's a decent place to eat in this filthy town, I'll take you to dinner. Lucille can show off her new dress. And, Jim, you and I will show off your wife.'

'Oh, but we can't,' Lucille said. 'You have dinner with us. We can't go off and leave the baby.

'Baby? Baby? You have a baby? What a lot of trouble you have in store! May I see the little devil?'

Jim began to glow. Billy could sense it in the next room. 'That's what he is, all right,' he said. 'A little devil.'

'He is not,' Lucille said stoutly. 'You'd cry, too, if you were wet or hungry and couldn't help yourself. He's in here, Nick.'

They trooped in to the bassinet, and Billy, who could see as long as the object wasn't too close to his eyes, examined the stranger with a belligerent stare.

He was a slim and dapper old man, with white eyebrows, a stiff white beard, yellow eyes, and a face full of dark humour. He returned Billy's stare unblink-ingly.

'He's a queer little character,' Old Nick commented.

'How?' Lucille Roberts demanded. 'He's perfectly normal.'

'Ah, yes, my dear. He is normal, now. But wait until he grows up. He's about half demon I should say.'

'Well,' Jim Roberts said with complacence, 'he comes by it honestly. I did my share of hell raising when I was a kid.'

'Yes,' Old Nick mused, 'he will take a leaf from your book and add a few of his own.'

In that instant, Billy Roberts sensed his own power. He was alone, owing allegiance to none. Old Nick, he could see, expected loyalty and obedience, and his remarks were for Billy's benefit rather than for the couple whose name he bore. Old Nick was accustomed to obedience.

Billy glared steadily into the yellow eyes, vowing never to yield any part of himself save that which pleased him to yield. He must be cautious, he knew. He must never exhibit precocious talents. He must appear to be an ordinary boy. But his double heritage gave him twofold powers, and he was equal to any threat against his independence.

Lucille caught her breath. 'How funny! He looks as if he doesn't like you, Nick. As if he were . . . well, thinking. It can't be, of course, but it's a little strange.'

'He,' Old Nick said with amusement, 'is telling me to go to the devil.' He smiled, added, 'Coals to Newcastle. I imagine, my dear, you'd be surprised if you could see inside your son's mind. No,' he amended, 'I suppose you wouldn't. Human beings never believe what they are not conditioned to believe.'

Billy closed his eyes. He'd made his point. Old Nick knew it was war from this time on. The form that war would take and on what fronts it would be waged would have to wait until he grew up. There were many things to learn.

They spoke of a town. He'd heard talk of 'the world.' These were some of the things he must learn. But the main fact was clear; he would not give in to Old Nick, or to anybody.

'He's asleep,' Lucille said.

'He's plotting,' Old Nick amended. 'He's figuring a means to do me in the eye.'

Jim and Lucille chuckled at the fantasic notion of a handful of baby engaged on such a project. 'Isn't he silly?' Lucille said. 'What would you like for dinner, Nick?'

'I won't stay, thank you. I must attend to a few matters. Concerning this child, I don't mind telling you.'

They jumped to the obvious conclusion. 'You're so generous, Nick,' Lucille said.

And, 'Yeah,' Jim added, 'don't put yourself out.'

'You *will* come back, Nick?' Lucille asked.

His eyes travelled over her, like fingers reading Braille. 'Yes, my dear, I'll be back. For one reason, this youngster and I are going to have a showdown one of these days. I have never been defied in this particular fashion. I find it fascinating.'

They chuckled again at the fantastic picture he evoked. 'He makes the baby sound like a young Machiavelli,' Lucille said. 'I'm sure he'll grow to like you, Nick, the way we seem to. We never saw you before you came in the door a few minutes ago. Never even heard of you. But it seems as if I've known you all my life. How about you, honey?'

'I feel the same way,' Jim said, flicking a glance through the door at his new automatic rifle. 'I sure do.'

A smile twitched Old Nick's beard. 'I grow on people,' he murmured and went away.

TWO

Billy Roberts spent the first eight years of his life obeying an ancient admonition: in learning to know himself. In doing so, he impressed the fact of his existence on the village residents somewhat more keenly than his playfellows.

The playfellows themselves were responsible for this notoriety, for they carried home tales of Billy's prowess.

They said he could make himself invisible, for in such games as Hide and Seek, Cops and Robbers, Cowboys and Indians, he excelled in a puzzling manner. The grown-ups chuckled indulgently at these tales, concluding that Billy was skilled in woodcraft. The youngsters, eager to discard the theory of invisibility, came to adopt this latter view.

They said he was as fleet-footed as a deer, which was true, and that he could catch in his bare hands that most elusive of birds, the bobwhite quail.

They were completely silent about his prowess in boyhood fights. If Sammy Jones blacked their eyes or rubbed mud in their hair, they ran home to their mothers with the garbled story. But not one boy ever told what happened to him when he tangled with little Billy Roberts.

The important fact escaped them, was never mentioned: whenever anyone came into contact with Billy, that person got into trouble. But trouble is a habit with children, a burden which they soon learn to carry with all possible equanimity. They never traced it to its source.

But the village thought of Billy Roberts more often than any of its other progeny. He was different. The difference was not important enough to launch investigation, but just enough to arouse a vague civic pride in the boy who showed promise of greater things.

He was not a prodigy. He remained with his own age group in school. True, he seemed to have more leisure time, he worked his lessons more quickly than most, but he did not surge ahead into old groups in the combined grade-high school of Mulveta.

At eight, then, in the third grade, Billy Roberts had explored his nature and capabilities to such an extent that he felt ready to give direction to his activities. He had received no interference from Old Nick or any others of whose existence he alone in the village was aware. He had not asked for guidance on those rare occasions when Old Nick brought him toys; he had remained aloof and independent.

His first move, too, was his own idea. It involved, indirectly, every person in Mulveta, but it involved particularly his teacher, young Miss Elkins, Marlin Stone, Fred Roth, and the principal of the school, Gary Fargo.

Miss Elkins was young, darkly beautiful, fresh out of State Normal, and fearfully anxious to make good on her first teaching job. She liked her twenty students in the third grade, and they were attentive when she addressed them on that day in the autumn term.

She didn't patronize them, she treated them as intellectual equals. 'Several of you,' she said in her soft, low voice, 'have shown promise in your drawing exercises. I have hopes that one or more of you will enter the Community Chest poster contest about which I am going to tell you.'

She explained the Community Chest organization in terms they could understand. She showed them posters which had been used in other years. She explained the purpose of the posters.

'I'll help you in selecting your materials if you like,' she said, 'and give you all the advice you want. I don't expect all of you to enter a poster, but I do think Frederick Roth, William Roberts, and Samuel Jones should try. All the other classes will have entries, and I'd like my class to be represented. The artist who makes the best poster will receive a ten-dollar prize and a free trip to the county seat where his or her poster will be entered in competition with the winning posters from other schools.'

Nobody in the room doubted who would make the best poster in the third grade. Fred Roth had shown an amazing facility with crayon, brush, and charcoal. His drawings had perspective, feeling, and form. If others wished to try, it was for second best; they all knew this.

The larger picture eluded them; they confined the contest to their own room. Even Billy Roberts, with his superior faculties, was hard put to imagine more than the city-wide aspect of the matter. He knew about county seats, but the fact that a nation-wide contest was in progress never entered his head.

But nonetheless, he should have proceeded as he did even if he had known. When he walked home with Marlin and Fred that afternoon, and Marlin said, 'Gee! Ten dollars and a free trip to the county seat!' Billy knew what he was going to do.

When they reached the gate of the Roth bungalow, Fred returned Marlin's books to her and cantered into his yard.

'I'll see ya in the barn right away,' Billy called.

'O.K., hurry,' Fred answered.

'Can I come, too?' Marlin asked.

'Naw,' Billy said. 'We got sumpin' private. You go home and make a poster.'

Her blue eyes clouded. 'I don't know if I can.'

'Sure ya can. I'll help ya. Maybe you'll win th' prize.'

'Will you help me, Billy? Honest?'

'I said I would, didn't I?'

'If you will, maybe I can do a good one. We can work together easy, living next door to each other. Can you come over tonight?'

'You come over. If your father gets a call from the hospital, he won't let us stay there by ourselves, and my family don't care how long you stay at our house.'

'I wish I had a mother,' she said wistfully. 'Then I wouldn't have to stay with people all the time when daddy's operating.'

'Don't you like to stay at our house? You don't have to, you know.'

'Oh, sure I do. Only I'd like to have a mother to make cocoa and cookies, too.'

He was impatient. 'Well, so long. See you tonight.'

'So long.'

He was soon in Fred Roth's barnloft, which alternated as the office of the F.B.I., a Western saloon, a robbers' roost, a cattle ranch, and Fred's studio.

He soon had the dark, intense youngster mixing thick poster paints while Billy outlined his idea for the poster.

You saw it, no doubt, during the '20s. The baby, with two teeth, not quite smiling, with the barest suggestion of hunger? With the legend: THAT THESE MAY LIVE! GIVE! It was very nearly three-dimensional, wholly so in its effect, and thousands upon thousands of prints adorned billboards, telephone poles, barns, fences, and windows.

Billy drove Fred each afternoon, and directed Marlin each night on a similar poster. Fred finished long before Marlin, which was well, because his unsigned poster disappeared one night, less than a week before the contest closing date. Billy did not allow Fred to become morose, and cut his tears of disappointment short to begin another, different in theme and subject matter.

Fred's second poster was good, far above average, but it was merely the work of a talented, not gifted, eight-year-old.

Principal Gary Fargo finally came to the point of the general assembly. He had introduced the bigwigs on the platform, from the *Sentinel* editor, Joe Wakeman, to that leader of local society, Mrs. Byington-Hill, while students squirmed in the filled auditorium and Old Nick, who was present with Jim and Lucille Roberts, eyed the nubile girls in the senior class.

Principal Fargo gave Miss Elkins, in the audience among her students, a fleeting look that flushed her dark cheeks, and introduced the principal speaker.

'All of us know and admire that outstanding man in our community, Mr. Elvin Markham. Mr. Markham, will you tell them the news?'

Markham heaved his two hundred and twenty pounds to his small feet and came laboriously to the centre of the platform. His flabby face took on a look of fatuous pleasure as he polished silver-rimmed spectacles, and everyone in the audience, adult and minor alike, felt patted on the head.

'Ladies and gentlemen,' he began, 'and I mean the little ladies and gentlemen as well as the parents and teachers present.' He paused for the laugh. 'This school—which we are very proud of, I'm sure you'll all agree'—he paused for a scatter of handclaps—'took part recently in a nation-wide contest.'

He described the contest in superlatives, dramatized the spectacle of students burning midnight electricity in the interests of charity. He did this at some length.

'And so we judges, Mrs. Byington-Hill'—a bow to the lady, who returned it—'Mr. Wakeman'—a nod, which got a grin from Joe Wakeman—'and myself met to consider the entries. We had difficulty, I don't mind telling you. Not difficulty in selection, for the winning entry is far better than its competitors, but difficulty in believing that an eight-year-old girl could do such marvellous work.'

A murmur ran over the auditorium. Necks craned.

'The winner was submitted late,' Markham continued. 'A little boy brought it to the judges late at night, explaining that its youthful creator had barely finished and had no time to submit it through her teacher, as the others had been submitted. The judges considered eliminating it on these grounds, but the drawing was so excellent that in the interests of our fair city and the artist herself we could not but award it first prize. I take great pleasure, therefore, and it is a signal honour to do so, in announcing the winner, daughter of our young physician, Dr. Stone, Miss Marlin Stone! And here is her poster.'

A thunder of applause greeted the poster. Marlin, sitting beside Billy, caught her breath.

'It's mine! But'—she looked hard at the drawing—'mine wasn't that good.' She started to her feet, and Billy grabbed her arm.

'Shut up!' he hissed. 'I fixed it for you.'

She sank back, while the applause continued.

Miss Elkins was familiar with Marlin's artistic prowess, and knew that the little girl could not have produced the finished work on display. It seemed too professional for even Fred Roth. But Miss Elkins was young, and shrank before the platform full of community leaders. She owed it to her integrity to raise the issue, but she simply couldn't do it. Not there and then.

Fred Roth recognized his drawing, but he would not have faced all those people for a thousand prizes. In addition, he would have given that picture or anything else he owned, to Marlin if it would bring her pleasure.

Yet the hurt was deep. The picture had disappeared from his barnloft studio, and reappeared here as Marlin's. The inference was obvious. She had stolen it. She didn't have to, he thought as he fought back tears, she didn't have to; she could have had it if she'd asked for it. All she had to do was ask.

And so the prize was awarded to a speechless Marlin. Miss Elkins cursed herself for inaction as the farce went too far for interference. Once the prize was given, she was powerless to speak. They would ask why she hadn't said anything when it was first announced. And why hadn't she? Because she was shy and afraid of her job. Now she must hold her tongue.

Pride and bitterness mingled in Fred Roth's mind as he watched the proceedings. His tongue, too, was tied. He couldn't tell anyone that he was the artist, for such a declaration would react harmfully on Marlin. Nor, he supposed, could Billy tell, for the same reason.

Billy Roberts sensed some of these overtones, but he could not foresee the far-reaching effects of his action. He had been interested simply in creating confusion and unhappiness. He looked first at Miss Elkins, then at Marlin and Fred and knew that he had achieved his ends. But it remained for his father, on a night some weeks later, to explain the full significance of his act—

He knew it was midnight when he awoke, though he had no clock in his room; he just knew. He also knew that the creature who was dim in the darkness was his father. He couldn't have said how he knew, but he did.

His first thought was for Jim and Lucille Roberts, asleep in the next room.

'They won't hear, my son. Even if they were in this room, they wouldn't know that I am here.'

'What do you want?' Billy whispered.

'I want to tell you how proud I am of you!' his father said. 'What you have done has a touch of genius. When the time comes, you will achieve an eminence denied even to me and my kind, because you have a twisted understanding of human values that I never had.'

It didn't make sense to Billy. 'I didn't do anything,' he said. 'I just got the prize for Marlin. She really thinks she drew the picture, now.'

Billy's father chuckled. 'Ingenious, too. It will be fascinating to watch those you have involved when that poster is awarded first national prize and brings a measure of fame to this little village.'

Billy was silent. He didn't understand what his father was driving at, but the creature seemed disposed to talk.

'With one simple act, my son, you have gained credits that I was years in earning. You have shaken Miss Elkins' faith in herself, and she will consider herself not good enough for that young Mr. Fargo who desires her. She will throw him over, causing him to become embittered. This will make him suitable material for us. She, in turn, will become an old maid, harsh, self-righteous to the point of fanaticism, and will also be suitable for us.'

Billy's father broke off to chuckle again.

'As for the boy, he will never paint again. He will not fulfil the destiny which the Others meant him to fulfil. He will go frustrated through life, and that frustration will drive him into our arms. The girl will observe this, and her suspicion that she was not responsible for the excellent drawing will grow to conviction. She will be reminded of her defalcation on all sides, for that poster will be used for years. This will drive her to excesses that will bring her inevitably to us.

'But this,' Billy's father went on, 'is only the small part of the larger scene. Each of these persons will meet hundreds of others during their lives, and have his effect on each. It's almost impossible to calculate the extent to which your ingenuity will affect mankind as a whole. For the effect widens, like a pebble dropped in a pool. I tell you, the words or thoughts don't exist with which properly to express my pride in you. Your heritage is stronger than I thought.'

Billy began to understand, dimly. One part of himself exulted; another felt sorrow. And all of him felt dissatisfaction.

'I didn't mean to do all that,' he said slowly. 'It was a joke. I was just trying out something.'

His father vented his weird chuckle again. 'That's what I meant about heritage, son. You can't help yourself. You must do things like that, as I must, and all the others of us. But you, with your instinctive grasp of human values, accomplish the greatest harm with minimum effort.'

Billy caught at the core of his dissatisfaction. 'What do you mean, I can't help myself?'

'Exactly that. You are powerless against certain factors in your make-up. These are even strengthened by your native cunning. Oh, it was a happy day when I conceived this plan!'

Billy stuck to the point. He rose up in bed and glared at the creature whose outlines were so vague in the darkness. 'You mean I was meant to do that? You planned it? Or Old Nick?'

'Nick will be pleased,' his father answered cheerfully. 'He'll probably bring you a new bicycle.'

Black anger surged through Billy. He had vowed independence, only to find that what he thought was that desirable quality was merely conforming to a behaviour pattern over which he had no control.

'New bicycle, huh?' he muttered. 'I'll throw it in his face. You get out of here! I don't want to see you any more. I'll show you! And Old Nick, too.'

THREE

Dr. George Stone watched Billy Roberts through the window of his study. The little boy sat atop a pile of sand in his own back yard and dipped into it with moody fingers. His short blond hair stirred in the Indian-summer breeze, and though all about him on the neighbouring hills was riotous autumnal death, the boy had no eyes for vivid trees and brown grasses. He looked at the sand, obviously deep in thought.

Dr. Stone remembered that he, not too many years ago, had been a dreamy child given to solitary meditation. The so-called joys of childhood had become too much for him at times, and he had wandered off alone to think. Was Billy Roberts another of those unfortunates going through life wrapped in the mantle of his own secret dreams?

Unfortunate was the word. Separated from his fellows by sensitivity, self-consciousness, and fear of ridicule, Dr. Stone had driven straight towards his destiny along a solitary and rigorous path. He was to be a great surgeon, by his own effort. Every fibre of him knew this.

And yet—this was a thing of sadness—he wanted the camaraderie of his fellows. Perhaps the very shyness which made this impossible was responsible for his inherent greatness, but the goal was not wholly desirable—now.

His dark lean face twisted and his intense eyes softened as he remembered when it had been wholly desirable. His narrow hands clenched as he tried to recall, literally recall, the time when his life had been touched with magic.

She had had beauty of form, true; but it was an overall beauty of character that had made Marilyn Webb his alter ego, had filled his days and nights with a sense of completion. She had wanted him to achieve his end for his own sake, not for whatever reflected glory might come her way as his wife.

His striving had taken on impetus, direction, and perspective. Each small success was a major triumph, each loss a spur towards perfection, intensified when they knew she was going to have a child.

Then she had died.

Dr. Stone winced as he thought of the following period. He had acted badly for a while. Though the nurse he had hired was voluble in praise of little Marlin's ability to sleep twenty-two hours each day, though the baby progressed from incubator to bassinet to crib in perfect health, his thoughts of the tiny bundle were venomous.

Then, as she grew, he began to see flashes of character remindful of her mother. He and she became friends, but never more than that.

His calling was responsible. He saw so little of her. She should have someone to care for her, and he couldn't afford to hire a nurse constantly.

Bitter memory clenched his hands again. Other mothers had lived; why had Marilyn been singled out to die in premature birth? Lucille Roberts had lived, Verna Byington-Hill had lived, and all the others. Why not Marilyn?

He did not like to think it had been the late Dr. Grimes' fault. it wasn't ethical. True, the man had been in his sixties, but he had delivered thousands of babies. Dr. Stone shrugged these thoughts away; the old man had gone and he, George Stone, had replaced him. His record in the operating and delivery rooms had so far been brilliant.

He came back abruptly to the purpose which formed in his mind while he looked through the window of his study at Billy Roberts. He must talk to Billy. He shrank from the necessity; hence the train of thought he indulged while shrinking. He could sit here all afternoon and recast his entire life and postpone the interview again. But he had procrastinated too long.

He tried to name the reason why he continued to postpone his talk with the little boy next door. He had always felt a trifle queer about that child he had delivered seven-eight years before. At the moment when he had held the tyke by his heels and spanked his bottom, he had felt a momentary flash of discomfort. Others had felt it, too, he could tell by their first quick look at Billy's face, the fleeting frown, the second look, the relaxation. There was nothing wrong with the boy's face; he was quite handsome, as a matter of fact. It was that—well, it took a second look to see him clearly.

Dr. Stone sighed. Procrastination again. With an abrupt gesture he put away the book of anatomy he had been studying and called through the window.

'Oh, Billy!'

The boy turned with a start, looking towards the window, and to Dr. Stone his face seemed to set.

'Come over, will you?'

The boy smiled, and Dr. Stone thought: handsome is hardly the word. He's going to raise hell with some damsel's heart some day.

'Sure,' Billy said, and came.

When the boy was seated in the big chair for consulting patients, with milk and a bowl of cookies on the table beside him, Dr. Stone said casually:

'It's sort of lonesome around here without Marlin, isn't it?'

'Sure,' Billy said.

'How's school, Billy?'

Billy bit off half a cookie, chewed and swallowed before answering. 'Same old stuff.'

'Billy, I'd like to talk to you about this prize that Marlin won. Do you mind?'

'Nope. I knew that's what you wanted.'

Dr. Stone thought: then I was right. This must be cleared up. Marlin has that same high sense of justice her mother had.

The telephone interrupted him. He nodded politely to Billy, said 'Excuse me,' and took it up in both hands.

It was Mrs. Byington-Hill. 'George . . . er, Dr. Stone!' she said fearfully. 'It's Gloria. She came home from Miss Petty's school for the week-end, and the little darling has something the matter with her throat.'

Ordinarily, Dr. Stone would have asked no questions. He would have gone. But Verna Byington-Hill had a tendency to hysteria, went into a tizzy if seven-year-old Gloria stubbed one of her aristocratic toes, and he had to get to the bottom of the truth about Marlin.

So he asked for symptoms, and after weeding out useless biographical data, decided the case was not serious.

'Have her gargle salt and soda in warm water,' he prescribed. 'If that doesn't bring relief, call me again.'

'Now,' he said, returning to Billy, 'about Marlin. Maybe you know her better than I do. You probably do. But I have a different slant, and I want to tell you about her. She likes things to be right, Billy, and when they are, she's happy. But when they're not, she's sad. See what I mean?'

'Sure.'

'Well, then. Now it was quite an honour for Marlin to win that poster prize, and she should have been pleased. Oh, she was, and she was very excited when she won the county award and went to the State capital. But she wasn't as pleased as the ordinary little girl should have been. Do you know why?'

Billy gave Dr. Stone a steady look. 'Nope.'

Dr. Stone tried another tack. Perhaps, he thought, he was being too precipitous. You don't pry things out of little boys. You suggest.

'Marlin's a pretty good artist, huh, Billy?'

Billy shrugged. 'Pretty good.'

'I have some of her drawings here.' Dr. Stone took a sheaf of paper from a pigeon-hole of his desk. 'Now I think they're the ordinary drawings a child of her age would make. They don't show exceptional talent. This house, here. Sure, it's a house, but nothing special. And this cow, I never saw horns like these on a cow, did you?'

Billy smiled. 'They're funny all right.'

'Exactly. But this poster which she entered. You saw it. You helped her, I believe?'

'Some.'

'Well, Billy, the whole drawing is too mature, too grown up, that is, for Marlin. It's a picture that could only be drawn by a full-grown artist, a good artist. Now, what I want to know is, how did Marlin come to draw something she couldn't have?'

Billy studied. He took a drink of milk. He looked at the floor. He looked up at Dr. Stone.

'She said it was hers, didn't she?'

'Yes, but she sounded as if she weren't sure.'

Billy shrugged. He said nothing.

'Do you like to draw, Billy?' Dr. Stone hoped that the sudden change of tactics might surprise a revealing answer.

'Some,' Billy said. 'I'm not much good.'

Dr. Stone decided that maybe you don't suggest things, maybe you come right out, man to man, and get an answer that way.

'Billy, I don't think Marlin drew that picture. I don't think she's that much of an artist in the first place, and I don't believe that she has a sufficient grasp of values to have conceived that slogan. Did she draw it?'

Billy looked a trifle bored. 'You can ask my folks. She was over to my house at night. She had a picture of a baby, and the words we got out of a book.'

Dr. Stone's telephone rang again. So Gloria's throat was worse, he thought. He apologized for the interruption again, and answered. It was a colleague at the county hospital who wanted advice on a certain case. The conversation was long and technical, and Billy was restive before Dr. Stone could return to his questioning. He decided he had shilly-shallied long enough.

'Billy, Marlin didn't make that picture. Who did? I don't want any more evasions.'

Billy's wide mouth set in a thin line. He glowered at Dr. Stone. He said nothing.

The telephone rang again. 'Dr. Stone!' It was Mrs. Byington-Hill. 'I've been trying to call you for fifteen minutes, but your phone was busy. Gloria's worse!'

She described symptoms, and Dr. Stone's free hand reached for his emergency kit. 'I'll be right there,' he said crisply.

'Hurry, doctor!' There was real agony in this, real human suffering.

He hung up, jumped up. 'I should have gone, but I wanted to talk to you, Billy. Run along now, and you might say a prayer for little Gloria Byington.'

It was a streptococcic throat, and the little girl was strangling as he ran into the big hilltop mansion left to the young widow by her late, second husband. Dr. Stone felt an old despair as he looked at the suffering child, and he felt the surge of hope, too. There was always a chance, and the fever of that knowledge guided his hands in swift, incisive moves.

Within three minutes he had a hole in her windpipe and a tube through that hollow cartilage. This let air into her labouring lungs while he went to work on the throat.

He won. After four hours of unremitting work, he knew he had won. And it was not just another piece of brilliance to swell his numerical success, it was a human achievement that lifted him out of the trough of exhaustion to a level of emotion that approached ecstasy.

He left the nurse, who had been summoned from the hospital, in the child's bedroom, and washed up in the ornate guest bathroom. Then he went downstairs to the frantic mother.

The moment he looked at her, he saw her in a new light. Heretofore she had been Verna Byington-Hill of unimpeachable reputation, social arbiter of the community, given to well-publicized works of charity. Verna the indomitable, who had sniffed at local schools and artisans and sent her daughter to Miss Petty's, imported her clothes from European capitals.

Now she was a mother, with no thought of her appearance or ancestry. Her strong, long face twisted with anxiety, her classic hands clenched in suspense.

She was beautiful, he thought.

He didn't give her a chance to ask the question. 'She'll be all right,' he said. 'Sit down. Relax. You'll be the next patient if you don't.'

She didn't sit, she sank. He caught her as she fell and put her on the divan before the great fireplace. He gave her a small jolt of brandy.

Presently she rose to a sitting position and looked into the flickering little fire. There was no artificiality in her now, he thought as he watched. She was real. Perhaps, he thought, all those things she had done for him in the last three years had been real, too. He hadn't considered her as a human being, and had resented her small gifts to Marlin, the special preparations she had sent over occasionally by her cook. They had been, to him, just part of her 'good work' for the needy. But perhaps they had sprung from a real warmth, a desire to bring pleasure to her friends.

He could see evidence of this warmth in her face as the fire threw wavering, exciting shadows on it.

She looked at him. 'I don't know how to thank you, George. But you can ask anything of me. Anything.'

He didn't question the source of his impulse. The fact that Marlin could be provided for here didn't even enter his mind—consciously.

He said, 'Will you marry me, Verna?'

Old Nick came to dinner laden, as usual, with presents. A box of cigars for Jim, a box of candy for Lucille—whose waistline was beginning to show traces of former boxes—and an air rifle for Billy.

Billy took the nickelled, shiny gun gingerly. Since his mother's eyes remained fixed on him, he muttered grudging thanks.

'Is that any way to treat your uncle Nick?' she demanded. 'He never comes here but what he brings you something nice. I don't know,' she said to Nick, 'what's the matter with him. He's never polite to you, even, unless he has to be.'

Old Nick's yellow eyes were amused. 'He declared war on me the first day I saw him. Remember?'

They thought back over the years. Jim Roberts twisted his thin, lined face with mental effort. Lucille's beautiful wide eyes clouded with thought.

'That's right,' Jim said. 'Remember how we laughed about it? That was the day you brought me that swell rifle.'

'And,' Lucille breathed, 'the purple dress.'

Billy had slipped off to his room, where he stood the air rifle negligently in a corner. He was aware, and he knew that Nick was aware, that a day of reckoning was approaching. But, he thought furiously, he was only a boy. He didn't have the maturity necessary to try his steel against such an antagonist.

Too, it wasn't smart to tip his hand to the old devil. Why let him know that he, Billy, was aware that they had pushed him around in this matter of the poster. He could rectify such small damage as had been wrought more easily if he worked secretly than if he declared his intention of doing so.

Not, he thought, that the damage was anything serious. He would fix things as soon as Marlin came back. She mustn't know, of course, but he wanted to see how she was taking this success before he made a move.

'Bill-eee?' called his mother at this moment, and he stumped down to the dinner table.

'Well,' Old Nick said, 'I suppose you've heard the gossip.'

Jim and Lucille looked blank. Billy felt a sense of impending disaster.

'Dr. Stone and Mrs. Byington-Hill will legalize their newly discovered passion for each other.'

'You mean they're going to get married?' Lucille gasped.

Old Nick looked at the wall clock, but seemed to listen rather than note the time. 'At this moment they are becoming . . . er, wife and man.' Old Nick grinned. 'Which is the proper way to say it in this case, I believe.'

'For Marlin's sake, I'm glad,' Lucille said. 'She'll have new clothes now. But how did it happen?'

Old Nick seemed to be amused and disposed to philosophize. 'As it always happens,' he said directly to Billy. 'An unwary man—or woman—caught up in an apparently aimless series of coincidences, trapped in a net of circumstance.' He turned to Lucille. 'The good doctor dallied too long today. Heroic measures were then necessary to save little Gloria's life.' After a thoughtful pause, he added, 'He had a great future.'

'Had?' Jim echoed. 'What do you mean, had? Why, his picture is in the State medical journal right now. There's a long piece about him. I didn't read it, but it shows he's going places.'

Old Nick smiled at Billy. 'Can't you just see the effect of all that money on him? And the social whirl? He'll wear white ties and develop a paunch, don't you think?'

Billy stared at his plate. Had they planned this, too? Had he merely been an instrument used in an extension of the poster incident to deny Dr. Stone a destiny designed for him by those 'Others' his father had mentioned. What would happen now?

'Will Marlin move up there?' Billy asked.

'That should be interesting to watch,' Old Nick said, grinning diabolically. 'A girl with strong character and a strong-willed stepmother.'

Lucille seemed to be puzzled. 'The way you talk, Nick, one would think you knew what's going to happen to everybody. You can't know.'

Old Nick smiled. 'I am a keen student of human psychology.' To Billy, he added, 'I have to be.'

FOUR

Fred Roth pointed his trombone at the ceiling, and into the murk of cigarette smoke and fumes of cheap gin poured a cascade of golden sound. All chatter at the crowded tables of Harry's Roadside Tavern stopped. Boys and girls—it was mainly a high-school crowd—listened to the singing magic of the horn.

Fred stated the theme in eight bars, with the five-piece band backing him in a tricky sound pattern. Then the 'reefers' took hold on his imagination, and he was off on a wild improvisation, a sermon of frenzy that found converts in twitching shoulders and restless hips.

The trombone was like a firewalker. It capered around the melody on the orchestra's hot counterpoint. It zoomed to a high G-sharp, fluttered down an agonized series of minors, writhed through eccentric arpeggios, uttered a wild sweet cry of triumph, and cut.

The darkness of the ill-lighted room pulsed for a moment. That music had been troubling, and eyes met furtively to shift away. There was no passion—yet. That was to come with the next number. But everybody needed a drink. Flasks came from pockets, young hands poured into glasses furnished by—and charged for—by Harry.

Marlin Stone nodded thanks as her escort poured into her glass a strong potion. She didn't really take her attention away from Fred Roth as she did so.

Funny, she thought, what happened to people. Freddie, for instance. He had ignored her for years, and now all of a sudden he was camping on her doorstep. He hadn't liked her since they were kids in grade school together, but now he was broken out in a rash of desire. She found it exciting, and she wondered what he'd do about her coming here with Jerry Folsom. He'd do something, if that burning look he sent her through the haze meant anything. His eyes were funny tonight. That was love, maybe, and not the weed that Gloria, the little prude, had said he smoked.

Fred's innards churned as he watched her from the platform. She was classy, all right. His mind skirted the word 'lovely,' accepted it. It was not a word he customarily used, but it applied to Marlin. No lack of masculinity was implied by using it in connection with Marlin. Jerry Folsom would use it without hesitation. But then Jerry was president of the senior class, the jerk, and could get away with it. Something should be done about Jerry. First, though, he had a song to play for Marlin.

It didn't have a name, this song. It didn't have anything, not even form. It wasn't born yet, but it was being born—in desire. It would play itself as it went along. He got to his feet and sent Marlin a twisted little smile.

He dropped softly into the melody and let it play itself, this sweet and terrible ache in his heart. The gay despair and bitter love of adolescence, the joyful sadness of a night in white December, the creeping swiftness of mad spring days, the innocent wisdom of youth, and, above all, the slow swoop of the Dark Angel himself—all these were in his nameless little tune.

Sammy Saltzer felt his hackles rise. A slow, sweet chill flickered along his spine as he raised his clarinet and blew a soft, high wail, a stinging stream of silver to the trombone's golden croon.

Rocky Flood looked back across the years, at all the empty glasses, at all the panting blondes, at all the papered walls, the cheap carpets, the creaking stairs of sad hotels. His left hand caught the beat with simple chords, but his right twisted a treble snare from the piano keys, a snarl at middle age and failure.

Ray Blochner lifted his saxophone and saw, spread out before him, a future as empty as his past as this boy made magic with his horn; a future purply-touched with madness, no love, no hate, no evermore, but liquor, drugs, and hypodermic shots in the arm of happiness. He whispered into his horn a reeling, drunken counterpoint to the clarinet's high wail.

Slappy Hacks flicked the strings of his bull fiddle and thought of a little flower, a little blue flower blooming all alone in the cow pasture last year when he was still a boy. He had picked it and had taken it that night to the girl on the neighbouring farm. She had cried, for nobody had ever given her a flower before. Now, hearing wizardry flowing from Freddie's golden horn, Slappy cried as he remembered, leaving her beautiful and lonely like the little flower had been. He took the beat from Rocky Flood and made each note a tonal footstep of Time, marching to that precipice which is the end of Time and of everything.

And even though a few of the boys and girls there were tone deaf, even though clean harmonic patterns meant nothing to their untrained ears, all were caught up in the resistless force of this music. Tension mounted, silence fell, and all felt that something was going to happen. Hands gripped glasses, eyes fixed on space, shoulders tightened, stomach muscles grew rigid. Something *had* to happen; the human frame could not hold such emotions as were aroused by this jigsaw of sound.

It happened. It happened quickly, and nobody knew how, or why, or who did it.

When the music ended on a complicated chord, Fred Roth put his horn in its rack and walked to Marlin's table. He was followed by the rest of the band, except for Slappy Hacks, for a variety of reasons. Ray Blochner went along because Freddie looked as if he might start something interesting; Sammy Saltzer because he was still caught up in the restrained frenzy of that last number and followed Freddie in person as he had on his clarinet; Rocky Flood because he had a fuddled sense of responsibility.

'Where you going, kid?' Rocky had said when Freddie stepped off the platform. Getting no reply, Rocky laid hold of Freddie's arm. 'Wait, kid. Take it easy, whatever it is.' When Freddy had flung off his hand, Rocky went along. The kid was so young, and some day Rocky must caution him about using so much 'tea.' It was bad for you at that age.

Only Slappy Hacks remained on the platform, salting his memories with tears of despair.

Fred was drugged by marihuana and by the ache in his heart. Not even he could reconstruct that maelstrom of thought which swirled inside his head. Something had to be done about Jerry; that was the simple motivation.

And either he, or Ray Blochner, or Sammy Saltzer, or Rocky Flood, or all of them together—did it.

Fred stood stiffly beside the table and fixed glazed eyes on Jerry Folsom. A long lock of black hair fell down over his forehead and he brushed it back with a slim, shaking hand.

'Leave my girl alone,' he said evenly.

'Now take it easy, kid,' Rocky said into his ear.

Jerry was instantly on his feet, and Marlin sprang between them. 'Stop it!' she cried. 'Freddie, go back to the bandstand. Don't start anything!'

He flung her aside with impersonal negligence, and she fell against the wall. Jerry Folsom started a roundhouse swing. Rocky Flood caught at Fred. Ray Blochner picked out an inoffensive youth at the next table and hit him on the ear. Sammy Saltzer blinked uncertainly.

And at that instant, Harry, bulking behind his soda fountain, switched off the lights.

He shouldn't have, of course. There was no point in it when just kids were brawling. But Harry had been conditioned in pre-prohibition bars on water fronts, in mining towns, and in lumber camps, and his action was instinctive. Many times in the past a quick finger on the light switch had saved lives.

But there was no shooting here, though the crack of Jerry Folsom's neck sounded like a pistol shot above the confused babble. When the lights were up again, the musicians were gone, Jerry lay dead, and nobody knew how it came about.

Fred Roth walked blindly along the street. Something had happened; he knew that. But what, or to whom, or by whom, were mysteries. His only clear knowledge was the need for flight, though innate caution checked his pace to an innocent amble. He spoke to none that he met or passed, and the bearded stranger who accosted him under a street lamp had to speak twice, sharply, before he halted.

'Going far?' the stranger asked casually.

Fred blinked in an effort to bring the questioner into focus. It looked like—it was old Yellow Eyes who visited the Robertses now and then. Nick, Billy called him.

'What's it to you?' Fred growled.

'Nothing, nothing,' Old Nick said pleasantly. 'I have a natural mild interest, but it isn't burning. Good night.'

Fred walked on. He didn't pause when Old Nick called after him, 'I'll be seeing you—some day.'

Marlin had to try her door key three times before she could enter the big hilltop house which she had referred to as home for eight years and thought of as a place to cache her stockings. Light filtered through the crack of an upstairs door, her father's door. She thought, with a bitter despair, that something like this had to happen before she came home while somebody was still up.

She put knuckles to the door softly, entered when Dr. Stone said, 'Come.'

He looked, she thought, exactly the sort to whom you'd take a problem like this. Rather soft with good living, steady-eyed, distinguished, with grey-flecked hair, and his long dark face carried a hint of cynical wisdom. He was impeccable, as always since he had married the lady of the manor, even in dressing gown and pyjamas.

He turned from the open medical journal on his desk as she entered, said with quiet sarcasm, 'Home already?'

It was a complete statement of complaints of her behaviour for the past several years, and yet it carried a hint of bewilderment, a touch of sadness. This daughter of his, so piquant in sweater and skirt, with a certain hardness in the youthful face framed in masses of red-gold hair, hadn't turned out too well, and he didn't know whether it was his fault or not. He didn't know. He had done what he could, he felt smugly certain, but had it been enough, or as much as he should have done?

Then he saw that she was on the verge of hysteria. She twisted her hands, there was fear around her whitening mouth, and her eyes were overwide.

Her voice was steady with effort. 'I'm in trouble, father.'

She could see him age. Lines deepened around his mouth, which was beginning to lose its tightness; his eyes, once clear with high resolve, clouded with pain.

'Again?' he said wearily. 'What now?'

'The boy I was with was killed at Harry's tonight.'

Once the words were out, she seemed ready to collapse, and he helped her into a chair.

'Killed?' he cried.

She was trembling. 'Jerry Folsom. He was my date, and I feel responsible to a certain extent. I . . . I don't know what to do, father!'

There was agony in her cry, and uncertainty. He put a hand on her head. 'Tell me about it quietly, Marlin.'

She told him the sequence of events. She mentioned no names, save Jerry Folsom's.

'Everybody ran away,' she said. 'I won't be drawn into it if I just keep my mouth shut. But somebody killed him, and I know it was one of four, or all of them. I've got to tell the constable, because nobody else will. They're all scared to death. All of us were there—' She hesitated, flicked him a look of embarrassment mingled with defiance, began again: 'You might as well know. Everybody will soon. We were out there drinking bootleg gin, and if it comes out, there'll be a terrible scandal. But I've got to be honest. I've got to tell what I know. And I need—somebody to go along.' She almost broke down. 'I'm afraid to go by myself.'

Dr. Stone's mouth drooped at one corner. His face twisted with real pain and distaste.

'It would be very unwise for you to become publicly involved,' he said slowly.

'Because of Verna?' she flared. 'And Gloria? Can't you think of anybody but yourself? Sure, they'd tell you what a rotten daughter you have, but a boy's dead!' Her voice rose. 'A boy's dead, do you hear?'

'Marlin!' he said sharply. 'Control yourself!'

She twisted a wry smile at him. There was contempt in it. 'I'm all right now,' she said quietly.

He turned away, wrung out a cry of despair. 'Marlin! Marlin, why have you done these things? You have a home here, more comfortable than others, but you've been dissatisfied ever since we came. You've made a name for yourself. The wild Marlin Stone. I don't know,' he said, 'what makes you do it.'

'Home!' she snorted. 'Homes are supposed to have warmth. You're supposed to be friends with people in your own home. Every breath I draw around here is examined—down somebody's nose. I hate this place! Look what it's done to you.'

He blinked uncertainly, but there was no uncertainty in his heart. He knew what she meant, and flinched as she went on to say it in the harsh, brutal words of youth.

'You were going to be a surgeon once,' she said bitterly. 'Now you're a society doctor. You dress up Verna's parties and get big fees from bored women who need a good spanking. So you give 'em pills. You've thrown away everything you've ever wanted, just because that woman liked to have a man around the place. Well, I'm glad you're some use to her. You've never been any use to me!'

Dr. Stone revived an old memory. This came about, he thought, warily, because I believed once that Marlin was taking something she didn't deserve; and Heaven help me, I still believe it.'

'Let's get out of here, father!' Marlin went on passionately. 'It isn't too late! Let's go back to our little house. We got along all right there. We can do it again. You've still got years ahead of you. Let's get out, father, now!'

Dr. Stone looked at his hands. Once they had been magical, swift, sure, and tender. Now they were just hands.

And yet this was not the main consideration. He knew it too well. He could regain facility. Not all, but enough. He could be a surgeon again. But there was Verna. What would people say if he left her? What would she say, what would she do? He knew she would never let him go. She just wouldn't. She clung.

'It's too late,' he said. There was despair in it.

'So?' Marlin said with quiet scorn. 'All right, it's too late. But not for me. I'm going. Now.'

From some inner recess, Dr. Stone acquired a measure of parental sternness and philosophy. 'Marlin, you're still young. Troubles seem overwhelming at your age, and you are inclined to act rashly without consideration of the future. Where will you go if you leave?'

'To the police, first,' she grated. 'Here we sit gabbing about our own little troubles, and Jerry Folsom lies dead on a speakeasy floor. Where will he go?'

'But what good can you do?' her father protested. 'You can't bring him back to life. All you can accomplish is to get yourself—and all of us—embroiled in a scandal. You can't do anybody any good.'

'Maybe I want to turn over a new leaf,' she replied evenly. 'I've helped to bring about conditions that caused Jerry's death. Maybe I can prevent others. You . . . you won't go with me?' she asked with quiet finality.

'Sleep on it, Marlin,' he pleaded. 'There is no need to go tonight.'

She gave him a look, but no answer. Then she was out of the room and the sound of hurried feet down the stairs came back to him. Dr. Stone jumped to his feet. He half started after her, but caught himself in time. If he went out like this, Verna would be displeased.

He pulled on some clothes hastily, and ran outside. Marlin had disappeared. He started down the road towards the village, but halted after a few steps. His shoulders slumped, and he turned back.

'Good evening, Dr. Stone,' said a voice.

Dr. Stone started, looked towards the voice, recognized that old visitor of the Robertses. Nick, they called him.

'Good evening,' he replied. He fidgeted for a moment when Old Nick said nothing. Then, 'Excuse me,' he said brusquely. 'I haven't time for a chat tonight.'

'Surely,' said Old Nick. 'There'll be plenty of time—later.'

FIVE

There was a deep, underlying pattern of tragedy and Bill Roberts recognized it, felt it. But he could not quench a flickering inner amusement as he waited for Marlin outside the courthouse, watched the crowd pour out in a gabbling stream, caught snatches of low-voiced comment.

'They had to hush it up, I tell—'

'—ought to be horsewhipped, letting kids—'

'What will this younger generation—'

'Well, my daughter was safe at—'

He was not outwardly amused. His long face was as grim as theirs, his wide mouth was straight, his blue eyes as solemn. The cynicism was inside, a slight contempt for civic pride which had quashed Marlin's testimony, had moved the coroner's jury to bring in a verdict of 'death by misadventure.'

Jerry Folsom, he reflected, was one more sacrifice on the altar of prohibition now. Just as militant Drys had made much of similar events before the Eighteenth Amendment was passed, so did they now cloak this incident in a mantle of community righteousness. If a report of the ruckus at Harry's should hit press association wires, the nation would brand Mulveta as a sink of iniquity, and the growing movement towards repeal would take impetus from the fact that this little town had screamed loudly of a man's right to take a drink in the open.

So there would be no investigation. Harry would be warned to stay out of the community, and parents would be more vigilant in regulation of their children's movements—for a while. But the name of Mulveta would not be blackened in the land. That fair flower of negation would continue to bloom whitely though its roots were set in death.

Presently Marlin came, stony-eyed, bitter-mouthed, clenched hands swinging against her plaid skirt. Billy fell in beside her and waited until they were alone on the noon-baked street before he spoke.

'Welcome back,' he said.

She started, eyed him with surprise. 'Oh, it's you. What did you do, throw away your veil?'

'I'm back in circulation,' he admitted.

'That gladsome sound,' she sneered, 'is the hearts of maidens, leaping. The hermit has come out of his cave. How do you like our little town, now that you've taken a public look?'

'How do you like it,' he countered, 'now that you've been dragged back to it?'

'Oh, I love it. I've got a beautiful room in my prison with a view. My keeper is something that was a man once. You must come up and see the new bars on my window.'

'They had a legal right to bring you back,' he pointed out. 'You're not eighteen yet. What were you running from, anyway?'

'To,' she corrected. 'I was running to. When they told me I was not to tell exactly what happened at Harry's, I ran off to find some place that cared more for a life than civic virtue.'

'Did you find it?'

'I guess not,' she said wearily. 'I guess any other place would be the same. What difference does it make? What do you want, anyway? Must be something brewing to make you come out of your shell.'

'Where's Fred?'

'How should I know? Why do you want to see him? You've been enemies for years now.'

Billy put his new resolution into words for the first time. 'I want to straighten out something that happened a long time ago.'

Marlin stopped, fixed her dark eyes on his. They looked wordlessly at each other. She wanted to ask questions, to bring an eight-year suspicion into the open, but she couldn't. She couldn't bear to know finally that she had not painted the poster which had brought her national notice.

'Have you tried his home?' she asked finally.

'He hasn't been there since the night at Harry's.'

She frowned down at her black and white shoes. 'There's a little dive over at Elton,' she said slowly. 'He took me there once. It has rooms upstairs. I was headed there, to make him come home and tell what happened to Jerry, but father caught me. You might try it. Blackie's, it's called.'

'Thanks.' He turned away and walked towards the interurban line which ran between Mulveta and the county seat.

'Billy,' she called after him. He halted. 'Are you sure you're—doing the right thing?'

'I'm sure,' he said, and went on.

Billy had to confess, as the interurban rattled through green fields and across Turkey Creek towards Elton, that he was not sure at all. But the experiment should be interesting.

He looked through the window at old Kirby's stand of young corn, and compared himself to the slender green stalks reaching to the sun. They were tended, supervised in their struggles towards maturity, but he was on his own. Nobody would offer him support in this move against his father and Old Nick.

He tried to imagine what forces would be brought to bear against him, so that he could protect himself, but what acts his own would inspire were beyond imagination. He must wait and see. One thing he did know: he was going through with this as long as he had life.

Man or demon, demon and/or man, Billy Roberts was not going to be pushed around any longer.

He had fought a losing passive fight; now he was going to carry the battle into their camp.

Jerry Folsom's death had awakened his dormant resolve, dormant because he had not felt capable of outright rebellion—he had been too young. That feeling of youthfulness had been responsible for eight years of procrastination. He had not known how to act wisely when honour after honour was heaped upon Marlin until it was nation-wide in scope. So he had waited, kept quiet.

Not altogether, for parental heritage was too strong. There had been the time Jim Roberts had taken him to St. Louis to buy his first long trousers, and he had misdirected a frantic man in the railroad station.

The man had leaped on the wrong train as it moved out. Billy had giggled. It had been a good joke.

But he had learned, in one of the midnight visits of his father, that the man had not reached an important conference in time to prevent chicanery that was to involve millions of innocent people.

He had been further embittered when he had learned this. A normal childish impulse had played into their hands again.

Childish impulse. He had thought about this. Other children, young and old, had played and would play practical jokes. Were such acts diabolic in origin?

He thought not. They stemmed from a streak of human cussedness, and he doubtless had his share. But he had been assured once by his father that he was the only one of his kind. He was an experiment, endowed with a conscious will to destroy moral fibre. If he submitted to that side of his heritage and took advantage of certain special abilities, he could throw a comparatively large section of humanity into such confusion that highly desirable excesses, from his father's point of view, would result.

Then others like him would be produced, an organized cabal of evil, bent upon destruction of morale and morality.

Which was all right with Billy. He cared nothing for the moves and countermoves of Old Nick and the Others mentioned occasionally by his father. But he did resent being a tool, and had fought against it for eight years.

He had not succeeded altogether, for there had been other incidents like the man and the train. But he had succeeded in the main, for he had withdrawn from contact with others. The Hermit, schoolfellows called him. Sure, he was lonesome, plenty. But he had had to think his problem through, and at the same time not contribute to the aims and purposes of his father and Old Nick.

Passive stubbornness had been the only weapon Billy knew how to use, and he had used it against his father, who had come to exhort him at midnight, against Jim and Lucille Roberts, who were honestly worried about his seclusive habits, and against Old Nick, who pretended solicitude with an amused gleam in his yellow eyes. And he had won out to some extent; his father hadn't appeared for a long time, Jim and Lucille as well as the townspeople came to accept his self-enforced solitude as part of his nature, and Old Nick left him alone.

But the death of Jerry Folsom drove him to action. He recognized it as one of the ramifications of that childhood incident which had diverted a few lives from intended channels. He recognized also that it would not end there. He could not change effects already wrought, but he could try to restore to their destinies Fred Roth, Dr. Stone, Miss Elkins, and Gary Fargo.

He rapped on Blackie's locked door, and presently a panel slid back to reveal a face.

'I want to see Fred Roth,' Billy said.

'Never heard of him,' the face replied.

'He's here,' Billy said. 'I know he's here.'

He did know, too. He couldn't have told you how, because that was part of his heritage you couldn't understand, but he knew.

The face didn't reply. It withdrew, and the panel closed.

Billy looked about him. Men and women were abroad, and doubtless one or more had him under unconscious observation. He eyed the office building across the street. Idle eyes might be on him there, too. Roving glances touched him, also, from passing cars. This was the wrong entrance for him to use—that way.

He walked leisurely to the corner, left to the alley, up it to Blackie's back door. After he made certain nobody was watching him, he simply walked through the door and upstairs to the dingy hall. Rooms opened off this. When he came to the door of Fred Roth's room, he knew he was in for trouble.

The voice that had denied knowledge of Fred Roth was speaking. 'And if he knows you're here, so do other people. You got to blow.'

Billy identified it with some surprise as the voice of a woman. He listened for the answer. It came from a stranger, to him.

'With the most exquisite pleasure, my dunghill rose. But we can't go out in nothing but pants. Give us the rest of our clothes, Blackie.'

A third voice made derisive comment. 'Give, Blochner? Blackie wouldn't *give* us a second thought. She'd charge for it. Huh, Blackie?'

'I'm not in this business for my health, Sammy Saltzer,' Blackie replied harshly. 'I get a hundred bucks, you get your duds.'

'Oh,' said another voice wearily, 'go take a bath. Or open a window. We haven't got a hundred dollars.'

'No dough, no duds,' Blackie said firmly. 'And you can put that on your thumbnail and sniff it, Rocky Flood.'

'But on the other hand,' Ray Blochner put in, 'no duds, no dough, my essence of garbage. Stalemate.'

'Stale or not,' Blackie retorted. 'Gonna get my dough. And you cokies are gonna blow.'

'How do you *like* that?' Sammy Saltzer said to the world at large. 'What a brain, what a brain!'

Billy put knuckles to the door, saw it nearly jerked off its hinges to reveal a huge female with lank grey hair, undersized eyes and oversized chin.

One of her large red hands leaped at Billy's throat, and a small flicker of surprise touched her eyes when the hand closed on air. She blinked, looked at him closely.

'Whadda you want?' she snarled.

'Fred Roth,' Billy said quietly.

'Snap out of it, Freddie,' Sammy Saltzer said behind Blackie. 'The marines are here now.'

'How'd you—' Blackie began. She broke off, thought for a second, and demanded vehemently, 'How *did* you get in?'

'Probably,' Ray Blochner observed quietly, 'through the holes in the plaster. Most anybody could.'

'I want Fred Roth,' Billy repeated.

'You get a kick in the stomach,' Blackie growled, 'if you don't scram outa here, punk.'

Billy saw Fred raise himself on the bed and turn a look of tired resignation towards the door. 'Who is it, police? Oh, hello, Bill. Come on in.'

Blackie made a blocking motion, but before it was completed, Billy was inside the stale-aired room. Blackie stared at him, at her hands, and her loose face seemed to come to pieces for a second. Then she stood very still, watching intently.

'Get your clothes,' Billy said; 'we're going home.'

'You got a C note?' Blackie demanded. 'That's what it takes to get him outa here.'

A small, contemptuous rage began to flicker in Billy. It was a new sensation to him, full of exhilaration and promise of wild excitement. What a pleasure it would be to give these clods an experience that would haunt them to their graves! To provide them with a strange illusion that would shatter moral fibre. Something they could not believe, but dared not doubt.

There lay his true destiny, and he knew it in a sudden surge of flaming hatred for these and their kind. They were created for his own amusement, and no greater joy existed than to see them broken slowly, exquisitely; to see them and their million brothers break themselves by futile resistance to forces they could never know or comprehend; to see them die, old and empty, unknowing of what had gone before or what was still to come.

Yes, and to see hope wither on its stem, and bitterness flower sullenly as they forever reached for a goal held slyly beyond their groping; to see them subside at last back into the morass of circumstance in whose creation they never had a hand.

He threw off these thoughts abruptly, for they were his father talking. To accede to their urging was to remain a tool, and he had come here to break their hold. He looked in some astonishment at the expressions of Blackie, Ray Blochner, Rocky Flood, and Sammy Saltzer. Fred Roth had apparently dropped his head into his cupped hands, but the others looked at him in—not exactly awe, or fear, or worship, but something of all these were in their widened eyes.

Had he been transformed by his own thoughts? Surely not, for this shell was a human body, bound by familiar laws.

He could consciously apply certain formulas known instinctively to himself to create phenomena, but so could they, if they knew. Surely, thoughts alone, whether born in passive contemplation or driving emotion, could not change him.

Apparently something had, or they thought it had. But now their eyes began to change. Relief grew, as if they had wakened from a realistic dream. Now they recognized it as a dream, but still some of its effect remained.

'Get your clothes,' Billy said to Fred Roth.

He raised his young, utterly weary face and looked at Blackie with a question. She answered abstractedly, with a trace of fear.

'I'll get 'em,' she said quietly, and went away.

Fred blinked, looked at Billy, at the others. 'What goes on here?'

They didn't answer. They looked away, at the spotted walls, at the peeled ceiling. Billy waited quietly.

Blackie returned with a pile of coats, shirts, socks and shoes. She flung them on the floor.

'Now get out of here,' she said hoarsely.

While they dressed, Billy recounted events up to and including the inquest.

'Nobody's looking for you,' he said. 'It's all over. You guys, though, had better go somewhere else. Fred stays here, at least till I get through talking to him.'

They nodded in agreement. Rocky Flood put on his shoes and kicked out the single windowpane.

'The foul air,' he explained, 'was beginning to get me. I was seeing things.'

Sammy Saltzer and Ray Blochner seemed to leap at this explanation. Puzzlement went out of their eyes. They smiled.

They didn't see Blackie as they clattered downstairs and out to the street. Sammy, Ray and Rocky shook hands with Fred. They went off on separate ways.

Fred stared after them, turned to Billy. 'Did I miss something? They act awful funny. And Blackie, the old—'

'Never mind,' Billy said. 'Let's go home. I got things to say to you.'

Old Nick was on the interurban. Billy pretended not to see him, but all the way to Mulveta he could feel amused yellow eyes on the back of his neck.

SIX

Billy's father came that night, with words as bracing as an icy shower. Billy lay in the midnight blackness with his eyes closed, listening. He no longer attempted to get a clear look at this creature; his appearance was no longer a matter of interest. But his words were, tonight.

'Now you have tasted it,' his father said. 'You know the thrill of your heritage, and you will never let it go. The memory of your brief experience this afternoon will drive you to rages more transforming than today's flicker. By the judicious use of hate and anger, you will come into your own.'

His own? Billy wondered what that might be, specifically. He had never had a clear picture of what he was meant to do or become; all his father's comments and all his own thoughts had dealt with rather broad generalities.

But he didn't interrupt to ask. He lay with his eyes closed, remembering the delicious excitement of the afternoon, when he had become—well, Something. He couldn't say what, for he had not been conscious of change. Neither could he interpret the expressions of those who had seen the transformation.

'I come to praise you again,' his father continued. 'You brought a change into the lives of four persons this afternoon that will affect large sections of mankind. Moral dissolution had already begun to set in, and by driving them out into wider fields you will have extended the effects of that dissolution to important proportions. The three musicians will join separate organizations. By their virtuosity they will command the respect of their fellows, and by their conduct lead them into excesses which will inject madness into their music. All who hear them will be stimulated to develop habit patterns which we can view with delight.

'As for the woman, she will go into business in a large centre of population. Haunted by what she saw today, she will seek wilder and wilder diversions. She will be highly successful in attracting larger and larger crowds, because of entertainments she will provide for their senses. She will be imitated by other entrepreneurs until the impact of what you have done today will spread across the civilized world.'

'So,' Billy thought. 'So. Whatever I do, I play into their hands. Still a tool, that's Roberts. Too late now to stop Blackie, Ray, Sammy, and Rocky. That's done, and they'll go right out and have their effect. But these others, these four, Fred, Dr. Stone, Miss Elkins, Mr. Fargo. They can be put back on their paths.'

His father shrugged Fred off into the future. 'I must confess, my son, that your plan for the boy Fred Roth seems obscure. But, as I have remarked before, you have an instinctive grasp of human values that I cannot have. So I wait and watch—all of us do—with fascination.'

Billy's emotion changed from wariness to tentative triumph. Was this possible? Heretofore, his father had been able to analyse the motives behind any of his acts in detail. But that was when Billy, consciously or unconsciously, had the same broad aims as his father. Now that the aim and purpose were radically opposed to his father's, that creature did not understand.

It was too soon to say with certainty that such was the case, but it was not too soon to watch, to analyse, to plan.

'Frankly,' his father went on, 'your treatment of his case this afternoon aroused some criticism, and suggestions for corrective measures were made by—some. But I counselled that we wait and watch. You have brought my predictions to brilliant reality in the past, and there exists no reason why you should not continue to do so. There is every reason why you should.'

Billy interrupted with a small trial deceit. 'I just told Fred that he really painted that poster, and that he'd be a sap not to take up art again. He believed it, because it's true. You got to tell enough truth to make people take whatever else you want to tell 'em.'

There was a small, fragile silence in the darkness. Billy's father broke it with a dry chuckle.

'I see. I see, my son. In your first awareness of power, you are experimenting with elaboration, with complex misdirection. You have the ability to succeed, and results are so much more gratifying than those obtained with simple acts. There will be no more criticism. There will be no corrective measures. You have my word on it.'

Billy wanted to ask about these corrective measures. But he did not, for to display too much interest might arouse suspicions of his critics, of whom there were apparently some in his father's circle. He said:

'What did you mean, come into my own?'

His father hesitated for a long moment. 'The steps by which you will develop to full stature will depend upon how you apply yourself to chosen tasks, and cannot be told now. I may say, however, that as a reward for what you accomplished today, your tongue has been—ah, touched. From now you will say exactly the right word at the right time. This power has heretofore been granted only to those who wished to sell their souls. They are not many, I am sorry to say. It has been fascinating to see the uses to which they put this power. At present there is only one, a house painter in some European country, Austria, I believe. But this is a gift to you, and you can become a leader of men if you choose.'

Billy lay in the darkness, smiling to himself after his father had gone. A new poise, a new confidence, was solid and calm within himself. His was now a power with unlimited uses. He felt that he could even turn it against Old Nick and his father if he liked. That would be pleasant, he thought.

* * *

Cynthia Elkins had been ready for an hour. She glanced at her watch for the fiftieth time, and for the twentieth time left the front window of her little cottage to give a last look at herself in the bedroom mirror.

She couldn't see much more than her head and shoulders in the oval glass, but she searched her image as if it were an examination paper she suspected of containing an undotted 'i.' She smiled at herself. 'You don't *look* twenty-nine,' she thought. 'Old Lady Elkins, indeed! It's just that the cruel little brats call everyone Old Lady This or Old Man That. No, your eyes and hair are dark and shining, your face and throat are smooth, and you look a little wicked with that fancy collar against the dark-blue dress. Why, you're blushing! Well, it's nice to *look* a little wicked—for him. He'll notice. He notices everything. He'll even notice—

'Quit starting guiltily! This is your own house, and you're alone in it. Go ahead and look at your legs if you want. They're yours, aren't they? You can stand on that chair and get a pretty good look in the mirror. There! Hike the skirt a little. No, too high. People would talk. They'll talk anyway.

'But why should they? You're performing an act of kindness. He's lonely, and would like an evening of intelligent conversation. He said so. It's an act of kindness. You can get down off the chair now.

'No, no lipstick. Do you want to look like a painted hussy? Do you want to look like that Marlin Stone? No lipstick. What if she does attract people? You know you'd rather spend the rest of your life alone than attract them the way she does. You would, too. Stop looking stricken.

'Why doesn't he come on? Well, he *could* be early.

'What was it he said to call him? Oh, you mustn't, though. Not in public, anyway. It might be all right in private, but not where anyone could hear you.'

She leaned nearer to the mirror, and imagined another head beside hers, distinguished, worldly, white-haired, and with a very impressive beard.

'Hello, Nick,' she whispered, blushing.

Gary Fargo put aside the crime-action magazine, and the crackle of Tommy-guns died slowly inside his head. Death comes to the arch criminal. As it should, he said hastily to himself. As it should. You can't let them break either legal or moral codes with impunity. Die they must, and like the rats they are.

But—

Yes, but. One taste, one short excursion into that life would compensate for the deadly dullness here. To have a keen, incisive brain—which he felt he had—to make lightning decisions, to protect his men, to . . . to have a moll.

Yes, to have a moll. Someone like . . . like . . . well, like Marlin Stone, dammit. Not to be seen in public with her, of course, but in the night, privately. In the hide-out. One couldn't face one's townspeople after being seen in public with such a one, but one could face these spring twilights with a heady sense of waiting, by the gods!

No, on second thought, no. He was principal of Mulveta's school, a position of responsibility and importance. He was getting something done. He was guiding the young. Some regret was to be expected in renouncing that other, colourful, existence, but in the end it was worth it.

These springs nights, though—

He got to his feet and walked around his study, the length of his stride taxing his short legs. His round eyes touched a stack of papers on his desk and moved away. They were to be read and corrected, for it was important that students in his civics class receive proper guidance, but not now, not now.

Not while twilight lay on the town, and a half moon rode at the zenith. A man had to have something.

He examined himself in the wall mirror. He took off his spectacles, polished them with gleaming linen. He put them back and looked again. He took a little comb from his vest pocket and combed brown hair over his growing bald spot. He put his hat on, adjusted it to a sober angle. He straightened his tie. He examined his fingernails. He went out.

He looked at the moon. He didn't smile at it, he didn't sneer. He just looked. Then he dropped his head and strolled along the street, white-lined with spring blooms.

In the next block was the little cottage with the baby-blue trim where Cynthia lived. Would she see him tonight, hail him from her front door? They could meet at her gate for a few moments of decorous conversation. They never had, but they could. That wouldn't offend the proprieties. Even if the neighbours were watching, that would be all right.

'Cynthia,' he thought, 'are you going to let your youth rot here? Are you going to let me rot here?'

He stopped. Three doors ahead—from Cynthia's door—an exodus was being made. She was on somebody's arm. This somebody had an air. A man of the world. You could tell by the way he walked that he was the epitome of the exciting male. A little pain touched Gary Fargo's heart as the couple came through her gate and turned towards him.

'I've come to lure you,' Old Nick said. 'To ply you with wickedness. You've been softened up by now.'

Cynthia took her hand from his and frowned slightly. This wasn't the note to be struck—not yet. What did he think she was? What would people say if they could hear? Or if they knew how her heart was hurling blood along her veins? She could feel it in his fingertips, and her temples.

'Won't you sit down?' she said coldly. 'May I take your hat and cloak?'

'Won't you get your hat?' he countered. 'I don't suppose you'd dare go out without it?'

'Are you—going out?'

His yellow eyes gleamed. 'Certainly. You'd be uncomfortable here, when I'd tell you all the things you've missed, all the things you should know. You can listen, and dream, and laugh publicly at ideas you'd shrink from in privacy. Sad, but true.'

Miss Elkins blinked. Perhaps it would be better to go out, after all. And, yes, she'd not dare go without a hat.

'Excuse me,' she said, and went to put it on.

He took her arm as they walked to her gate. The touch of his fingers just above her elbow sent delicious little ripples of sensation clear to her toes. Her eyes, she thought, must be very pretty now.

Why, there was Gary . . . er, Mr. Fargo. How awkward. What would he think? That Mr. Nicholas was an uncle? He didn't look like an uncle, he didn't act like one. No. Mr. Fargo didn't think he was, either. You could tell by that stricken look. Oh, dear, what can you say? You've got to say something.

'Good evening, Mr. Fargo.'

The slight bow, the slight tipping of his hat. You could tell what he was thinking, all right. Well, let him think! He symbolized this little dot on the map. Never step out of the straight and narrow.

They walked on. Funny that Mr. Nicholas didn't say anything. She stole a sidewise glance at him. He seemed to be amused, as if he were reading her thoughts.

They walked on towards the interurban line. Miss Elkins didn't nod at the half dozen persons they met as they passed Forbes' confectionery, Riker's drugstore, and Runt's pool hall. They didn't speak to her.

But she looked sharply at a youth who eyed them as he approached along the sidewalk. It was that Roberts boy, and he had a strange expression on his narrow face. She couldn't cut him dead.

'How do you do?' he said to both of them.

'Good evening, Billy,' she answered. She felt suddenly ashamed. She didn't know why. It was some overtone in his voice. It brought home to her the responsibilities she had accepted when she became a schoolteacher.

Mr. Nicholas didn't speak to the boy. She flicked another sidewise glance, and saw the yellow eyes twinkling at the boy and—yes, at her, too.

Billy spoke directly to her companion. 'Bored?' he asked. That was all. He bowed slightly and went on.

Old Nick and Cynthia Elkins went on.

The interurban line came nearer and nearer. It began to loom in her mind like an unwelcome temptation. If that Roberts boy hadn't come along with his sly insinuations. No, they weren't insinuations. They were true. Truth is truth and that's all there is to it. One simply didn't do certain things. Especially with . . . with an old rake. Oh, dear! How could she live with herself after this? She stopped, turned to Old Nick.

'I don't expect you to understand, Mr. Nicholas. But goodbye. I must go home. I've got to go home. Good night.'

He didn't answer, he didn't bow. She carried with her a small anger at his obvious amusement. Let him laugh! Right was right and wrong was wrong, and there was no compromise. It was all right for him and his kind, who had no sense of responsibility, to flout certain conventions. But those conventions were the basis of right living, and you either conformed or you were not the right kind of person.

And she hadn't intended to flout them in the first place, she told herself. Curiosity had been her motivation. She had wanted to know, so that the knowing would give her a broader grasp of people, a broader understanding.

But you didn't have to go through some things to know. There were fundamental eternal truths that you knew by instinct. If you had a sense of responsibility, you abided by them.

Oh, there he was. Mr. Fargo had not returned home. He was coming towards her along the path she had so lightly trod a moment before. She slowed her headlong pace. She touched her hair to make sure it was not disarranged. She smoothed the front of her dark-blue dress, and smoothed it over her hips.

'Mr. Fargo,' she said with a breathlessness that was not altogether the result of her hurrying. 'I'm a little frightened. Will you see me home, please?'

He blinked. His round face began to beam. 'With pleasure,' he said gravely.

'It won't inconvenience you?' she asked anxiously.

'Not at all, not at *all*.'

They strolled along the quiet street. She looked up. There was a moon. She hadn't noticed.

SEVEN

It was not his father who appeared in Billy's room that night. Even before the creature spoke, Billy knew this. There was not only an alien *feel* to it, but an ominousness. This was the enemy.

'All right,' it said harshly, 'let's have it.'

'Have what?' Billy asked.

'What's your game? You're up to something. So let's have it.'

Billy smiled. 'Or else?'

'Yes! Or else.'

'Did Old Nick send you?'

'Nick!' the creature snorted. 'What does he care? He says it doesn't matter in the end, and we can play our games. But this is no game, my bucko. You can't play fast and loose with us and get away with it. You're a serious experiment, and you've got to act like it. Why did you throw those two together again?'

'Who?'

'And don't play dumb! You're not fooling anybody. I know you're almost as smart as Nick himself. Almost. The old maid and the old fool, that's who.'

'I didn't throw them together.'

'Now look,' his visitor said patiently, 'I'm not even listening to what you say, because you could probably talk me out of it. I know your tongue's been touched. But I want to know what's going on. If you're pulling a fast one, let me tell you—don't. You won't like what happens.'

'What could happen? What could you do?'

'Listen, I'm not a show-off. I didn't come here to bandy tortures with you. I'm asking you one more time, what's up?'

'What could be up?' Billy countered. 'I was told I couldn't help doing whatever I do. It's born in me.'

'Your old man talks too much. Besides, he's a dreamer. That's why he never advanced any further than he has. You know and I know you can try anything you please. But you can't get away with double-crossing. I'll see to that. Or be damned for it.'

'Are you my old man's boss? You're not a dreamer?'

'I didn't get to be a supervisor sticking pins in old ladies. I work on a big scale, not with individuals. But I'm gonna work on you, bud. You're important, if you pan out. So that's why I want to know. You did something you weren't supposed to do. Why?'

'Whoever or whatever this creature is,' Billy thought, 'he talks a lot. Maybe that's all he does. Maybe he won't really do anything.'

'I don't have to tell you,' he said.

There was a little silence.

Then, from all sides gigantic shapes of terror lunged at him. They could not actually be seen, but, like figures in a nightmare, could be sensed. Billy could neither discern nor divine their real shapes, but he felt a frantic need to escape, to beat them off.

For they gibbered. It wasn't words, but obscene threats drooling from great mouths.

He tried to move and could not. Like the dreamer of a nightmare, he was frozen in his bed. His arms were leaden, his neck rigid. He couldn't even cry out the terror that had him in a cold sweat, that was driving him to madness.

The pressure eased, and he gasped. 'I'll tell you!'

The pressure went away, the unseen shapes vanished.

'I hate that sort of thing,' his visitor said. 'I think it's silly. Impish. Not grown up. But sometimes it's necessary. Now tell.'

'The trouble with you,' Billy said, 'is you can't wait to see what happens. You want everything right now. Listen. What I've done already to Mr. Fargo and Miss Elkins is only the beginning. I'm gonna do lots more to them and some others. But it'll come out all right in the end. You'll see.'

'Hm-m-m,' his visitor said dubiously. 'I don't know what to say. I know you're clever. I ought to, the way your old man bubbles over you. But you could get things in a mess if you wanted to, and what the Auditors would say I don't know. I don't want to know. And I don't feel that I can trust you.'

'What could I do? Old Nick is around all the time.'

'I told you,' his visitor snapped, 'that he doesn't care about details. He takes the long view. He didn't try to stop you tonight, did he? No, he thinks it's funny. He thinks everything's funny. No sense of sobriety, that's Nick. All he wants is results, and he enjoys getting 'em, no matter how long it takes.'

'Well, I've told you. If you don't believe me, I can't help it.'

'In my business, bud, you don't believe anybody. You should hear some of the stories I get. Some of 'em say, 'Oh, but I don't belong here, really. There must be a mistake.' And the things they can dream up to make it sound good! Listen, I wouldn't believe Nick himself, on a pile of Pit cinders.'

'Then do whatever you want to, and beat it,' Billy said. 'I got to go to school tomorrow, and I'm sleepy.'

Silence fell. It lengthened, and lengthened, and lengthened. There was a troubled sigh, and then Billy knew he was alone.

Had he won? Well, he hadn't been hurt, he hadn't been stopped, he hadn't given out any information. But still—

It was a sense of things to come, unpleasant things, that kept him awake in the dark.

Where would it end? If he could stall long enough, he could straighten out the mess he created as a child, as far as its principals were concerned. But what then? What would they do, or try to do, to him? How could he protect himself against them?

He shivered, thinking of those shapes that lunged at him out of the darkness. All the while it had been happening, he had known it was a trick, but his terror had been tangible almost. It was a terror you could have weighed, or bitten. And that had been off the arm. It wasn't planned, or elaborate. What could they do when they really tried?

But he was going ahead with it until they stopped him. What they had done to him wasn't fair. It was as if they had given him wings and told him not to fly outside his own room. If his every act were to be dictated by Old Nick and his kind, why should he exist at all?

He could be a leader of men, his father had said. Sure, like that goat in the stockyards that led the sheep to the slaughter pen. But who wanted to be a goat? Not all your life, anyway.

He thought of Fred Roth, how Fred had reacted when he confessed that he had turned in the poster under Marlin's name.

'I was just a kid, Fred,' he'd said, 'And she wanted it. I wanted her to have it. I'm sorry it caused you all this trouble.'

The strange fact was that he had been sorry. Fred hadn't gone in much for the simple joys of youth. He'd fallen in with older musicians, and had learned to play like an angel. He'd driven himself towards a sophistication that was as false as it was damaging.

It was only natural that he had gravitated into that bunch at Harry's. They were seeking sensations, too, though their reasons were different. They'd had their day. They were just trying to hang on to it, whereas Fred was trying to create one.

But maybe Fred was straightened out now. What was it he'd said?

'I guess it was yours to give, Bill. You gave me the idea and told me how to do it.'

'But *you* painted it, Fred. I didn't do that.'

'Yeah. That's right. I'm glad I know that.'

'You can paint others, too, Fred. You really got something.'

'Maybe. It's more fun than blowing a horn, anyway. Look, Bill, I've had a bad time. I'm sorry about Jerry, I don't know what to do.'

'Paint pictures. That's what you want to do. Sure, you're sorry about Jerry. Who isn't? But it's done. So paint.'

'Maybe I will. Come over some time?'

'Sure thing.'

Billy thought of that promise with warmth. It would b nice to have a friend—again.

Well, that took care of Fred, it seemed. Leave it alone now, and stall these midnight visitors when they got curious.

And Miss Elkins and Mr. Fargo were straightened out, too, apparently. Else why this visit tonight from the 'supervisor'? Remaining was Dr. Stone. And Marlin?

Funny, his father had never gone into that question. Had Marlin become what she was as a result of his act? But what was she? She was honest, that was sure. It was true that she did not conform to patterns laid down by school authorities, but how could she, cooped up in that big house with Verna and Gloria? That would drive anybody to drink, and worse. But the question was, had she been intended to grow up this way or had she been jolted out of her destined channel by Billy Roberts?

He couldn't say. Of one thing he was certain, though: he would surely like to do something about Marlin. She was all right.

Principal Gary Fargo touched his head to see that his bald spot was covered when his secretary announced that Marlin Stone had answered his summons. He arranged his round face in an expression of disapproval and removed all but a faint spark from his eyes as she sauntered through the door in a blue blouse matching her eyes and setting off honey-coloured hair, a jaunty skirt revealing smooth knees, and white, high-heeled shoes.

He repressed his desire to spring up and offer a chair, to touch her bare arm, perhaps, as he helped her into it. As he shifted his eyes from her clear, level gaze, a fleeting memory bothered him. He had been thinking of her only a few days ago, but in what connection? It seemed to him that it had occurred on the night he had met Cynthia and taken her home, but the reason why he had been thinking of Marlin eluded him. Well, it was of no importance.

'Please sit down,' he said without expression.

Her full mouth twitched at the corners. 'I'll stand.'

'As you please.' He gathered his thoughts, reviewed in his mind the stormy teachers' meeting of the preceding night. 'Miss Stone, as you are possibly aware, we, who are instructors, have a grave responsibility towards our charges.'

She said nothing to this. The pause began to be embarrassing, and he hurried on:

'We must instill in them an awareness of their obligations to others and to themselves. It is no small task, I assure you. Youthful spirits are inclined to . . . ah, break over the traces.' He smiled apologetically for the slang phrase. 'We are inclined to excuse infractions of codes of behaviour so long as they do not become habitual, for they bespeak healthy growth. Corrective measures, however, are necessary at times. Do you follow me?'

She smiled tolerantly.

Fargo flushed, continued: 'I regret that such an occasion has arisen . . . er, that such an occasion is . . . ah, that is to say, an incident which has been brought to our attention seems to warrant such treatment. But we do not act hastily. We should like to hear your version of the incident. You know, of course, to what I refer. Have you anything to say?'

Marlin twisted her mouth down at one corner and looked at him until his eyes shifted. 'You've made up your mind, Mr. Fargo. I heard about your little party last night. How you and your girl friend swung the others in line.'

'Miss Stone!'

'All right, how you and Miss Elkins carried the banner. Go ahead and kick me out. Get it over with.'

'Our constitution,' he said firmly, 'grants every person the right to hear and defend himself against charges. That is why you are here. You are charged with smoking on school property. Have you anything to say?'

'Nope.'

'You admit it?'

Marlin shrugged. She felt a certain bitter amusement, remembering how she had gone into the girls' locker room and found Lucy Belle Wethers sneaking a smoke. How she had told Lucy Belle, the class ranking student, that Miss Elkins was close behind. How Lucy Belle had shoved the cigarette at her with an 'Oh, deah, do something with it!' And how Miss Elkins had come in and found her. The situation itself was beside the point, of course, if she were to be honest.

'I have smoked on school property, as about ninety per cent of my class have. It's no secret, is it, that we students smoke? It couldn't be, or there wouldn't be any rules about it.'

'We have seen no evidence,' Mr. Fargo said evenly, 'that your classmates indulge such habits. We do have evidence in your case. You must admit that such incidents are not examples of good conduct?'

'Look, Mr. Fargo. Will you be honest?'

He made a gesture like a pigeon ruffling its feathers. 'I believe,' he said haughtily, 'that I have such a reputation.'

'Do you? Well, then, answer me this. Would it do me any good to defend myself? Really?'

'Miss Stone! Every person has the right to defend himself. Your question reflects to my discredit. It implies that I am not open-minded.'

'Well, are you? You and Miss Elkins fought to have me expelled. Then you fought to get you the right to use your own judgment. Hadn't you made up your mind before I got here? Honest?'

'I had not!' he snapped. 'I am rapidly coming to a decision, however, as a result of your insinuations.'

'Then lay on, MacDuff,' she murmured.

'You leave me no alternative, Miss Stone. Once,' he said, 'you distinguished yourself, and brought nationwide credit to this school. But that triumph seemed to stultify you. You made no further efforts along artistic lines, and—'

'I'm no artist,' she interrupted. 'Miss Elkins knew it then, I could tell.'

'That is beside the point. Since that time you have broken rule after rule. These infractions have been overlooked because of your fine background—'

'My stepmother's money, you mean.'

'Please! We have reached our limit. Unless you take an oath to give up the injurious habit of using tobacco in any form and apply yourself to your studies, I must expel you.'

'I won't make any such promise, Mr. Fargo. I don't think it's important, whether I smoke or not. And I think it's my business, not yours. I may not be of age, but I'm old enough to decide certain things for myself.'

'Then I must regretfully inform you, Miss Stone, that you are no longer a member of this student body.'

Old Nick twinkled across the dining table at Billy and helped himself to scalloped potatoes. 'What else could you expect?' he asked. 'Medals?'

'But why pick on Marlin?' Billy demanded. 'Almost everybody smokes.'

'Billy!' Lucille interposed. 'You don't?'

'Once in a while. Why?'

'Oh, Billy,' she wailed. 'You're just a baby.'

'You'd better not let me catch you,' Jim Roberts said. 'You're not old enough yet. When you're eighteen, we'll talk it over.'

'All right,' Billy said impatiently. 'I'll quit. Buy why pick on her?' he asked Old Nick again.

'You are aware,' Old Nick said humorously, 'that a new alliance has been . . . well, not consummated, I assure you, but formed. Miss Elkins and Mr. Fargo have converged on each other after several years of moving along separate paths. During those several years, they developed certain mental habit patterns. They convinced themselves that a certain rigorousness was the laudable and satisfying factor in living. When they formed their spiritual merger, they were strengthened in their rigid appraisal of conduct. Like the dog in the manger, they are prevented by themselves from enjoying certain lapses, and their code becomes the righteous code. Singly, neither of them would have prosecuted the case against Marlin with such fervour. But in their new-found strength, they will wage war to the death against what from their viewpoint is evil. Whose name is Legion.'

'But,' Billy persisted, 'why pick on Marlin?'

'Surely it's simple,' Old Nick replied. 'Marlin is everything Miss Elkins cannot bring herself to be: honest, beautiful, curious, and courageous. She is everything Mr. Fargo cannot have: excitement, adventure, the prize of conquest. So they ganged up on her. They'll be even stronger in this respect,' Old Nick mused, 'after their coming emotional . . . uh, union. It won't be very satisfactory to either.'

Once again, Billy thought, he had played into Old Nick's hands. The future actions of Elkins-Fargo would bring results gratifying to Nick. You could tell that by the pleasure in his voice. Was it going to be thus, always?

EIGHT

Gerald Folsom, Sr., posted another entry to customers' accounts, and glanced at the clock. Three minutes to five. He put one elbow on his desk, spread his hand horizontally and laid his mild grey face in it.

Jerry, he thought. Jerry used to drop in around this time and walk home with him. While he finished the tag end of the day's work, Jerry would loaf out in the main office and kid around with Miss Holman. Jerry wasn't ashamed that his old man was merely a bookkeeper for the department of water and power. Jerry wasn't ashamed to appear on the street with him, though he was grey and a little stooped after fifteen years of bending over rows of figures.

Jerry had a great future. Had. That account at the bank, that special account, had three thousand four hundred eighteen dollars and twenty-six cents in it, not counting accrued interest falling due next week. It would have sent Jerry to college.

Jerry's future would have been his, too. His and Martha's. They would have watched him become the school basketball star, president of his class, editor of the school paper. They had discussed it, even before he was born, had planned it in detail. They had both worked towards one end, making their son a success.

All for nothing. All the years of skimping, doing without new clothes, using old furniture long past its day, not going to shows because of the cost—wasted. Washed out in one little moment of violence.

For six weeks now, they had sat silent at night, listening. Not that they expected to hear him come whistling up the walk, to burst in the front door, toss his cap on the couch and demand something to eat. No, he was dead and buried. They knew he wouldn't come back. But they sat listening.

There was nothing to talk about. They had been in the habit of totting up expenses, paring where they could, deciding how much they could put in the special account next week. Sometimes it would come to only fifty cents, but once it was as much as eight dollars less a few cents. They thought of that one magnificent week when everything broke right as the time they put in almost eight dollars. Not as more than seven. It seemed larger the other way, and that meant more comfort for Jerry in the end.

A stark realization of finality came to him as he sat with his face in his outspread hand. His life was over, too. His and Martha's. They had nothing to talk about any more, except the past; and the past was too painful to consider.

No, they couldn't talk about the exciting day, when they were already middle-aged, when they knew he was coming. They couldn't talk about the plans they'd made, or how he'd got hilariously drunk the day Jerry was born and brought home a complete football outfit. Or how he'd sheepishly returned it the next day and got his money back so they could buy him a crib.

They couldn't talk about it, because it didn't mean anything any more. Jerry was gone. And they couldn't tell each other again that he was a smart kid and popular, too.

They couldn't talk about the future, because it was just bending over this desk, shielding his eyes with a green eyeshade, posting entries, making out bills, sending second notices. Ten years of it to come. Then, retirement. For what? They'd planned that Jerry would have been self-supporting by then, perhaps married to a nice girl, and they could sit on the front porch for the rest of their lives waiting for the mailman to bring them news from their 'children.' And perhaps grandchildren, before they died.

The five o'clock whistle blew, and Gerald Folsom, Sr., straightened. With automatic motions, he closed his ledgers, tidied his desk, removed the eyeshade, shucked into his shiny coat, and put on his hat. These acts did not register on his conscious mind, for he was thinking of what he was going to do.

It wasn't fair that he and Martha should have all the suffering. He had decided that on the day of the coroner's inquest. But the inquest itself had given him nothing. Not a name, not a hint.

Afterwards, he had learned the true nature of Harry's Roadside Tavern, but by then it was closed and Harry was gone. He had debated a few days on whether to quit his job and run Harry to earth and kill him, but he wouldn't have known how to go about it. Besides, that wouldn't bring any suffering to anybody. It was doubtful if Harry's parents were still living, more doubtful that they would sit around their living room, empty, if Harry should die.

Then, a whisper here, a hint there, and he had built the picture of the incident. Freddie Roth. He had parents. He had been in the centre of things when it happened. Little Freddie, but not too little to bring suffering and death.

Justice was all Gerald Folsom, Sr., wanted. And there was no justice in a situation where only he and Martha sat night after night, listening. Surely no man could call that justice.

He muttered grave good-evenings at his fellow workers and went out into the street. He walked woodenly, with his slight shuffle, shoulders stooped, to Pete Worley's hardware store.

Pete's weather-bitten face sobered as he saw the old man enter. Damn it, how could you tell the nice little guy you were sorry his son got killed in a speak? Maybe if you just kept still you wouldn't have to say anything. You could just wait on him. You could quit twisting your hands, too, you big ox.

'I . . . . I would like to buy a gun,' Mr. Folsom said hesitantly.

'Goin' huntin'?' Pete asked jovially.

'Why . . . why, yes.'

'Got just the thing for you, then. Now you take this—' He took a double-barrelled shotgun from a rack, handling it as if it were a pretty girl. 'It shoots where you point it. Parker. Very good make. Full choke left, half choke right barrel. Knock a rabbit off at a hundred yards.'

'Why . . . I, uh, had something smaller in mind.'

Pete looked over his display. 'Well, here's a Remington sixteen, repeater. Can't go wrong on it.'

'No, I mean . . . a little gun, a pistol.'

'Can't do much huntin' with a pistol. Rats, maybe.'

'Yes,' Mr. Folsom said.

'Well, then! Here's the thing. Twenty-two target. Eight shot. Feel that balance.' Mr. Folsom took the gun gingerly and, after some fumbling, hefted it. Pete waxed enthusiastic. 'Sweet little gun, that. Point it like your finger. Hair trigger. Shoot the knobs off a horny toad at twenty paces.'

Mr. Folsom pointed the gun at the wall, closed his eyes and pulled the trigger. He opened his eyes, gazed through his spectacles with disappointment.

'Nothing happens.'

'Oh, you got to cock it. It's single action. Pull back the hammer. No, here. Lemme show you.'

Pete demonstrated. Mr. Folsom tried it.

'I'll take it, Will you load it?'

'Sure. How many shells you want?'

'Just what the gun holds.'

Pete frowned. 'You can't do much shootin' with eight shells. Besides, I can't break a box.'

'I'll pay for the box,' Mr. Folsom said mildly. 'But I want only enough to fill the gun.'

'O.K.,' Pete said, shrugging.

'You sure get some funny ones,' Pete thought, as he watched Mr. Folsom shuffle away with the gun in his pocket. 'If the little guy isn't careful, he'll fool around and shoot off one of his toes.'

Mr. Folsom, in his wooden fashion, walked up Main to Elm and turned toward Roth's. It was fitting that he had drawn a cheque on the special account to pay for this. He had invested part of Jerry's future in evening the score.

Somehow, that fact seemed to impart poetic justice to what he was going to do.

When he had come to the wooden swinging gate in the Roths' picket fence, he stood quietly for a moment and eyed the two-storey house. It was somewhat larger than his own, but not enough to matter. Mr. And Mrs. Roth would be no more lonely than he and Martha.

That was all he wanted—to even up matters. He assured himself again on this point. His was not a mission of revenge, for he knew that vengeance was not his. *Vengeance is mine, saith the Lord*. He had read it many times. But it didn't say anything about justice, or balancing accounts.

He opened the gate.

As he did so, he detected movement in the barn, out back by the Bellefluer apple tree. He had eaten those apples, a little flash of memory told him; Mrs.

Roth had given Jerry a basketful once, and Martha had made apple dumplings. While he recalled the incident, his eyes fixed on the loft window and identified the source of the movement. It was Fred.

'This way is better,' he thought as he skirted the house and shuffled towards the barn. 'No need to ask where Fred is. The shock will be greater if they just find him without any warning.' That was the way it had been in Jerry's case. No warning. This was the way of justice.

When he put a foot on the bottom step of the staircase mounting to the loft, Fred called out from above:

'That you, Billy? You'll have to hurry, while there's still light enough. What took you so long?'

Mr. Folsom went up. When his head projected above the loft door level, he saw Fred standing at an easel before the big north window, brush in one hand, palette on the other arm. Fred didn't turn until Mr. Folsom was clear of the stairs.

Then, 'See what you think of—' Fred began. He identified his visitor. 'Why, Mr. Folsom,' he said, puzzled.

Mr. Folsom said nothing. He moved nearer, put his hand on the gun that sagged his coat pocket, and concentrated on what he must do. Pull the hammer back until it clicks. That's it. Now take out the gun and point it like a finger.

'What you doing?' Fred cried, fear and bewilderment in his voice. 'Don't do that? Don't—'

Mr. Folsom pulled the trigger. Fred clapped a hand to his chest. His dark, intense face went slack with astonishment. 'You—shot me!' he said in a voice of wonder.

Mr. Folsom pulled back the hammer again, pulled the trigger again. This time, Fred jerked as the bullet hit, and fell to the floor. He lay there moaning, twisting in agony, and Mr. Folsom returned the gun to his pocket.

Mr. Folsom began to mutter a little monologue. It had no words, it was just sound. There was something tender in it, like the gurgling of a baby. He retraced his way carefully down the stairs and went away, crooning his meaningless monologue softly to himself.

Billy Roberts walked the few blocks to Fred Roth's deep in thought. How much time did he have before Old Nick would crack down? How long could he stall his father and the 'supervisor'? Now that Fred had begun in earnest to paint, he expected action, for they were watchful.

As he cut across a back yard along boyhood ways to the Roth barn, he saw a stooped little man going away. Mr. Folsom. What was he doing here?

A sudden premonition sent Billy over the Roths' back fence without touching it. He streaked in full flight to the barn and burst up the stairway.

Fred's face was covered with blood from a crease along the side of his head. Blood oozed between fingers clamped against his stomach. He was unconscious, but alive.

Billy ran to the house, found the telephone, and had Marlin on the phone when

Mrs. Roth came to investigate the commotion. Her kindly face was puzzled and questioning but when Billy waved her to silence she stood quietly, waiting.

'Is your father home?' Billy snapped into the telephone. He listened, interrupted. 'He can't go out. Keep him there. . . . I don't care if he's supposed to have dinner with the President. . . . You stop him. Tell him to get ready for an operation. . . . Fred Roth. . . . I'll get a hearse from Collins.'

He hung up, called the Collins Mortuary.

'What . . . Fred?' Mrs. Roth asked incoherently. 'What happened? Where's my boy?'

'He's bleeding to death in the barn,' Billy said brutally.

Mrs. Roth promptly fainted. That was good. She wouldn't clutter up the—

'Collins Mortuary,' a soft voice purled into the receiver. It was hopefully mournful, and you could hear in it the rubbing together of sad, black gloves.

'I know you haven't got an ambulance,' Billy said, 'so send a hearse with a stretcher over to Fred Roth's. Hurry! He's bleeding internally.'

'But we do not—' the voice began regretfully.

'I know it isn't good business for you,' Billy cut in, 'but you can save a boy's life if you step on it. And if you don't, how much business do you think you'll get from this town afterwards?'

'We're on our way,' the voice said briskly, 'Roth's? Two minutes.'

Billy took a quick look at Mrs. Roth. She was coming to, but maybe she'd be out for another two or three minutes and not be in the way. He ran out to the front fence and, not caring if anyone was watching, tore out a section large enough to let the hearse through.

It came screaming up Elm, the voice of succour in the trappings of death, and he motioned it through the gap to the barn. As it hurtled through, he leaped on the running board. He had the stretcher out and halfway up the stairs before the sombre car had come to a complete stop. The driver came flying after him.

Gloria Byington thought:

'Gosh, he's cute. You'd think he might be a college man. He does the same things to you when he talks. But really super. Not at all like those *boys* that Miss Petty imports for dances. Will he still be downstairs when I finish dressing?'

She examined herself in the mirror. 'Well,' she thought, 'you really are sort of lanky, but you're not a complete waste. Your skin is clear, and your eyes are pretty. Better wear a scarf over that scar on your throat. Yes, it's exciting, and several boys have wanted to kiss it, but it's best not to distract him tonight. He has a lot on his mind.

'Marlin would be simply furious if you took him away from her. She can pretend all she likes, but she's interested in him. So are lots of other girls. Woman hater, is he? Men have been cured of that before, mother says.

'A red scarf. It's better with straight black hair. There. That does something for you. You look well in green and red.

'Mother says men are simple. You just have to do something nice for them, and they follow you around. She's going to be angry at Dr. Stone, though. She doesn't like to see an opera alone.

'But who could have resisted him? I wanted to do the operation myself, when he got through talking. So did Marlin, I could see. How exciting he is. And how clever. He got Fred up here in eight minutes, he said.

'You can bet Dr. Stone will save him. He just has to, after the way Billy talked.'

'Will I be popular! The Junior Auxiliary of the Mulveta Browning Circle won't read much Browning tonight. A shooting, an emergency operation. They'll hang on my story. They always do, of course. It's nice to be envied. It's nice to own a bank. Well, it will be mine when I come into my money.

'That would be a good career for Billy. I must speak to Mr. Andrews.

'Now, you look all right, and you don't have much time. You've got to stop and say hello to him. The black fur, I think. It makes your hair shine. Here we go, then, ready or not.'

'How is he?' she asked Billy, who was sitting on the edge of the divan in the downstairs living room.

'I don't know. They're still in there,' he replied, running his eyes over her in a quick, appreciative appraisal.

'Did the nurse come?'

'Yes, Marlin's cleaning up, I guess. She helped Dr. Stone until the nurse got here.'

'Who shot him, Mr. . . . . er, Billy?'

'Mr. Folsom, I guess. I just talked to the constable on the phone. They picked him up with a gun on him. He was mad. He went out of his mind.'

'Quietly, no doubt,' Marlin said from the doorway. She came into the room, pale, strained. 'The way he always has done everything.' She examined Gloria. 'My! The plush horse. Very fancy, friend.'

'Thank you,' Gloria said frostily. 'Where are you going to spend the night tonight, Marlin?'

Marlin grinned. 'I'm going to spend the night with a man, dear.'

'How's Fred?' Billy interjected.

'You can tell the papers,' Marlin said, 'that our brilliant local physician and surgeon, Dr. George Stone, extracted the slug. It was lodged in his spinal column. He's going to be all right. Yep, Dr. Stone came through again. If Mrs. Roth keeps out of his hair, he'll finish up nicely. One thing,' Marlin added, 'Dr. Stone is now married, and so is Mrs. Roth. There won't be another mistake along *that* line.'

'I resent that,' Gloria said.

Marlin looked at her. 'Me, too, kid.'

Gloria consulted her jewelled watch. 'I must run. Shall I leave the light on for you, Marlin, when I come in?'

'Why waste the electricity?'

'Very well. Good night, Billy.'

'So long,' Billy said.

When Gloria was gone, Marlin looked solemnly at him. 'Billy, I—' She paused.

'Well, it was swell of you to talk daddy into it. I didn't like what I had to do in there, especially after Mrs. Roth came and saw all the blood, but I liked what it did to daddy. It made him a man again. Thanks.'

Billy rose. 'I hope it lasts. If everything's O.K. now, I better be going. You wouldn't like to go to a show, would you?'

'Yes, very much. But I've got to sit up all night with Freddie. The nurse has to go back to the hospital as soon as he's out of danger. Tomorrow, maybe?'

'That'll be swell, Marlin.'

NINE

What was it his father had said?

He couldn't quote it exactly, but it was something like: 'The girl—Marlin—will be constantly reminded of her defalcation, and be driven into our arms.'

It came back to him, sitting beside Marlin in the theatre. While Rod la Roque and Vilma Banky progressed hurriedly along separate paths to that inevitable meeting of lips, arms, and bodies on the screen, it came back to him.

Marlin had been marked down as their quarry, then. If he were to thwart them, he had better begin.

Why, he asked himself, why this burning necessity to block them? Was it strictly to declare his independence, or was it because—

No, not that. He didn't care anything about people. Or did he? There was Fred, for example. He liked Fred. He was honestly glad that Fred was going to pull through all right. He liked the way Dr. Stone had reacted: with a friendly hopefulness that Bill knew what he was talking about, that his faith was justified. He had liked the way Gloria had looked at him last night. He liked the shy, knowing smiles Miss Elkins gave him in the halls at school.

Was that it? Was his human heritage so strong that he could not let that other side dominate?

He didn't know. He knew only that he must do what he must do. He knew that he liked Marlin's hand in his here in the darkness.

He knew that he didn't want them to get Marlin. As far as the others were concerned—Miss Elkins, Mr. Fargo, Fred, Dr. Stone—it was more a matter of principle. This was personal. In this shadow stirring of desire, it was suddenly important that Marlin be put beyond their reach.

Why was it, he wondered, that he was inarticulate with Marlin? Why didn't the right phrase leap instinctively to his lips? He could talk to others. Witness that impassioned plea to Dr. Stone yesterday. But with Marlin he didn't know quite what to say, quite what to do with his hands.

His tongue had been touched, his father had said. But were there circumstances where that fact was of no avail? Did that other person his father had mentioned, whose tongue also had been touched, have trouble in talking to girls? Or to a girl, a special girl?

He could talk others into doing what he wished. He knew this, felt it. But when it came to something he really wanted, he didn't know what to say. Was this new power so valuable, then, if it didn't work all the way? Was that the kind of gifts they made, glittering on the surface, but mud deep inside?

For the first time, Billy began to believe that trickery had been employed. Certainly the facts seemed to bear out this theory. They had provided him with a troublemaking heritage, and he could not use it for his own amusement. He had played into their hands until a few weeks ago when he had gone to Elton for Fred, and even on that occasion results had been partly what they desired. Those musicians had gone out, his father said, missionaries of madness, and would make converts all over the world. He could not imagine their ultimate effect; he could only guess.

He had not intended that. He had wanted to restore Fred. But it seemed that his intentions had little to do with effect. This was a matter for resentment.

He was like a play. He began to see this now. He was being tried out in the sticks. If he made a hit, he would open on the Broadway of Old Nick's activities. If the run there were successful, road shows would be formed—others like himself—and sent all over the world.

But if he should flop? What then?

Where was the Cain's warehouse in the realm of devil's drama? The sets and props of a 'turkey' wound up in Cain's warehouse. But he was sets, props, and actors in this play. Would a part of him be sent off to some storehouse, and the rest—the actors—dismissed?

But how could he fail?

He had had a glimmering of successful failure in the 'supervisor's' reaction to his exhorting Fred Roth to paint again. Apparently the supervisor could not conceive that he would deliberately fight his heritage. They—the 'supervisor,' his father, the others—regarded their own conduct as a matter of course. They regarded him, Billy, as one of their own. And so, he must carry on the programme of confusion as a result of heritable characteristics. That was the path of failure—deceit.

He didn't know the film had ended until Marlin removed her hand and the lights went up. She looked at him mistily as patrons began to file out.

'I'm a sucker for these things,' she said. 'Did you like it?'

'Sure. That what's-her-name is pretty.'

'Oh, do you think so?'

Her slight coolness angered Billy. There it was. He'd said the wrong thing, not struck exactly the right note. Why? Surely it was an inoffensive remark? He wouldn't have made it, though, to anyone else. To Gloria, for example. He'd have said just the right word automatically, and she'd have glowed. She wouldn't have drawn away, as Marlin had. His tongue was touched, indeed. It was tied, where Marlin was concerned.

'What do you want to do?' he asked.

'Whatever you want to.'

'Do you want a soda, or something?'

'Why not?'

Her indifference told him that he had failed again. But what should he have suggested? What did she want? A walk in the moonlight? Stronger fare than a soda? If that were it, he'd have nothing to do with it. He didn't know why, exactly. But he knew that he didn't want to contribute to Marlin's reputation as . . . as, well, face it, as one who was 'fast.' The reason for this escaped him, too.

As they passed Runt's pool hall, he knew that he could go into the back rooms and get a bottle of gin, for Runt catered to the high-school crowd. But not for Marlin.

The Sweet Shop was crowded, as usual after a show, with noisy groups of boys and girls chattering about the movie, about coming events, teachers, dates. A trio of boys in flapping corduroy circulated among the tables, now and then pinching a girl who squealed with mock terror. Three girls whispered to each other about those present.

When Billy and Marlin entered, an absolute hush fell for a few seconds. All present regarded the unprecedented appearance of Billy Roberts in public with a girl.

He saw their eyes, and suddenly knew why he would not get a bottle of gin for Marlin. Into the eyes of the girls came a sort of sympathy for him; the boys eyed him with a knowing envy. They didn't like Marlin.

She was different. She had been expelled from school. Though she had been reinstated a few days later, and though her 'crime' was shared by the majority of those present, she was different. Not only because of her expulsion, Billy knew, but because she had broken codes of conditioned behaviour when she felt like it, and had regarded such infractions as unworthy of comment.

It was not active dislike. It was resentment, perhaps unconscious, at her because she was not of the pack. She walked her own way alone.

Billy wanted her to be liked. That was the simple fact. And that was the reason why he would not be a party to furthering her isolation. Along that path lay the excesses his father had mentioned. That path led to Old Nick.

Yet it was more than that. He wanted her to be liked for herself, because he liked her.

A buzz of whispers became normal gabble again as Billy and Marlin found vacant stools at the counter and ordered. Marlin took a packet of cigarettes from her gay purse.

'Don't smoke,' Billy said quietly.

She turned astonished blue eyes on him. 'Why not?'

'Just—because. Please.'

'Don't be a sil,' she said. 'Have one?'

'No. And you're not, either.'

'Who do you think you are, anyway? I will so have one.'

She did. Billy stared miserably at the soda jerk who assembled their orders with deft acrobatics. He did not look up when the trio in flapping cords called at him in tones of implied obscenity:

'Hey, Bill! Hot stuff, huh?'

For the remark was not made to him; it was made to those present. He was alien. If he had been one of them, they would have called him aside and whispered the remark, added suggestive comment.

He felt very much alone. He hadn't known before this desire to be accepted. What was happening to him? he asked himself fiercely. Where was that glib contempt of people? How was he changing?

'We might as well go,' Marlin said, 'before you bust out crying.'

'O.K.,' he snarled. 'I'll take you home.'

'If it's too much trouble, you needn't bother.'

'I need the exercise, anyway. Come on.'

On the street they ran into Old Nick. Billy glared at the jaunty figure, started to push on by without speaking. Nick blocked the way, doffed his rakish hat to Marlin.

'How you've developed, my dear,' he said pointedly.

'What do you want?' Billy growled.

'Oh, I'm on the prowl. Looking for victims. Speaking of which—' His yellow eyes caressed Marlin—slowly.

She looked up at him with calm amusement. 'Sorry,' she said. 'I wouldn't be interested.'

'A pity,' Nick murmured.

'You might try inside,' she suggested. 'Lots of fresh young stuff there.'

'Thank you. I may. Let me warn you, though, about Master Billy. He has ideas of his own. They may be'—he paused, twinkled at Billy—'dangerous.'

'I can handle him,' Marlin said.

Billy looked sullenly at Old Nick. 'Can you?' he asked. 'Can you handle me?'

'I?' Old Nick said mildly. He turned to Marlin. 'He's in a bad humour. What's the matter with him?'

'I think he's ashamed to be seen in public with me. He tried to preach, inside.'

'Ah?' Old Nick's eyebrows raised. He tipped his hat again. 'Good night.'

Billy maintained a furious silence as they started up the hill. He hadn't handled himself well in that encounter. He had practically declared his intentions, and had aroused no reaction to guide him. Old Nick had merely been amused. As usual. If he would only fight back—

A tiny chill touched Billy's spine. That very objectivity which Old Nick maintained was a little frightening. It gave you no hint. You couldn't tell what Old Nick thought, or what he might do. This was dangerous ground.

'Are you bored?' Marlin asked. There was no resentment in the question. It implied that she didn't really care.

'No, I'm not bored,' he said crisply.

She didn't reply. They strolled along the moonlit road between whispering trees. The lazy breeze carried the damp odour of fresh blooms and the eternal query of a far-off owl. Something scurried away from the crunch of their feet.

'Listen,' Billy said presently, and there was no rancour in his voice now. 'I wish you'd snap out of it.'

'Out of what?'

'Oh, these things you do that people don't like. I want you to be—well, good.'

'My goodness,' Marlin murmured in astonishment. 'I'm not hurting anybody. What's eating you?'

'Nothing. Nothing, I guess. Skip it.'

'No, I want to know. All I do is have fun. I do what I want when I want to. I don't lie to people. I don't gossip. I don't tell tales out of school. Is that bad?'

'Well,' Billy fumbled, 'you drink, you smoke—'

'And go out with the boys? I don't see anything wrong in that, as long as I don't hurt somebody else. Do you?'

'Well, people talk.'

'But they're people like Gloria. She'll bar somebody from her club because she was born on the wrong side of the tracks, she'll gossip about others, she'll tell lies. That doesn't hurt me as long as I like myself, does it?'

'Well, it seems to. Look at those girls in the Sweet Shop. They hardly spoke to you.'

'They're just jealous, Billy. They do the same things I do, but they don't come out in the open. They're afraid to, and they turn against anybody that does.'

Billy was out of his depth. He had felt like a small boy all evening, he thought angrily.

'All right, skip it. Well, here we are.' They stood at Marlin's gate. A little expectant silence fell. Billy twisted his hands. 'Can I . . . would you . . . that is—'

She cut into his floundering. 'I think I'd like to kiss you good night, Billy. You're sweet, in a funny sort of way.'

He went home in a glow of pleasure that was dampened with doubts, fears, and misgivings. These were crystallized somewhat by his midnight caller.

'My son,' his father said, 'I am here more in sorrow than in anger. I am afraid that I don't understand you.'

'You and me, too,' Billy thought.

'I informed you recently, my son, of certain, ah, criticisms. These have increased sharply. Naturally, I upheld you. I counselled patience. I was overruled. But I secured an extension. Before corrective measures are applied, you may declare your intentions and explain your conduct.'

Billy pretended weariness. 'What have I done now?' Beneath the pretence, however, was wariness. Maybe he would get a clue, a signpost.

'Only one of your actions is specifically criticized. This is your saving of the boy, Fred Roth.'

Billy was startled. 'But I couldn't just let him lie there and bleed to death.'

'And why not?'

Billy was stunned by the tone. It was not cold-blooded, callous, or heartless. It was just mildly curious.

'Why . . . why,' he stammered, 'it wouldn't be right.'

'And why not?'

'Whadda you mean, "and why not"?'

'I mean that he was ready for us, my son. You had prepared him, made him ready. Then, with a touch of genius, you had shown him vistas of pleasure. He had glimpsed that goal again for which he was originally bound. Then, before he had entered the path to it, he was shot—a further consequence of your original act. He would have died. He would have been ours. But you snatched him away from us. Why?'

Billy was helpless to answer for a moment because he was trying to adjust his perspective to his father's. Was he expected to have stood by without emotion and watch Fred die? Fred, who had asked him to come over? Fred, who was a good guy? Apparently he was. His father seemed to regard it as the natural thing to do. Protestations of humanitarian impulses would not impress this creature, because he couldn't grasp them. He could grasp cunning, however.

'Well?' his father asked.

Billy still was silent. He recalled the emotions he had experienced in Blackie's. He had hated man, wished him slow tortures, wished that human hope would die slowly, painfully. That was something his father could understand.

'Look,' Billy said finally. 'When this thing first started, the only people involved were Miss Elkins, Mr. Fargo, Fred, Dr. Stone. Right?'

'That is correct.'

'All right. They got jolted out of the thing intended for them by the Others you talked about. Well, I've got 'em all back on the first road again. Well, wouldn't it be a lot more fun to jolt 'em out of it again just when they get really going on something they like? Wouldn't the effect be greater on the world in the end?'

His father was silent for a moment, then vented his strange, dry cackle.

'Then I was right. I knew, my son, that I could depend on you. I knew that you would not show filial ingratitude, after all I've done for you. Oh, you're a chip off the old block, all right. Now I'll have something to tell them! Will they hang their horns in shame! Thank you, my son. You've made a worried father very happy. You're damned with the worst of us; I'm proud of you.'

His father disappeared, and Billy lay excitedly in the dark. The proposal he had made was a humming in his veins, and he wondered if it wouldn't be pleasant, after all.

TEN

Billy knew that the supervisor would come again. As weeks blended into months and his new philosophy developed, he knew that it was inevitable. His attitude wasn't right.

Dr. Stone walked erect and briskly these days, and did his trick in the Elton Hospital surgery; Miss Elkins and Mr. Fargo went around in a kind of roseate glow; and Fred Roth made plans to attend a Chicago art institute after graduation. Billy observed all this with fond, paternal eyes.

They deserved their chance. That was his new philosophy.

It developed when his schoolmates showed themselves as shyly eager to accept him as he was to be accepted. That careless slap on the shoulder, that 'Hiya, Bill,' those pleasant feminine smiles which he received these days brought a warmth, a sense of belonging which was as strange as it was gratifying. He liked people.

He saw them as fundamentally friendly. If you gave them a chance, they'd go out of their way to be nice. If you didn't hold them off in contempt, they came to you with smiles, with invitations, with camaraderie.

And he, who had been lonely to a degree they couldn't grasp, became whole, became human. There were parties, there were dances, there were picnics. A whole new world of adolescent activity opened before him, and if he wallowed a little in it he felt that it was only to be expected. He had remained aloof for so long.

And Marlin. Not that she had changed her attitude or her activities. But it was a common sight now to see Billy and Marlin together—at parties, at dances, walking home from school. Because of this, her excesses were fewer, he told himself. He felt excited inside when he thought of Marlin. The way she looked at him, the way she spoke.

He came finally to the conclusion that foisting him or others like him on these essentially just and fair beings was unforgivable. Besides, acting in the interests of evil—evil from the human standpoint, not Old Nick's—was a lonesome job. Regardless of where he got it, Billy Roberts had the desire to be liked, accepted.

But reprisals must come. The supervisor hewed to the line.

They were longer in coming than he anticipated, with the result that he lay awake at midnight night after night and lost a great deal of sleep. The expectant waiting wore him down. Perhaps this was by design, he thought, when finally he felt a presence. He was tired, irritable and defiant because of the waiting. His judgment might be warped.

'This is no game, bud,' the supervisor said bluntly. 'We don't like the way you're carrying on. We want to know what goes.'

'You can go to hell,' Billy snapped.

'Where else?' the supervisor asked, puzzled. 'What has that got to do with it?'

Billy welcomed the confusion. He had flared up too quickly. That was not the way. Relax. Wait.

'Nothing, I guess,' he answered. 'What's wrong now?'

'Why don't you get a cross?' There was venom in the supervisor's snarl. 'Why don't you hire a church? You're acting like a holy fool!'

'Why don't you give me a chance?' Billy retorted. 'I'm not ready yet.'

'You muffed one chance, bud. Look at Fred Roth. He's healthy as a hog and ready for art. If he isn't stopped, he'll get at it one of these days and we'll lose him. You ought to hear the Others rejoice when we lose one. It's sickening. And look at Dr. Stone. He sleeps with a scalpel these days. And the fool teachers. They fairly drip love and good-fellowship. And Marlin Stone. She hasn't been on a decent drunk in two months. What are you trying to do?'

'I've already said what I was trying to do,' Billy replied stoutly. 'You know about it.'

The supervisor made a sound of disgust. '*Agh!* Your old man! You could wind him around your little finger. I'm tired of getting set up for these dopes—for nothing. I've prepared for Fred Roth twice. But you had to give Dr. Stone a pep talk that kept his knife from slipping. Now give out, and give out straight, bud.'

'Would you believe me, whatever I say?'

'Certainly not. But I'd like to hear it.'

'Then nuts to you. What are you going to do about it?'

The supervisor said, 'O.K., boys.'

This time there were no unseen shapes. He could see them this time. First, there was a squad of busy little 'things.' They gagged him and trussed him.

They weren't very gentle.

These went away, leaving behind a memory of teeth and white eyes. They were replaced by something that Billy refused to picture to himself. Even though he looked at it, its shape and form failed to register on his mind. It was alien. It conformed to no rules of form or shape that he knew. His mind rejected it in a revulsion of unknowing.

It made sounds.

His brain refused to record these sounds, they were so far beyond the bounds of experience. He could never recall them to mind, later. They remained a blankness of—not loathing, or terror, but something of both.

It went to work on him.

He remembered that. He was meant to remember. The things it used for tactile exploration—not hands; things—reached down inside his body, trailing a foulness, a filth. There were pains, but these were not designed to reduce him to abject agreement. They were sharp and hard to bear, but were as nothing to his knowing what was being done to him.

He rejected that, too. The censor of his sanity threw a block between knowledge and consciousness, but memory leaked through. It was unformed, vague around the edges, but nauseating to an unimaginable degree.

After a hundred centuries of unbearable disgust, the thing withdrew, went away. Billy hated himself. He cried a little in the darkness. Hot tears of self loathing dribbled down on to his pillow. He couldn't move, he couldn't speak, but he could hate.

'Let that be a sample to you,' the supervisor said. 'There's plenty more where that came from. Let me tell you something, bud. You're going to come through. There's no "or else" about it. You're important to the future of futility, and you're going to pan out. Your old man hadn't had an idea for centuries, but when he dreamed you up he was really dreaming of brimstone. Now look, bud.'

The supervisor's tone changed. It took on a note of cajolery. Billy had to listen. He was helpless in the darkness.

'Think what it means, bud. One of the reasons we get so many is that human beings are unbalanced. They haven't got perfect perspective. There's some cruelty in 'em, and they'll do something—even as trivial as giving out a wrong phone number—which causes a shift in somebody's life. That sort of thing can mean more damned than you can shake a fork at. But look what you got. You got awareness. And you got power. Listen, you can make yourself anything you like.

You haven't got the power of life or death over 'em, but you got the power of after-life. Don't that make you want to stand up and cheer? Honest, bud, you don't know what you're missing. Listen.'

Another wave of self-loathing swept over Billy, and he couldn't shudder. This was the most painful experience of all; he was bound in such a fashion that a shudder was impossible. But he listened.

'I was a host in seventeenth-century England, bud. All I ever did was to smother the rich guests of my inn—Sign of the Unicorn, it was called—and rob 'em. I was smart, sure. I took their corpses miles away and left 'em. Nobody ever caught on. Nobody but the one who cut my throat, that is. But what I mean is this. When I became a demon, first grade, I saw what I could have done if I had known some of the things I do now. And you know 'em. Bud, you can do more good than any demon-to-be that ever lived. And you just stand around, watching.

'I'm telling you, bud, you'll never get this opportunity again. One of these days you'll kick off and be like the rest of us, just taking advantage of those imperfections in human beings. Now I'll admit that you've done good work. One of these days there's going to be a mess as a result of it. People will get caught up on the wave of frenzy you started right here in this little hole, and every country in the world will feel the effect. But you're slackening. You're not doing as much as you can.

'Believe me, bud, I don't like to do what I've just done to you. But you need a lesson. And I'm not playing. If you don't snap out of it and accomplish some of the good you're able to accomplish, you'll regret it. Just some of it, that's all I ask now. You're young yet. When you get right in there pitching—no pun intended—you'll be able to make the Others look at their hole card.'

The monologue ended. Billy was alone. Alone and bound in such a fashion that not even a muscle could be moved. He couldn't even blink his eyes. His lungs could expand and contract in breathing, but all the rest of his body was rigidly immobile. He had a moment of panic. Was he to be left here helpless, forever?

He tried to picture results in that case. Jim Roberts and his mother would come in tomorrow morning after they decided something was wrong. And they would be helpless. All they could do would be to stand and look. They couldn't untie bonds they couldn't see—he was sure the bonds that held him were invisible—and they couldn't loose an invisible gag. He would be, to all intents and purposes, hopelessly paralysed.

Suppose it went on and on. He would die, eventually, from lack of food. He thought of steaks. His mouth could water all right. That part of him wasn't paralysed.

There was a kind of *'phut.'* The supervisor was back.

'All right, boys,' he said. To Billy, he went on apologetically: 'I forgot you, bud. I didn't mean to leave you like this.'

The busy little things loosed him. They went away. The supervisor went away.

At breakfast, Billy looked at his mother with new eyes. Was it from her that he received this stubbornness that overrode his desire to proceed along lines outlined by his father and the supervisor? She was mild, she was pretty. She ran the house with a minimum of effort. He decided that he didn't know much about this Lucille Roberts who had borne him.

He had been too engrossed with his own problem to pay much attention to Jim or Lucille. He had had no occasion to call upon them for assistance—they could have given none, anyway. He had eaten with them, for nearly seventeen years. About all he knew was that Jim liked to spend quiet evenings at home reading or listening to the new radio which had vacuum tubes instead of a crystal, and that Lucille was on tap when needed.

She mended his socks and shirts. She saw to it that he was clean and fed. She was quietly insistent on both points.

Maybe that was where he got it, this strength had upheld him despite what he had gone through last night. Certainly he hadn't inherited it from his father, for that creature was weak. Compromise was his meat and drink. This had been proved.

His father had been willing to believe, had counselled a waiting game to Billy's critics. He did not like to face an issue, and so had earned the contempt of his associates and his son.

So if the human side of himself were the stronger, here was food for thought. Could these powers, inherited from the paternal strain, be used for purely human purposes? Could he combat Old Nick, win over him?

Not without difficulty. That had been proved, too. Billy shuddered into his breakfast food, remembering that vague horror of the night before. He had been helpless then. But was there a way to fight that sort of thing, to make himself stronger than it?

He would investigate, today.

He went to the public library, missing his first class, and asked to see books on magic. The village library boasted only one work, badly written and uninformative. But he pored through flowery chapter after chapter until he came upon one fact which seemed useful. After he had made a mental note of it, he felt a touch on his shoulder.

'Hi, Bill,' Fred Roth whispered. 'What you doing here?'

'What are you?' Billy countered.

'Oh, I got an idea.' Fred exhibited a book labelled 'Commercial Drawing and Illustration.' He smiled regretfully. 'It takes a long time and a lot of money to become a really fine artist. But I could do this stuff, like Arthur William Brown, and McClelland Barclay, and James Montgomery Flagg. I could make some money, and then study serious art.'

Billy glared. 'You dope,' he whispered fiercely. 'If it doesn't mean anything to you, O.K. We'll say no more about it. But if it does, then get at it. The serious stuff, I mean. You can be another Grant Wood, if you got the guts.'

'But I only thought—'

'Nuts! You're just lazy. That's O.K. with me, you understand. I don't care. It's up to you.'

'But, Billy, I'll go for years without getting anything out of it. I'll have to eat somehow.'

'They did,' Billy pointed out. 'They didn't starve.'

'Well, I thought it was an idea,' Fred replied. 'All right, have it your way.' He returned the book to the desk.

Billy walked to school with Fred. 'What if you don't get rich at it?' he demanded. 'Remember a guy named Da Vinci? And Michelangelo? And Donizetti? I don't know enough about 'em to know whether they made a lot of money or not, but look how they've lived. They've done a lot of good. Well, who's going to remember the drawings of magazine illustrators a hundred years from now?'

'O.K., O.K.,' Fred grunted.

'What's the matter with you?' Billy asked fiercely. 'Are you gonna be an artist or not?'

'I said I was, didn't I? All right, you just watch.'

'That's more like it,' Billy conceded.

After school he tried to buy what he wanted at Riker's, but was told that it would take a few days. It had to be ordered from Kansas City.

At the dinner table, Jim Roberts opened the conversation which was to change Billy's life.

'Guess who came into the garage today to talk to me,' he asked with an air of pride.

Billy and Lucille looked up.

'Well?' Lucille demanded. 'Are you going to tell?'

'Mr. Andrews, that's who,' Jim said triumphantly. 'What do you think of that?'

'We're not overdrawn at the bank, Jim?' Lucille asked anxiously.

Jim's long, lined face was contemptuous. 'Naw. He wanted to talk to me. Maybe you think I didn't feel like a fool. I was putting rings in old man Archer's car, and I was grease all over when he called down in the pit at me. He was dressed like J. P. Morgan, or somebody, and I—'

'What did he *want?*' Lucille cried.

Jim's face went blank. 'Huh?' he said absently. He shook himself. 'Oh. He wants to make a banker out of Billy.'

'He—what?' Lucille asked.

'Yeah. Our kid. Whadda you know? Howd'ya like that, son?'

Billy suspended a bit of roast beef halfway to his mouth. 'I don't know, dad. I hadn't thought about it. Why me?'

'Oh, he said he'd been watching you. Said you were a good, bright kid, just the kind who makes a success in that game. You could work Saturdays now, learning the ropes. Then, when you're out of school, you could start as a bookkeeper. He allowed you wouldn't be one long.'

His mother, Billy thought, watched him anxiously, as if she hoped he'd say no.

'Well, I don't know,' Billy said. 'I guess it'd be all right.'

'All right?' Jim cried. 'I hope to tell you. The most solid business in this town. You could really be somebody after you worked up to it.'

'What's this town?' Lucille asked with scorn. 'A wide place in the road. He's got better things in him than that. I know it. He's different. Aren't you, baby?'

'Different, how?' Jim demanded. 'He's just like the rest of the boys. Quieter than most, maybe, but coming out of it lately. And what's the matter with this town, I'd like to know? It was good enough for your father and mine. We sent a State senator from here once, Senator Higgins. My dad used to talk about it.'

'Well, Billy's getting big enough to decide things for himself,' Lucille said slowly. 'If that's what he wants to be, I won't say anything. But I had hoped that he would be something really big. I wanted him to be a psychiatrist.'

'A what?' Jim asked.

'A mind doctor. Like Freud.'

'Never heard of him. Floyd? Who's he?'

'Freud,' Lucille said. 'He can tell you what kind of person you are by what you dream.'

'*Agh!*' Jim said scornfully. 'That stuff's for old women. Anybody can buy a dream book for a dime, and I don't hold with it, anyway.'

'It isn't like that at all!' Lucille flared. 'It's scientific. And Billy's got something special; don't think I haven't seen it.'

'Well,' Jim said dubiously, 'maybe so. I don't know what you're talking about, but I guess it's all right. But it is up to him. Whadda you say, son?'

Billy twisted a sad little smile at his plate. He felt like crying. Each of them wanted him to become great according to their notion of greatness. And it was out of their hands, really.

'I don't care,' he said. 'Whatever you think.'

'Well, then,' Jim said, 'why don't he go to work at the bank on Saturdays? Then if he don't like it, he can go out and be like this guy Floyd.'

'Freud,' Lucille murmured.

ELEVEN

Among the customs of Mulveta High School was an assembly of the senior class sometime in the last three months before graduation to 'Look At Life.' The class sponsor—Gary Fargo in this instance—always made an admonitory speech containing most of the trite and hackneyed advice which students are subjected to at that time of their lives; and a student of the class was selected to make another address.

Billy Roberts made up his mind that he should be this student. He was in possession of facts which his fellow students could not be expected to know. And although he could not give them a bald statement of these facts—they wouldn't believe him—he could give his conclusions. These might save them difficulty in later life, might thwart Old Nick to some extent.

That was the root of the matter. What had started out long ago to be a declaration of his own independence had now become a campaign against Old Nick. There would be consequences; he was sure of this. But he had taken steps to protect himself, and awaited the bell which would send the senior class into the study hall with some measure of serenity.

The means of his protection had finally arrived at Riker's. He could pick it up on the way home from school. It had required a month of writing to herb companies, but a Chinese store in New York had finally come through with five pounds of the dried leaves of English rue. According to what he had been able to find in books, that was protection.

It was with a spirit of defiance, that he faced his class after Mr. Fargo had mumbled the expected bromides. With a spirit of accomplishment, too, for he had laboured over the writing of this speech, and had spent days in committing it perfectly to memory.

'I want to talk on the subject of ''Obligations,'' ' he began to the bored students. 'There are many types of obligations, but all of them can be lumped under the general heading of ''Obligations to Society.''

'Men found out a long time ago that rules of behaviour had to be drawn up, and that these rules of behaviour had to be followed. Otherwise, they'd be shooting each other all the time. These rules are called laws, and they provided for the enforcement. You'll find out about laws. The quickest way is to break one.

'But they didn't write all of 'em down. They figured they didn't have to, because they exist implicitly in society. I'm talking about obligations that you don't find in the law books.

'Now there isn't any law that says you've got to tell the truth about what you did last night. That's a good thing, sometimes. And there isn't any law that says you have to meet your girl friend at the corner of Main and Elm, even if you did tell her you would.

'Because, look. If you don't meet her, she'll be sore. At least, the girls I know will. All right. So she waits around until she gives you up. She's got nothing to do, so she starts something she hadn't planned.

'The point I want to make is that that might change her whole life, and the lives of lots of others she comes into contact with. While she's angry, she'll be ready for things she wouldn't have considered otherwise, and those things sometimes wind up in scandal you never live down.

'You have an obligation, therefore, to do what you say you'll do. If your word's no good, you're a weak plank in the basic platform of society.

'Here's another point, even more important than the last one. Now all of us know it's fun to play jokes on people. Now that's all right, as long as people know it's a joke as soon as it's over. But half the fun is in not telling until they find it out by themselves.

'I'll tell you about one. There was a kid about nine years old, or, maybe he was twelve, it doesn't matter. Anyway, he was in the Union Station in St. Louis. A man in a big hurry ran up and asked where a certain train pulled out. The kid didn't know, but he knew that the train he'd come in on wasn't the train the man wanted. So it was a good joke to direct him to that train. The kid had a good laugh.

'But he found out later that the man was headed for a big conference. When he got on the wrong train, he was delayed so long in getting back on the right one that the conference was over. The stuff he had in his brief case would have changed the decision of that conference, would have prevented a big company from folding up, would have stopped a couple of men working a stock deal that ruined thousands of people who had put their money into the company. He was ruined along with them, and his children didn't receive the education they would have.

'Sure, it was a good joke to the kid, because all he saw at the time was a man pelting down to catch the wrong train. It wasn't much of a joke when he learned what happened.

'So there's another obligation to society. Don't bring confusion and mix-ups into the lives of others. And insist that nobody does it to you. Insist that they keep their word, and you keep yours.

'A practical joke can cause more damage than you might think. Don't play 'em, unless you let people know it is a joke as soon as it's over.

'Look, accidents are bound to happen, and sometimes they ruin people's lives. You can't prevent accidents. But you can prevent the sort of thing I've mentioned. I could give you other examples, but that one is enough to tell you what I mean.

'It isn't enough just to do unto others what you'd like them to do to you. There are loopholes in that. But if you do what you *ought* to, in the interests of society as a whole, you'll get along all right.'

The final bell rang at this point, and Billy's audience began to stir. They gathered their belongings under arms and set themselves for a quick dash for the door as soon as they were dismissed.

Billy said, 'I guess there's no use going on with this. You wouldn't remember, anyway. That's all I have to say.'

His speech hadn't come off. Marlin and Fred told him as much, walking home from school.

'Well, anyway,' Marlin said, 'it meant as much as Mr. Fargo's speech. And that was absolutely nothing. What do you think we're going to do, go around the rest of our lives pushing little ducks in the water for a laugh?'

'Here comes old man Whitaker,' Fred said. 'Let's tell him it's Tuesday instead of Friday, and then Bill can finish his speech.'

'Never mind,' Billy said wearily. 'I should have known better, with a bunch of morons.'

Here was further evidence of his being tricked, he thought. He had wanted to tell them to be careful, that evil eyes watched, evil forces waited; that outside the ken of their imagination were creatures poised to pounce on the slightest misstep and turn it to advantage. He had wanted them to understand that excesses—that is, any departure from the norm—led surely down the path of destruction. But he hadn't used the words. He hadn't known the words. The ideas he had wanted to disseminate were at odds with Old Nick's philosophy. So he hadn't known the words.

Perhaps it was true that his tongue had been touched. This had been demonstrated when he put Dr. Stone back on the path he had been intended to tread. That hadn't meant much to Billy, and it *could* have been a step towards the eventual dissolution of Dr. Stone. But when all the cards were down—as when he was speaking to Marlin, or his classmates—his words fell short.

Very well, then. Why have any truck with the whole works? Why not throw it over—if he could.

He could try.

'I've got to stop in at Riker's,' he said. 'You want to wait outside here for me?'

He went in. Mr. Riker peered over his glasses, pored through them at a bill of lading.

'Just a minute, Billy.'

The old man limped into the back room, returned with a bulky, boxed package. He set this on the counter, told Billy the price. Billy paid, and started to pick up the package.

A feeling of nausea ran through him before he picked it off the counter. His stomach turned over. He was repelled from the brown box. It had no odour, it had no objectionable appearance. But he couldn't touch it. If he did, he would lose his dinner.

He backed away sharply, as if he had been struck in the face, and the nausea went away. If he stayed beyond reach, the package didn't seem to affect him.

'I'm sick,' Billy said. 'I've got to go. I'll have Fred Roth pick this up. I've got to—'

He ran outside. He leaned panting against the store. He hadn't counted on this.

Still, it was logical. He was part demon. It should react against him. And the sickness that swept over him wasn't of the fatal variety. If he carried the box, he would vomit, yet. But what would be its effect on the supervisor? Surely it would be more acute?

'What's the matter?' Marlin asked. 'Did you swallow a worm?'

'Nothing. I'm just sick.'

'Why? What happened?'

'Nothing.' He looked at Fred. 'Will you pick up that package in there and carry it home for me? I've got to go.'

Billy ran off alone. He didn't want to get close to that package, except in the privacy of his own room.

Fred brought it to him, dumped it on the floor.

'Want me to open it, Bill?

'No, thanks. I'll do it.'

Now came the hard part. He had to circle his bed with the leaves. He tried. He was sick in the bathroom.

He tried again. He was sick again.

Finally, he opened the box, retching constantly. But it had to be done. He placed the leaves tip to tip under the carpet around his bed and then crawled into it, hoping he would die.

He was beyond the effect of the leaves that encircled him, but his sickness had been so violent that he had no energy whatever. He lay back on his pillow, fully clothed, pale, breathing loudly.

He knew that he could never step over that circle. He was trapped here. He had felt the increase in the effect of the rue when the circle had been completed. It had literally flung him back against his bed. Of course, he could ask Jim Roberts or his mother to lift up the carpet and break the circle, but he shrank from that.

They thought he was sick. They wanted to call Dr. Stone. Billy dissuaded them. He didn't want a doctor. He wanted to be left alone. After some argument, they acceded.

Then came the task of waiting for midnight. The hours crept, but they passed. As they passed he became more and more aware of the circle of dried leaves around his bed.

First, there had been a sense of great relief, being in the centre and beyond reaching distance of the limits of the circle. Then had come a faint, almost imperceptible discomfort. This had increased slowly until he had no appetite. The thought of food sickened him. Nausea remained at this level until his visitor arrived.

'My son!' it gasped. 'What have you done? What are you trying to do?'

'You can't get through,' Billy said.

His father became grim. 'A serpent's tooth,' he grated. 'Oh, ungrateful son! You will pay, and pay, and pay to the end of eternity. Think you to scorn your heritage, throw it aside, with impunity? Not so, not so! You . . . you *angel!*''

With this vituperative exclamation, his father vanished. He was not alone for long.

Shadow shapes appeared. There were millions, it seemed. They clustered, they pressed long noses against the invisible barrier created by the herb. They sniffed, they looked for an opening. Billy watched, uncomfortable and uneasy, as the fantastic shapes flitted about his bed trying to break through. But triumph still persisted. They couldn't get at him.

Then the supervisor came.

'Now look, bud,' he said. 'If you give up, we'll be easy on you. And you might as well. You can't get away with it. We'll get you in the end. You'll get sicker and sicker as each day goes by until you finally starve to death. Then we'll have you. It won't be very easy then, let me tell you.'

'Go away,' Billy said.

'Sure, sure. But look, bud. Why make it tough for yourself? All right, so you don't like what you are. You can be different. We'll help you. But not if you act like this. We're your friends, bud. You can trust us.'

'Go away.'

'But don't you see what it's going to do to you? You'll be in a mess in hell, and I'm not kidding. Give up now, break that circle, and everything will be rosy. You have my word on it.'

'Go away.'

'Well, if you're going to be difficult,' the supervisor sighed. 'Come and get him, fella.'

There had been millions before. There was one now. This was a weird-looking creature of an incredible age. What was designed to be its face was wizened, puckered, shrunken. The hands, or what passed for hands, were twisted and green. Its body was a nightmare of skinny bones.

It made passes. It chanted gibberish.

With each pass, with each unintelligible phrase, Billy jerked. It felt as if he were prodded with white-hot irons. He had no muscular control whatever.

This went on for some time.

If only, Billy thought desperately, he knew where the next prod was coming from. But they struck from unexpected angles, and he was whipped back and forth in his bed like a rag in the wind.

But it couldn't get through the circle. Billy clung to that thought. He must cling to it, through everything.

They didn't go away and leave him alone as before. They stayed the night, one torturer relieving the last. They gave him sensations of needles and swords, of kicks and blows, of heat and cold, the long night through. When day broke, they desisted in their torture, but they waited outside the circle for the next night to come.

They waited unseen, malevolent, when Lucille and Jim came in to find Billy almost unconscious from lack of sleep. They waited while Dr. Stone examined him and recommended hospitalization. They became alert when this suggestion was made.

They remained alert while Billy fought leaving his room.

'I won't go, I won't go!' he moaned over and over.

'But, Billy,' Dr. Stone said mildly. 'You're ill, boy. You're seriously ill. I can't determine the cause of it here, but we could locate it in the hospital and cure you.'

'I won't go, I won't go, I won't!'

'But, Billy!' Lucille said anxiously. 'You're our baby. We don't like to see you sick. You might even—'

'They won't kill me,' Bill cut in. 'They're scared to. I got right on my side.'

'Delirium,' Dr. Stone murmured. He became persuasive again. 'Billy, I owe you a great deal. I'd like to repay you. Come along now, won't you, while you're still strong enough?'

'I'm going to be all right,' Billy groaned. Beads of sweat popped on his forehead with the effort to be lucid. 'Please go away and leave me. I can sleep sometime today. I'll get better, honest.'

'Well,' Dr. Stone said, 'keep him here and watch him. Let me know if there's any change. His condition isn't serious enough to override his wishes. If he becomes worse, we'll take steps, naturally.'

They left him alone. He slept, after a fashion. Not well, because of the growing nausea, and the consciousness of those things just beyond the wall of rue.

He couldn't eat anything that day, and it was with a great deal of difficulty that he persuaded his mother and Jim Roberts to go to bed that night.

'If you get sick in the night,' Lucille said in traditional phraseology of that part of the country, 'call us. Will you?'

'Sure, sure. I'll be all right, though.'

He wasn't all right. The tortures on the preceding night were a curtain raiser to what they did now. These pains were not bold and straightforward, like those of the night before. They were slow, heavy, subtle, sapping at his energy.

He had rebelled, and aroused the fury of Hell.

Could he possibly expect to beat them off, one boy against a myriad angers? He didn't know. He knew that he would try. He might die, but it would be worth it to show Old Nick that you couldn't make anything you liked of human nature no matter what the odds. Some vestige of resentment would flare up, and defeat Old Nick and his kind. So he might lose, but he would never be defeated.

He came very near it, on that second night. That dull heavy pain which lay inside him very nearly reached the unbearable point. At times the supervisor appeared to taunt him, to demand surrender. Billy wasted no strength to deny him. He kept his silence, but he wanted to cry, 'Enough.' The morning came, and they let up.

Morning came, and with it came Old Nick.

TWELVE

Old Nick didn't come inside. He stood in the doorway while Jim and Lucille came to Billy's bedside. Lucille felt his forehead; Jim looked on helplessly.

Billy shot a contemptuous glance at the bearded, dapper visitor. 'You can't get to me, Nick. You can't come in.'

Old Nick was amused. 'There are many ways to skin a cat.' To Lucille and Jim, he said, 'It's rather . . . uh, close in here. If you'll carry him out, Jim, I'll see that he's cured.'

'No!' Billy cried weakly. 'Don't let him get me!'

'Why, Billy!' Lucille admonished. 'Nick's our friend.'

'Nuts!' Billy snorted. 'He's the—'

He broke off. Why make them think he was out of his head? He filled with despair. He had lost, after all. He was more than a match for the minor minions, but Old Nick had the edge. Old Nick could do what he liked—except approach the bed. Even that was no advantage. It became apparent, immediately.

Jim slung Billy over his shoulder and carried him into the front room. Billy's nausea increased sharply as they crossed the circle, hidden under the carpet, then vanished once they were outside. Jim put him on the couch in the front room and stood back.

'He's feeling better,' Jim announced. 'The colour's coming into his face.'

'Yes,' Old Nick murmured. 'The atmosphere in there was not exactly healthy. What he needs now is a sulphur bath.'

Billy relaxed. What did it matter now? He had lost.

A worried frown formed between Lucille's blue eyes.

'I don't see how we can manage it,' she said dubiously. 'I guess we could borrow some money from the bank. He'd have to go to Wyoming, I guess.'

Old Nick held up a hand. 'This one is on me,' he said. 'I'll have him back tomorrow.'

'Tomorrow?' Lucille said. 'You'd have to fly. That's expensive. We couldn't let you do it, Nick.'

Old Nick silenced her with a negligent hand. 'Don't worry about it. I'd do anything to straighten him out. Come on, Billy.'

'Wait till I pack a bag for him, then.'

'That won't be necessary,' Old Nick said.

Billy lay quietly on the couch, and strength surged back into him. It was strictly physical strength, however; he had no energy or will to fight Old Nick. It was so futile. He could see that now.

'Come on, Billy,' Old Nick said again and with a sense of compulsion, Billy followed him out of the house.

He cast back a look at the little cottage, and at Jim and Lucille on the porch.

'Goodbye,' he said.

Goodbye and goodbye. It had been a noble experiment. It had failed. He had not been able, in the last push, to hold them off. They had made him strong, but not strong enough. They had tricked him with false hope.

He paid little attention to the way they trod, he and Old Nick. What did it matter? The fight was done, the battle lost.

The final part of the way was a twisting path through flickering lights. It led at last into a great throned chamber.

Before the throne was a five-pointed platform, and Old Nick bade Billy to stand on it. Then Old Nick took his seat on the throne. Billy looked at him with dull and weary interest, noting the new aspect without shock, without surprise.

He was still Old Nick, yes. Amusement flickered in his yellow eyes. But he was black and shining now, magnificent with a touch of sadness. The Black Prince in exile.

The high-domed chamber began to glow. The hidden light source brought glitter and a savage splendour. Billy and Old Nick were alone, one wearily defiant, the other sadly amused.

The throne room began to fill. First came others fashioned like Old Nick, but lacking the regal mien. They formed a dark and shining phalanx beside the throne.

Then came hundreds to fill the floor. They were not frightening, despite furious expressions, for they had familiar shapes. Among them was his father, Billy knew, though he could not pick the creature from the angry ranks. Among them was the supervisor, too.

Once, these had been men. Now they were servitors. Was this to be his fate also?

He faced them without fear from the raised pentagram. He faced them with contempt. He had lost, but he had lost honourably. He was outnumbered, hundreds to one. No stigma of defeat attached to his circumstance; no stigma of surrender, either.

Old Nick spoke to the glowering mass as he had spoken to men, with a touch of contemptuous amusement.

'In the interests of harmony, I have acceded to the request of your committee. I have brought Billy Roberts to trial. Who wishes to bring charges?'

'I do!'

One stepped forward out of the ranks. He strode furiously towards Billy, re-coiled just before he touched one of the points of the pentagram. He glowered. He was the supervisor.

'We had a good thing in this punk, Nick. His old man's a dope, all right, but he was cooking off the top coals when he pulled this one out of his stovepipe. And the punk fell in with us. He knew what he was meant to do, and he did it—for a while. Then he doubled on us. So we slapped him around a little, and he fell in line again. To do what? To get cute, that's what. He read a book, the scut. But he lied, and that's the main thing. He said he was cooking up a mess of trouble for the little bunch he jolted out of their paths in the first place. He got 'em back in that groove, and I'm . . . well, I'm blessed, Nick, if he didn't leave 'em there. Then he gives us the brush-off. Now what can you do with a rat like that? All I ask is, give him to me. My squad will figure something to do—for a long time.'

The hush that fell was presently broken by an angry mutter of agreement among the ranks of those who had been human. This welled up until the great chamber shivered. Old Nick cut it short with a raised hand.

'I have rather idly wondered for a long time,' he told them dryly, 'who was the stronger, you or human beings. We have an answer here, of a sort.'

Old Nick stood, his robe of office shining in the light. He paced across and back on the dais of his throne. He spoke mildly.

'You may remember that when this experiment was first proposed, I said that it didn't matter how it turned out. It has mattered in this respect: I have an answer to my idle question.

'I gave you permission to experiment because I thought it might be entertaining to watch. It was. I saw him as an infant swear eternal independence. I watched his first deceits. I saw the demonic strain dominate—for a while.

'I enjoyed his awkward failures at bringing order out of the confusion he had created. Then I observed what should serve here as an object lesson—the emer-gence of the human strain. There were some lapses, but on the whole this side of him gained steadily. He looked on his fellow creatures and, like his mother, found them good. What he did for a short time was not in his own interests, but in theirs. This brought results which he desired, for the motivations were at odds with those in the other facet of his heritage; which brought only confusion and eventual residence here.'

Old Nick's tone changed. It became sharper, admonitory. He flashed the ranks a dark look.

'If you had let him be, we should have seen the next phase. He would surely have brought confusion and damnation again to those he was trying to save, for his motivation no longer stemmed from human traits. He was out simply to do me in the eye. A characteristic I have seen here, somewhat to my annoyance.'

The ranks surged back from the crack of Old Nick's voice. Billy sensed their fear again. It was abject, pitiful.

'But no,' Old Nick went on scornfully. 'You were not content to let matters take their course. In your, er, damned adolescence you had to plunge ahead. My aeons of waiting, of accepting what comes my way, of grasping such opportunities as present themselves—you gained nothing from them. You ignored my counsel.

'And so he has beaten you, at your own game by your rules. It is not he who should be punished; it is you.'

Old Nick paused reflectively, and Billy could feel the cold fear which settled over the ranks, the breathless fright.

'As I remarked,' Old Nick went on, 'it has satisfied my idle curiosity. Human beings are the stronger. They will always beat you, when your opposition is active. Enough of them will come to Hell in their own hand basket, but when that prerogative is threatened they will turn and destroy the tangible threat to their independence.

'I have told you time after time that the imbalances of human nature will bring our share to us. They are like the horse: you may lead him to drink, but you cannot always drive him.

'It was a beautiful theory, this scattering of focal points of confusion throughout humanity, but it fails in practice because human beings are stronger than you. They walk their own road, whether that be to an insipid glory or to damnation.

'Wait! Watch! It is the greatest show on earth. When opportunity offers, sow your seed of temptation. It is not only gratifying to do so, but sometimes offers high sensual pleasure.

'Now to the point. You ask that this boy be turned over to you. I say he is not ready, that you will never break his spirit. And if you do not break it, you have failed. The Council will decide'—he nodded at the dark and shining phalanx—'but my advice is to leave him alone.'

'But, Nick,' the supervisor cried. 'You mean, let him go back?'

'I do.'

'But think what it would do to prestige! If human beings ever learn that they are stronger than we are, we're cooked. We might as well shut up shop and go fishing. And he's just the boy to tell 'em, after what's happened.'

'Hm-m-m, yes. Perhaps.'

'That'd be a grace of a note!' the supervisor exclaimed. 'We work our tails off here, and, if you let him go, we're ruined. You don't want the Others to win, do you?'

'I think we should provide against the contingency that puts you in such a blather. How about it, Billy? What do you think?'

A sense of unreality had begun to come over Billy while Nick, impassive and sardonic, addressed the assembled horde. Surely this was not happening? Surely it was out of his fevered imagination? He was sick in bed at home; this was a nightmare.

These were phantasms. If he could only wake up, they would vanish.

He stood erect on the pentagram. He swept them with arrogant eyes.

'I'm not afraid of you,' he said. 'You can't do anything to me. All I have to do is open my eyes and *p-f-f-f-t!* you're gone. You're just something I dreamed up. I'm a human being. I don't lie. I keep my word. And if somebody else lies, I don't want anything to do with him. Even if I ever was part demon, I'm not any more. I'm not afraid. You hear? I'm not afraid. You can't be real, you just can't!'

'This is interesting,' Old Nick commented. 'You've known since you were a baby that part of your heritage lay here. If you can throw all that aside in one moment, I'd like to know the mental processes behind it.'

'Look at 'em!' Billy snarled. He waved at the massed ranks on the floor of the glowing chamber. 'You say I'm like them? They're like whipped dogs. They shiver when you say "boo" at 'em. I couldn't be like 'em. They're filthy. They're dirty inside. They're—bad!'

The loathing in his voice was like a lash across their faces. They stirred, muttered, moved a step towards him.

'Come on!' he cried. 'You're two hundred to my one, and that makes it about even.' He whirled on Old Nick. 'I never was like them! They gang up. They pick on somebody who can't stand up to 'em. Then, when somebody does, they run for help.'

Old Nick flashed the ranks a smile full of teeth. 'He has you there, boys.' To Billy: 'But I thought all this wasn't real. You speak now as if it were.'

The voice was so quiet, so objective, that a little tongue of fear flickered in Billy. He looked long and hard at Old Nick. The image he saw was sharp and clear. He looked at the others, the dark and glittering, the evil horde.

It was real.

His shoulders slumped. 'I don't know,' he said in a small voice. 'It seemed for a minute I was dreaming. I wanted it that way. But I remember. All my life, people have had to look at me a second time before they could see me clearly. They never mentioned it, because they got used to it. I've seen 'em do it to you, and I can see you all right. I guess that proves something.'

He was silent. There was no movement anywhere.

'I guess,' he went on dully, wearily, 'you got me. Do what you want. I won't try to fight you, Nick, because you've always been stronger than me. I didn't ask to be born the way I was, but that doesn't matter, does it? You always had the edge. But as for them'—he straightened his shoulders, looked at the ranks with flashing eyes—'come and get me, then, you—scum! I'm better than you are, and you know it!'

A sharp, eerie cry went up from their midst. 'Oh, my son, my son!'

Billy spat, exclaimed in revolted horror, *'Phtaaa!'*

The ranks surged forward. They rolled across the bright floor in a wave of fury, red and fiery eyes flaming with hatred.

Billy planted his feet widely apart, brought clenched fists to his waist. One good sock, that's all he wanted.

They never reached him. When they came to the pentagram, they recoiled, yelping with pain. The front ranks fell to the gleaming floor, were trampled by those who in turn fell and in turn were trampled until knowledge of futility pene-trated and they stood back. Those on the floor scrambled up. All faced Old Nick in fearful trembling.

He chuckled. 'Naturally, I protected him. Back to your places!' This was un-adulterated savagery, and they fell back as if before a whip.

There was a short, contemplative silence.

'You have suggested the solution, Billy, to this rather awkward situation,' Old Nick said. 'I am sure the Council will take it into consideration. It would be better, I think—better from my viewpoint, you understand—to place a Cone of Silence around you while the Council deliberates.'

Instantly a soundless void closed around Billy. He could see, but could hear nothing.

He saw the dark, glittering beings confer. He saw Nick speak to them, smoothly, suavely. He saw the impassioned supervisor gesture at them. He waited. Presently a spokesman from the Council spoke briefly.

Old Nick nodded with dark pleasure. He waved his hand again, and—

They were at Billy's gate. Lucille and Jim came out to meet them.

'Hello, mother,' Billy said cheerfully. 'Hello, dad. Mr. Nicholas had the right treatment, all right.'

Old Nick clapped Billy on the shoulder. 'We shall see, we shall see,' he said.

THIRTEEN

He signed the foreclosure notice and, as usual, liked the looks of his signature. 'W. J. Roberts, manager.' One of these days it would read 'president,' as soon as weakwilled, doddering old Andrews kicked off. He was the youngest manager in the history of the bank, he should be its youngest president.

W. J. That was a matter of pride, too. Nobody called him Billy any more, except his mother. He thought idly of his mother.

He really should get over to see her more often. It was probably true that she was lonely, now that Jim had died in that automobile wreck last year. But the future of the bank and the future of Mulveta took nearly all of his time. When he became president, he would have more opportunities for duty calls.

If old Andrews would only hurry and get it over with. The bank would be better off without him. Look at the way he'd acted over this foreclosure. Sure old Kir-by's wife and daughter had died, and it had been expensive to bury them. But was that the bank's affair? It was not. Collecting the mortgage payments was the bank's only business with Kirby.

But the directors had come around, though it had been like pulling teeth to make them agree to put Kirby off the land. You'd think that grown men would have out-grown the disgusting softness they displayed in the meeting yesterday. Besides, if that canning factory came here, old Kirby's farm would be the perfect site, and the bank would make another profit. That wasn't the main point, though. He liked the way he had told those men, all at least twice his own age, what the main point was.

'Society,' he had said, 'is built around the premise that agreements will be carried out by both parties. The bank loaned Kirby money on his farm. That was the simple, legal fact. Drought, mismanagement, misfortune, or any other reasons behind the need for that loan were not the affairs of the bank. But Kirby's signed agreement to repay that loan by a certain time was the affair of the bank. He has failed to do so. To grant him an extension is merely to confess our disbelief in the basic plank in the platform on which society is built. We must believe in it! We must keep that platform solid!'

Oh, he had brought them around, in the end. It was a matter of pride that he could bring almost anybody around. Maybe he could be a State senator, after all, as soon as he was old enough. Then this country should see things!

There would be no shilly-shallying then, once he was in the Senate. This country would learn not to meddle in the affairs of other nations, and the government would learn to keep its hands out of private business.

Gloria would like being the wife of a senator.

There was a small, discreet cough. Billy raised his eyes, and his mouth dropped open as he saw that he had a visitor. He blinked, for the figure was slightly out of focus. He looked again. It was Old Nick, dapper, white-bearded, white-haired, yellow-eyed.

'How did you get in here?' Billy demanded. 'My secretary had orders—'

'I slipped past her and came through the keyhole,' Old Nick said blandly. 'How are you, Billy?'

'I'm going to fire that girl. If she'd sleep at night like decent people should, things like this wouldn't happen. Well, since you *are* here—though I still can't see why I didn't hear the door—what can I do for you? I'm pretty busy.'

'I won't keep you long,' Old Nick said. 'It's been six years since I saw you last, and since I was coming through here I thought I'd drop in and see how my ex-protégé was doing.'

'Protégé?' Billy said. 'I pride myself on the fact that I'm self-made. Nobody helped me.'

'You married Gloria,' Old Nick pointed out.

'But I was the manager of the bank first, and she had nothing to do with my promotion. Why, I hadn't seen her more than three times before I was running things here.'

'I see,' Old Nick murmured. 'May I sit down? This looks like a comfortable chair.'

'I'm afraid I—' Billy began. He stopped, frowned as a memory formed, then smiled without mirth. 'Yes, go ahead. I have something to tell you.' He reconstructed pictures in his mind. 'I had a nightmare about you, once, Nicholas. It seemed we were in a big place, and you were judging me. I hadn't thought of it since, until you popped in here. Silly, isn't it?'

'It *was* silly,' Old Nick said.

Billy blinked. Why had he told the old fool about that dream?

'What did you want to see me about?' he asked coolly.

'Why, I ran into two friends of yours. I saw Fred Roth in New York. He doesn't like his job.'

'Fred's a fool,' Billy snorted. 'He studied art for five years all over Europe, and what did he intend to do with it? He wanted to come back here, get a job as janitor, and paint landscapes! Ye gods! Landscapes! Not only that, but he had refused a good job in a New York advertising agency, where he could make some money and amount to something. Well, I showed him the error of his ways. It took me a week, but he finally agreed it was time he started making a place for himself in society.'

'You needn't worry,' Old Nick said, 'about his ever painting. He spends all his spare time playing in a band. The leader used to play here. Sammy Saltzer. You may remember him.'

'No. Well, I'm through with Fred. I saved him twice, once from the law, and that time the crazy old coot . . . what was his name, Folsom? . . . shot him. Though God knows why I took him to Stone. It was just luck the old fool didn't kill him.'

'Speaking of Dr. Stone—' Old Nick said. 'But first, how is he?'

'He's a drunken wreck,' Billy said with contempt. 'I don't know where he gets the liquor; there's not a drop in Mulveta except in the private cellars of some of the better element, but he gets it. My mother-in-law very justly kicked him out some five years ago. I saw to it that young Dr. Ames, who came here shortly after that, got ahead. Dr. Stone doesn't have any patients now except some riffraff down by the water works. And they're the lowest kind of charity cases.'

'I see. I saw another friend of—'

Billy's telephone rang. 'Hello,' he said. 'Oh, hello, Mr. Fargo. I'm glad you called. Did you read Joe Wakeman's editorial this morning? . . . Well, he quoted my speech to the Business Men's luncheon. He put me in the position of hounding that Evans girl, er, Mrs. Melville she is now. . . . Yes, I'm in full agreement with you on that. She should not be allowed to associate with the decent element here. If she wants to marry a notorious playboy like Melville, that's her business. But I say to keep her tainted affairs out of this city. . . . What? . . . No, he didn't say a word actually, about me, except to print my speech. The insult was in the caption, "The Quality of Mercy Is Not Strained." . . . It made me boil, too. . . . I agree with you. I can't take part openly in black-balling him out of the club, but I'm with you all the way. Thank you. Goodbye.'

He hung up, stared grimly at the phone. His long, youthful face showed deep lines on either side of his mouth. 'People might as well learn now,' he said aloud, 'that moral turpitude hasn't a chance in this town. Or learn it the hard way, from me and the Fargos!' He turned to Old Nick, blinked, focused cold, hard eyes. 'Did you want anything else?'

'I saw Marlin, too,' Old Nick said quietly.

A pang hit Billy's heart. It was momentary, gone with the instant, but it evoked memories. It evoked something else, too. His eyes softened, took on a faraway look.

'How is she?' he asked. It was almost a whisper.

'Oh, the same as ever,' Old Nick said easily. 'She does what she enjoys, sees whom she likes, sends her father money which she earns as a model. She goes her own way. I have wondered why you didn't marry her. You could have, you know. She sent you her love, incidentally.'

'I suppose I could have,' Billy assented.

Old Nick's tone indicated that he was speaking to a very gay dog, indeed. 'You could have. You had a way with women, Billy.'

Billy flushed, smiled complacently. Then his eyes were hard again. 'Marlin was hardly the, er, type for me. She was really no better than she should be. People were right about that. So it just wouldn't do for me to have married her. I tried to make her change. She wouldn't, so she went her way, and I went mine. It's best that way.'

'No, Marlin will never change,' Old Nick agreed. 'That is one of my sorrows. People like her, who take their destiny in their own two hands, are rare. Nothing affects them but their own sense of rightness. A pity.'

'You're pretty old to make a play for a girl of her age,' Billy said in a half growl.

Old Nick shrugged. 'Age wasn't the reason for my failure, or yours. Marlin's own integrity was the reason. We need not have bothered. Ah, well,' He got to his feet. 'I can wait for the next one. I have found that if I wait long enough, I usually succeed.'

'You're an old rake, Nick,' Billy said with heavy joviality.

Nick twinkled at him. 'Well, I'll get along. I must say, Billy, that I am pleased with you. Highly pleased.'

'It was nice of you to drop in,' Billy said politely. 'When will you be back?'

'I doubt very much,' Old Nick said, 'if I shall come here again. It was curiosity that brought me. I watched you grow up, you know. You were unique, as a boy.'

'I—guess so,' Billy said hesitantly, 'I don't remember very much about it. People say I've changed a lot, but I don't see it. Why, Joe Wakeman called me inhuman the other day.'

Old Nick chuckled. 'Oh, you're human. Wholly human. I saw to that, six years ago, when you were sick.'

'You *did* help me,' Billy said. 'I had forgotten. But all you did was take me some place to be cured. A sulphur spring in Wyoming, wasn't it— But you didn't do anything to *me*.'

'No,' Old Nick agreed. 'You had already formed a pattern of conduct. Human conduct, the kind I like. You can tell Editor Wakeman he's mistaken.'

'I'll tell him to go to hell.'

'Good!' Old Nick said. 'The more the merrier.'

There was a pause. Billy shuffled the foreclosure notice around on his desk. 'Well, uh—since I won't see you again, Nick, goodbye.'

'Oh, I'll see you,' Old Nick said. He went to the door, paused, added pleasantly, 'Some day.'

MALCOLM JAMESON

Blind Alley

Nothing was further from Mr. Feathersmith's mind than dealings with
streamlined, mid-twentieth-century witches or dickering with the Devil. But something *had* to be done. The world was fast going to the bowwows, and he suffered
from an overwhelming nostalgia for the days of his youth. His thoughts constantly
turned to Cliffordsville and the good old days when men were men and God was
in His heaven and all was right with the world. He hated modern women, the
blatancy of the radio, That Man in the White House, the war . . .

Mr. Feathersmith did not feel well. His customary grouch—which was a by-
word throughout all the many properties of Pyramidal Enterprises, Inc.—had hit
an all-time high. The weather was rotten, the room too hot, business awful, and
everybody around him a dope. He loathed all mention of the cold war, which in
his estimation had been bungled from the start. He writhed and cursed whenever
he thought of priorities, quotas and taxes; he frothed at the mouth at every new
government regulation. His plants were working night and day on colossal contracts that under any reasonable regime would double his wealth every six months,
but what could he expect but a few paltry millions?

He jabbed savagely at a button on his desk, and before even the swiftest-footed
of messengers could have responded, he was irritably rattling the hook of his
telephone.

"Well?" he snarled, as a tired, harassed voice answered. "Where's Paulson?
Wake him up! I want him."

Paulson popped into the room with an inquiring, "Yes, sir?" Mr. Paulson was
his private secretary and to his mind stupid, clumsy and unambitious. But he was
a male. For Mr. Feathersmith could not abide the type of woman that cluttered up
offices in these decadent days. Everything about them was distasteful—their bold,
assured manner, their calm assumption of efficiency, their persistent invasion of
fields sacred to the stronger and wiser sex. He abhorred their short skirts, their
painted faces and their varnished nails, the hussies! And the nonchalance with
which they would throw a job in an employer's face if he undertook to drive them
was nothing short of maddening. Hence Mr. Paulson.

"I'm roasting," growled Mr. Feathersmith. "This place is an oven."

"Yes, sir," said the meek Paulson, and went to the window where an expensive air-conditioning unit stood. It regulated the air, heating it in winter, cooling

it in summer. It was cold and blustery out and snow was in the air; Mr. Feathersmith should have been grateful. But he was not. It was a modern gadget, and
though a touch of the hand was all that was needed to regulate it, he would have
nothing to do with it. All Paulson did was move a knob one notch.

"What about the Phoenix Development Shares?" barked the testy old man.
"Hasn't Ulrich unloaded those yet? He's had time enough."

"The S. E. C. hasn't approved them yet," said Paulson, apologetically. He
might have added, but thought best not to, that Mr. Farquhar over there had said
the prospectus stank and that the whole proposition looked like a bid for a long-
term lease on a choice cell in a Federal penitentiary.

"*Aw-r-rk,*" went Mr. Feathersmith, "a lot of Communists, that's what they
are. What are we coming to? Send Clive in."

"Mr. Clive is in court, sir. And so is Mr. Blakeslee. It's about the reorgani-
zation plan for the Duluth, Moline & Southern—the bondholders' protective committee . . ."

"*Aw-r-rk,*" choked Mr. Feathersmith. Yes, those accursed bondholders—always yelping and starting things. "Get out. I want to think."

His thoughts were bitter ones. Never in all his long and busy life had things
been as tough as now. When he had been simply Jack Feathersmith, the promoter,
it had been possible to make a fortune overnight. You could lose at the same rate,
too, but still a man had a chance. There were no starry-eyed reformers always
meddling with him. Then he had become the more dignified "entrepreneur," but
the pickings were still good. After that he had styled himself "investment banker"
and had done well, though a certain district attorney raised some nasty questions
about it and forced some refunds and adjustments. But that had been in the 30's
when times were hard for everybody. Now, with a war on and everything, a man
of ability and brains ought to mop up. But would they let him? *Aw-r-rk!*

Suddenly he realized he was panting and heaving and felt very, very weak. He
must be dying. But that couldn't be right. No man of any age kept better fit. Yet
his heart was pounding and he had to gasp for every breath. His trembling hand
fumbled for the button twice before he found it. Then, as Paulson came back, he
managed a faint, "Get a doctor—I must be sick."

For the next little while things were vague. A couple of the hated females from
the outer office were fluttering and cooing about the room, and one offered him a
glass of water which he spurned. Then he was aware of a pleasant-faced young
chap bending over him listening to his chest through a stethoscope. He discovered
also that one of those tight, blood-pressure contraptions was wrapped around his
arm. He felt the prick of a needle. Then he was lifted to a sitting position and
given a couple of pills.

"A little stroke, eh?" beamed the young doctor, cheerily. "Well, you'll be all
right in a few minutes. The ephedrine did the trick."

Mr. Feathersmith ground his teeth. If there was anything in this topsy-turvy
modern age he liked less than anything else it was the kind of doctors they had.
A little stroke, eh? The young whippersnapper! A fresh kid, no more. Now take
old Dr. Simpson, back at Cliffordsville. There was a doctor for you—a sober,

grave man who wore a beard and a proper Prince Albert coat. There was no folderol about him—newfangled balderdash about basal metabolism, X-rays, electrocardiograms, blood counts and all that rot. He simply looked at a patient's tongue, asked him about his bowels, and then wrote a prescription. And he charged accordingly.

"Do you have these spells often?" asked the young doctor. He was so damn cheerful about it, it hurt.

"Never," blared Mr. Feathersmith. "Never was sick a day in my life. Three of you fellows pawed me over for three days, but couldn't find a thing wrong. Consolidated Mutual wrote me a million straight life on the strength of that and tried their damnedest to sell me another million. That's how good I am."

"Pretty good," agreed the doctor with a laugh. "When was that?"

"Oh, lately—fifteen years ago, about."

"Back in '28, huh? That was when even life insurance companies didn't mind taking a chance now and then. You were still in your fifties then, I take it?"

"I'm fit as a fiddle yet," asserted the old man doggedly. He wanted to pay this upstart off and be rid of him.

"Maybe," agreed the doctor, commencing to put his gear away, "but you didn't look it a little while ago. If I hadn't got here when I did . . ."

"Look here, young man," defied Mr. Feathersmith, "you can't scare me."

"I'm not trying to," said the young man, easily. "If a heart block can't scare you, nothing can. Just the same, you've got to make arrangements. Either with a doctor or an undertaker. Take your choice. My car's downstairs if you think I'll do."

"*Aw-r-rk,*" sputtered Mr. Feathersmith, but when he tried to get up he realized how terribly weak he was. He let them escort him to the elevator, supporting him on either side, and a moment later was being snugged down on the back seat of the doctor's automobile.

The drive uptown from Wall Street was as unpleasant as usual. More so, for Mr. Feathersmith had been secretly dreading the inevitable day when he would fall into doctors' hands, and now that it had happened, he looked out on the passing scene in search of diversion. The earlier snow had turned to rain, but there were myriads of men and lots of equipment clearing up the accumulation of muck and ice. He gazed at them sourly—*scrape, scrape, scrape*—noise, clamor and dirt, all symptomatic of the modern city. He yearned for Cliffordsville where it rarely snowed, and when it did it lay for weeks in unsullied whiteness on the ground. He listened to the gentle swishing of the whirling tires on the smooth, wet pavement, disgusted at the monotony of it. One street was like another, one city like another—smooth, endless concrete walled in by brick and plate glass and dreary rows of light poles. No one but a fool would live in a modern city. Or a modern town, for that matter, since they were but unabashed tiny imitations of their swollen sisters. He sighed. The good old days were gone beyond recapture.

It was that sigh and that forlorn thought that turned his mind to Forfin. Forfin was a shady fellow he knew and once or twice had employed. He was a broker of a sort, for the lack of better designation. He hung out in a dive near Chatham Square and was altogether a disreputable person, yet he could accomplish strange things. Such as dig up information known only to the dead, or produce prophecies that could actually be relied on. The beauty of dealing with him was that so long as the fee was adequate—and it had to be that—he delivered the goods and asked no questions. His only explanation of his peculiar powers was that he had contacts—gifted astrologers and numerologists, unprincipled demonologists and their ilk. He was only a go-between, he insisted, and invariably required a signed waiver before undertaking any assignment. Mr. Feathersmith recalled now that once, when he had complained of a twinge of rheumatism, Forfin had hinted darkly at being able to produce some of the water of the Fountain of Youth. At a price, of course. And when the price was mentioned, Mr. Feathersmith had haughtily ordered him out of the office.

The doctor's office was the chamber of horrors he had feared. There were many rooms and cubbyholes filled with shiny adjustable enameled torture chairs and glassy cabinets in which rows of cruel instruments were laid. There were fever machines and other expensive-looking apparatus, and a laboratory full of mysterious tubes and jars. White-smocked nurses and assistants flitted noiselessly about like helpful ghosts. They stripped him and weighed him and jabbed needles in him and took his blood. They fed him messy concoctions and searched his innards with a fluoroscope; they sat him in a chair and snapped electrodes on his wrists and ankle to record the pounding of his heart on a film. And after other thumpings, listenings and measurings, they left him weary and quivering to dress himself alone.

Naked as he was, and fresh from the critical probing of the doctor and his gang, he was unhappily conscious of how harshly age had dealt with him after all. He was pink and lumpy now where he had once been firm and tanned. His spindly shanks seemed hardly adequate for the excess load he now carried about his middle. Until now he had valued the prestige and power that goes with post-maturity, but now, for the first time in his life, he found himself hankering after youth again. Yes, youth would be desirable on any terms. It was a thoughtful Mr. Feathersmith who finished dressing that afternoon.

The doctor was waiting for him in his study, as infernally cheerful as ever. He motioned the old man to a chair.

"You are a man of the world," he began, "so I guess you can take it. There is nothing to be alarmed over—immediately. But you've got to take care of yourself. If you do, there are probably a good many years left in you yet. You've got a cardiac condition that has to be watched, some gastric impairments, your kidneys are pretty well shot, there are signs of senile arthritis, and some glandular failure and vitamin deficiency. Otherwise, you are in good shape."

"Go on." Now Mr. Feathersmith knew he would have to get in touch with Forfin.

"You've got to cut out all work, avoid irritation and excitement, and see me at least weekly. No more tobacco, no liquor, no spicy or greasy foods, no late hours.

I'm giving you a diet and some prescriptions as to pills and tablets you will need . . .''

The doctor talked on, laying down the law in precise detail. His patient listened dumbly, resolving steadfastly that he would do nothing of the sort. Not so long as he had a broker on the string who could contact magicians.

That night Mr. Feathersmith tried to locate Forfin, but Forfin could not be found. The days rolled by and the financier felt better. He was his old testy self again and promptly disregarded all his doctor's orders. Then he had his second heart attack, and that one nearly took him off. After that he ate the vile diet, swallowed his vitamin and gland-extract pills, and duly went to have his heart examined. He began liquidating his many business interests. Sooner or later his scouts would locate Forfin. After that he would need cash, and lots of it. Youth, he realized now, was worth whatever it could be bought for.

The day he met with his lawyers and the buyers' lawyers to complete the sale of Pyramidal Enterprises, Inc., Mr. Blakeslee leaned over and whispered that Forfin was back in town. He would be up to see Mr. Feathersmith that night. A gleam came into the old man's eye and he nodded. He was ready. By tomorrow all his net worth would be contained in cash and negotiable securities. It was slightly over thirty-two million dollars altogether, an ample bribe for the most squeamish demonologist and enough left over for the satisfaction of whatever dark powers his incantations might raise. He was confident money would do the trick. It always had, for him, and was not the love of it said to be the root of all evil?

Mr. Feathersmith was elated. Under ordinary circumstances he would have conducted a transaction of the magnitude of selling Pyramidal with the maximum of quibbling and last-minute haggling. But today he signed all papers with alacrity. He even let Polaris Petroleum & Pipeline go without a qualm, though the main Polaris producing field was only a few miles south of his beloved Cliffordsville. He often shuddered to think of what an oil development would do to a fine old town like that, but it made him money and, anyhow, he had not been back to the place since he left it years ago to go and make his fortune.

After the lawyers had collected their papers and gone, he took one last look around. In his office, as in his apartment, there was no trace of garish chromium and red leather. It was richly finished in quiet walnut paneling with a single fine landscape on one wall. A bookcase, a big desk, two chairs and a Persian rug completed the furnishings. The only ultra-modern feature was the stock ticker and the news teletype. Mr. Feathersmith liked his news neat and hot off the griddle. He couldn't abide the radio version, for it was adorned and embellished with the opinions and interpretations of various commentators and self-styled experts.

It was early when he got home. By chance it was raining again, and as he stepped from his limousine under the marquee canopy that hung out over the sidewalk, the doorman rushed forward with an umbrella lest a stray drop wet his financial highness. Mr. Feathersmith brushed by the man angrily—he did not relish sycophantism, he thought. Flunkies, pah! He went up in the elevator and out into the softly lit corridor that led to his apartment. Inside he found his houseboy, Felipe, listening raptly to a swing version of a classic, playing it on his combination FM radio and Victrola.

"Shut that damn thing off!" roared Mr. Feathersmith. Symphonic music he liked, when he was in the mood for it, but nothing less.

Then he proceeded to undress and have his bath. It was the one bit of ritual in his day that he really enjoyed. His bathroom was a marvel of beauty and craftsmanship—in green and gold tile with a sunken tub. There was a needle bath, too, a glass-enclosed shower, and a sweat chamber. He reveled for a long time in the steamy water. Then, remembering that Forfin might come at any time, he hurried out.

His dinner was ready. Mr. Feathersmith glowered at the table as he sat down. It was a good table to look at, but that was not the way he felt about it. The cloth was cream-colored damask and the service exquisitely tooled sterling; in the center sat a vase of roses with sprays of ferns. But the crystal pitcher beside his plate held certified milk, a poor substitute for the vintage Pommard he was accustomed to. Near it lay a little saucer containing the abominable pills—six of them, two red, two brown, one black, and one white.

He ate his blue points. After that came broiled pompano, for the doctor said he could not get too much fish. Then there was fresh asparagus and creamed new potatoes. He topped it off with fresh strawberries and cream. No coffee, no liqueur.

He swallowed the stuff mechanically, thinking all the while of Chub's place, back in Cliffordsville. There a man could get an honest-to-goodness beefsteak, two inches thick and reeking with fat, fresh cut from a steer killed that very day in Chub's back yard. He thought, too, of Pablo, the tamale man. His stand was on the corner by the Opera House, and he kept his sizzling product in a huge lard can wrapped in an old red tablecloth. The can sat on a small charcoal stove so as to keep warm, and the whole was in a basket. Pablo dished out the greasy, shuck-wrapped morsels onto scraps of torn newspaper and one sat down on the curb and ate them with his fingers. They may have been made of fragments of dog—as some of his detractors alleged—but they were good. Ten cents a dozen, they were. Mr. Feathersmith sighed another mournful sigh. He would give ten thousand dollars for a dozen of them right now—and the ability to eat them.

Feathersmith waited impatiently for Forfin to come. He called the operator and instructed her to block all calls except that announcing his expected guest. Damn that phone, anyway. All that any Tom, Dick or Harry who wanted to intrude had to do was dial a number. The old man had an unlisted phone, but people who knew where he lived called through the house switchboard notwithstanding.

At length the shifty little broker came. Mr. Feathersmith lost no time in approaches or sparring. Forfin was a practical man like himself. You could get down to cases with him without blush or apology.

"I want," Mr. Feathersmith said, baldly, "to turn the hand of the clock back forty years. I want to go to the town of Cliffordsville, where I was born and raised, and find it just as I left it. I propose to start life all over again. Can you contact the right people for the job?''

"Phew!" commented Mr. Forfin, mopping his head. "That's a big order. It scares me. That'll involve Old Nick himself . . .''

He looked uneasily about, as if the utterance of the name was a sort of inverted blasphemy.

"Why not?'' snapped the financier, bristling. "I always deal with principals. They can act. Skip the hirelings, demons, or whatever they are.''

"I know,'' said Forfin, shaking his head disapprovingly, "but he's a slick bargainer. Oh, he keeps his pacts—to the dot. But he'll slip a fast one over just the same. It's his habit. He gets a kick out of it—outsmarting people. And it'll cost. Cost like hell.''

"I'll be the judge of the cost,'' said the old man, stiffly, thinking of the scant term of suffering, circumscribed years that was the best hope the doctor had held out to him, "and as to bargaining, I'm not a pure sucker. How do you think I got where I am?''

"O. K.,'' said Forfin, with a shrug. "It's your funeral. But it'll take some doing. When do we start?''

"Now.''

"He sees mortals only by appointment, and I can't make 'em. I'll arrange for you to meet Madame Hecate. You'll have to build yourself up with her. After that you're on your own. You'd better have plenty of ready dough. You'll need it.''

"I've got it,'' said Mr. Feathersmith shortly. "And yours?''

"Forget it. I get my cut from *them.*''

That night sleep was slow in coming. He reviewed his decision and did not regret it. He had chosen the figure of forty deliberately. Forty from seventy left thirty—in his estimation the ideal age. If he were much younger, he would be pushed around by his seniors; if he were much older, he wouldn't gain so much by the jump back. But at thirty he would be in the prime of physical condition, old enough to be thought of as mature by the youngsters, and young enough to command the envy of the oldsters. And, as he remembered it, the raw frontier days were past, the effete modernism yet to come.

He slept. He dreamed. He dreamed of old Cliffordsville, with its tree-lined streets and sturdy houses sitting way back, each in its own yard and behind its own picket fence. He remembered the soft clay streets and how good the dust felt between the toes when he ran barefoot in the summertime. Memories of good things to eat came to him—the old spring house and watermelons hung in bags in the well, chickens running the yard, and eggs an hour old. There was Sarah, the cow, and old Aunt Anna, the cook. And then there were the wideopen business opportunities of those days. A man could start a bank or float a stock company and there were no snooping inspectors to tell him what he could and couldn't do. There were no blaring radios, or rumbling, stinking trucks or raucous auto horns. People stayed healthy because they led the good life. Mr. Feathersmith rolled over in bed and smiled. It wouldn't be long now!

The next afternoon Forfin called him. Madame Hecate would see him at five; and he gave a Fifth Avenue address. That was all.

Mr. Feathersmith was really surprised when he entered the building. He had thought a witch would hang out in some dubious district where there was grime and cobwebs. But this was one of the swankiest buildings in a swanky street. It was filled with high-grade jewelers and diamond merchants, for the most part. He wondered if he had heard the address wrong.

At first he was sure he had, for when he came to examine the directory board he could find no Hecate under the H's or any witches under the W's. He stepped over to the elevator starter and asked him whether there was a tenant by that name.

"If she's on the board, there is," said that worthy, looking Mr. Feathersmith up and down in a disconcerting fashion. He went meekly back to the board. He rubbed his eyes. There was her name—in both places. "Madame Hecate, Consultant Witch, Suite 1313."

He went back to the elevators, then noticed that the telltale arcs over the doors were numbered—10, 11, 12, 14, 15, and so on. There was no thirteenth floor. He was about to turn to the starter again when he noticed a small car down at the end of the hall. Over its door was the label, "Express to 13th Floor." He walked down to it and stepped inside. An insolent little guy in a red monkey jacket lounged against the starting lever. He leered up at Mr. Feathersmith and said, "Are you *sure* you want to go up, pop?"

Mr. Feathersmith gave him the icy stare he had used so often to quell previous impertinences, and then stood rigidly looking out the door. The little hellion slid the door to with a shrug and started the cab.

When it stopped he got off in a small foyer that led to but a single door. The sign on the door said merely, "Enter," so Mr. Feathersmith turned the knob and went in. The room looked like any other midtown reception room. There was a desk presided over by a lanky, sour woman of uncertain age, whose only noteworthy feature was her extreme pallor and haggard eyes. The walls were done in a flat blue-green pastel color that somehow hinted at iridescence, and were relieved at the top by a frieze of interlaced pentagons of gold and black. A single etching hung on the wall, depicting a conventionalized witch astride a broomstick silhouetted against a full moon, accompanied by a flock of bats. A pair of chairs and a sofa completed the furnishings. On the sofa a huge black cat slept on a red velvet pillow.

"Madame Hecate is expecting you," said the cadaverous receptionist in a harsh, metallic voice. "Please be seated."

"Ah, a zombie," thought Mr. Feathersmith, trying to get into the mood of his environment. Then as a gesture of good will, though he had no love for any animal, he bent over and stroked the cat. It lifted its head with magnificent deliberation, regarded him venomously for a moment through baleful green eyes; then, with the most studied contempt, spat. After that it promptly tucked its head back in its bosom as if that disposed of the matter for all eternity.

"Lucifer doesn't like people," remarked the zombie, powdering her already snowy face. Just then a buzzer sounded faintly, three times.

"The credit man is ready for you," said the ghostly receptionist. "You'll have to pass him first. This way, please."

For some reason that did not astonish Mr. Feathersmith as much as some other features of the place. After all, he was a businessman, and even in dealing with the myrmidons of Hell, business was business. He followed her through the inner door and down a side passage to a little office. The fellow who received him was an affable, thin young man, with brooding, dark-brown eyes, and an errant black lock that kept falling down and getting in his eyes.

"A statement of your net worth, please," asked the young man, indicating a chair. He turned and waved a hand about the room. It was lined with fat books, shelf after shelf of them, and there were filing cases stuffed with loose papers and photographs. "I should warn you in advance that we have already made an independent audit and know the answer. It is a formality, as it were. Thought you ought to know."

Mr. Feathersmith gazed upon the books with wonderment. Then his blood ran chill and he felt the gooseflesh rise on him and a queer bristly feeling among the short hairs on the back of his neck. The books were all about *him!* There were two rows of thick volumes neatly titled in gold leaf, such as "J. Feathersmith—Private Life—Volume IX." There was one whole side of the room lined with other books, in sets. One set was labeled "Business Transactions," another "Subconscious Thoughts and Dreams," and then other volumes on various related aspects of their subject. One that shocked him immensely bore the horrid title of "Indirect Murders, Et Cetera." For an instant he did not grasp its import, until he recalled the aftermath of the crash of Trans-Mississippi Debentures. It was a company he had bought into only to find it mostly water. He had done the only thing to do and get out with a profit—he blew the water up into vapor, then pulled the plug. A number of suicides resulted. He supposed the book was about that and similar fiascoes.

He turned to face the credit man and was further dismayed to see that gentleman scrutinizing a copy of the contract of sale of the Pyramidal company. So he knew the terms exactly! Worse, on the blotter in plain sight was a photostat copy of a will that he had made out that very morning. It was an attempt on Mr. Feathersmith's part to hedge. He had left all his money to the Simonist Brotherhood for the propagation of religion, thinking to use it as a bargaining point with whatever demon showed up to negotiate with him. Mr. Feathersmith scratched his neck—a gesture of annoyance at being forestalled that he had not used for years. It was all the more irritating that the credit man was purring softly and smiling to himself.

"Well?" said the credit man.

Mr. Feathersmith had lost the first round and knew it. He had come in to arrange a deal and to dictate, more or less, his own terms. Now he was at a distinct disadvantage. There was only one thing to do if he wanted to go on; that was to come clean. He reached into his pocket and pulled out a slip of paper. There was one scribbled line on it. "Net worth—$32,673,251.03, plus personal effects."

"As of noon, today," added Mr. Feathersmith, handing the paper across the desk.

The credit man glanced at it, then shoved it into a drawer with the comment that it appeared to be substantially correct. Then he announced that that was all. He could see Madame Hecate now.

Madame Hecate turned out to be the greatest surprise so far. Mr. Feathersmith had become rather dubious as to his ability to previse these strange people he was dealing with, but he was quite sure the witch would be a hideous creature with an outjutting chin meeting a down-hanging beak and with the proverbial hairy warts for facial embellishments. She was not like that at all. Madame Hecate was as cute a little trick as could be found in all the city. She was a vivacious, tiny brunette with sparkling eyes and a gay, carefree manner, and was dressed in a print housedress covered by a tan smock.

"You're a lucky man, Mr. Feathersmith," she gurgled, wiping her hands on a linen towel and tossing it into a handy container. "The audience with His Nibs is arranged for about an hour from now. Ordinarily he only comes at midnight, but lately he has had to spend so much time on Earth he works on a catch-as-catch-can basis. At the moment he is in Germany—it is midnight there now, you know—giving advice to one of his most trusted mortal aids. No doubt you could guess the name, but for reasons you will appreciate, our clientele is regarded as confidential. But he'll be along shortly."

"Splendid," said Mr. Feathersmith. For a long time it had been a saying of his that he wouldn't wait an hour for an appointment with the Devil himself. But circumstances had altered. He was glad that he had *only* an hour to wait.

"Now," said the witch, shooting him a coy, sidelong glance, "let's get the preliminaries over with. A contract will have to be drawn up, of course, and that takes time. Give me the main facts as to what you want, and I'll send them along to the Chief Fiend in the Bureau of Covenants. By the time His Nibs gets here, the scribes will have everything ready."

She produced a pad and a pencil and waited, smiling sweetly at him.

"Well, uh," he said, a trifle embarrassed because he did not feel like telling her *quite* all that was in his mind—she seemed such an innocent to be in the witch business. "I had an idea it would be nice to go back to the town of my boyhood to spend the rest of my life . . . ."

"Yes?" she said eagerly. "And then . . . ."

"Well," he finished lamely, "I guess that's about all. Just put me back in Cliffordsville as of forty years ago—that's all I want."

"How unique!" she exclaimed, delightedly. "You know, most men want power and wealth and success in love and all that sort of thing. I'm sure His Nibs will grant this request instantly."

Mr. Feathersmith grunted. He was thinking that he had already acquired all those things from an uninformed, untrained start in that same Cliffordsville just forty years ago. Knowing what he did now about men and affairs and the subsequent history of the world, what he would accomplish on the second lap would astonish the world. But the thought suggested an addendum.

"It should be understood," he appended, "that I am to retain my present— uh—wisdom, unimpaired, and complete memory."

"A trifle, Mr. Feathersmith," she bubbled. "A trifle, I assure you."

He noticed that she had noted the specifications on separate sheets of paper, and since he indicated that was all, she advanced to a nearby brazier that stood on a tripod and lit them with a burning candle she borrowed from a sconce. The papers sizzled smartly into greenish flame, curled and disappeared without leaving any ash.

"They are there now," she said. "Would you like to see our plant while you wait?"

"With pleasure," he said, with great dignity. Indeed, he was most curious about the layout, for the room they were in was a tiny cubicle containing only a high desk and a stool and the brazier. He had expected more demoniac paraphernalia.

She led the way out and he found the place was far more extensive than he thought. It must cover the entire floor of the building. There was a long hall, and off it many doors.

"This is the Alchemical Department," she said, turning into the first one. "I was working in here when you came. That is why my hands were so gummy. Dragon fat is vile stuff, don't you think?"

She flashed those glowing black eyes on him and a dazzling smile.

"I can well imagine," he replied.

He glanced into the room. At first sight it had all the appearance of a modern chemical laboratory, though many of the vessels were queerly shaped. The queerest of all were the alchemists, of whom about a dozen sat about on high stools. They were men of incalculable age, bearded and wearing heavy-rimmed octagonal-lensed eyeglasses. All wore black smocks spattered with silvery crescents, sunbursts, stars, and such symbols. All were intent on their work. The bottles on the tables bore fantastic labels, such as "asp venom," "dried cameleopard blood," and "powdered unicorn horn."

"The man at the alembic," explained the witch, sweetly, "is compounding a modified love philter. You'd be surprised how many star salesmen depend on it. It makes them virtually irresistible. We let them have it on a commission basis."

She pointed out some other things, such as the two men adjusting the rheostat on an electric athanor, all of which struck Mr. Feathersmith as being extremely incongruous. Then they passed on.

The next room was the Voodoo Department, where a black sculptress was hard at work fashioning wax dolls from profile and frontview photographs of her clients' most hated enemies. An assistant was studying a number of the finished products

and occasionally thrusting pins into certain vital parts. There were other unpleasant things to be seen there and Mr. Feathersmith shuddered and suggested they
pass on.

"If it affects you that way," said the witch, with her most beguiling smile,
"maybe we had better skip the next."

The next section was devoted to Demonology and Mr. Feathersmith was willing
to pass it by, having heard something of the practices of that sect. Moreover, the
hideous moans and suppressed shrieks that leaked through the wall were sufficient
to make him lose any residual interest in the orgies. But it was not to be. A door
was flung open and an old hag tottered out, holding triumphantly aloft a vial of
glowing violet vapor.

"Look," she cackled with hellish glee, "I caught it! The anguish of a dying
hen! He! He!"

Mr. Feathersmith suffered a twinge of nausea and a bit of fright, but the witch
paused long enough to coo a few words of praise.

She popped her head into the door beyond where a senile practitioner could be
seen sitting in a black robe and dunce's cap spangled with stars and the signs of
the zodiac. He was in the midst of a weird planetarium.

"This is the phoniest racket in the shop," she murmured, "but the customers
love it. The old guy is a shrewd guesser. That's why he gets by. Of course, his
horoscopes and all these props are just so much hogwash—custom, you know."

Mr. Feathersmith flicked a glance at the astrologer, then followed her into the
next room. A class of neophytes appeared to be undergoing instruction in the art
of Vampirism. A demon with a pointer was holding forth before a set of wall
charts depicting the human circulatory system and emphasizing the importance of
knowing just how to reach the carotid artery and jugular vein. The section just
beyond was similar. It housed the Department of Lycanthropy and a tough-looking
middle-aged witch was lecturing on the habits of predatory animals. As Mr.
Feathersmith and his guide looked in, she was just concluding some remarks on
the value of prior injections of aqua regia as a resistant to possible silver bullets.

He never knew what other departments were in the place, for the witch happened to glance up at one of the curious clocks that adorned the walls. She said
it kept Infernal time. At any rate, His Nibs was due shortly. They must hurry to
the Apparition Chamber.

That awesome place was in a class by itself. Murals showing the torments of
Hell covered the long walls. At one end was a throne, at the other a full-length
portrait of His Nibs himself, surrounded by numerous photographs. The portrait
was the conventional one of the vermilion anthropoid modified by barbed tail,
cloven hoofs, horns, and a wonderful sardonic leer. The rest of the pictures were
of ordinary people—some vaguely familiar to Mr. Feathersmith.

"His Vileness always appears to mortals as one of their own kind," explained
the witch, seeing Mr. Feathersmith's interest in the gallery. "It works out better
that way."

Two imps were bustling about, arranging candles and bowls of incense about a
golden pentagon embedded in the black composition floor. There were other ca-

balistic designs worked into the floor by means of metallic strips set edgewise, but apparently they were for lesser demons or jinn. The one receiving attention at the moment was immediately before the throne. The witch produced a pair of ear plugs and inserted them into Mr. Feathersmith's ears. Then she blindfolded him, patted him soothingly and told him to take it easy—it was always a little startling the first time.

It was. He heard the spewing of some type of fireworks, and the monotone of the witches' chant. Then there was a splitting peal of thunder, a blaze of light, and a suffocating sulphurous atmosphere. In a moment that cleared and he found his bandage whisked off. Sitting comfortably on the throne before him was a chubby little man wearing a gray pin-striped business suit and smoking a cigar. He had large blue eyes, several chins, and a jovial, back-slapping expression. He might have been a Rotarian and proprietor of a moderate-sized business anywhere.

"Good morning," he said affably. "I understand you want transportation to Cliffordsville of four decades ago. My Executive Committee has approved it, and here it is . . ."

Satan snapped his fingers. There was a dull *plop* and an explosion of some sort overhead. Then a document fluttered downward. The witch caught it deftly and handed it to His Nibs, who glanced at it and presented it to Mr. Feathersmith.

Whether the paper was parchment or fine-grained asbestos mat, that gentleman could not say. But it was covered with leaping, dazzling letters of fire that were exceedingly hard to read, especially in the many paragraphs of fine print that made up the bulk of the document. Its heading was:

COMPACT *between His Infernal Highness Satan, known hereinafter as The Party of the First Part, and one J. Feathersmith, a loyal and deserving servant, known as The Party of the Second Part. To wit:*

The perusal of such a contract would have been child's play for the experienced Mr. Feathersmith, had it not been for the elusive nature of the dancing letters, since only the part directly under his eye was legible. The rest was lost in the fiery interplay of squirming script and had the peculiar property of seeming to give a different meaning at every reading. Considered as a legal document, thought Mr. Feathersmith out of the depths of his experience, it was a honey. It seemed to mean what it purported to mean, yet . . .

At any rate, there was a clause there that plainly stated, even after repeated readings, that The Party of the Second Part would be duly set down at the required destination, furnished with necessary expense money and a modest stake, and thereafter left on his own.

"The compensation?" queried Mr. Feathersmith, having failed to see mention of it. "You'll want my soul, I presume."

"Dear me, no," responded Satan cheerily, with a friendly pat on the knee. "We've owned that outright for many, many years. Money's all we need. You see, if anything happened to you as you are, the government would get about three quarters of it and the lawyers the rest. We hate to see that three quarters squandered in subversive work—such as improved housing and all that rot. So, if you'll kindly give us your check . . ."

"How much?" Mr. Feathersmith wanted to know, reaching for his checkbook.

"Thirty-three million," said Satan calmly.

"That's outrageous!" shouted the client. "I haven't that much . . ."

"There was to be 1 per cent off for cash, Your Vileness," reminded the witch sweetly.

Mr. Feathersmith glared at both of them. He had been neatly trimmed—right down to chicken feed. His first impulse was to terminate the interview then and there. But he remembered that, given youth and opportunity, he could make any number of fortunes. He also had in mind the dismal future forecast for him by the doctor. No. The transaction had to be gone through with. He meekly signed checks for his full balance, and an order on his brokers for the delivery of all other valuables.

There was one more thing to do—sign the pact.

"Roll up your left sleeve," said the witch. He noticed she held a needle-tipped syringe in one hand and a pad dampened with alcohol in the other. She rubbed him with the cotton, then jabbed him with the needle. When she had withdrawn a few cubic centimeters of blood, she yanked the needle out, unscrewed it and replaced it by a fountain-pen point.

"Our practitioners did awfully sloppy work in the old days," she laughed, as she handed him the gruesomely charged pen and the pact. "You have no idea how many were lost prematurely through infection."

"Uh-huh," said Mr. Feathersmith, rolling down his sleeve and getting ready to sign. He might as well go through with it—the sooner the better.

"Your transportation," she added, handing him a folding railroad ticket with a weird assortment of long-defunct or merged railroads on it, queer dates and destinations. But he saw that it ended where and when he wanted to go.

"Grand Central Station, Track 48, 10:34 tonight."

"Better give him some cash," suggested Satan, hauling out a roll of bills and handing them to her. Mr. Feathersmith looked at them with fast-rising anxiety; the sight of them shook him to the foundations. For they were large, blanketlike sheets of paper, none smaller than a fifty, and many with yellow backs. Satan also handed over a coin purse, in which were some gold pieces and six or eight big silver dollars. Mr. Feathersmith had completely forgotten that they used such money in the old days—pennies and dollar bills were unknown in the West, and fives and tens in paper so rare as to be refused by shopkeepers. How much else had he forgotten? It rattled him so that he did not notice when Satan disappeared, and he allowed himself to be ushered out in a mumbling daze by the little witch.

By train time, though, he had cheered up. There was just the little journey halfway across the continent to be negotiated and the matter of the forty years. No doubt that would occur during the night as a miracle of sorts. He let the redcap carry his luggage aboard the streamlined flier and snugged himself down in his compartment. He had not had to bother with having clothes of the period made to order, for the witch had intimated that those details would be taken care of automatically.

His next job was to compose the story he was going to tell to explain his return to Cliffordsville. Besides other excellent reasons, he had chosen the particular time for his rejuvenation so as not to run foul of himself in his earlier personality or any of his family. It had been just at the close of the Spanish War that both parents had died of yellow fever, leaving him an orphan and in possession of the old homestead and the parental bank account. He had lost little time in selling the former and withdrawing the latter. After that he had shaken the dust of Cliffordsville from his feet for what he thought was to be all time. By 1902 there was no member of the Feathersmith family residing in the county. His return, therefore, would be regarded merely as an ordinary return. He would give some acceptable explanations, then take up where he had left off. Sooner or later he would pull out again—probably to Detroit to get in on the ground floor with Henry Ford, and he thought it would be a good idea, too, to grab himself some U. S. Steel, General Motors and other comers-to-be. He licked his lips in anticipation of the killing he would make in the subsequent World War I years when he could ride Bethlehem all the way to the top, pyramiding as he went, without a tremor of fear. He also thought with some elation of how much fun it would be to get reacquainted with Daisy Norton, the girl he might have married if he had but stayed in Cliffordsville. She was cold to him then, but that was because her father was a rich aristocrat and looked down upon the struggling Feathersmiths. But this time he would marry her and the Norton acres under which the oil field lay. After that . . .

He had undressed automatically and climbed into his berth. He let his feverish anticipations run on, getting dozier all the time. He suddenly recalled that he really should have seen the doctor before leaving, but dismissed it with a happy smile. By the time he had hit his upper twenties he was done with whooping cough, measles and mumps. It had been all these years since, before he required the services of a doctor again. He made a mental note that when he next reached sixty he would take a few precautions. And with that happy thought he dropped off into sound sleep.

The Limited slid on through the night, silently and jarless. Thanks to its air conditioning, good springs, well-turned wheels, smooth traction, rock-ballasted roadbed and heavy rails, it went like the wind. For hundreds of miles the green lights of block signals flickered by, but now and again another train would thunder by on an eastbound track. Mr. Feathersmith gave no thought to those things as he pillowed deeper into the soft blankets, or worried about the howling blizzard raging outside. The Limited would get there on time and with the minimum of fuss. That particular Limited went fast and far that night—mysteriously it must have covered in excess of a thousand miles and got well off its usual route. For when Mr. Feathersmith did wake, along toward dawn, things were uncannily different.

To begin with, the train was lurching and rocking violently from side to side, and there was a persistent slapping of a flat wheel underneath. The blizzard had abated somewhat, but the car was cold. He lifted the curtain a bit and looked out on a snow-streaked, hilly landscape that strongly suggested Arkansas. Then the train stopped suddenly in the middle of a field and men came running alongside with lanterns. A hotbox, he heard one call, which struck him as odd, for he had not heard of hotboxes for a long time.

After about an hour, and after prolonged whistling, the train slowly gathered way again. By that time Mr. Feathersmith noticed that his berth had changed during the night. It was an old-fashioned fore-and-aft berth with an upper pressing down upon it. He discovered he was wearing a flannel nightgown, too—another item of his past he had failed to remember, it had been so long since he had changed to silk pajamas. But by then the porter was going through the car rousing all the passengers.

"Gooch Junction in half a' hour, folks," he was saying. "Gotta get up now— dey drop the sleeper dere."

Mr. Feathersmith groaned and got up. Yes, yes, of course. Through sleepers were the exception, not the rule, forty years ago. He found his underwear—red flannel union suit it was—and his shirt, a stiff-bosomed affair with detachable cuffs and a complicated arrangement of cuff holders. His shoes were Congress gaiters with elastic in the sides, and his suit of black broadcloth beginning to turn green. He got on the lower half of it and bethought himself of his morning shave. He fished under the berth for his bag and found it—a rusty old Gladstone, duly converted as promised. But there was no razor in it of any type he dared use. There was a set of straight razors and strops and a mug for soap, but he would not trust himself to operate with them. The train was much too rough for that.

But he had to wash, so he climbed out of the berth, bumping others, and found the lavatory. It was packed with half-dressed men in the process of shaving. The basins were miserable affairs of marble and supplied by creaky pumps that delivered a tablespoonful of water at a time. The car was finished in garish quartered oak, mahogany, mother-of-pearl and bright woods fitted into the most atrocious inlays Mr. Feathersmith could have imagined. The taste in decoration, he realized, had made long steps since 1902.

His companions were "drummers"—heavy, well-fed men, all. One was in dry goods; one in coffee, tea and spices; another in whiskey; and two of the rest in patent medicines. Their conversation touched on Bryan and Free Silver, and one denounced Theodore Roosevelt's imperialism—said it was all wrong for us to annex distant properties like the Sandwich Islands and the Philippines. One man thought Aguinaldo was a hero, another that Funston was the greatest general of all time. But what worried them most was whether they would get to Gooch Junction at all, and if so, how much late.

"We're only an hour behind now," said the whiskey drummer, "but the brakeman told me there's a bad wreck up ahead and it may take 'em all day to clear it . . ."

"Many killed?"

"Naw. Just a freight—engine crew and brakeman and about a dozen tramps. That's all."

"Shucks. They won't hold us up for that. They'll just pile the stuff up and burn it."

It was ten when they reached the Junction, which consisted of only a signal tower, a crossing, and several sidings. There was no diner on, but the news butcher had a supply of candy, paper-thin ham sandwiches on stale bread, and soda pop. If one did not care for those or peanuts, he didn't eat. Dropping the sleeper took a long time and much backing and filling, during which the locomotive ran off the rails and had to be jockeyed back on. Mr. Feathersmith was getting pretty disgusted by the time he reached the day coach and found he had to share a seat with a raw farm boy in overalls and a sloppy old felt hat. The boy had an aroma that Mr. Feathersmith had not smelled for a long, long time. And then he noticed that the aroma prevailed in other quarters, and it came to him all of a sudden that the day was Thursday and considerably removed from last Saturday and presumptive baths.

It was about that time that Mr. Feathersmith became aware that he himself had been unchanged except for wardrobe and accessories. He had expected to wake up youthful. But he did not let it worry him unduly, as he imagined the Devil would come through when he had gone all the way back. He tried to get a paper from the butcher, but all there were were day-old St. Louis papers and the news was chiefly local. He looked for the financial section and only found a quarter of a column where a dozen railroad bonds were listed. The editor seemed to ignore the Orient and Europe altogether, and there was very little about Congress. After that he settled down and tried to get used to the temperature. At one end of the car there was a pot-bellied cast-iron stove, kept roaring by volunteer stokers, but despite its ruddy color and the tropic heat in the two seats adjacent, the rest of the car was bitter cold.

The train dragged on all day, stopping often on bleak sidings and waiting for oncoming trains to pass. He noticed on the blackboards of the stations they passed that they were now five hours late and getting later. But no one seemed to worry. It was the expected. Mr. Feathersmith discovered he had a great turnip of a gold watch in the pocket of his waistcoat—a gorgeously flowered satin affair, incidentally—and the watch was anchored across his front by a chain heavy enough to grace the bows of a young battleship. He consulted it often, but it was no help. They arrived at Florence, where they should have been before noon, just as the sun was setting. Everybody piled out of the train to take advantage of the twenty-minute stop to eat at the Dining House there.

The food was abundant—fried ham, fried steaks, cold turkey, roast venison and fried chicken and slabs of fried salt port. But it was all too heavy and greasy for his worn stomach. The fact that the vegetables consisted of four kinds of boiled beans plus cabbage reminded him that he did not have his vitamin tablets with him. He asked for asparagus, but people only looked amused. That was stuff for the rich and it came in little cans. No, no asparagus. Fish? At breakfast they might have salt mackerel. They *could* open a can of salmon. Would that do? He looked at the enormous, floury biscuits, the heavy pitchers of honey and sorghum molasses and a bowl of grits, and decided he would have just a glass of milk. The butter he never even considered, as it was a pale, anemic salvy substance. They brought him an immense tumbler of buttermilk and he had to make the best of that.

By the time they were back in the cars, the brakeman was going down the aisle, lighting the Pintsch lamps overhead with a lamplighter. The gas had a frightful odor, but no one seemed to mind. It was "up-to-date," not the smelly kerosene they used on some lines.

The night wore on, and in due time the familiar landscape of old Cliffordsville showed up outside the window. Another item he discovered he had forgotten was that Cliffordsville had been there before the railroad was run through. On account of curves and grades, the company had by-passed the town by a couple of miles, so that the station—or depot—stood that distance away. It would have been as good a way as any to approach the town of his childhood, except that on this day the snow had turned to drizzling rain. The delightful clay roads were all right in dry weather, but a mass of bottomless, sticky, rutted mud on a day like this. Mr. Feathersmith walked out onto the open platform of the car and down its steps. He viewed the sodden station and its waterlogged open platform with misgiving. There was but one rig that had come to meet the train. It was the Planter's Hotel bus— a rickety affair with facing fore-and-aft seats approached from the rear by three steps and grab-irons, à la Black Maria. The driver had his storm curtains up, but they were only fastened by little brass gimmicks at the corners and flapped abominably. There were four stout horses drawing the vehicle, but they were spattered with mud up to the belly and the wheels were encrusted with foot-thick adhesions of clay.

"Stranger here?" asked the driver, as he gathered up his reins and urged the animals to break the bus out of the quagmire it had sunk down in.

"I've been here before," said Mr. Feathersmith, wondering savagely why— back in those good old days—somebody had not had enough gumption to grade and gravel-surface this road. "Does Mr. Toler still run the hotel?"

"Yep. Swell hotel he's got, too. They put in a elevator last year."

That was a help, thought Mr. Feathersmith. As he remembered the place it had twenty-foot ceilings and was three stories high. With *his* heart, at least for the first day here, he was just as happy at not having to climb those weary, steep stairs. And, now that he thought of it, the Planter's Hotel *was* a darn good hotel for its day and time. People said there was nothing like it closer than Dallas.

The drive in took the best part of two hours. The wind tore at the curtains and gusts of rain blew in. Three times they bogged down completely and the driver had to get out and put his shoulder to a wheel as the four horses lay belly-flat against the oozy mud and strained as if their hearts and backs would break. But eventually they drew up before the hotel, passing through streets that were but slightly more passable than the road. Mr. Feathersmith was shocked at the utter absence of concrete or stone sidewalks. Many blocks boasted no sidewalks at all; the others were plank affairs.

A couple of Negro boys lounged before the hotel and upon the arrival of the bus got into a tussle as to which should carry the Gladstone bag. The tussle was a draw, with the result that they both carried it inside, hanging it between them.

The hotel was a shattering disappointment from the outset. Mr. Feathersmith's youthful memories proved very false indeed. The lobby's ceiling was thirty feet high, not twenty, and supported by two rows of cast-iron fluted columns topped with crudely done Corinthian caps. The bases and caps had been gilded once, but they were tarnished now, and the fly-specked marble painting of the shafts was anything but convincing. The floor was alternate diamond squares of marble—black with blue, and spotted with white enameled cast-iron cuspidors of great capacity, whose vicinity attested the poor marksmanship of Cliffordsville's chewers of the filthy weed. The marble-topped desk was decorated by a monstrous ledger, an inkpot and pens, and presided over by a supercilious young man with slicked-down hair neatly parted in the middle and a curly, thick brown mustache.

"A three-dollar room, of course, sir?" queried the clerk, giving the register a twirl and offering the pen.

"Of course," snapped Mr. Feathersmith, "the best. And with bath."

"With bath, sir?" deprecated the young man, as if taking it as a joke. "Why, there is a bath on every floor. Just arrange with the bellboy."

The old financier grunted. He was forgetting things again. He glanced over his shoulder toward the rear of the lobby where a red-hot stove was closely surrounded by a crowd of drummers. It seemed to be the only spot of warmth in the place, but he was intent on his bath. So he accepted the huge key and tag and followed the boy to the elevator. That proved to be a loosely woven, open-cage affair in an open shaft and operated by a cable that ran vertically through it. The boy slammed the outer door—there was no inner—and grasped the cable with both hands and pulled. There was a throaty rumble down below and the car began gradually to ascend. Inch by inch it rose, quivering, at about half the speed of a modern New York escalator. Mr. Feathersmith fumed and fidgeted, but there was no help for it. The elevators of forty years ago were like that. It was just too bad his room was 303.

It was big enough, twenty by twenty by twenty. A perfect cube, containing two gigantic windows which only a Sandow could manage. The huge double bed with heavy mahogany head and foot pieces was lost in it. Several rocking chairs stood about, and a rag rug was on the floor. But the *pièce de résistance* of the room was the marble-topped washstand. On it rested a porcelain bowl and pitcher and beside it a slop jar. Mr. Feathersmith knew without looking what the cabinet beneath it contained. He walked over to it and looked into the pitcher. The water had a crust of ice on top of it. The room had not a particle of heat!

"I want a bath. Right away," he said to the bellboy. "Hot."

"Yassir," said the boy, scratching his head, "but I ain't know ef the chambermaid's got around to cleaning hit yit. They ain't many as wants bath till tomorrow. I kin go look and see, though."

"I've got some laundry, too. I want it back tomorrow."

"Oh, mister—you-all must be from New Yawk. They ain't no such thing here. They's a steam laundry, but they only take up Mondays and gita it back on Sat-

'day. My ma kin do it fer you, but that'll have to be Monday, too. She irons awful nice. They's mighty little she ever burns—and steal!—why, white folks, you could trust her with anything you got. Now'n then she loses a hand'chuf er some little thing like that, but steal—nossir.''

"Skip it," snorted Mr. Feathersmith, "and see about that bath." He was re-learning his lost youth fast. There had been times when metropolitan flunkyism had annoyed him, but he would give something for some of it now. He pulled out a dime and gave it to the boy, who promptly shuffled out for a conference with the maid over the unheard-of demand of a bath on Friday afternoon.

One look at the bathroom was enough. It was twenty feet high, too, but only eight feet long by three wide, so that it looked like the bottom of a dark well. A single carbon filament lamp dangled from a pair of black insulated wires, led across the ceiling, and gave a dim orange light—as did the similar one in the bedroom. The bathtub was a tin affair, round-bottomed and standing on four cast-iron legs. It was dirty, and fed by a half-inch pipe that dribbled a pencil-thin stream of water. In about two hours, Mr. Feathersmith estimated, his bath would be drawn and ready—provided, of course, that the maid should remove in the meantime the mass of buckets, pans, brooms, mops and scrub rags that she stored in the place. One glance at the speckled, choked other piece of plumbing in the place made him resolve he would use the gadget underneath his own washstand.

"I kin bring hot water—a pitcher ur so," suggested the colored boy, "ef you want it."

"Never mind," said Mr. Feathersmith. He remembered now that a barber shop was just around the corner and they had bathtubs as well. It would be easier to go there, since he needed a shave, anyway, and pay an extra quarter and get it over with.

He slept in his new bed that night and found it warm despite the frigidness of the room, for the blankets of the time were honest wool and thick. But it was the only crumb of comfort he could draw from his new surroundings.

The next morning Mr. Feathersmith's troubles truly began. He got up, broke the crust of ice in his pitcher, and gaspingly washed his face and hands. He waited tediously for the slow-motion elevator to come up and take him down to breakfast. The meal was inedible, too, owing to its heaviness. He marveled that people could eat so much so early in the morning. He managed some oatmeal and buttered toast, but passed up all the rest. He was afraid that grapefruit was unheard of; as to the other fruits, there were apples. Transportation and storage had evidently not solved the out-of-season fruit and vegetable problem.

It also worried him that Satan had done nothing so far about his rejuvenation. He got up the same gnarled, veiny hands, florid face, and bald head. He wished he had insisted on a legible copy of the contract at the time, instead of waiting for the promised confirmation copy. But all that was water over the dam. He was here, so, pending other developments, he must see about establishing his daily comforts and laying the foundation for his fortune.

There were several things he wanted: to acquire the old Feathersmith homestead; to marry Daisy Norton; to bring in the Cliffordsville oil field—wasn't there already Spindletop, Batson and Sour Lake making millions?—then go back to New York, where, after all, there was a civilization of a sort, however primitive.

He took them in order. Representing himself as a granduncle of his original self, he inquired at the local real-estate man's office. Yes, the Feathersmith place was for sale—cheap. The former cook, Anna, was living near it and available for hire. It did not take Mr. Feathersmith long to get to the local livery stable and hire a two-horse rig to take him out there.

The sight of the place was a shock to him. The road out was muddy in stretches, and rocky and bumpy in others. At last they came to a sagging plank gate in a barbed-wire fence and the driver dragged it open. The great trees Mr. Feathersmith had looked back on with fond memory proved to be post oaks and cedars. There was not a majestic elm or pecan tree in the lot. The house was even more of a disappointment. Instead of the vast mansion he remembered, it was a rambling, run-down building whose porches sagged and where the brown remnants of last summer's honeysuckle still clung to a tangle of cotton strings used for climbers. They should have a neat pergola built for them, he thought, and entered.

The interior was worse. One room downstairs had a fireplace. Upstairs there was a single sheet-iron wood stove. What furniture that was left was incredibly tawdry; there was no telephone and no lights except kerosene wick lamps. The house lacked closets or a bath, and the back yard was adorned with a crazy Chic Sale of the most uninviting pattern. A deserted hog-pen and a dilapidated stable completed the assets. Mr. Feathersmith decided he wouldn't live there again on any terms.

But a wave of sentimentality drove him to visit Anna, the former cook. She, at least, would not have depreciated like the house had done in a paltry two years. He learned she lived in a shack close by, so he went. He introduced himself as an elder of the Feathersmith family, and wanted to know if she would cook and wash for him.

"I doan want no truck with any kind of Feathersmith," she asserted. "They're po' white trash—all of 'em. The ole man and the missus wan't so bad, but that young skunk of a Jack sold out before they was hardly cold and snuck outa town twixt sundown and daylight an' we ain't never seed ur heard tell of him since. Jus' let me alone—that's all I ask."

With that she slammed the cabin door in his face.

So! thought Mr. Feathersmith. Well, he guessed he didn't want her, either. He went back to town and straight to the bank. Having discovered he had three thousand dollars in big bills and gold, a sizable fortune for Cliffordsville of the period, since the First National Bank was capitalized for only ten, he went boldly in to see Mr. Norton. He meant to suggest that they jointly exploit the Norton plantations for the oil that was under it. But on the very moment he was entering the portals of the bank he suddenly remembered that the Cliffordsville field was a very recent one, circa 1937, and therefore deep. Whereas Spindletop had been discovered by boring shallow wells—a thousand feet and mostly less—later-day wells had depths of something over a mile. In 1902 the suggestion of drilling to six thousand feet and more would have been simply fantastic. There was neither the equipment nor the men to undertake it. Mr. Feathersmith gulped the idea down and decided instead to make a deposit and content himself with polite inquiries about the family.

Mr. Norton was much impressed with the other's get-up and the cash deposit of three thousand dollars. That much currency was not to be blinked at in the days before the Federal Reserve Board Act. When money stringencies came—and they did often—it was actual cash that counted, not that ephemeral thing known as credit. He listened to Mr. Feathersmith's polite remarks and observed that he would consider it an honor to permit his wife and daughter to receive the new depositor at their home. Personally fingering the beloved bank notes, Mr. Norton ushered out his new customer with utmost suavity.

The call was arranged, and Mr. Feathersmith put in his appearance at exactly 4:30 p.m. of the second day following. Ransacking his mind for memories of customs of the times, he bethought himself to take along a piece of sheet music, a pound of mixed candies, and a bouquet of flowers.

The visit was a flop. Befitting his new status as an important depositor, he took a rubber-tired city hack to the door, and then, to avoid the charge of sinful extravagance, he dismissed the fellow, telling him to come back at five. After that, bearing his gifts, he maneuvered the slippery pathway of pop bottles planted neck down, bordered by bricks and desiccated rosebushes. He mounted the steps and punched the doorbell. After that there was a long silence, but he knew that there was tittering inside and that several persons pulled the curtains softly and surveyed him surreptitiously. At length the door opened cautiously and an old black mammy dressed in silk to match let him in and led him into the parlor.

It was a macabre room, smelling of mold. She seated him in a horsehair-covered straight chair, then went about the business of opening the inside folding blinds. After that she flitted from the room. After a long wait Mrs. Norton came in, stately and dignified, and introduced herself. Whereupon she plumped herself down on another chair and stared at him. A few minutes later the giggling Daisy came in and was duly introduced. She also bowed stiffly, without offering a hand, and sat down. Then came the grandmother. After that they just sat—the man at one end of the room, and the three sedate women in a row at the other, their knees and ankles tightly compressed together and their hands folded in their laps. Mr. Feathersmith got up and tried to manage a courtly bow while he made his presentations, thinking they were awfully stuffy.

He thought so particularly, because he had formerly had Daisy out on a buggy ride and knew what an expert kisser she could be when the moon was right. But things were different. He introduced various possible topics of conversation, such as the weather, the latest French styles, and so forth. But they promptly—and with the utmost finality—disposed of each with a polite, agreeing "Yes, sir." It was maddening. And then he saw that Daisy Norton was an empty-headed little doll who could only giggle, kiss, as required, and say, "Yes, sir." She had no conception of economics, politics, world affairs . . .

"Aw-r-rk!" thought Mr. Feathersmith. The thought took him back to those hellcats of modern women—like Miss Tomlinson, in charge of his Wall Street office force—the very type he wanted to get away from, but who was alert and alive.

He listened dully while Daisy played a "Valse Brilliante" on the black square piano, and saw the embroideries her fond mother displayed. After that he ate the little cakes and coffee they brought. Then left. That was Daisy Norton. Another balloon pricked.

On the trip back to the hotel he was upset by seeing a number of yellow flags hung out on houses. It puzzled him at first, until he remembered that that was the signal for smallpox within. It was another thing he had forgotten about the good old days. They had smallpox, yellow fever, diphtheria, scarlet fever, and other assorted diseases that raged without check except constitutional immunity. There was the matter of typhoid, too, which depended on water and milk-supply surveillance. And it came to him that so long as Satan chose to keep him aged, he must live chiefly on milk. Cliffordsville, he well remembered, annually had its wave of typhoid, what with its using unfiltered creek water and the barbarian habit of digging wells in the vicinity of cesspools. Mr. Feathersmith was troubled. Didn't he have enough physical complaints as it was?

He was reminded even more forcibly of that shortly afterward when he came to, sitting up on the floor of a barroom with someone forcing whiskey into his mouth.

"You fainted, mister, but you'll be all right now."

"Get me a doctor," roared Mr. Feathersmith. "It's ephedrine I want, not whiskey!"

The doctor didn't come. There was only the one, and he was out miles in the country administering to a case of "cramp colic"—a mysterious disease later to achieve the more fashionable notoriety of "acute appendicitis." The patient died, unhappily, but that did not bring the doctor back to town any quicker.

The next morning Mr. Feathersmith made a last desperate effort to come back. There was a bicycle mechanic in town who had recently established a garage in order to take care of Mr. Norton's lumbering Ford and Dr. Simpson's buggylike Holtzmann. Those crude automobiles thought it a triumph to make ten miles without a tow, had to be cranked by hand, and were lighted at night by kerosene carriage lamps or acetylene bicycle lamps.

"Why not devise a self-starter," suggested Mr. Feathersmith, recalling that millions had been made out of them, "a gadget you press with the foot, you know, that will crank the engine with an electric motor?"

"Why not wings?" asked the surly mechanic. He did not realize that both were practical, or that Mr. Feathersmith had seen better days. The trouble with Mr. Feathersmith was that he had always been a promoter and a financier, with little or no knowledge of the mechanical end of the game.

"It works," he insisted solemnly, "a storage battery, a motor, and a gilhookey to crank the motor. Think it over. It would make us rich."

"So would perpetual motion," answered the garage man.

And that was that.

Dr. Simpson, when contact was made, was even a poorer consolation.

"Ephedrine? Vitamins? Thyroxin? You're talking gibberish—I don't know what you mean. Naturally, a man of your age is likely to get short of breath at times— even faint. But shucks, Mr. Feathersmith, don't let that bother you. I've known men to live to a hundred that didn't stack up as well as you. Take it easy, rest plenty with a nap every afternoon, and you'll be all right. We're only young once, you know."

When Mr. Feathersmith found that the good doctor had nothing to offer better than a patented "tonic" and poultices for his rheumatism, he thereafter let him strictly alone. The situation as to vitamins and glandular extracts was worse than hopeless—the dieticians had not got around yet to finding out about calories, let alone those. Mr. Feathersmith worried more and more over Satan's inexplicable delay in bestowing youth befitting the age, for Forfin had insisted the Old Boy would fulfill his promise if the price was paid. But until that was done, the old financier could only wait and employ his time as profitably as he could.

He kept ransacking his brains for things he could invent, but every avenue proved to be a blind alley. He mentioned the possibility of flying to the circle that sat about the lobby stove, but they scornfully laughed it down. It was an obvious impossibility, except for the dirigible gas bags Santos-Dumont was playing with in France. He tried to organize a company to manufacture aluminum, but unfortunately no one had heard of the stuff except one fellow who had been off to school and seen a lump of it in the chemical laboratory. It was almost as expensive as gold, and what good was it?

Mr. Feathersmith realized then that if he were in possession of a 1942 automobile no one could duplicate it, for the many alloys were unknown and the foundry and machine-shop practice necessary were undeveloped. There was nothing to paint it with but carriage paint—slow-drying and sticky. There were no fuels or lubricants to serve it, or any roads fit to run it on.

He played with other ideas, but they all came croppers. He dared not even mention radio—it smacked too much of magic—or lunacy. And he most certainly did not want to be locked up as a madman in an insane asylum of the era. If standard medicine was just beginning to crawl, psychiatry was simply nonexistent. So he kept quiet about his speculations.

Since life had become so hard and he was cut off from any normal intercourse with his fellow townsmen, he yearned for good music. But, alas, that likewise was not to be had outside one or two metropolitan orchestras. He went once to church and heard a home-grown, self-taught soprano caterwaul in a quavering voice. After that he stayed away. He caught himself wishing for a good radio program—and he had altered considerably his standards of what was good.

A week rolled by. During it he had another stroke that was almost his last. The New York doctor had warned him that if he did not obey all the rules as to diet and other palliatives, he might expect to be taken off at any time. Mr. Feathersmith knew that his days were numbered—and the number was far fewer than it would have been if he had remained in the modern age he had thought so unbearable. But still there was the hope that the Devil would yet do the right thing by him.

That hope was finally and utterly blasted the next day. Mr. Feathersmith was in the grip of another devastating fit of weakness and knew that shortly he would be unable to breathe and would therefore fall into a faint and die. But just before his last bit of strength and speck of consciousness faded, there was a faint plop overhead and an envelope fluttered down and into his lap. He looked at it, and though the stamp and cancellation were blurred and illegible, he saw the return address in the corner was "Bureau of Complaints and Adjustments, Gehenna." His trembling fingers tore the missive open. A copy of his contract fell out into his lap.

He scanned it hurriedly. As before, it seemed flawless. Then he discovered a tiny memorandum clipped to its last page. He read it and knew his heart would stand no more. It was from the cute little witch of Fifth Avenue.

DEAREST SNOOKY-WOOKY:

His Nibs complains you keep on bellyaching. That's not fair. You said you wanted to be where you are, and there you are. You wanted your memory unimpaired. Can we help it if your memory is lousy? And not once, old dear, did you cheep about also having your youth restored. So that lets us out. Be seeing you in Hell, old thing.

Cheerio!

He stared at it with fast-dimming eyes.

"The little witch—the bad, badgering little . . ." and then an all-engulfing blackness saved him from his mumbling alliteration.